Publications

Of

The Colonial Society of Massachusetts

VOLUME LXXIX

THE CORRESPONDENCE OF

John Cotton Junior

THE CORRESPONDENCE OF
John Cotton Junior

EDITED BY

Sheila McIntyre & Len Travers

Boston: The Colonial Society of Massachusetts, *2009*

Distributed by the University Press of Virginia

DEDICATION

Joanna, Carolyn, and Michael: patient spouses.

ISBN 978-0-9794662-2-9
Printed from the Income of the Sarah Louise Edes Fund

Contents

Contents

Introduction

"My Father," remembered Josiah Cotton, "was a man of Universal Acquaintance & Correspondence, so that he had & wrote (phaps) twice as many letters as any Man in the Countrey."[1] Fortunately for scholars, hundreds of those letters survive, and they are compiled in this volume, many appearing in print for the first time. Rev. John Cotton Jr. (1640–1699), pastor of the church at Plymouth from 1667 to 1697, does indeed appear in the letters as a person of "universal acquaintance," with both famous and lesser-known correspondents in all the New England colonies and several in England. His surviving correspondence far outweighs that of his more illustrious father, who on occasion asked that his letters be burned—something that it is difficult to imagine John Jr. requesting.

The letters printed here begin in 1664, when Cotton was a young divine trying to survive scandal, and cover the years of his ministry in Plymouth almost without interruption. Those years included his energetic revival of the Plymouth church, the continuance of his missionary work among the region's Natives, first begun on Martha's Vineyard, the vicious conflict known as Philip's (later King Philip's) War, intrigues among the colonies and the royal government, the demise of Plymouth Colony, and the controversial end of his ministry. Most of his letters were written to and from colleagues in the ministry and in government and, as he grew older, to and from his children settled in distant towns. Cotton's correspondence reveals both his powerful family connections—Mathers, Saltonstalls, Rosseters—and his extraordinary dedication to remaining informed. Filled with often-intimate detail, the letters in this collection will be of particular interest to students of early American family history as well as of political, military, and church history.

Born 15 March 1639/40, John Jr. was the second son and namesake of John Cotton (1585–1652), the minister of Boston's First Church, renowned for his part in the founding of Boston and the Antinomian controversy and for his pamphlet warfare with New England's *enfant terrible*, Roger Williams. John Jr. attended Harvard College, graduating in 1657 and embarking then on a kind of "apprenticeship" calculated to prepare him to follow in his father's (and older brother Seaborne's) ministerial footsteps. He traveled to Hartford, in the Connecticut colony, to live with the Reverend Samuel Stone, his father's former colleague. When an opening appeared in the pulpit of nearby Wethersfield in early 1660, Cotton, no doubt with Stone's recommendation, received an invitation to the pastorate there, which he promptly accepted. Apparently confident of passing the customary probationary period, in November of that same year he married Joanna Rosseter of Guilford. He was twenty years old, rather young for such a step (most New England men waited, or had to wait, until their mid- to late twenties), but Cotton's future looked bright. He was already a member of the most esteemed profession in the land, a freeman of the colony, and so respected as to be given the sober responsibility of executor for the estate of Connecticut's lately deceased governor, Thomas Welles.

Cotton's bright prospects vanished in the wake of sexual scandal, when he reportedly became overly familiar with several women in Wethersfield. He soon faced serious charges. In early 1662 a court-appointed committee that included his former mentor Samuel Stone was ordered to sort things out. Although cleared of a charge of "sinfull striving" with a woman not his wife, Cotton displayed a propensity for impulsive, reckless speech during his defense that would resurface periodically over the course of his career. His judges may not have believed him guilty of fornication, or even of sinfully striving toward that end, but they were convinced that he had not conducted himself with complete propriety, especially given his position. Specifically, they censured him sharply for "sinfull Rash unpeacabell" words "of a very high defaming nature" (the latter reference concerned remarks he made to Gov. Welles's daughter!).[2] Cotton's hopes of occupying a pulpit in Wethersfield or anywhere else in Connecticut were dashed. With Joanna and his year-old son, John, Cotton retreated to Guilford, perhaps staying with Joanna's physician father, Bryan Rosseter.

Cotton's humiliation was not yet complete. By March 1664 Boston's First Church, where his father had been minister and of which he was still a member, was demanding his appearance for disciplinary action in connection with his Connecticut misadventures. On 1 May he was excommunicated for "lascivious uncleane practices with three women and his horrid lying to hide his sinne." Cotton made a "penitential acknowledgement openly confessing his sinnes" and his membership was reinstated five weeks later, but the damage to his reputation had been done.[3] The only occupation for which he had been trained must have seemed closed to him for the foreseeable future.

Closed, that is, unless he were willing to start again, and at the bottom. Before the 1640s, the English in the northern colonies undertook little missionary work in comparison to the religious of the French and Spanish colonies. John Eliot, pastor of the church at Roxbury, was by the mid 1660s the most famous of the few Puritan pastors who had taken up the challenge. According to a contemporary chronicler, it was he who suggested Cotton's next move.[4] The island of Martha's Vineyard, south of Cape Cod, had a small English settlement at Great Harbor (now Edgartown) whose pastor, Thomas Mayhew Jr., had been lost at sea seven years before. Mayhew had also been an energetic and highly competent missionary to the island's Native people. If Cotton were willing to take up both duties and to remove himself and his family to what was arguably the most remote English community in New England, the job would be his.

Under the circumstances, Cotton was more than willing. Late in 1664 he moved his family to the island and set to work ministering to the small congregation. He also prepared for his new role as a missionary. Employing English-speaking Native interpreters to teach him, he studied the local Native dialect so that in little more than a year, as Cotton wrote in March 1666, "I preached my first sermon to the Indians in theire owne language."[5] For the following twenty months, Cotton seems to have satisfied the island's Christian Indians, preaching all over the Vineyard except at Aquinnah/Gay Head, where the Natives showed little interest in, and even some hostility toward, missionary efforts. Cotton's relations with his congregants at Great Harbor were likewise positive. Following the usual trial period, the church members invited him to stay and he accepted. The town secured him a modest parsonage, voted £40 for his annual salary, and began to raise funds for a new meetinghouse. Forty pounds was about half of what he might have received on the mainland, but with an additional £30 a year from the Society for the Propagation of the Gospel in New England for his missionary work and £10 allowed his wife by the same body for attending to the Natives' medical care, the Cottons were back on their feet.

Despite his outwardly successful ministry, however, Cotton was restless and unsatisfied. When he could, he made excursions to the mainland, especially to Boston, where he sounded out friends and relations to learn of job prospects. He obviously felt the Vineyard's isolation keenly, having been brought up amid the bustle and intellectual challenges of Boston and Cambridge. He particularly missed the comparatively simple mainland network of exchanges via correspondence—significantly, we found no letters to or from Cotton from the Martha's Vineyard years. His frustration also may have exacerbated his deteriorating relations with the island's proprietor. Thomas Mayhew Sr., father of the dead missionary, increasingly regarded Cotton's growing influence with the island Natives as a threat to his own authority—at least, that is how Cotton saw it. In his missionary journal the young minister recorded several instances of Mayhew's professional jealousy as related to him by tattletale Natives. Cotton's impulsiveness may have been getting the better of him again, or perhaps he was becoming confident of a new appointment, for matters between him and Mayhew developed into such an impasse that the Commissioners of the United Colonies had to step in. In September 1667 both he and Mayhew were rebuked by the

Commissioners for their "mutuall Contensions and Invictives one against another," which "undid what they taught the Natives."[6] Although there was no repairing the breach and Mayhew, as proprietor of the island, was not going anywhere, by this time Cotton had other options. His networking efforts on the mainland had paid off, and he had received several offers from communities there in need of ministers. The Commissioners strongly suggested that he accept one of them. Two months later Cotton and family were back on the mainland in the Old Colony town of Plymouth.

Cotton's new home was a quiet agricultural town, a far cry from the boisterous commercial center of his childhood years. Plymouth, the oldest English town in New England and the genesis of Plymouth Colony, had never had great success in attracting and keeping suitable ministers. The colony made do without one for its first nine years, and those who came afterward were lackluster at best. During the late 1650s Plymouth, again without a minister, found itself handicapped in combating the "Quaker invasion" spiritually, but vigorous civil authorities kept the aggressive dissidents a safe distance from the town. By the time Cotton arrived, the church was in a moribund state, with baptisms and membership in marked decline. Plymouth was not Boston, but for Cotton it was at least on the right side of Vineyard Sound, and he launched himself into his new responsibilities with an energy that the Plymouth church had not seen since its early years. Formally ordained the last day of June 1669, he and ruling elder Thomas Cushman "made it their first special Work together to pass through the whole Town from Family to Family to enquire into the State of their Soules, and according as they found the Frames either of the Children of the Church or others, so they applied Counsels, Admonitions, Exhortations and Encouragements."[7] This "Service was attended with a Blessing," for within the year the church's membership rose almost threefold, from twenty-seven to seventy-four. In the next three years thirty-seven more persons joined, and nearly a hundred more would become members by the end of Cotton's ministry.[8]

Cotton may have benefited from a demographic shift in the town—a relatively large number of young people reached sufficient age for church membership about this time—but by all accounts the young minister, not yet thirty at the time of his ordination, was popular and attractive, physically and temperamentally. His son Josiah remembered him as a man of "a handsome ruddy yet grave countenance, of a sanguine complexion, a middling stature and [probably referring to his later years] inclined to fatness." He was also "of a strong healthy constitution, so that (if I mistake not) he was not hindered by sickness for above one day from his public labours for 20 or thirty years together."[9] Cotton's robust nature seems to have extended to his ministerial work. Although he wrote out his sermons (none of which have come to light), he did not read from the manuscripts, which allowed him to keep eye contact with his listeners. He was relaxed in his delivery, with a strong, clear voice and a "noted faculty in sermonizing and making speeches in public." Additionally, he had a "good gift in prayer and inlarged much therein as there was occasion," whether in the public meeting or with individual parishioners. As the first Harvard-trained minister in the colony, Cotton must have impressed the people of Plymouth with "his vast and strong memory, in so much that if some of the words of almost any passage of Scripture were named to him he could tell the chapter and verse, or if chapter and verse were named, he could tell the words." He was, his son insisted, "a living Index to the Bible." Although "a competent scholar . . . divinity was his favorite study."[10] His talents seemed to suit the struggling Plymouth church perfectly.

Cotton began holding catechisms for children every two weeks, initiated monthly meetings of the church for "religious Conference," and tidied up the loose ends of church business, issuing formal dismissals to members who had long since moved to other towns. In short, the new pastor was hard working, charismatic, knowledgeable, sincere—and young, with his best years still before him. The Plymouth church seemed at last to have found in Cotton a minister who was a comfortable fit. For his part, Cotton had found a place where he was clearly needed and appreciated, and where his blemished past appeared not to matter. By 1670, Cotton seemed justified in calling for a day of thanksgiving specifically for "the settlement of God's ordinances after soe long a vacancy, & the good success of the Gospel amongst them."[11]

The satisfaction that Cotton demonstrated in his ministry, however, belied a growing feeling of isolation. Much of his correspondence during his thirty years in Plymouth focused on needing, requesting, receiving, and sharing information. Living in Plymouth meant that Cotton, like other ministers far removed from Boston, not only looked to the Bay Colony capital but to a regional network of clergy for current news, copies of recently-published tracts and broadsides, intellectual stimulation, and doctrinal information. Many of these clergymen had begun their careers together as part of a vital intellectual community at Harvard. Being scattered in remote pulpits challenged their efforts to remain part of the intellectual life they once shared. Letters helped bridge the distance between them.

Historians of King Philip's War (1675–1676, or to 1677 if the conflict in northern New England is included) have long recognized the value of Cotton's correspondence. Since his arrival in Plymouth, Cotton had cultivated relationships with neighboring ministers, just as he had maintained regular correspondence with leading clergy in Boston and Cambridge. Cotton's ties in both directions—into the backcountry and out to the coast—enabled him to gather and distribute information as few others could. Cotton's information spread throughout a ministerial letter-exchange network that recognized the importance of rapid information diffusion, especially during crises. As the fighting raged in Plymouth Colony, Cotton appealed to his colleagues for news of intensifying attacks and counterthrusts by both Native and English forces. One of Cotton's frequent correspondents at this time was Rev. Noah Newman of Rehoboth. Newman's location in the western part of Plymouth Colony gave him access to late-breaking news from the officers and soldiers who filled his town and church on their way to or from the fighting in Rhode Island. Newman interviewed participants, read personal letters that others shared with him, questioned military postal riders, and ministered to the soldiers. He and other informants passed on much of this information to Cotton, who in turn related the news to others in his network, even copying letters verbatim so that readers might "hear" news unedited as it changed hands. Cotton's letter exchange during King Philip's War traveled far beyond the small agricultural and frontier towns of Plymouth Colony. Some of Boston's leading ministers wrote to Cotton to obtain reliable information about the conflict and came to rely on his newsletters. Joshua Moodey, a minister settled in Portsmouth, New Hampshire, wrote to Cotton on 1 April 1676, thanking him for "ye Intelligence" about the Medfield attack.[12]

This devastating war tested the faith of many English settlers who feared that their own sinfulness had provoked God's wrath and brought about "so dreadfull a judgement" upon them. Like other New Englanders, lay and clerical, Cotton saw in the English settlers' worldliness and religious complacency an explanation for the war. Hoping that fervent prayers to God might check Philip's successes, Cotton turned to the traditional ordinances. He called for formal days of humiliation and prayer on four occasions during the war to help the members of his congregation confront their sins and joined them with the churches of other Plymouth and Massachusetts towns in a region-wide day of humiliation on 29 June 1676. The list of sins that Cotton read to his congregation included missing church meetings, losing their love of the Bible, abandoning the godly life, "polluting" the Sabbaths, and "frequenting such places & companyes not becoming christians." By these errors, Cotton told his listeners, "wee have provoked the Lord God . . . by our sins [we] have had a deep hand in procuring these calamities."[13] The correspondence also reveals the efforts of some ministers, including Cotton, to use the spiritual crisis to inspire recommitment to church discipline and fellowship. Under his guidance and leadership, the Plymouth church renewed its founding covenant, it members pledging anew "to walke in all our wayes according to the Rule of the Gospel . . . in mutuall love to & watchfulness over one another, depending wholly & only upon the Lord our God to enable us by his grace hereunto."[14]

At the conclusion of the fighting in southern New England, Cotton was happy to return to his regular ministry and to his missionary work, which had been interrupted by the war. Local (and sometimes even distant) clergy sought Cotton's help with a variety of questions, and Cotton and his colleagues debated theological and social concerns in their letters to one another. The aftermath of war brought new anxieties concerning, in particular, New England's frosty relationship with post-Restoration England. Since the 1660s the Crown government under Charles II had been trying to reassert its authority in England's American colonies. The disruption brought about by King Philip's War (an obvious embarrassment to the New England governments) gave the Crown new opportunities to affirm its primacy. After the tumultuous years of the Dominion of New England, the subsequent Glorious Revolution, and the establishment of additional colonial settlements, Plymouth Colony finally lost its autonomy in 1692. Cotton's correspondence from these years constitutes a vital resource for the study of this period in New England, especially the parts played by Plymouth civic leaders.

Together with politics, family matters dominate the letters of the 1680s and 1690s. The activities of Cotton's wife, Joanna, and of his maturing children at once bound the family to its community and connected it to the towns and churches beyond Plymouth's boundaries. In addition to raising her children and sometimes accompanying Cotton in his pastoral work, Joanna served her neighbors as a midwife and healer. Her father, Bryan Rosseter, was a physician in Connecticut, and he may have sparked her interest in medicine, which she enhanced throughout her life by studying medical books that she received from relatives and friends in England. During Cotton's ministry on Martha's Vineyard, Joanna had practiced "Phisicke and Surgery" among the Natives and perhaps among the English there as well. Cotton's letters frequently refer to his wife's concerns and responsibilities: providing advice to her children, medicines sent and received, treatments for postnatal care. Like most fathers, Cotton worried about the health, safety, and education of his children. "My father," remembered son Josiah, "never aimed at laying up for, or leaving a great Estate to his Children, but yet he took special Care of, and was at great Charge about their Education, which is better than an Estate." This he somehow did "without ye Advantage of a school in the Town" except for a short-lived one in 1672.[15] When sons John and Rowland seemed ready for higher education, Cotton sought the advice and help of his step-brother, Increase Mather. While Cotton felt confident that he could begin their education, he knew that Mather could better instruct his sons as they matured. Increase sent his own son, Cotton Mather, to Plymouth to tutor the Cotton boys in preparation for Harvard College. Ultimately, all of Cotton's sons who survived to adulthood—John, Rowland, Josiah, and Theophilus—graduated from Harvard and became ministers, and daughter Elizabeth married Salisbury minister James Allin and, after he died, his successor Caleb Cushing.

By the end of 1696, Cotton's spirits were soaring. Another clergyman son was ordained in November, his missionary work brought him continued satisfaction, his salary arrived regularly, and he enjoyed frequent travel to Boston. Late in the year, he was even invited by the Boston clergy to deliver the Wednesday sermon in Boston's Old South meeting house. His listeners apparently liked what they heard; as Cotton related in a letter to his son Rowland, six hearers swore their saving testimony and became church members "while I was in the pulpit."[16] It must have been a moment of great satisfaction when Cotton was sought out, welcomed and honored in the town where he had been shamed thirty years before. But if it was the high point in his career, he would not enjoy it for long.

For three decades Cotton had been an effective and generally popular minister to the Plymouth church, "and yet," son Josiah wrote, "what man is there without his failings?" As a younger man in Connecticut and on Martha's Vineyard, Cotton had displayed an unfortunate propensity for injudicious speech, and he did not suffer those whom he considered fools lightly. As Josiah admitted, "He was Some what hasty & perhaps Severe in his Censures upon some Persons & Things, which he thought deserved it; And that possibly Occasioned some Hardships he met with, & ye violence of some People against him."[17] In 1695 Cotton had opposed the invitation of a Plymouth church member to become a teaching elder at a church in the northwestern part of the town. To some in his congregation his opposition looked like unwarranted ministerial interference in the laity's business. Whether Cotton spoke or acted undiplomatically is not known, but the controversy continued over several years and Cotton was unable, or perhaps unwilling, to prevent several members from withdrawing from communion over the incident. There were probably other factors not recorded in church records that contributed to the congregation's discontent, but the result was an anti-Cotton faction of unknown size but significant influence eager to see Cotton gone.

Cotton was also convinced that the actions eventually taken against him were politically motivated: retaliation for his indirect support of the 1692 Massachusetts Bay charter. The new charter, which grafted Plymouth Colony onto its larger neighbor, was extremely unpopular among Plymouth residents. Cotton wrote to Joanna of his fears on 6–7 July 1698. According to him, when his step-brother Increase Mather, the agent for Massachusetts, returned with the charter "taking in Plimouth, our people were all in a rage at him." Many influential men "from their godly zeale & reall Conscience) did raile at him & revile him for falsenesse, treacherous dealing yea & wickednesse to take them in to be slaves." They felt particularly betrayed because it appeared to be their "seeming" friend, Mather, who had orchestrated Plymouth's demise. Cotton defended Mather: "my spirit & my respect to my deare Brother ingaged me to give many a severe rebuke to such things & upon that account these persons that have bin most against me were provoked at me ever since." While his fellow residents were claiming that, "old Mather would goe to hell shortly for all his wickednesse," Cotton tried to support his step-brother and claimed that his own enemies sought to get rid of him because of it: "I know & soe doe many more that for this I . . . suffered much prejudice with many." Hiding behind claims of political conspiracy would have been convenient, but given the powerful reaction that Plymouth residents had to the charter, Cotton's suspicions cannot be dismissed.

On 18 June 1697, thirty-five Plymouth church brethren met to "consider the sad & scandalous reports that hath bin raised & spread abroad." The allegations concerned "some miscarriages in the Pastor towards Rebekah Morton," a married woman. The details of the case are murky; "miscarriages" implied improprieties of a sexual nature, but just what form these might have taken, or how accurate the allegations may have been, we cannot now know. The church meeting heard "her charges & the Pastors particular vindications of himselfe from all those scandals," but also of "his confession of one." Again, whether the latter remark refers to an earlier allegation, or even to the decades-old Connecticut incident (as Josiah seemed to think), and what Cotton was actually "confessing" are unclear. The church's response in this matter appears to have been a vote of confidence, at least a tentative one; the brethren unanimously voted to ask Cotton to "carry on the Lords worke among them as formerly."

But Cotton's enemies were now in full cry. While the Plymouth church saw no reason to take disciplinary action, the same Boston clergy who had praised Cotton six months earlier now called for his dismissal. A council of ministers from four towns tasked with settling the matter was unable to effect a reconciliation, or perhaps they found the evidence against Cotton too damning; on 30 September 1697 they recommended that Cotton "ask a Dismission, and the Church to grant it," with expressions of "Love and Charity." There was little "Love and Charity" evident in the conclusion, however; his forced resignation came as a "great Grief of a Number in Church and Town, who earnestly desired his Continuance." Others, in language that Cotton himself might have approved, called Cotton's ejection "a Base piece of villainy" and noted that "Mr. Cotton had as much Injustice done him in that Abominable Proceeding against him as those other innocent men who were Murdered on account of the Pretended Witchcraft" of 1692.[18]

Had the fifty-seven year-old Cotton transgressed—again? Samuel Sewall certainly accepted his guilt and in his famous journal described Cotton's stubbornness in confessing his errors—certainly a consistent pattern in Cotton's personality. Even Increase Mather (again in hearsay recorded by Sewall) "declared among the Ministers that they had dealt too favourably with Mr. Cotton."[19] Nevertheless, before he left Plymouth a year later, Cotton made his peace with the church, "making a full and penitential acknowledgement of those evils" of which the council had convicted him, "and desired forgiveness of God and the Church." Cotton seemed finally to be confessing his guilt, but again, of what? Familiarity with another man's wife? "Undue Carriage in chusing Elders" (Sewall's judgment)? Stubbornness and pride?

If Cotton's step-brother Increase thought the church council insufficiently harsh, nephew Cotton Mather seemed more sympathetic. He confided to his diary his "extreme Anguish of mind, from the terrible and amazing Circumstances, of my poor Uncle at Plymouth (condemned the last week, to Silence, by the just sentence of the Council.)." The younger Mather may have agreed that the council's action was "just," but he obviously felt compassion for "the deplorable Condition of my fallen Uncle."[20]

After losing the pulpit he had filled for so long, Cotton journeyed to Yarmouth and Sandwich, spending time with his sons who lived nearby. Naturally, Cotton could no longer count on his modest salary from Plymouth for serving as the church's minister.

Joanna moved in with their son Rowland's family in Sandwich. Josiah Cotton remembered his mother as a woman of a delicate emotional constitution; she may have left Plymouth in part due to feelings of shame, whether or not she believed her husband to be guilty (once more?) of indiscretion. In any case, Joanna and John's frequent separations in the wake of the second adultery scandal encouraged painful rumors about their marriage. John referred to the gossip in his letter to Joanna of 8 July 1698; she had recently returned to Plymouth after a long stay at Rowland's, and he was then staying in Yarmouth: "I spake with mercy Dunham at Mr Whippo's, & since I came hither Mr M: telles me, she hath vindicated you & me from some considerable aspersions, grounded upon your living soe long at Sandwich."[21] For his part, Cotton returned to Plymouth to settle his affairs and prepare for his future—all the time awaiting an invitation from another congregation.

When it came, the invitation was from an unexpected, almost outlandish, quarter: Charlestown, South Carolina. Cotton had never journeyed out of New England, and Carolina was nearly as far from his home as it was possible to be while still on the British colonial mainland. Yet there were advantages to the offer worth considering. Charlestown was founded in 1680 to serve as the commercial and political hub of the new proprietary colony. Although the religious makeup of the inhabitants there was not as homogenous as New England's (the dominant persuasion was Anglican), there was a considerable Congregationalist population in the town, and a pastor with Cotton's proven ministerial gifts might do well there. Certainly, Cotton might have felt that he was more wanted and needed in Charlestown than in his current situation. In addition, if Cotton retained any fondness for the vitality of an important seaport town, Charlestown might have proffered satisfaction in that regard; located at the convergence of the Ashley and Cooper rivers, Charlestown was an ideal location for trade.

It was also an ideal habitat for disease-carrying mosquitoes. As late as 1708, the population of the entire Carolina colony was only 8,000, and more than half of these were slaves. Dysentery, malaria and yellow fever gave Carolina the highest mortality rate in the mainland colonies. Cotton must have understood the risks but realized that another opportunity like this one might not come. Just as God had seemed to provide a place for him at the time of his earlier disgrace, so now He might be holding out one last opportunity for redemption. Some Boston ministers wrote letters of support for his candidacy, which may have settled the matter in Cotton's mind; he did not take long to accept the position. Approaching old age, Cotton now contemplated a change as sudden, as radical, and as hazardous as any he had experienced. "I sit down astonished," he reflected to his wife, "& am musing whether it be a beginning of mercy & deliverence, or a lightning before death."[22] He left Plymouth in mid November 1698 and reached Charlestown three weeks later.

He arrived without his wife. Joanna chose not to accompany him for reasons that we must guess. Her health had declined and she may have felt unable to make the trip. Perhaps she simply was unwilling to leave home and children behind for an unfamiliar place with such an unhealthy reputation. She may have contemplated joining her husband later; certainly Cotton desired this. But also, there is the possibility that she believed the more serious allegations against her husband and the two had not yet found a way to heal the emotional wounds. Son Rowland wrote to his father, "mother seems not to know what to do abt coming to you . . . I suppose sheel write you her mind."[23] Joanna did write, keeping up as regular a correspondence as conditions permitted, and some of the last letters in this collection indicate that husband and wife had switched roles, with Joanna quietly assuming the job of news correspondent to her now remotely-settled husband.

"My Father," Josiah recalled, "had all ways a strong Impulse upon his spirit, that he should not dy in Plymo[uth] (as no Ministr had before him) which accordingly happened."[24] Cotton applied his customary energy to his new situation. By March 1699 he had helped to gather a church in Charlestown and become its pastor. He set about his work after the fashion of his early years in Plymouth, catechizing, preaching, and organizing fasts and private meetings. He "opposed gainsayers, satisfied the doubtful," and won new members. But there could be no repeat of his Plymouth successes in the southern colony. When yellow fever struck the town in August, the virulence and lethality of the outbreak matched those of any smallpox epidemic experience Cotton remembered from New England; at least 179 of the town's inhabitants succumbed to the disease. When Cotton himself became sick he lasted only three days, dying on 17 or 18 September 1699. The last letters in the collection tell how his family in New England received the news.

Cotton Mather's reaction was to believe that his uncle had atoned for past sins: "I have Reason to give great thanks unto Heaven, in that the Lord accepted that poor Man, to dy in the Service of the Church, After the Death which there had been upon all hopes of any such matter, by his Abdication from his work at Plymouth."[25] Even as he died in body Cotton, too, may have hoped that he had redeemed himself before God. Perishing along with his faithful in Charlestown, far from his home and without the comforts of family, Cotton nevertheless could feel that he had fulfilled the ministerial calling that had directed his life, despite the obstacles that his own weaknesses had thrown in the way. God's blessing surely flowed to him through the souls of the converted.

Editorial Method

OUR GOAL IN THIS EDITION IS TO PRESENT all known correspondence to and from John Cotton Jr. in chronological sequence and faithful transcription. All letters and documents are printed in full, excepting text lost through the deterioration of the archival material. Unlike many collections, these transcriptions also include notes made on the letters' address side. Cotton frequently indicated how long letters took in transit, and scholars of communications may find this data useful. We have striven to preserve the style and forms of Cotton and his contemporaries to the degree that this is possible in print, believing this approach to be important to scholars. We have likewise tried to minimize editorial intrusions in the documents, adding our marks only when necessary for clarity. We have provided footnotes for each document where required, to identify individuals and places, to clarify vague textual passages or to help contextualize letters within events of the period. Our purpose is to assist the reader's understanding and appreciation for the documents without unduly altering the original writers' creation.

Lofty purposes must occasionally bow to practicality and publishers' protocols, however, and the written word cannot be perfectly rendered in print. For the correspondence we have adopted the following rules and methods.

Presenting the Text

IN THE COURSE OF EDITING THE LETTERS passing to and from Cotton, we noticed patterns of correspondents and content analogous with distinct phases of Cotton's life and career. Accordingly, we have prefaced groups of letters, and some individual letters, with explanatory remarks to provide context and continuity.

Each letter or document begins with a heading that briefly indicates the origin, recipient, and date. In the transcriptions, dates are kept as written. We make no adjustments for "Old Style" or "New Style" dating. In the headings only, "split" dating for items generated between January and March is rendered in modern form, as "1694" for "1693/94," and so on. If dates are missing from the original or the original is misdated, presumed or corrected dates appear in brackets.

The great majority of letters in this collection followed a similar format; our standardization reflects that dominant configuration. All datelines appear at the right margin, salutations to the left. Writers rarely indented paragraphs in the seventeenth century; indents appear in this edition only if Cotton or his correspondents used them. Closings to the letters are placed on separate lines at the left margin, while signatures are also placed on separate lines, to the right. Postscripts begin following the signature line, at the left margin. A descriptive/provenance note follows each document preceding the footnotes and contains the names of the source institution and collection, the address on the manuscript (if a letter), the endorsement, notes by previous editors, and Cotton's remarks on letters he received. The document's condition is described if it is relevant.

We have retained original spelling, punctuation, and errors such as inadvertent repetitions. Cotton and his correspondents frequently used colons and semicolons where today would appear periods and commas. We have inserted a space following each of these marks, whether or not the writer seems to have done so. The capitalization of letters appears as written. Determining capitalized letters is often a matter of judgment, and while we cannot claim our judgments are definitive, we have made every effort to render these correctly. If the abbreviations of words are unclear, we supply the missing letters in brackets the first time they appear in a letter. There were relatively few thorns used for an initial "th" in an article or pronoun; we have retained these thorns, rendering them as the letter "y," which they resemble, and brought them to the line, thus using "y^e" for "the," "y^s" for "this," "y^m" for "them," and so forth. We have kept the seventeenth-century use of "i" for "j" as written. On the other hand, it is often difficult to tell when a writer intended to use "v" for "u" ("ovr" for "our"), as there is little difference in their appearance in the manuscripts. We have employed modern spellings for consistency. Some of Cotton's correspondents abbreviated "our" to "o^r." Tilde marks, indicating missing letters, appear only occasionally in this collection, and the missing letters are silently supplied. Brevigraphs raised above the line, often used in the names of months, are retained, as, "$Decemb^r$" or "$octb^r$."

Superscriptions and interlineations have been retained. Crossed-out words are enclosed in angle brackets and italicized, for example, <*had not*>. If letters of a word are missing or illegible but are easily identified by the word's context, we supply the remaining letters in brackets, as "bro[th]er." If no conjecture can be made, we leave the brackets empty and insert a number of spaces indicating the number of letters that appear to be missing. If a word is missing and not conjecturable, the missing word is indicated by brackets enclosing an ellipsis of three periods: "[. . .]." Two missing words are indicated by brackets enclosing four periods: "[. . . .]." A missing passage of more than two words is indicated by "[. . . .]" followed by a footnote estimating the amount of missing matter. Illegible words are designated "[illeg.]" or "[several words illeg.]." Conjectured words are enclosed in brackets with a question mark: "[church?]."

Acknowledgements

We incurred many debts to fellow scholars and friends in creating this collection. If, in the lines that follow, we have failed to acknowledge any of these we must, like Cotton, confess our guilt and beg pardon.

Many of the letters in this collection bear the marks of historian and Congregationalist minister Thomas Prince (1687–1758, H.C. 1707).[26] Throughout our notes to these letters, the phrases "Prince notes" or "In Prince's hand" reveal our great debt to him for preserving and annotating Cotton's correspondence. Cotton's letters probably owe their very survival to Prince's deep love of New England's history. Prince was from Sandwich on Cape Cod, once part of Plymouth colony, and his family corresponded with Cotton—letters from and to Prince's maternal grandfather, Gov. Thomas Hinckley, and his maternal grandmother, Mary Hinckley, appear in this collection, and his parents, Samuel and Mercy, and brother, Nathan, appear repeatedly as subjects, informants, and bearers, as does young Thomas himself. Three modern archival collections that bear Prince's name account for dozens of the letters in this volume: the Cotton-Prince Papers and the Prince Library at the Boston Public Library and the Thomas Prince Papers at the Massachusetts Historical Society. Prince's distinctive scrawled annotations also appear on dozens more letters scattered throughout other collections, such as in Miscellaneous Bound at the Massachusetts Historical Society.

Although Prince read history avidly beginning as a child, in 1728 he began work in earnest on a comprehensive chronology of New England's history. Drawing on his own extensive correspondence network, he asked ministers throughout New England to send him information, which augmented his own extensive reading.[27] Critics of *A Chronological History of New England* have noted that he did not use much of the local content that he requested but instead focused on crafting a medieval chronicle, beginning with Genesis and ending with the earliest days of New England in 1630.[28] He had hoped to reach the centennial year of 1730 in his coverage, but he never did.

A second attempt in 1755, published serially, yielded no better result despite a second round of letter inquiries and was discontinued after the third installment. But Prince's devotion to preservation makes his lackluster literary reputation seem insignificant; in the process of collecting materials for the *Chronological History*, he saved countless scribal and print manuscripts from destruction, including several documents crucial in American history, such as William Bradford's Letter-Book and *History of Plimoth Plantation*. A few of Cotton's letters survive only because Prince made manuscript copies of them, for the originals have since disappeared.[29] It is Prince's obsession with accurate dating—the hallmark of a chronicle—that appears most frequently in the Cotton letters; he patiently worked to date news within letters by referring to other letters or events with a known date. He carefully showed the trail he followed in his annotations, justifying a particular date based on its significance to other people and events. While we have often corrected Prince's work, his diligence is inspiring to anyone trying to tell the many stories that any personal letter contains.

Although Prince willed his vast documentary collection to his church, Old South in Boston, the contents were scattered quickly after his death in 1758, thanks in part to well-intentioned but forbidden borrowing, a sale by his son-in-law Lt. Gov. Moses Gill and, perhaps, marauding bands of Loyalists and Redcoats, if the often-told stories prove true. The Boston Public Library holds much of what remains of the printed material, and the manuscripts are scattered in many collections, primarily at the Massachusetts Historical Society.

Many libraries and archives have allowed us to publish from their manuscript collections. Their curators and reference librarians were unfailingly generous while we collected, copied and transcribed the letters and led us in many useful directions as we tried to annotate them as fully as possible. We thank Libby Bouvier of the Massachusetts State Archives; Peter Drummey and his redoubtable staff at the Massachusetts Historical Society; Thomas Knowles of the American Antiquarian Society; Eugene Zepp of the Rare Books Room at the Boston Public Library; the Guildhall Library, London; and the reading room staffs of the New England Historic Genealogical Society and Harvard's Houghton Library for their assistance. The Mayflower Room in the Plymouth Public Library was home for many months of annotation research, and we are grateful that Plymouth continues to support such an excellent collection for historians and genealogists alike to use freely. Kenneth Minkema generously and meticulously read the manuscript and offered great advice. His critique came at a crucial time; he praised the manuscript that we thought was complete but suggested some reasons why it was not quite finished, and the book is much the better for his wisdom. Kate Viens saved us from sloppy formatting, misplaced commas, incomplete citations and clumsy turns-of-phrase more often than we would like to recall. Her keen editing has made us better writers and more careful storytellers, and we are deeply grateful for her devotion to this project. John Tyler of the Colonial Society of Massachusetts enthusiastically supported our project from its inception and has shown infinite patience with us, knowing full well that this was going to take longer than we thought. We hope the result will have proven worth the wait.

SHEILA MCINTYRE & LEN TRAVERS

---

1. Josiah Cotton, "Account of the Cotton Family," 36, Houghton Library, Harvard University.
2. See "Report of Committee to General Court of Connecticut Colony," 20 March 1662.
3. *Publications of the Colonial Society of Massachusetts* 39 (1961): 60-61.
4. Daniel Gookin, *Historical Collections of the Indians in New England* (New York, 1972), 50-51.
5. For Cotton's missionary work on Martha's Vineyard, see Len Travers, "The Missionary Journal of John Cotton, Jr., 1666–1678," *Proceedings of the Massachusetts Historical Society* 109 (1999): 52-101.
6. *Records of the Colony of New Plymouth in New England,* ed. Nathaniel Shurtleff and David Pulsifer, 12 vols. (Boston, 1855–61), 10:329.
7. Publications of the Colonial Society of Massachusetts *Collections* (hereafter *CSM*), 22 (Boston, 1920), 144.
8. The records of the Plymouth church during Cotton's tenure are printed in *CSM,* 22:144-86.
9. Josiah Cotton, "Account of the Cotton Family," 47.
10. Josiah Cotton, "Account of the Cotton Family," 46.
11. *CSM,* 22:146.
12. See the letter from Joshua Moodey, 1 April 1676.
13. *CSM,* 22:150, 151.
14. *CSM,* 22:148.
15. Josiah Cotton, "Account of the Cotton Family," 36.
16. To Rowland Cotton, 8 and 9 December 1696.
17. Josiah Cotton, "Account of the Cotton Family," 47.
18. Arthur Lord, "Rev. John Cotton of Plymouth," Publications of the Colonial Society of Massachusetts *Transactions* 26 (1924–26): 79-81.
19. *The Diary of Samuel Sewall, 1674–1729*, ed. M. Halsey Thomas (New York, 1973), 1:378. If Cotton had gotten wind of Mather's remarks, he might understandably have regretted his defense of Mather six years earlier.
20. "The Diary of Cotton Mather, 1681–1708," ed. Worthington Chauncey Ford, *Massachusetts Historical Society Collections*, 7th ser., 8 (Boston, 1911), 236-37.
21. To Joanna Cotton, 8 July 1698.
22. To Joanna Cotton, 8 July 1698.
23. From Rowland Cotton, 25 April 1699.
24. Josiah Cotton, "Account of the Cotton Family," 37.
25. "Diary of Cotton Mather," 23 October 1699, 1:319-20.

26. "Thomas Prince" in John Langdon Sibley, *Biographical Sketches of Graduates of Harvard University, In Cambridge, Massachusetts* (Boston, 1873–), 5:341-68.

27. Thomas Prince, *A Chronological History of New England in the Form of Annals, Being a summary and exact Account of the most material Transactions and Occurrences relating to This Country, in the Order of Time where in they happened, from the Discovery by Capt Gosnold in 1602, to the Arrival of Governor Belcher in 1730, with an Introduction Containing A brief Epitome of the most remarkable Transactions and Events Abroad from the Creation; Including the connected Line of Time, the Succession of the Patriarchs and Sovereigns of the most famous Kingdoms & Empires, the gradual Discoveries of America, and the Progress of the Reformation to the Discovery of New England* (Boston, 1736).

28. John Van de Wetering, "Thomas Prince's *Chronological History*," *William and Mary Quarterly*, 3d ser., 18 (1961): 546-57.

29. See below, for example, John Cotton to Rowland Cotton, 31 January 1691.

Personal Notes

IN THE NINETEENTH CENTURY, when gentlemen scholars painstakingly collected and published the letters of so many early American correspondents, Cotton escaped largely unnoticed. Maybe the adultery accusations simply made him too hot to handle, especially since he was the son of the great spiritual founder of New England. No one even collected Cotton's letters into a "papers of" manuscript collection. Most of his letters sit in broad collections, such as those at the Massachusetts Historical Society, in "miscellaneous bound" or in the collected papers of someone else, such as the Curwen Papers at the American Antiquarian Society. Whenever I presented papers that included quotations from Cotton's correspondence, someone in the audience would enquire, "where are those letters?" So, in an appropriate reflection of Cotton's own habits of collaboration, this project was conceived at the suggestion of a few senior scholars after I delivered a conference paper on Cotton at the annual meeting of the Organization of American Historians in 1998. My thanks to Richard Brown, Ken Minkema and Mary Beth Norton for encouraging me to put my unfinished monograph on the shelf and dive into Cotton's world. Realizing that the task was too huge to tackle alone, I invited Len Travers, then of the Massachusetts Historical Society, to join me (he probably grew to regret that decision). Len's editing of Cotton's missionary journal may have hooked him on Cotton's infectious prose (and comparatively easy handwriting). My deep gratitude goes to him; he kept this project rolling when I feared it would never see print, and his dedication, wisdom and long-suffering devotion to "the fabric of our lives" never ceased to amaze me.

I have taken the Cotton project with me on several moves, and I am particularly grateful to Brian McKillop of Carleton University and my colleagues at SUNY Potsdam, especially Jim German and Geoffrey Clark, for their interest in my work. The Social Sciences and Humanities Research Council of Canada supported this work through a two-year postdoctoral fellowship. The late Sargent Bush and David Hall offered kind words of encouragement at an early stage of the project. Alan Taylor's and Emily Albu's friendship is invaluable, even as their prolific writing is humbling. Jonathan Shev and Louise Mundstock of UC Davis supplied the Latin transcriptions for the post-1680 letters. Dr. Jonathan Dann of the University of Michigan's Clements Library helped to decipher some particularly nebulous passages in the letters from Joseph Lord. John Huffman re-raised the superscriptions that had mistakenly become lowered (thanks to technology) in dozens of letters from the Boston Public Library on very short notice.

Michael von Herff, a historian temporarily in exile in the corporate world, reminds me that "Love carrys through many difficulties easily & makes heavy burdens light," as John wrote to Joanna. His constant good humor and support made the work possible, and my gratitude and love are written into every word. I understand Cotton's fear, pride and love for his children much more vividly since becoming a mother; William, Silas and Lucy von Herff have been the best excuse to leave the quiet of the library and play. My family, especially my mother, has listened patiently to all my stories about Cotton and spent many days taking care of my children so I could spend countless hours in the seventeenth century.

During a lunch break at the MHS with some other early Americanists, I admitted that when I read these manuscript letters I actually "heard" the writer's voice, which made the difficult handwriting and language easy for me to understand. Believing that they all shared this experience, I was surprised when they laughed and warned me not to circulate that too broadly. Ignoring their advice, I hope that readers also "hear" Cotton's voice when they read this volume. Reading someone else's mail always carries an illicit thrill. Cotton was naive enough to gossip and share his emotions with both intended and unintended readers, even when his candor often got him into trouble. Bringing his letters to a wider audience is exactly what Cotton would have wanted—he thrived on the notoriety that his letter-writing connections gained him—and I hope that modern readers will enjoy the correspondence of the "bad boy of the Cotton clan" as much as we did.

Sheila McIntyre

Personal Notes

CONTRARY TO WHAT DR. MCINTYRE SUGGESTS, my only regret concerning this project is that I did not think of it first. As Sheila relates, I was busy with Cotton's Indian missionary journal at the same time that she was exploring the informal news nexuses of seventeenth-century New England, to which, of course, Cotton was an important contributor. I was also familiar with Cotton's correspondence touching upon the King Philip's War years and relating to my particular interest, the history of Plymouth Colony. But it was Sheila who approached me with the idea of getting Cotton's entire correspondence into one volume. We two had a nodding acquaintance from our graduate school days at Boston University, but it was this tragic, yet eminently familiar and approachable figure from the past, and those others whose experiences he preserved in writing, who made us friends. We have become "gossips" ourselves, in the antique form of two who eagerly share news about others—only our subjects are long dead. I have enjoyed my part in this endeavor immensely, but without Sheila's initial proposal for the project, Cotton might still reside in that literary limbo to which nineteenth-century historians (for whatever reason) consigned him. It is just as well that neither she, nor I, knew at the time what claims Mr. Cotton *et al* would make on our lives. We'll know better next time.

In addition to the acknowledgments we have made above, I too must confess my ignorance of Latin and thank my one-time mentors Joseph Scionti and Kevin Hargreaves for translations of certain passages in the pre-1681 letters. Mark Peterson, a scholar of the Old Colony church and one of our readers, provided much encouragement and saved us from at least one embarrassing gaffe. Doug Winiarski, who has his sights set on another member of the Cotton family, likewise shared information and insights generously. Nathaniel Philbrick alerted me in the nick of time to a letter I would otherwise have overlooked. And the Rev. Peter Gomes, when I have been fortunate enough to steal a few minutes of conversation from that wise and very busy man, has inspired me with his eagerness to hold the finished volume in his hands. That makes three of us, at least.

And if we may be allowed to dedicate this volume, we think it appropriate to do so to the patient, longsuffering spouses—Joanna, Carolyn, and Michael—for all of whom we have acquired ever-greater regard over the course of this project.

LEN TRAVERS

ONE

Failure in Connecticut 1662–1664

FITTINGLY, PERHAPS, THE FIRST DOCUMENTS in this volume illuminate what was arguably the defining period of Cotton's life. His alleged misconduct and subsequent fall from grace in Connecticut deprived him of a promising career in that colony and indirectly led him to semi-exile on Martha's Vineyard, to missionary work, and to Plymouth Colony—almost certainly not the career path he envisioned when he graduated from Harvard College. By leaving Connecticut when he did, however, Cotton may have been spared difficulties of another sort. By 1662, the commencement of Cotton's personal troubles, Gov. John Winthrop Jr. had obtained a royal charter for his colony of Connecticut that engrossed the neighboring New Haven colony. Several years of protest ensued before New Haven grudgingly accepted the all but inevitable. John Davenport, a founder of New Haven and an old friend of Cotton's father, was bitterly opposed to the union and to the decisions of the New England synod of that year, which adopted new strategies to promote full church membership (what nineteenth-century scholars dubbed the "Half Way Covenant"). Cotton's Connecticut mentor, the Reverend Samuel Stone of Hartford, favored both union and the synod's recommendations. There was no love lost between Stone and Davenport, and Cotton eventually would have had to choose his camp. Perhaps he had done so already; his own father-in-law, Bryan (Bray) Rosseter of Guilford, New Haven Colony, openly despised and defied the Davenport faction.

A committee of two magistrates and two ministers including Stone met to determine the facts surrounding the complaints against Cotton. Although the committee's report, printed here, found reason to fault most everyone involved in the complicated affair, its conclusions were most damaging to Cotton. The committee members seemed more annoyed with Cotton's demeanor than with his alleged misdeeds. Cotton even complained that *he* was the victim in this case and that the imputed sexual impropriety was in fact of another party. It may be significant that the party in question, as well as another of Cotton's accusers, were of the family of the recently deceased Gov. Thomas Wells, for whose estate Cotton was executor, and that some Wells family members had complained of Cotton's stewardship. Whatever the case, the committee clearly felt that Cotton was not telling them the whole truth and was at least guilty of astonishingly poor judgment. The report's harshest words were for the young minister, pointing to his "sinfull Rach unpeacabell" speech, "espeasially Considering his place and [charge]."

Report of Committee to General Court of Connecticut Colony

20 MARCH 1662

Whear as We whose names are subCribed wear appointed by the Cort & desiered by the partis Conserned to hear and determin the maters Controversall between them apone our patient hearing serious Consideration of all things aleged on both sides we doe give in our determination as follows
first as to Steven Scott his Charge aganst mr Cotten as first yt he minds noe Lectuers nothing but his wife & drinking & secondly in reading goodwife rights acknowledgement yt left out or put in as he pleased in these to we find him uterly to falle as to Scotte 3d Carge viz that the Judgment or Curse of god Would not Remove frome Wetherfield whilst mr Cott aboad ther[1] this we doe not se sufiCiently proved therfor desier him to <*exspres for the time to Come a due Christian wach ouer him selfe Respecting any such Behauer Conserning ye Mor*> acknowledg his great sene ther in Conserning mr Cottens going into mis Chittendins[2] Chamber with good wife right pretending mearly to see the furnituer of the hous we aprehend A foolish Curiosity and a mater of noe good Report and desiering him to exsprese for the time to Come a due xts[3] wach ouer himselfe Respecting any such behauour Conserning the more grose acte mentioned in goodwife wright testimony Respecting mr Cotten we se not sufficient euedenc to ConClude the sam Respecting the Carge laied to mr Cotten that hee so spack on Purpas to wex[4] mis wells[5] we judge his exspresions hear in to be sinfull Rach unpeacabell espeasially Considering his place and Carge to mr Cottens Carge of mr Samu wells[6] Respecting his testimony that it was fals thoe he Retracts his words & diverts them to another senc we Judge his speach hearin as indiscret Rach & inConsiderat as to mr Cottens Carge of mis wells to bee guilty of lisiueous whorich practises this we do sentence as a Carge of a veary high defaming natuer Rashly spoken and in no way Proued by him against her, to the sinfull striving aleged by mis wells against mr Cottene with her we se not evedenc to Conclud it whereas ther was

a seming or intimated Charge of m^{r} Cotten in publick aganst m^{rs} wells as if she strove with hime as Joseph m^{is} did with Joseph[7] m^{r} Cotten doth befor us uterly Renounc the same namly all aperanc of any such Carge and therfor wee doe desiere the partis Conserned to Rest satefied her in wee do allso being deply sensabell of the Chastisinge hande of the Lord not only apon the partickuler Plac in the which the Parsons aboue Conserned lives but apon the holle Contery By Reasone of the Conteneued often Reneued: & greatly umbeling Deferances that haue aRose at wetherfield doe ernestly desier that all ther in & spesialy the Parsons now att warianc to Consider them self in quier why the allmighty Contendeth with them & Cloeth them with Peac & umbelnes of Mind & to exersis themselfs Daily to keep truth and love that the Weary God of Peac may be with them

Sam. Wilis=[8]
Sam. Stone=[9]
Sam. Hocker=[10]
John Allen:=[11]

March 20th 61=
62=

Andrew-Eliot Papers, Massachusetts Historical Society.

---

1. Wethersfield was already a troubled town by the time Cotton arrived there. In 1659 some townsmen, disgusted with the church's changing baptismal policies, left Wethersfield and, along with Hartford dissidents, formed the Connecticut River town of Hadley in Massachusetts. Not all of the dissenters went, however, and lingering resentments may have fueled the impression that the town was subject to a "Judgment or Curse of god." Samuel Harrison Rankin Jr., "Conservatism and the Problem of Change in the Congregational Churches of Connecticut, 1660–1760" (Ph.D. diss., Kent State University, 1971), 21, 36.

2. Probably Joan Sheaffe Crittenden (d.1668), widow of William Crittenden of Guilford and New Haven. An influential man, Crittenden had been one of the founders of the New Haven church, a lieutenant in the colony's militia, and a magistrate. James Savage, *A Genealogical Dictionary of the First Settlers of New England*, 4 vols. (1860–62; facsimile reprint, Baltimore, Md., 1990), 1:382.

3. Christian.

4. Vex.

5. Elizabeth Deming Foote Wells, widow of Nathaniel Foote and second wife of Gov. Thomas Wells. Savage, *Genealogical Dictionary*, 4:478.

6. One of the sons of the late Gov. Thomas Wells, who with his siblings had recently made complaint to the court at Hartford concerning Cotton's handling of Gov. Wells's estate. Samuel was admitted a freeman of the colony in 1657 and in the year before had been named ensign for the Wethersfield militia. J. Hammond Trumbull, *The Public Records of the Colony of Connecticut* (Hartford, 1850), 1:297, 311; *Records of the Particular Court of Connecticut 1639–1663, Collections of the Connecticut Historical Society,* 22 (Hartford, 1928), 242.

7. A reference to Gen. 39, in which Joseph spurns the sexual advances of his master's wife and is accused by her of the wrongdoing.

8. The names of the committee members are all entered in the same hand as that of the report. Samuel Willis (1632–1709) was chosen a magistrate in Hartford shortly after his graduation from Harvard in 1653; he held the position until 1685. A sometime commissioner to the United Colonies of New England and later an assistant to the Connecticut General Court, he was also actively engaged in trade, frequently traveling to the West Indies. John Langdon Sibley, *Biographical Sketches of Graduates of Harvard University, In Cambridge, Massachusetts* (Boston, 1873–) (hereafter *Sibley's Harvard Graduates*), 1:323-25.

9. Rev. Samuel Stone (1602–1663). In 1637 he negotiated with Natives to purchase the Connecticut land that became Hartford, where he was minister until his death. Allen Tolman and Dumas Malone, eds., *Dictionary of American Biography* (New York, 1957) (hereafter *DAB*).

10. Rev. Samuel Hooker (1635–1697), son of the famous Rev. Thomas Hooker, founder and first pastor of Hartford. Samuel preached in Plymouth Colony in about 1657; in 1661 he declined the pastorate of Springfield in favor of that of Farmington, Connecticut, where he remained until his death. *Sibley's Harvard Graduates,* 1:348-52.

11. A lieutenant in the Hartford militia, John Allen was nominated for the magistracy in October 1661 and elected in May 1662. Trumbull, *Public Records of the Colony of Connecticut*, 1:373, 378.

From John Davenport — 23 March 1663

Ultimately, the committee's recommendation for a peaceful resolution did not prevail, either with the Connecticut people or with Boston's First Church, of which Cotton was still a member. The following letter from his father's old friend probably did little to cheer him. Although a year had passed since the committee's investigation, Cotton's troubles had not abated, in part, it seems, due to his stubborn reluctance to publicly acknowledge and repent his transgressions.

To M^r^ <*John Cotton*>

DEARE S^R^,

Y^rs^ dated ye 17th. of ye 11th. m.[2] I received ye 9th. day of ye 12. m. And having so good an opportunity, by so safe an hand as M^r^. Sam: Streete,[3] I returne such Answer as I can to y^r^ Letter. wherein I observe wth thanckfullnes y^r^ kinde acceptance of my loving freenes in expressing my deepe sense of y^r^ sinfull miscarriages. I could not have approved my faithfulnes to God, to you, & to my owne Conscience, if I had neglected such a season of so speaking to you, as I did, y^t^ being ye first opportunity wch was given me of treating wth you, ore tenus,[4] about such matters as were not fit to be committed to wrighting, wch might fall into other hands, to ye blemishing of y^r^ name, wch I desired to preserve unspotted, by me, while I sincerely endeavoured y^e^

healing of y^{r} soul. how often have I fervently desired y^{t} as you beare boath y^{r} fathers names. so you might hold forth ye virtues of Christ, in ye spirit & Conversacon, wch eminently shined in him! Thus you would be knowne to be his son, morally, by imitacon, as well as naturally, by generacon, wch would have given you a double interest, in ye hearts of Gods people, who knew, loved, & highly honoured y^{r} blessed Father, who being dead would thus have lived in you, as worthy Mr. Hooker, doth in his good son, at Farmington.[5] Nor am I out of hope y^{t} yet it may be so, if ye Lord convince you powerfully of y^{r} former sins, & humble you effectually for y^{m} to Justifie wisdomes Counsels by y^{r} holding forth publickly y^{r} unfeined repentance, as I told you Origen[6] did, wth many teares, y^{t} scandal might be removed, wch while it remains, will be *to katechon*,[7] to hinder ye acceptance of y^{r} exercise of guifts in preaching, wth men, & ye blessing of it from God. You promised y^{t} you would send me a Copie of y^{r} publick acknowledgemt, wch is reported to be slight, & unsatisfying, & y^{t} you would propound some things in reference to y^{r} case, for further advise.

But you have done neither. whereby I am dissadvantaged from giving you y^{t} helpe, wch otherwise I might have done, wth Gods assistance. It is a temptacon from satan, to hinder you from propounding y^{r} case, upon a secret expectacion, to see more of God in it, hoping y^{t} God, who helped me before to speake as if I had knowne ye inward frame of y^{r} heart, will againe direct me to speake some thing to ye troubles of y^{r} heart, though I be not fully acquainted wth y^{m}. For though if you had acquainted me wth y^{r} troubles, & ye grounds of y^{m}, & the effects, my bowells would have bene troubled wth you, & for you, & from a true sympathy I should have endeavoured to asswage y^{r} greife, or to direct y^{r} apprehencons, or otherwise to speake suitably to y^{r} case; yet it is not God's manner, nor may you expect it, to reveal to his serv^{ts}, by immediate inspiracion, the cases of others, w^{ch}, by his ordinances, they aught to expresse, y^{m}selves & seeke helpe in from others, y^{t} ye communion of saints may be preserved & exercised among y^{m} mutually. Thus you see how satan tempteth you to tempt God. As for me, be you assured y^{t}, in any way of God, you shall finde me really ready, upon all occasions, to be helpfull to you as ye case may require. Farewel & account me, as I am,

Y^{r} true freind in ye Lord,

John Davenporte

N. H. ye 23: of ye 1st. m. 1662./3.

S^{R},

I thanck you for my letters to y^{r} Father, wch you sent me, according to my desire & y^{r} promise. some I rec^{d}. by Edm: Toolie,[8] & some by Jacob molines,[9] wth y^{r} letter. If any yet remaine wth you; you will further oblige me if you send y^{m} to me. iterum Vale.[10]

Mather Papers 1:29, Prince Library, Rare Book and Manuscripts, Boston Public Library.

---

1. Rev. John Davenport (1597–1670) was vicar of St. Stephen's, London, when John Cotton Sr. fled his parish in 1632. The elder Cotton apparently stayed with Davenport while arranging transport for himself and his wife, John Jr.'s mother. Davenport emigrated five years later, in time to participate in the Antinomian controversy. He left Boston in 1638 to be pastor of New Haven. He strenuously opposed both the 1662 synod's recommendations (dubbed the "Half Way Covenant" by later historians) and the 1665 union with Connecticut. His controversial return to Boston as the fourth pastor of First Church in 1668 led to the withdrawal of a group of members who then founded Third Church (Old South) *DAB*.
2. Not found.
3. Samuel Streete (c. 1635–1717) had not yet finished his degree at Harvard at this time but was of an age not to be styled the "Sir" customarily applied to younger matriculating students. Following his graduation in 1664 he taught the Hopkins Grammar School in Hartford and was ordained pastor of the Wallingford church in or about 1674. *Sibley's Harvard Graduates,* 1:160-62.
4. "Up to that point."
5. Samuel Hooker.
6. Origen of Alexandria (c. 185–253), a Greek Christian father, who supposedly asserted the ultimate probable salvation of all souls, including those of the fallen angels.
7. "The obstacle."
8. Edmund Toolie or Tooly of New Haven (d. 1685). Savage, *Genealogical Dictionary*, 4:312.
9. Jacob Moline of New Haven.
10. "Again, hail."

To John Winthrop Jr.,[1]

8 March 1664

Ultimately, it may not have mattered whether Cotton had confessed his sins or not; there was an influential and tenacious faction in Wethersfield that wanted Cotton gone, and by early 1664 he had lost his pulpit there. He was also in deep trouble with the First Church. In the four letters that follow, Cotton solicits John Winthrop Jr.'s aid in facing the Boston brethren's disciplinary actions. With each letter, Cotton seems more intent on justifying himself, tenaciously rejecting certain levels of submission beyond what he felt strictly necessary. It seems a small wonder, then, that the church did not accept his first, apparently half-hearted repentance and excommunicated him. By the time of his last letter to Winthrop, in November of that tumultuous year, he was still jobless but may already have been preparing for his new position in Great Harbor (Edgartown), where he took his family in January 1665. There is no evidence that Cotton ever wrote to Winthrop again.

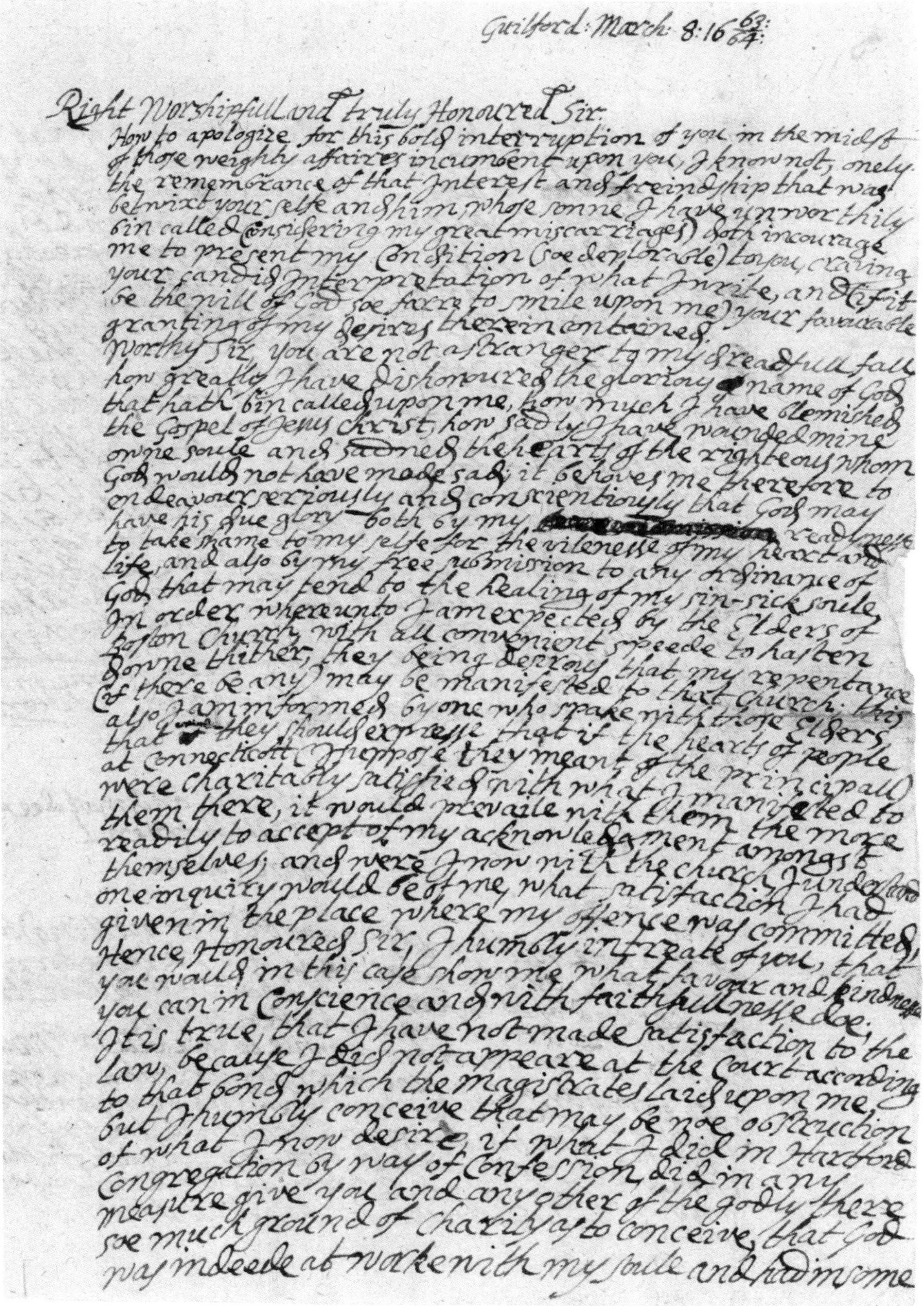

Guilford: March 8: 16 63/64:

Right Worshipfull and truly Honoured Sir.
How to apologize for this bold interruption of you in the midst
of those weighty affaires incumbent upon you, I know not, onely
the remembrance of that Interest and freindship that was
betwixt your selfe and him, whose sonne I have unworthily
bin called (considering my great miscarriages) doth incourage
me to present my Condition (soe deplorable) to you, craving
your candid interpretation of what I write, and (if it
be the will of God soe farre to smile upon me) your favourable
granting of my desires therein contained.
Worthy Sir, you are not a stranger to my dreadfull fall
how greatly I have dishonoured the glorious name of God
that hath bin called upon me, how much I have blemished
the Gospel of Jesus Christ, how sadly I have wounded mine
owne soule and sadned the hearts of the righteous whom
God would not have made sad; it behoves me therefore to
endeavour seriously and conscientiously that God may
have his due glory both by my [redacted] readinesse
to take shame to my selfe for the vilenesse of my heart and
life, and also by my free submission to any ordinance of
God that may tend to the healing of my sin-sick soule,
In order whereunto I am expected by the Elders of
Boston Church with all convenient speede to hasten
downe thither, they being desirous that my repentance
(if there be any) may be manifested to that Church: this
also I am informed by one who spake with those Elders
that they should expresse that if the hearts of people
at Connecticott (I suppose they meant of the principall)
were charitably satisfied with what I manifested to
them there, it would prevaile with them the more
readily to accept of my acknowledgment amongst
themselves; and were I now with the church I understand
one inquiry would be of me, what satisfaction I had
given in the place where my offence was committed,
Hence, Honoured Sir, I humbly intreate of you, that
you would in this case show me what favour and kindnesse
you can in Conscience and with faithfullnesse doe.
It is true, that I have not made satisfaction to the
Law, because I did not appeare at the Court according
to that bond which the Magistrates laid upon me,
but I humbly conceive that may be noe obstruction
of what I now desire, if what I did in Hartford
Congregation by way of Confession, did in any
measure give you and any other of the godly there
soe much ground of charity as to conceive, that God
was indeede at worke with my soule and had in some

John Cotton Jr. to John Winthrop Jr., March 8, 1663/64.
Courtesy of the Massachusetts Historical Society.

GUILFORD: MARCH: 8: 1663/64

RIGHT WORSHIPFULL AND TRULY HONOURED SIR.

How to apologize for this bold interruption of you in the midst of those weighty affaires incumbent upon you, I know not, onely the remembrance of that Interest and freindship that was betwixt your selfe and him, whose sonne I have unworthily bin called (considering my great miscarriages) doth incourage me to present my Condition (soe deplorable) to you, craving your candid Interpretation of what I write, and (if it be the will of God soe farre to smile upon me) your favourable granting of my desires therein contained.

Worthy Sir, you are not a stranger to my dreadfull fall, how greatly I have dishonoured the glorious name of God that hath bin called upon me, how much I have blemished the Gospel of Jesus christ, how sadly I have wounded mine owne soule and sadned the hearts of the righteous whom God would not have made sad; it behoves me therefore to endeavour seriously and conscientiously that God may have his due glory—both by my [. . . .][2] readynesse to take shame to my selfe for the vilenesse of my heart and Life, and also by my free submission to any ordinance of God that may tend to the healing of my sin-sick soule, In order whereunto I am expected by the Elders of Boston Church, with all convenient speede to hasten downe thither, they being desirous that my repentance (if there be any) may be manifested to that church; this also I am informed by one who spake with those Elders, that they should expresse that if the hearts of people at Connecticott (I suppose they meant of the principall) were charitably satisfied with what I manifested to them there, it would prevaile with them the more readily to accept of my acknowledgment amongst themselves; and were I now with the church, I understand one inquiry would be of me, what satisfaction I had given in the place where my offence was committed, Hence, Honoured Sir, I humbly intreate of you, that you would in this case show me what favour and kindnesse you can in Conscience and with faithfullnesse doe; It is true, that I have not made satisfaction to the Law, because I did not appeare at the Court according to that bond which the Magistrates Laid upon me, but I humbly conceive that may be noe obstruction of what I now desire, if what I did in Hartford Congregation by way of Confession, did in any measure give you and any other of the godly there soe much ground of Charity as to conceive, that God was indeede at worke with my soule and had in some measure affected my heart with the sense of my great transgressions; the signifying of something of this nature, <I hope> by letter to the Elders or church of Boston, I hope would be a service acceptable to God, and that which would exceedingly oblige a poore, distressed creature to you. If God move your heart hereunto, I should hope both Mr Allyns,[3] Capt: Talcot[4] and Mr Richards[5] Deacon Migatt[6] would concurre with you herein (or at least some of them.) Sir, Could I obtaine that favour of you as to conferre with these or some of them as you have any occasion, with what speede you can, or any others whome you shall Judge meete to acquaint with the matter, as from yourselfe, It will be a courtesy, I hope I shall never forget to be truly thankfull for; I know something of this kinde, if any thinge be attaineable, will be expected by the church, and of what use it may be by Gods blessing, I beleve you easily see. Sir, I have noe doubt of your concealing these lines. I leave the case with you humbly begging of God to guide you therein, and beseeching of your earnest prayers to God for me, that He would effectually remember his mercy to me, in the deepe humbling of my soule for sin, and soe fitting me for all the grace I neede.

I rest, Sir, your obliged, and most deepely distressed friend

John Cotton

SIR,

I purpose within this moneth (God willing) to goe for Boston by the Seaside, if you please soe farre to condescend as to informe me what may be done, it will greatly incourage me to hasten thither.

My Mother presents her service to you and Mris Winthrop[7] she earnestly desires you to tender her condition with the rest of the family, her husband and son being soe violently torne from her by soe threatning a Providence, that you would improove the power God hath betrusted you with, for their comfortable and safe restoring to the family againe which is truly distressed for the want of them.

The Winthrop Papers 12:48, Massachusetts Historical Society. Addressed "These For the Right Worshipfull, his worthily Honoured freind, John Winthrop Esquire, Governour of the Colony of Connecticott, at his house, in Hartford." Endorsed "Mr. J: Cotton.

---

1. John Winthrop Jr. (1606–1676), eldest son of Gov. John Winthrop of Massachusetts Bay, was named governor of the Connecticut plantations by founders lords Saye and Sele and Lord Brooke in 1635. After some years of moving among Connecticut, Massachusetts, and New Haven, he settled permanently in Hartford after being elected governor in 1657. He served in that office continually until his death. On a mission to England from 1661 to 1663, Winthrop was made a member of the prestigious Royal Society and won a surprisingly liberal charter for Connecticut that annexed the New Haven colony. *DAB*.
2. Two or three words crossed out.
3. Probably Matthew Allyn, a magistrate and moderator of the General Assembly. Trumbull, *Public Records of the Colony of Connecticut*, 1:425.
4. Capt. John Talcot of Hartford was made Major of the Hartford County militias. George M. Bodge, *Soldiers of King Philip's War* (1906; reprint, Baltimore, Md., 2000), 467.
5. Possibly James Richards of Hartford, merchant and Commissioner to the United Colonies of New England. Henry R. Stiles, *The History of Ancient Wethersfield, Connecticut* (New York, 1904), 1:291.
6. Probably Joseph Mygatt or Mygate of Hartford, who frequently served as a juryman for Connecticut's Particular Court. *Records of the Particular Court of Connecticut*, 20-199 *passim*.
7. Winthrop Jr. married his second wife, Elizabeth Reade, in 1635. *DAB*.

To John Winthrop Jr., 28 March 1664

GUILFORD: MARCH: 28: 1664:

[RI]GHT WORSHIPFULL AND TRULY HONOURED SIR.

About three weekes since I made bold to trouble you with a few lines, the contents of which I neede not now to repeate. God by his Providence giving one opportunity more of sending up, before my going into the Bay,[1] I could not omitt the reiterating of my request to you, that if you can doe any thinge in uprightnesse that may tend to Gods honour and to the alleviating at the least, the burthen, which otherwise may fall and lye more heavy upon me, [. . . .][2] that you will please now to doe it; I shall account your kindnesse herein a reall smile from heaven, and a reall obligation of your poore, distressed friend to you: Sir, I purpose the next weeke, at the furthest to begin my Journey to the Bay and to goe by the seaside, a word from you before that time, will be very acceptable, if you please soe farre to condescend to me; you may command my service to carry letters for you to the Bay, I purpose to call at your son Newmans[3] as I goe to Hampton. Sir, By my father Rosseter,[4] you may convey letters hither. I beg your prayers for me,

In haste, I rest, Sir, your distressed, unworthy friend

John Cotton[5]

The Winthrop Papers 12:49, Massachusetts Historical Society.

---

1. Massachusetts Bay.
2. Four or five words crossed out.
3. Winthrop Jr.'s eldest daughter, Elizabeth, married Rev. Antipas Newman of Wenham, Massachusetts, in 1658. Robert C. Black III, *The Younger John Winthrop* (New York and London, 1966), 187-88.
4. Bryan Rosseter, Cotton's father-in-law. See the letter of 24 September from Bryan Rosseter, below.
5. Despite whatever help Winthrop may have provided, Boston's First Church excommunicated Cotton for "lascivious uncleane practices with three women and his horrid lying to hide his sinne." Humiliated, Cotton made a "penitential acknowledgment openly confessing his sinnes" and was reinstated to church membership five weeks later. *Publications of the Colonial Society of Massachusetts* 39 (1961): 60-61.

To John Winthrop Jr., 11 October 1664

GUILFORD: OCTOBER: 11: 1664:

HONOURABLE SIR

I am bold once againe to trouble you in this kinde, with reference to that satisfaction etc formerly spoken of. God by his good hand of Providence soe disposed, that two of the persons principally concerned in this matter, were Lately at this towne, I noe sooner heard of their being here; but I immediately attended the tendring of satisfaction to them, God soe farre appeared therein, as that the woman declared her selfe to be fully satisfied; soe did the man also, onely he added this Condition, viz, if I had sent up such letters as were to be communicated to the Congregation, and to particular persons; I lookt at my selfe as principally ingaged to indeavour the satisfaction of these above mentioned, for some reasons not fitt to be written, and therefore acknowledge it to be the good hand of God, to give me soe farre an opportunity of soe speaking with them; But the mans Condition being such, it confirmes me the more strongly in the apprehension of the necessity of reading that letter publickly. Mr Ston is now here, who informes me of your Journey to wethersfield etc for which I desire to blesse God, and to acknowledge my reall thankfulnesse to your selfe for soe great a kindnesse; By what replyes, I understand, you had from one, I am still more and more inclinable to beleve, that everyone concerned will not manifest actuall satisfaction, If God soe dispose, I desire to submitt to his will therein; however, that is not soe fully expected at Boston, all they Looke to heare of, is, that I have regularly tendered my acknowldgements to them, this being done and testified will comfortably issue matters there, and without this, I feare I shall be greatly damnifyed, not onely upon spirituall accounts, but temporall also, for I am informed by letters lately received from the Bay, that there is a considerable summe amongst my friends there, privately collected and intended for me, but it will not be sent to me till they heare what I have done for the satisfaction of offended persons at Connecticott: Sir, I know the Generall Court is now soe neere,[1] together with other weighty affaires that may lye upon you, that it is not for me to expect you can have the least opportunity of consummating this matter for me, but when those occasions are ended, I would humbly beg of you to be further mindfull of me, that soe I may obtaine Testimony to show at Boston, that I have answered their expectations.[2] If the persons, at whose house you were, or any others should say, that what is done should satisfy them, if I would come up, and speake soe much my selfe face to face, I pray, Let it be dasht, and their expectations of any such thing, for I have some spetiall reasons within my selfe, that doe wholy take off my minde from any inclination to come up as yett, besides I have heard that some in wethersfield doe but waite for such an opportunity of my being there, for the venting of the old prejudices of spirit against me; (sub sigillo[3] be it spoken) which makes me feare my coming up, would proove greatly to my dammage; But if any should persist in such a motion, I would intreat you, having tendred the letters, to desert the businesse, onely with your Test. that such and such acknowledgements have bin presented to them. If you should have any opportunity to speake with those, to whome I spake at this towne, I doubt not but they will owne the truth of what I have now written, and soe you will be capable of asserting that also; my purpose is, God willing, to goe to Boston, the next moneth by the seaside, but I may not, I must not goe thither till this spetiall matter be effected; worthy Sir, I beg pardon for my greate boldnesse with you, knowing your wonted bowels, towards persons in distresse, doth thus farre embolden me; I beg your earnest prayers for me, resting,

Sir, yours much obliged

John Cotton

The Winthrop Papers 12:49, Massachusetts Historical Society.

---

1. The Connecticut General Assembly met at Hartford on 13 October 1664. Trumbull, *Public Records of the Colony of Connecticut*, 1:431.
2. Cotton's restoration to the Boston church apparently came with the condition that he make every sincere effort to mend fences in Connecticut.
3. Literally "under the seal." Cotton probably means that he has learned of rumors to the effect.

To John Winthrop Jr., 2 November 1664

Guilford: November: 2: 1664

Right Worshipfull

I have bin bold to trouble you very much already, but am enforced once more to beg of you to tender my deplorable condition soe farre as to consider what further may be done, after soe many unsuccessfull indeavours, for the more full issuing of this soe uncomfortable a businesse; I was in good hopes you would have returned home this way, and then I should have had an opportunity of more full discourse with you; I have mett with Mr Allyn here, and have informed him how the case stands, as farre as I know of it; and he is fully of the minde, that there would be noe danger, but much advantage by reading of that letter to the Congregation publickly; what though M^r^ welles[1] be not satisfied, and it may be some others more remotely concerned of the like minde? that cannot in the least prejudice me at Boston; for the

Elders and others did expresse themselves that they did not expect to heare that all concerned were actually satisfied; it would be enough to them, that I did verbally or by writing make such acknowledgements as carried with them the nature of a Just satisfaction. Therefore, worthy Sir, I would humbly beg of you that you would forward the reading of that letter, if it be possible, the next sabbath; I cannot goe to Boston, till that be done, with out apparent hazard from the church there, there is an absolute necessity, for my comfort, that it should be soe; Now when the letters are read, I desire John Allyn to send them both to me, wi[th] your testimonies that M^{r} M: and [. . .] and their wives are fully satisfied, and that acknowledgments were read in publick [&] communicated in private, and then I leave it with Boston to Judge, whether I [have?] not fully attended the rule, I have gr[ounds?] enough to think, it will give full cont[ent] to them there: Honoured Sir, I must [beg the?] hastning of this, for I stay for nothi[ng but?] this: I am ready for my Journey [. . .] and dare not step one foote forward [. . .] till this be done at wethersfield, the c[old] weather is neere, and I am afraid to [wait?] above one weeke longer or ten dayes a[t] furthest, least winter should stop m[y] Journey, or make it very uncomfort[able.] Good Sir, I crave pardon for my bo[ldness?] and beg your granting my desire wi[th all?] possible expedition, and let me t[hough?] unworthy have the benefit of your da[ily] prayers;

I rest, Sir, yours affectionately ob[edient]

John Cotton

The Winthrop Papers 12:49, Massachusetts Historical Society. The left margin was trimmed sometime after the letter was written, cutting off some right-margin words and letters on the reverse.

---

1. Samuel Wells.

TWO

Plymouth's New Minister
1669–1674

A PERIOD OF NEARLY FIVE YEARS separates Cotton's last letter to John Winthrop Jr. and the beginning of this second cycle of correspondence. This gap, the longest in this volume, is particularly unfortunate, for it comprises nearly three years that Cotton spent on Martha's Vineyard, ministering to the English there and developing his new role as a missionary to the island Natives. There again, Cotton fell afoul of authority, quarreling with island proprietor Thomas Mayhew and forcing the Commissioners of the United Colonies of New England to arbitrate the matter. As had happened in Connecticut, the authorities found Cotton to be most at fault; or at least, it was his removal to Plymouth in late 1667 that afforded the easiest remedy to the clash of personalities.[1]

In Plymouth, Cotton found a church much in need of a shepherd's guiding hand, and the letters that follow give some idea of the range of tasks facing a young minister who takes over the direction of a somewhat dilapidated church. With characteristic energy, Cotton launched himself into his work, reenergizing church members and their families with frequent visits and home catechising and restoring church discipline. His sincerity and charisma, coupled with the fact that Plymouth had lacked a minister and the sacraments for some years, attracted dozens of new members to the church. Some of his correspondence at this time clearly concerned church "housecleaning," such as tracking down former members who had drifted away from the town without formally terminating their church affiliation. Formal dismissals or transfers to new churches usually followed these transactions. A necessary part of Cotton's job involved building relationships with his colleagues who were ministering to the other churches of Plymouth Colony, most notably Thomas Whalley of Barnstable and Noah Newman of Taunton. Those letters in which the ministers exchange advice on thorny matters of doctrine and discipline make clear just how important these relationships were. It is interesting to note how Cotton's lineage, and the relative prestige of being pastor

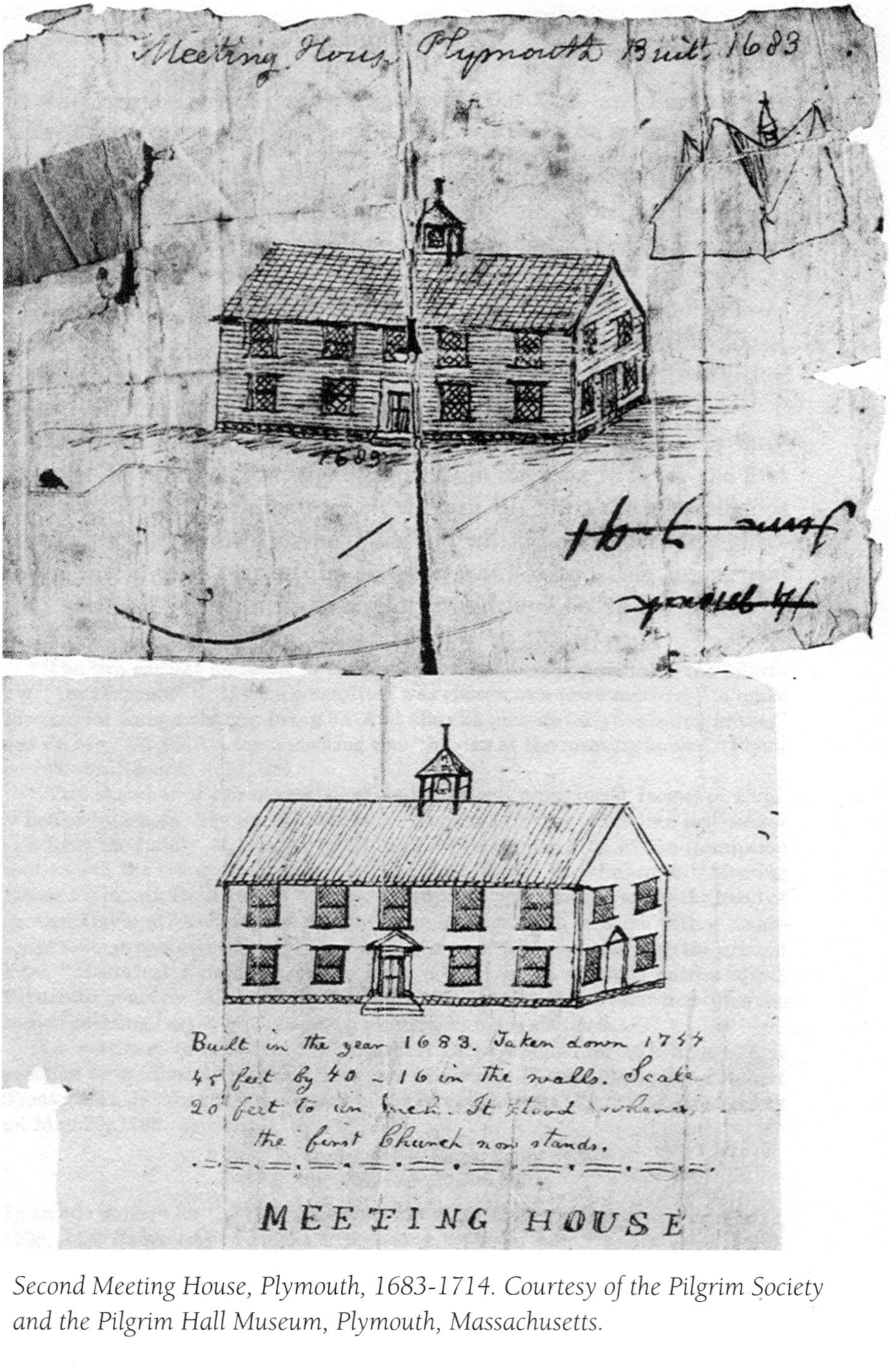

Second Meeting House, Plymouth, 1683-1714. Courtesy of the Pilgrim Society and the Pilgrim Hall Museum, Plymouth, Massachusetts.

of the "parent" church of Plymouth Colony, seems to have commanded deference for the young pastor from colleagues more than twice his age. Cotton weighs in on the problem of orthodoxy in the religiously diverse western parts of the colony and even resumes his father's old feud with Rhode Island's Roger Williams.

In these letters, Cotton also announces the resumption of his Native missionary work, this time to the nearby mainland Wampanoag. The General Court of the colony turned to Cotton to facilitate days of humiliation and prayer in times of trouble and to help with a fund drive for Harvard College in Cambridge, Massachusetts Bay (although we can be sure of Cotton's support for the latter enterprise, Plymouth's contribution was embarrassingly small). Even as Cotton became accustomed to his duties and at last found broad community acceptance, his letters to and from family members left behind evince the hardship of separation from loved ones in times of stress, especially during an age in which transportation was difficult and unreliable. Even maintaining contact by letter was problematic, as Cotton reveals through his frequent references to the challenges of securing reliable delivery.

---

1. Len Travers, "The Missionary Journal of John Cotton, Jr., 1666–1678," *Proceedings of the Massachusetts Historical Society* 109 (1999): 52-101.

From Bryan Rosseter,[1] — 24 September 1669

Cotton's father-in-law had a controversial career in the sometimes rough-and-tumble politics of Connecticut. In this letter, however, he reveals an uncharacteristic frailty and near-despondency as he describes the devastating effects of an epidemic.

Dear & Lo. Son & Daughter-

My hand trembles & Pen is unsteady in the very thoughts of Writing unto you, Great is the Ld & greatly to be feared, None is so sovereign as He, It becomes poor tabernacled Man to Sit Silent, be dumb, & not to open his Mouth at the Lords Doings tho he should break in Pieces by the Blow of his hand, & consume our Beauty like a Moth, Surely Every Man is vanity;[2] When Jobs Friends heard of his sore Afflictions, they came to Mourn with him & to Comfort him, but when they saw the Greatness of his Misery & sore Afflictions, & that his Grief was so very Great, it was Amazing so that they wept & rent their mantles & sprinkled Dust on their heads & sat down silent seven Days;[3] There is no other Hope nor Refuge but in the Ld. that hears Prayer, gives Ear to Cries, & holds not his peace at Tears, therefore I will say unto ye Ld. as David, I also am a stranger with thee & a sojourner as all my Fathers were, oh spare Me that I may Recover Strength before I also go hence, & am seen no more[4]—Must I now step forth with sad Tidings as the Messenger of Job, One tiding after Another (as it is said a 3 fold Cord is not easily broken) so trebled sad & sorrowfull Tidings Cont: break in Pieces. I must say with the Prophet I will weep bitterly, Labour not to Comfort me,[5] tho. with some Check I would fain say with Job in Patience of Spirit & silent submission to his Will that is God only Wise; Naked came I into ye World and Naked shall I return out of the World. The Ld gives & the Ld takes & blessed be his Name. We have had a sore visitation again by Sickness & Mortality here in Guilford this summer as the last, Our Graves are Multiplied & fresh Earth Heaps increased, Coffins again & again have been carried out of my Doors, I have taken up a Lot amongst ye Tombs in ye midst of them; yr Sister Sarah[6] died august 10th Her Mother[7] was overborn with Grief that for 10 Days she refused to eat what was necessary to Sustain nature, & spent that time in Sighing & bitter Mourning to ye Decay of strength and ye Distemper Seized on her & she died Augst: 29th. Then the 2d Day of the Week following ye young Daughter Sarah[8] Sickened, & the 4th Day Convulsion ffits followed her & she died Septr 8th—The Same Day Joasias[9] came home from Kellingsworth very Sick under ye Sentence of Death in himself & lay very dangerously hazardous for many days but is newly Recovered, that is a mercy. Yet I must Return to sighs & sorrows saying as Naomi did, Call me Marah, Call me Marah,[10] I was full but now am empty, I will weep bitterly—the good Lord Support your Hearts when these Sad Tidings come to You—Sarah Rosseter pofrest [profest] long before taken Sick that she should dy this summer, Exprest so much to Several; When Death Seized her, her mother desired her to give some testimony by Sign of her good hope if she could not speak, She fixed her Eyes up to Heaven & Smiled, so died, & when dead lay with a Smiling Countenance—to the admiration of ye Neighbours that were present, that is comforting—yr Mother had clear & full assurances of Gods Love Days before her Death & held it to the last, & spent much time in Prayer for her Children, strongly pleading ye Covenant & was strongly pswaded & believing that God had Eternal Mercy in store for them all. She was willing nay desirous to dy, & could look Death in the face with constant Resolution, until she had obtained the Conquest through his dear Redeemer that had conquered Death & the Grave. These are rich & comforting Mercies, but the greater my Loss, I can Rejoice in her & their Gain but Mourn over my Loss, the Loss of a Sweet companion yt had been so long a comforting companion in all my Tribulation, I will weep bitterly—I might have enlarged in many things—But I can hold it no longer—Pray Pray Pray for us, so rests yr Lo. ffather

Bryan Rosseter

Guilford Septr. 24th 1669

Plymouth's New Minister, 1669-1674

Josiah Cotton, Manuscript "Account of the Cotton Family," 18-22, Houghton Library, Harvard University.

---

1. Bryan (Bray) Rosseter (d. 1672), Cotton's father-in-law, was among the first of the English from Massachusetts Bay to settle the Connecticut colony in 1636; here he served as a magistrate and recorder until 1652. His grandson Josiah Cotton wrote that Rosseter had a degree in "Physick" and that he was also a feisty character. When he first brought his family to Guilford, "it was under the Government of New-Haven," and not liking "some Proceedings that were very rigid & arbitrary," he signed a petition to the King for a union with Connecticut. "In which (altho lawfull for every subject) his House was beset by a Company of armed men Who surrounded the House day & night, But being a Man of good Courage he stood upon his Guard, till he made his Escape to Hartford." When Rosseter returned to Guilford in 1664, boisterously confident of Connecticut's consolidation, John Davenport and Nicholas Streete of New Haven complained that he "hath been long, and still is a man of a turbulent, Restless, factious spiritt." He died in Guilford on 30 September 1672. "Memoirs of Prince's Subscribers," *New England Historical and Genealogical Register* (hereafter *NEHGR*) 9 (1855): 336-37; Josiah Cotton, Manuscript "Account of the Cotton Family," 17-18; Isabel MacBeath Calder, ed., *Letters of John Davenport, Puritan Divine* (New Haven, 1937), 237.
2. Ps. 39:11: "When thou with rebukes dost correct man for iniquity, thou makest his beauty to consume away like a moth: surely every man is vanity. Selah."
3. See Job 2:11-13.
4. Ps. 39:12-13: "Hear my prayer, O LORD, and give ear unto my cry; hold not thy peace at my tears: for I am a stranger with thee, and a sojourner, as all my fathers were. O spare me, that I may recover strength, before I go hence, and be no more."
5. Isa. 22:4: "Therefore said I, Look away from me: I will weep bitterly, labor not to comfort me, because of the spoiling of the daughter of my people."
6. That is, Joanna's younger sister Sarah.
7. Joanna's mother, Elizabeth.
8. This was apparently Sarah's daughter.
9. Josias, or Josiah, Rosseter (d. 1716), Joanna's brother, became a magistrate and recorder like his father and a member of the upper house of the Connecticut Assembly from 1701 to 1711. "Memoirs of Prince's Subscribers," 337. See the letter of 14 February 1683.
10. Ruth 1:20: "And she said unto them, Call me not Naomi, call me Mara: for the Almighty hath dealt very bitterly with me."

To Sarah Mather, 27 & 29 December 1670

Cotton's mother was Sarah (Hawkridge) Story, the widow of William Story, who married John Cotton Sr. in 1632. The elder Cotton died in 1652; she then married the Reverend Richard Mather (1596–1669) "shortly after" he was widowed in 1655.[1] John Jr. wrote this awkward consolation to his mother, who had lost her third husband only the year before.

Plymouth December: 27: 1670:

Deare and much Honoured Mother

The last weeke I received your letter with all the things you sent, for your love & care in which wee heartily thank you & our cousen: I was very sorry when I heard you were left alone this winter season, but, Deare Mother, you know very well that it is many yeares God hath bin weaning you from Creature comforts & teaching you, to be above them, to place your heart & your hopes upon a higher & more steady object; how many times, alas how many times, have you found the streames to be dryed up, but <*yet*> you never yet found the fountaine to faile you, when your flesh & your heart hath failed you, the father of mercies & God of all comfort hath still bin your portion, your rock both for protection from evill & for supply of all needfull good: And you know he hath said, I am Jehovah I change not,[2] all creatures are changelings, there is noe trusting in them, but God is the same for ever, he alwayes abideth faithfull & cannot deny himselfe. & therefore although you are alone, yet you may have most of the best company, even of him who delights to be most neere to his poore children when they are most destitute of Creature comforts & supports; The truth is, I am soe sensible of your lonesome Condition, that I would come downe on purpose to visit you, but that I feare the weather that is soe uncertaine & hazardous in the winter season: you have a rich treasury of Gospel promises to resort unto, & I beleve God will helpe you more & more to remember, that a Christian whilest in this world must live by faith & not by sight.

I write this letter not knowing as yet by whom to send it, but I hope I shall meete with some body ere long, My wife intends by him that brings this letter, to send you a pound of flax; That 3 shillings I send to buy my bootes,[3] I now write to my Brother Mather[4] to take them to himselfe to pay for Lockyers pills:[5] I would entreat you to buy for me 2 skaines of black silk 3 yds of black cotton ribband 6 yds of green galoom,[6] 4 yds of black strong course ribbon if you take them up at Mr Atwaters shop,[7] & adde them to my account for the cloake, I will pay him for all together in the spring; my wife is very well satisfyed with her cloake; The things I write for I intreat you send by him that brings [. . .] letter, whom I will desire to call upon you for them[.] mine & my wives duty to you with Love to Coz; Simo[ ] I humbly beg your daily prayers to God for me, that he would keepe me in his holy feare, & delight to doe me good, though unworthy, that I may be a blessing in my generation; I rest,

Your Dutifull Sonne,

John Cotton

pray send me a peice of sealing wax:
If any letters for us at Mr Atwaters from Connecticott, pray send them

Dec: 29:

I meeting with young Kempton that lives at my Cousen Coopers, I send my letter by him, I hope it will not be long before I shall meete with some body that may call upon you to take them & bring them to me:

Mather Papers 1:43, Prince Library, Rare Books and Manuscripts, Boston Public Library. Addressed "These For his Deare and much Honoured Mother, Mris Sarah Mather, at her house, in Boston." Letter mutilated along center fold.

---

1. Allen Tolman and Dumas Malone, eds., *Dictionary of American Biography* (New York, 1957) (hereafter *DAB*), s.v. "Mather, Richard."
2. Mal. 3:6: "For I am the LORD, I change not; therefore ye sons of Jacob are not consumed."
3. A line and a half crossed out.
4. Cotton's sister Maria (1642–1714) married Increase Mather (1639–1723) in 1662.
5. Lionel Lockyer (1600–1672) was famed in his day as an apothecary and physician, especially for the supposed efficacy of his cure-all pills, sold in latten boxes of about 100 pills each. In support of (and to market) the product, he wrote *An Advertisement, Concerning Those Most Excellent Pills Called, Piluæ Radiis Solis Extractæ, Being an Universal Medicine* (1664). It is not clear whether Cotton (or his wife) acquired the book or the pills themselves, but clearly Lockyer's fame had reached across the Atlantic. His tomb at Southwark Cathederal, featuring a sculpture of a reclining Lockyer and an inscription of notably bad verse, remained a favorite of monument tourists through the nineteenth century (http://www.southwark.anglican.org/cathedral/tour/lockyer.htm); see also Charles J. S. Thompson, *The Quacks of Old London* (London, 1928).
6. A close-woven ribbon or braid made with gold, silver, or silk threads and used for trimming garments.
7. Most likely the premises of Joshua Atwater (d. 1676), "a busy trader" from New Haven who moved to Boston in 1659. James Savage, *A Genealogical Dictionary of the First Settlers of New England*, 4 vols. (1860–62; facsimile reprint, Baltimore, Md., 1990), 1:76.

From Noah Newman,[1]

10 January 1671

Beginning in the 1640s, the remote western reaches of Plymouth Colony attracted religious mustangs, particularly Baptists and, in the 1660s, Quakers. There, far from the easy reach of Plymouth but close to the dissenters' haven of Rhode Island, those seeking religious alternatives found room for experimentation. Most Plymouth Colony towns lacked the means to attract dynamic orthodox clergymen of Cotton's caliber, and without the firm powers of enforcement enjoyed by the magistrates of Massachusetts Bay, the General Court could only do so much to discourage pluralism. In several of the letters that follow, we see evidence that Cotton jumped into the fray, hoping to check the activities of a Baptist preacher and to neutralize what he clearly considered the odious influence of Roger Williams.

Janaury: the 10th. 70

[D]eare Sir.

[....] respects promised to yourselfe & yours. Having this opportunity [....] mrs. Esthers Indian bearer whom she sends to Namasacut[2] if not to Plimouth for her dismission which I told her would not bee like to Come by any other way in respect of the winterlinese of the season; I am willing to gratifye your desire, in returning you what account I can of our prsent affaires[.] You are pleased in yours to desire mee to let you know what we have done with our recanting woman, wch Question ase matters are att this instant Circumstanced wth us, hath some ambiguity in it, because there is one recanting from us & another recanting to us, the tearm recantation is more applicable to the latter, yet my thoughts have been you intend it to ye former, (viz) Elizabeth Bullocke,[3] who is rebaptised, by mr. Miles.[4] Now Concerning our proceedings wth her I shall give you this breife account. when there was att first some waverings in her mind about ye point of baptisme, falling in Conjuction wth some Convictions shee was then under touching her spirituall Condition, she was by the advice of some friends mooved to speke wth mee, wch shee made some attempts unto, but being providentially disapointed shee too hastily as I understand drew up this Conclusion that shee was out off her way to seeke it, & surely the voyce of God was in her being so disappointed Calling her to desist, or to that purpose as she sayd; Altho she came to the towne but twice (Living att mr Browns)[5] & one of these times; she might allmost Conclude shee should not find mee att home. It being upon plimouth Election weeke;[6] but by this meanes I had no speech wth her till shee was propounded to mr Miles his Church for as I understand shee did pretty soone attaine unto a ripenes of assurance touching her spirituall & eternall well being & was not long before she was stedfastly perswaded of her need of a further Baptisme then shee had yet received; Now upon what I had heard of her procedure in that way, I proposed it to the Churches Consideration, what was our duty in the Case before us, upon wch it was determined she should be sent for, to come to my house, where one or two of the brethren wth my selfe should debate wth her. at wch time I demanded of her the grounds upon wch she went in the repetition of her infant Baptisme so she Layd downe two objections, upon wch I told her there was but one that did relate to the subjects of Baptisme, the other had respect to ye manner; therefore we would goe through one first Namely who were the subjects of Baptisme & as God helped me I showed her the emptines & ungroundednes of her objection & layd before her severall arguments for the validity of her first Baptisme <*what*> & told her what she did not see backt wth plaine Scripture shee should reject. I beseeched her in her owne language to tell me of any impertinentcy in those answers I gave her or those scriptures I alledged, somtimes shee would plead weaknes & say shee Could not reason out the point wth mee, somtimes shee would say God had so perswaded her heart, & shee must walke according to the light shee had received—I desired she would but promise mee to ponder the things I had sayd to her, but she would not. finally shee Came to the result That she Could not owne any relation shee stood in, to this Church by her parents membership Nor any baptisme she had received amongst us, that was acc[....] Neyther was she willing (as she sayd) to hear or Consider [....] her from her present perswasion; & so I left her w[....] her I would leave w^{t}h her, since I mooved the Church againe about [....] sent too to understand the frame of her spirit, (wch seemes to be as formerly [....] know that we did yet Looke after her [&] should proceed further wth her when opp[ortunity] served, wch doth not Now in respect to her remoteness it being winter season living a matter of 8 or 9 [miles?] from us If I mistake not; I am very thoughtfull what issue we ought to put to such a Case tho I perceive the C[hurch] excepting 2 or 3 are very tractable in the busynes. I therefore Crave yor: advice by the next opportunity—

Touching the other recanter (It is the wife of one Jarrat Ingram,[7] who wth her husband were members of m^{r}: Miles his Church both rebaptized, she formerly recieving baptisme in this or weymouth Church; Now it is about 2 year since she fell into heavy desertions & temptations, both wth respect to her spirituall Conditio^{n} & her relation unto them; by reason of wch she hath had as I understand very hard measure from them being threatned wth falling into Judas his Case. & wth denying the Lord of Life & glory in denying the baptisme she had received amongst them, by which you have some tast of their spirits and of that weigh[t] they lay upon their administrations what ever become of ours; but in short upon her addresse to mee, after a pretty Large experience of the frame of her spirit I have proceeded to propound her to this Church; having been a Constant hearer here (by her living in the towne) this 2 year or upwards, yet nevertheles in her being Called to an account att Swancy shee is Charged wth the sin of forsaking the assemblys of the Saints; she now stands propounded since the last sabbath. & Now having given you this account of ours, give me leave to aske you what you have done or will doe wth yor: recanting woman;

I mean m^r^. Howland's daughter that marryed to Jonathan Bozworth,[8] who is Joyned to m^r^: Miles his Church & rebaptized; there is another also that Came from your p^lc^ whose maidens Name was Paddocke marryed to Zech: Eidee[9] that I thinke hath proceeded as far, but I know not what her relation is to your Church. Those things my thinkes rightly & duely Considered speakes an inconsistence in our Communion wth them. If my heart faile mee not I Could be willing to exercise as much Charity as any towards m^r^ Miles or others of that opinion, yet Moses his answer to Phar: will not be out of my mind. Shall we sacrifice the abomination of the Egyptians before their eyes & will they not stone us.[10] so shall we see that which we professe to be an ordinance of Jesus xt[11] trampled under foote in so manefest a manner, & must we be silent, nay must we give Countenance to it. &c. Touching m^rs^ Esther's motion I suppose you understand the successe of it by her request for her diss:, & therefore say no more but wish ye blessing of God there w^th^; tho' for my own p^t^ I have noe more aptnesse to it, then as I find it undenyable in a way of order, that is upon some Considerations, Not to Cast any aspersions upon her pson or qualifications [in?] the Case, Thus wth dearest salutations I rest wth ye hearty request of yor prayers,

Yo^r^ assured friend & Brother.

N. N.

Pray when opportunity serves p^r^sent my service to our Hon^d^: Governour[12] my respects to the Elders [. . . .][13]

God hath given me a young son Henery In the memory of his Now glorifyed grandfather[14]

Cotton Family Papers 6:1, Prince Library, Rare Books and Manuscripts, Boston Public Library. Addressed "To the Reverend His truly Esteemed Friend m^r^. John Cotton Pastor of the church in Plimouth, these." Endorsed "from Mr Newman January, 10: 1670:" Some words, especially on the reverse, have been lost to a tear in the upper left hand corner.

---

1. Rev. Noah Newman (d. 1678), son of Rev. Samuel Newman of Rehoboth, assumed his late father's ministry in 1668. George H. Tilton, *A History of Rehoboth, Massachusetts: Its History for 275 Years 1643–1918* (Boston, 1918), 58, 88.

2. Nemasket, or Namassaket, in what is now Middleborough, Massachusetts.

3. Eliz. Bullocke, possibly Elizabeth Billington, second wife of Richard Bullocke or Bulluk, married 21 September 1660. Samuel N. Arnold, comp., *Vital Records of Rehoboth, 1642–1895* (Providence, R.I., 1897), 67.

4. John Miles or Myles (c.1621–1683), "a learned preacher of the Church of England," took advantage of the atmosphere of religious experimentation and, sometime during Cromwell's protectorate, became a Baptist and gathered a following. Ejected from his place after the Restoration, in 1662 he and some

supporters emigrated to Dorchester in Massachusetts Bay. Probably realizing there would be no tolerance there for his views, Miles moved to Rehoboth. He apparently did some preaching in the area but in 1667 removed with some likeminded people to the western part of the town (now Swansea) to form a separate, Baptist worship with himself as pastor. After the destruction of Swansea in King Philip's War, Miles established a Baptist gathering in Boston but returned to his rebuilt town in 1680 and died there three years later. Otis Olney Wright, ed., *History of Swansea, MA 1667–1917* (Swansea, Mass., 1917), 197-98. See the letter of 6 January 1685.

5. Probably James Brown (1623–1710), a prominent resident and son of one of the town's original proprietors, who was Rev. Miles's brother-in-law, a founding member of Miles's church, and an assistant to the Plymouth General Court. Wright, *History of Swansea*, 200.

6. At this time the Plymouth election court was held in the first week of June.

7. Jarret Ingraham (d. 1717) lived in Rehoboth as early as 1665, when his child Mary was born. Arnold, *Vital Records of Rehoboth*, 653, 840.

8. Hannah Howland (b. c. 1637), the sixth child of *Mayflower* passengers John Howland and Elizabeth Tilley, married Jonathan Bosworth in 1661. It is probably to her that Cotton refers in an entry in the Plymouth church records for 1670: "A child of this chh who had bin here baptized, removing to Swanzey was rebaptized by the Pastor there, which the chh being informed of, did unanimously declare it to be a matter of offence, & sent letters to those concerned in that action to signify that such a practice would be a barre to our Ecclesiasticall communion & desired they would doe soe noe more." Eugene Aubrey Stratton, *Plymouth Colony: Its History & People 1620–1691* (Salt Lake City, Ut., 1986), 310-11; Publications of the Colonial Society of Massachusetts *Collections* (hereafter *CSM*), 22 (Boston, 1920), 146.

9. Zachariah Eedy married Allice Paddock on 7 May 1663. Nathaniel B. Shurtleff, ed., *Records of Plymouth Colony*, 13 vols. (Boston, 1855–59), 8:23.

10. Exod. 8:25-26: "And Pharaoh called for Moses and for Aaron, and said, Go ye, sacrifice to your God in the land. And Moses said, It is not meet so to do; for we shall sacrifice the abomination of the Egyptians to the LORD our God: lo, shall we sacrifice the abomination of the Egyptians before their eyes, and will they not stone us?"

11. Christ.

12. Thomas Prence (c. 1600–1673) was governor of Plymouth Colony from the death of William Bradford in 1657 to his own death on 29 March 1673. *CSM*, 22:147; Stratton, *Plymouth Colony*, 340-41.

13. Two or three words illegible.

14. Henry Newman (b. 1670) graduated from Harvard College in 1687 and was the librarian there from 1690 to 1693. Sometime after 1695, he moved to London, where he lived with the Duke of Somerset's family and served as the agent for both Harvard and the New Hampshire colony. He was also a corresponding secretary for the Society for the Propagation of the Gospel. John Langdon Sibley, *Biographical Sketches of Graduates of Harvard University, In Cambridge, Massachusetts* (Boston, 1873–) (hereafter *Sibley's Harvard Graduates*), 3:389-94.

From Hannah Johnson and Mary Blake,[1]

20 February 1671

As Cotton contemplated his response to the threat of Rev. Miles, he was also busy locating church members who had drifted away from Plymouth and granting them formal letters of dismissal.

Reverant [and B]eloved in Christe Jesus

Some months since we Receved a leter from you[u2] intimatinge to us the desire of the Church wth the Care the Church hath for us in Regard of our prsent standing and the desire the Church hath of our prsent and eternall good; ffor Answere to yor Letter we have the longer defurred it because there was hope of the unitinge and Closing of these Churches but as yet we doe not see it wch Causeth us yet to Crave of the Church a littell longer time before we doe settle and pick unto wch Church we shall joyne and somethinge in Regard that neather of our husbans are yet Resovld unto wch Church to joyne, soe that we would faine Chose if possible where they joyne; Now Consideringe the intent of yor writinge that it is in love and your Care of us therein, having this opportunitie we dare not omite it any longer feeringe it may be judged a: disregardinge of the Church, but we hope the Church will not soe judge of us; for you are in our harts much Respected in the Lord Christe, desiringe yor prayers for us that God would please to settell us where he may have moste glory and we may have Comfort in our settellinge[.] thus wth or due Respects to you and our prayers to god to direct you in all yor ways we take our leave and humbly Rest & shall ever Remaine

yor Lovinge Sisters in Christe

Hannah Johnson
mary Blake

Boston this 20th of ffebruary 1670.

Cotton Family Papers 6:2, Prince Library, Rare Books and Manuscripts, Boston Public Library. Addressed "To the Reverant Mr. John Cotton pastor of the Church of Christ in Plimouth these [are] sent."

---

1. In the Plymouth Church records for the year 1670, Cotton wrote,: "Some persons, a brother & 2 sisters that had formerly walked with his chh being now removed & not owning their chh-relation, the chh agreed & it was openly declared by the Elder in the name of the chh, that wee esteemed them noe longer to be members of us." *CSM*, 22:146.

2. Not found.

To John Myles, 14 March 1671

Sir

you are not ignorant how much your desires have bin manifested by word & writing, of having & maintaining Communion with the churches of Christ in this wildernesse, & in particular with the church here; The Consideration of which, makes us greatly to marvell at the newes of any such actings of yours as doe, (at least to our present apprehensions) bespeake an utter *<impossibility>* improbability of our regularly Ecclesiasticall communicating with you in any way: To tell you the very truth of our hearts, when the motion of Communion with you was first stirring amonge us, such was the Largenesse of our charity to you, as that wee really desired the agitations thereabouts might issue in a gratification of your request upon that account, & wee apprehended an inclination in the bretheren also thereunto, wee being in great hopes, that by some discourse with yourselfe the grace of Christ would soe appeare in your answers to what wee had to say to you as that all obstructions of our mutuall brotherly communion would have bin removed; but the onely wise God (whose awfull dispensations of providence in this respect wee desire to adore) disappointing our intended Conference a first & a 2ond time with his owne immediate hand, wee had thereby granted us from the Lord a longer opportunity of more serious & deliberate thoughtfulnesse what conclusive answer to give to such a motion; In this Interim, while our thoughts were unsettled & undetermined, it pleased God to bring to our eares the sad tidings of your pollution of the Holy ordinance of Baptisme, by reiterating the eternall administration of it to divers of the children of the Churches hereabouts, & in particular to one of our owne; hereupon our Church meeting together, it was unanimously declared that this practice of yours is very offensive, & puts in such a barre of Communion as wee are not able for the present to remove: Sir, wee beseech you to consider, how it is possible for us to hold any Communion with you, or you with us, when your principles lead you to such practices as tend to destroy the very foundation of our Church order, (the doctrine of Baptisms being a foundation of truth, Heb: 6: 1: 2:)[1] Doth not your Covenant one with another utterly exclude a very considerable part of the federall members of Christs visible Kingdome from having any interest therein? & doth not this re-washing of persons formerly baptized in true Churches of x^{t} & by true Ministers (as you your selfe acknowledge) plainly inferre that their first Baptisme was a nullity & to be rejected if the subject thereof soe please[?] Can a chast heart, sincerely affected to the faith & order of the Gospel patiently endure to see the pretious blood of our Lord Jesus Ct (that is solemly represented in that sacred ordinance of Baptisme) to be soe lightly esteemed? Wee would not be soe void of Charity to you, as to thinke that a *<spirit>* prophane spirit acts you in this matter, wee rather hope your soe acting proceeds from Infirmity of minde & from want of a due consideration of the ill consequences of such a course. Wee doe therefore beg of God on your behalfe, that he would open your eyes to see the great evill of this way of yours whereby the name of God (that is called upon his Churches & ordinances[)] is dishonoured, the hearts of those in Church fellowship (who have with great comfort beheld the gratious fruits of this Initiatory seale of the Covenant to themselves & theirs) much sadened, & a wide doore opened to loosenesse & all sin in our youth, for if they are not under the bond of the holy Covenant of God sealed to them in Infancy, then the sons of God may be as bold in wayes That are vitious & prophane, as the children of men are, & who shall check or controll them? it is manifest that you Judge there is noe Eclesiasticall restraint can be laid upon them, which God forbid: wee shall not enlarge on this hand, only beare with us, if wee be zealous for our God, & for the preserving in peace & purity those holy priviledges & blessed ordinances he hath betrusted us withall, lest if wee should altogether hold our peace at such a time & upon soe sad an occasion as you have given us, the Lord should be provoked ag^st^ us to lay all our pleasant things waste; wee would entreat of you not to palliate & excuse this evill action of yours to one of ours, by saying, that you force noebody to desire baptisme of you, every one is left to their owne liberty, she desired it of you, & you are bound in conscience to answer such desires of your members, these are but fig leaves & will not be a sufficient covering, when the Lord shall call you to an account for the same; meanwhile wee cannot but lay it sadly to heart that wee see that which hath a tendency to undermine any one of the ordinances of Jesus x^t^ so long established amongst us; & therefore that wee may doe what in us lyes to prevent your future progresse in a way soe irregular, wee declare with reference to any others, the Children of our Church residing with you, that you cannot without manifest breach of rule, & great offence to our Consciences administer your baptisme to them; wee hope, that rule, 1 Cor: 10: 32:[2] will not be unminded by you, as to this matter; & wee doe hereby charge any that stand in such relation to us not to dare to renounce their Baptisme formerly reçeived amongst us, or to desire any new administration of it from you; As for what is past, could wee see a spirit of Repentance & Humiliation in you & her for the same, wee hope wee should be ready to forgive the great wrong you have done us, till then wee are offended with you; wee shall adde noe further, but our prayers are to God to save his poore Churches from Apostacy, & from any ensnarements by such examples as may tend to alienate hearts from the thruth received, & in his Infinite mercy reduce you from errour & helpe you to walke in the way of truth, resting

yours according to truth

J: C: [&] T: C: with the Consent of the Church:

Plym: 1st m: 14 d: 1670: 71:

Cotton Family Papers 6:3, Prince Library, Rare Books and Manuscripts, Boston Public Library. Addressed at bottom of letter "These For the Reverend Mr John Myles Preacher of the word at Swanzey:" This appears to be Cotton's edited draft copy of the letter sent to Rev. Myles.

---

1. Heb. 6:1-2: "Therefore leaving the principles of the doctrine of Christ, let us go on unto perfection; not laying again the foundation of repentance from dead works, and of faith toward God, of the doctrine of baptisms, and of laying on of hands, and of resurrection of the dead, and of eternal judgment."
2. 1 Cor. 10:32: "Give none offence, neither to the Jews, nor to the Gentiles, nor to the church of God."

From Roger Williams,[1] 25 March 1671[2]

Williams had engaged Cotton's father in an increasingly personal pamphlet debate in the 1640s and early 1650s. We cannot be certain why Cotton chose to come to his father's defense at this point, nearly twenty years after the debate ended. However, placing this letter in the context of Noah Newman's letter of 10 January, printed above, and Gov. Thomas Prence's letter cited below, it seems clear that Cotton's missing letter to Williams, and this reply, are part of a renewed debate on religious toleration, made more immediate to Cotton by the activities of Rev. John Miles and his followers in Swansea.

Providence 25 March 1671 (So Calld)

S^R,

Lo: respects premised. About 3 Weeks since I recd Yo^rs dated in 10^br [December]:[3] & wonder not y^t Præjudice, Interest & passion have lift up Your Feete thus to trample on me as on some Mahumetan Jew or Papist, Some Common Thiefe or Swearer, Drunckard or Adulterer, imputing to me ye Odious Crimes of Blaspheamies, Reproaches, Slanders Idolatries to be in ye Devills Kingdome, a Graceless man &c And all this with out any Scripture, Reason or Argum^nt wch might inlighten my Conscience, as to any Erro^r, or offense to God or Yo^r deare Father.

I have now much above 50 years humbly & Earnestly begd of God to make me as vile as a dead Dog in mine owne eye,[4] So y^t I might not feare what Men should falsly Say or Cruelly doe ag^nst me: & I have had Long Experience of his mercifull Answer to me in Mens false Charges & Cruelties ag^nst me to this Hower.

My great offense (you So often repeate) is My Wrong to Yo^r dear Father Yo^r glorified Father &c[5] But ye truth is, ye Love & Hono^r wch I have alwayes shewed (in

Speech & writing) to y[t] Excellently learned & holy Man Yo[r] Father, have bene so great y[t] I have bene censured by divers for it. God knowes y[t] for Gods Sake I tenderly loved & honoured his pson (as I did the psons of y[e] Magistrates, Ministers & Members whome I knew in old England, & knew their holy Affections & upright Aimes & great Selfe deniall to enjoy more of God in this wildernes) And I have therefore desired to Wave all psonall Failings &c & rather mencion their Beauties, to prevent y[e] Insultings of y[e] Papists or Prophane Protestants who use to scoff at y[e] Weakenesses Yea & at y[e] Divisions of those they used to brand for Puritants The holy Eye of God hath seene this y[e] Cause why I have not said nor writ what abundantly I could have done, but have rather chose to beare all Censures, Losses & Hardships &c

This made y[t] hon[rd] Father of y[e] Bay m[r] Wintrop to give me y[e] testimony not only of Exemplary Diligence in y[e] Ministry (when I was Satisfied in it,) but of Patience allso, in these Words in a Letter to me [S.[r] We have often tried Yo[r] Patience, but Could never Conquer it.][6]

My humble desire is still to beare not only what You say but when Power is added to Yo[r] will, an hanging or burning from You as You plainly intimate You would long since have serv'd my Booke,[7] had it bene Yo[r] owne, as not being fit to be in y[e] Possession of any Christian as You write.

Alas Sr what hath this Booke merited above all y[e] many thouhsands full of Old Romish Idolls names &c & New Popish Idolatries w[ch] are in Christians Libraries, & use to be alleadged in Testimonie, Argumnt & Confutation?

What is there in this Booke but presseth Holynes of Heart Holynes of Life, Holynes of Worship & Pitie to poor Sinners & Patience toward them while they breake not y[e] Civill peace.

Tis true, my first booke y[e] bloudy Tenent was burn[t] by y[e] Presbiterian Partie (then prevailing):[8] But this booke, whereof We now speake (being my Reply to Yo[r] Fathers Answere,) was recd with Applause & Thancks by y[e] Armie by y[e] Parlmt, professing y[t] of Necescity, Yea of Christian Equity, there Could be no Reconciliation, Pacification or Living togeather but by pmitting of Dissenting Consciences to live amongst them: In So much y[t] y[t] excellent Servant of God m[r] John Owen (Calld Do: Owen)[9] told me before y[e] Generall, (who Sent for me about y[t] very busines) y[t] before I Landed, Himselfe & many others had answered m[r] Cottons booke allready.

The first booke, & y[e] Point of Permitting Dissenters his Ma[ties] Royall Father assented too,[10] & how often hath y[e] Son our Soveraigne declared himselfe indulgent toward Dissenters notwithstanding y[e] Clamors & Plottings of his Selfe Seeking Bpps?[11]

And S[r], (as before & form[r]ly) I add, if your Selfe or any in Publicke or Private shew me any Fayling ag[nst] God or Yo[r] Father in y[t] Booke, you shall find me diligent & faythfull, in Waighing & in confessing or Replying in Love & Meekenes.

Oh you say Wrong to a Father made a dumbe Child Speake &c S[r] I Pray forget not y[t] Yo[r] Father was not God but man Sinfull & failing in many things as we all doe saith ye Holy Scripture: I Presume You know ye Scheme of m^r Cottons Contradictions (about Church discipline) presented to ye World by m^r Dan: Cawdrey, a man of Name & Note[12] allso S^r take heed You Prefer not the Earthen Pot (though Yo^r Excellent Father) before his most High Eternall Maker & Potter:[13] Blessed y^t you were borne & proceeded from him if You hono^r him a more for his Humilitie & Holynes, then for outward Respect wch Some (& none shall justly more then my Selfe) put upon him.

Sr You Call my 3 Proposalls &c[14] abominable, false & wicked: But (as before[)] Thouhsands (High & holy too Some of them) will wonder at you: Capt: Gookins from Cambridge writes me Word[15] y^t he will not be my Antagonist in them being Candidly understood: Yo^r hon^rd Govr tells me there is no Foundacion for any dispute with Plymmouth about those Proposalls for You force no mens Conscience:[16] But Sr You have Yo^r Libertie to prove them abominable false & wicked & to disprove y^t wch I have presented in ye Booke Concerning ye N. E. Churches to be but Parochiall & Nationall, though Sifted with a finer Sive & Painted with finer Coulo^rs.

You are pleased to Count me Excommunicate & therein You deale more cruelly with me then with all ye Prophane Protestants & Papists too, with whome You hold Communion in ye Parishes to w^ch (as You know) all are forced by ye Bps,. & yet you Count me a slave to ye Devill, because in Conscience to God & Love to God & you I have told you of it: But S^r, ye truth is (I will not say I excommunicated you but) I first withdrew Communion from Yo^r Selves for halting betweene Christ & Antichrist, ye Parish Churches & Christian Congregations:[17] Long after when you had Consultations of killing me, but Some rather advised a Drie Pyt of Banishm^nt: m^r Peters[18] advised an Excommunication to be Sent me (after ye manner of Popish Bulls &c[)] But the same man in London embraced me, & told me he was for Liberty of Conscience & preacht it & Complaind to me of Salem for excommunicating his distracted wife & for wronging him in his Goods wch he left behind him.

S^r, You tell me my Time is Lost &c because (as I conceave you) not in ye function of Ministrie: I Confesse the offices of Christ Jesus are ye Best Callings but (generally) they are ye worst Trades in ye World, as they are Practiced only for a Maintenance, a Place, a Living a Benefice &c God hath many Employm^nts for his Servants: Moses 40 Years & ye Lord Jesus 30 Years were not idle: though litle knowne what they did as to any Ministry. And ye 2 Prophets Prophesie in Sackcloth[19] & are Christ Jesus his Ministers though not owned by ye Publike Ordinations: God knowes I have much & long & Conscientiously & mournfully waighed & digd into ye Differences of ye Protestants themselvs about ye Ministry: He knows what Gains & Præferm^nts I have refused in Universitie, City Countrey & Court in Old Eng, & Something in N. E. &c to keepe my Soule undefiled in this Point, & not to act with a douting Conscience &c

God was pleased to shew me much of this in Old Engl: And in New being unanimously chosen Teacher at Boston (before Yo^r deare Father came divers yeares) I conscientiously refused & withdrew to plymmouth, because I durst not officiate to an unseperated people, as upon Examination & Conference, I found them to be: At plymmouth I spake on y[e] Lords days & weeke days, & wrought hard at y[e] How [Hoe] for My Bread (& so afterward at Salem) untill I found them both Professing to be a Seperated people in N. E. (not admitting y[e] most Godly to Communion without a Covenant) & yet out Communicating with y[e] Parishes in Old, by their members repairing on frequent occasions thether.

Sr I heartily thanck You for Yo[r] Conclusion wishing my Conversion & Salvation without w[ch] Surely vain are our priviledges of being Abrahams Son Enjoying y[e] Covenant, holy Education, holy Worship holy Church or Temple, of being adorned with deepe understanding miraculous Faith, Angelical Parts & utterance, y[e] Titles of Pastors or Apostles Yea of being Sacrifices in the Fire to God.

S[r] I am unworthy (though desirous to be)

You[r] Friend & Servant

Roger Williams

Jeremy Belknap Papers, Massachusetts Historical Society. Addressed "To M[r] John Cotton at his house in N. Plymmouth these pres[nt]." Endorsed "From M[r] Roger Williams March 25: 1671:"

---

1. Roger Williams (c. 1603–1683), the famous founder of Providence Plantation. His brief and troubled career as teacher to the Salem church ended with his expulsion from Massachusetts in 1635. Williams traveled to the head of Narragansett Bay and negotiated with Narragansett sachems for land on which to settle. Other dissidents followed and formed the colony of Rhode Island and Providence Plantations, whose autonomy the neighboring New England colonies frequently threatened. Time and again, Williams proved instrumental in defending the colony from its detractors. *DAB.*

2. Glenn W. LaFantasie included this letter in his edition of *The Correspondence of Roger Williams*, 2 vols. (Providence, R.I., 1988), 2:627-33. While the letter appears in the present edition with some changes, these are chiefly matters of style. See LaFantasie's notes for an excellent analysis of Williams's more confusing passages and references.

3. Not found.

4. A reference to David's self-abasement in 1 Sam. 24:14: "After whom is the king of Israel come out? after whom dost thou pursue? after a dead dog, after a flea."

5. Cotton's father had been one of those who attempted to turn Williams from his "errors" before his banishment. The elder Cotton remembered that he "spent a great part of the Summer [of 1635] in seeking by word and writing" to dissuade Williams from his defiance of the Massachusetts General Court. Ultimately, Cotton and the rest of the Bay Colony ministers approved the court's sentence of banishment later that year. Cotton and Williams's correspondence continued for a short while afterward but broke down and ceased after some mutual recriminations. Cotton's last, admonishing letter to Williams found its way into print in 1643 (apparently without Cotton's approval), arousing Williams to his own defense in *Mr. Cotton's Letter Lately Printed* (1644), then to an attack on the "New England Way" in *The Bloudy Tenet of Persecution* of the same year. Cotton countered with *A Reply to Mr. Williams* and *The Bloudy Tenet Washed*, published together in 1647. Williams made the final thrust with *The Bloody Tenet Yet More Bloody* in 1652, the year Cotton died. The initial volleys in this war of print debated the justice of Williams's banishment, but Williams quickly raised the stakes, blasting what he

considered the orthodox New England colonies' intolerance, the impurity of Puritan churches, and the inappropriate partnership of church and state in New England. The language of the letters is often personal and acrimonious. For full texts of these works, see James Hammond Trumbull et al, eds., *The Complete Writings of Roger Williams*, 7 vols. (New York, 1963), vols. 1-4.

6. Williams's brackets; letter from Winthrop not found.

7. Apparently Cotton was upset by Williams's final entry in the debate with his father, *The Bloody Tenet Yet More Bloody,* citing "wrong" done to his father in print. However, Williams's letter suggests that Cotton may not even have read *The Bloody Tenet Yet More Bloody* until recently.

8. The reaction of the House of Commons to Williams's *Bloudy Tenet of Persecution* was swift; on 9 August 1644 the House ordered the pamphlet to be publicly burned. James E. Ernst, "Roger Williams and the English Revolution," *Rhode Island Historical Society Collections* 24 (1931): 12.

9. John Owen (1616–1683) left Oxford University in 1637 rather than submit to Archbishop Laud's demands for clerical conformity. He wrote a blistering critique of the Anglican Church, *Display of Arminianism,* and became an Independent in thought and practice, even tending toward antinomianism. He served in several civil offices during Cromwell's Protectorate and pleaded for religious liberty after the Restoration. *Dictionary of National Biography*, ed. Leslie Stephen and Sidney Lee, 63 vols. (London, 1885–1900) (hereafter *DNB*).

10. Charles I. As LaFantasie points out, it is difficult to understand how Charles could have agreed with Williams's convictions, if indeed he actually read them. LaFantasie, *Correspondence of Roger Williams*, 2:632.

11. Bishops.

12. Daniel Cawdrey (1588–1664), a nonconformist cleric, inclined toward the Presbyterian party during the English Civil War and signed a petition condemning any harm to the captured Charles I. Rewarded with the offer of a bishopric after the Restoration, however, he declined, and he refused to submit to the 1662 Act of Uniformity. Despising both Anglicans and Independents, Cawdrey wrote two pamphlets attacking the liberal tenets of John Owen. *DNB*.

13. Isa. 64:8: "But now, O LORD, thou art our father; we are the clay, and thou our potter; and we all are the work of thy hand."

14. Cotton had apparently seen a letter from Williams to Gov. Thomas Prence and Maj. John Mason dated 22 June 1670, in which Williams offered to debate three points in Hartford, Boston, and Plymouth: "First that forc't Worshipp stincks in Gods Nostrills. 2 That it denies Christ Jesus yet to be come, and makes the Church yet National, figurative and Ceremoniall. 3 That in these flames about Religion, as his Matie his Father, and Grandfather have yielded, there is no other prudent Christian Way of preserving peace in the World but by permission of differing Consciences." LaFantasie, *Correspondence of Roger Williams*, 2:617.

15. Not found.

16. Possibly a reference to Thomas Prence's reply to Williams (of July 1670?), printed in LaFantasie, *Correspondence of Roger Williams*, 2:625-26. If so, Williams interpreted Prence's response oddly.

17. Failing to win ordination as pastor of the church in Salem, Williams moved to Plymouth in late 1631. Recounting the year 1633, William Bradford summed up Williams's experience at Plymouth: "Mr Roger Williams (a man godly and zealous, having many precious parts, but very unsettled in judgemente) came over first to the Massachusets, but upon some discontente left that place, and came hither, (wher he was friendly entertained, according to their poore abilitie,) and exercised his gifts among them, and after some time was admitted a member of the church; and his teaching well approoved, for the benefite wherof I still blese God, and am very thankfull to him, even for his sharpest admonitions and reproufs, so farr as they agreed with truth. He this year began to fall into some strang opinions, and from opinion to practise; which caused some controversie betweene the church and him, and in the end some discontente on his part, by occasion wherof he left them some thing abruptly. Yet after

wards sued for his dismission to the church of Salem, which was granted, with some caution to them concerning him, and what care they ought to have of him." William Bradford, *History of Plymouth Plantation*, 2 vols. (New York, 1968), 161-63. Another Plymouth eyewitness added detail to Bradford's restrained account, asserting that Williams actively recruited adherents to his "singular opinions," some of whom were also dismissed from the church and left with him. Nathaniel Morton, *New England's Memorial* (1854, reprint, Bowie, Md., 1997), 102.

18. Hugh Peter (1598–1660), the famous Puritan divine, came to Massachusetts Bay in 1635 and became pastor of the Salem church after Williams left. Returning to England in 1641, he became a chaplain of the Puritan armies in England and Ireland and the personal chaplain to Oliver Cromwell. He urged the trial and execution of Charles I in 1649, and for this he was tried and executed after the Restoration. *American National Biography*, ed. John A. Garraty and Mark C. Carnes (New York and Oxford, 1999) (hereafter *ANB*).

19. A reference to Rev. 11:3: "And I will give power unto my two witnesses, and they shall prophesy a thousand two hundred and threescore days, clothed in sackcloth."

To the Elders of the First Church of Boston,[1]

10 April 1671

Reverend & highly Honoured in the Lord,

Some of the children of our Church Living in Boston have Lately desired our consent to their Joyning with the third Church,[2] many serious thoughts wee had what answer to returne to their desires, being utterly unwilling to doe any thing that might [be] grievous to yourselves whom wee greatly love & reverence, & at last concluding it would bee noe matter of offence to you because of that Candour (wee heare) you have manifested to the leaders of that society, & readynesse to give them the right hand fellowship in your private treaties with them; & also considering the necessity of a speedy answer, in regard that one of the woemen is very neere to her time of restraint, wee have therefore consented to them in this their motion, heartily pouring out our supplications to the God of Peace, that he would in his abundant mercy perfect that Reconciliation betwixt yourselves & your brethren that may comfort all our hearts & the hearts of all that truly fear God & tend soe greatly to the glory of his name in Jesus Christ,

In whom wee rest yours sincerely & respectively

J: C: [&] T: C:[3] with the Consent of the Church

Plimouth:
Apr: 10: 1671:

Cotton Family Papers 6:4, Prince Library, Rare Books and Manuscripts, Boston Public Library. Addressed at bottom of letter "To the Revd Elders of the 1st ch: of X^t in Bost: these present." This appears to be Cotton's edited draft copy of the letter sent to the elders.

---

1. First Church, or Old Church, was gathered at Charlestown in 1630 and relocated to Boston that same year. It was situated at Cornhill, opposite the Town House.
2. Third Church was formed in 1669 by a group that split off from First Church over the controversial 1662 synod. It was known locally as South Church, later as Old South Church.
3. Thomas Cushman (1608–1691) became Ruling Elder of the Plymouth church in 1649, succeeding the venerable William Brewster. Stratton, *Plymouth Colony*, 276-77.

To the Elders of the Third Church of Boston, 26 June 1671

To the third gathered Church of Christ in Boston Grace, mercy & peace from God our father; & from our Lord Jesus Christ, be multiplyed.

Reverend & Dearley Beloved in the Lord

whereas by the Providence of the only wise God, in whose hand are all our times & wayes, our beloved brother & sister, viz Mr John Winslow & Mary his wife[1] have their setled habitation amongst you, & wee seeing noe hopes of their returne unto us, they having also manifested unto us their desires to Joyne themselves unto you, in order to the regular participation of all the ordinances of Xt in his church, wee doe therefore by these our letters dismisse them to your holy fellowship, beseeching you to receive them in the Lord as it becometh saints into the bond of your holy Covenant, & in all Christian Love & faithfullnesse to watch over them, & administer to them those blessed ordinances of Christ, for their further ædification in faith & holinesse; our prayers to God for them are that they may be fruitfull & profitable amongst you by their exemplary walking according to the rules of the Gospel, for the glory of God & the furtherance of your & their Consolation in Christ Jesus, to whose grace & blessing wee commend them & you in all your holy administrations; beseeching God even our father to adde to you daily such as shall be saved, & that you may stand compleat in all the will of God; craving also your prayers for us, wee take leave & subscribe ourselves,

Your truly Loving Brethren in the order & fellowship of the Gospel

J: C: [&] T: C: with the Consent of the Church

Plymouth
June 26: 1671:

Such of their children also as live with you whether adult or inadult wee commend to your care & watch in the Lord & to be received by you according to their capacity desiring of the Lord to accompany the dispensation of his holy word to them for their effectuall Regeneration that in the Lords good time they may become Living stones in his holy Temple.

Cotton Family Papers 6:5, Prince Library, Rare Books and Manuscripts, Boston Public Library. Addressed at bottom of letter "For the Revd Elders of the 3[d] gathered ch: of Xt in Boston, these." This appears to be Cotton's draft copy of the letter sent to the elders.

---

1. Mary Chilton (1607–1679) arrived in New England on board the *Mayflower* in 1620. She married John Winslow (1597-1674), who arrived the year after. They removed to Boston in 1655. Stratton, *Plymouth Colony*, 262, 374.

From the General Court of Plymouth Colony, August 1671

In the spring of 1671, rumors spread that Philip (Metacomet), sachem of Pokanoket (on Plymouth Colony's western boundary) was preparing a surprise attack on the English settlements. Although only weakly substantiated, the rumors jolted the Plymouth government into a flurry of preemptive activity. The General Court proceeded to pass ordinances demanding that Natives surrender all European weapons, and deliver "engagements of fidelity" to Plymouth authority. At its July 1 meeting, the Plymouth General Court ordered a call-up of the town militias for a military expedition to force compliance with the terms of disarmament from the Saconnet Indians (in the area of modern Little Compton, Rhode Island), "upon a supposition that they would not accept of the tearmes proposed." A contingent from the eastern towns of the colony was to set out on August 8 and march to Assonett (modern-day Freetown, Massachusetts), there to rendezvous the next day with men from the western towns. The force was to consist of 102 men, including forty Natives. The Court ordered that the colony's churches observe "a sollemne day of humilliation" on 9 August, "to seeke the presence and favor of God, and his blessing on us in the entended expedition." Before that could happen, however, the Saconnet sachem Awashunks came to Plymouth and on 24 July agreed to submit to Plymouth's terms. Although the mission against Saconnet was scrubbed, the Court insisted that the call-up go forth, in order to intimidate other recalcitrant Natives, and rescheduled the day of humiliation for 16 August. In September, the Plymouth authorities managed finally to extract humiliating concessions from Philip, including disarmament.[1]

Plymouth

To m^{r} John Cotton Pastor and m^{r} Thomas Cushman Elder [of the] Church of Christ att Plymouth to be Comunicated to that Congregation wth all Convenient Speed

Beloved bretheren and frinds wee p^{r}sume it is not unknowne unto you that the Ind[ians of] Saconett were and are found Coep^{r}tenors[2] in Complyance with Phillip the Cheif Sac[hem of] Poconakett in his late Conspiracye against us which appeers as otherwise; soe by being p^{r}sonally with him att mount hope[3] on that accoumpt; and alsoe appeered with him, sundry [....] armes att Taunton; on Consideration wherof and other p^{r}ticulars Concurrent wee thought meet to Require some of the Cheif of them to give [illeg.] att Plymouth in order unto a settlement of matters between them and us Relating to [the p]^{r}mises and to bring in all theire English Armes; both which they Refused to doe; Notwithstan[ding] wee have sent unto them letters and Messengers severall times with assurance of their [peace]able Coming and Returning; and in stead of an answare suitable to our expectations; they have [sent] us Divers Insolent Returnes manifesting therin great Refractarynes and adversnes to our termes of Complyance; on Consideration wherof our Councell of Warre Concluded to send some smale force under the <*hand*> Comand of Major Josias Winslow;[4] to Reduce them to a more Rationall and peacable Demenior and Carriage; and wee did appoint the eight Day of this Instant August, to be observed by the severall Congregations of this Juridiction [ac]tively in fasting and prayer to seeke the presence of God and his blessing with us in soe [illeg.] an enterprise; but soe it was the good Pleasure of God to Dispose [otherwise?] Awashunckes the Cheif Sachem of Saconett; hath bine lately with us and [several words illeg.] life and peace with us; which hath given us Renewed [cause?] to [Reflect?] on our former agitations and Conclusions about the p^{r}mises; and Notwith[standing] wee saw Cause to lett her Returne in peace and safety; on such Conditions as have [been] Indented between us; yett withall wee see Reason to Retaine our former Resoluti[on] [...] Reference to a sending forth as aforsaid; to Reduce such a p^{r}ty of the said Salvages [....] make head against us. and therfore the Majestrates of this Jurisdiction do sev[ ] Comend the 16th Day of this Instant unto the severall Congregations in this Gov^{r}ment [...] sett apart and observed as a sollemne Day of humiliation to seeke the face and favor [....] that hee would please to Continew our lives and liberties without a goeing fourth or efus[ion] of blood; <or *in case Nessesitie Require a*> a foretast wee have by the submision of the said S[achem] but incase that be not attained; that hee would please to succeed us and prosper us in our expedition so as his name may have the Glory and wee and ours after may have Cause to Rejoyce in the mercy and salvation that hee may worke for us [....] soe that providence Disposeth that there be noe Nessesitie of a goeing forth we Desire [....] [12?] Day of this Instant may be observed as a Day of thanksgiving unto God for his [...] mercy in that behalf;

The Desire of the [....] of this Jurisdic[tion] [....] p^{r}: Nathan[iel Morton][5]

[....] of the sixt month (71)

Cotton Family Papers 6:6, Prince Library, Rare Books and Manuscripts, Boston Public Library. Mutilated on left and right margins.

---

1. *Records of the Colony of New Plymouth in New England,* ed. Nathaniel Shurtleff and David Pulsifer, 12 vols. (Boston, 1856–61) (hereafter *PCR*), 5:74-75.

2. Copartners.

3. Mount Hope, or Montaup, now in Bristol, Rhode Island, was the home of Metacomet (Philip).

4. Maj. Josiah Winslow (c. 1629–1680), eldest surviving son of Edward Winslow, founding member and governor of Plymouth Colony. Josiah served as Plymouth Colony Assistant (1657–1673) and as Commissioner for the United Colonies (1658–1672). In 1657 the General Court named him "Commander in Chief," or Major, of the colony's militia companies. *DAB.*

5. Nathaniel Morton (c. 1613–1685), the nephew of Gov. William Bradford, became Secretary (later Clerk) of the General Court of Plymouth, a post he held until his death. His access to colony records, and his uncle's papers, facilitated his publication of *New England's Memorial* in 1669. Stratton, *Plymouth Colony*, 330-31.

To the Elders of the First Church of Boston, 1 AUGUST 1671

TO THE FIRST CHU[RCH] [....] GRACE & PEACE [....] & FROM OUR LORD [....]
REVEREND, MUCH HONORED & [....] LORD JESUS,

our Beloved Sister M^{ris} Hannah Joh[nson][1] having bin by the providence of God many yeares since removed from us unto you, in all which time of her residence amongst you she hath had the benefit of Communion with you, by virtue of her church relation here, wee thought it her duty to Joyne in Covenant with your selves, that she might be under your *<speciall>* Christian care and watchfullnesse for the advancing of the spirituall weall of her soule, & therefore advised her to be in the use of meanes for attaining soe choice of favour, which Counsell she hath regularly hearkned unto; and desired our letters of dismission to you; wee doe therefore by these commend & dismisse this our Sister to you beseeching you in the Lord to receive her into your holy fellowship, as saints ought to be received, & to administer to her the pretious blessings of the house of God for her spirituall growth in grace & further quickening and enlargement in walking in the wayes of God.

Thus Commending her unto God, whose grace alone can enable to walke worthy of soe great mercies, & *<begging>* desiring that you may be more & more inriched with the blessings of truth, holinesse & peace, *<desiring>* [c]raving also your fervent prayers for us, wee take Leave, subscribing our selves,

Your Affectionate Bretheren in the faith & fellowship of the Gospel

J: C: [&] T: C: with the Consent of the chu[rch]

Plymouth
6 mo: 1st d: 1671:

Cotton Family Papers 6:7, Prince Library, Rare Books and Manuscripts, Boston Public Library. Addressed at bottom of letter "To the Reverend, our truly Honoured friends & Bretheren the Elders of the first gathered church of christ in Boston, these." Cotton's draft copy. Substantial tear in top margin.

1. See the letter from Hannah Johnson and Mary Blake of 20 February 1671, above.

To the Elders of the First Church of Boston, [1 August?] 1671

[....] in Boston [....]muel [....] Reve[rend] [....] [br]etheren in our Lod Jesus christ.[....] Mary Blake,[1] having bin by the [providence of Go]d many yeares since removed from us & thereby uncapable of enjoying that Christian Communion with & helpe from us, which soe solemne a relation doth oblige unto, wee therefore advised her to seeke some regular Establishment in one of the Churches of Christ in the place where now she lives, which counsell of ours she hath <*regularly*> orderly hearkned unto, & desired our letters of dismission unto you;

wee doe therefore by these commend and dismisse this our sister unto you, beseeching you in the Lord to receive her into your holy fellowship, as saints ought to be received, & to administer to her the pretious blessings of the house of God, with all due watchfullnesse over her in the Lord, for her spirituall growth in grace etc all the rest as on the other side. & superscription also, mutatis mutandis.

Cotton Family Papers 6:7, Prince Library, Rare Books and Manuscripts, Boston Public Library. Cotton's draft copy, written on the reverse of the last letter. Substantial tear in top margin.

---

1. See the letter from Hannah Johnson and Mary Blake of 20 February 1671, above.

To the Commissioners of the United Colonies, 7 September, 1671

Cotton appears to have sincerely enjoyed his missionary work with the Natives of Martha's Vineyard, but there he had the advantage of beginning with a congregation that had, in some cases, nearly two decades of instruction and study under Rev. Thomas Mayhew. As Cotton relates below, the situation on the mainland was very different.

Worshipfull & truly Honoured Gentlemen

Although by the Providence of God, in whose hand are all our times, I was called from that place where I had for a time some liberty to attend the worke of God amongst the Indians, as also considerable Encouragement from your selves to further me therein; yet I have ever since retained a firme resolution of heart to endeavour the best good of poore Indians, if it would please God soe far to smile upon me, as to open the doore for such a service where now I live; Accordingly I did endeavour by going twice or thrice to Josiah[1] in his life time, but the Interest of the world was more deare to him then any thing of a better life then I could present him with; not long after this his refusall of such a motion, God tooke him from all his worldly Enjoyments: About the beginning of october last I attempted againe with some Indians that live, some 8, some 12 miles from my house, wherein it hath pleased God to give me some good successe, to whom I desire to give the praise of it; There was not one praying Indian when I began with them, but in one meeting after another, they have encouraged my heart to be constant in the worke with them, there being now Thirty praying Indians amongst them; & this I doe finde that every sermon leaves them with desires of another; there are divers more hearers, whose coming on to the wayes of God I hope for & expect continually; Thus much I thought it my duty to acquaint your worships withall, as knowing that your hearts are sincerely desirous of the prospering of this worke of God among these desolate soules: I have not further to adde, but my humble & earnest request, that I may have an Interest in your daily prayers to the God of heaven, that he would accept of me, owne & blesse me in his service; & therewith I take leave, subscribing myselfe, Gentlemen,

your worships humbly & sincerely devoted

John Cotton

Plimouth,
September 7: 1671

The New England Company Original Correspondence (MS 7936), Guildhall Library, London. Addressed "These For the Right Worshipfull, the Commissioners of the United Colonies, in Boston."

---

1. Probably Josias Wampatuck, a Massachusett sachem living at the Mattakeesett Ponds in Plymouth Colony (modern-day Pembroke, Massachusetts). Although his mother had received a Christian burial, Josias was reluctant to embrace the new religion; even the "Apostle to the Indians," John Eliot, had been rebuffed by Wampatuck. In 1669, Josias led a Native contingent against the Mohawks and was killed in battle. Russell Herbert Gardner, "Last Royal Dynasty of the Massachusetts," *Bulletin of the Massachusetts Archaeological Society* 57 (1996): 19.

From Simon Bradstreet,[1] et al, 13 September 1671

As had been the case on Martha's Vineyard, Cotton received modest renumeration for his missionary work in Plymouth Colony from the Society for the Propagation of the Gospel in New England, through its agents among the Commissioners of the United Colonies.

Boston: Sept: 13th: 1671

Sr:

We received yours dated the 7th: Instant By wh[ich] we are informed of the Renewall of your Labours In Endevoringe The Conversion of the Natives in That part of the Country where God in his providence hath now desposed your habitation. and shall be glad To heare of your further progresse in yt Good Worke. And for your Encoragmt: Wee have appointed mr. Hizk. Usher[2] to pay you tenn pounds wh: you may have In mony or Goods wh: you like best, upon all demands. Thus desiringe ye Lord to succseed and blesse your Endevours <*To*> herin we rest.

Your Lovinge Freinds

Simon Bradstreete
Thomas Danforth[3]
Samuel Willis

Cotton Family Papers 6:8, Prince Library, Rare Books and Manuscripts, Boston Public Library. Addressed "These For our Lovinge Freind mr John Cotton, Minister at plimoth present." Endorsed "from the Commissioners of the United Colonies: September, 13: 1671:"

---

1. By the time Simon Bradstreet (1604–1697) retired from public office in 1692, he had amassed the longest record of public service in colonial New England history. He arrived with the Winthrop fleet in 1630, as secretary of the Massachusetts Bay Company, and after 1636 was elected magistrate every year except those of the Dominion of New England. He lived in Ipswich during most of this time but moved to Boston in 1672, after the death of his wife Anne, the famous poet. In 1678 he was deputy governor, and he became governor the next year. In the New England political spectrum he was a moderate Puritan and was frequently criticized for his moderation. When royal officials arrived after the suspension of the Massachusetts charter in 1684, hard-line Puritans denounced him for his apparent obsequiousness, but Bradstreet refused to serve in the Dominion government. It was to Bradstreet that colony leaders turned after the overthrow of Gov. Andros in 1689; he served as interim governor until the arrival of William Phipps in 1692. *ANB.*

2. Hezekiah Usher (d. 1676), merchant of Boston, was one of the founders of the Old South Church. He had been a selectman for the town since 1659 and was a member of the prestigious Artillery Company.

3. Thomas Danforth (1623–1699), emigrated to Massachusetts in 1634 and settled in Cambridge. He was a commissioner of the United Colonies, assistant to the General Court 1659–1679, and deputy governor when he sat on the court of Oyer and Terminer during the 1692 Salem witchcraft trials. *ANB.*

From Increase Mather,[1] 5 December 1671

Dear Brother

I R'd yr MSS. for wch I thank you. I am sory to hear of yr affliction in Rowlands[2] griefs. The Lord pitty hime for his covenants sake. God hath bin gracious to my wife in restoring her to a comfortable measure of strength again. The Lord help us to walk answerably before him, according to what his willing & grt delivering dispensations have bin. Through ye wonderfully good providence of God, I enjoy my health in as good measure as at any time since my coming to N. E. pray ernestly yt God would Continue yt mercy & help me to improve it as shall be most for his glory, & my owne injoying at ye great day. The good Lord be gracious to you in my sister, & continue her a blessing & comfort to you, I rest

Yor true brother

I Mather

Boston. 5. Decr. 1671.
5. Dec. 1671[3]

Cotton Family Papers 6:9, Prince Library, Rare Books and Manuscripts, Boston Public Library. Addressed "These For ye Revd. my dear Brother mr John Cotton Pastor of ye Church in Plymouth." Endorsed "from my Brother Mather December, 5: 1671:"

---

1. Increase Mather (1639–1723), the famous Puritan divine, was Cotton's step-brother and brother-in-law, having married Maria Cotton (b. 1642) in 1662. After taking his degree at Harvard in 1656, Increase traveled to Dublin, where his older brother Samuel was minister. He took his MA at Trinity College and preached at several places in England and on the island of Guernsey. He rejected the conformity required after the Restoration and returned to New England in 1661. He was besieged with offers for employment, but he accepted a position at Second Church in Boston's North End and was ordained there in 1664. He initially opposed the baptismal practices advocated by the synod of 1662, but gradually came to tolerate the measures. He was prone to illness from his youth, and his son Cotton described a fever in 1669 as so complicated by "that Comprehensive Mischief which they call, The Hypocondriacs Affection, that he lay confined all the Winter." Active in religious and intellectual pursuits and a prolific writer, he also played a crucial role in colonial politics. When Crown authorities demanded the return of the Massachusetts charter in 1683, Mather exhorted the Boston freemen to instruct their deputies to the General Court to reject the order. When the charter was annulled, Mather was chosen an agent to present colony grievances to the court of James II. After the 1688 revolution, Mather worked to get a new charter from William and Mary, a charter that ultimately subsumed Plymouth Colony under Massachusetts. Mather was allowed to nominate the first governor under the new charter, the Maine-born adventurer Sir William Phipps. *Sibley's Harvard Graduates*, 1:410-70.

2. This appears to refer to Rowland Cotton (1667–1722), the dutiful second son of John Cotton and Joanna Rosseter, who was nearly four years old at this time. If so, the "griefs" are presumably connected to some childhood malady. A graduate of Harvard in 1685, Rowland accepted the call of the Sandwich church in 1692 over the invitation of Dedham, in part "being willing to live near his parents who were then at Plymouth." Adapting to the local religious environment, he preached several lectures to the

Increase Mather painted by John van der Spriett, 1688.
Courtesy of the Massachusetts Historical Society.

town's Quakers when their speaker died and also preached once a month to nearby Natives, whose language he learned. Rowland achieved the worldly success that had eluded his father. Despite his large family and modest salary, "his excellent wife's industry," combined with timely legacies and prudent management, allowed his family to live in moderate wealth, "much of a gentleman in his garb and customs." Perhaps in consequence of his lifestyle, he became fat and gouty in his last years. *Sibley's Harvard Graduates*, 3:323-26.

3. Line added by Prince.

From Thomas Walley,[1] [March] 1672

Reverind and dearly beloved in o^{R} Lord Jesus

As for my Comming to Plimoth I feare it will be to soon for me to journey abroad but if I am well and the weather Encouraging I shall endeavor it: the business of [m^{r}.] Miles I feare will prove troublesom I can say little [in it] I desire ye Lord may direct it he have noe regard to the peace of the churches they need not be forward to have Communion wth him as for yor questions to the first whether admonition be a church sensure. I judg it is yor honoured father in the way of the churches of N: E:[2] p 91. Calls it a sensure and m^{r} Hooker in his survey[3] 3 part chap: of sensures Calls it a sentence and the sensure of admonition. it is used for the same end that excommunication is if admonition nor suspension are not church sensures then there are noe church sensures <*there*> but only excommunication .

As for suspension many things are sayd Pro & Con the pson under the sensure of <*Excommuni*> admonition is a knowne sinner and the people of God should not willingly ptake wth such lest they pertake of theyr sins and psons under that sensure Cannot ptake wthout giving offense the 2 Thes: 3. 14. 15[4] sayth soe much for suspention that I wonder how any should think it reasonable publikly to object agst it. though there should be different apprehentions ye thing being disputable and Crcomstantiall the dispute about it should have bin privat. publik objecting is only of use when daingerouse errors are preached. this publik objecting when frequent and about lesser things in my opinion savours of greate imprudence if not of blind Zeale and prid. it puts stumbling blocks in the way of the ignorant & weak a meanes to fill Congregations with Contention and helps the divil to steale away the good seed lately sowen. and yet it is o^{r} duty to take heed of giving any just occasion to those that are forward that way. and to beare with those that through weakness Cannot take right seasons to doe Gods work. Deare Brother I scribbled these things in hast they are scarsly worth yor reading. only I would not have you discouraged in yor work neither much Contend wth those that differ from you in these lesser things I never Knew a need of suspension for psons being under admonition being advised not to offend have followed advice but this but my owne experience.

yor last papers I have now [re]ceived I thank yo^{u} for them I shall bring y^{m} or send them next weeke my hea[rty] love to yor selfe & m^{rs} Cotten, my servis to ye Governor

praying [illeg.] in haste I rest
y^{rs} in o^{r} Lord Jesus

Tho: Walley

Cotton Family Papers 6:10, Prince Library, Rare Books and Manuscripts, Boston Public Library. Addressed "ffor the Reverend, and my much honoured friend m^{r} John Cotten Pastour of the Church of Christ in Plimoth these present." Endorsed "From Mr Walley Received, March, 4: 1671:

---

1. Thomas Walley (1618–1679) was "driven from the exercise of his ministry in London" after the Restoration, according to Cotton Mather, and arrived in New England about 1663. Shortly thereafter he was ordained minister of the church at Barnstable, which had been "miserably broken with divisions" begun by Quaker-inspired dissent in the mid 1650s. Walley seems to have been temperamentally suited to the task of healing the wounds in the religious community. Mather reports that he possessed a "charming wisdom," a proper Christian humility, a capacity for independent thinking and a "well-bounded toleration" of "those that peaceably differ from the generality of God's people in lesser things." Walley was present at Cotton's ordination and delivered "a solemne Prayer" for the occasion. Cotton Mather, *Magnalia Christi Americana, or The Ecclesiastical History of New-England* (1852, reprint, New York, 1967) 599-601; *CSM*, 22:144.
2. John Cotton Sr., *The Way of the Churches of Christ in New England* (London, 1645).
3. A reference to Thomas Hooker, *A Survey of the Summe of Church-Discipline* (London, 1648).
4. 2 Thess. 3:14-15: "And if any man obey not our word by this epistle, note that man, and have no company with him, that he may be ashamed. Yet count him not as an enemy, but admonish him as a brother."

From the General Court of Plymouth Colony, 9 March 1672

Plymouth Colony is famous today for a legendary thanksgiving, but days of humiliation and prayer, to sound out the possible causes of God's displeasure, were just as characteristic of the reformed Protestant communities there. The first such occasion recorded had been in 1623, in response to a near-disastrous drought, and others occurred sporadically in Plymouth and other New England colonies throughout the colonial period. Usually these occasions named specific issues for consideration, as in the example here.

To Mr John Cotton [....] and Mr Thomas Cushman Elder[....] at Plymouth [....] [co]mmunicated to that Congregation with [....]

Beloved

Wheras by the good [Provid]ence of God the Revolution of the yeare [....] as our seed time Draweth on and [....] hath pleased God in severall yeares past [....] such Respect by Depriv[....] all of the fruites of the earth in gr[....]asting [....] and that also a sperit of Prophanes Doth more actively appeer th[....]ouly Generally in the land but also in this our Collonie in p^{r}ticular; In speciall in Re[spect? ....]eanes[1] which hath more than ordinarily broken out amongst us the yeare past [....]lsoe in Consideration of the many sad afflictions which the people of God doe suffer in other prtes of the world the p^{r}mises Considered with severall other *<thinges>* p^{r}ticulars that might be named, and wee hope will not be omitted this Court thinkes meet to propose to the severall Congregations within this Jurisdiction to sett apart the first fourth Day in the next month which wilbe the third Day of the month to be observed as a solleme Day of humilliation throughout this Collonie; to seek the Lord for the Continuance of his p^{r}sence with us and Removing and preventing evills from us or towards us and a supply of such blessings as wee stand in need of both speritual and temporall soe as may be to his praise and our Comfort.

By order of the Court

Nathaniel: Morton Secretary.

Plymouth March the 9th 1671,

Cotton Family Papers 6:11, Prince Library, Rare Books and Manuscripts, Boston Public Library. Two large tears on the top margin.

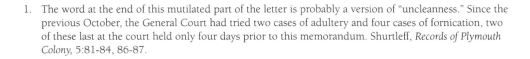

1. The word at the end of this mutilated part of the letter is probably a version of "uncleanness." Since the previous October, the General Court had tried two cases of adultery and four cases of fornication, two of these last at the court held only four days prior to this memorandum. Shurtleff, *Records of Plymouth Colony,* 5:81-84, 86-87.

From the General Court of Plymouth Colony, [5 July] 1672

To MR John Cotton Pastour and MR Thomas Cushman Elder of the Church of Christ att Plymouth to be Improved as is beneath enserted;

Wee being Informed that it is upon the hartes of our Naighbours of the Massachusetts to support and Incurrage that Nursary of Learning att harverd Colledge in Cambridge in New England;[1] from whome have through the blessing of God Issued many usefull p^{r}sons for publicke service in Church and Comonwealth; being alsoe Informed that divers Godly and well affected in England are Reddy to Assist therin by way of Contributeing Considerable sumes provided the Country heer are forward to promote the same; and that the severall Townes in the Massachusetts have bine very free in theire offerings, therunto wee alsoe being by letters from them <*Invigh*> Invited and Insighted to Joyne with them in soe good a worke; and that wee may have an Interest with others in the blessing that the Lord May please from thence to Convey unto the Countrey; this Court Doth therfore earnestly Comend it to the Minnesters and Elders in each Towne that they takeing such with them; as they shall think meete; would p^{r}ticularly and earnestly move and stir up all such in theire severall townes as are able to Contribute unto this worthy worke, be it in mony or other good pay; and that they make a Returne of what they shall effect heerin unto the Court that shall sitt in <u>October next</u> whoe will appoin^{t} meet p^{r}sons to Receive the Contributions and faithfully Dispose of the same for the ends proposed;

By order of the Court

Nathaniel: Morton Secretry

Plymouth the 5th <u>1672</u>[2]

Cotton Family Papers 6:14, Prince Library, Rare Books and Manuscripts, Boston Public Library.

1. The Old College building at Harvard was so decrepit by 1671 that the college governors decided to begin a subscription drive for a new building. The appeal went out to every town in the Bay Colony but apparently was extended to other New England colonies as well. Predictably, perhaps, Plymouth's response was meager; though several towns pledged funds, there is no record that the college ever received them. By the end of the year the drive had raised £2280 in pledges. New College, or Old Harvard Hall, was sufficiently finished by the summer of 1677 to be used for Commencement. Samuel Eliot Morison, *Harvard College in the Seventeenth Century* (Cambridge, Mass., 1936) 2:376-77, 423-25.
2. Morton left out the month, but it is probably July. The Plymouth General Court met on 5 July in 1672, and a letter from that court to the Commissioners for the United Colonies of New England dated 9 September 1672 declares "there is alreddy a contribution made" to the college "according to our low condition." Shurtleff, *Records of Plymouth Colony,* 10:354-55.

From John Freeman, et al, 31 July 1672

Cotton's Boston connections were obviously regarded as an asset for a struggling church on Cape Cod.

Rewerent and well belowed in the Lord Jesus Christ[1]

that late experience that we have had of your redines and wilingnes to be hellpfull to us in your good advise to the well managin of the apointments of god: for the which our desier is to render you many thanks: as allso the blessing of god upone your indewars[2] with the rest of oure Honored Rewerent and belowed friends, doth inwit and imbolden us farther to improve our intrust in you: being aquanted that you are sencibell of our sad Condition: being so long destitut of a minister in ofise amongst us: to goe in and out before us and break the bread of life unto us.[3] which our solles doe ernestly long after: and being informed you are spedily to goe to Bostoune and Cambridg where wee question not but you will hafe opertuniti to Conwers and adwise with those that will be abell to informe you, and to inquier out a sutabell person for us: you so well knoing our Condition and state, our ernest request to you is that you wolld so far fawour us if it be posibell to enquier out som sutabell person for us:[4] and by the furst opertuniti to let us here from you hou far god hath apered in your indewours: by which you shall forewer obllige us youre Loveing brethren in the faith and feloship of the gospell: in the be hallfe and with the Consent of the Church.

John ffreeman[5]
Tho Crosby
Daniell Colle[6]
Samuel ffreeman[7]

Eastham [July 31]:[8] 1672

Cotton Family Papers 6:13, Prince Library, Rare Books and Manuscripts, Boston Public Library. Addressed "To the Rewerent and well be Lowed Mr John Cotton Pastor of the Church of Christ in Pllimworth. these Present with Care." Endorsed "From the Church of Eastham July, 31: 1672:."

---

1. The writer consistently uses the letter *w*, when non-initial, as a double *v*.
2. Endeavors.
3. Thomas Crosby, a member of the "search committee" and whose signature appears below, had been ministering to Eastham but had not been ordained. He later turned up as "merchant" in neighboring Harwich. Frederick Lewis Weis, *The Colonial Clergy and the Colonial Churches of New England* (Baltimore, Md., 1936), 64; *Sibley's Harvard Graduates,* 2:370-79.
4. Samuel Treat began preaching in the town that year. Weis, *Colonial Clergy*, 208.
5. John Freeman (1627–1719) was a prominent resident of Eastham and of Plymouth Colony. He came to New England with his father in 1635 and married Mercy, the daughter of Gov. Thomas Prence, in 1650. By the time of this letter he had been a selectman for nine years and also served intermittently as a deputy to the General Court, assistant governor, and in a variety of town and colony offices. In King Philip's War he was a captain, afterwards rising to the rank of major. Mary Walton Ferris, comp., *Dawes-Gates Ancestral Lines: A Memorial Volume Containing the American Ancestry of Mary Beman (Gates) Dawes* (private printing, 1931), 2:356-61.
6. Daniel Cole (1614–1694) was one of three brothers who emigrated to New England in 1633 and settled in Plymouth Colony. At this point he was both an Eastham selectman and a deputy to the General Court. Frank T. Cole, *The Early Genealogies of the Cole Families in America* (Columbus, Oh., 1887), 32.
7. Samuel Freeman (1638–1712), no relation to John, was deacon of the church. *The American Genealogist* 11:73-80, 171-79.
8. The day and month are obliterated. Beneath, in what appears to be Thomas Prince's hand, is the date "July 31."

From Increase Mather, 15 July 1673

BOSTON 15. 5^M. 1673

DEAR BROTHER

Just now I rec'd yor tre.[1] My Father hath noth. on y^t Q. you propound, y^t I know of. I th [think?] Mr Tillinghast hath a discourse on y^t subject,[2] whether it be in my study I can not certaynly tell, nor hav time to looke. In a wrd. [word?] I Conceive that ye worke of ones generation, is to attend to y^t wch Peter calls the p^r sent Truth 2 Pet: 1:12:[3] wch doth vary according to ye several ages men live in. In the primitive Times, y^t great work was bearing witness to ye greatest of Truths Revealed in ye Gospel, y^t Jesus of Nazareth is ye son of God & Savior of ye world, ag^t Jews & Heathens who all denyed it After y^{t} ye great work was To bear witness to y^{t} Truth concerning ye Eternal generation & God head of Christ, wch ye Arians raysed such bitter p^{r}secutions against. After y^{t} bearing witness ag^{t} Antich^{t}. First in asserting ye truths concerning prophetical & Priestly office of C^{t}, we were oppressed by Papists that brought in Traditions, Transubstanciation, Masse &c And now the great work is to enquire into, (& bear witness accordingly) ye Truths relating to ye Kingly office of Christ, both as to y^{t} government he hath appoynted in his church, wch hath not bin much minded nor generally known to ye world, till ye last age; & y^{t} glorious Kingdome wch he will one day (at his 2d Coming) have over all ye world; ye glory of y^{es} Truths, (& so of those Pphesies concerning ye utter Ruin of Antichrist, & Conversion of ye Jews, fullness of ye gentiles &c.) is broke forth of late more y^{n} in former ages. Therefore I am pswaded y^{t} a diligent searching into, & giving or Testimony as to all y^{es} matters, is ye work ye Lord calls up y^{s} generation for. And inasmuch as Times of great Light should be Times of much Holiness, therefore ye Lord expects from y^{s} generation, Holiness to ye Lord as Zach. 14. 20.[4] And inasmuch as y^{s} are times of much division, so ye practice of ye duty of Love to brethren, is ye special work of y^{s} Time. And inasmuch as y^{r} is a great & unusual decay as to y^{e} [Pwrs?] of godliness amongst C^{htns} every where, The last age had less light but more Zeal & devotion y^{n} y^{s} hath. so our work is to pick up & live up ye power of godliness, & interest of practical Holynes &c. R^{ts} to my sister. The Lord be wth you

I am yor lov: brother

I Mather

Cotton Family Papers 6:16, Prince Library, Rare Books and Manuscripts, Boston Public Library. Addressed "These For ye Revd m^{r} John Cotton Pastur of ye Church in Plymouth." Endorsed "From my Brother Mather July, 15: 1673:."

---

1. Not found.
2. Perhaps one of the published sermons and discourses of John Tillinghast (1604–1655), English preacher and Fifth Monarchist. *DNB*.
3. Biblical reference superscribed by Cotton. 2 Pet. 1:12 reads: "Wherefore I will not be negligent to put you always in remembrance of these things, though ye know them, and be established in the present truth."
4. Zech. 14:20: "In that day shall there be upon the bells of the horses, HOLINESS UNTO THE LORD; and the pots in the LORD'S house shall be like the bowls before the altar."

To George Shove,[1] 6 October 1673

To the ch: of ct: at T:[2] Gr: M: & P: fr[om God] our f: & from our L: J: C: be mult:[3]Rev: & dearly bel: in our Lord JesusBeing made acquainted with the desire of Eliz: Williams daughter of Br: Walter to injoy com: with G: in all his ord: in Ch: fel: wch you where div: prov: hath ordered the place of her abode, wee cannot but acknowledge the Lds goodnes and cov: faith: in stirring the hearts of any of his cov: seed to rememb: & to give up themselves to him. & do therefore rejoyce in this motion & desire the furtherance thereoff, & doe by these letters of dismission give her up unto you and the Lord, desiring your acceptance of her according as you finde the Lord satisfying your counc: by her profes: & Conver: that she is one whom xt hath received; wee pray you to watch over her for the best good of her soule & to administer to her the holy things of God soe as may best conduce to her sprituall edif: & eter: salv: Thus praying unto God that you may be a blessing unto her & that she may be soe blessed of God as to be a bles: amongst you, & that the L: would inrich you all more with the blessings of truth, hol: & pe: craving also your prayers for us, wee rest,

your Lov: bre: in the fa: & fel: of the Gosp:

J: C: [&] T: C: with the Cons: of the Ch:

Plim:
oct: 6: 73:

Cotton Family Papers 6:17, Prince Library, Rare Books and Manuscripts, Boston Public Library. Addressed at bottom of letter "To the Revd Mr Shove Pastour of the ch: of xt at Taunton, these." This is apparently Cotton's copy of the letter of dismissal.

1. Rev. George Shove (1634–1687), born in Dorchester, was ordained third minister of the church at Taunton in 1665. He was brother-in-law to another Cotton correspondent, Noah Newman, having married his sister Hopestill Newman (1641–1674). Samuel Hopkins Emery, *History of Taunton, Massachusetts, from its Settlement to the Present Time* (Syracuse, N.Y., 1893), 1:183-86; Tilton, *History of Rehoboth*, 49.

2. "To the church of Christ at Taunton."

3. "Grace, Mercy, and Peace from God our Father and from the Lord Jesus Christ be multiplied," a standard greeting for church correspondence adopted from the New Testament epistles.

From Thomas Danforth, et al, 26 December 1673

Rev^rnd Sir

not hearing any thing by L^tr p^rsented to our consideration from you we only ordered m^r Usher to pay your sallery of 20£ as formerly and for as much as a pticuler acc^ott. of the pgresse and successe of y^r work, wth others amongst ye Indyans, is very acceptable to the Gentmen of ye Corporation for that affayre in England; it is therefore desired you would please (p the first convenient opertunity) to send to the Commissioners here what you judge meet may by them be transmitted to the s^d Gentmen for theire better satisfaction therein: not elce but wth our loving respects to you p^rsented and prayers to God for his rich blessing on y^r pious Labors in the Gospell for ye good of those poore darke natives we take leave & rest

y^r affectionate ffrinds

Thomas Danforth
William Stoughton[1]
Thos Hinckley[2]

[Bos]ton decb 26. 1673

Cotton Family Papers 6:19, Prince Library, Rare Books and Manuscripts, Boston Public Library.

---

1. William Stoughton (1631–1701) became one of the most powerful men in late seventeenth-century Massachusetts. His family emigrated to the colony in its earliest years (it is not clear whether William was born in England or America) and settled in Dorchester. In 1644 his father returned to England to fight with the army of Parliament, and after William graduated from Harvard College in 1650, he followed him there. William studied at Oxford for a ministry in England but lost his support soon after the Restoration. In 1662 he returned to Massachusetts where, despite a talent for preaching and some offers of a ministerial position, he pursued a life as a landowner and magistrate. He was an assistant at the General Court from 1671 to 1686, served as a commissioner for the United Colonies, and when the Dominion of New England was formed, held positions in the unpopular government. This last notwithstanding, he survived the downfall of the Dominion, and under the 1691 royal charter government was named lieutenant-governor and chief justice of Massachusetts. To most scholars today he is notorious as the chief justice of the Court of Oyer et Terminer during the Salem witchcraft trials, of which he was an unrepentant supporter. He continued as lieutenant-governor until his death in 1701. *ANB*.

2. Thomas Hinckley (1621–1706), last governor of Plymouth Colony, emigrated from his native Kent to join his father, Samuel, at Barnstable, on Cape Cod, in 1639. He became a deputy to the General Court in 1645 and an assistant from 1658. In June 1681 he was chosen governor of the colony after the death of Josiah Winslow, and he served in that capacity until Plymouth's absorption by Massachusetts Bay in 1692. As governor, he strongly supported missionary efforts in the colony. Edward Randolph (see 20 December 1679) characterized him as "a rigid independent" in terms of his religious temperament. Certainly he was no friend to Quakers and other dissidents in the colony: he strongly advocated, and enforced, a 1677 law establishing a general tax for the support of properly ordained ministers. This policy, and his position as governor, were suspended during the years of the Dominion of New

England (1686–1689). Hinckley accepted a position in the Dominion government but resumed his gubernatorial duties when the Dominion collapsed and Gov. Andros was deposed. Hinckley allowed himself and Plymouth Colony to be drawn by Massachusetts Bay into a series of failed operations against the "Eastern" (Maine) Indians and Canada in the opening years of King William's War. The high taxes levied to support the war led to a breakdown in colony authority, as strapped towns refused to pay their assessments or carry out directives of the General Court. Unable to marshal enough support for a new colony charter, Hinckley became resigned to Plymouth's absorption by Massachusetts, made official by that province's charter, 7 October 1691. He continued to serve as a council member in the new government and died at Barnstable in 1706. Jacob Bailey Moore, *Lives of the Governors of New Plymouth and Massachusetts Bay; From the Landing of the Pilgrims at Plymouth in 1620, to the Union of the Two Colonies in 1692* (Boston, 1851), 201-32.

To Daniel Gookin,[1] 14 September 1674[2]

Worshipfull & Honoured Sir:

Mr. Bourne[3] haveing been long in the Indian Worke, and acquainted wth ye Indian language, in Several parts is most able to give you a Satisying account of the worke of god; and its progresse among the Indians of this Colony, I have not long lived here, but in this time I began to preach The word of God to a Company of Indians at a place Called Kitteaumut,[4] Since w^ch^, through the blessing of God, the number of praying Indians is forty males & females, as yett they have no Indian Teacher; but on the Sabbath dayes they usually go to heare one of m^r^ Bournes Indians, at ye nearest place to them.

About 10 of these Can read the English bookes,[5] and many more are very desirous to learne to read the word: but here is very great want of Indian Primers & Bibles, I much desire y^t^ the Commissioners would take Some Speedy Course, to supply that defect, I sometimes preach to ye Indians upon the Cape, at Several places & at Namassekett, whether Come the praying Indians of Assawomit & ketchiquut[6] of those Indians m^r^ Bourne gives you the acount,[7] When the Courts are here, theire are usually great multitud's of Indians from all parts of the Collony, at those Seasons I preach To them, wch I mention because God hath so farre blessed it, as to make it a means to encourage Some that live very remote to affect praying to God (viz) Manmanewat Sachem of Sakonett[8] & Some principall Indians of Coquitt,[9] who made theire Confessions, and declared theire willingnes to Serve God, and they Do Improve all the oppurtunityes they Can gett to heare the word, they Come to heare me at Acushnett,[10] when I preached theire, and do desire further means of Instruction. I desire you^r^ prayers for me & mine and rest Sir,

you^r^ worships in any Service for X,

John Cotton

Plimouth Sep: 14: 1674.

When I lived at the vineyard the praying Townes were Chappaquidgick,[11] Nashamoiess,[12] Sengekontakit,[13] Toikiming,[14] Nashuakemmiuk, Talhanio,[15] one Church there gathered long before, but no officers Since I lived here, I went over wth m^r^. Eliot[16] thether, & Hyacomes[17] was ordained pastour, John Tokinosh[18] Teacher, John Nanoso[19] & Joshua Mummeecheeg[20] ruling elders, Since I heare they are become Two Churches, the pastour & one Ruling elder for Chappaquidgick, the teacher & the other Ruling elder for the other Church, (wch hath some members (If I mistake not) in all the other townes above mencioned, hands were Imposed in ordination, by m^r^ Eliot, m^r^ Mahew[21] & my selfe, the church at Marshpaug,[22] was Gathered & m^r^ Bourne ordained pastour of it, hands Imposed by m^r^ Eliot & I & one of the messengers of Natick church & one of the vineyard Major Winslow (now our Governour)[23] m^r^ Southworth, m^r^ m^r^ [sic] Hinkly and m^r^ Bacon were the magistrates present, Mr Walley, m^r^ Arnold, m^r^ Shove, m^r^ Thornton, m^r^ Homes, m^r^ Newman, wth bretheren from all our Churches. How these Churches have increased I Cannot Informe.

Att Nantucket according to my best Intelligence: there are 3 praying townes & praying Indians about 300 males & females; one Church, the Pastour is John Gibbs,[24] the men in Church ffellowship are about 20, the women, 10, there Children are all baptised the English upon that Island who are about 27 families & many of them Anabaptists, did at first seeke to hinder them from administring baptisms to infants, but now they are quiet & meddle not wth them, Caleb[25] is preacher to one Towne there.

Daniel Gookin, "Indians Converted or Historicall collections of the indians in New england," Massachusetts Historical Society. Addressed "These for the Worshipll: Capt Daniel Gookin Magistrate living in Cambridge."

---

1. Daniel Gookin (1612–1687) settled in Virginia as early as 1630 and later served in the House of Burgesses. A zealous Puritan in a predominantly Anglican colony, Gookin emigrated to Massachusetts in 1644. He became a Deputy for Cambridge to the General Court in 1649, was a magistrate (1652-1686), and superintendent of Natives living in Massachusetts "praying towns" from 1656 until his death. *DAB.*

2. Gookin copied this letter, in parts, in chapters 8 and 9 of his manuscript "Indians Converted or Historicall collections of the indians in New england," dated 1674, which was first printed as "The Historical Collections of the Indians of New England," in *Collections of the Massachusetts Historical Society* (1792). In Gookin's manuscript, the letter appears in segments on three different pages, but Gookin identifies all as bearing the same date. The segments appear here in the order in which Gookin copied them. The original letter has not been found.

3. Rev. Richard Bourne (c. 1610–1682), minister of Sandwich, was an active missionary to Natives on Cape Cod, and served as pastor of the Native congregation at Mashpee. Mary Farwell Ayer, "Richard Bourne, Missionary to the Mashpee Indians," *New England Historic and Genealogical Register* 62 (1908): 139-43.

4. Kitteaumut was the area southward from modern-day Manomet, in Plymouth, to Buzzard's Bay. William T. Davis, *Ancient Landmarks of Plymouth* (Boston, 1883), 152.

5. Gookin's margin note reads "10 of them can read Indian."

6. Namassaket, Ketchiqut/Kuhtiticut/Titicut, and Assowampsett were neighboring Native communities in what are now Middleborough and Lakeville, about halfway between Plymouth and Philip's village at Mount Hope. Thomas Weston, *The History of the Town of Middleborough, Massachusetts* (Boston and New York, 1906), 18.

7. See the letter of Richard Bourne to Daniel Gookin, 1 September 1674, also in chapter 8 of Gookin's manuscript.

8. Mamanuett was a sachem of Sakonet, modern-day Little Compton, Rhode Island. Shurtleff, *Records of Plymouth Colony*, 5:224-25.

9. Probably Coksit, or Coakset, in modern-day Westport, Massachusetts.

10. The Native Acushnet was located at the head of what is now called the Acushnet River in southeastern Massachusetts, currently the border between New Bedford and the town of Acushnet.

11. Modern-day Chappaquiddick, an islet at the east end of Martha's Vineyard separated from the larger island by a narrow channel.

12. An area on the eastern shore of Edgartown Great Pond.

13. An area around what is now known as Sengekontacket Pond, between Edgartown and Oak Bluffs.

14. Takemmy is in modern-day West Tisbury.

15. Nashuakemmuk and Talhanio are locales in modern-day Chilmark, near Menemsha.

16. John Eliot (1604–1690), minister of Roxbury, was New England's most famous missionary and the publisher of numerous texts in the Massachusett dialect. *DAB*. See Eliot's letter to Cotton of April 1680.

17. Hiacoomes (d. c.1690), the first and most famous of the Reverend Thomas Mayhew's converts, lived near Great Harbor (Edgartown) when the English arrived there in 1642. He learned to read English and began preaching to other Natives in 1646. Hiacoomes continued preaching after his mentor's death in 1657, and when the Native church organized in 1670, John Eliot and John Cotton ordained him pastor and teacher. Experience Mayhew, *Indian Converts or Some Account of the Lives and Dying Speeches of a Considerable Number of the Christian Indians of Martha's Vineyard in New England* (London, 1728), 1-12.

18. John Toquenosh (Tockinosh, d. 23 Jan. 1683/4) became teaching elder of the first Native church in 1670. A persuasive preacher, "he was reckoned to exceed Hiacoomes both in his natural and acquired abilities." Mayhew, *Indian Converts*, 14-16.

19. John Nahnosoo, "one of the first called among the Indians" of Martha's Vineyard, was ruling elder of the 1670 Native church, staying with the Vineyard contingent after the church split. Mayhew, *Indian Converts*, 17-18.

20. When the Martha's Vineyard Natives formed their first church in 1670, they chose Joshua Momatchegin (d. c. 1703) to be their ruling elder. When the church later split between the converts of Chappaquiddick and of Edgartown, Momatchegin stayed with the former. According to Experience Mayhew, he struggled valiently, but futilely, to arrest the declension and drunkenness that descended on both the English and the Natives on the islet in the 1690s. Mayhew, *Indian Converts*, 34.

21. Thomas Mayhew Sr. (1593–1682) became the sole English proprietor of Martha's Vineyard in the early 1640s. After his son, the Reverend Thomas Mayhew (b. 1621) was lost at sea in 1657, Thomas Sr. attempted to carry on his son's missionary work to the island Natives.

22. Mashpee, on Cape Cod.

23. Josiah Winslow became governor of Plymouth Colony in 1673 upon the death of Gov. Thomas Prence.

24. Gookin identifies John Gibbs's Native name as Assasamoogh. Gookin, "Indians Converted," Massachusetts Historical Society.

25. Caleb also taught school for the Christian Indians of Nantucket. "He earnestly desires to learn to read and understand English; and entreated me to procure him an English bible, which accordingly he had by order of the Commissioners." "Indians Converted," Massachusetts Historical Society.

From Noah Newman, 8 December 1674

Tanton. Decemb: 8. 74.

Reverend & Dear Si[R].

This oppertunity invites me to an acknowledgement of your Constant respects towards mee, Having long waited for a Convenient bearer, I hope't' you had my apologie by my Brother Shove, unto w[m] I hardly gained time to scribble a line or two when he was upon his Journey to Plimouth, but putting it into y[e] hand of a Swanzy bearer my seale was uncivelly broke, & my letter being found by a freind returnd to me againe a weeke after y[e] delivery, Such an incivillity as I scarce ever met wth. but by that means you mist my excuse & have been put upon y[e] greater exercise of Charity towards me. I perceive my Broth[s]. busynes goes forward, & hope God will follow it wth his blessing; your willingness to accompany my Brother his next Journey I take as a kindnes to my selfe, who would have waited upon him cheerfully had I not been so throng'd w[th] other hurrys at this time; I have a reall desire to se Barnstable & my Good freinds there, & yet I Can but assigne one Journey in my life to them, which I shall be very willing to performe If God permit, as a Testimony of my hardy accord w[th] y[e] p[r]sent matter depending. Sir I have something upon my breast Concerning your letter to Mr. D[1] & thô: I have rol'd it up in much charity it [w?]on't digest freely but by times I feel its fretting relique, espeacily when I remember from whom it was & of whom & to whom. Dear Si[r]. I hartyly Congratulate m[rs] Cot[s]. recovery of which I hear by my Bro. I perceive my Brother purposeth his Journy ye next weeke & expects yor. Company wth him thro[h] to Barnsta: upon ye second day, I am now wth him at Tanton upo[n]. a visit hearing ye last weeke of his illness, thô thrô God's mercy he is Comfortably recovered; pray faile him not the next weeke. Thus w[th] Respects to yo[r] s: & M[rs] Cotton w[th] y[e] rest of yo[rs] Craving yo[r]. mindfullness of me in yo[r]. best desires, I rest

yo[r] Assured freind

Noah Newman

my Brother Shove & Newman p[r]sent you w[th] their Respects

Cotton Family Papers 6:20, Prince Library, Rare Books and Manuscripts, Boston Public Library. Addressed "To the Reverend m^r^. John Cotton Pastor to the church of Christ in Plymouth these." Endorsed "From Mr Newman December, 8: 1674:."

---

1. Not found.

From Thomas Walley, 19 December 1674

REVEREND SIR

my hearty Love to yor selfe and M^rs^. Cotton I hope you got home well I bless God we are in health I thank you for yor good Company with us my Daughter is now wholly and cheerfully m^r^ shoves he may be welcome in the midst of ffebruary to finish his work I am now in hast god Allmighty bless yo and yo^r^s I am

yor truly Loving ffriend and Brother in o^r^ Deare Lord

Tho: Walley

Barnstable
Dec. 19: 1674

Cotton Family Papers 6:21, Prince Library, Rare Books and Manuscripts, Boston Public Library. Endorsed "From Mr Walley December, 19: 1674:."

THREE

King Philip's War
1675–1676

In the interim between Thomas Walley's friendly letter above and the somber proclamation introducing this section, dramatic events moved the colony and Philip's (Metacomet's) Wampanoags to the point of open warfare. And again, the unusual absence of Cotton correspondence dating from this pivotal period is maddening, for Cotton was undoubtedly privy to, and instrumental in, some of the critical decisions made by the Plymouth government.

While Cotton had been settling into his Plymouth pulpit, relations between the English of Plymouth Colony and the non-Christian Wampanoag under Philip had worsened. Fearful of rumors that linked the sachem to other Native groups plotting armed resistance, Plymouth authorities had forced a humiliating submission from Philip in 1671. In January 1675, the body of a Christian Indian named John Sassamon was discovered under the ice of Assowampsett Pond, in modern-day Lakeville. Only days before, Sassamon had reportedly informed Gov. Josiah Winslow of an impending attack by Philip's men. An examination of the body seemed to indicate foul play, and later a Native witness came forward to identify three other Natives as the murderers, at least one of whom had close ties to Philip. For their trial in Plymouth on 1 June, the court established a six-man panel of Natives to advise and (ultimately) concur with the all-English jury's guilty verdict. The Native men on the panel were almost certainly Christian converts; three of them appear by name in Cotton's missionary journal. When the court needed "some of the most indifferentest, gravest, and sage Indians" for the job, they undoubtedly turned to Cotton for his recommendations.[1] Two of the convicted were hanged on 8 June; the third, who received a temporary reprieve, was shot a month later. Soon after, fighting broke out in the western part of the colony, and historians generally credit the controversy surrounding the trial and subsequent executions with inciting the outbreak of King Philip's War.

Nowhere is Cotton's role in an inter-colonial network of correspondence more evident than in the letters that follow; the contacts he had made through his ministry

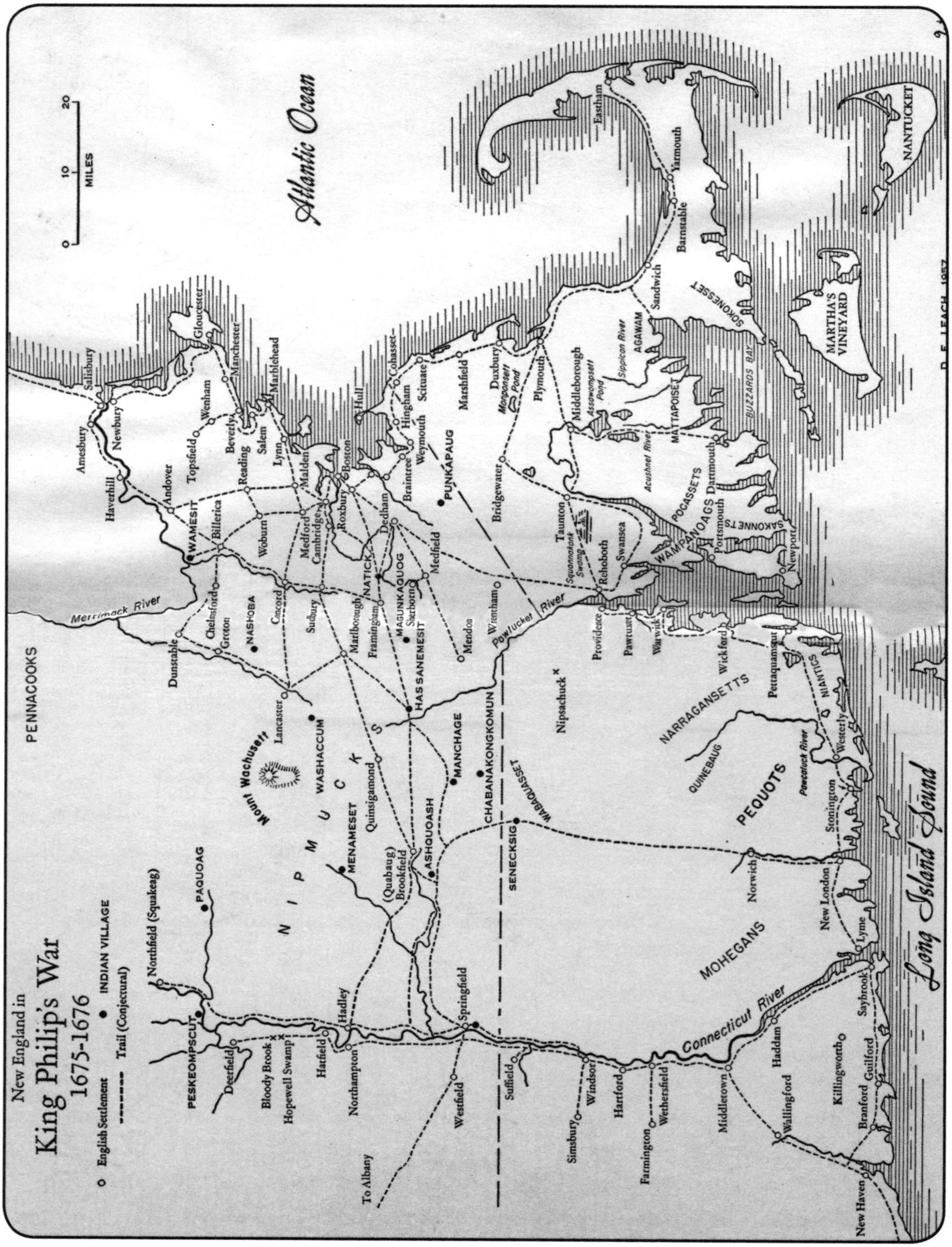

From Flintlock and Tomahawk: New England in King Philip's War *by Douglas Edward Leach. Copyright © 1958 and renewed 1986 by Douglas Edward Leach. Used by permission of W. W. Norton & Company, Inc.*

now served him well. As the letters clearly show, the rapid flow of events in a war that quickly went seriously wrong for the English left them anxious about loved ones, desperate for news, and searching for explanations for shocking setbacks. Detailed reports of the English disaster at Bloody Brook near Deerfield reached Cotton in eleven days, reports of the indecisive Great Swamp Fight in nearby Rhode Island, much sooner. The letters below demonstrate a critical element of the process of information sharing in late-seventeenth-century New England: replication. Cotton actively solicited news from colleagues and acquaintances, then transcribed portions of letters, or even letters in their entirety, for transmission. Plymouth's pastor and his correspondents refer to many letters that have not survived and others that, for whatever reason, did not reach their destinations.

Little more than a month into the war, Cotton and his friends in the ministry were arguing the origins of the conflict. Cotton seems to have been firmly in the camp of providentialists who considered the bloodshed and destruction to be divine judgement for New England's sins. Cotton complained that the colonists placed "too much confidence in an arm of flesh" and not enough in the arm of the Lord. He viewed the costly English raid at the Great Swamp, which some considered a victory, as "God's frowne upon the Army," perhaps in part because of his obvious anxiety for his friend, William Bradford Jr., who was seriously wounded in the engagement. As the war became increasingly nasty, with the summary execution & enslavement of Native prisoners a growing response to vicious raids, Cotton seems to have shared some of Thomas Walley's disgust at the "severity shewed towards the Squaws that are sent away," though at the end of the war he would take a part in one of the victors' more infamous deliberations.

Cotton's letters show that he did more than merely pass on news during this period. As English communities were destroyed, their people left homeless and families shattered, Cotton was busy with relief efforts to assist the hundreds of refugees who fled the beleaguered western towns. Always mindful of the causes of the war as he construed them, Cotton was also instrumental in introducing the novel practice of renewing church covenants to refresh the faith of church members and encourage new membership. And as is always the case in these letters, Cotton revealed his own family's concerns.

1.. *Records of the Colony of New Plymouth in New England,* ed. Nathaniel Shurtleff and David Pulsifer, 12 vols. (Boston, 1855–61), 5:117, 168.

Proclamation of the Plymouth Colony Council,

22 June 1675

Open hostilities between English colonists and Wampanoags loyal to Philip broke out on 20 June 1675, when some of the latter's young men looted and burned abandoned houses in Swansea. On the 23d, the day after this proclamation was issued, an English youth reportedly shot and killed a Native, and Philip's followers retaliated the next day, killing or mortally wounding nearly a dozen English men.[1]

To <*MR Co*> the Elders of the [Churches of] Plymouth

The Councell of this Colony taking into the[ir ser]ious Consideration the awfull hand of God upon us in permitting the heathen to carry it with great in[solenc]y & rage against us, appearing in their great hostile preparations & also some outragious carriages as at all other times soe in spetiall the last Lords day to some of our neighbours at Swanzey to the apparent hazard if not the reall losse of the lives of some already, doe therefore Judge it a solemne duty incumbent upon us all to lay to heart this dispensation of God, & doe therefore commend it to all the Churches, ministers & people of this colony to set apart the 24th day of this instant June, which is the 5th day of this weeke wherein to humble our soules before the Lord for all those sins whereby wee have provoked our good God soe sadly to interrupt our peace & Comforts, & also humbly to seeke his face & favour in the gratious continuance of our peace & priviledges, & that the Lord would be intreated to goe forth with our forces & blesse, succeed & prosper them, delivering them from the hands of his & our enemies, subduing the heathen before them & returning them all in safety to their families & relations againe, & that God would prepare all hearts humbly to submit to his good pleasure concerning u[s & o]urs.

By order of the Councell of w[ar]

Nathaniel Morton Secretary

Plym: June 22 1675

Cotton Family Papers 6:24, Prince Library, Rare Books and Manuscripts, Boston Public Library. The text of the proclamation is in Cotton's hand, but the salutation, closing and authorizing signature are that of Secretary Morton. Apparently the Council asked Cotton to write the announcement of this emergency day of humiliation, with Morton adding the rest later.

1. Douglas Edward Leach, *Flintlock and Tomahawk: New England in King Philip's War* (New York, 1958), 36-43.

From William Bradford, 21 July 1675

After the fighting at Swansea, a combined force of Plymouth, Massachusetts, and Native soldiers sealed off the Mount Hope peninsula upon which Philip's people lived, hoping to contain the conflict. By the time the colonial army made its sweep down the peninsula, however (June 30), the sachem and his followers had withdrawn by boats to Pocasset (modern-day Tiverton, Rhode Island), on the eastern shore of Narragansett Bay. The English were then forced to redeploy and hunt for their enemy in the difficult terrain around the Pocasset Swamp.

HON^D^ SIR

After my Best respects psented to y^r^ selfe & m^rs^ Cotton this is to Certify of my health (Blessed be god) though I may say wonderfully pserved by Especiall providence, we ralled forth from roade iland the last weeke with our one[1] peopell on the maine as far as Cokset[2] & att o^r^ returne we found the track of the Enimi we follow it to a great Swampe Entered it but they oute rane us, onli fond[3] thire habitations wch we burned and tow old men whome we dispaced.[4] tow dayes after we marched agane and found them hid in an hidious Swame,[5] we Entred had a hard dispute wth them they shot on all sides att us, we followed home to them beate them of thire place, fired thire wigwams Slew aboute seven of them, they wounded foure of ours and one of our owne men lost by accidentall providence by one of our owne peopell, here we found thire lugage gote divers pots & kitles of thires, then we returned to mount hope to refresh our selfs met wth the bay forces come from Naraganset, then to-gether the last munday[6] marched up into the Cuntry, after halfe a days march met wth the Enimi, who Charged upon our Forlorne,[7] kiled tow of ours we followed on and in a great Swampe[8] we found thire body we Entred in, the bay forces first, Emi[9] seing it, betooke them selfs to trees & thickets fired thicke upon us we drafe[10] them from thire first station, but sudine the hand of god seemed to be against us we had many slaine and wounded, fife slaine and six wounded & some of them i feare mortall & of these most were Capt Mosles[11] men & tow of Capt hinchmans[12] men So we retreated to the water side wth o^r^ wounded men we toke an old indian in the Swame, who tolds us that Philipe & the Squa Shachem were both thire wth thire men.

Sir this is the Substance of things that hath happenned and what the lord calls us furder to do we are weighting upon hime, desiring to lay o^r^ selfs low before hime who will exalt us in his due time, i am a fraid we [. . . .]ow much in o^r^ owne strenght, thirefore [is?] th[. . . .]d of providence upon us, we are now gowing to make another garison on pocasset Side towards Roade Iland to keepe the Enmi from thire Corne & the water side wch Capt hinchman hath undertaken, we & the Bay have written home for furder advice, for we are at a stand, the good lord direct us, all our plimoth men are well. I pray remember me to all my frinds Especalli to my deare deare wife & Childen, to home i shall not have now time to write

pase by my speling for i write in great hast

yo[r] yo[r] sarvant & loving frind

Will Bradford

from hount [mount] hope
21 Juli 75

Addressed "For the Revent m[r] John Cotton att Plimoth Deliver Theses." Printed, with photographic facsimile, in A Letter from Major William Bradford to the Reverend John Cotton: Written at Mount Hope on July 21, 1675, and containing an Account of the Operations leading up to an unsuccessful Attempt to Capture Metacom alias King Philip the Wampanoag Chieftain *(Providence, R.I., 1914). The facsimile shows a tear in the top of the second page obscuring words on the top two lines. The original letter, reported in 1914 to be at the John Carter Brown Library at Rhode Island Brown University, is currently unaccounted for.*

---

1. Own.
2. Coksit, or Coakset, corresponds to the area around modern-day Westport, Massachusetts, and Little Compton, Rhode Island.
3. Found.
4. Dispatched.
5. Swamp.
6. 19 July.
7. I.e., advance guard.
8. Pocasset Swamp.
9. Enemy.
10. Drave (i.e., "drove").
11. Captain Samuel Mosely (1641–1680) commanded a company of volunteers recruited in Boston that included captured pirates and assorted n'er-do-wells. Though an effective fighting force, Mosely and his company soon became notorious for their brutal treatment of Natives, regardless of their loyalties. Jenny Hale Pulsipher, "Massacre at Hurtleberry Hill: Christian Indians and English Authority in Metacom's War," *The William and Mary Quarterly* 53 (1996): 459-86.
12. Daniel Henchman (d. 1685) first appears in Massachusetts records of 1666. A year later, he helped Daniel Gookin and others establish the plantation at Quinsigamond Ponds (Worcester). Made a freeman of the colony in 1672, he was appointed captain of the Fifth Boston Company in May 1675. He died 13 October 1685 in Worcester. George M. Bodge, *Soldiers of King Philip's War* (1906; reprint, Baltimore, Md., 2000), 47-48.

From Thomas Walley, 25 July 1675

The next few letters from Thomas Walley indicate the impact of the adverse military situation on at least some of the clergy and other settlers of Plymouth Colony, as they struggled to interpret the divine significance of the war's events.

July 25. 1675.

Reverend Sir and my Dear ffriend

we are here much engaged to yo^{u} for yor Love and paines I feare we shall never make due recompense but I have bin forced to put the Lord to reward many of my friends and I trust he will reward yor Love at present I can only returne yo^{u} hearty thankes. it is a sad and dark Day I feare it may be long, but in the Evening time it will be light and o^{r} deliverance may Come when we lest think of it. who is able to give an account of the sin or sins god is now dealing with us for I may say as Jer: 9. 12.[1] a discovery of it that might Convince all men were of more worth then the treasures of India if I knew what it were I hope I should doe my duty a Quaker told me it was for my saying in my sermon they were blasphemers and Idolators and for the psecution they have had from us[2] but I judg we may as well feare it is o^{r} suffering in the publik exercise of theyr false worship which for ought I know is suffered only in this Colloney what ever o^{r} reformation is the high places remaine a[nd?] yet the hand of god hath fallen upon us We find in scripture that when there hath bin some publik judgment, there hath bin some peculier work for the magistrate to doe the Lord discover his will I hope they would be ready to doe theyr duty theyr zeale if for god might be a spetiall meanes to turne away gods anger. we have great Cause to be humbled under this mighty hand of god if it should Continue till we Could agree in o^{r} humiliations and for a reformation I feare it would last long and Cost deare—there is nothing but mercie Can save us and help us it will be well if the judgment be removed and Gods anger at once otherwise the worst will Come at last we may now Guess why god hath taken away soe many of o^{r} worthies of late[3] sure it was from the Evill to Come and to make way for this scourge yet I hope there is a remnant left to stand in the Gap who Can prevaile wth god.

Sir I pray yo^{u} put a Candid Construction upon these hasty lines and give me yor opinion of them I am willing to be Corrected in my judgment – and I allsoe desire you will Continue our intelligencor for we are allwayes longing for yor letters. let us Continue to pray for each other I am

yo^{r}s in o^{r} Deare Lord

T: W

Cotton Family Papers 6:25, Prince Library, Rare Books and Manuscripts, Boston Public Library. Addressed "ffor the Reverend and my much esteemed ffriend m^{r} John Cotten Pastour of the Church of christ at Plimoth these dd." Endorsed "From Mr Walley July, 26: 1675:."

---

1. Jer. 9:12: "Who is the wise man, that may understand this? and who is he to whom the mouth of the Lord hath spoken, that he may declare it, for what the land perisheth and is burned up like a wilderness, that none passeth through?"
2. Quaker dissidents first appeared in Plymouth Colony in the mid 1650s. The colony government enthusiastically participated in their subsequent persecutions until it was restrained by the restored King Charles II in 1661. Thereafter, Quakers found havens on Cape Cod and in the western towns of Plymouth Colony. They made themselves no more popular when, at the beginning of the war, they claimed that English reverses and losses were God's judgement for having previously persecuted them.
3. So it might have seemed to historically-minded settlers; fifty-five years after Plymoth's founding, many of the leading lights of the colony's early days were dead, elderly, or had moved away. Most recently, Gov. Thomas Prence, that "terror to the ungodly," had passed away in 1673.

From Thomas Walley, 2 August 1675

Reverend Sir and my dear ffriend

I must still renew my thanks for yor Continued labor of Love god I trust will reward yor kindness to me and preserve us in this Evill day I hope god is bringing down o^{r} enemies I have not doubted of theyr fall but they may be brought to ruin and the anger of god not turned away. as to the Causes of gods displeasure with us I know my owne weakness to be such that I dare not adventure to expose my thoughts to publik *<view>* sensure. though new England hath many sins to be humbled for and to reforme yet I feare gods Controversy with us is for breach of Cov^{t} with him there are two sects Eminently guilty those that have pfessed religion and Apostatized have rejected ye Lord and his wayes wch many are totally guilty of and many others that Continue with the churches have Lost theyr zeale for truth and plead for Baal are indulgent to any thing that is against the truth many of the pfane are more orthodox then som pfessors of religion it grieves me to say soe

the other sort that violate the lords Cov^{t} are the rising generation that know not the god of theyr fathers but Carry proudly and harken not to the word of the lord and in the best sort of pfessors the love of the world prevailes and they give the world to much Cause to be jealouse of their sincearity which is a greate stumbling block Covetuousness is a mother sin (if I mistake not) among pfessors of religion we ministers as we have o[r] many sins to be humbled for soe I feare this is one we have bin unwilling to displease some of our Church members and have not bin soe faithfull to god and them as we ought to have bin

as for o[r] honoured magistrates and deputies though I have a high esteeme of them and honor them & obey them yet I feare yet I feare [*sic*] the old zeale for truth is decayed and truth is not such a jewel as it hath bin the Lord give them one heart and make them valiant for the truth

I am not for Cruelty yet I judg there should at least be a restraint of all publik false worship and the walls of Jerusalem should be built though the times are troublesome for many will think this is not a [season?] to reforme but I feare the displeasure of god more than the displeasure of men for [illeg.] I could trust god with the event.

when yo[u] goe to Boston I pray you remember my love to yo[r] relations I am greatly in debt to yo[r] Brother Mather I present my thankes to him for his usefull and seasonable labors and for his love to us w[ch] I Cannot requite and I pray you visit my relations and remember my love to them and give them the letter inclosed. Sir I have many letters to write to the Army we have divers that savour of godliness and theyr letters are Comfortable let us Continue to pray for each other I am in haste but am

yo[r] humbly loving ffriend and Brother in the work of or Lord

Tho: Walley

Aug: 2. 1675.

I pray you present my hearty love to m[r] Hull[1] to who[m] I am much engaged

Cotton Family Papers 6:26, Prince Library, Rare Books and Manuscripts, Boston Public Library. Addressed "ffor the Reverend and my much esteemed ffriend m[r] John Cotten Pastour of the Church of christ in plimoth these present." Endorsed "From M[r] Walley August, 2: 1675:."

---

1. John Hull (1624–1683), silversmith and goldsmith, was one of Boston's most esteemed citizens. He was appointed in 1652 to coin money for Massachusetts—the famous "pine tree" currency. A ship owner and substantial property holder, he was colony treasurer in 1676 and a member of the Court of Assistants from 1680–1683. His diaries are among the most valued personal papers of early New England history. *DAB.*

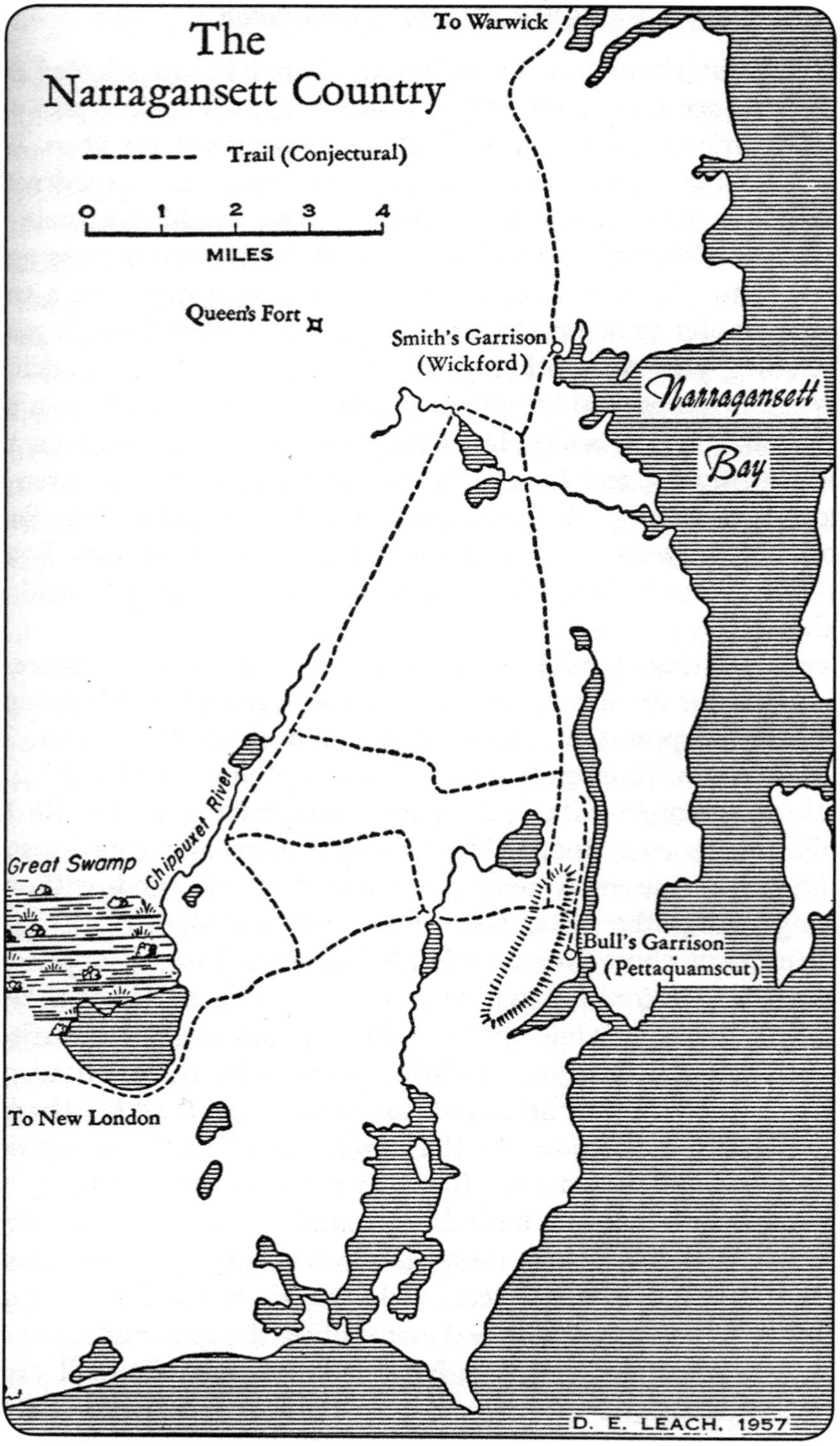

From Flintlock and Tomahawk: New England in King Philip's War *by Douglas Edward Leach. Copyright © 1958 and renewed 1986 by Douglas Edward Leach. Used by permission of W. W. Norton & Company, Inc.*

From Thomas Walley, [20 September 1675]

Reverend and worthy Sir

I have this week received two letters from yo^{u}[1] for wch I returne thanks and see we have still Cause to acknowledg the goodnese of god to a poor sinfull Land if god would reforme us we should have peace and health restored—yo^{u} have sent to me for my notes upon Jam: 5: 14:[2] and truly I am ashamed to send them to yo^{u} for they are as all that I doe is very imperfect and this being a limited subject there being scarsly any paralel scriptures there is little more in it than a Collection of what others have don my Commen[tators] speak allmost the same thing and all most in the same words I have not time to mend it if I could I pray yo^{u} Cover my weakness and send my notes againe by m^{r} Hinkly or some other as soon as yo^{u} Can. as for my Journey to Boston it is spoiled god hath sent me a wife home to me and saves [me] the Labor of a tediouse Journey the Last day of the Last week I Came to a resolve to stay at home and not to look after a wife till the spring the next morning I heard mrs Clark of the Iland was Come to our Towne who had bin motioned by some of my friends the providence of god hath soe ordered it that we are agreed to become one. I have had waighty reasons in [my?] owne opinion moving me to it I desire yo^{u} will pray that the blessing of god may be with us shee is one of o^{r} members and I judg hath escaped the polutions of the place where shee Lives and of wch shee is a weary.[3] I pray yo^{u} present my service to o^{r} honoured Governor I give him humble thanks for his Kind invitation and to yo^{u} for all yor Love with my hearty Love to yor selfe and good mrs Cotton Committing you to the Lord I [illeg.]

yo^{rs} in o^{r} Deare Lord

A Hand Letter I had by [Mr Clark?]
we are like to marry next week pray for us but we invite few excuse mee

Curwen Family Papers, American Antiquarian Society. Addressed "ye Rev^{d} & my Truly Loving Friend m^{r} John Cotton Plimouth." Endorsed "From Mr Walley. 7^{br} 20 Receiv^{d}." Several small holes along right margin and bottom edge.

---

1. Not found.
2. James 5:14: "Is any sick among you? let him call for the elders of the church; and let them pray over him, anointing him with oil in the name of the Lord."
3. According to Walley's will, Mrs. Clark's Christian name was Sarah; no marriage record has yet come to hand. "The Island" frequently appears as shorthand for Rhode Island, certainly a place of religious "polutions" to Walley and Cotton, but considering Walley's position on mid Cape Cod, he may mean the much closer island, Martha's Vineyard.

To [Thomas Walley?], 23 September 1675

By the late summer and fall of 1675, the war had spread far beyond the borders of Plymouth Colony. After burning several towns in the western part of Plymouth, Philip and his followers headed north and west into central Massachusetts. Other Native groups, nursing old grudges against the English and probably inspired by the actions of Philip's people, began attacking Massachusetts settlements in the Connecticut Valley and on today's Maine coast.

Boston Sep: 23: 1675:

[Re]verend & Honoured Sir

Mr Hinckley hath written to you soe that I need not write of many things occurring before I came hither. on Sep: 12: the Sabbath, Capt Appleton[1] at Dearefeild deserted one of the 3 garrison-houses to goe to meeting at one of the other, only left one man there; in the time of worship the Indians asaulted that house, burnt it, the man in it not heard of since; Capt Appleton did with his Company come upon the backside of the Indians & drave them away. Capt Lathrop[2] with about 46 men went to Dearefeild with Carts to fetch away their thresht Corne, wheat etc. in their returne with Carts & people they were set upon by the Indians, Capt Lathrop slaine & all his men, only two, 18 men of Dearefeild slaine also, the Indians cut the bags of wheate in pieces & the beds; Capt Mosley came up to the fight, 2 of his men slaine & 11 wounded, the Indians said to him, come Mosely, come, you seeke Indians, you want Indians, here's Indians enough for you, Mosely fought them from 11 a clock till the Evening, he had with him about 70 men, he Judged the Enemy were about 1000, Mosely did retreat[.] Major Treat[3] with about 100 souldiers & Monheagin Indians[4] came up to the fight [&] drave away the Indians, the Monheags did very good [ser]vice & are much commended for it, on the last sabbath [t]hey did bury our dead: About Quaboag[5] noe Indians have bin seene these many weekes, only 1 old man was espied among corne, they pursued him, he ran, they overtooke him, he would confesse nothing, they laid him downe, Cornelius, the [D]utch man[6] lifting up his sword to cut off his head, the Indian [lif]t up his hand betweene, soe his hand was first cut off [& par]tly his head, the second blow finished the Execution: yesterday newes from the Easterne parts[7] that 4 or 5 [....] beseiged with the Enemy who were about 500, the townes are Castine[,] Saco, Scarborough, & (I think) Wells, they are in expectation [....] cutt off by the Enemy every houre, & those places are soe [....] that it is very probable they will be destroyed: The I[ndian] Prisoners here are first indicted by the Grand-inquest,[8] the [....] Petty-Jury, one is found guilty of Confederacy with the Ene[my] [....] supposed the verdict will this day be the same for all the [....] yesterday one litle John who was accused for shooting [...] Stoughton at Taunton,[9] was hanged here. noe newes yet

[....] Last night here was an Alarm through all this towne & p[....] Country, all the Cause as yet knowne is, that some of Mald[en] [...] late discharged a gun: yours are well here. My dearest [....] feverish, I intreat your prayers for her & me & all ours [....] through mercy, is very well. Due Salutations, etc

I am, Sir, yours unfainedly

John Cotton

Cotton Family Papers 6:27, Prince Library, Rare Books and Manuscripts, Boston Public Library. Mutilated on left margin; some words on reverse of letter lost or obscure.

---

1. Samuel Appleton (1624–1696) of Ipswich commanded English forces in the upper Connecticut River valley but lacked adequate numbers either to protect the western Massachusetts settlements or to prosecute an offensive war against the Natives. Leach, *Flintlock and Tomahawk*, 96-97; Bodge, *Soldiers of King Philip's War*, 142-58. See the letter of 29 May 1695.

2. Captain Thomas Lathrop emigrated to Salem in 1634. He and eighty men were helping to evacuate the village of Deerfield when they were ambushed at Muddy Brook, five miles south of the village, on 18 September. Seventy-one soldiers and teamsters were killed, Lathrop among them. The stream was renamed Bloody Brook, the designation it bears today. Leach, *Flintlock and Tomahawk*, 88; Bodge, *Soldiers of King Philip's War*, 133-41.

3. Major Robert Treat (c. 1622–1710) commanded Connecticut forces in the upper Connecticut River valley. *DAB*.

4. Mohegan Indians of Connecticut, allied with the English.

5. Quaboag, or Brookfield, was abandoned soon after a devastating attack and siege by Nipmuck Indians. Leach, *Flintlock and Tomahawk*, 81-84.

6. This is probably Cornelius Anderson, one of a number of Dutch privateers or pirates captured by Captain Mosely and reprieved in exchange for joining Mosely's company to fight against the Wampanoag. Nathaniel Philbrick, *Mayflower: A Story of Courage, Community, and War* (New York, 2006), 238-39.

7. Massachusetts settlements in Maine came under attack beginning in September 1675. The colony government was forced to divert troops and supplies to that theater through 1677.

8. On 16 September 1676 the Massachusetts General Court gave the Council the discretion to dispose of all Native prisoners, advising that "such of them as shall appeare to have imbrued their hands in English blood should suffer death here, and not be transported into forreigne parts." Nathaniel B. Shurtleff, ed., *Records of the Governor and Company of the Massachusetts Bay in New England (1628-86)*, 6 vols. (Boston, 1853–54) (hereafter *Mass Bay Recs*), 5:115.

9. "Litle Jno Indian yt Came as a messengr from [blank] being prooved to be a murderer of the English in ye warr was Condemnd to be hangd & was executed accordingly [21 September 1675]." *Records of the Court of Assistants of the Colony of the Massachusetts Bay 1630–1692*, 3 vols. (Boston, 1901–28), 1:53. The Stoughton in question may be a relation of Nicholas Stoughton, who married Elizabeth Knapp in Taunton in 1673. Savage, *Genealogical Dictionary*, 4:214.

From Zechariah Walker,[1] 23 SEPTEMBER 1675

STRATFORD SEPT: 23. 1675

LOVING BROTHER

& sister, yours of ye 26th of August[2] I lately received, w^{r}by wee were certified of ye health & welfare of yor selves & yours, wch newes though alwaies welcome, yet had now a double welcome considering what dangers have lately been neer you by ye indians. my self, wife & children are through ye mercy of god all in good health, & do send hearty salutations according to capacity, to you both, & all yo^{r}s. I have spoken wth bro: Rossiter[3] since my receipt of yours, concerning what you proposed, but he did not apprehend it safe to betrust ye writings of such concernm^{t} wth a person so related, as y^{t} if ye mony be detained from us, may be likely to injoy it himself: he being likewise wholly a stranger to all of us; he y^{r}fore rather inclines to send by some other person. But if in ye mean time Governor Leverit[4] will so far gratify you, as to bestow a few lines, in way of perswasion to o^{r} aunt, not to detain from ye fatherless, w^{t} she hath over & over under hand acknowledged to be y^{r} due, it may possibly save further trouble both to her, & us. We think long to hear how god hath dealt with sister, in her lying in, wch by yor letter we conclud to be either past, or now present[5] I hope you will take ye first opportunity to inform us. I cannot at ye present inlarge, but with hearty Salutations to all friends with you y^{t} shall inquire after us, to desire yor prayers for us, & remain

yor ever Loving brother

Zechariah Walker

Curwen Family Papers, American Antiquarian Society. Addressed "For ye reverent Mr John Cotton, pastor of ye church of christ at Plimouth These deliver." Endorsed "From Mr Zecha Walker [illeg] 1675."

---

1. Rev. Zachariah Walker (1637–1700) was one of seventeen students who left Harvard College without a degree in 1655. He took up a ministry at Jamaica, Long Island, in 1662, but moved to Stratford, Connecticut, six years later. While in that place he married Joanna Cotton's sister Susannah (b. 1652). The church in Stratford was divided into two factions; each was allowed its own minister. Walker was pastor for one of the parties, which eventually formed the town of Woodbury. Walker continued to minister at both places until 1678, when he moved permanently to Woodbury. John Langdon Sibley, *Biographical Sketches of Graduates of Harvard University, In Cambridge, Massachusetts* (Boston, 1873–) (hereafter *Sibley's Harvard Graduates*), 1:567, 2:84-86.

2. Not found.

3. Joanna's brother Josias Rosseter.

4. John Leverett (b. 1616), governor of Massachusetts from 1673 until his death in 1679. *DAB*.

5. Joanna gave birth to her eighth child, Josiah, 10 September 1675.

From Thomas Walley, 18 November 1675

Reverend Sir and my deare ffriend

I still returne the poor pay of thanks for yor continued Labor of love which hath bin a great refreshing to mee and others. I am glad it hath pleased god to returne you and yo^{rs} in safty to yor owne habitation in which place I wish yo^{u} much of the presence of god. as to the news Concerning o^{r} honoured Govr going forth to war[1] in regard of his fraile body and our need of him at home I am troubled yet who knows but god will make him a saviour to this poor distressed land set aside his weakness and our need of him I Know noe man fitter for this great servis we must doe what we can to keep him alive and in health by our prayers if god Call him forth his Call will be his warrant. if our enemies be not subdued we shall have noe need of magistrates in a little time we have now need of such [souldiers as] god will bless. I much lament that rash Cruelty of our English toward Innocent Indians.[2] I have never heard what those 64 things are that are agreed upon[3] for information the good Lord carry [several words illeg.] sir at present I am not very [several words illeg.] messenger is in hast my hearty lo[ve] [illeg.] good m^{rs} Cotten and to all yo^{rs} [illeg.] prayers for each other that we may have hearts sutable to the times and o^{r} worke I am

yo^{rs} in o^{r} deare Lord Jesus

Tho: Walley

Nov 18 1675

Curwen Family Papers, American Antiquarian Society. Addressed "ffor the Reverend and my much esteemed ffriend Mr John Cotten Pastour of the Church of Christ at Plimouth these dd." Endorsed "Mr Walley [nove] mber, 18: 1675." Large stain in lower right quarter.

---

1. The Commissioners of the United Colonies elected Gov. Josiah Winslow to command the inter-colonial army that would invade the Narragansett country.

2. The war had gone badly for the English, and despite the fact that Christian Indians had fought with the colonists against Philip's forces from the outset, by late summer English settlers were suspicious of Christian Indian loyalty. Instances of harassment, intimidation, and violence against these people increased ominously through the fall and winter of 1675–76.

3. Reference unclear.

From Noah Newman, 16 December 1675

Colonial leaders became convinced that the Narragansetts of southwestern Rhode Island were giving aid and comfort to Philip's people; they grew increasingly fearful these Natives would openly join the Wampanoag leader, throwing their substantial human, material, and strategic resources against the English. There was, and is, no direct evidence that the Narragansetts seriously considered this second possibility, but in the late autumn/early winter of 1675, the English commanders decided to mount a major show of force that turned into a pre-emptive attack on the Narragansett homeland. An inter-colonial force of more than a thousand men made its way to certain rendezvous points, one of which was the Plymouth Colony town of Rehoboth, on Rhode Island's border. The army's destination was the little settlement of Wickford, on the western shore of Narragansett Bay.

REHOB: DECEMB^{R} 16: 75

REVEREND & DEAR SI^{R}:

Hearing of some that were intending towards yor parts I called to mind your faithfull & brotherly remembrance of me at Boston from whence I had the fullest & surest intelligence of the Northern war, which being now Come weest, by my present situation I consider my selfe to have ye oppertunity though not the ability of a retaliation. Decemb. 10 All the forces of mass: & Plim: arived wth us & Billeted amongst us y^{t} night only Capt. Prentice[1] & the most of his troope being wth us the night before past over to Providence. Some of Prov: coming over that night brought intelligence of some few wigwams neer them wch might be conveniently surprized that night by a pty sent over or otherwise they escaping would give intelligence to the rest of ye Armies approach. upon wch the Gen ordered Capt. Johnson[2] wth as many of his men as he could muster up that night to passe over & possesse himself of the sayd wigwams accordingly he went but ye Indians were escaped a considerable time before as appeared by the snow y^{t} was faln since. Decemb: 11 The army past over from us to Prov: at the Narrow passage upon a raft made of Cannows & bands over them I tooke my leave of the Hon^{d} Gen: His chaplins &c only Capt Mosely & his company were to passe over in sloopes to Nar:[3] Decemb: 12 The army quartered about Pautuccksett:[4] They had intelligence that Pumham[5] & his crew were upon Pautuccksett river[6] by wch means they addressed thems. to surprize him upon the sabba: day at night but he was gone In their passage thence to Nar: they discovered 30 Indians an howr or 2 before day, & finding them a sleep tooke them wthout the losse of a man. they are reported to be the enemys scout to give them intelligence of the English army—who have given our Eng an account of the place where ye ememy is & their designes upon wch our army tooke their march to m^{r}. Smiths[7] & found all well saved fro^{m}. the enemy wch they were affraid of woud have been consumed by fire before they came this intelligence Mr Ame gave to m^{r} Browne. & m^{r} Browne sent to me, I have as yet no thing of certainty concerning o^{r} Coneticot forces, Thus far our God hath been pleased to appear for us, we are eagerly waiting to hear w^{t} god hath further to do wth us, what we may next hear he only knows, my hearts desire is if God hath a blessing for us it may be given us in such a way as no flesh may glory in it selfe but all glory may be given to God thus wth dearest respects from my selfe & wife to yor. s: & yo^{rs} craving the constant helpe & benefit of yor. prayers I rest

yor. Assured friend Noah Newman

Decembr. 17 A post came from Narrag: through our Towne wth serverall Letters from the army, The news above mentioned about the 30 Indians is not so punctuall as before related. The Late & f^{mr} intelligence you have in ye enclosed as it came by Letter, only the bearer doth credibly informe us that Jere Bulls[8] is burnt 22 psons or thereabouts killd & serverall houses of petequamscut fired, which he was an eye witnes too Just before he left the army, The vessell expelled from Boston was not arived and various reports about Coneticote forces

Pray Enquire of Jonathan Barnes[9] for a horse that was left wth him by one of yarmouth y^{t} is now in ye army I forget ye mans name but I thincke I mistake not ye place of his living. The horse is a bay horse an ambler wth a halter gall behind his ear & upon his goale. a Roxbury R upon his shoulder he belongs to m^{r} Lamb of Roxbury that marryed m^{rs} Mary alkocke.[10] the horse being formerly her fathers, he was unjustly carryed away from these [pts?] & if you Can by any means recover him & send him to ye owner you will do a kindnes to therein to yor frend

N: N:

Curwen Family Papers, American Antiquarian Society. Addressed "To the Reverend His Dear Freind m^{r} John Cotton Pastor to the church of christ in Plimouth these." Endorsed "From Mr Newman December, 16: 1675."

---

1. Capt. Thomas Prentice of Cambridge (c. 1620–1709) commanded a troop of mounted soldiers in the Narragansett campaign. Bodge, *Soldiers of King Philip's War*, 80.

2. Isaac Johnson of Roxbury (d. 1675) was captain of the Artillery Company of Boston in 1667 and commanded a company of Roxbury and Weymouth men in the Narragansett campaign. He was among the first to be killed in the attack on the Narragansett fort, falling just inside the obstacle-strewn entrance. Bodge, *Soldiers of King Philip's War*, 159-61.

3. Narragansett.

4. Pawtuxet was a settlement near the mouth of the river by the same name (see note 6, below).

5. Pomham was sachem of the Shawomet Indians, near modern-day Warwick, who had been tributaries to the Narragansetts. In 1643 Pomham submitted himself and his people to the authority of Massachusetts Bay in order to terminate his obligation to the Narragansetts. When the war came, however, he sided with his former overlords and was killed in battle 27 July 1676 near Dedham. Samuel G. Drake, *Biography and History of the Indians of North America* (Boston, 1837), book 3:75-76.

6. The Pawtuxet River flows easterly into Narragansett Bay between Providence and Warwick, Rhode Island.

7. Richard Smith kept a trading post at Wickford, on the western shore of Narragansett Bay south of Warwick. The colonial army used it as an advance base during the campaign. Leach, *Flintlock and Tomahawk*, 122.

8. Jireh Bull's stone garrison house stood at Pettaquamscutt, on the western shore of Narragansett Bay. It was to have been a rendezvous for the colonial army but was destroyed by Indians on or just before 16 December. Leach, *Flintlock and Tomahawk*, 127.

9. Jonathan Barnes (1643–1714) inherited most of the considerable estate of his father, John Barnes, one of Plymouth's few general merchants. Jonathan married Elizabeth Hedge (1647–1731) in 1665 and was elected constable of Plymouth in 1677. *Vital Records of Plymouth, Massachusetts to the Year 1850*, comp. Lee D. Van Antwerp, ed. Ruth Wilder Sherman (Camden, Me., 1993), 665; Shurtleff, *Records of Plymouth Colony*, 5:231.

10. Joshua Lamb (1642–1690), Roxbury merchant, owned lands in Roanoke, Virginia, which he had purchased from Sir William Berkley. Lamb married Mary Alcock (1652–1700) of Roxbury. Bowen, *Early Rehoboth*, 2:50; Clarence Almon Torrey, *New England Marriages Prior to 1700* (Baltimore, 1865), 448.

From George Shove, 31 December 1675

From Wickford, the colonial army set out to find and destroy the fortified Narragansett village deep in the Great Swamp, in what is now Kingston, Rhode Island. In the "Great Swamp Fight" that ensued on 19 December, the Natives were driven from the village while sustaining great losses and the village was destroyed; however, the English also suffered heavy casualties in the assault, and many subsequently died of mortal wounds. Although badly hurt by the English raid, the Narragansett threat had not been extinguished; in fact, the colonists' actions transformed the formerly neutral survivors into committed enemies.

TAUNTON DEC. 31. 75.

REVEREND & DEAR S^R^

This Letter from my Brother Newman[1] hath Lyen at my house for a passage ever since Saturday was sevenight: Jam. Hoskins Came since tis true but Called not for it, yet knew a weeke before of my desier to send. I suppose he had forgotten it. we sent a man to R. Island this weeke that we might be informed of the Armye & of o^r^ owne men in perticular a list of the slain and wounded I have sent to you & [request ?]

request you having perused it to thrust it into the Letter I have sent to father Walley. since the ingagem^{t} 19 instant, o^{r} Army visited Pumhams Quarters found noe Indians burnt 60 wigwams & returned. it is reported our Generall hath sent a Letter by a skawe[2] taken Captive, to the Sachems the Answer we yet hear not. Capt Bradforthe is wounded[3] as we formerly heard, but we hope not Mortally. I heard from him [illeg] Night his wound as I heer is in the back, a little under one shoulder, the shaft not got out, but the Surgeon hopes his recovorye I have sent a line or two to his wife & desire yor Care for the Conveyance of it because I know not her Name to distinguish it. My Brother Newman went on tuesday to R Island to visit the wounded I have not heard from him since. one of our men is slain 3 wounded but not mortallye viz Serj^{t} witherell, James Bell, Joseph white[4] of particulars I have noe more not having yet spoken with the man y^{t} Came. if he bring any information of yours, I will inform it to morrow. It Appears though the Enemie have received Considerable damage yet his power is not yet broken. the Lords hand is yet against us we are not prepared for mercye, pray pray, pray My hearty Salutations to yo^{r}selfe & Mi^{rs} Cotton farwell S^{r}

Yo^{r} Assured freind

GS.

This Letter had come on Saturday but y^{t} the weather hindered

Curwen Family Papers, American Antiquarian Society. Addressed "To ye Reverend his verye good freind Mr John Cotton Pastor of the Ch. of Christ in N. Plimouth these prsent." Endorsed "[From Mr Shove] December, 31: 1675:" Stain across center fold.

---

1. Probably the preceding letter from Noah Newman.

2. Probably "squaw."

3. Captain (later Major) William Bradford (1624–1705) of Marshfield, son of Plymouth Colony governor William Bradford, served as assistant for many years and commanded the Plymouth contingent during the campaign. See 5 July 1676.

4. William Wetherell was a sergeant in the Plymouth regiment's second company. Peleg Sanford of Rhode Island later presented a bill to the Plymouth court for "8 yds of Duffle to Sergt. Witherly, James Bell and other Taunton men that came wounded to my house December 24th," "cash to James Bell, to bear his charges home," and "To Serg't Witherell, James Bell & Joseph White for their diett lodging and attendance two of them for one month and one of them three weeks at 8s. per week." Bodge, *Soldiers of King Philip's War*, 183, 427; Samuel Hopkins Emery, *History of Taunton, Massachusetts, from its Settlement to the Present Time* (Syracuse, N.Y., 1893), 1:404.

The Great Swamp Fight. A nineteenth-century illustration.

To Increase Mather, 3 January 1676

Plimouth January, 3: 1675:

Deare Brother

I desire you to blesse God with me for healing mercy to me & mine: Mr Holmes died, Dec: 24:[1] The poore people are desolate, I have many serious thoughts what the meaning of the Providence of God is in his death, I meane espetially as to the season of it; he being one of those who imp[ute] these dreadfull frownes of providence to our dealing [with] the Quakers, & the late publick Fast Dec: 2:[2] (which was h[is last] publick worke), except the sabbath after) he said in his sermon he was of the same minde as to that matter as formerly, but he heard not of Gods frowne upon the Army, Jan: 19:[3] the newes coming to us but the same houre he dyed: I wish I could heare you prophesy good to this land, I should then beleve these wars may have an end, the Lord fit us for his good pleasure; if wee loose Capt Bradford, wee loose a great part of our glory, & I most of my comfort as to man I beseech you pray earnestly for his life if it be not too late. My selfe & wife salute you & our sister & Cousen Cotton, desiring your prayers for us, I rest,

your Affectionate Brother

John Cotton.

many persons & families are here still sick, & deaths renewed.

Mather Papers 2:21, Prince Library, Rare Books and Manuscripts, Boston Public Library. Addressed "These For the Reverend, his Deare Brother, Mr Increase Mather, Teacher of a Church of Christ at Boston." Endorsed "B^r J. C. Jan. 3. 1675/6."

---

1. Rev. John Holmes, minister of Duxbury (1658–1675), died 24 December 1675, remembered as "a godly man . . . efficacious in the great and honorable work of preaching the Gospel." Justin Winsor, *A History of the Town of Duxbury, Massachusetts, with Genealogical Registers* (Boston, 1849) 178-79; E. Waldo Long, ed., *The Story of Duxbury 1637–1937* (Duxbury, Mass., 1937), 45.

2. At their 2 November meeting, the Commissioners of the United Colonies urged the the constituent governments to appoint Thursday, 2 December "as a sollemne Day of Prayer and humilliation; to supplycat the Lords p^rdoning Mercye and Compasion towards his poore people; and for successe in our Indeavours for the Repelling the Rage of the enimy." Nathaniel Shurtleff, ed., *Records of Plymouth Colony*, 13 vols. (Boston, 1855–59), 10:358.

3. Prince's note: "Dec." The reference is to the Great Swamp Fight, 19 December 1675.

To [Thomas Walley?], 8 JANUARY 1676

PLIMOUTH JANUARY, 8: 1675:

REVD SI[R]

In Sat[urd]ay's hast. I cannot [...] transcribe for you Mr Hinckleys letter to the Treasure[r][1] Capt Bradford in a hopeful way to d[o]e well through Gods great mercy, (a sentence I love to write) I know not yet who of ours are slaine or wounded. our forces have had some action since the fort fight: viz, assaulted Pumhams towne,[2] burnt 150 wigwams, tooke some corne, but the Indians fled: our Troop was sent to discover whether the Indians remained at the [....] because of your [....] hardly think I shall [....] after the sabbath; many sick at [....] G: Da[ ]ett is dead, old G: [....] his [....] have their wives setled wi[....] men Indians left at Mattake[....] likely to dye) all of us salute you, God [....] soe prayes your Lov[....]

very few of our wounded men [...] there will hardly be time [....] the frost, our Southerne force[....] of Sep: 14: or 15: Let God order it [....]

I am, Sir [....] your Bro: by him

Cotton Family Papers 7:1, Prince Library, Rare Books and Manuscripts, Boston Public Library. Letter badly mutilated across middle; lower right-hand portion missing. No signature survives, but the handwriting is that of Cotton.

---

1. Not found.
2. After the Great Swamp Fight, the colonial army retired to Wickford. In late December the English raided Pomham's deserted home village, destroying it.

From Noah Newman, 10 January 1676

Rehoboth. Jan. 10. 75

Reverend & Dear Sir

I last night received yo^{r}s[1] having wth some impatiency waited for an oppertunity to hear from you or send to you; when I tooke my Journey to the Island to visit the wounded wch I heard was come thither I was presented with an oppertunity of going to Narragansett: wch I tooke hold of tho. where I found the Gen: well: & cheerful wth the rest of his attendance: when I was there this enclosed was presented me by a Plimouth man unto wch I [....] refer you for particular intelligence. Att that time they were [...] for the return of a Sqaw whom they brought wth them fro^{m} the fight & [...] children: she was sent leaving her children behind to get some understanding of the enemys losse. I am informed she is not returned [the?] reason I know not, since that there hath been an Eng: Scout sent out which broght in 2 Indians, who Informe that the Indians lost 300 of their cheife fighting men in the ingagem^{t}. besides women & childr: & old men. When the English were upon their march towards them all the sachems were together to veiw the fortification then making. but the alarum being given all wthdrew to another place but aquanapin.[2] who was shot through his thigh: The body of Indians are drawne off fro^{m} the ground they fought upon about 6 miles not further from but wide of ye head Quarters of the English. the Indians tell them there are 16 Engl: bodyes amongst the slain of the Indians, most the Indians Dwellings were burnt they render there Condition to be full of streights, & desire of parlying wth the Engl: If with safty. upon wch one of the says Indians was sent to [acquaint?] the sachems wth the Engl: their acceptance of a treaty provided they would come such a time viz Jan^{r} 1. wch proving stormy the sachims could not come & after durst not come till they had further order from the English. whereupon [illeg.] that time was prefixt, since wch I hear nothing; a post past by the Last week in wch Mr Dudly was but called not here, the sume of what I here relate I hrd from one that met them upon the rode. more strength went up the Last weeke from the Massachusetts. under the Command of Capt. Brocklebank of Rowley. Capt. Sill of Cambridge. Capt. Wadsworth of Milton.[3] Some of their men was tutcht wth the frost by the extreamity of the season & are left behinde at warentum,[4] & 2 here, others were very hearty & cheerfull & marcht from us Jan: 8.—I suppose the Number of men lost the last fight will amount to about 70. besides such as any wounded some of whose lives may yet be in suspence. I heard the Last weeke Capt. Sealy[5] was dead. I Looke every day & hour for certaine intelligence of things both at ye Iland & Narrag: by some gone from us to visit them. There is of late some losse by fire at Narragan: but I heare it so variously reported, I dare say no thing till I have better information—when I was wth Capt Bradford he was very cheerfull & hopefull, yet much affected wth M^{r}. Holms his death wch I first brought him the intelligence off; I had the rumor of that mortallity that was in y^{r} parts but not ye distinct account till I received yours. The Lrd humble us under his mighty hand & Sanctifye to us that cup he is causing to passe round amongst us—I desire to blesse God wth you for his mercy to yor family To whom the Lord Continue the same, through the mercy of our God my famiy is in health, & to use an usuell saying of my mother now in heaven The Lord still holds a Course of kindness wth this poore plantation, Not one person being slaine & but one considerably wounded who is in a hopefull way of recovery. oh that we could answer the tender mercy of our God in thankfullnes & fruitfullnes. wherin helpe is wth yor prayers. Thus wth my Loving respects to yor s: yor second selfe & all yo^{rs}. my wife Saluting you all, wth desier of mutall prayers. I rest

yor Assured freind

Noah Newman

Remember my Loving respects to Goodwife Followay[6] if living & others inquiring after us.

Curwen Family Papers, American Antiquarian Society. Addressed "To the Reverend His Dear freind Mr John Cotton Pastor to the church of christ in Plimmouth these." Endorsed "From Mr Newm[an] January, 10: 167[6]." Small hole in top center.

---

1. Not found.

2. Narragansett sachem Quinnapin was a well-connected, prominent war leader of the Narragansetts. He was a nephew of the renowned Miantonomo, a brother-in-law to sachem Philip by his first marriage, and husband of the powerful Pocasset sachem Weetamoo. He was captured in August 1676, tried in Newport, and shot 25 August 1676. Bodge, *Soldiers of King Philip's War*, 385.

3. Capt. Samuel Brocklebank (c. 1630–1676) of Rowley, Capt. Joseph Sill (1639–1692) of Cambridge, and Capt. Samuel Wadsworth (d. 1676) of Milton commanded reinforcements sent from camps at Dedham and Rehoboth. Brocklebank was a deacon of the church in Rowley and captain of the town's militia company. Sill had served nearly from the outset of the war and narrowly escaped destruction with Capt. Richard Beers's detachment on 4 September 1675 near Northfield. He returned to the Connecticut River area in the spring of 1676 and served in the "Eastward," or Maine, operations in the autumn, after the war in southern New England had wound down. He moved to Lyme, Connecticut, after the war and died there at the age of 53. After garrisoning the Marlboro-Milton area through the winter, Wadsworth and his company of seventy men, including Brocklebank, were drawn into an ambush near Sudbury on 21 April 1676. Only thirteen English escaped the slaughter; Wadsworth and Brocklebank were not among them. Leach, *Flintlock and Tomahawk*, 140; Bodge, *Soldiers of King Philip's War*, 206, 218-31, 266-72.

4. Not identified.

5. Savage, *Genealogical Dictionary*, 2:138-39.

From James Oliver,[1]

14 January 1676

This rich and detailed "letter from the front" was apparently compiled from a journal or orderly book. Cotton's transcription, which immediately follows Oliver's letter, is much easier to read, as Cotton largely corrected Oliver's phonetic spellings and added some punctuation and capitalization. For this reason, we do not annotate every dubious word or phase in this letter, but if the reader employs a literal pronunciation of Oliver's spelling, the meaning likely will become clear.

Narowgansett 14: 11. 1675

Mr Cotton

[A]nd loving frind yours Cam to hand yesterday in answer to it to ad to what you hav heard I well know not after a tegous[2] march in a biter Cold nigt that folowd the sabath 12 10^{m}.[3] we hoped our pilot would have led us to pumham by break of day but how it Cam to pass we wer mis led and so mist a good opertunity 13 day 10^{m} we Cam to m^{r} smith, and that day took. 35 p^{rs}[4] 14 of that m^{o} our generall[5] went out with hors and foot I with my Company was left to keep garis[6] I sent out 30 of my men to scout ab[road] who kiled 2 Indans and brought 4 prisoners on of which was beheaded that Eving our army Cam hom at night kild 7 and brought in 9 more yong and old 15 instant 10^{m} december Cam in john a roug[7] with a pretence of peac and was dismist with the arant[8] that we might speake with sachems that Eving and was not gon ¼ of an hour befor his Company that lay hid behind a hil kild 2 salem men within a mile of our quarter and wounded a 3rd that [....] and at a hous [....] [ther?] I had 10 men tha kiled 2 of them [illeg.] man [illeg.] instantly Captain mously my selfe and [...] gardener of salem[9] we wer sent to fetch [in] <*Captain*> major apltons Company that kept [...] mils ½ of and Coming back tha lay behind a ston wal and fired on us in sight of the garison we kild a Captain that kild the sale[m] men and had his Cap on that night tha burnt jery bul's hous and kild ther 17 yong and old 16 instant 10mo Cam that news 17: instant Cam news that Conetycot forcis wer at petyswamscut kild 4 indans, and took 6 prisoners that day we sold Captain Davenport[10] 47 indyan yong and old for 80 in mony 18 d we marched to petyswamscut with al our for[ces] only a garison left that night proved a snowy night we lay a thousand in the open fei[ld] that long night covring our [selves] with hay in the moring 19 being Lords day we marched [at?] 5 a Clock in the morning between 12 and 1 we Cam up with the Enymy and had a sore fight f[or] 3 hours we lost that are dead now about 68 and had 150 wounded many of which ar[e] recoverd we [illeg.] that long snowy Cold night [we] had about 18 mils to our Qarter with 210 dead and wounded we lost 8 ded behind the fort we had but 12 dead when we [Cam] from the [swamp] beside the 8 we lost many dyed by the way and as soon as tha wer brought in so that we buryed that [illeg.] being 20 d in on grave 34 and next day 4 and next day 2 next day 2 and non sinc her dyed at road Iland an att petyswamscut 2 lost in the woods and kiled 20 day as we heard sinc som say 2 mor dyed 5 of this number was kiled befor as I have written 19 d by the best intelygenc we have we kild 300 fighting men that 19 day a prisoner that we tooke last 6th day saith 3 [illeg.] and abov 300 weomen and Children we burnt abov 500 houses of ther then al that was ther but 9 with all their Corne that was in baskets, great stor our signall mer[cy] that night not to be forgot was when we drew of with so many dead and wounded that tha did not persue us which the yong men would hav don but the sachems would not Consent tha had but 10p powder left our generall with about 40 lost our way and wandered al that night and Cam [several words illeg.] til 7 a Clock next morng its thought we we[re] within 2 mils of the Enymy againe but god kept us to him be the glory we have kild now and then on sinc and burnt abov 200 wigwams m[ore][11] [several words illegible] we killed 9 last [6th?] day we fetch in their Corn dayly and that undoes them this is as neer as I [last words on page illegible] I read the narrative to my ofisers in [my?] tent who all asented to the truth of it I am tow long only I am wiling to tell you as mch as I can if oppertunyty present [illeg.] bro dexter saith my bro wilyams son [go on?] well from stoningtown last night Cam [illeg.] master treat [....] hear with 350 horse and foot the 27: instant men of the mohegens nor peaquids tha proved very fals fired into the aire and sent word befor tha Cam that tha would do so but got much plunder guns and ketls we shal persue the Enymy then who are fled a great part of what [illeg.] is written was atested by Joshuah tife[12] an inglishmen who larned indyn maryed a indan a wampanog who shot 20 times at us in the swamp he was taken att providence 14 instant brought to us 16 instant and after his Confesyn was hanged drawn and Qartered 18 instant a sad wretch he never hear a sermon he said but on this 14 year [so?] his father going to recal him bak sinc [illeg.] ther lost his head and lys unburyed he said he never heard of the Name of Jesus Christ [a line along left margin illegible] Sir I am yr Lo friend

Ja[me]s Oliver

Cotton Family Papers 7:2, Prince Library, Rare Books and Manuscripts, Boston Public Library. The date of this letter is problematic. While the dateline clearly indicates the 14th of January, Oliver's narrative refers to events occurring as late as the 18th of that month. This apparently led Prince to assume that the dateline was incorrect, for he dated the letter 26 January (see descriptive note to following letter). It seems most likely that Oliver began his narrative on the 14th but, either lacking conveyance or awaiting further events, did not finish it until after the execution of the unfortunate Tifte. Oliver's handwriting is awful and made more difficult by the condition of the letter: two of the four pages are badly faded, and all margins are mutilated.

1. James Oliver (d. 1682), son of Thomas Oliver, the ruling elder of Boston's First Church, was made a freeman of Massachusetts Bay in 1640, was captain of the Artillery Company in 1656 and 1666, served in several town offices, and was captain of the First Military Company of Boston c. 1673. Appointed to command a Boston company in the Narragansett campaign, he was discharged in February 1676. The following September a would-be lynch mob approached him to obtain his support for the jailbreak and unlawful execution of some Native prisoners. Although generally no friend to Natives, an indignant Oliver reportedly drove the ringleaders off with his walking stick. In a 1680 petition in which he prayed to be released from further service, he described himself as aged and infirm. The petition was granted, and Oliver died two years later. Bodge, *Soldiers of King Philip's War*, 173-78.
2. Tedious.
3. I.e., tenth month (December).
4. Prisoners.
5. Josiah Winslow.
6. Garrison.
7. I.e., "John, a rogue," probably "Stone-wall John," a Narragansett who had lived with the English before the war and apparently had learned stonemasonry. He led a parlay on 15 December, which the English suspected was a ruse to stall the attackers. Bodge, *Soldiers of King Philip's War*, 181.
8. Errand.
9. Capt. Joseph Gardner of Salem, in the thick of the Great Swamp Fight, was killed instantly by a bullet through his head, apparently from indiscriminate "friendly" fire. Benjamin Church, "Entertaining Passages Relating to Philip's War," in Richard Slotkin and James K. Folsom, *So Dreadfull a Judgement: Puritan Responses to King Philip's War, 1676-1677* (Middletown, Conn., 1978), 413.
10. Capt. Nathaniel Davenport (b. c. 1632) of Boston was killed just within the breach in the Narragansett fort. Leach, *Flintlock and Tomahawk*, 129; Bodge, *Soldiers of King Philip's War*, 168.
11. The following line, ending with "undoes them" is written in the margin but seems to have been intended to go here. At least, that is how Cotton read it; see his transcription, which follows.
12. Joshua Tifte, a former resident of Pettaquamscutt, had apparently been living with the Narragansett for some time, to the disgust of his family—his father cut him out of his 1674 will with the bequest of only a shilling. Captured near Providence and interrogated, Tifte admitted that he was present in the Narragansett fort during the 19 December battle and probably fighting against the English. Convicted of treason, the notorious renegade was hanged and quartered at Wickford on 18 January 1676. Leach, *Flintlock and Tomahawk*, 139-40.

From James Oliver, 14 January 1676 (Cotton's transcription)

Na[rra]gan[sett]675:

After a taedious <*night*> march in a bitter cold night that followed the sabbath, Dec: 12: wee hoped our Pilot would have led us to Pumham by break of day, but soe it came to passe wee were misled & soe mist a good opportunity: Dec: 13: wee came to Mr Smiths, & that day tooke 35 prisoners. Dec: 14: our Generall went out with horse & foot, I with my company was left to keep Garrison, I sent out 30 of my men to scout abroad who killed 2 Indians & brought in 4 prisoners, one of which was beheaded, our Army came home [...] night, killed 7 & brought in 9 more young & old: Dec: 15: ca[me] John a Rogue with a pretence of peace & was dismist with [illeg.] Errand that wee might speake with Sachims, that Evening he not being gone ¼ of an houre, his company that lay hid behind a hill killed 2 Salem men within a mile of our quarters & wounded a 3^{d} that he is dead & at a house 3 miles off where I had 10 men they killed 2 of them; Instantly Capt Mosely, myselfe & Capt Gardner were sent to fetch in Major Appletons company that kept 3 miles & ½ off, & coming they lay behind a stone wall & fired on us in sight of the garrison, wee killed the Capt that killed the Salem men & had his cap; on that night they burnt Jery Bulls house & killed 17: Dec: 16: came that news. Dec: 17: came newes that connecticutt forces were at Petaquamscutt, killed 4 Indians & tooke 6 prisoners, that day wee sold Capt Davenport 47 Indians young & old for 80 pd in mony. Dec: 18: wee marched to Pettaquamscott with all our forces only a garrison left, that night was very snowy, wee lay a 1000 in the open field that long night: in the morning Dec: 19: Lords day at 5 a clock wee marched betweene 12 & 1 wee came up with the Enemy & had a sore fight 3 hours, wee lost that are now dead about 68 & had 150 wounded many of which are recovered, that long snowy cold night wee had about 18 miles to our quarters, with above 210 dead & wounded, wee left 8 dead in the fort, wee had but 12 dead when wee came from the swamp besides the 8 wee left, many dyed by the way & as soone as they were brought in, soe that Dec: 20: wee buried in a grave 34 & next day 4 & next day 2, next day 2 & none since here; 8 dyed at R: Island, at Petaquamscut, 2 lost in the woods & killed Dec: 20: as wee heard since some say 2 more dyed, by the best Intelligence wee killed 300 fighting men. A prisoner wee tooke [....]50 & above 300 woemen & children, wee burnt above 500 houses; left but 9, burnt all their corne that was in baskets, great store: our signall mercy that night not to be forgotten, viz, that when wee drew off with soe many dead & wounded they did not pursue us which the young men would have done but the Sachems would not consent, they had but 10 pd of powder left. our Gen: with about 40 lost our way & wandered till 7 a clock morning before wee came to our quarters [...] thought wee were within 2 miles of the Enemy againe, [...] God kept us, to him be the Glory: wee have killed now & then

[...] since & burnt above 200 wigwams more: wee killed 9 last [ ]day, wee fetch in their corne daily & that undoes them. [Thi]s is as neere as I can a true relation, I read the Narrative to my officers in my tent who all assent to the truth of it. Monhegins & Pequots prooved very false, fired into the aire & sent word before they came they would doe soe, but got much plunder, guns & kettles; a great part of what is written was attested by Joshua Tifte, who married an Indian a wampanoog, he shot 20 times at us in the swamp, was taken at Providence Jan: 14: brought to us, 16: executed 18: a sad wretch, he never heard a sermon but once this 14 yeares, he never heard of the name of Jesus Christ, his father going to recall him lost his head & lyes unburied.

Cotton Family Papers 7:3, Prince Library, Rare Books and Manuscripts, Boston Public Library. The text is in Cotton's hand. Prince's note: "NB On the Top of ye Other page it was wrote by the Same Hand Thus—Narragenset. 26. 11. 1675." See descriptive note regarding the date of Oliver's narrative preceding this letter. Additional note in unknown hand: "N.B.—The above is a copy of the preceeding & is by James Oliver.

To Thomas Walley, 4 February 1676

Christian Indians, especially in Massachusetts, were generally treated shamefully, facing harassment, lynchings and displacement by fearful or bigoted colonists. Some, as reported below, offered their services in dangerous assignments in exchange for better treatment for themselves or their families.

Plimouth February, 4: 1675 :

Reverend Sir

From Mr Hinckley I transcribe, dated Jan: 31:[1]

James an Indian spy (sent hence with one Job[2] thought to be lost) came in last Tuseday, he sayes they met with 7 Indians about wanexit,[3] they took them & carried them 20 mile crosse connecticutt path northward of Quebaug where were 3 townes, in all 300 fighting men well armed, they threatned to kill them because they were spyes, English brothers, though they had before told them they lived poorly at Dear Island[4] had little wood & soe came away; at last they going to one eyed Johns[5] wigwam Sagamore of Nashaway & their capt he told this James he was glad to see him he was his freind & a lusty man, had helpt him to kill Mohauks & charged his gun & said he would kill whomsoever should kill him: some of them said he had killed Philips counsellors at mount hope & Philip had hired some to kill him with some others that helpt the English against him: They told them on inquiry, that they durst not goe to Boston & soe knew not what English were gon to Narroganset; they spake of sending him to Philip, he excused it because he was a lusty man and must first goe out & get some English heads to carry with him before he durst goe to Philip: Job & he pretended to goe out ahunting, killed 3 deare quickly & perceiving they were dogged by some other Indians went over a pond & lay in a swamp till before day & when they had prayed together he run away, Job being desirous if he could to get away his children who were carried away with many others as they were gathering corne (of which wee heard heretofore) & were not knowne whither till now; & he would excuse James his running away because the Indians threatened to kill him; he says they have not much corne but store of beife, pork & venison, they within 20 days after the wednesday before intended to fall upon Marlborough, Lancaster, Groton etc Matoonus[6] is one of them, other Nipmug, Quabaug & Nashua Indians: A Narroganset brought to them 1English head they shot at him & said they were the English friends all last summer; afterwards 2 messengers with 12 heads craving their asistance, they then accepted them; A messenger to them also from Philip who is with Hadley Indians within halfe a days Journey of fort Albany (this seems to concurre with New York Governours Intelligence)[7] the Mohauks help them with Ammunition from Albany; the Mohauks will not (they say) fight with the English; but will fight the Monhegs (the English brothers) in aid of the Narrogansets: The Narrogansets inform Quabaug Indians that they killed 200 *<Indians>* English, lost but 40 fighting men, 300 old men, woemen & children in the wigwams burnt: one Pepper of Roxbury[8] an Englishman with Quabaug Indians being taken when Capt Beeres was slaine; Philip hath 2 more; Peppers master tells him he shall have Liberty to goe home in the spring; Quabaug Indians promise to send 20 to see how it is with the Narrogansets Haecille scripsit.[9] He also told G: Paybody that at a farme 5 miles beyond Sudbury, (the man of the house being at Boston for Ammunition) the Indians came & killed his wife & 7 children & 2 lads killed or lost. from Mr Shove I transcribe not, concluding he hath written as largely to you as to me by Will: Mayo.[10] These Mutineers & Runnagado's filled the spirits of people with base prejudice against the Generall, I dread the consequence of soe wicked a frame: Gods Anger burns agst this poore land, what will become of us? craving your prayer for me & mine,

I rest, Sir, yours

J: C:

Cotton Family Papers 7:4, Prince Library, Rare Books and Manuscripts, Boston Public Library. Addressed "These For the Reverend his much Honored Freind Mr Thomas Walley Pastour of the Church of Christ, at Barnstable."

1. Hinckley's letter to Cotton (not found) contained the report relayed by Cotton that follows, based upon the testimony of James Quannapaquait, recorded by Daniel Gookin, 24 January 1675/6. The original relation is at the Connecticut Archives; the most recent transcription appears in Neal Salisbury, *The Sovereignty and Goodness of God by Mary Rowlandson, with Related Documents* (Boston, 1997), 24, 118-28.

2. James Quannapaquait, a.k.a. James Rumneymarsh of Nashaway, and Job Kattanannit were Nipmuck men released from internment on Deer Island to spy for the English. They pretended to be enemies of the English and successfully infiltrated the insurgents' camps. On 24 January James brought Daniel Gookin word of an imminent attack on Lancaster, Massachusetts. Gookin was unable to persuade authorities of the report's authenticity, however, and by the time Job brought confirmation on 9 February, it was too late; Lancaster was attacked the next day. Daniel Gookin, *An Historical Account of the Doings and Sufferings of the Christian Indians in New England in the years 1675, 1676, 1677* (New York, 1972), 486-90.

3. Wamesit, a Pawtucket "praying town" on the Merrimack River.

4. James and Job were hardly exaggerating. The Christian Indians suffered terribly on the bleak island that winter. Some 400 were incarcerated there by March 1676. By that time, many more had died of exposure and privation. Leach, *Flintlock and Tomahawk*, 150.

5. One-eyed John, a.k.a. Monoco, led an attack on Lancaster the previous August and was shortly to lead another. He was captured in the final days of the war. Leach, *Flintlock and Tomahawk*, 164-65.

6. Matoonus was a Nipmuck war captain who led the first attack against a Massachusetts town, Mendon, at the beginning of the war. In late July 1676 another Nipmuck, Sagamore John, handed him over to Massachusetts authorities when he submitted himself and his followers. Matoonus was then executed by a Nipmuck firing squad on Boston Common. Leach, *Flintlock and Tomahawk*, 223.

7. New York Governor Edmund Andros kept a close eye on the war, especially since King Philip had come to seek help from the Mohawks in the winter of 1675–76.

8. Capt. Richard Beers of Watertown and a company of about thirty-six men were ambushed on 4 September 1675 near Squakeag, north of Deerfield on the Connecticut River. Robert Pepper, a young soldier, was wounded and taken captive at that time. Leach, *Flintlock and Tomahawk*, 87.

9. "Here ends the account."

10. William Mayo (1654–1691), son of John Mayo and Hannah Reycraft of Eastham. Shurtleff, *Records of Plymouth Colony,* 7:26; Savage, *Genealogical Dictionary*, 3:189.

From Thomas Walley, 16 February 1676

FFEB 16 1675

REVEREND AND DEARE SIR

the Letters that yo^u^ have favoured me with have bin a refreshing to me in this Sad time. the world grows old and withered and affords little Comfort. I have great Cause to Complaine of my owne heart I want wisdom patience a humble spirit I feare I am vexed rather then grieved at the frowardness and discontents that are among to many at this day the sins that god afflicts us for we are multiplying and adde to them dayly who shall live when god shall deale with us for our transgressions Can we expect that we shall prospor against our enemies when nothing likes us that god doth we please not god neither Can men please us. we Know not the dutys of an inferior state we shall all seek to raigne till Tirants raigne over us. god will certainly humble this Land gods providences seeme to preserve our enemies to be thornes in our sides this news from Lancaster is exceeding Sad[1] and should greatly humble us I long to heare how it fares with the rest of that Towne and what the enemie hath don there from theyr first Comming to it for we have uncertaine reports when yo^u^ see o^r^ honoured Generall I pray yo^u^ present my servis to him I long to heare of his health and hope the Lord will keep up his spirit under all discouragements – we know noe man in the place he hath sustained that Could have preservd his honor in the servis of this Cuntry better then he hath don his for it is difficult to be in a high place in New England. Sir the Last Lords day it was agreed by the Elders and Brethren of o^r^ church to set apart 5th day Come seaven nite wch will be the 24th of this month I pray yo^u^ faile not to be with us it had bin this week but that we desire yor help—the mercie of god to o^r^ place is soe greate that it was a dispute whether it should not be kept as a day of thanksgiving but the pvidences of god being mixed I hope we shall endevour to [ ]e them the Lord fitt us my Love to yor selfe and yo^rs^

I am yor truly loving ffriend and Brother

Tho: Walley

Washburn Papers 14:1, Massachusetts Historical Society. Addressed "ffor the Reverend and my much esteemed ffriend Mr John Cotton Pastour of the church of christ at Plimoth these DD." Endorsed "From Mr Walley, February, 16: 1675:."

---

1. Lancaster, Massachusetts, was attacked 10 February by a combined force of Narragansett, Nipmuck and Wampanoag warriors. They killed at least fourteen and captured twenty-three, one of whom was the now-famous Mary Rowlandson.

Copy of an order by the General Court of Plymouth Colony, 7 March 1676

ORDER OF COURT FOR A FAST, DATED MARCH, 7: 1674/75 FOR PLIMOUTH CONGREGATION[1]

[Thoug]h wee have abundant cause to take notice with Thankfullnesse, of the great kin[dness &] mercy of God vouchsafed to us in soe gratious preserving us & soe many of our townes hitherto [in] the midst of many dangers [f]rom those miseries & desolations which our sins have deserved, & also in saving [the] lives of soe man[y of] our souldiers who were greatly hazarded in the Engagements with the enemy & by the blessing of God gave such a check to them, & espetially in the preservation & gratious returne of our honoured Governour & magistrate notwithstanding all threatening appearances of the contrary, for all which expressions of divine favour let praises waite for our God in Sion. Yet considering that the Lords hand is still stretched out against us in the war continued betwixt us & the Heathen, who still continue to doe mischeife in sundry places, even to the consuming of habitations, estates & lives of many, & not knowing how neere wee also may be to such deadly dangers, the Lord also contending with us by deadly sicknesse which hath caused divers families to mourne for their awfull bereavments, Divine Providence also threatning us with scarcity of bread, an usuall effect of war, the Governour & Councill doe therefore seriously commend it to all the Congregations in this Colony, to set apart the 29th of this Instant to be solemnely observed as a day of publick Humiliation, wherein to humble our soules before God for all those evills whereby wee have provoked our good God to write such bitter things against us, & to seeke Attonement & Reconciliation with him through Jesus Christ, & that he would please to worke in every one a true spirit of Reformation in their severall relations, & thereby fit us for the mercy of deliverance out of these afflicting troubles, & that the Lord would guide those his servants, whom it doth not eminently concerne, in a right way for the attainement of soe good an end, & that he would in due time restore our peace succeed our armes blesse the labours of our hands & crowne this yeare with his goodnesse, for his names sake.

Nath: Morton Secretary.

Cotton Family Papers 7:5, Prince Library, Rare Books and Manuscripts, Boston Public Library. This copy is entirely in Cotton's hand, including Morton's signature.

1. This heading appears to have been appended some time after the text was copied and misdated at that time. From the context the actual date seems clear.

From Noah Newman, 14 March 1676

Those Native bands fighting the English were growing desperate: short of food, unable to encamp for very long, and with women and children to care for. Nevertheless, they were still quite capable of taking the offensive. In the early morning hours of 21 February 1676, a Native force estimated at 300 to 400 warriors infiltrated "every part of the town" of Medfield, Massachusetts, set fire to houses and outbuildings, and then shot inhabitants and soldiers as they responded to the alarm. Although the town contained about 200 English soldiers and militia, these were scattered in quarters throughout the community and no effective watch had been set. The result was a stinging and embarassing defeat for the English; about forty houses, nearly half of those in the town, were destroyed, and twenty people were killed or wounded. To add insult to injury, the attackers withdrew across the Charles River toward Sherborn and burned the bridge behind them in the face of the tardy pursuit.[1]

REHOBOTH. MARCH. 14. 16756 [sic]

REVEREND & DEAR SI[R]

I received yo[r]s[2] w[ch] should have come (as you say by Goodman Sabin) returning thanks for your remembrance of me therein, desiring to sympathize w[th] you in the Continuance of those tryalls you are yet under by the prevailing sicknes. As to yo[r] desire of the Hystory of the medfield tragedy as you well call it, I shall give you the Best account I can, The time of it was febru: the 21 being the 2d day in the morning, It seemes probable that the enemy had Logd himselfe secretly in most of their barns, & waited for the first appearance of day, intending to take persons at their first Looking out at their doores in the morning, w[ch] accordingly they did, some troopers Lodging at Ephr: Wiswalls one was killd being one of the first that was killd in the Towne: viz) [sic] one Jackson of Newtowne. The Indians bounc't at Goodman Dwights house to provoke him to Looke out & when he did Looke out shot him thorugh the shoulder, who is dead since I was their. At widow fishers the ordinary keeper Joshua Fisher her Grandson going out the doore was shot att. the bullet passing through some flesh about his choller bone grazed upon his throat & Left a scar. he stepping backe & raising the house Leift Henery Adams[3] stept but over the threshould, & was shot through the windpipe & fell downe dead. Goodman Bowers & his son was Kild Thomas Mason & his son kild, Sergeant Thomas Thurston Lodging at—Brigdstreet & his wife up in the Towne at Seth Smiths she was stricken dead to the enemys apprhension, & a child Layd at Each hand of her dead as they thought they stript her & tooke of her head cloths, she afterward came to her selfe went into the house got a blanket & run to M[r]. Wilsons, Though as he told me a frightfull spectacle they not knowing who she was her hair hanging downe & her face covered wth blood.[4]—her children had both life in them & one was living when I was there she had another daughter shot through both her thighs another carryed captive Samuel Smiths wife being big wth child & another child in her arms was crossing over an open feild to a Garrison house & was over taken by the enemy & Kild, & her child left alive, found standing by its dead mother where they thought it had stood neer an hour when they found her & it—

The sight of this poore people was very astonishing in the morning, fires being Kindled round about them, the enemy numerous & shouting so as the earth seem'^{d} to tremble, & the cry of the terrifyed persons very dreadful oh what a sudden Calamity was this, & what an emblem of the sud^{n} & dreadfull appearance of the great Judge of the world when he shall Come to render vengeance to the wicked, few when they Lay downe thought of such a dolefull morning.

I doubt[5] their was too much Confidence in an arm of flesh If there was the Lord hath Let them see what a poore thing flesh is, The souldiers could get into no body for ye resistance of the enemy, the Capt^{s} walked up & downe wthout any men Considerable, & yet 3 Cap^{ts}. in the Towne, viz Capt. Barbar of ye Towne, Capt. Jacobs Capt Oaks.[6]—There was about 50 houses & barns burnt, of wch about 29 dwelling houses, I cannot give you an exact number of the persons killd nor their names, I askt the Question 2 or 3 times when I was there & Mr Wilson Could not resolve me, he told me they had been in such a distraction he had not injoyned himselfe since, to take or give any exact relation Capt Jacobs told me he Judged there was about 16 dead y^{t} was kild & had dyed since, there was severall wounded that Lay at Mr. Wilsons (viz old More that somtime lived at Mendham, one Bumsted of Boston who [was] thigh broken. Dan clarke of medfild, Ephr: wrights wife who was arm Broken Seargent Thur: wife whose head had been peirct wth one of their Tomheags one of her daughters shot through the thigh & one of her child strucke on the head. yet she sayd all her afflictions was Swallowed up in the Losse of her poore child gone into Captivity. The enemy as Mr Wilson told me he thought was something surprizd, wth their great Guns & such a Number of men wch they percieved was amongst them & therefore gave their watchwords to draw off, their passage away was over Brigstreet bridge wch they fyred, & for awhile encamped on the other side, & from thence past away a writing was found at ye foot of the Bridge wth this impost & Quakere Language Thou English man hath provoked us to anger & wrath & we care not though we have war wth thee this 21 years for there are many of us 300 of wch hath fought wth thee at this time, we have nothing but our lives to loose but thou hast many faire houses cattell & much Good things. this is the summe. they were seen By Boggastow[7] people march away. a Company & Carriages of plunder another Company & their Carriages of plunder & in y^{t} order they marched away & were Judged by them to be Numerous more than they themselves give an account. oh that our hearte Could tremble at ye Consideration of these things, It is surely a day of great tryumph wth them; the Lord grant it may be a day of deep humiliation wth us; The last weeke a man kild at Groaton & another Carryed away the man carryed away is old Blood—M^{r}. Brattle going up to enquire after the army & [assist?] them when at Malburough, by the accidentall discharge of a Gun Mr Ransforths son was Killd & had but time to make his will & wthout sealing it he dyed:—this brings to my mind a nother remarkable providence at Med: Henery Adams, his wife going up into Mr Wilsons Chamber to get some repose after her great losse & there being layd downe upon a bed, a gun went accidentally off below, & shot through the chamber floore & through the bead & her body off wch she dyed wthin 24 hours.[8] Thus Sir, being at the end of my paper wth Respects to Mr Bradforth, yor s: M^{r}s Cotton, wid. fallowell & the rest of my good freinds, Desiring mutuall prayers I rest

Sir yor Assured Freinde

N. Newman

Curwen Family Papers, American Antiquarian Society. Addressed "To The Reverend Mr John Cotton Pastor to the church of christ In Plimouth These." Endorsed "From m^{r} Newman March, 14: 1676:" In a different hand: "Ind^{n} assault."

---

1. Gookin, *Doings and Sufferings*, 493-94.
2. Not found.
3. Henry Adams commanded the town's militia and was killed in the attack. Gookin, *Doings and Sufferings*, 493; Bodge, *Soldiers of King Philip's War*, 284.
4. One historian asserted that Mrs. Thurston had "probably" been partially scalped, but Newman's second-hand account (the only source for this incident) will not support that conjecture. A simpler explanation is found further on in this letter, when Newman names some of the wounded, including Sgt. Thurston's wife, whose "head had been peirct wth one of their Tomheags." Jill Lepore, *The Name of War: King Philip's War and the Origins of American Identity* (New York, 1998), 92-94.
5. I.e., "suspect."
6. Capt. John Jacob (d. 1693) emigrated with his parents to Hingham in 1633. A veteran of the Narragansett Campaign, he commanded a company of eighty soldiers at Medfield when it was attacked. Lieut. Edward Oakes commanded twenty mounted troopers, also quartered in the town. Gookin, *Doings and Sufferings*, 493; Bodge, *Soldiers of King Philip's War*, 283.
7. Boggestow was the area of the Charles River valley between Medfield on the east and Medway and Sherborn on the west. William S. Tilden, ed., *History of the Town of Medfield, Massachusetts 1650–1886* (Boston, 1887), 24.
8. Gookin relates that on the night following the attack that had left her a widow, Mrs. Adams was killed by none other than Capt. Jacob: "having a gun in his hand half bent [half cocked], with the muzzle upward towards the chamber, he being taking his leave to be gone to his quarters, by some accident the gun fired through, and shot floor, mat, and through and through the body of the Lieutenant's widow." Gookin, *Doings and Sufferings*, 494.

From Noah Newman, 27 March 1676

More tragedy awaited the English in this "winter of despair," and this time it was Plymouth's turn to suffer. In March 1676, Capt. Michael Pierce of Scituate led a contingent of sixty-five English and twenty Natives from Plymouth Colony on a search-and-destroy mission against Narragansett Indians. The English crossed the Pawtucket River on 26 March about 5 miles north of Providence to attack a band that Pierce had learned was in the vicinity. They encountered a far stronger force than they had expected, probably led by the sachem Canonchet, or Nanuntenoo. The colony soldiers were soon surrounded and very nearly wiped out; fifty-two English, including Pierce, and eleven allied Natives were killed.[1]

REHOBOTH: 27. OF THE FIRST 76

REVEREND & DEAR S^R^

I received yo^r^s Dated the 20 of this Instant[2] wherein you gave me a dolefull relat[ion] of what had happened wth you & what a distressing Sab: you had p[. . .] I have now according to the words of yor owne Letter an oppertun[ity] to retaliate yor account wth a Relation of what yesterday Happ[ened] to the great sadning of all our hearts filling us wth an awfull expect[ation] of w^t^ further evills it may be antecedaneous too both respecting our [. . .] & you. upon the 25 of this Instant Capt. Peirce went forth wth a small party of his men & Indians wth him, & upon discovery of the [ene] my fought him w^th^out damage to himselfe, & Judged that he had Con[sidera]bly damnifyed them. yet he being of no greater force chose rather [to] retreate & goe out ye next morning wth a recrute of men & ac[ording]ly he did taking Pilots from us that were acquainted wth ye ground But it pleased the Soveraigne God so to order it y^t^ they were [. . .] wth a great multitude of the enemy wch hath slaine 52 of [our?] Engl: & 11 Indians—The account of their Names is as follows: From Scituate 18 of wch 15 slaine (viz) Capt: Peirce: [Samuel Russell][3] Benj: Chittington John. Lathrope. Gershom Dodson. Sam Prat Thom: Savery. Joseph Wade Will: Wellcome. Jer: Bastow. John [Ensign] Joseph Cowwen, Joseph Perry John Perry John Rowse

Marshfeild 9 slaine. Tomas Littell John Ems Joseph Whitg John Burroughs Joseph Phillips. Sam: Bump. Jothr Low. [More ___] John Brance. Duxburough 4 slaine. John Sprage. Benj: [Soal] Thomas Hunt. Joshua Phobes.—Sandwich 5 slaine. Benj: Nye David Bessey. Caleb. Blacke Job, Gibbs. Stephen Wing.—Barnstable 6 slaine Leiuft Fuller. John Lues Eliezir [Clapp] Sam: Lenurt. Sam. childs Sam. Boreman.—Yarmouth. 5 [slaine] John Matthews John Gage Will Gage Hen: Gage Hen: Gold. Estham. 4 slaine, Joseph Nesserfeild: John: Walker John [M___] Nathaniall Williams. of Rehob: slaine 4. John Read. Benj: [...] John Fitch Junir. John Meller Junir. & Thomus man is [...] returned wth a [sore] wound:—Thus Sir. you have a sad account of the Continuance of Gods displeasure against us yet still I desier [steadfastly] to looke unto him who is not only able but willing to save all such as are fit for his salvation It is a day of ye wickeds tryumph but the sure word of God telles us his Tryumphing is but [...] oh that we may not lengthen it out by our sins.—The Lord helps to Joyne Issue in our prayers Instantly & Earnestly for ye healing & helping of our Land, our Extreamity is Gods oppertunity—

Thus wth our dearest respects to yor S:, M^{r}s Cotton & such sorrowfull freinds as are wth you I rest

yor ever Assured freind Noah Newman

Since the writing of this letter, John Matthews & sam: Linnit are found alive;[4]

Curwen Family Papers, American Antiquarian Society. Addressed "To the Reverend His Dear Freind Mr John Cotton Pastor to ye church of christ in Plimouth, these." Endorsed "From Mr Newman March, 27: 1676:" In another hand, "Newman shove Walley <maj^{r}. *Bradford*> capt oliver <*Heath*> In. Mather. <*Nath Mather*>. Incr. Math^{r}. Seab^{n} Cotton [illeg.] <*Moodey*> Mr Newman Read." Cotton noted at the bottom of the page, "since the writing of this letter, John Matthews & Sam: Linnit are found alive." Another note in a modern hand: "An incorrect copy of the within Letter is printed in Mr Dean's history of Scituate page 122—." Badly torn along right margin.

---

1. Leach, *Flintlock and Tomahawk*, 167; Bodge, *Soldiers of King Philip's War*, 347-49.
2. Not found.
3. Owing to the present condition of the letter, some names are missing or illegible. Names in brackets are supplied by Bodge, *Soldiers of King Philip's War*, 349-50. Bodge worked from the same letter a century ago, when it was presumably in better shape, but even then he reported that it was "much worn and mutilated."
4. This postscript is in John Cotton's hand.

From Joshua Moody,[1]

1 April 1676

Ports^{o} 1. (2.) mo <u>76</u>

MR Jno Cotton

[...] & Rev^{D} S^{R}

I rec^{d} [several words lost] week wth ye Enclosed, unto wch I have [several words lost] wch y^{u} may please to convey, [...] Busines wil be don as I have sent him word.—

I thank you for yor Intelligence. I have read it & showed it unto many who have pused it wth great Sympathy, & hope it hath been of some good use. If anything remarkeable of like natr occurr among you for ye future (wch ye L^{d} in his mercy p^{r}vent) your handing it to us w^{d} be matter of great Satisfaction y^{t} wee might know things pticularly & truly. Reports are so many & various y^{t} one knowes n^{t} what to believe we had heard a Report of ye Solemn Tragedy before yo^{rs} came, but it was noth^{g}: so satisfactory. I may say (as in ye beginng of yo^{rs} y^{u} doe) hitherto things have been quiet among us y^{s} winter & spring, but what I may send y^{u} in ye Close of my letter (if a speedy Conviance p^{r}sent not of wch I am n^{t} certain) is wth ye Lord. The Indians about us are many of y^{m} come in & more coming. theyr words are very good & fair. ye L^{d} only knows w^{t} is in y^{r} Hearts, thô as yet theyr Actions are not contradictory to y^{r} words so farr as wee know. There is no trusting of y^{m} they often mean worst w^{n} they speak best. wee have no Cause to think o^{r} Troubles over, tho some seem to run high in y^{r} Thoughts y^{t} way O^{r} Indians say y^{t} ye Eastern Indians (except those y^{t} are on ye other side of Kennebeck) are like minded wth y^{m}selves, & all for peace wth ye English. There is noth^{g}: new among us. The Burn^{g} of Mr Dummrs house at York[2] lately I p^{r}sume y^{u} have heard of, himselfe w^{s} in o^{r} Town ye while It was don by ye Hay-stack wch caught fire (as its thought) fro^{m} some sparks remain^{g} after burn^{g} of some Rubbish to clear ye ground in ye Garden. Hee lost most of w^{t} hee had, all his Library pvisions, beds except one. The L^{d} help us to watch & pray alwaies y^{t} wee may bee acc^{td} worthy to stand, w^{n} ye son of man shall come. In him I am

Yo^{r}s in w^{t} I may

Jo Moodey

Curwen Family Manuscript Collection, Box 1, Folder 3, American Antiquarian Society. Addressed "To the Rev^{d} m^{r} Jno Cotton Pastor of ye Church of x^{t} at Plymmouth p^{r}st." and "For ye Revd John Cotton Plimth." Endorsed "From Mr Moodey April, 1: 1676:" Mutilation along fold near top of the page and along the right margin.

1. Joshua Moodey (1633–1697), Harvard class of 1653, began his ministry in Portsmouth, New Hampshire, in 1658. Following a falling out with Lt. Gov. Edward Cranfield in 1684, Moodey was convicted on a charge of refusing to administer sacraments according to the Church of England liturgy. He was

imprisoned for thirteen weeks and forbidden to preach in the province again. He found succor in Boston and was reportedly one of the "Five Ministers of Boston" who participated in the downfall of Sir Edmund Andros in 1689. Cotton's son John III was called to the Portsmouth church in 1691 but stepped aside when Moodey expressed an interest in his old post. Moodey defended Philip and Mary English during the Salem witchcraft trials of 1692 and encouraged their flight to avoid certain conviction. He then returned to Portsmouth, Cranfield having left in disgrace in 1685. Upon traveling to Boston in 1697 for medical help for "a Complication of Distempers," he died and was buried there. *Sibley's Harvard Graduates* 1:367-80.

2. Shubael Dummer (1636–1692, HC 1656) was a classmate of Increase Mather's at Harvard. His mother, Mary, had been "led away into the new opinions in Mrs Hutchinson's time," after which his father moved to Newbury. Dummer began preaching at York (in what is now Maine) in 1662. Dummer lost only his house and possessions on this occasion; he was not so lucky the next time. On 25 January 1692, "divers hundreds" of snowshoe-shod French Canadians and Indians assaulted the town. As many as forty-eight English were killed and seventy-three were taken captive. Rev. Dummer was reportedly shot dead near his doorway as he was mounting his horse. *Sibley's Harvard Graduates* 1:471-75.

From Thomas Walley, 17 April 1676

Walley seemed more concerned than most about the harsh treatment accorded enemy captives, particularly women and children. In this letter he reveals the damaging effects of English policies and military reverses on the attitudes of the initially supportive Native populations of Cape Cod.

Reverend and Deare Sir

it hath pleased god of Late to visit me with sickness my health is much impaired but the Lord is good and I have Cause to bless him and through his grace submit to his will and waite upon him. I am greatly afflicted in my spirit to see the dainger we are in and the Confusion and Sad disorder that we are fallen into New England must prepare them selves for what yoke the Lord will lay upon them for god will not beare the prid and Stubbornese of this generation there is non to help us in this day of our trouble a pverse spirit is among us by the righteouse judgment of god. that we are soe secure soe Carelese of our owne safty is not only our sin but it is our punishment and what it will <*worke for*> worke in the end god knows—we had Some hope the Indians with us might have proved faithfull and bin a help to us but they see our weakness and our Confusion and take great notice of the severity shewed towards the Squaws that are sent away[1] Some of them much grieved others I feare pvoked they see we Cannot soe easily raise Armes as send away poor Squaws the Country about us is troubled and grieved at this action accounting it very unseasonable and what the effect will be god only knows I Could wish our honored Governor would send for them back and returne them to theyr friends I judg it would be very acceptable to this part of the Cuntry for there is much discontent about it some feare we have payd deare for former Acts of severity and how deare we may yet pay god knows [...] now in hast if you Can doe any thing for th[....] of this act you will doe good servis [....] our honored Governor doe [....] Consider our [position?] it will not be thought unreasonable that they should be returned again sir my hearty Love is to you and m^rs^ Cotten I pray you p[ray fo]r me present my Servis to Cap: Bradford

yo^r^s in o^r^ Lord

Tho: Walley

April 17 1676

John Davis Papers, Massachusetts Historical Society. Addressed "For ye Rev^d^. & much Hon^d^ Friend m^r^. John Cotton Plimth." Endorsed "From m^r^ Walley: April: 17: 1676:." Prince's note: "about sending Captive squaws out of the Country."

---

1. The colonies increasingly resorted to enslaving Native prisoners, in part to defray the staggering costs of the war. Scores, perhaps hundreds, were sent to English Caribbean colonies. The practice, especially when used against Native women and children, obviously disgusted even English-allied or neutral Natives. James D. Drake, *King Philip's War: Civil War in New England 1675–1676* (Amherst, Mass., 1999), 136-39.

To Thomas Walley, 17 April 1676

Plimouth April: 17: 1676

Reverend & much Honoured Sir

Though I know not this morning of any opportunity of sending to you, yet I am willing to get ready for one. The Enclosed came to my hand on Saturday; Mr Moodey writes to me of a readynesse to pay the 10 pd, & if I might counsell in the matter, I would say that 10 ^pd^ in Silver is farre better then 10 ^pd^ in goods at Pascataquay; & seeing through my hands letters have had soe speedy a conveyance to & fro, & the buisnesse [*sic*] is soe ripened for accomplishment, I am willing (presenting my love to G: Hamlin & his wife) to tender my service yet further, if they please to accept it; Intending, God willing, for Boston next Monday by water, I suppose at the Election[1] I may meete Mr Moodey there, & if G: Hamlin sends me the Receipts desired, I may then take the money & deliver them to him. if a speedyer way present to attaine the end he will doe well to take it.

For publick newes, Mr Moodey thus writes to me

"The Indians about us are many of them come in & more coming, their words are very good & faire, the Lord only knowes what is in their hearts, though as yet their actions are not contradictory to their words soe farre as wee know, there is noe trusting of them, they often meane worst when they speak best; wee have noe cause to thinke our Troubles over, though some seem to run high in their thoughts that way: our Indians say that the Eastern Indians, (eccept those that are on the other side of Kennebeck) are like minded with themselves & all for peace with the English; Mr Shubael Dummer, Pastour at Yorke, while himselfe was in our towne, his house was casually burnt by the Haystack which caught fire (as its thought) from some sparks remaining after burning some rubbish to clear the ground in the garden, he lost most of what he had all his library, provisions, beds except one.["] Haecille.

Andover was assaulted at nooneday,[2] one man wounded, & cattell driven away: The rumour of souldiers out of o: E: is yet uncertaine: April: 9: on the Sabbath, the Indians beset Belerica round about,[3] when they were at meeting as yet noe account of the successe: this to G: Blush fell accidentally into my hands I know not whence it comes. Sir, if you have Dugards Rhetorick,[4] pray helpe me to it. worthy Sir, with reference to the transactions of the last weeke, I am exceedingly afflicted to thinke, that wee should soe reele & stagger in our Counsells as drunken men, & that soe pretious a people as Rehoboth should be soe forsaken by us for our owne selfish-interests, if I were in your study alone I would tell you, how much blemish some have gotten for being soe backward to maintaine a garrison at Rehoboth. This morning the Govr (being much incouraged by Capt Bradford & the Treasurer thereunto) hath sent 2 men post to Rehoboth, to signify that if they will come off, an army from us shall guard them, but if they will stay & Judge it necessary for their safety, they shall have from us 40 or 50 men to keepe garrison with them etc[5] & truly Sir if your Southerne men shall faile in this, it will be Just matter of reproach to them, however it is resolved, helpe shall be sent them if they accept it: Good newes in Letters from stonington to Boston. on the Lords day, Apr: 9: some connecticutt forces, Capt George Denison[6] being cheife, tooke & killed 42 Indians, of which Quanonshet was one, who was taken in that Coat he received at Boston,[7] his head is sent to Hartford, his body is burnt; then also was killed one Hostage that run from Hartford, & some cheife counsellors; also 3 sachems & 3 capts were taken & killed neere Patuxet: There was also a fight Apr: 2: by those forces with the Narrogansets, the issue of that I have not a particular account of: Apr: 12: one woman & 2 children were killed at wooburne: At Boston the votes for nomination of Magistrates, for divers old ones run very low; Capt Gookins hath 446 which is but 5 more then major Savage hath who is the last in nomination of the 18: Mr Dudly hath 651: An Indian at Boston who was improoved as a messenger to the Enemy being returned, affirmes that Capt Peirce & his killed scores of the Indians that Sabbath day: I must now conclude this letter having sundry things to transcribe for you, which Just now I received from Boston: our church hath set apart this following wednesday for Humiliation & prayer,[8] I am much straitned for time, but my Respect to you obliges me to transcribe the Enclosed: with our service to you presented, & due salutations to all as if particularly named, craving your earnest prayers for us

I rest, Sir yours sincerely devoted in what I may

John Cotton

2 houses burnt last weeke about Braintree at Monaticutt[9] & some at Bridgwater, as Edward wanton[10] told us last Saturday.

Cotton Family Papers 7:6, Prince Library, Rare Books and Manuscripts, Boston Public Library. Addressed "These For the Reverend, his much Honoured Friend, Mr Thomas Walley, Pastour of the Church of Christ, at Barnstable."

---

1. The Massachusetts election court was held 3 May 1676. *Mass Bay Recs.*, 5:77.
2. Andover was attacked "in the beginning of April"; one man was killed, a house was burnt, and several animals were killed or mutilated. Increase Mather, *A Brief History of the Warr with the Indians in New England*, in Slotkin and Folsom, *So Dreadfull a Judgement*, 115.
3. On 9 April, Increase Mather reported, "sundry of the enemy were seen at Billerica, and (it seemeth) had shot a man there." Mather, *A Brief History*, 115.
4. Probably *Rhetorices Elementa: quaestionibus et responsionibus explicata* (1657) by William Dugard (1606–1662), English schoolmaster, state printer, and friend of John Milton. *DNB*.
5. The Rehoboth men declined the offer to abandon their town, citing their concern that "we should in soe doing be wanting to the name of God and the interest of Christ in this place, and bewraye much diffidence and cowardice, and give the adversarye occasion to triumph over us, to ye reproach of that great and fearful name of our God." Thomas Cooper et al to Thomas Hinckley, 14 April 1676, printed in "The Hinckley Papers," *Collections of the Massachusetts Historical Society*, 4th ser., 5 (Boston, 1861), 2-4.
6. Capt. George Denison of Stonington and Capt. James Avery of New London, Connecticut, commanded a force of forty-seven English and eighty Natives. Early in April they surprised a band that included the Narragansett sachem Canonchet, son of Miantonomo and presumed leader of the group that had demolished Pierce's company the month before. Some of Denison's Native allies captured the sachem and offered to spare his life if he would urge his people to surrender; this Canonchet steadfastly refused to do. He was taken to Stonington and executed there by the Mohegan Oneco (or Oweneco) and two Pequot sachems of equal rank. In an ambiguous passage, Mather's account suggests that the English "caused" the allied Natives to shoot Canonchet, then cut off his head, in order to drive a permanent wedge between the Indians of Connecticut and the Narragansetts. Canonchet's captors probably needed no prodding, however; Oneco was the son of Uncas, Canonchet's old enemy, and the Pequots likewise had little reason to love the Narragansetts. Bodge, *Soldiers of King Philip's War*, 383; Mather, *A Brief History*, 115.
7. Canonchet reportedly received a silver-laced coat in October 1675, when he and other Narragansett sachems, then in Boston, pledged not to participate in the war against the English. According to a chronicler of the war, Canonchet was wearing this coat when his band was surprised, and in his flight he threw off first his blanket, then the distinctive and encumbering coat. William Hubbard, *The Present*

State of New-England, Being a Narrative of the Troubles with the Indians of New England (Boston, 1677) reprinted in Samuel G. Drake, ed., *The History of the Indian Wars in New England from the First Settlement to the Termination of the War with King Philip, in 1677,* 2 vols. (1865; facsimile, New York, 1969), 1:182, 2:58.

8. In the Plymouth church records Cotton wrote, "The war continuing & also sickness, the chh set apart April, 19: for fasting & prayer, & also May, 30: for the same grounds." Publications of the Colonial Society of Massachusetts *Collections* (hereafter *CSM*), 1:148.

9. Today's East Braintree, on the north side of the Monatiquot River.

10. Edward Wanton (d. 1716), Boston shipcarpenter, moved to Scituate in 1661. Savage, *Genealogical Dictionary*, 4:406.

From Noah Newman, 19 April 1676

From the beginning of the war, Rehoboth was vulnerable to sudden attack due to its relative remotemess. Rev. Newman's letter describes a settlement virtually in a state of siege, with a determined corps of colonists grimly refusing to abandon what remains of their community.

Rehoboth. Aprill 19. 76

Reverend & Dear S^r^

This day I received yo^r^s of the 11 of this instant[1] & am glad of an oppertunity by the same post that brought it to returne you this answer; Thanks be to god we have yet the most of our lives given us as a prey though many of our habitations are desolate & in ashes, the losse of wch is not so much to be taken to heart by us as our sins wch occassioned the same. oh that we could truly humble our selves under the mighty hand of God who can & will exalt us in due time; I cannot but often reflect upon the patience & long sufferance of our most mercyfull father who made our enemys stay so long for their comissions to do us any harm, & had not our God seen it needfull for us they have never had it to this day; & truly by that disturbance & astonishment that I have seen in some mens spirits since the late tryall I fully discerne wee had need of it, to convince us of our security who were ready to thinke such things would not befall us, but why we should promise our selves such [immunity?] I know not, Nor why that wch our sins hath been so long p[...] of, & so visibly drawing on upon us for so long a time should so much startle & astonish us being come I know not; Sundry amongst us upon the desolation [made] by fire began to conclude their was no subsisting, but I have not yet received it that God calls us to a remoovall unlesse we could leave our sins behinde us, wch I se little likelyhood of at present; If it should be the pleasure of God to bring this country universally loe & that the Lord by his providences (having truly humbled us) should un^r^take any thing further for a remnant uniting, & y^t^ our spirituall advantage as well as our Temporall might be designed therein this would be more taking wth men then any thing I have heard yet. But for men still to goe about wth this Question Who will show us any Good argues still an old frame. & an aptnes to thinke that if the p^r^sent distresse be but avoided all is well, & I likewise fear a remoovall will involve us in such new cares & hurryes y^t^ we shall forget the Lords Controversy wth us. Our freinds at ye Cape hath made us a motion of drawing downe that way, it was considered by us the last weeke & ye answer returned in the Negative;[2] As to yor invitation given me & my family I returne you most hearty thanks & reckon you one of my Dearest freinds with whom I could willingly live & dye, but at the p^r^sent I much respect the publiq interest, The Lord reward you for all yor former kindnes & p^r^sent care & love; if I should not take heart & be incouraged at such a time as this is who should? for I perceive my wealth increaseth & I find more fell into my lap then I can possibly improove. The other day it was disputed by some whether they should give me this one house that I now live in & Now I have more houses given me then I know what to doe wth & many intreaties to use them; If it were not so I have no cause to mistrust the care & faithfullnes of the Lord God of my fathers who hath ever done for me more then I could aske or thinke; In answer to yor desire about our desolation, The 28 of march the Enemy appeared[3] early in the morning very numerous & overspread our towne & fell presently to fyring of empty houses & burnt about 35 houses that had familyes belonging to them besides four other vacant houses y^t^ had no inhabitants & Barnes—they also slew one man gone at a distance from his Garrison early in the morning. they killd severall Cattell & burnt much hay they drew aside in the evening & pitcht their camp by the side of ye towne, rose up at day light the next morning tooke their walke over to providence & there did likewise—my great trouble was that not w^th^standing all fair warnings wch they had yet things were too much unsettled wth us, so y^t^ they [illeg.] more provision & other treasure especially at Providence then we should have [...]ed to have left y^m^, if we had not been unreasonably secure. Providence though they saw us in a flame incouraged themselves the enemy would steer some other course & by that means exposed a 100 bushels of corn & meal much goods & money to ye enemy wch was all taken away. The buryall of the slaine tooke us 3 days the burden of it lying upon our towne the 3^d^ day we had some from Dedham & Medfeild that afforded their helpe therein ye first day their was 17 English & 3 Indians buryed; The 2d day that I might Expresse my respect to Capt. Peirce & Leift: Fuller who dyed so Honorably I went forth & y^t^ day we buryed 18 English & one Indian; ye 3^d^ day they buryed 7 or 8 Eng: & one Indian since searche hath been made but no more can be found I know not but some may wander & perish in ye woods being strangers. when the Indians were at Provid: they Called to speake wth one [Valentine] Whitman,[4] Mr Williams hearing of it called to them & told them if they would parly he would parly wth them, wch they did & he had an hours discourse wth 3 of them, they told him the great God was against us & wth them, & that English men were like Women & that there was [three words crossed out] fifteen hundred of them that had burnt our towne & was burn[ing?] of theirs, he offered himselfe to be instrumentell to procure a treaty between them & ye English, they told him they would say more after a months time & another suggested that they intended to spend a month upon Plimouth Colony for the burning of that.—yesterday one of our Towne being abroad wth a teame alone was shot at but was not hit his oxen one was kild & the oth[er] wounded, he carelessely went forth both alone 3 miles from ye towne & w^th^out any gun, I hope it will be a conviction to him & others of such p^r^sumption. we are at p^r^sent generally visited wth a sudden & sore cold, the Lord sanctifye it to us & teach us to se how soone he can take us into his owne hand who are ready to thinke If we escape but the enemy we are out of the vaile of danger.

Dear s^r^ Let us have ye benefit of yor prayers that we may be refined [by] our burning & that God would not cease afflicting us till he hath accomplished his good pleasure upon us in making us a people to his praise, Goodman Miles[5] whose house barnes & Tan house is burnt & some of his stocke lost returns you wth his wife many thanks for yor kind offer & know not but If oppertunity offer that one of their sons about 14 or 15 years old might come to you & be wth you it might do them a kindness, & if you want a maid servant they have a daughter to dispose of.—Thanks be to God my family are Compet[ant]ly well recovering out of their colds my wife singulerly well contented to stay in the place she is in, & in no wise discouraged from a dependance upon God to cary us & ours thrô such ensuing difficulties as seem to be before is, I account it a very great mercy & canot be sufficiently thankfull for it. M^r^ M[...] is gone to ye Iland & Mr Brownes family is there his pson [two words illeg.] ye Iland & Swanzy, many of the Inhabitants gone & others [line faint, illeg.] cause that I do not write being in such straites of time. I no yor ever to [...] of him. I am sorry there is so great a [reflection?] upon authority in ye army mooving but I am discouraged the more as to our Conditon, for my hearts desire & prayer to God is y^t^ I may be above all disappointments of that nature, but so much as to be mooved at them, & to looke at all insufficientcy & uncertainty [...] Creature to be most like it selfe. The first day that any English blood was [shed was?] a fast, & my subject was psal. 46. 10[6] Be still & know that I am God: wch I desire ever to have in mind for my incouragemt in the worst times—The Good Lord incourage & strengthen all our hearts in himselfe & make us perfect in every good word & worke, hithertoo we have suffered little, I fear there are greater & sore evills behinde the Lord fit us for them, & instruct us by them. Let me hear from you as oft as may be as you shall from us. Thus wth affectionate salutes craving the continuance of mutuall prayers I rest [line illeg.]

[Noah Newman]

I canot but condole yor & our losse in the death of that good old [paster?][7] ye Lrd sanctify such breaches to us.—

Curwen Family Papers, American Antiquarian Society. Addressed "For the Revd & much Respectd Friend mr John Cotton Plimth." Endorsed "From mr Newman April 19: 1676." Several small holes along right margin and darkened lines along fold marks.

1. Not found.
2. Cape Cod, far removed from the fighting, was unquestionably the safest place for English and allied Native refugees.
3. Rehoboth was attacked 28 March. There was no apparent loss of life, as the people were holed up securely in the town's garrison houses. This left the attackers free to burn deserted homes, barns, and mills, confiscate food stores, and drive off or kill the town's cattle. Leach, *Flintlock and Tomahawk*, 168.
4. Valentine Whitman (c. 1627–1701) of Providence was a deputy, town treasurer, and an interpreter who had facilitated land transactions with Native peoples. Richard LeBaron Bowen, *Early Rehoboth: Documented Historical Studies of Families and Events in this Plymouth Colony Township* (Rehoboth, Mass., 1948), 3:18.
5. Probably John Myles, son of the controversial Reverend John Myles. Bowen, *Early Rehoboth*, 3:18.
6. Ps. 46:10: "Be still, and know that I am God: I will be exalted among the heathen, I will be exalted in the earth."
7. Probably a reference to the death of Rev. John Holmes of Duxbury the preceding December; see 3 January 1676.

To Thomas Walley, 10 June 1676

During the final stages of the war in southern New England, Native bands, their resources depleted and hungry from months on the run, began trickling back to their homelands in search of food caches and forage in familiar territory. This left them open to detection and attack by English forces, eventually the fate of Philip and his followers themselves.

Plimouth June, 10: 1676:

Reverend & much Honoured in the Lord

Before you were gone out of sight I was ready to set pen to paper to informe you of the newes from Boston Govr to ours: A squaw came into Roxbury & was examined last thursday, she saith Allumps[1] with 300 men are at a place neere warwick, called Watchu,

& there they plant, they are soe neere that when they goe to gather groundnuts they heare the English dogs bark on wednesday last Capt Henchman spied a considerable party of the enenmy [enemy] about 5 miles from Nashaway, & was very likely to doe them much mischeife, but that 2 of the Indians in a canoe discerned the English, & alarmed the Indians who presently fled, the English pursued them, killed 7, tooke 29 prisoners, (of which 2 were men) much fish, kettles [&] rescued 1 English captive, a boy; the English received not the least hurt, our Indian friends behaved themselves very faithfully & couragiously: Capt Pittymee[2] had the barrell of his gun damnifyed, & that was all the damage in this encounter, blessed be God:

one coming from New Yorke put in at Milford, Major Treat told him that the Mowhawks had within 5 weekes killed 70 of the Enemy:[3] The Posts from Taunton not yet returned. Deare sir I returne you hearty thanks for your good company, pretious labours, & particular kindnesses to me & mine, the Lord reward you; this hath bin a sad day with my servant, I intreat your prayers for him: wee long to heare of your safe arrivall being sensible that windes were not very advantagious for you: My selfe & wife heartily salute you, craving a constant interest in your prayers; service to [...] m[....]ey, [...] due remembrances to all friends as if particularly named; I rest, Sir,

your much ingaged friend

John Cotton

[...] Sir, forget not my [....]

Cotton Family Papers 7:9, Prince Library, Rare Books and Manuscripts, Boston Public Library. Addressed "These For the Reverend, his much Honoured Friend, Mr Thomas Walley, Pastour of the Church of Christ, at Barnstable." Some mutilation toward bottom of letter.

---

1. A Narragansett by birth, Allumps (a.k.a. Hyems or James) was also related to Uncas, the influential sachem of the Mohegan people. Partly through Uncas's influence, Allumps became sachem of Quinnebaug as early as 1644. Dennis A. Connole, *The Indians of the Nipmuck Country in Southern New England, 1630–1750* (Jefferson, N.C., 2001), 144-45.

2. Andrew Pittimee was one of the Massachusett Christian Indians removed to Deer Island. He was subsequently recruited to scout for the English forces. His wife and two sisters were among a group of noncombatants killed by some of Capt. Moseley's men on 7 August 1676; Pittimee was among those who discovered the bodies two days later. See Gookin, *Doings and Sufferings*, 501, and Jenny Hale Pulsipher, "Massacre at Hurtleberry Hill: Christian Indians and English Authority in Metacom's War," *The William and Mary Quarterly* 53 (1996): 459-86.

3. During the winter of 1675–76, Philip and his followers traveled to Schaghticoke on the Hudson River in hopes of engaging the aid of his traditional enemies, the Mohawks. Whether at the urging of New York's Gov. Edmund Andros or for their own reasons, the Mohawks instead attacked Philip's band, inflicting devastating casualties. Drake, *King Philip's War*, 122.

From Thomas Walley, 26 June 1676

REVEREND SIR AND MY DEARE FRIEND

yor Last I received for wch I give yo^{u} thanks as for all others. the engagement[1] was propounded to the people Lords day was Seaven[ight] it is was strongly opposed wth weak arguments by one of the Brethren and only one man appeared to joyne wth him my desire was to put it off as you have don but the Chiefe wth us were for doing it upon the day of humiliation and then it was don but I feare by to few for some I suppose absented them selves and others declined it—Good men in o^{r} daies doe more to hinder reformation than the pfane (I meane some good men) the reliques of a ridged seperatis dwell wth some w^{o} think to take some other time to see who else will engage we had news the last day of ye week from sea John Huckins[2] being a fishing and meeting wth a fishing Boat that the week before the United forces had Killed between 2 and 300 Indians[3] we suspend o^{r} faith till we heare from yo^{u} but sure of late god hath given us some tokens of favor for wch we have great Cause to be thankfull I am at present not well and indeed seldom have good health my hearty Love to yor selfe and Good m^{rs} Cotton I Commend you to o^{r} good God and rest

yor truly affectionat ffriend

Tho: Walley

June 26 1676

we hope before Long to heare news from good Capt Bradford

it was well my Letter was inanimate otherwise it might have bin set in ye stocks

Curwen Family Papers, American Antiquarian Society. Addressed "For ye Rev^{d} & much Respected friend Mr John Cotton [...] Plimth." Endorsed in a contemporary hand other than Cotton's "Walley June 26: 1676." One small hole in letter.

---

1. A reference to a proposed renewal of the church covenant, a practice supported by both Cotton and Walley. Cotton had better success convincing his Plymouth congregation; see the letter of 19 July 1676 to Thomas Walley, below.

2. John Huckins (d. 1678) of Barnstable was a son-in-law to Elder John Chipman. Savage, *Genealogical Dictionary*, 2:487.

3. Probably a reference to the surprise English attack at Peskeompscut (Turner's Falls) on 18 May, though the estimate of Native casualties is probably greatly inflated. The large number of remaining Natives counterattacked, and in the course of their retreat the English lost nearly one quarter of their men. Leach, *Flintlock and Tomahawk*, 201-4.

From William Bradford, 5 July 1676

REHOBOTH. 5 JULI 76.

HONOURED SIR

with all my due respects continually remembered unto you, and m' Cotton i know you looke for a few lines from me, but indeed they must be few att this time, the occurrences of affaires require it. i thanke god we are all in good health except Elcanah Chusman[1] whome we left not wel att rood iland, but i procurred a woman who promised me to have a great Care of hime. we have been upon the persute of Philipe, but canot yet find his lurking places, Capt Prent[ice] & forscore horse with wagones are here with us, upon the expedecion we have sent for more forces out of the bay, & also sent a post over to Major Talcot but nether he nor good m' fish that is wth them would pswade them to come over the river: they were so leaden wth plunder, the Mohegs i meane, the English leave willingly. the last friday above Coweset[2] they Slew & toke almost 2 [hundred] men women & children, & the[....] [s]uden: god gracious goeth wth them blessed be his Name, the last Munday in [...] [illeg.] they had another fight, for the gunes were heard to providence in all the afternone; the lord stile prosper them if be his blessed will we are at a stand, all the body of Indians are neere us on munday, when we were gone out, feched of many cattle from Ingrams necke, burned 3 or 4 more houses we persued them found where they kiled thiere Cattle, but they when to their quarters about Taunton in a hideous Swampe as we are informed, wee are upon Motion after them the lord direct us & blesse our indevors if it be his blessed will & increase my faith & patience, my helpe is only in hime. Continue to pli the Throne of grace for me that god may be my present helpe in time of need as he hath been, And concernig the disposing of my last wifes children[3] i cannot come to a conclusion here if that Mach be reall, if it be of god i will not hinder it; i heare that thiere is Suppli of Corne come in a Charatable worke in deed, from frinds of Coniticut[4] the lord be blessed in storing up theire harts & blesse them 7 fold for it. if i have any concernment in it as i have heard my advise to you is that a great part of it be laide saved up that according to need it may be disposed <*of to those that have need*>, for we know not what need their yet may be: Sir i must break of, you see bi my Scripling; i am in great hast and in deed, the many ocurences are so y^{t} if the lord did not support, i should sinke under them But i trust in the lord who is a god seen in the Mont, my portion for ever & who giveth wisdom to them that aske in faith. give me wisdom & understanding show to god through this great worke, and returne me in saufty to you, to his Name shall be the Everlasting praise. remember me to all frinds, especialy to Elder Chusman to m' [Secretari?]. I [...] where i [heare?] the Burgomasters have degraded, if so i would know, if my other Commander be [degraded?] also:

youre Ever Effeccinate frind

William Bradford

m' floid is her[ ]es in the Army

Curwen Family Papers, American Antiquarian Society. Addressed "for his honoured frind m' John Cotton in Plimouth." Endorsed "From Major Bradford July, 5: 1676:" Two small holes in the middle.

---

1. Elcanah Cushman (1651–1727), the fifth child of elder Thomas Cushman and Mary Allerton.
2. An area on the west shore of Greenwich Bay, now Warwick, Rhode Island.
3. For his second wife, Bradford married a widow whose name may have been Wiswall, nee Fitch. Robert S. Wakefield and Lee D. Van Antwerp, comps., *Mayflower Families in Progress: William Bradford of the Mayflower and his Descendants for Four Generations* (Plymouth, Mass., 1987), 3.
4. There is no mention of this boon in the Plymouth colony or Plymouth town records, but it is acknowledged in Plymouth Church records and is consistent with Connecticut's subsequent actions. When news of the war's devastation reached Ireland, sympathizers raised £1000 "for the reliefe of distressed persons" in the New England colonies. A grateful Plymouth church "set apart April, 26 [1677] to be kept as a day of thanksgiving for peace, health, supplyes of corne & provision by contribution from Connecticott & from Dublin in Ireland." More help was to come. Connecticut had been spared most of the fighting, and its General Court, citing "good reason moveing them thereunto," decided on 10 May 1677 to "remitt theire part of the Irish charaty to the distressed persons in the Massachusetts Colony and Plymouth Colony." Trumbull, *Public Records of the Colony of Connecticut*, 2:304, 483, 496-97; *CSM*, 22:153.

From George Shove, 6 July 1676

TAUNTON. JUL. 6. 76.

DEAR SR

[...] deprived of opportunity to write to you by o[r] deputies, it being [...] posed upon me to give the Govern[r] an account of the affairs [...] which I doubt not you are now better informed by Benj Church [...] throughout [rest of line illeg.] am desired to write to you in bahalfe of some[....] [...]rne, that they may have a share in the bountye of o[r] brethren [inland?] [...] Committed to your trust to dispose of to such as are distressed. Now I Confesse [...] that Mendicant spirit that is too visible at this time. yet I must [...] saye the Influence of the warr hath been such upon this place that [...] almost awonder they have subsisted as they have. God hath [...] been [...] in doing for us above o[r] thoughts. the dammage of o[r] crops the loss [...] were judged to amount to 1500 bushells of corn, besides o[r] Charges [...]ing of Souldiors (which for ought I percieve the people have been very [....] o[r] people [...] bought by M[r] Keiths Account above [...] bushells, 40 bushells they had Came from the westward to Rehoboth &

[....] hath been bought of R. Island. yet the povertye of many [....] to be set on worke for a supplye to preserve the [...] of many [...] of a supply in your hands were willing to [....] Cast themselves upon yor Chartye & have Come without any further [...] [n] couragm^{t} & [illeg.] to the number of 20 or more whose distresses are [su]ch that they have neither Corn nor bread nor any thing to buye with [...]but I thought that would be too unseemly an obstruction or Imposi[tion] upon one soe charitable: & I doubt not but you finde recievors Enough nearer home. Neverthelesse I have Encouraged a fewe to [...]e & present presuming you will afford them some reliefe & if [...] finde that you can minister to the reliefe of any more they may [...] theire turn afterward. There are noe lesse then five familees in my garrison that Cannot all make up 5 bushels of Corn of any sorts three [...] have none at all. by y^{t} you may judge of the straits of manye [...] in the place & for some there be that have any to spare that they [...] been able to make any rate for me this year (I speak it not [...] my selfe in for any share I have bought at Bridewater already^{e} [...]ing to buye more) for that a reliefe at home they Cannot have, [...] [m]ust feele it alreadye. if you Can therefore spare to ye reliefe [...] give me an account what you are able to due & I will accordingly [...] order for ye Conveyance hither. if you finde my post [in?] ffrancis [...] hands you will doe me a great kindnes to [get it?] brought [....] Care with bread. News we have not any. I present my Love & re[spects] with my wifes to yourselfe & Mi^{rs} Cotton & desiring we may [mu]tually pray each for other & joyntly for o^{r} Land, I Remaine, S^{r}

Your affectionate brother & serv^{t} in the Lord

George Shove

[...] Names of those y^{t} are sent to you [...] here subscribe [...] Phillips his son whose father is slain & Mother a helpless widdowe [...]ell Fisher whose familee is very poore [....] Thomas Caswell. William Brigs [...] John Gold. Sam. Hoskins. Joseph Graye. Andr Smith [...] you may be pleased to Enquier of them y^{t} Come of ye familees & of [...] Condition of the place

verte

S^{R}

Upon the tidings of Phillips designe to Assault [...] our neighbours are frustrated at present & I am [....] from you first. I intreat you to give [....] [three lines faint, illeg.]

Curwen Family Papers, American Antiquarian Society. Addressed "For ye Revd mr [...] Cotton Plimth." Left margin badly frayed and whole document stained.

The Death of King Philip by N. C. Wyeth, Harper's Magazine, ***June 1883***.

From Thomas Walley, 18 July 1676

REVEREND AND DEARE FFRIEND

yor Continued Love Labor and Care multiplies engagements upon me for thankfullness. I hope I am much affected with the greate goodness of god to this poor afflicted Cuntry and that god is pleased to give us any smiles from him selfe. we dayly long to heare from our Army oh that god would pardon theyr sins and ours and make us all humble that good may Come unto us a frame of heart sutable to gods Dealings with us would give assurance of Deliverance but we are (I feare) far from it which Causeth many sad thoughts of heart but god Can <*save him*> glorify him selfe in Saving an unworthy people. I am glad of the success Ben: Church hath[1] it is the good friut of the Coming in of Indians to us those that Come in are Conquered and help to Conquer others—I observe through out the Land where Indians are imploied there hath bin the greatest success if not the only success which is a humbling pvidence of god that we have soe much need of them and Cannot doe our work with out them it should teach us to be wise in our Carriage towards them. as for the Corne that is in yor hand to dispose of I desire m^{r} Hinkly and yo^{u} will [ ]er it when yo^{u} are together it is a great merc[ie], that god stirs up the hearts of any to help this poor Cuntry god that raiseth us friends I trust will be our friend to help us in all our difficulties the news from England (if true) is straing the Lord pity his people there I Doubt not but when yo^{u} have news from our Army yo^{u} will take the first opportunity to acquainte us with it I pray you present my hearty Love to good m^{rs} Cotton and when yo^{u} write to Major Bradford present my servis to him I Comitt yo^{u} to the Lord I pray Dayly for yo^{u} I beg yo^{r}s for me I am

yor truly Loving ffriend and Bro: in Christ

Tho: Walley

July 18th 1676

John Davis Papers, Massachusetts Historical Society. Addressed "To ye Revd. & much Estemed Friend mr John Cotton Plimoth." Prince's note[?]: "abt. ye Indns being more successful as to Philip then the English."

---

1. Benjamin Church (1639–1718) of Duxbury had moved to Sakonnet (modern-day Little Compton, Rhode Island) just before the war began. He participated in the early campaigns and in the Great Swamp Fight. In the summer of 1676 he was given command of a mixed force of English and Natives from Plymouth Colony. Even before he took the field, Church was instrumental in persuading the Sakonnet sachem Awashonks to surrender herself and her followers to the colony government. Church recruited some of the Sakonnets to join his force, which captured several bodies of enemy Indians in the Middleborough-Monponset Pond area only days before Walley's letter. Leach, *Flintlock and Tomahawk*, 208-10, 216-17. See also 13 January 1691.

From William Bradford, 18 July 1676

Deare Sir

After my harty salutations to you wth thanks for [....] remembrance by letters to me wch i am not so ab[le] [....] you nor so often as my desire is bec of the th[....] & troubles that attend me, but being now at Taunt[on] [...] good to informe you in breefe the lord dealings to[....] been in much Mercy ever since I came forth (blesse[d] [....] it was longer then I thought it would be before we [c]ould beat up Philips quarters, but we had such Cautions given us that he was of great strength & we to weake, but as soune as the Bay forces Came up we March to the place where the Negroe left hime,[1] & by the way we cute of Many Scouts of the Enimie & one especally well knowne to be a Notorious villan, caled Ruben a Stoute fellow & one of Philips Champions: & we tooke a prisoner that Carried us through a thicke Swampe directe to Philips residence, but he was fled wth all his compani but thire we cute of Some Stranglars, so we beate down the Necks towards the Sea, and upon Mataposet[2] we litt of a parsel of them & thire we tooke aboute 20 or 30 of them by the sea side we incampt all Night, & Marched up the Nex day into the woods, and by the way we toke a prizoner who undertooke to cary us to Philips residence, so he carried us into a hidous swampe where he had been that Morning but he was fled, we psued, Many Miles, killed by the way Many of the Enimy, Neere 15 or 16. Most old persons that was not so able to follow, aboute the after Noune they dispersed them selfs in a plane that we lost thire Maine Tracke the Nex day we persued them againe found thire Tracke, wch led us into a dismale Swame, wch we Entred and about 3 mile in the Swampe we met wth them aboute 3 hundred. but Philipe was parted from that company the day before as we were informed & So we left hime behind, as we judge, but we fell upon that Company, & kiled, & tooke as the Indians guive an account aboute 76 the rest dispersed Every way, thire was kiled as the Indians Informe us tow Cheefe one of Philip's Brother daughters one of g[re]at accoun[t] amon[g] them & the other a young Shachem of Naragan[set] Qenapins Brother.[3] truly Sir I must need say th[...] Lord as done Much for us, remembring us in o[ur] [....] Estate *<of>* his Mercy for Ever indureth [....] of his returning [....] humble peopell [....] the lord in Mercy, for his poore peopele [goe?] on if it be his blessed will, if tis he y^{t} fighteth for us he cane onli bring downe thire stoute harts & if the cheefe knot of them were broken & Philipe taken I hope in the lord Time it will be but we must weight u[pon] the lord who by his one way) & *<illeg.>* I am pswaded will doe more immediately by his owne power) the war would soone end: and we injoy our former peace: and for that end it is for the peopel of god to continue thiere prayers to hime in faithe, for I am pswaded & do verily beleive that by the Many prayers of his and thire sights & grones, he hears in heaven & will grant for our Mediator sake the returne of his gracious presence to his pore peoplell. we are very much ingaged to the Massachusetts for thire helpe att this time, we being so lowe, and in deed theire Commanders caries exceeding well, and are godly & well accomplised gentle the Indians are a great helpe to us & goe on very courageously the English allwayes backing of them. the lord also as undoubtedly you have heard prospers Coneticute forces, M^r^ fich was wth them i had not the hapiness to se though they lay wth in 6 miles of us one Night. they tooke 50 guns as was reported going [...] besids many killed & taken neere Warwicke.

Most of our forces came to Taunton on Saturday night Capt Brattle & my selfe came in on lord Noone we are now this day Marching out againe, the lord guide us in our way & his gracious presence be stile wth us, help us in your prayers for we have great need of them. Sir heere is divers of Taunton, as you had Information y^t^ have need of sup[ply] of Corne as Mr Shove will informe you, & i shall adde unto it that you Suppli thire needs wth Corne, and also that m^r^ Shove hime selfe have Some Supply for [he] hath been Much burdened in respect of the war w^th^ [...] that have lyen wholly upon [...] & hath psent need [....] you be very Carefull [....] come by lose [....] hier men to [....] tend it before [....] to any lose if pos[....] here breake of in [....] have no time to [....] [s]ecretary remember [...] to hime. Salu[...] Respects to m^r^ Cotton [....] to m^r^ Clarke [...] returned to you [....]

To my Cousen whittny, my love to my Sone John Bradf[ord][4] [....] & to all frinds, desiring stile to you all properity yor ever Assur[...]

Will Bradford

Curwen Family Papers, American Antiquarian Society. Addressed "for his Much Respected frind Mr John Cotton Deliver this In Plimoth." Endorsed "from Major Bradford Received, July 18: 1676:." Right and bottom margins badly frayed.

---

1. A reference to Jethro, slave of Hezekiah Willet of Swansea. On 30 June Willet was killed in a raid on that place and Jethro was captured, but he soon escaped and found, or was found by, Bradford's men. During his captivity he had learned of Philip's plans for an impending attack on Taunton. Bradford detached some soldiers to warn and help protect the town, so that when the attack came on 11 July, Philip' warriors found the town too well prepared and withdrew. Leach, *Flintlock and Tomahawk*, 210, 215; Emery, *History of Taunton*, 1:388.
2. Not the modern-day town on Buzzards Bay, but Mattapoisett Neck in Swansea.
3. I.e., Quinnapin's brother; see the following letter to Thomas Walley.
4. John Bradford (1653–1736), eldest son of William Bradford and his first wife, Alice Richards (c. 1644–1671). Wakefield and Van Antwerp, *Mayflower Families in Progress*, 2.

To Thomas Walley, 19 July 1676

With William Bradford's colonial forces operating southwesterly out of Taunton and Benjamin Church's mixed force of English and Native allies probing westward from the Buzzards Bay region, it seemed as though it would be only a matter of time until one of them caught up with Philip's dwindling band. In fact, after the chastening winter and spring months, English successes probably contributed to a religious revival in the colony, as Cotton describes here. Many of the missing or obliterated words of Bradford's preceding letter are supplied here by Cotton.

PLIMOUTH JULY, 19: 1676:

REVD & WORTHY SIR

Its not forgetfullnesse of you that I have not written to you since saturday,[1] but the church setting apart yesterday for solemne Humiliation & renewing our Covenant,[2] I could not spare the time from necessary preparation thereunto: through the rich grace of God the worke was solemnely & comfortably carried on, the Lord give us a heart to performe our vowes: I read a paper to the church in full communion containing an acknowledgment of sundry Violations of our covenant & a renewall of our engagement for Reformation, they unanimously manifested their consent by Standing, both brethren & sisters: then a paper was read to the children of the Covenant mentioning sundry of their evills & desires of Reformation, unto which they all in like manner manifested their consent. Sir, I intreat you by the first opportunity to send that History the secretary lent you,[3] my Bro: Mather desires earnestly to see it & I would shortly carry it to him.

By Indians I doubt not but you have heard of the successe of our Army, from Major Bradford at Taunton dated July, 17: I transcribe.

"Gods dealing to us have bin in much mercy ever since I came forth (Blessed be his name) it was longer then I thought it would be before wee could beat up Philips quarters, because wee had such cautions given us that he was of great strength, but as soone as the Bay forces came up wee marched to the place where the Negroe left him & by the way wee cut off many scouts of the Enemy & one well knowne to be a notorious Villaine, Reuben, a stout fellow & one of Philips champions, & wee took a prisoner that carried us through a thick swamp directly to Philips residence, but he was fled with all his company, there wee cut off some straglers; then wee beat downe the necks towards the sea, & upon Mattapoysett wee met with a parcell, & tooke about 20 or 30 of them; by the seaside wee encamped all night, & next day marched up into the woods & by the way tooke a prisoner who undertooke to carry us to Phillips residence, he brought us into a hideous swamp where Philip had beene that morning but he was fled, wee pursued many miles, killed by the way <*many*> of the Enemy, 15 or 16:

most old persons that were not soe able to follow, about the afternoone they dispersed themselves in a plaine that wee lost their maine track, the next day we pursued them & found their track which led us into a dismall swamp which wee entred & about 3 mile in the swamp wee met with them about 300, but Philip was parted from that company the day before as wee were informed, & soe wee left him behind as wee Judge, but wee fell upon that Company & killed & tooke about 76, the rest dispersed every way, the Indians informe us that one of Philips Brother's daughters was then killed, one of great account among them & a young sachem of [Narragansett] Quinnapins Brother. truly I must needs say the Lord hath [done? .... kindness?], remembring us in our low estate, for his mercy indures for ever, & I look upon these as smiles & tokens of his returning againe to us if wee can be a humble people & our sins prevent not, the Lord in mercy for his poore people goe on if it to be his blessed will, it is he that fighteth for us he can only bring downe their stout hearts, & if the cheife knot of them were broken & Philip taken the war would soone end & wee enjoy our former peace, I hope in the Lords time it will be, but wee must waite upon the Lord who will worke by his owne way & I am perswaded will doe more immediately by his owne power; & for the end it is for the people of God to continue their prayers to him in faith, for I am perswaded & doe verily believe that by the many prayers of his & their sighs & groanes he heares in heaven & will grant for our mediators sake the returne of his gratious prescence to his poore people: wee are very much ingaged to the Massachusets for their helpe at this time wee being soe low & indeed their commanders carry exceeding well & are godly & well accomplisht Gentlemen; the Indians are a great helpe to us & goe on very couragiously the English alwayes backing of them: Connecticutt forces tooke 50 guns, in their returne home, with the Enemy; most of our forces came to Taunton on saturday night, Capt Brattle & my selfe came in on Lords day noone:" Haecille.

connecticut men tooke 7 guns & killed & tooke many persons in their returne after the 190 of which wee heard before:

on Monday they marched forth, our forces on the East side of the River[4] & Massachusets on the west: About 37 captives are coming hither from Taunton, & that wicked Cuinam[5] who went among our friends with Major Bradford, but being accused by the murtherers at mr Clarks[6] to be an incourager & directour of Totoson in that villany, he was sent for by the Govr & is coming: I cannot but greatly wonder at the Lords pitty & compassion to his poore people manifested in his Late providentiall smiles, ever since this Godly Major went forth & from the time & that the churches have bin thoughtfull about renewing their Covenant, the Lord help us to walke worthy of his goodnesse: my selfe & Dearest present due respects to you, craving your prayers for us, I rest,

Sir, yours in strongest bonds

John Cotton

Ben: Church went on monday night with about 40 English & Indians to seeke for the Enemy about Dartmouth & 8 hogsheads of bread then went hence to Taunton for the Army; this weeke from Taunton 20 men came to me for corne, they carried away 62 Bush: their wants are very great:

our army found an English youth (belonging to the Bay Army) greivously mangled who had been sorely tortured & killed by a squaw on Thursday: 3 more belonging to the Bay taken by the Enemy, not a man of ours killed or wounded, a distinguishing mercy; one bullet touched an Indians belly & at the same grazed on the thigh of an English man but noe damage.

July: 20: The carts returned Last night, in going to Taunton, some of our Indians desiring to separate & to goe by Namasket river, they espied some of the enemy reaping John mortons[7] Rye; one of ours run to tell Ben: Church of it, who with most of his still accompanyed the bread, but sent back 3 English who with our Indians killed 1 man, & tooke 3 captives & carried them to Taunton They saw about 20 of the Enemy, & but 1 gun, will: Tuspaquin[8] was one

Bridgewater men, July, 19: went out, having seene tracks of Indians, & tooke a squaw & 4 children & killed a man Rob: Badcock, an Indian well knowne to us, & tooke 3 guns & severall kettles & other Indian trade; the English spoiled all their provision, they had 12 Bush: of Roots & had killed an English Beast: the squaw says they are about 80 of which 10 men, & they had a greate debate about coming into the English, but could not agree

Cotton Family Papers 7:10, Prince Library, Rare Books and Manuscripts, Boston Public Library. Addressed "These For the Reverend, his much Honoured Friend, Mr Thomas Walley, Pastour of the Church of christ at Barnstable."

---

1. Letter not found.
2. An account of this event, written by Cotton for the Plymouth church records, is printed in *CSM*, 22:148-53.
3. Probably Gov. William Bradford's manuscript history of Plymouth Colony. See the letter to Increase Mather, 24 November 1676, below.
4. Taunton River.
5. Cuinam (spelled Keweenam in Plymouth Colony records) was implicated in the assault on the Clark garrison house by Indians who had already been condemned for the killings (see the following note). He was found guilty and "immediately accordingly executed" by beheading. Shurtleff, *Records of Plymouth Colony* 5:205-6.
6. William Clark's garrison house, located on the Eel River three miles south of Plymouth center, was attacked about 9:00 a.m. on 12 March, a sabbath day. Clark was not at home, but his wife and two neighbors were killed in the raid. Totosan or Tatoson, "one of the most notorious of our enemies," was accused of complicity in the murders along with ten others. Three of these, plus one informant

who did not actually take part in the raid, were executed, but Tatoson was still at large two years later. Shurtleff, *Records of Plymouth Colony*, 5:204-6, 209.

7. John Morton (1650–1718), son of one of the original purchasers of Middleborough, moved from Plymouth to take up residence there in 1669. Although he lived in Middleborough for the rest of his life he never transferred his church membership from Plymouth. Weston, *History of the Town of Middleborough*, 49-50. See 30 January 1688 and 9 July 1688.

8. Wantowapuct, or William Tuspaquin, was the son of Tuspaquin, known to the English as "the Black Sachem," and Amie, Philip's sister. The senior Tuspaquin was sachem of the Indians at Assawompsett and one of Philip's chief followers. He was captured by Benjamin Church's rangers and put to death at Plymouth in September 1676, but Wantowapuct apparently escaped capture. This is the last reported sighting of him; although previous chroniclers have assumed that he was killed in the final stages of the war, there is no evidence that this was the case. Ebenezer W. Peirce, *Indian History, Biography and Genealogy* (North Abington, Mass., 1878), 211.

From William Bradford, 24 July 1676

TAUNTON, 24 JULY, 1676.

HONRD SIR:

I received yours, wherein I take it as an exceeding great kindness to be so open hearted to me. I take it as a friendly acceptation. I am heartily glad of the good successes of any that are instruments of God against your enemies. I am glad of the successes of my Cousin [Church][1] The Lord yet continue it, and give him more and more, and the grand enemy also: I shall in no wise emilate any man. The Lord give him and us, or any that have successes on the Enemy, to be humble, and give God the only praise for his power, goodness, mercy to his poor people, who hath been mightily seen in it, who hath been our only hope, and hath given the enemy into our hands by His especial grace. I now in a good chonscious Answer before God and man I have done my duty and neglected no opportunity to face upon the enemy, and I am verily persuaded that if we should [have] adventured without the Benj[2] Forces, we had either been worsted or also lost many men. He had placed himself in such an advantaged place; and I had rather be accounted a slow person or what man may please, Yea, even a coward, than to adventure the loss of any of my soldiers. To have been worsted by the enemy would have been a great discouragement to any. You know the state of thing when I came first out. I should have been glad if any would have tooke it in my roome, and I know there is many that would have managed it better than myself. But now we have many commanders that are very forward and think themselves the only men. We are going forth this day intending Philip's head-quarters. I shall not put myself out of Breath to get before Ben Church. I shall be caucious, still I cannot outgoe my nature. I will leave the issue with God, but truly, Sir, I see some frowns of God towards our Army, but we are many weake, and strike with strange blows, yea, some of our commanders, Captain Sparrow,[3] my lieutenant, but I hope the Lord will forgive them, are returning home with many others, so that we are left as an army. The Lord be our helpe, I am mightily engaged to friends, especially to those that have given me such a large gift. The Lord give it largely into their bosoms. I hope to see you the latter end of the week, if the Lord give me life. Mr. Arnol[4] and Mr. Shove presents theire respects to you, and myself to Mrs. Cotton and all friends.

I ever remaine, your asssured
For ever,

Will Bradford

Pray remember me to all my family, whom I hope are well. I have a great desire to see them.

Printed in the Providence Journal, *15 January 1876, with the following explanatory note: "The original letter of Major Bradford was found by the present possessor, Gen. C. C. Van Zandt, among the papers of his great uncle, Hersey Bradford, who was the youngest son of Gov. William Bradford, of this State, the latter being a direct descendant of the Plymouth Bradfords. Gov. Bradford presided as speaker in Rhode Island, more years than any other man, save his great grandson, our late Lieutenant-Governor. The style of writing of this old relic is exceedingly curious, so much so, that it is impossible for any ordinary reader to understand it. This led Hon. Albert G. Greene, late president of the Rhode Island Historical Society (who was the father of Mrs. Van Zandt) to endeavor to make a copy of it. He succeeded, and it is from his copy that the above was taken. . . . The letter is addressed, 'For his much Respected Friend, Mr. John Cotton. Deliver these In Plimoth.'" The bottom of the* Journal *article is signed "F. G. H." The whereabouts of the original, if it is still extant, are unknown; there is no copy at the Rhode Island Historical Society.*

---

1. "Carsh" in the *Providence Journal* transcription, but the intention is "Church," i.e., Benjamin Church, who was related to Bradford by his marriage to Alice Southworth.
2. Undoubtedly the word here was "Bay" in the original, i.e., the Massachusetts forces. These obvious errors in transcription, together with the apparent modernizations of capitalization and spelling (see Bradford's other letters to Cotton for comparison), underscore how unfortunate it is that the original letter is unavailable.
3. Jonathan Sparrow (d. 1707) had come to New England as a child with his parents in 1632. The family settled in Eastham on Cape Cod, where Jonathan married and became active in town affairs. He served numerous terms as deputy to the General Court and married a daughter of fellow townsman Gov. Thomas Prence. He was promoted from ensign to lieutenant in October 1675, but apparently had achieved the rank captain by the time he [Bradford] wrote this letter. Mary Walton Ferris, comp., *Dawes-Gates Ancestral Lines: A Memorial Volume Containing the American Ancestry of Mary Beman (Gates) Dawes* (private printing, 1931), 2:765-68.
4. Presumably Samuel Arnold (1622–1693), minister of Marshfield.
5. Not found.

6. Noah Newman was married to Joanna Flynt, daughter of Rev. Henry Flynt of Braintree. *Sibley's Harvard Graduates*, 3:390-91.

7. Probably the same Jethro mentioned in the letter of 18 July from William Bradford, above.

8. Thomas Shepard, minister of Charlestown. See letter from Daniel Gookin, 16 December 1677, below.

From Noah Newman, 3 August 1676

Tanton Aug: 3. 76

Reverend & Dear Sir

I have received severall of yo^{rs} since I saw you & It hath been no small trouble to me that no returne hath been made but it hath been a time of [ ]ligs hurryes wth us ever since, & oppertunities slipt by me unheard off till too late to improove, the last night I came to Tanton hoping there to have an oppertunity of writing to you, when I came thither I was intertained wth yor Last of July 31.[1] Now thought I I shall be chidden by my Good freind & lasht to my worke; but found you still very favourably & charitably treating me; Therein I accord with you in the thanks due to God for the bounty of his servants, the Complaints & indeed the murmurings of some amongst are for ye p^{r}sent unexpectedly silenced by such provedentiall supplies as hath been cast in upon us from our freinds about us. some undertooke to p^{r}dict a famine to us especially in this place when they saw ye p^{r}valentcy of ye enemy; I am not wthout feares such a scourge may follow, but If it doe God will bring it at a time & by such means as we think least off; The Lrd prepare us for his pleasure I desire we may have a discerning of his goings amongst us both in [way?] of Judgment & mercy; I was ye Last night welcomed when I came [here?] wth ye News of Capt: Chur: victories, the Lord sanctify such successe to him & us, I am very thoughtfull of Gods meaning in it. yet our deliverance seems to sticke in the birth, I fear we are not ready to receive w^{t} God is ready to bestow.—we here received from the westward 140 & odd bushell of Indian 19 bush: of pease—40 of wch went to Tanton; It hath been a great releife to us, the Lrd make us duely thankfull—The dole you speake of that is Coming to me I thankfully accept. & Judge it will Come the best to me from Boston If you Can procure it there & it would doubly accomodate me if it were ground we having no mill. It may be if my mother Flint[2] hear of it she will be helpfull therein. pray p^{r}sent my service to Majo^{r} Bradford excuse my not writing to him being in hast. I rejoyce in his p^{r}servation & safe arrivall, pray faile not to intreate him to remember my Brother flints earnest desire concerning Jethroe[3] (viz) that if he be to be sold he may have him, If he be set fre y^{t} he might be sent to him; I would intreate you If you goe quickly into the bay to certify my Brother Flint w^{t} ye major will doe about him in answer to his desire:—The Coneticot army is now here & undetermined wch way to returne whither directly to Rehoboth or to drive ye necks as they Goe—returne me thanks to Mr Mather, Th: Shep:[4] as you have oppertunity for their remembrance of me.—Thus wth due respects to yor s & Good Mrs Cotton returning you thanks for yor. Last kind intertainmt desiring the continuance of mutuall prayers I rest

yo^{r}s Assuredly in all Love

Noah Newman.—

Curwen Family Papers, American Antiquarian Society. Addressed "For the Rev^{d} his Dr Friend Mr John Cotton Plimth." Two small holes along right margin.

---

1. Not found.
2. Noah Newman was married to Joanna Flynt, daughter of Rev. Henry Flynt of Braintree. *Sibley's Harvard Graduates,* 3:390-91.
3. Probably the same Jethro mentioned in the letter of 18 July from William Bradford, above.
4. Thomas Shepard, minister of Charlestown. See letter from Daniel Gookin, 16 December 1677, below.

FOUR

Recovery and Imperial Politics 1676–1680

PHILIP, THE "GRAND ENEMY" OF WHOM William Bradford wrote in his 24 July letter, was finally hunted down by Benjamin Church's men and killed on 12 August 1676. In two of the most famous ironies associated with this tragic conflict, Philip died at Mount Hope, the scene of the war's opening skirmishes, and at the hand of a Native soldier in Church's mixed force.

Even as the final campaigns unfolded, New England's secular and religious leaders were writing histories of the conflict, largely with a London audience in mind. Ipswich minister William Hubbard got to the press first; his *The Present State of New-England* seemed to place much of the blame for the war on the Plymouth government, even as he apparently dismissed the colonists' missionary efforts and the capacity of the Natives to profit from them. Increase Mather, Cotton's step-brother, was working on his own version of the events, *A Relation of the Troubles Which Have Happened in New-England*, which stressed the English colonists' spiritual decay as the reason for God's wrath, and the obvious lesson that New England's trials constituted a call from God for revival.[1] Mather sent a copy of Hubbard's history to Cotton to inquire about certain facts that Mather obviously doubted. As the above correspondence reveals, Cotton was decidedly in Mather's camp with regard to historical causation, and after consulting with some of the major Plymouth actors in the war, he wrote to support his step-brother, expressing himself freely on the subject of Hubbard's "errors"—as usual, perhaps too freely. In the meantime, while the historians argued, fighting in northern New England continued (historians now consider King Philip's War to have been the southern phase of a much larger New England conflict) and Cotton remained a conduit for news from the front, all the while continuing to coordinate relief efforts for those communities hit hardest by the war.

In this role, Cotton rendered valuable service. Many of Plymouth's churches, which offered their communities everything from spiritual solace to material relief, had been seriously disrupted. The war affected churches directly, as their membership suffered casualties and communities scattered. But in addition, the churches experienced attrition among members of the clergy. Duxbury's minister died in 1675, and Cotton lost two of his closest colleagues and correspondents, Thomas Walley of Barnstable and Noah Newman of Rehoboth, a few years later. Attracting new ministers for Plymouth congregations was not easy, as the colony was poor and almost crushed with unaccustomed debts, which were the result of prosecuting the war. Finally, as the following letters show, Cotton's associates thought that an orthodox front was needed in the face of a new movement promoting the toleration of dissident churches. Some of the radicals apparently attributed the devastating Boston fire described by Increase Mather, as well as outbreaks of smallpox, to the colony government's stiff-necked opposition to heterodoxy.

As always, personal matters find expression in letters to and from friends and family. The Cottons fret about a son beginning his career at Harvard, asking Increase Mather to keep an eye on the boy. In return, Increase's son Cotton comes to stay with his Plymouth aunt and uncle, in part it seems to "take the waters" for his health. As if the devastation of war were not enough, Boston suffers a major fire and an outbreak of smallpox, both of which touch the Mathers very nearly. The loss of a child brings the Cottons letters of sympathy and consolation, and it becomes Cotton's turn to console when congregations are bereft of their ministers. Cotton also resumes his missionary work while making a valuable contribution to John Eliot's second edition of his Massachusett-language Bible. Finally, Cotton and his correspondents sense the stirrings of royal politics in New England, as Crown agents attempt to enforce greater conformity with England's navigation laws and bring the colonies into the imperial fold. While Massachusetts Bay in particular vigorously resisted cooperation, Plymouth's governors exhibited a more compliant disposition—a strategy that seemed to pay off, as the last letter of this section suggests.

---

1. For a fuller account of this literary contest, see Anne Kusener Nelsen, "King Philip's War and the Hubbard-Mather Rivalry," *The William and Mary Quarterly*, 3d ser., 27 (1970): 615-29.

To the Commissioners of the New England Confederation, 7 September 1676

As coordinated Native resistance in southern New England sputtered out, the English worked to rebuild their shattered communities and make sense of the devastation left by the war. One of the thorny problems to settle was the disposition of King Philip's wife and son, captured by the English shortly before the sachem was killed. This section opens with a memorandum to the Plymouth Colony government in which Cotton and a colleague summarize the Biblical case for executing the boy as a "child of death." The memorandum gives support to both sides of the issue, but it is not clear which course of action Cotton favors.

The Ques: being propounded to us by our Honoured Rulers, whether Philips Son be a child of death?[1] our Answer hereunto is, That wee doe acknowledge that Rule, Deu: 24: 16:[2] to be Morall & therefore perpetually binding, viz, that in a particular act of wickednesse <*which is*> thought capitall, the crime of the parent doth not <*charge?*> render his child <*with?*> as child of punishment by the civill magistrate yet <*wee*> upon <*our most*> serious consideration <*& mature deliberation,*> wee humbly conceive, that the children of notorioius Traitors, rebells & murtherers, espetially of such as have bin the principall leaders & actors in such horrid villanies & that agst a whole country, yea the whole Interest of God may be involved in the guilt of their parents, & may salva republica[3] be adjudged to death. as <*espetiall*> to us seems evident by the scripture Instances of <*the priority of*> Saul, Achan, Haman. the children of whom were cut off by the sword of Justice for the transgressions of their parents, although concerning some of these children <*at least,*> it be manifest, that they were not capable of being co-actors therein <*with them*>

Samuel Arnold
John Cotton

September 7: 1676:

John Davis Papers, Massachusetts Historical Society. This is apparently Cotton's original draft, written on both sides of a small strip of paper, much edited and entirely in his handwriting, including the two signatures.

---

1. On 1 August, Church's men surprised Philip's band along the Taunton River in Bridgewater. Philip escaped, but his wife and son of about nine years were captured. A debate ensued over whether the boy's life was forfeit according to Old Testament law. Douglas Edward Leach, *Flintlock and Tomahawk: New England in King Philip's War* (New York, 1958), 230-31.

2. Deut. 24:16: "The fathers shall not be put to death for the children, neither shall the children be put to death for the fathers: every man shall be put to death for his own sin."

3. Either "for the good of the republic" or "without transgression of the republic."

From Thomas Walley, 9 October 1676

Reverend and deare ffriend

I heard of yo[r] being at Boston otherwise I had not bin soe long with out a letter from yo[u] nor yo[u] with out one from me and now I have little to write but only to tell yo[u] that I soe like my new Condition that I desire to be thankfull to god for it[1] I think I Could not have had a better wife the pvidence of god hath ordered this business I trust in greate mercie to me. pray that god will every way turne it to my good and make us blessings one to another and to o[r] family and the place we live in I hope it is the answer of my prayer though my son and daughter are Come from Boston to visit us they have brought us scarsly any news what yo[u] have I pray you send me and when you write to Reverend M[r] Mather I desire yo[u] would in my name give him thanks for the book he sent me and wish the <*exhortion*> Exhortation he hath annexed to it were written upon All hearts in new England he seemes to me to be a man very faithfull to god to his people and to the whole Cuntry the Lord bless his Labors and make them Effectuall to many. if yo[r] selfe and M[r]s Cotten will give us a visit though I cannot make her mistris of my house yet I will entertaine you both as my loving ffriends I present my harty Love to you both and pray that god will bless you with all needfull blessings I am

yo[r] truly Loving ffriend and Brother in o[r] Lord

[Thom: Walley]

Octob: 9: 167[6]

Curwen Family Papers, American Antiquarian Society. Addressed "To The Rev my Much Honrd Friend m[r] J Cotton Plimth." Endorsed in a contemporary hand other than Cotton's "From M[r] Walley 8[br] 9: 1676." Torn along bottom margin.

---

1. Walley had married the year before; see his letter of 20 September 1675.

From James Keith,[1] 30 October 1676

If Cotton were equivocal in the matter of Philip's son, some of his fellow ministers were less so. James Keith, the author of this letter, favors more merciful scriptures as a guide.

Bridgwater Octob 30 1676

Reverend & deare Sir.

Being still denyed opportunity of personall converse much desired & longed for. I must intreat your acceptance of these few lines by which I do cordially salute you & yours in the Lord. elder Brett[2] wt my self did fully intend, about 3 weeks ago to h[ave] givin you a visit together wt our frends at Dukesburrough & Marshfeild but were prevented, my self being takin ill, about y^t^ time, having severall fits of the fever, & some other bodily infirmityes upon me, whereby I was hindered, one sabbath in the publick exercise of my ministry, god hath now restored competent health to my self & my family, & likewise to our people in generall, blessed be the name of the Lord. I long to heare what becomes of Philips wife & his sone, I know there is some difficulty in y^t^ ps 137. 8. 9.[3] though I think it may be considered, whether there be not some specialty, & somewhat extraordinary in it: y^t^ law Deut 24. 16.[4] compared w^t^ the commended example of Amasiah—2. Chron. 25. 4[5] doth sway much w^t^ me in the case under consideration, I hope god will direct those 2 whom it doth concern to a good issue let us joyn our prayers at the throne of grace, wt all our might, that the Lord would so dispose of all publicke motions & affairs y^t^ his Jerusalem in the wilderness, may be the habitation of justice & the mountain of holines, y^t^ so it may be also a quiet habitation, a tabernacle y^t^ shall not be takin down. deare Sir I know not when I shall see you, though I so earnestly desire it, I purpose, god willing, to go down to Boston the next week, I should be heartily glade to meet you there, if your o[cc]asions lead y^t^ way, however let us pray one for another, w^t^out ceasing. I pray Sir present my service to the much honoured governour & the rest of the honoured bench, if you have opportunity, present my true love & respects to Mr Arnold[6] when you see him, my respects to your elder & other freinds, I hope you will favour me w^t^ a line or 2. by the bearer if time permit, not else at present, my cordial respects presented to your self & Mistris Cotton, praying the lord to be wt you through all changes, & to preserve you in his everlasting arms, I rest

Your very affectionate friend to serve you in the lord

James Keith

John Davis Papers, Massachusetts Historical Society. Endorsed "[F]rom Mr Keith october, 30: 1676:"

1. Rev. James Keith (c. 1643–1719), first minister of the Bridgewater church, was educated at Aberdeen and emigrated to Boston in 1662. Introduced to the Bridgewater congregation by Increase Mather, he was ordained in 1664. Nahum Mitchell, *History of the Early Settlement of Bridgewater in Plymouth County, Massachusetts* (1840; reprint, Bowie, Md., 1997), 43-44, 207.
2. William Brett (d. 1681) emigrated to New England by 1645. Described as "a grave and godly man," he was made ruling elder of the Bridgewater church shortly after Keith's ordination. Mitchell, *History of the Early Settlement of Bridgewater*, 45, 120.
3. Ps. 137:8-9: "O daughter of Babylon, who art to be destroyed; happy shall he be, that rewardeth thee as thou hast served us. Happy shall he be, that taketh and dasheth thy little ones against the stones."
4. Deut. 24:16: "The fathers shall not be put to death for the children, neither shall the children be put to death for the fathers: every man shall be put to death for his own sin."
5. 2 Chron. 25:4: "But he slew not their children, but did as it is written in the law in the book of Moses, where the LORD commanded, saying, The fathers shall not die for the children, neither shall the children die for the fathers, but every man shall die for his own sin."
6. Samuel Arnold of Marshfield; see his letter of 3 April 1677, below.

To Increase Mather, 24 November 1676

Mather's *A Brief History of the Warr with the Indians in New England* was printed in Boston shortly after Philip's death in August. It apparently was not well received. This letter reveals that Mather had already commenced his longer, more reflective work, *A Relation of the Troubles Which Have Happened in New-England* (Boston, 1677) and was soliciting information for its composition. Cotton obliges but also asks for his step-brother's help regarding one of the Cottons' sons.

PLIMOUTH NOVEMBER, 24: 1676:

REVD & DEARE BROTHER

I have bin very sollicitous to answer your desires with reference to matter for your History, & did therefore goe on purpose to our Govr with your letter last wednesday who then promised me to devote the next day to waite upon you in looking for what he might have usefull in that respect, & speedily to write to you concerning Alexander[1] etc & also he hath in his keeping something drawne up by our secretary, which he intends to send you, or what is meet out of it; also I have desired & obtained of Major Bradford a Booke in Folio written by his father[2] which I shall send by the first opportunity by water, if I cannot send it by land: The Journall of Plimouth beginnings[3] I could send you, but I thinke it needs not for you told me some passages in it, whence I conclude you have that booke: Major Bradford hath another printed

Booke which he thinks would well contribute to you, its title is, Good newes from P: in N: E:[4] but he cannot finde it, he will doe his endeavour speedily to helpe me to it, if he doe you shall soone have it. I told the Govr, the matter required hast, I hope you will very suddenly heare from him:

My Dearest being sagacious, did immediately conjecture something was amisse, which necessitated discovery, the fruit of which was & is, much greife & bitternesse of heart; after some houres of secret lamentation God brought to her that, 1: Tim: 1: 15;[5] with some power, which sustaines her heart in hopes, that even that gratious word may finde accomplishment on this subject, Amen, Amen: once a weeke at least be intreated to send for him & converse with him, who knowes, but God may make you his father?[6]

I could intreat earnestly of you that you would write a Cordiall letter to my afflicted wife, to quiet her heart & strengthen her faith in God that one soe deare to her may be saved from sin & be accepted into mercy: our soules are troubled for him, wee heartily wish his hastening out of the schoole that he might be under your roofe & Eye, etc I durst not be soe bold as to urge for it this winter, but I hope in the spring it may be attaineable, & that your sophisters may be good Tutors to him, you being Præsident; I hope you are not supplyed with a Barrell of Beefe, & therefore doe put aboard for you out of my owne store a Barrell of choice Beefe, which may be with you the next faire winde; I now set noe price upon it, neither doe I desire you to pay me any mony for it; I hope my child may ere long bring me much more into your debt, & I shall make Conscience, God helping, to send to the full for your satisfaction in Butter & other necessaries for a family; & I hope about this time twelve-moneth to save you much trouble in laying in your winter-provisions, & halfe in halfe of the prizes you now pay upon those accounts:

My selfe & wife heartily salute you & yours, with our kinde love to our Cousens, I thanke you for my late Courteous Entertainement with you; wee beg your prayers for me & mine; A strong man dyed here this weeke, 2 or 3 men more are Judged neere death, the Lord awaken us before it be too late. I rest, Sir,

your Affectionate Brother,

John Cotton

The Major hath found the booke, Mr clark posts away this saturday sunset, I hope on monday a man will bring you the books.

Mather Papers 2:28, Prince Library, Rare Books and Manuscripts, Boston Public Library. Addressed "These For the Reverend, his very Deare Brother, Mr Increase Mather, Teacher of a church of christ at Boston, present." Endorsed "B^r^ J. C. Nov. 24. 1676."

1. Wamsutta (d. 1662), son and successor of sachem Massasoit of Pokanoket. In 1660, Wamsutta and his younger brother Metacomet adopted the English names Alexander and Philip, respectively, at least in dealings with the English. *Records of the Colony of New Plymouth in New England,* ed. Nathaniel Shurtleff and David Pulsifer, 12 vols. (Boston, 1855–61) (hereafter *PCR*), 3:192. The issue regarding Alexander will come up again; see the letter to Increase Mather of 19 March 1677, below.

2. A reference to Gov. William Bradford's manuscript history of the colony, known today as *Of Plimoth Plantation*. Portions of the history appeared in print as early as 1669, but it was not printed in its entirety until the middle of the nineteenth century.

3. [G. Mourt et al.], *A Relation or Journall of the beginnings and proceedings of the English Plantation setled at Plimoth in New England, by certaine English Adventurers both Merchants and others* (London, 1622).

4. Edward Winslow, *Good Newes from New England A true Relation of things very remarkable at the Plantation of Plimoth in New-England* (London, 1624).

5. 1 Tim. 1:15: "This is a faithful saying, and worthy of all acceptation, that Christ Jesus came into the world to save sinners; of whom I am chief."

6. The object of the Cottons' concern was their eldest son, John (1661–1706), then at Harvard, from which he graduated four and a half years later. After graduation he preached in Exeter, New Hampshire, for about six years, during which time he apparently took part in an armed protest against the unpopular Gov. Cranfield's policies. "By reason of the Indian War, &c." of 1690–91, he moved his family to his parents' house in Plymouth and occasionally preached at Scituate. In 1691 he went to Yarmouth to assist Rev. Thomas Thornton, and when Thornton moved to Boston two years later, Cotton succeeded him as pastor. In 1704 he "was taken off from public service by a paralytic disorder," and less than a year later, "being under weakness of body and mind," he resigned. He resembled his father in one particular way: his brother Josiah descibed him as "of a loving liberal nature, but of a quick spirit so that his haste too often veiled his prudence." John Langdon Sibley, *Biographical Sketches of Graduates of Harvard University, In Cambridge, Massachusetts* (Boston, 1873–) (hereafter *Sibley's Harvard Graduates*), 3:212-15.

From Increase Mather, 13 December 1676

Dear Brother

I re^{d} yo^{rs} of 4th Instant,[1] whereby I perceive yor readiness to sympathize wth me, in ye mercifull affliction, w^{h} ye only wise & faithfull God hath seen meet to inflict upon me & my poor Family. I see y^{t} Hee is a tender hearted & Loving Father, in y^{t} He doth correct me wth so much gentleness, notwthstanding all my unworthy walkings before him. He hath shewd peculiar Loving kindness to me (however vile & sinfull) in this dispensation. It is true y^{t} my House is burnt;[2] & winter provision is all consumed, for no one went into ye cellar. Nor did anyone goe into ye garrets to save w^{t} was there. So y^{t} Trunks & clothes there are perished. Also a box of my Fathers letters w^{h} was there disposed; & my Mothers Trunk of writings. I am also told since the fire, y^{t} you had a [blacke?] cloake therin & I think I am troubled for ye loss of y^{t}, y^{n} for any thing of my owne. Lumber in ye house, is mostly consumed, as bedsteads Tables &c yet ye Lord hath spared to us all [o^{r}] beds & bedding & most of ye chairs in ye Houses & most of o^{r} Linnen. Plate is mostly melted, & some of it, not yet found. But <*ye greate*> behold yet greater mercy. My Bookes & M.SS. are most of y^{m} safe. God (& I beleive his Angels) did so influence y^{t} I could not sleep y^{t} morning w^{n} ye fire broke forth; but I smelt ye fire, before ye cry was made in ye streets (about 2 hrs before day) & rose, & looked out of ye windows, & y^{n} some began to cry Fire. My first wishe was to gett ye children out of ye House, since ye wind brought ye flames directly up ye street where I lived. There I went into my study, & tooke ye M.SS wch were of greatest value & gave y^{m} to my Cotton & bad him goe away wth y^{m}. Then my Cousin John & I threw Bookes down ye stairs as fast as wee could, & people carried y^{m} away. I had (through ye wonderfull & tender mercy of ye most High,) Time to throw down almost all my Bookes, but before I could quite clear my study, some called to me, & told me I was a dead man if I stayd any longer. So I departed Letters are burnt so are my old notes p^{r}pd in E. & in Guernsey, & in Boston [page ends, most of letter missing]

Mather Family Papers, American Antiquarian Society. Addressed " These For ye Rev^{d} my dear Brother Mr John Cotton, preacher of ye gospell in Plymouth." Endorsed "From my Brother Mather December, 13: 1676: about the fire at Boston which was, November, 27:"

---

1. Not found.

2. Boston's second great fire (the first was in 1653) began on the morning of 27 November 1676. Samuel Sewall wrote an account of the blaze in his famous diary, noting especially that "the House of the Man of God, Mr. Mather, and God's House were burnt with fire. Yet God mingled mercy, and sent a considerable rain, which gave check in great measure to the (otherwise) masterless flames; lasted all the time of the fire, though fair before and after. Mr. Mather saved his Books and other Goods." Samuel Sewall, *The Diary of Samuel Sewall 1674–1729*, ed. M. Halsey Thomas, 2 vols. (New York, 1973), 1:28.

From Thomas Walley, [1676?]

REVEREND & DEAR S^{R}

My hearty salutations to y^{r} self^{e} & Mrs Cotton rejoycing to hear of the repairing of her then impayred health when I was last with you

S^{r} I was willing to present you with a few lines having so opportune a season as by one of y^{r} own houshold: I did & doe lament truly my providentiall obstacles y^{t} we could not convenire in uno tertio[1] on ye last Kindnes to Barnstable in whose service ye past day I have been engaged

the lord by solemn & tremendous strokes on sundry of our poor flock y^{t} dwell solitary in ye woods did interrupt my attendance of service at Barnstable for whom in subserviency to our comon lord and master i hope i have an engaged heart: the lords stroke indeed is solemn by smiting sundry in their intellectuals in a strange & unusual manner if my novice apprehension fayl me not; though not according to the form of a diabolical possession as some may apprehend: as also ye day following ye sole[mni]ty at Barnstable we had a town mee[tin]g injoyned into the concernments & agitations of wch conventicle, did apprehend my self not to be a little engaged as did afterwards appear concerning the canonical ground on which the meeting house to be errcted should stand[2] the [town?] being [du?] in their interest [apper?] [...] recommend y^{e} [...]

Curwen Family Papers, American Antiquarian Society. Endorsed "Mr Walley." Bottom margin torn and missing.

---

1. A grammatically suspect phrase, the sense of which is apparently "meet the three of us as one"; that is, Walley with Cotton and his wife.

2. The first meetinghouse in Barnstable, erected in 1646, was replaced in 1681 by a larger building on Coggin's Pond, near Thomas Hinckley's house. Donald G. Trayser, *Barnstable: Three Centuries of a Cape Cod Town* (1939; reprint, Yarmouthport, Mass., 1971), 12-13.

From Thomas Walley, 16 & 28 January 1677

Reverend and Deare Sir

I am sensible of the affliction that it hath pleased god to exercise you and yor deare wife with[1] it is a Day in which god is Correcting and trying his people in this wilderness the affliction you have at present is noe new or straing affliction but that which is Common to the children of god and may therefore be the more easily borne our children that are dead are not lost Jobs children were not doubted we shall goe to them our Children are more the lords then ours and therefore he may dispose of them they are his children but he sets them to us to nurce the nurce often Loves the Child but when the parents send for it it must goe home a greate part of or obedience lies in or submission to the will of god and being graciously quiet under his hand we have more to losse then what we have los[t] [...] all we have is at gods dispose god hath more to give then yet he hath given us and the way to have much is to be Content with his dealings our tryall not like the tryalls of others Job had all his children taken from him many have theyr children taken away when they are grown and when they are sinning as Aarons sons and Absolome Dear friends be of good Comfort this affliction as well as others shall be for good and Know that when god hath manifested his will we are to be quiet to hold our peace.

I am glad god hath graciously recovered preciouse mr Newman yor motion for a meeting of our Brethren in the ministry I could like but it is not now a season and I Dare not be soe bold as to desire them to meet at my house but were it theyr Desire they should be welcome I much feare that zeale for religion decays where god expects it most and we are secure though not delivered we are a silly dove without heart for god There have bin some that have stood in the Gap if some others be not found in their Roome Ruinating Judgments will Come if it please god to lift up the hearts of or Magistrates and ministers in the waies of God things will goe well with the cuntry Luther sayth nunuquam poriclitadur religio visi inter Reverendisemos[2] [I] may adde inter honorabiles[3] those that walked in the first waies of David were the best Kings it is good for us to look oft upon or patternes

if our Judges be as at the first gods Dealings will be towards us as at first. I highly prize or present magistracy and ministry yet am jealouse I hope with a Godly jealousy that religion is not our interest as in times past that we are become to indifferent in [the] matters of God or want Courage to doe duty. but god I trust will not leave us but recover life and spirit in his people I know the more men appeare for god the more god will honor them when we account it our best wisdom to please god then it will be well with us. Sir you Continue yor labor of Love to me and I Continue my thankfullness to you the Lord help us to serve him and one another in Love and I trust the good Lord will give you and yor wife his Consolations in the Day of yor affliction and Continue and bless yor remaining mercies my hearty Love is to yor selfe and good m^rs Cotton we in my family are in health pray for us I am

yor truly Loving ffriend

Tho: Walley

Jan: 16. 1676

When yo^u write to Tanton I pray yo^u remember my Love to my Son and Daughter Shove.[4]

This Day I received yo^rs Dated Jan: 16th.[5] the Lord Causeth many to mourne in our Daies my desire is that god will Cloth his mourners with garments of joy and gladness and though god withhold joy yet labor to be quiet he that gives us blessings may take them from us and Espetially such blessings as he never promised to keep with us it is mercie enough that he hath given us him selfe his son his spirit that he hath given us grace and many other abiding mercies our best mercies are our surest mercies—

a child is gon but god is not gon grace is not gon nor yet the child lost it is a more blessed thing to endure affliction then to Continue in prosperity god Loves us when he afflicts us and Loves to see us beare his hand patiently—yor child was not taken from yo^u by the hand of Barbarouse Indians but by the hand of a graciouse father and you had yor child as Long as god saw it good for yo^u to have it this is our greate privileg nothing we have is taken from us till it is best for us to be without it—but Deare Sir yor letter hath two requests in it and I am truly sorry that I Can answer yo^u in neither as for my notes upon Jam: 5. 11.[6] allthough I Could find them I should not send them it is true I did Run over the Epistle of James but only gave a briefe explication and some observations and short vses[7] except upon some verses I know what I have Don upon this text is soe little soe meane and soe unsutable to yor thoughts that I Dare not send it when I Drew toward the end I hastened and sayd little to any thing I pray yo^u in this excuse me.

As for the other yor Daughters Comming to us I should gladly answere yo^u in it but it is a work my Daughter Dare not undertake and shee hath much business and at present without a maide and allwaies in a Cumber with her children and providing for Indians that her husband imploies.

yor engaged ffriend

Tho: Walley

Jan: 28.

Yo^r Last letter[8] I received for wch I give yo^u thanks but have noe opportunity to adde any thing

I pray you[u] present my Love to yo[r] godly Elder I doubt not but god will support him and Comfort him

Cotton Family Papers 7:13, Prince Library, Rare Books and Manuscripts, Boston Public Library. Addressed "ffor the Reverend and my much honoured ffriend m[r] John Cotton Pastour of the Church of christ in Plimoth DD." Endorsed "From m[r] Walley January, 18: 1676:"

---

1. The Cottons' eighth child, Josiah (b. 10 September 1675), died 9 January 1677.
2. A confusing passage, but given the context it is probably "Religion never used to be in danger among clergymen."
3. "Or among respectable persons."
4. Hopestill Newman Shove, the wife of Taunton minister George Shove, died 7 March 1674. Rev. Shove married Hannah Bacon Walley, the widow of Rev. Thomas Walley's son Thomas, on 18 February 1675. *PCR*, 8:65; *Sibley's Harvard Graduates*, 1:554.
5. Not found.
6. James 5:11: "Behold, we count them happy which endure. Ye have heard of the patience of Job, and have seen the end of the Lord; that the Lord is very pitiful, and of tender mercy."
7. Verses.
8. Not found.

To Increase Mather, 19 January 1677

PLIMOUTH JANUARY, 19: 1676:

REVD & DEARE BROTHER

I wrote to you last weeke[1] by Mr Smith who was once schoolm[r] at your End, & informed you of Gods holy hand in bereaving us of our deare litle one; it pleased God last saturday to lay a sore Affliction also upon our Good Elder, bereaving him of his daughter,[2] who had bin married 11 moneths & was delivered of a living son & dyed within 6 houres after, she was godly & in full communion 4 or 5 yeares ever since she was 17 or 18 yeares old: the good man begs your prayers for him, who indeed never met with such an affliction before: I hope you have received mine by way of Hingham,[3] & desire to heare from you, you may write by M[r] John Alden[4] who intends to returne this way to his vessell early next weeke; I pray looke also for the paper of Quaeries I sent you about Nov: 27:[5] & please to returne some breife answer to them; & if you have opportunity, desire M[r] Thatcher[6] to give you the letters he had prepared to send me which came not, My lads went once & againe to his house but he was absent, & though that child by Gods soveraigne hand be removed, yet directions in such a case (lying by us) from persons of skill, may by Gods blessing save the lives of many others, & therefore I desire his lines, & pray present my due respects to him with desires for his prayers for us.

Capt Church is gone with some to Road Island, his Leiftenant, Jabez Howland[7] with others are to meete him at Rehoboth next Tuseday, they intend to be about an 100 English & Indians, the Lord succeed them: Your Jether is a pretty litle boy, about June next he is 7 yeares old; it will be some time before he doe you service, but I hope he will be soon capable of good Instruction, he can truly answer that Ques: who made him?[8]

My selfe & Dearest heartily salute you & yours[;] she is most desolate and pensive, & did yesternight fall afresh to mourning, as if she had nothing else to doe, I hope your lines may come for her direction & comfort, & for mine also; our Love to our Cousens, Let us have your earnest prayers for a sanctifyed fruite of this Affliction, I rest,

your Affectionate Brother,

John Cotton

Mather Papers 1:44, Prince Library, Rare Books and Manuscripts, Boston Public Library. Addressed "These For the Reverend, his Deare Brother, Mr Increase Mather, Teacher of a Church of Christ, at Boston. Per Capt: Paige." Endorsed "B^r^ J. C. Jan. 19. 1676/7." Some mutilation along center fold.

---

1. Letter not found.
2. A reference to Cushman's fifth child, Fear (b. 1653). Hubert Kinney Shaw, comp., *Families of the Pilgrims* (Boston, 1956), 36-37.
3. Not found.
4. Not the famous "Pilgrim" but his "marrinor" son (c. 1626–1702), who moved to Boston before 1669. Esther Littleford Woodworth-Barnes, comp., Alicia Crane Williams, ed., *Mayflower Families through Five Generations*, vol. 16 (Plymouth, Mass., 1999), 27, 30, 33.
5. Not found.
6. Probably Peter Thatcher. See the letter to Increase Mather of 15 & 16 July 1678, below.
7. Jabez Howland (b. c. 1644–1712), eighth child of *Mayflower* passengers John Howland and Elizabeth Tilley. Shaw, *Families of the Pilgrims*, 108.
8. Jether/Jethro/Jebber, who appears infrequently in the letters that follow, was a Native lad, perhaps one of the many captive Native children who were given to English settlers after the war. Cotton was obviously preparing the boy for service in Mather's house.

Increase Mather to Joanna Rosseter Cotton, 22 January 1677

Dear sister

I Cannot chuse but heartily sympathize wth you in this bitter day wch is come upon you, in respect of ye death of y^{t} Dear little one whom it hath pleased ye only wise & faithfull God to take from you I trust, he will give you grace to carry it wth Patience & moderation in respect of grief as becomg a christian otherwise you will despond [illeg.], & wrong yor selfe yor Family, yor body, yor soul, & it may be provoke ye Lord to bring a [two words illeg.] upon ye Fa[ ] The main thing y^{t} should quiet yor spirit, is y^{t} ye blessed will of god is done, [Isa?] 39. 8.[1] And truly y^{ts} heaven upon earth, when we can bring o^{r} wills into a perfect subjection to ye good pleasure of ye Almighty, who doth all things well. Yet there are other Considerations, wch should Cause you to let yor moderation (in respect of natural forms under such a bereavment) be known to all men. e.g. The Lord might have dealt more bitterly wth you He hath taken away one Hee might have taken all, as from Job; & from many in N. E. since ye late troubles on ye land. yor child dyed under the visitaton of ye lords more imediate & mercifull hand, w^{ras} many precious ones, y^{ir} children have fallen into ye hands of men cruel & skillful to destroy.[2] you have moreover reason to conclude, y^{t} ye child is blessed, since christ himselfe hath sayd, y^{t} of such is ye kingdom of Heaven. Had hee lived, you would have bin caring for him but christ hath provided Infinitely better for him y^{n} ever you could have done. would you not have rejoyced to have seen y^{t} child outstrip you in grace? And why should you not rejoyce y^{t} hee is got before you to glory? yea rejoice in y^{t} God hath made you an instrument to replenish heaven, & bring forth an heir for ye kingdome of God. Hath christ taken a son out of your boosom, and layd it in his owne boosom? should that aggrieve you? Remember also ye Resurrection. when there was a good woman y^{t} had lost her son, & one y^{t} was grown up to mans estate, (& y^{n} its harder to part wth y^{m}) I can only say; ye Lord Jesus was compassionate towards her and bid her not to weep, for her son should rise again. Luk. 7. 13.[3] so I say to you, though yor son shall not rise again so soone as hers did, yet it will be ere long, & his Resurrect^{n} farr more glorious then that was. Besides, if you humbly address yourselfe to God in Jesus Christ, who knows how much of Himselfe Hee may communicate to you now Hee hath taken a creature comfort from you? There is a memorable Passage [entered?] in y^{t} Booke called ye fulfilling of scriptures[4] (p. 491.) of a good man who w^{n} his son was dead, Hee went alone to pour out his soul unto god, & afterwards was cheerful (as Hannah you know was no more sad after she had prayed) some wondred at him for it but Hee told y^{m}, y^{t} if he might but enjoy such another manifestation of God, as in y^{t} private prayr, Hee had met wth Hee could be Content to bury a son every day. Now ye Lord give you ye good of this affliction, & be yor everlasting comforter. To him I commend you & rest

yor Loving Brother

Increase Mather

22 of 11 ^m.^ 1676.

Cotton Family Papers 7:14, Prince Library, Rare Books and Manuscripts, Boston Public Library. Addressed "These For the Rev^d^ my dear Brother m^r^ John Cotton, Pastor of ye Church in Plymouth." Endorsed "F[rom m]y Brother M[ather] January, 22: 1676:."

---

1. Isa. 39:8: "Then said Hezekiah to Isaiah, Good is the word of the LORD which thou hast spoken. He said moreover, For there shall be peace and truth in my days."
2. The "consolations" of this last passage, in particular, echo themes found in the above letters of Thomas Walley.
3. Luke 7:13: "And when the Lord saw her, he had compassion on her, and said unto her, Weep not."
4. A reference to *Fulfilling of the Scripture: Or, An essay, shewing the exact accomplishment of the word of God in his works performed & to be performed* (1669), by Robert Fleming (1630–1694), Scottish divine.

From James Keith, 29 January 1677

Bridgwater Jan: 29 —76.

Reverend Sir & deare brother in the lord

I received yours of the 15. of this instant,[1] which brought me the sorrowfull tidings of your bereavement: though I have ben hitherto exempted from trials of that nature, yet I hope I have in some measure learned to sympathise wth brethren under such affliction. deare Sir faint not under these rebukes of god, it is the lord that hath done it, as in a way of soveraignty & holines so also in faithfulnes in loving kindnes & mercy. you may be apt under such a severe stroake to say as sometimes Jacob all these things are against me,[2] but deare Sir give me leave to minde you of those sweet & solemn truths by you described. on ps. 119 it is good for me that I have bein afflicted:[3] it is a great comfort to godly parents concerning theire children, that however they are bereaved, yet still they have them in the promise, it is no insignificant thing that our Lord Jesus hath said suffer little children to come to me, he is the great & good shepherd, who hath a favour for poor children & doth gather the lambs unto his bosom—deare Sir be of good comfort. it is not long before god will wipe away all teares from our eyes, the time is short & therefore it remaineth that they that weep be as though they wept not. our people here have ben visited this winter wth the jaundice & some wth the fever, but still the lord doth correct us in measure blessed be the lord who hath taken us into his own hand & hath not suffered us to fall into the hands of men deare Sir pray for us that all the visitations of god may be in mercy to us. I cannot now enlarge being in more then ordinary haste. my true love & respects presented to your self & Mistris Cotton, praying the Lord to be a comforter to you both. I rest

Your assured & affectionate friend to serve you in the lord

James Keith

Cotton Family Papers 7:15, Prince Library, Rare Books and Manuscripts, Boston Public Library. Addressed "To The reverend his very affectionate friend Mr John Cotton pastor of the church of christ in Plimouth." Endorsed "From mr Keith January, 29: 1676:."

---

1. Not found.
2. A reference to Gen. 42:36: "And Jacob their father said unto them, Me have ye bereaved of my children: Joseph is not, and Simeon is not, and ye will take Benjamin away: all these things are against me."
3. Ps. 119:71: "It is good for me that I have been afflicted; that I might learn thy statutes."

To Increase Mather, 19 & 20 March 1677

In this letter Cotton betrays some classic male helplessness in the temporary absence of his wife as he frets over Jether, the servant he is grooming for Mather. Amid this laundry-list of local news and historical debate about the recent war, the fate of Philip's son is barely apparent. The boy was not killed but may have suffered as bad a fate.

Plimouth march, 19: 1676:/77:

Revd & Deare Brother

I could have desired to have kept your booke[1] a few days longer, whereby it might have bin filled with marginall notes of Errata's, our Govr & magistrat[es] had some cursory perusall of the booke, the mistakes are Judged to be many more then the truths in it: our Govr & mag: doe affirme that Alexander was got home before he dyed.[2] I am in a great straite abo[ut] your boy, the Treasurer hath obtained a sutable boy for your service, & the litle one is re[turn]ed to Ben: Church againe: My wife being gone westward I cannot cloath this Jether as she would: I am in doubt whether it be best to send him now or not. I incline to send him, partly because he is now fit to cut your wood, & goe to mill, which service you now want, & Thesaur:[3] goes now to Boston, who I suppose will see you, you will not faile to give him great thanks & acknowledgments for his respect to you in it: I decline sending him, because I have not yet an order from you soe to doe, What I shall resolve in the morning I know not; if he come I suppose the Boatman will expect 2 or 3 shill: for his passage, though they tell me not soe, nor will they take ought of me, nor aske ought of you, but I thinke such a summe must be profered, & if it be taken I am glad it costs you noe more: I received him meanely clad, & cannot put on him more then these black rags for want of my wife: I send my sister a few Egges; by the last boat I sent her some Cabbages & Cranberries, I feare for want of a written order, my John[4] might take them home, but know not how it is.

Hearty remembrance to you & sister, the Lord give her a good time. pray for your Lov: Br:

J: C:

march, 20:

Dear Brother, upon after thoughts, it seems to me best at present not to send your boy, because you desired me to keep him till you had occasion to send for him, therefore by these I only informe you that the [. . .] shall be readily sent you, when you please to send for him:

I now send your imperfect History:

Good Mr newman preaches our Election sermon, it is not his turne, but because he is newly come out of the fire,[5] ergo he was chosen.

Philips boy goes now to be sold:[6]

If you have more Almanacks then one etc. if not I desire it not.

Major [Br]adford confidently assures me, that in the Narrative de Alexandro [there a]re many mistakes, & fearing lest you should through misinformation print some mistakes on that subject, from his mouth I thus write:

Reports being here that Alex: was plotting or privy to plots against [the E]nglish, Authority sent to him to come downe, he came not, whereupon [Ma]jor winslow was sent to fetch him, Major Bradford & some others went with him, at munponset river[7] (a place not many miles hence) they found Alex: with about 8 men & sundry squaws he was there about getting Canooes: he & his men were at Breakfast under their shelter, their guns being without, they saw the English coming, but continued eating, & M: Winsl: telling their businesse, Alex: freely & readily without the least haesitancy consented to goe, giving this reason why he came not to the court before, viz., because he waited for Capt Willets returne from the Dutch[8] being desirous to speake with him first: they brought him to Mr Colliers[9] that day, & Govr Prince then living remote at Eastham, those few Magistrates who were at hand issued the matter peaceably, & immediately dismissed Alex: to returne home, which he did part of the way, but in 2 or 3 dayes after, he returned & went to Major winslows house,[10] intending thence to travell into the Bay & soe home, but at the Majors he was taken very sick, & was by water conveyed to Mr. Bradfords, & thence carried upon the shoulders of his men to Tetehqut river, & thence in canooes home, & about 2 or 3 dayes after, dyed:[11] After this there was great Solemnity in the congratulating Philips coming to the crowne, by the flocking of Multitudes of Indians from all parts, sachems & others, with great feasting & rejoycing at Mount Hope; this caused the Govr to call a meeting on purpose, Aug: 6. to do as the memoriall saith.[12]

Mather Papers 1:52, Prince Library, Rare Books and Manuscripts, Boston Public Library. Addressed "These For the Reverend, his Deare Brother, Mr Increase Mather, Teacher of a Church of Christ at Boston." Letter somewhat mutilated at edges.

---

1. Actually, Mather's copy of William Hubbard's *The Present State of New-England, Being a Narrative of the Troubles with the Indians of New England* (Boston, 1677). Mather apparently sent his copy to Cotton for comment as he was working on his own *A Relation of the Troubles Which Have Happened in New-England* (see letter to Increase Mather, 24 November 1676, n. 1). Hubbard's book first appeared sometime after 16 February 1677, the date of Hubbard's dedicatory letter printed with the volume. A later printing contained an endorsement of the book, dated 29 March 1677, by Boston magistrates Simon Bradstreet, Daniel Denison and Joseph Dudley. Mather and Hubbard (1621–1704), the minister of Ipswich, were rivals in the print-war of words to interpret the significance of King Philip's War. See Nelsen, "King Philip's War and the Hubbard-Mather Rivalry," 615-29.
2. See the fuller account to which this refers, below in this letter.
3. I.e., "Treasurer"?
4. John Cotton, still at Cambridge.
5. Perhaps a reference to Newman's exposed position in Taunton during the war.
6. This is the last known record indicating the fate of Philip's son.
7. Monponset Pond, in present-day Halifax, Massachusetts.
8. Thomas Willet (c. 1607–1674) was captain of the Plymouth company of militia in 1648, a frequent assistant after 1651, and a commissioner of the United Colonies for Plymouth. His connections with the Dutch at Manhattan apparently spanned some years, for in 1654 he was chosen to advise English colonial forces who were preparing to support an attack on the Dutch colony by Cromwell's government. The assault never materialized, and after the war Willet carried on with business there. When an English squadron seized Manhattan in 1664 and renamed it New York, Willet became the first English governor of the city. He later returned to Plymouth, residing in Seekonk, where he was buried on 3 August 1674. Eugene Aubrey Stratton, *Plymouth Colony: Its History & People 1620–1691* (Salt Lake City, Ut., 1986), 371-72.
9. William Collier (d. c. 1671), one of the original Merchant Adventurers of Plymouth Colony and one of the few to emigrate to New England, in 1633. He lived in Duxbury and served the colony in several high-ranking offices. He was an assistant at the time of this incident. Stratton, *Plymouth Colony*, 268.
10. In Marshfield, Massachusetts.
11. Rev. Hubbard's account, taken from an unknown source or sources, differs significantly from Winslow's relation. See Hubbard, *Present State of New-England,* 1:49-51.
12. Morton's *New England's Memorial* outlines the main points of the General Court held on 6 August 1662, where Philip appeared at the insistence of the worried English. The record says that there he reaffirmed his friendship with the Plymouth government and acknowledged himself to be a subject of King Charles II. Nathaniel Morton, *New England's Memorial* (1854, reprint, Bowie, Md., 1997), 187; see also *PCR,* 4:26.

From James Oliver, 27 March 1677

Boston 27 march 1677

m^{r} Cotton sir after kind respects promised to you and mis Cotton yesterday arived m^{r} Jno Philips of Charls toune[1] from Scotland 5 weeks pasage, brings news of m^{r} danfort son the scoler death of the small pox in London[2] m^{r} stoughton and m^{r} Buckly[3] I did see both ther letters to frinds for m^{r} stoughton to m^{r} tayler m^{r} burke to m^{r} Edward who find hard worke in england worse then tha expected both [of] them have been il of a Cold but mendi[ng] [...] but in that meal of dis[ ] [....] I beleve wil be seen m^{r} Jno Lof[ ] [....] 29: instant [....] m^{r} n[ ]land [....] hath a [....] stay no Lete[ ] [....] since I began [....] James [....] be lost by [....] point our [....] thus the [....] peopl [....]

Cotton Family Papers 7:18, Prince Library, Rare Books and Manuscripts, Boston Public Library. Addressed [To the] rev^{d} John Cotton att plimoth." Endorsed "[....] March, 27: 1677:." The handwriting is that of James Oliver. Bottom half of letter badly mutilated.

---

1. John Philips (c. 1633–1726) was a master mariner of Charlestown who parlayed his success at sea into prominence on land. He was made a freeman in 1677; became first a lieutenant, then captain, of the Artillery Company; was a representative to the colony legislature from 1683 to 1686; and served on the Committee of Safety in the revolt against the Andros government. James Savage, *A Genealogical Dictionary of the First Settlers of New England*, 4 vols. (1860–62; facsimile reprint, Baltimore, Md., 1990), 3:412-13.

2. Samuel Danforth (1652–1676), the eldest son of Deputy Governor Thomas Danforth, was a classmate of Samuel Sewall's at Harvard. Amid some controversy, he was elected Resident Fellow, or Tutor, of the college in 1675. He contracted smallpox on a trip to London and died there on 22 December 1676. *Sibley's Harvard Graduates*, 2:369-70.

3. Peter Bulkley (1643–1688), deputy from Concord, and William Stoughton (1631–1701), Norfolk County justice, left for England in October 1676 on a mission to answer a complaint that Massachusetts had usurped the proprietary rights of John Mason and Sir Ferdinando Gorges to lands between the Merrimack and Naumkeag Rivers. There were other complaints as well, emanating from the "odious and rapacious" Edward Randolph and from Quakers charging continued persecution in New England. In the event the agents could do little, as the Court was preoccupied with the Popish Plot and other political matters. Bulkley and Stoughton returned to Boston in late 1679, after three years of fruitless lobbying. *Sibley's Harvard Graduates*, 1:194-96; 2:68-69.

From Thomas Hinckley, 2 April 1677

REVRD SIR

These are only to give cover to the enclosd desiring your care to convey the 13$^{£}$ therewth to m^{r} Newman p some fitt opportunity being p^{te} of our Towns Contribution last fast wch wth about 14 or 15$^{£}$ more in clothing & cattell is wth us to send p convenient opertunity for y^{e} releif of those most-sufferrers [by?] y^{e} cause of y^{e} heathen espetially at Rehoboth though also if any in like strayts by suffering from the enimy at Swaunsey who abode by theire stations as y^{e} other did at Rehoboth to be considered in the distribution thereof, by m^{r} newman & m^{r} Browne: who have y^{t} trust committed to y^{m}: m^{r} Brown being assigned 3$^{£}$ of y^{e} money for himself & m^{r} Newman 4$^{£}$ thereof for himself I wish it had beene more for him & more in y^{e} whole for y^{e} rest from us who have beene so signally p^{r}tected from those suffrings wch our betters have felt [y^{e}] smart of but it is as it is—not elc y^{e} messenger staying but wth thanks for your care & traiell about ye pease I committ you & yours to ye keep^{r} of his Israel desiring your prayers for him who rests Sir

y^{rs} obliged in effect as in affection.

T. Hinckley

Barnestabl 2^{d} Aprill. 77.

Miscellaneous Collections, Massachusetts Historical Society. Addressed "These ffor the Revrd and his much esteemed good ffrind mr John Cotton Plimoth dd." Endorsed "From mr Hinckley April, 2: 1677:" In a different hand: "Contributn for sufferers by Indians at Rehoboth [illeg.] abt: 28£."

From Samuel Arnold,[1] 4 April 1677

Reverend Sir My hearty salutations being presented to you I p^{r}ceiving by skipper Watson your desire to be informed of the event of Mr Clerkes answer to the widdow.[2] we found it better than we expected. my wife going with me to her I after declaring the desperatenes of the case; after a little pause she gathered up her spirits & declared that she was better satisfyed and hoped she should so remaine, then she could have been had she not understood that he was an obliged man to neither, I was glad things being as they were that she was not sent to [illeg.] to him & hath borne up since with considerable cheerfulnes. Sir I have sold your booke & sent your mony, I bles god I have found some reviving since I saw you for which I pray you be thankfull to god in my behalfe although I dare not yet resolve upon my lecture If I do I shall indeavor your being acquainted with it. our general Gov:[3] I hope is mending, enjoying much more [ease?] then formerly threw gods mercy I pray you present my love to Mr Clarke & gratefull remembrance of his last kindnes my due respects to your elder & m^rs^ Cotton when you see them which god mercifully grant in his due time, craving your dayly prayers to the Lord for me I rest

Sir Your cordiall friend & brother in the Lord

S. A.

Marshfeild Aprill 4th . 77

Cotton Family Papers 7:19, Prince Library, Rare Books and Manuscripts, Boston Public Library. Addressed "To the Reverend m^r^ John Cotton Pastor of the Church of Christ in Plymouth." Endorsed "From Mr Arnold April, 4: 1677:."

---

1. Samuel Arnold (1622–1693) lived in Sandwich in the 1640s, then in Yarmouth as early as 1653; there he was elected deputy in 1654 and 1656. He was ordained Marshfield's third minister in 1658 and served in that capacity until his death. Charles F. Swift, *History of Old Yarmouth* (Yarmouth Port, Mass., 1884), 67.
2. The editors were unable to learn more about the situation to which Arnold here refers, but it sounds intriguing.
3. Gov. Winslow; see below.

From James Oliver, 10 April 1677

10: Aprill 1677

Mr Coten yours Cam to hand yesterday[1] I am sory for yours govornors pains and ilnes and am glad of your several Charytys to rehobo in habitants for your other Enquiry m^r^. glover of sprinfeild[2] is Chosen to preach the artilery sermon. Deputys m^r^ stoder and major sevens[3] select men added to the former deacon Elyot and deacon alin[4] Constabls m^r^ John safin m^r^ [illeg.] Howord[5] m^r^ [illeg.] son in law [illeg.] dead John par[ ]ter Ephraim savage[6] young [illeg.] leiftant wils[?], for news from the eastward[7] our 2 vesels went awy this day fraught to releive Koosicke garison Last night Cam [news?] y^t^ 2 kild at wels[8] on taken alive 2 houses burnt at York and from blak Point[9] 5 men and on woman lately kild ther the last 5 day the remainder of winter harbor burnt[10] we ar in great fear of the next news from new York 9 kild and lost sertainly 2 escaped I spake with on of them m^r^ wilard is Quit gone from us to the south Church[11] to our greife but we must say the Lords wil be done your last lins about your dearest is a mistake as I supos Jesus Christ is the most and altogether Lovely and so is dearest after to morow I may send you the nomynatyn of Majestrat, I pray you present my servis to your governor, and my generall and to your treasuror, hope is learning to speake and her catycist y[r] L[o] frind and servt

James Holiver

Cotton Family Papers 7:20, Prince Library, Rare Books and Manuscripts, Boston Public Library. Addressed "To the Reverent m[r] John Cotton att Plimoth present."

---

1. Not found.
2. Peletiah Glover (1637–1692) attended Harvard College from 1651 to 1654 but did not graduate. He took up the ministry of Springfield, which Samuel Hooker had declined, in 1661. *Sibley's Harvard Graduates,* 1:558-59.
3. A meeting of the Boston freemen on 5 March 1677 chose Anthony Stoddard and Maj. Thomas Savage as deputies to the General Court. Stoddard (d. 1687) was a merchant and linen draper. Formerly a selectman, he was a member of the Artillery Company and, according to Sewall, "the ancientest shop-keeper in Town." *Diary of Samuel Sewall,* 1:134. Thomas Savage (1607–1682), who married a daughter of Anne Hutchinson, was a tailor and shopkeeper and a founder of the Old South Church. He had also been a selectman, held the rank of captain in the Artillery Company, and during King Philip's War had been a major of Massachusetts forces. Thwing Index of Boston Inhabitants, Massachusetts Historical Society, Boston.
4. Seven selectmen for Boston were chosen on 12 March 1677, including Henry Allen and Jacob Eliot. Allen (1627–1696), a housewright, held his office for ten years. Eliot (1633–1693) was a deacon in the Old South Church; upon his death, fellow member Samuel Sewall remarked, "We shall hardly get another such a sweet Singer as we have lost. He was one of the most Serviceable Men in Boston." *Diary of Samuel Sewall,* 1:312-13; Thwing Index.
5. Two curious choices for the office of constable. John Saffin (c. 1634–1710), originally from Plymouth Colony, was a merchant of Boston and later Speaker of the House of Deputies. Anthony Howard or Haywood (c. 1639–1689) was also a well-off merchant. Thwing Index. For Saffin, see also 19 October 1696.
6. Ephraim Savage (1645–1731) served in King Philip's War as a sergeant, became an ensign later in 1677, and eventually rose to the rank of captain. He was also town clerk of Boston. *Sibley's Harvard Graduates*, 2:128-30.
7. Although the war in southern New England was entering its last months, fighting had spread to the Maine settlements; this continued for nearly a year after Philip was slain. In October 1676, Samuel Sewall wrote to a cousin that though "the late massacre" had ended for most of New England, "yet there is some trouble and bloodshed still in the more remote Eastern parts." *Diary of Samuel Sewall*, 1:26.
8. Wells is on the coast of southern Maine, between the Piscataqua and Saco Rivers.
9. Black Point is in modern-day Scarborough, Maine.
10. Winter Harbor is part of today's Arcadia National Park, in Maine.
11. Rev. Samuel Willard (1640–1707) was pastor of the church in Groton, Massachusetts, when a series of Native assaults in March 1676 destroyed much of the town, leading to its evacuation by the English. Groton was resettled in 1678, but by that time Willard had accepted a call from Boston's South Church, where he was installed in March 1678. *Sibley's Harvard Graduates*, 2:13-14.

To Increase Mather, 14 April 1677

The controversy over the causes, and "blame," for King Philip's War, described in the introduction to this section, swept Cotton into its vortex. It was not an argument in which Cotton wanted to be involved, and he clearly suspected that some indiscretion on the part of his step-brother, one of the contestants, was to blame.

PLIMOUTH APRIL, 14: 1677:

REV^D & DEARE BROTHER

Soe much confidence I have in you, that I durst to put my life in your hands; how it comes to passe that you, my most intire friend, have endangered my losse of my best friends here, besides all that reproach those concerned in the Bay will lay upon me, you will enforme me in your next: I went last wednesday to visit our Govr, who had lately received letters from Mr Hubbert[1] & Mr Dudley:[2] informing thus: m^r Hub: saith, Mr John Cotton one of your preachers hath written to his Brother Increase Mather, that some of your magistrates said there were as many mistakes or untruths in the booke as lines, this he had from Mr Allen, & Mr Thacher[3] who said he heard the letter read, & 1 of these ministers advised him to send to the Govr for satisfaction: M^r. Dud: writes sharply & reproachfully of me for what I wrote to you: our Govr is angry, & sent for the Treasurer, the day before, & possessed him as if he were the maine man whom I intended: but when I came to the Govr, I told his honour, that divers magistrates spake of mistakes in the booke: M^r D: & M^r H: desire our Govr to put an Imprimatur, & to assert the truth of the book: I told the Govr; I hoped he would returne noe answer that should entrench upon the truth of my words, for I would assert that I had written nothing but the truth: the Govr said, the most considerable mistake he observed was about the taking of Peter, & Moseleys taking prisoners as he went to Narrogansett, for he tooke none, but went by water from Prov: or warwick, to m^r Smiths.[4] other mistakes were more circumstantiall: I am at a losse what to write at such a distance; my desire is that you would honestly tell me why you trusted J: A: having litle reason to expect but that he would make mischeife of it: I am certaine you intended noe harme to me, but if you doe not improove your piety & prudence to suppresse discourse of this subject,—I am hoping for your answer to my last de John: my selfe & wife heartily salute you & yours, longing to heare of God's dealing with her; pray for us & ours, I am,

your Affectionate Brother

John Cotton

I am in great trouble of spirit, & straitned for time, soe that I cannot write to you as I would about this matter, I lack to speake with you; I hope my letter you keepe close; I finde noe Magistrate disowne his words, & therefore truth is my friend, but I feare lest our Govr, write some kind of Attestation, etc I dare not write what I thinke: pray write to me, what the very sentence is,[5] which I wrote about mistakes, verba[tim.]

Mather Papers 1:56, Prince Library, Rare Books and Manuscripts, Boston Public Library. Addressed "[Th]ese For the Reverend, his Deare Brother, Mr Increase Mather, Teacher of a Church of Christ at Boston." Endorsed "Br J. C. April. 14 1677." Lower left corner of letter torn.

---

1. Hubbard.
2. Joseph Dudley (1647–1720), the son of Gov. Thomas Dudley, graduated from Harvard College in 1665. He began his career as a deputy from Roxbury in 1673, served in the campaign against the Narragansetts, and was chosen an assistant to the General Court in 1678. A vigorous supporter of closer imperial ties, in 1684 he was dropped from office by the voters. Under the Dominion government he flourished, however. He was president of the provisional royal government, and chief justice after Gov. Andros arrived. His part in the introduction of Church of England ceremonies to New England and his participation in the controversial land-grabbing schemes of the Andros government made him one of the most hated men in New England. Considered a traitor of the colony by the Puritan orthodoxy, in particular, he was deposed, imprisoned and ejected when the Dominion fell in 1689. Returning to the colony in 1692, he plotted continuously to become governor, an aspiration that he finally realized in 1702. *American National Biography*, ed. John A. Garraty and Mark C. Carnes (New York and Oxford, 1999) (hereafter *ANB*).
3. Probably Peter Thatcher. See the letter to Increase Mather of 15 and 16 July 1678, below.
4. Hubbard's history says that Mosely and his men took ship at Swansea, landed somewhere on the coast near Smith's garrison at Wickford, and on their way there "happily surprised thirty six *Indians*, one of whom he took along with him as a Guide, Peter by Name, that was at that Time under some Disgust with his Country-men, or his Sachim, which made him prove the more real Friend to our Forces in the Service." Hubbard, *Present State of New-England*, 1:138-40.
5. See the letter to Increase Mather of 19 March 1677, above.

From Increase Mather, 21 April 1677

Dear Brother

I am sorry to hear of w^{t} mr H. hath written to yor Govr concerning yor Letter to me, wch Hee never saw nor hath truly Reprted. If ye generality of Reprts in his Narrative, should be like y^{t} his Imprimatr, it is pitty. <*line crossed out*> You <*two words crossed out*> say indeed in yor Letter, y^{t} some of yor magistrates sd Hee was mistaken in affirming y^{t} Alexander dyed [2?] days &c before he came halfe way home. And also y^{t} some body (whether yor selfe or who it is you doe not express) judged y^{r} were many mistakes in all he had published. But you doe not write, y^{t} y^{r} were as many untruths as Lines in mr H Narrative; much less y^{t} yor Magistrates did any of y^{m} say so. mr H. hath therefore done wrong to you & others in so reproving of you—I did not divulge yor letter. onely mr Th. & mr A. (being concerned in giving [Letters of?] Impremat^{rs}[1] were desired by mr H. to enquire of [me?] w^{t} mistakes I observed in his Narrative, whrup^{n} I read to y^{m}, w^{t} you wrote, but did not mention yor Name, only y^{t} I had r^{d} ye Letter from a minister in Plymouth Colony.

I was forward to Encouraging mr H. in his worke. And of my owne accord gave a Large Imprimat^{r} to his Booke. but afterwards wthdrew it, partly because I understood y^{r} was more mistake in it (& I was lately informed y^{t} at Connecticott they find much fault wth it) y^{n} at first I thought ther had bin. And partly because Hee had ye printer set mr Allen his Name to my [Attestat^{r}?], & y^{t} mr A never saw it to this day, wch thing some take to be a degree of Forgery, had it bin done as was designed, Also because I percieve so much of Adulation (as it seemed to me) as caused his discourse to be Nauseous, & I believe modest & H^{m}ble Spirits can not but wish ye style had bin otherwise upon y^{t} account as to some persons yet living—for to Commend ye dead is no flattery. but to applaud persons alive & to y^{r} faces, whether they deserved it or no, I know not w^{t} else to call it. I hear y^{t} mr Bulkly hath written a farr more impartial Narrative, & I shal doe w^{t} I may to promote ye Publicat^{n} of it.

w^{n} you see yor Govr, prsent my service to him. I doubt not, but w^{n} He *<illeg.>* is rightly informed *<illeg.>* any hard thoughts wch mr H. may by his misreport have occasioned concerning himselfe will vanish.

The Lord be wth you.

I am, yor [Affecti]nate Brother

I Mather

Boston. 21. 2m 1677

Mather Family Papers, American Antiquarian Society. Addressed "These For ye Rev^{d} my dear Brother Mr John Cotton, Pastor of ye Church in Plymouth." Endorsed "From my Brother Mather April, 21: 1677:" Noted in a hand other than Mather's or Cotton's: "de Hubbard Indian Wars–valuable–."

---

1. Probably "Letters of Imprematr."

From Thomas Walley, 9 May 1677

Reverend sir

Yesterday all most at night I received yo[r] Letters by m[r] Bourn[1] they have Laine at Sandwich many daies soe that yo[u] may perceive that yo[r] Letters Came to late. as for yo[rs] to M[r] Lauthrop[2] I have not yet sent it to him but intend to doe it speedily I have advised with my Daughter Allen[3] about it who did suppose knew much of m[r] Clarks mind and is troubled at his Carriage toward this maid[4] and sayth his sister Lauthrop liked the maid and mutch only could have wished shee had bin older I am sorry m[r] Clarks Conscience is not more tender if he were here I doubt not but he would[5] what hath bin his sin and what is his Duty it may be M[r] Lauthrop may write to him if it be not to late. sir at present I am not well I have bin greatly distempered with a Cold and other weaknesses and am oft ready to think my daies to live are not many but my times are in hands of god and to his good will I freely submit I pray yo[u] pray for me I am sorry for the sicknese of our honoured Governor and good m[r] Arnal—Sir I have now spook wth m[r] Lauthrop and he hath read yo[r] Letter and doth like w[t] yo[u] have don and will as soon as he Can write to or speak wth W: C: Sir, I have bin all this day on my bed, as sick as at any time of late yeares my Love to yor selfe and mrs Cotton I am

yo[rs] in o[r] Lord

Tho: Walley

may 9th 1677

Sir I pray you dispatch this to M[r] Baker.[6]

Cotton Family Papers 7:22, Prince Library, Rare Books and Manuscripts, Boston Public Library. Addressed "For the Reverend M[r] John Cotton Pastour of the Church of Christ at Plimoth these."

---

1. Not found.
2. Barnabas Lothrop of Barnstable; letters not found. See the letter to Thomas Hinckley of 14 February 1679, below.
3. Walley's daughter Hannah (d. 1711) married Samuel Allen of Barnstable (d. 1726) on 10 May 1664. Savage, *Genealogical Dictionary*, 1:44.
4. It is not clear if this is the same Mr. Clark, or the same situation, referred to in Samuel Arnold's letter of 4 April 1677.
5. Word missing? "Own" or "admit"?
6. Probably Nicholas Baker, see the letter of 9 July from Nicholas Baker, below.

Letter of Dismissal for T: D:,[1] 28 May 1677

Rev^d^, Honoured & Beloved

G: in his prov: having soe disposed, as that our belov: bro: T: D: hath bin now for many yeares together removed far distant from us & improoved in the exersising of his gifts in Teaching the word of G: to those amongst whom he hath lived, & the same hand of divine prov: leading him forth by a renewed invitation to like service in a place remote from us whence he cannot injoy the benefit of comm: with us nor wee attend the duties of ch: relation unto him, wee have therefore Judged it meete & necessary to answer the desires of this our Bro: & doe by these our letters testify that he was regularly admitted into the fel: of this Ch: & hath continued in the relation of a member thereoff these many yeares, by virtue whereoff, wee doe on his behalfe request that he may have the priviledge of holy Comm: with any of the Ches of J. xt[2] where he may occasionally sojourne for his ædification in grace & holines; & also our desire is that his children be acknowledged in the Lord according to their capacity:

we doe also hereby further declare, that if the prov: of G: soe dispose as that our Bro: D: reside in any place where he may injoy setled Comm: in all the ord:s of xt in a way of ch: fel: wee doe now give him liberty to improove these our letters of a dismission of him to any such ch: of xt walking in the order of the Gosp: & desire their acceptance of him in the Lord, as becometh saints; our prayers to G: are for him that he may be kept in the way of G: & preserved blamelesse to his heavenly kingdome, & wee pray also, that walking in the feare of the Lord & in the Comfort of the H: G: there may be an increase of the ches of J: xt:

whose breth: wee are in the faith & fel. of the Gosp:

J: C: Pastour. T: C: Elder with the consent of the ch: of Plim:

May: 28 1677

Cotton Family Papers 7:24, Prince Library, Rare Books and Manuscripts, Boston Public Library. Addressed at bottom "Inscribed To any of the ches of xt to whom these letters may come The Ch of xt in Plim: wisheth Gr: & P: in our deare L: J: Noe superscr[iption]." Cotton's copy of letter.

---

1. Not identified.

2. I.e., "Churches of Jesus Christ."

To Increase Mather, 19 June 1677

In the aftermath of King Philip's War—perhaps even as a consequence of it—the annoying issue of religious toleration in Plymouth Colony surfaced once again. Nearly two weeks before Cotton wrote this letter to Mather, Plymouth's General Court "[desired] the elders of the severall churches in this collonie to give their resolution to the following query, viz: What are those due bounds and lymetts which ought to be sett to a tolleration in matters of Religion as may consist with the honor of Christ, the good and welfare of the churches and of the civill govment?"[1]

Plimouth June, 19: 1677:

Revd & Deare Brother

As I yet heare nothing from you in answer to any thing in my 2 last letters to you;[2] the Elder tells me, you say you have a paper of my fathers Concerning Toleration, I have it not, therefore I pray you not to faile of sending it to me by this opportunity, it may now be of some Considerable use to me & others: I thanke you for your booke, Major Bradford & Mr Southworth[3] returne you like thankes for theirs, this day I sent away Mr Hinckleys & Mr Walleys; the other 3 shall soone be sent also: I doubt if you had sent one to Mr Arnold he would not have had strength enough to have read it in his life; he is not yet dead, but told me last weeke he expected his great change before our day of Thanksgiving (which is on the morrow)[4] cease not to pray for him while he lives:[5] In thoughts about the Ques: propounded, some things occurre, which I desire your Judgment about; viz, whether a publick Confession might not be agreed upon & subscribed unto & none to be tolerated for publick worship but such as consent therein? whether they can be tolerated that in their publick dispensations declare it to be a sin or Antichristian for any of their members to hold Communion with any churches that are not of their perswasion? & whether such are to be tolerated who revile & reproach the Civill goverment, the churches or ordinances of Xt? other things are in my minde, I shall be glad to have your Judgment of these or any other things relating to this matter: I am perswaded God hath put an opportunity into the hands of the Elders of this Colony to doe some good service for his name, & though wee are very weake yet who knows but that God who made this poore Colony praesidentiall in renewing Covenant, may discover something of his minde here also about this matter, Revd m^r Walley is a holy man & will be our great leader, I perceive he is very studious about the Ques: pray earnestly for Gods prescence with him & with all engaged, that God may have some glory in the management of this solemne affaire: I perceive John is under your roofe,[6] I need not say, you know my soules desire to God & you on his behalfe: by a letter from Capt oliver yesterday[7] I understand that you preached a choice sermon June 10: in your owne meeting house; I hope you will not much borrow the helpe of young weake Preachers till you have warmed the new house with many a pretious sermon: Concerning Ger: Hobart[8] (because it may be he may sometimes helpe you) I will write a true narrative, & it may be you may doe me right at one time or other: He denyes to pay me rent sayes I owe him 30 shil: now Judge you: I desired him to preach for me, promised him some reward as God should enable me, but mentioned not a word of a particular summe, though in my heart I ever intended 10 shil: a sabbath: but because he was forced from his worke, I had such respect to him as to write to our Elder etc to move for a Contribution for him, upon my Motion they contribute & give him betweene 30 & 40 shil: in silver, & because they looke upon him as low, our Deacons added & gave to him 10 shil: in silver more out of the church-Treasury, & when he came to Boston I gave him 30 shil: in silver for his preaching here 3 Sabbaths, which was the utmost I could doe; & yet this disingenous man, though he had almost 4 ^{pd}, could malapertly charge me with owing him 30 shil: now, & till that is out he will pay me nothing, when I told him, I promised him noe particular summe, he replyed, the bargaine is then yet to Make: truth is, the case is soe with me, that I cannot forgive my rent, if ever ought be due to him for preaching for you, I must assigne you to take it, for I shall make conscience to pay you as fast as I can for Johns board: I write thus largly, being desirous that this letter made be findable in your study, if ever there the occasion to discourse G: H: thereabouts, either with or without me: my selfe & wife heartily salute you & yours; desiring your prayers for us & ours, & hoping for a good full letter from you, I rest,

your Affectionate Brother,

John Cotton

wee daily expect to have your call of your servant home:[9]

Mather Papers 1:69, Prince Library, Rare Books and Manuscripts, Boston Public Library. Addressed "These For the Reverend, his Deare Brother, Mr Increase Mather; Teacher of a Church of Christ at Boston." Endorsed "B^r J. C. Jun. 19. 1677."

---

1. Shurtleff, *Records of Plymouth Colony,* 5:233. For the response of the elders, see the letter of 12 July 1677 to the General Court, below.
2. Not found.
3. Constant Southworth (c. 1615–1679), stepson of Gov. William Bradford, was treasurer for the colony and an assistant to the General Court. Stratton, *Plymouth Colony*, 355-56.
4. There is no record of this event in Plymouth colony, town, or church records.
5. Rev. Arnold recovered from his illness and lived another sixteen years.
6. The Cottons were obviously relieved that their son was under his uncle's watchful eye.
7. Not found.

8. Rev. Gershom Hobart (1645–1707, H.C. 1667), son of Rev. Peter Hobart of Hingham, found work when the displaced residents of Groton, Massachusetts, returned to their abandoned town in the spring of 1678. He was ordained there in November 1679. *Sibley's Harvard Graduates*, 2:229-30. See also [11] August 1694.

9. Jethro, presumably.

To Increase Mather, 25 June 1677

PLIMOUTH JUNE, 25: 1677:

REV[D] & DEARE BROTHER

Mr Shove was this day at my house as he passed along to Barnstable, (for your booke he thankes you) & told me that in Mr H's history, things are strangely falsifyed, (I use his owne words) he much commends your History & sayes had Mr H: followed your Narrative he had showed more truth; my request to you is, that you will prudently of your owne accord (unlesse you see weighty reason to the contrary) write a letter to Mr Shove & desire him to acquaint you with the mistakes he knowes to be in that booke; I doubt not but he will readily grant your desires, for he freely asserts many things to be notorious—& if you had the particulars in writing, I beleive it would be of good use: If you see meete to write to him, pray doe it now by Mr clarke & send it hither, because here he will call next weeke & soe you may soone have an answer:

our due salutations to you & sisters & cousens, craving your prayers, etc., for me & mine, in great haste I rest,

Your Affectionate Brother,

John Cotton

Mather Papers 1:70, Prince Library, Rare Books and Manuscripts, Boston Public Library. Addressed "For the Reverend, Mr Mather Teacher of a Church, at Boston, present." Endorsed "Br J. C. Jun. 25. 1677."

From Thomas Walley, 26 June 1677

Edmund Andros, the royal governor of New York, had been instrumental in preventing King Philip from soliciting the aid of the Mohawk people, and indeed in encouraging the Mohawks to attack Philip's followers. But Andros was no friend to Puritan New England. At his sovereign's behest, he boldly moved to challenge the boundaries of the New England colonies, first in western Connecticut and, as described here, in the Massachusetts claims of today's Maine.

Reverend and deare Sir

I bless god we came safe to Boston ye ffryday last on ye morning. Upon Lords day Came the news of 4 vessels with 200 men in them and 16 peeces of ordnance fro^{m} Major Andros who are to take possessio^{n} of the Eastern parte and to build a strong fort[1] wch seemes to be a plot and a snare but god will have us depend upon him those vessels wer met at Cape Cod 200 Mohakes are to meet them Uncas son is taken by the Mohakes[2]—Major Clark is now ready to goe to the Eastward some say wth 300 men[3] what to doe I know not noe more news except I should tell yo^{u} that an old man was like to be whiped for Kiseing his wife

Sir I hope to be with yo^{u} at plimoth if I must preach I must if god help me I shall be willing pray for me but I think it is good for yo^{u} to be ready and then it is most meet yo^{u} should preach my hearty Love to yor selfe and m^{rs} Cotton I have written fro^{m} Barnstable I know not whether yo^{u} have received it I Committ yo^{u} to o^{r} good god I am

yor assured ffriend

Tho: Walley

June 26. 1677

Curwen Family Papers, American Antiquarian Society. Addressed "for the Reverend and my much esteemed friend Mr John Cotton Pastour of the church of christ at Plimouth these." Endorsed " From Mr Walley June, 26: 1677:." Noted in a hand other than Cotton's or Walley's: "minister of Barnstable before m^{r} Russell."

---

1. In June 1677, Edmund Andros sent 100 troops with cannon, a prefabricated fort and a year's supply of provisions by sea to the Maine coast in an attempt to end the fighting there and to secure the claim of the Duke of York to the region. Adding teeth to his diplomacy with the Wabenaki peoples was a large force of Mohawk and Oneida warriors that traveled overland from New York. Within a month, Andros and the Iroquois had persuaded the Wabenaki to make peace and to return English prisoners and several captured fishing vessels. Stephen Saunders Webb, *1676: The End of American Independence* (Cambridge, Mass., 1985), 387-88.

2. The Mohawks thoroughly distrusted Uncas and his son Oweneco. In June 1677 Oweneco was "surprised and taken from the English at Wegwanack & carried away captive," probably to ensure

Uncas's good behavior while Mohawk war parties were far away helping Andros. By May 1678 the Connecticut government helped to secure Oweneco's return. J. Hammond Trumbull, *The Public Records of the Colony of Connecticut* (Hartford, 1850), 2:499.

3. Maj. Thomas Clark (d. 1683), one of Boston's wealthiest merchants and an officer in the Artillery Company, led a Massachusetts force to Maine on 28 June. Like Andros, the Bay men aimed to neutralize the Wabenaki and to reassert English authority, in this case represented by Massachusetts. Clark and his men fared less well, however, suffering heavy casualties in an ambush at Black Point. Savage, *Genealogical Dictionary*, 1:401; Webb, *1676*, 388.

From Nicholas Baker,[1] [9 July 1677]

Scituate, a coastal town on Plymouth Colony's border with Massachusetts, had been one of the loci of trouble during the Quaker controversy of the late 1650s. Quakers actually made few converts in the colony, but their presence, and the General Court's heavy-handed response to their "cursed tenets," encouraged other dissidents who, as Baker's letter demonstrates, were never entirely quelled.

Reverend & much Respect Sir

These few lynes are in the first place to present my owne & my wives hearty love & due Respects to yo^{r}selfe & good m^{r}s Cotton: with o^r many & hearty thanks for yor late visit so kindly of us: & Espetially that m^{r}s Cotton should her selfe in her grate & undeserved love undertake such a voyage & Incourage yo^{r}selfe thereunto: the Lord Jeasus Recompense it you both: for whose sake we believe you did it: Sir I am in Respect of the Condition of my body much as I was when you were here: not in that Extremity of paine as some time formerly: I have now Eight Lords dayes together beene at meeting But no wayes able to come to you to Plymouth: which gladly I would if it were the Lords will: but I desier to submit to his good & holy will: & to praise his name that my pains now are so tollerable Sir I can not write much to you: writing is very troublesome to me: I pray present my due Rspects of my most hearty love to all the Reverend Elders that shall be present with you upon so good & necessery a business: I begge the prayer & praises of you all to god for me & myne: deare Sir I am very unfit & unable to give advise in so waighty a case: yet I must needs manifest myselfe greatly pleased with the good notion that is made & doe pray the Lord so to dyrect you all in giveing yor Resolution to the Query: & the court to doe something Effectually that may at last Restraine those that are mad with damnable Herisies: to the Subverting the Glorious gospel of the blessed god: & soules of men what in them lyeth: & under Conviction I Conceive it is more safe & Easy to say what is

Intollerable then to say what shall be tollerated: divers very sad Examples we have in o^r^ very towne: some woefully neglecting to Come to the publike worshipe of god on the Lords dayes: some not onely maintaining damnable & Blasphemious doct[rines] (the perticulars I need not mention they are Commonly knowen) [but?] also openly divulge them: carrying about & profirring [...] Hyreticall bookes: Inviting all sorts of persons Esp[etially] [the?] younger sort to their diabolicall worshipe: openly mee[ting] on the Lords day (a little from o^r^ meeting house & that Espe[tially] In the middle of the day between o^r^ Exercises that they may (as they doe) draw many unsettled & younger persons to their wayes: some times Coming in to o^r^ publike meeting while we are in o^r^ worshiping of god: & interrupting us therein: calling us false profits: & a company of Hypocrits: & persuading the people not to heare us preach the gospel: as have been lately done amongst us: & what doth it availe to Restraine such madness to lay such by the heels 2 or 3 houres: accuseing both court: & officers: & mynisters for Robers & Receivers of theire stolen goods when any thing is taken from them (according to the Lawes of god & man) to uphold the true worshipe of god amongest us: what doe these & such like but open their mouthes in Blasphemie against god To Blaspheme his name: & his tabernacle: them that dwell in heaven: Sir I hope I am fare from a harsh Ridged persecuting spirit against such as Erre through weakness in lessir matters Espetially being of a humble & peaceable spirit: nither have I beene a stirrer up of the majestrat to punish men for thir consciencs (as I have been accused) but being called at this time to give my advice: duty to god & those that god have set over me binds me to be obedient & Faithfull according to my ability: & I doe believe according to the screptures: that as its the duty of all to contend Earnestly for the faith: & as the Elders & churches are to doe it by doctrine, Conversation & discipline: so the magistrate is not to beare the sword in vain but to punish Evilldoers: & Incourage them that doe well: & to be nursing fathers to the churches of christ: [Howe] they are to act in such cases is not my place to determine: but [I pray] god give them wisdom: protection: & courage in gods cause [....] what I have written be taken in the better part: though [...] performed I am willing to be a friend to peace & truth: [....] not had an opportunity to see M^r^ witheral:

Sir I Remane yo^rs^ in all I am able

Nico^s^ Baker

I hope all will agree that open profonation of the lords day is Intollerable:

Curwen Family Papers, American Antiquarian Society. Addressed "These for the Revrd & his much Respected m^r^ John Cotton Pastor to the Church of Christ at Plymouth dd." Endorsed "From M^r^ [...] Baker of Scituate. Received July, 9: 1677:" Hole along outside margin.

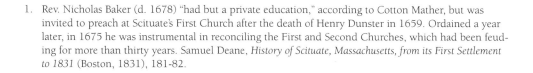

1. Rev. Nicholas Baker (d. 1678) "had but a private education," according to Cotton Mather, but was invited to preach at Scituate's First Church after the death of Henry Dunster in 1659. Ordained a year later, in 1675 he was instrumental in reconciling the First and Second Churches, which had been feuding for more than thirty years. Samuel Deane, *History of Scituate, Massachusetts, from its First Settlement to 1831* (Boston, 1831), 181-82.

To the General Court of Plymouth Colony, 12 July 1677

The leaders of the colony's churches responded quickly to the General Court's request for guidelines with regard to religious toleration. Only five weeks passed between the Court's query and the date of this report.

RIGHT WORSHIPFULL, WORSHIPFULL & HONOURED IN THE LORD

Your true piety expressed in a continuall respect had to the Interest of the [...] in this Colony (which wee esteem none of the least of those mercies God hath favoured us with) wee greatly rejoice in & desire to blesse God for Assur[ing] our selves therefore of your sincere desire to attaine to a right understandi[ng] of the minde of God in what relates to the preservation & propagation of the true Religion among us; wee have (though un[der] a deep sense of our many disadvantages thereunto) cheerfully under[taken] the discu[ssion] of that point by your selves proposed & give our answer as followeth

Quest: The Question being, what are those due bounds & limits which ought to be set to Toleration in matters of Religion as may consist with the Honour of christ, the good & welfare of the churches and of the civill Government?

Answer: The Answer is in these Propositions.

Prop: 1: That none be tolerated to set up any publick worship that shall refuse [to] subscribe or otherwise manifest their consent to the Confession of faith following.
2 Tim: 1:13:
Rom: 6: 7:

mar: 3: 1: Pet: 1: 25:
Col: 3: 16: 2: Pet. 1: 21:
2 Tim: 3: 15: 16: 17:
I beleive the scriptures contained in the old & new Testame[nt are the] word of God & are given by inspiration of God to be the rule of [...]

Deu: 6: 4: Jer: 10: 10:
1 Cor: 8: 4: 5: 6:
1 John 5: 7: Mat: 28: 19:

I beleive there is but one only living & true God & that in the [....]
godhead there be three persons of one substance, power & [...] God the Father, God the Son & God the Holy Ghost.

Gen: 1: per totum.

I believe this one God, Father, son & holy ghost made the w[hole?] w[orld & all?] things therein of nothing in the space of six days very [...]

Gen: 1: 26: 27:
Ecle: 7: 29:

I beleive God made man [in his] owne image in knowledg[e,] R[ight]eousnesse & true holinesse

Gen: 3: Rom: 5: 12:
& 3: 19: 23: Eph:
2: 1: 3: Gal: 3: 10:

I beleive that our first parents being seduced by the subtlety of sa[tan] & [eating?] the forbidden [fruit] sinned against God & fell from the [...] wherein they were crea[ted], & that all mankinde descending fr[om] them by ordinary generation sinned in them & fell with them [in] their first Transgression & soe were brought into a st[ate] o[f death?] & misery, loosing Communion with God & falling under his wr[ath]e.

Isa: 42: 1: 6: Joh: 10: 36:
1 Pet: 1: 19:
1: Tim: 2: 5: 6:
Act: 3: 22: 23: Ps: 110: 4:
Heb: 2: 17: Ps: 2: 6:
Eph: 5: 13:

I beleive that God in his eternall purpose chose & ordain[ed] Lord Jesus, his onley begotten son to be the one & only mediato[r] betweene God & man, the Prophet, Preist & King, the head & Saviour of his church.

Phil: 2: 6: Joh: 1: 1:
Gal: 4: 4: Joh: 1: 14:
Luk: 1: 35: Mat: 1: 23:
1 Tim: 3: 16:

I beleive that Jesus christ the second Person in the Trinity [is the?] very & eternall God, of one substance & equall with the Father[&] that when the fullnesse of time was come, the son of God, the second person in Trinity tooke upon him mans natur[e, was?] conceived by the power of the Holy Ghost, in the womb of [the] virgin Mary of her substance, soe that the Godhead & m[an] were Joyned together in one person, which person is [....] very man yet one christ, the only Mediator betweene Go[d & man.]

I beleive that the Lord J[es]us christ by his perfect obedience [....] of himself upon the [cros]se, hath fully satisfyed the Justi[ce of] his father & purchased [....] Reconciliation, but [....] all those [...] father [....]

[...] 5:13 Rom: 5: 19:
[....] 5: 10 He[b:]
[...] 14:

I beleive the Elect are made partakers of the Redemption purchased by Christ by the effectuall application of it to their soules by his word & spirit.

I beleive that Justification is an act of Gods free grace unto sinners in which he pardoneth all their sins, accepteth & accounteth their persons righteous in his sight not for anything wrought in them or done by them, but [...] for the perfect obedience & full satisfaction of Christ, by God [   ]uted to them & received by faith alone.

I believe Sanctification is a worke of Gods grace whereby the
Eph: 4: 23: 24: Elect are in time renewed in the whole man after the Image
1 Thes: 5: 23: Rom: of God & are enabled more & more to dye to sin & live to
6: 3: etc 1 Pet: 4: 1: 2: Righteousnesse.

I beleive that whosoever God have accepted in Jesus christ, effectually called & sanctifyed by his spirit, can neither totally
Joh: 10: 27: 28: 29: nor finally fall way from the state of grace, but shall certainly
Phil: 1: 6: 1: Pet: [....] percevere to the end & be eternally saved.

Joh: 13: 1: I believe the bodies of men after death turne to dust & all Corruption, but their soules (which neither dye nor sleep) having an immortall substance immediately returne to God who gave them, the soules of the Righteous being then made perfect in holines are received into heaven & the soules of the wicked are cast into hell.

I beleive the bodies of the Just & unjust shall be raised at the Last Day.

I beleive that God hath appointed a day in which he will Judge the world in Righteousnesse by Jesus Christ in which Day all persons that have lived on earth shall appeare before the Judgment seat of Christ to give an account of their thoughts, words & deeds, & to receive according to what they have done in the body whether good or evil.

That none be tolerated who revile & reproach the Civill
Joh: 2:6: Authority, the Churches & ordinances of Christ in them which
Prop: 2: are approved & established by this Government.

2 Pet: 2:10: That none be tolerated who receive into their Communion persons
[....] 5: 12: Ezek: that are excommunicated for Scandalous evills by the churches
they belong unto till they have made their peace with such
Prov: 3: churches or the sentence be declared unjust by other churches.

[....] 18: 17: 18: Those are not to be tolerated who declare that it is sinfull & Antichristian for any of their members to hold Communion with the churches of Christ approved by the Authority of this Colony.

That such shall not be tolerated who give disturbance to the approved churches of Christ in their publick administrations.

That such shall not be tolerated to set up any publick worship that upon pretense of Religion professedly or practically declare that they will not when the government requires give assistance as others doe, & shall be by law required for the preservation of the pe[ople] of the Country against the common enemies of it. Seducers to Heresie & Apost[ates] from the faith & order of the G[ospel & all] those whose principles [& practices tend directly] to the extir[pation of the C]hurches [as established are not to be tolerated.]

HONOURED WORTHIES

wee would not hereby be understood to arrogate to our selves the acura[te] decision of soe weighty a point, but in compliance with the call of God manifest by your joynt Concerned desires that wee should attempt the resolution of this question, it being a matter of extraordinary weight with us, that all possible meanes be used f[or] securing of that blessed Interest of the Gospel designed by our [fathe]rs the first planters of this wildernesse, whose very worke was here to build an Altar to the true God, with whom the Lord was signally present in accepting & succeeding their fervent prayers & paines for the laying a happy foundation for us survivors to build upon, wee have in submission to better Judgments made this our reply with a peculiar accommodation to the present emergencies before us, leaving such difficulties as may further appeare to after-disquisition: if wee have therein arrived at any thing amounting to y[our] satisfaction & direction wee desire God may have the p[raise.] That which our eye hath been upon is in obedience to the [...] of God, to maintaine a due contest for the faith once deliver[ed to the?] Saints against such as doe or may creep in unawares [...] the grace of God into Lasciviousnesse & denying the only Lor[d God] & our Lord Jesus Christ; yet avouching a tender respect to [...] in some things may difer from us, provided they doe a[pprove] themselves freinds to the power & purity of Godlines amongst [us?] Wee therefore unfainedly desire that all our hea[rts may be] sutably affected with the solemne engagements wee h[ave been?] under towards our God, & the great difficulty of the worke wee are called to in order to reall & thorough Reformation, [that our] poore endeavours may finde acceptance with you & s[ ] faithfull in our Israel, & that the God of wisedome may b[e] with you, strengthning your hearts & hands & prospering your worke,

HONORED PATRIOTS

<*which*> is the prayer of us who are ready to serve you in the Lord

George Shove — Tho: Walley
John Cotton — Tho: Thornton[1]
James Keith — John Smith[2]
Noah Newman — Samuel Treat
Tho: Cushman — William Brett

Plimouth July, 12: 1677:

wee whose names are here underwritten although by Gods providence detained from the meeting of the Reverend Elders in returning their answer to the above said Question, having perused & considered doe freely consent & subscribe hereunto

Samuel Arnold William Witherell[3]
Nicolas Baker Tho: King[4]
Henry Cobb[5] John Chipman[6]

Cotton Family Papers 7:30, Prince Library, Rare Books and Manuscripts, Boston Public Library. Addressed "These to the Honoured General Court assembled at Plimouth Present." The ministers' opinion on toleration is in Cotton's hand, written on both sides of a single sheet, mutilated on the right-hand and bottom edges; many Biblical references are illegible or obliterated. For some text now lost to mutilation, the editors relied on a handwritten transcription made earlier, when the document was presumably in better condition than it is currently; Cotton Family Papers 7:30 (photostat), Massachusetts Historical Society. The "cover letter" associated with the opinion is apparently Cotton's copy, as the entire text, including the signatures, is in his hand.

---

1. Rev. Thomas Thornton (c. 1607–1700) was educated for the ministry in England but was ejected from his pulpit there in 1662. He emigrated to New England and began preaching to the Yarmouth church in 1663, but was not confirmed there for another four years. Some residents had opposed his candidacy and had tried to discourage him. Apparently hard feelings remained, for after one of his sermons a listener declared, "half of it was lies" (he was later persuaded to retract his statement). Thornton also served the community as a physician and, like Cotton, ministered to Native congregations as well. Thornton moved to Boston in 1693, probably to live with his son Timothy, a merchant and representative. Swift, *History of Old Yarmouth*, 92; Marion Vuillemier, *The Town of Yarmouth, Massachusetts: A History, 1639–1989* (Yarmouth, Mass., 1989), 9-10, 243; Frederick Lewis Weis, *The Colonial Clergy and the Colonial Churches of New England* (Baltimore, 1936), 203; *Diary of Samuel Sewall*, 1:426.
2. John Smith left the Barnstable church about 1663, "being different in opinion from them." He sojourned in New York, returning to Barnstable in 1672. He assisted Thomas Walley in the pastorate until the latter's death, filling the office until 1688, when he retired. Trayser, *Barnstable*, 37-38.
3. Rev. William Witherell (1600–1684) moved from Duxbury in 1645 to become the pastor of Scituate's Second Church. Deane, *History of Scituate*, 190-92.
4. Thomas King (d. 1691), an early settler of Scituate, was an elder of the Second Church. Deane, *History of Scituate*, 301. See 3 October 1684.
5. Henry Cobb (d. 1679) was one of the early settlers of Scituate. He moved to Barnstable about 1641and became a deputy for the town and an elder of the church there. Stratton, *Plymouth Colony*, 265-66.
6. John Chipman (c. 1620–1708) was one of two men chosen to be ruling elders of the Barnstable church in 1670. Stratton, *Plymouth Colony*, 262-63.

From Increase Mather, 23 July 1677

Dear Brother

This is to Entreat y^{t} you would send My Indian lad to me p ye next vessel; for I have promised one in Dorchester tht Jether shall serve him untill winter, w^{n} I shall (if I live) need his service in my owne Family, & by y^{t} Time, I hope he will be able to speake English.

I suppose you have heard how ye Indians near C. Sables have taken many of o^{r} Fishing vessells[1]—About 50 souldiers are gone out of Salem to pursue y^{m}, w^{t} ye issue will be ye Lord knoweth. Sabbath day [illeg.] sevenights, ye women at Marblehead as y^{y} [Came?] out of ye Meeting House, fell upo^{n} two Indians y^{t} were brought in as Captives, & in a tumultuary way very Barbarously murdered y^{m}.[2] Doubtles if ye Indians heare of it, o^{r} Captives amongst y^{m} will be served accordingly. All these things are ag^{t} us.[3] R^{ts} to my sister. The L^{d} be with you, I am

Yo^{r} Afect. brother

I. Mather

Boston. 23. 5^{m} 1677.

I doe not hear of any one sick of y^{e} small pox since M^{r} [illeg.] death, but men may have received y^{e} $Infect^{n}$, & it not appear for 3 or 4 weekes. I think you had best defer Rowlands coming untill y^{e} Commencement, for fear of y^{e} worst.

Cotton Family Papers 7:31, Prince Library, Rare Books and Manuscripts, Boston Public Library. Addressed "These for ye Revd my dear Brother Mr John Cotton, Pastor of ye Church in Plimouth."

---

1. For a fuller account of the activities of the "Indian Mariners," see Hubbard, *Present State of New-England*, 2:238-40.

2. This harrowing incident, which occurred on 15 July 1677, is detailed in James Axtell, "The Vengeful Women of Marblehead: Robert Roules's Deposition of 1677," *The William and Mary Quarterly*, 3d ser., 31 (1974): 647-52.

3. A paraphrase of Jabob's complaint in Gen. 42:36.

From George Shove, 10 September 1677

REVER[D] & DEAR S[R]

I long to hear from you not having recieved any lines from you for a great while. I had Come Last wednesday to Bridgwater to hear you but that I was affraid to venture forth soe soon, having the Lords day before been Confined to my house by extream paine in my tooth & universall indisposition of bodye. Since that I had a sore broke in my jawe yet yesterdaye found noe in Convenience in my g[oing] forth or Labour. to day Simon Cooper[1] being sent for upon another occasion I have venturd to get the root of tooth drawn It troubled me being jealouse other wise of an Impostume[2] in my jawe which I am confermed in upon the sight of the tooth. I am yet under some indisposition by the paine of it but I hope the worst is past if I Can avoid taking Cold. the widow frith her son is dead & shee will be necessitated to return to Duxburye. the sicknes I hope is with us abated. I present my Love & respects with my wifes to yorselfe & yors & desiring that mutuall prayers may Continue I subscribe S[r]

yo[r] Assured friend

George Shove

Taunton Sept. 10. 77.

Cotton Family Papers 7:32, Prince Library, Rare Books and Manuscripts, Boston Public Library. Addressed "These for Reverend M[r] John Cotton Pastor of the Church in Plimouth Prsent." Endorsed "From M[r] Shove September, 10: 1677:"

---

1. Probably Simon Cooper, a Newport, Rhode Island, physician. Savage, *Genealogical Dictionary*, 1:454.
2. Abscess.

From Thomas Walley, 8 October 1677

Reverend Sir and my honoured ffriend

I have not given you[u] a visit in a greate while and now it is like to be but short I am often exercised with much weakness. this I have time to doe to give you[u] thanks for yo[r] remembrance of me to present my Love to yo[r] selfe and good m[rs] Cotton and to beg the Continuance of yo[r] prayers I have as much need of that help as ever I had. I am troubled at this new breaking out of the Indians and by reason of [not?] enough newes we are much in the dark about [th]e news it selfe what it is. the good lord grant [a]ll may issue well Poor new E. is in Dainger at home and abroad but god at his pleasure Can set Pvidences a foot for our good I have Cause to think my time is short in the world I waite for my last and great chaing my desire is to be faithfull and usefull while I live and that I may not be a burden but a blessing in my generation. I could make some Complaints but I had better doe it to god then to men and more hope of prvailing that way it is god must give all Sorts of helps. Sir when you[u] are at leasure I shall be glad to heare from you[u] for yo[r] Letters are a Comfort to me I am now in hast my prayers are to god for you[u] and yo[rs] and I am

yo[rs] in o[r] lord Jesus

Tho: Walley

Octob: 8th 1677

Cotton Family Papers 7:33, Prince Library, Rare Books and Manuscripts, Boston Public Library. Addressed "ffor the Reverend and my Loving ffriend M[r] John Cotton Pastour of the church of christ at Plimoth these DD." Endorsed "From M[r] Walley october, 8: 1677:"

To Increase Mather, 20 October 1677

Plimouth october, 20:1677:

Revd & Deare Brother

yours I received[1] & the bookes, 7 of those which came first are sold at Bridgwater, I will endeavour to sell all as fast as I can: I intreat you to returne by M[r] will: Clarke who is now at Boston an answer in writing to my following request which I affectionately make to you: viz, concerning my Cousen Cotton[2] your son, that he may live here with me this winter; God hath given him grace, & his learning is above what those of his standing have usually attained unto, whence he is able to doe good to others; &

you know it is recorded as the honour of your blessed father that at 15 yeares old he was called to be a Schoolemaster, & why may not his Grand-son have it put into the records of his life that before that age he was accounted worthy to be soe imployed: All the worke I would engage him to should be to be Tutor to my John, & Rowlands Teacher, he shall be sure, God helping, not only of a Comfortable board free of all charge, but returne in march (if soe you please) with 5 pd of silver in his pocket though none else should improove him: I doubt not but that many would be glad to improove his helpe for writing & Ciphering, & would give him a good reward for his paines, but I would not urge for more then you see meete at present, only assure you the reward abovementioned shall be faithfully paid for the service desired. most Deare Brother, I professe I have had many serious thoughts of this motion before I made it, & cannot frame any Arguments of weight in oppositurn; you cannot but thinke my wife & I (to both whom he is deservedly very Deare) shall be as tender of him as the hearts of his tender parents can desire, & although I cannot benefit him in his learning as you can, yet the Logicall & Theologicall notions of Mr Stone which I tooke in writing from him may I question not be of good use to him in his studies: I intended a more large & better studyed Invitation of my Kinsman, but coming this day from Taunton, & the boat going before morning, I am cut short of my purpose: my selfe & wife heartily salute you & yours & him, pray be intreated to send me a speedy & comfortable answer, I hope the motion is of God, my heart is much in it: pray for us, I am,

your Affectionate Brother,

John Cotton:

It may be his being here may prevent his having the small pox this winter: God knows:

Mather Papers 1:83, Prince Library, Rare Book & Manuscripts, Boston Public Library. Addressed "These For the Reverend, his very Deare Brother, Mr Increase Mather, Teacher of a Church of Christ, at Boston, present." Endorsed "B^r^ J. C. Octob. 20. 1677."

---

1. Not found; presumably not Mather's letter of 23 July, above.

2. Prince's note: "Cotton Mather was then 15 years old."

From James Oliver, 20 October 1677

20: 8: 77

m^{r} Cotton Sir after kind respect I had sent your wine by m^{r} greenwood order but a gros grained master woul not stay on minit for it—for news from england here arived m^{r} tuck 7 weeks pasage with 8 pasingers 4 ship[s] mor of ours may be Dayly Lookt for by [...] holen who Cam out 10 days before this and n[ews?] arrived was bad news for new england as m^{r} biseil marchant of M^{r} tuck afirm but i[n] that ten days the scale turned and goes hopfuly on our sid our patent now b[y] Lord Cheif Justis of England declared to be good and Confirmed to be good and our asent have much favor on this turne wi[th] the king and Counsel who atend the kings pleasur but not Like to Com this year they feare from hadly Last night Cam a post 19 indyan were ther 10 instant and [have?] burnt hadly mil[1] and the house [....] to it the enymy was persued by [....] kild on of the enymy and wou[nded] [...] more one of our men slightly w[ounded] our Court upon news from england yestir day ajurned til the 23 instant [...] have embarqed al vesels great small [...] til then 15 9^{ber} is a publick tha[nks][2] for many mercy

I am y^{rs} to Coma[nd]

James [Oliver]

Cotton Family Papers 7:34, Prince Library, Rare Books and Manuscripts, Boston Public Library. Addressed "To Reverent M^{r}. John Cotton dliver." Right-hand edge of paper mutilated, especially bottom half. Although part of the signature is lost, the handwriting is that of James Oliver.

---

1. More than a year after King Philip's War came to an end in southern New England, the upper Connecticut Valley was still a dangerous place. Natives raided Hatfield, whose people were "a little too secure," on 19 September. Several were killed and two dozen taken prisoner. "About a fortnight after," according to William Hubbard [actually 10 October], "the same Indians attempted to take a Mill at Hadley, two miles from the Town," but in Hubbard's account they failed. Hubbard, *Present State of New-England,* 2:239-40.

2. On 10 October 1677 the Massachusetts General Court ordered that the third Thursday in November would be held as a day of thanksgiving for "the great plentifull harvest, a cessation of the wrath and rage of the ennemy in great measure, &c." Nathaniel B. Shurtleff, ed., *Records of the Governor and Company of the Massachusetts Bay in New England (1628–86),* 6 vols. (Boston, 1853–54), 5:156.

From Thomas Walley, 19 November 1677

Rev. Walley's health clearly was failing. Both to assist him in his duties and to prepare a future pastor for Barnstable, Gov. Hinckley and others wooed a young Harvard graduate, Samuel Angier. Their efforts ultimately were unsuccessful, but the following letters suggest the difficulties that often factored in negotiations with prospective ministers, and with church members, especially in Plymouth Colony.

Reverend Sir and my Deare ffriend

I this Day he[1] received yo^rs[2] by a Son of Elder Coachmans for which I give yo^u thanks and truly yor Letters are worth more but the poor only acknowledg Kindnesses I am very glad of the book yo^u sent me for I had some desire to read it againe. I pray yo^u returne hearty thanks from me to that holy Laboriouse and Loving seat of god to whom I and many others are greatly obliged his works praise him happy are they that are of publik use in theyr generat^n As for Mr Angier[3] I should be glad of his Company and Labors but desire he may have some assurance of what shall be promised Mr Hinkly and Mr Huckins are forward in it I feare there will be but few more found to engage much but I would have nothing that I write hinder his Coming if he Could take a Journey hither in yor Company he would then the better Know what to doe—the Law yo^u write of for taking the oath of Allegiance[4] seems to have much policy in it I wish the event answere expectation many that have bin obedient subjects to the King have scrupled that oath more then the oath of supremisy—at present my body is fraile my health not soe good as it hath bin I have need of yor prayers and should be glad to see yo^u my hearty Love to yor selfe and Good m^rs Cotton I am
yo^rs in o^r deare Lord

Tho: Walley

Barnstable Nov: 19 1677:

Cotton Family Papers 7:36, Prince Library, Rare Books and Manuscripts, Boston Public Library. Addressed "ffor the Reverend and my Loving ffriend Mr John Cotton Pastour of the church of christ in Plimoth these."

---

1 I.e., "have."

2 Not found.

3 Samuel Angier (1655–1719); see the letter of 17 September 1679 from Thomas Cooper et al., below.

4 On 1 November 1677, the General Court enacted a law that "noe pson whoe hath Not taken the oath of fidellitie shall have libertie to voate in any Towne meeting untill he hath taken the aforesaid oath." *PCR*, 11:248.

From Thomas Hinckley, 10 December 1677

Rev^rd^ SirI rec^d^ yours of ye 8th instant[1] for wch I return you many thanks, & herewth acquaynt you how far there hath beene a prcedure as to ye affayre respecting m^r^ Angier viz: I pposed to ye Congregation on ye next Lords day after exercise, taking it for granted that they were sensible of ye great advantage wch wold accrew to have our children & youth brought up & educated in good literature & that now there was a probable opertunity to obtayn a meete pson to teach a grammer schoole & to write & sometimes to be helpfull to m^r^ Walley if need were & therefore desired for the more orderly managing of that affayre they wold please to meete at m^r^ Walleys ye next second day at even so many as cold, divers accordingly came but by reason of ye cold season & divers being absent on ye report brought of a house on fire there was not that full meeting as was to be desired, yet those p^r^sent from both ends <*of*> & middle of ye Towne manifested there good affection to that work (as a some others pticularly had also don who were not there) & there appeared six of them p^r^sent, willing to ingage to make up what shold be wanting of ye summe of 20^£^ in money (for this yeare) pposed: only as to his helping of m^r^ walley he shold be at his owne free pleasure whether once in 2 months more or lesse as he might see cause for his own privileg or advantage as to his better prperation in the work of ye ministry wch we suppose he is designed to in Gods time, wch was no further intended by my self in what I that way pposed to him, yet those p^r^sent (& I have reason to judge also many that were absent are of ye same minde) manifested theire readines (as reason requires) to a due further consideration of his labors in case Gods pvidence shold so order it that by reason of m^r^ Walleys bodily wekenes he shold be put on any constant or considerable improvements of his gifts amongst us: & though I cold have wisht he might have beene better pvided then at my house, yet at p^r^sent things seeme so farr as it he must be contended, if he come, wth such accommodation as we can afford. we had hoped to have had a more full meeting on ye day of thanksgiving but that proving so stormy few were p^r^sent, so that we wayt now for a more full meeting next 5th day at lecture or ye first convenient season provided an opertunity may be for more to manifest their good affection to prmote so good a work of wch from ye generality of our people I doubt not but to receive wch may possibly be more incouraging to him: after wch I intend to write to him & send you if your man be not gon before, but if he shold, if you please to write to him, it wold be very acceptable, if he wold come wth your son John to give you a vissit & you wth him to give m^r^ Walley a vissit (who is Desirous to have you both preach here) whereby m^r^ Angier might have opertunity also ye better to satisfy himself either they here to continue, or appoynt a time for his after coming if God please to incline his mynde thereto: howevr I hope his vissit should not be chargeable to him, some small matter will be conferred on him to beare his charges, not elce at p^r^sent (fearing the messenger may stay) but referr you to Geo: Huckins—who intends to visit you I with my respects & my wifes affectionatly to your self w[th] m[ris] Cotton & all frinds. craving your continued prayers. I Committ you to the keeper of his Israell & rest Sir

yours greatly obliged in effect as in affection

Thos Hinckley

Barnstable 10 of Decb. 77.

Sir there is like to be but about 6 schollers at p[r]sent to attend a grammer schoole whereby he will have lesse labor & more opertunity for his other studdies then where a schoole is more numeros. Possibly there may be a few more in winter time & but a [fe]w to learn to write & cipher. he may have the benefitt to himself of any schollers from any other Townes if any such present: only m[ris] Gorams son[2] who belongs to our church & hath accommodations in our Towne though at p[r]sent she live a littell wthout our lyne in yarmoth bounds, by reason of her myll standing there, is to be accoted as one of our Towne. in case Pvidence shold order its so that he cannot come this winter I could be heartily glad that he would aply himself to joyn in full communion w[th] y[e] church there it seeming most suitable that such who are to teche others to observe all things whatsoevr Christ hath commanded, shold themselves example them thereunto not doubting but his love to Christ will putt him on desire to seek & enjoy him in the use of all his ordinances &tc. my pen hath deceivd me in y[e] multiplication of these lines. vale Charissime dom[3]

Tui acmaentissime

T: H.

Cotton Family Papers 7:37, Prince Library, Rare Books and Manuscripts, Boston Public Library. Addressed "These ffor the Rev[rd] and his worthily esteemd ffrind m[r] John Cotten dd In Plimoth." Endorsed "From m[r] Hinckley December, 10: 1677:"

---

1. Not found.
2. Capt. John Gorham of Barnstable died 5 February 1676 of wounds suffered in the Great Swamp Fight the previous December. His son John led a company of men in the 1690 campaign against Quebec. Trayser, *Barnstable*, 107, 112.
3. "Hail, dear sir."

Cotton Mather engraved by Peter Pelham.
Courtesy of the American Antiquarian Society.

To Cotton Mather, 11 December 1677

Plimouth December, 11:1677:

Charissime Cognate[1] I am heartily ingaged to you for your love & respect manifested in your Epistles iterated & reiterated, I hope the next winter (if God till then spares us) wee shall not need to write to one another, but may vivâ voce discourse as now wee cannot: The power of Satan in hurrying soules to hell through divine permission is dreadfully amazing; a man of Sandwich about a fortnight since had his neck within the rope, but full execution was prevented by his Brother's timous[2] approach to loosen the rope: Dec: 4: before day & till some time in the night after was here such a dreadfull storme, as hath not bin knowne these 28: yeares, viz. Jan: 13:1649: the sabbath before your blessed uncle (now in heaven)[3] preached his first sermon in that meeting house lately consumed; In this town it blew downe one dwelling house, & one barne, & killed nigh an 100 geese, which were next morning by sundry taken upon the shoareside, it was with us a day appointed for publick Thanksgiving, but very few could attend it, a humbling providence! That man of Sandwich who the weeke before had almost killed himselfe, was by the fall of his owne house (the top of it) almost killed in this storme, but he is yet spared: I now send by Starkey for John to be with me a while this winter; your paper-messenger at their returne shall be very welcome: <*our*> though your Aunt have noe salutations from you, yet by me she heartily salutes you, soe wee doe both, & your father & mother. The God of your fathers love & blesse you forever,

soe prayes, your Affectionate uncle,

John Cotton

Houses & barnes many were blowne downe in other townes by this storme.

Mather Papers1:21, Prince Library, Rare Book & Manuscripts, Boston Public Library. Addressed "These For his Dearely Beloved Cousen, Mr Cotton Mather, at his fathers house, in Boston." Endorsed "Uncle J. C. Dec. 11. 1677." The back of the letter contains notes in Mather's hand.

---

1. "Dearest relation."
2. I.e., "timely"? The editors found no other record of this attempted suicide.
3. Samuel Mather (1626–1671) was the older brother of Increase Mather. Cotton Mather later wrote that his uncle was "the first that did Preach the Gospel to the North Church of Boston," but he left for England in 1650, never to return. He became minister to a church in Dublin in 1656 and died there at the age of forty-five. *Sibley's Harvard Graduates,* 1:78-87.

From Daniel Gookin, 16 December 1677

With the smallpox spreading in Boston and its environs, the Cottons obviously feared for their scholar son John's safety and requested that he be allowed to return home, bringing his studies with him. Gookin's letter reveals something of the workload of a Harvard student of the period.

REVEREND S^R

By ye lines I received from you ye last week I am informed of your desire that your son should come home, which m^r Oakes[1] with m^r [Cerles?] & my selfe did judge was expedient & could not bee pleaded against considering ye occasion, I hope it will bee noe disadvantage to him in ye least degree, since he will be under ye eye and inspection of a father & such a father. He is with his classe just entering upon ye study of ye Sacred tongue, they begun Schickards Grammar[2] ye last week I did purpose when they had once recited that, y^t y^y should begin <*theire*> ye hebrew Psalter with y^r Grammar ye Second time. In Greek they have made progresse so far as to finish theire Grammar and recite 8 or 9 cap. in ye Acts of ye Apost: I <*had*> purpose within 3 weeks or a moneth to putt y^m upon reading some <*poet*> Greek Poet afterwards (if God please) some of Isocrates orations, for Latin they have read a cunsiderable part of Tullies Oration pro & luentio.[3] I designe after y^r finishing of y^t Oration to Let y^m reade Horace for some time. And thus you have an account of such studies which per [...] y^e <*same hand*> first <*halfe yeare have*> entrance have ben wont to improve y^r time in, and wch I suppose will fill up your sons time this winter, y^r are only besides y^s readings and declamations, which S^r I need not to mind you of. I wish S^r y^t ye last may be attended by him as often (while he is from ye college) as can be with convenience—Sr Your Son was with mee since I received your letter, desired that he might have a Bithnea.[4] I (having your warrant for what I did) delivered it to him.

There is nothing further S^r I need trouble you withall. But humble service to your selfe & Virtuous Ladye, wishing that ye peace of God that passeth all understanding may dayly possess your soules, that he, who commands his blessing when & where & how he pleaseth may command it upon you & yours, I need not to say y^t I hope John will improve his time to ye best advantage.

I need only to adde y^t I hope I <*have*> shall have your prayers y^t ye Colledge shall have y^m, y^t All Gods people in y^s parts shall have y^m. The small poxks do spread at Charlestowne and Boston.

m^r Sheperd of Charlestowne[5] was taken very ill on friday night, It doth not yet appeare what his distemper is, but some do feare much y^t it may be y^t infectious distemper. I hope God will remember his people & shew mercy in y^t respect. Let us be helped by your prayers, and by all that love ye peace & welfare of our land.

Sr Pray parden my prolixity & every thing *<may>* that [...] bin tedious to you & thereby [...] mee to bee & to remaine to be yo[ur] [h]umble servant

[D]aniel Gookin Junr

Decemb. 1677

The worth of ye Bithnea is Eleven d. but ye price shall be but nine: Eight is ye lowest.—

Curwen Family Papers, American Antiquarian Society. Endorsed "From Mr Daniel Gookin Junior December. 16: 1677:" One large hole on final side of the manuscript.

---

1. Urian Oakes (1631–1681) graduated from Harvard in 1649. About 1654 he traveled to England, where he served as "Chaplain to One of the most Noted Persons then in the Nation," according to Cotton Mather. Bearing with the persecution of nonconformists after the Restoration, in 1671 he finally accepted the repeated invitations from the church in Cambridge to become its pastor. Along with Rev. Thomas Shepard of neighboring Charlestown, he opposed broad toleration in New England. *Sibley's Harvard Graduates,* 1:173-85.

2. Wilhelm Schickard (1592–1635), German astronomer and mathematician, is perhaps best known today for having devised a calculating machine in 1623. Also in that year, however, he produced *Horologium ebraeum*, a Hebrew grammar book that was popular at Harvard.

3. Possibly a work by Thomas Tully (1620–1676), English divine. *Dictionary of National Biography*, ed. Leslie Stephen and Sidney Lee, 63 vols., (London, 1885–1900).

4. Possibly a reference to letters of Pliny the Younger, who was governor of Bithnia, or Bithynia (later Byzantium) from 111 to 113. In one famous exchange, Pliny reported his actions against Christians to the emperor Trajen. If this is the reference, then presumably it is a small book used for the instruction of the scholars.

5. Thomas Shepard (1635–1677) was the second son of the famous Rev. Thomas Shepard of Cambridge. A graduate of Harvard College in 1653, he was ordained the teacher of the Charlestown church six years later. He supported the "Coercive Power" of the magistrates in matters of religious toleration, especially with regard to Baptists. During the smallpox epidemic of 1677–1678, more than ninety persons died in Charlestown. Shepard "went with his Life in His Hand," according to Cotton Mather, to "One of his Flock, who lying sick of this Distemper, desired a Visit from him." Shepard caught the disease and died on 22 December 1677. *Sibley's Harvard Graduates,* 1:327-35.

To Increase Mather, 1 January 1678

As this and some of the following letters make clear, towns in Plymouth Colony had been spared the smallpox epidemic only temporarily.

Plimouth January, 1: 1677:

Revd & Deare Brother

Those Gallants that said at Boston they would come & keep Christmasse, (you know where) were as good as their word; how it was celebrated I know not: our Govr is troubled with the gout: what God is doing with us I know not, soe God would have it that a Taunton man must take the infection at Boston & goe home, and 3 or 4 dayes after come downe to Plimouth & soe to Duxbury, & there in a few dayes dye of the small pox: wee doe not heare that it is begun with any else but the woman of that house where the man dyed hath bin ill these 2 dayes; The Lord fit us for his holy will: I intreate of you to spare my Cousen Cotton to buy these necessary things mentioned in the note, I know not who else to request such a kindnesse of, & it being a matter of life & death, pray gratify me herein: wee also earnestly request of you to send us your Judgment of this disease what is good to prevent it, & how persons visited with it must be ordered & attended, if any oyle of Tarre be to be had, if you send any I will send you money for it: my selfe & wife present due respects to you & yours, desiring your prayers for us,

I rest, your affectionate Brother

John Cotton

pray let my Cous: write & now send me an exact copy of Mr Page his bond: I must take some order about what shortly will be due to me therein. I send forty three shil: in silver to buy what the note mentions:

Mather Papers 2:30, Prince Library, Rare Books and Manuscripts, Boston Public Library. Addressed "These For the Reverend, his Deare Brother, Mr Increse Mather, Teacher of a church of Christ, at Boston." Endorsed "Br J. C. J[...] 1677."

To Increase Mather, 7 January 1678[1]

[Top of page torn; several lines lost] as soone as he hath delivered it because my wife hath not set her hand to the deed; I kno[w] not tricks in law, but that 25 pd which he is to deliver for me at your house this next Feb: 17: is noe sooner given into your hands but is really yours at your service, & therefore you may lawfully keep it as your owne:

That family in which the Taunton man dyed of the small pox at Duxbury is now sorely visited with that desease, the man & his wife & 2 children & their 2 servants all downe at once, & some of them exceeding bad: one man in Plimouth (the Treasurers son) hath these 2 dayes had dangerous symptomes, & my starky this last night complai[ned] of paine in his head & universall Coldnes, he saith he smelt a very ill savour being neere the dead corps of mr Paine[2] (who I suppose is not at all a kin much lesse brother to Moses Paine) what God is doing with us I know not, I earnestly desire your hearty remembrance of us before the Lord that wee may be prepared to meete God in the way of his judgements: our need of divine pitty & help is much the more, considering my wife is neere her time[3] [p]ray [for] her.

[Top of page torn; several lines lost] [N]ewhaven [. . . .] reconcile tha[t] [. . . .] what he mentions in his letter to Govr winslow (in that ship which brought the Contribution) of his brother Cotton living neere him, which letter of his was (as he saith) sent 3 moneths before mine (directed to Newhaven) he writes that Papists are more numerous in that Citty then Protestants & seemes to have some awfull expectation of changes, if any evill there have bin designed since I perceive it is noe more then what he looked for:

I am glad I wrote to him upon his mentioning my name to our Govr (though happily he thought it was my Bro: Cotton[4] that lived neere him) I hope you have sent that letter with yours to him before now) please to informe me when you will have an opportunity to send to him againe, for seeing he is pleased to desire lines from me I esteem it my duty to answer him therein: our kinde Love to Sister & Cous: Cotton etc with due respects to you, I rest,

your Affectionate Brother

John Cotton

I expect to send these by Leift: way[5] at his returne

[Top of page torn; several lines lost] white they are [. . . .] money, it is all pro[. . . .]re stored taken to about 30 sh[il:?] the wronged [. . . .] suspect a man, discourse him, exa[. . . .] he denys the fact, Home comes every [. . . .] others about the Theft & their suspi[. . . .] partners who sustained the wron[g] [. . . .] suspected man with them, bef[ore?] som[. . . .] he denys Guilt, & soe they cease, only [. . . .] after all this

I having heard much di[. . . .] lest there might be secret guilt in the [. . . .] wrath to follow him, I secretly obtained [. . . .] solemnly with him, as you may appre[. . . .] hopes of attaining the end, he did reque[. . . .] the partyes & promi[ ] as soone as he [. . . .] this from him to open triall: Q: Is n[. . . .] I pay not the money? & if I be urged [. . . .] was stolen, what answers may best be [. . . .] to such inquirers, suppose a Magis[. . . .] for your Answer:

Yours,

J: C:

I have noe witnesse, but in heaven, that th[. . . .] promised to repay, he may deny again [. . . .]

Mather Papers 2:31, Prince Library, Rare Books and Manuscripts, Boston Public Library. Addressed "These For the Reverend, his Dear[e] Brother, Mr Increse Mat[her,] Teacher of a Church of Christ; at Boston." The top and left side of the paper is torn away, apparently at the folds.

---

1. Prince's note: "Plimouth. Jan. 7. 1677/8."
2. Cotton's contemporaries believed that some diseases could be transmitted by "miasmas," foul odors such as those caused by decaying vegetation (for example, in swamps) and flesh.
3. The Cottons' ninth child, Samuel, was born 10 February 1678 and died 23 December 1682.
4. Seaborn Cotton; see the letter from Seaborn Cotton of 4 February 1679, below.
5. Possibly Richard Way (d. 1697), cooper of Dorchester, member of the Artillery Company and lieutenant at Castle Island. Savage, *Genealogical Dictionary,* 4:440-41.

From Thomas Walley, 16 January 1678

REVEREND SIR

for yo^{rs}[1] I give yo^{u} thanks if m^{r} Mathers news be true it is very good but we are doubtfull there was some mistake in figures or some other way one of our vessels Came home but 2 or 3 days before January that brought other news—as to my selfe I think I am somthing better then I have bin but still weak and often ill but I have Cause to be thankfull god is good to me. as to yor question or Case[2] I Can say little—only this

1 it is not safe upon the account of the Law to divulge what is Confessed to yo^{u} alon suppose the man deny it againe how will yo^{u} prove it

2 if any man out of trouble of Conscience Confess his sin privatly provided the Crime be not Capitall and that noe Innocent pson Suffer for want of the discovery of the <*crime*> same I judg it may and ought to be kept secret but if at last the pson falls into the Same Sin againe and againe then the sinner hath brooken his promis: of reformation and god by his pvidence hath discovered him

but if there be 2 or more witnesses that have heard yo^{u} say he Confessed to yo^{u} then yo^{u} have betrayed yo^{r}selfe but I have heard of noe such thing

for the money though yor paying of it will strengthen theyr suspition yet yo^{u} need not Care if they will not receive the money upon yor tearmes Let them stay till they are willing—yor book I have sent yo^{u} and give yo^{u} thankes for the lent of it it is a good book and many choice things in it Sir I present my hearty Love to yo^{r}selfe and m^{rs} Cotton the Lord bless yo^{u} and yo^{rs} pray for me I am

yor affectionate and truly Loving friend

Tho: Walley

Jan: 16th 1677

Sir I have sent yo^{u} some trouble by Mr Howland if he Canno^{t} doe it him selfe wch is to send money I have sent sealed in a bag to my son at Boston which I pray yo^{u} doe for me with his letter when yo^{u} have opportunity

Curwen Family Papers, American Antiquarian Society. Addressed "ffor the Reverend and my much honoured ffriend m^{r} John Cotton pastour of the church of christ in Plimouth these dd." Endorsed "From Mr Walley January, 16: 1677."

---

1. Not found.
2. The details of Cotton's "case," to which the mutilated postscript in the previous letter may also refer, is unknown to the editors. In the following letter, Increase Mather appears also to be giving Cotton advice on the matter.

From Increase Mather, 8 February 1678

yor tur[....] I [....] in time [....] .1. A man [....] his [promise?] [....] unlawful [....] be [....] ^{y}s [illeg.] shold be [joined?] to ye Publick [illeg.], [....] 2. These scriptures w^{ch} [illeg.] faithfullness in keping secrets &c to bind ye Conscience in ye case. 3 No man should wthout necessary cause divulge ye sin & shame of his Neighbor. 4 A ministers breast ought to be sacred, & none should think y^{t} that is by a Troubled Conscience Committed to him may be divulged by him. I am much grived to hear of m^{r} walleys sickness. God in mercy spare & restore him if it be his will. His death would be a black omen of new troubles hastning up^{n} ye Colony. I suppose you may hear y^{t} m^{r} Norton is dead m^{ris} (Anthony) Chicly was buried y^{s} day. The small pox is in 5 or 6 Houses in Boston at both [ends?] of ye Town. I hear y^{t} 32 fishing Boates were driven away from Marblehead 30 [illeg.] in ye storm. Tis feared y^{y} are generally cast away. one was found neer Boston, ye men being dead. R^{ts} to my sister. The Lord ye great deliverer give her a good [illeg.] To his grace in christ, I Comm^{d} you, & rest

yor affectionate Brother

I Mather

Febr. 8. 1677.8.

Cotton Family Papers 8:1, Prince Library, Rare Books and Manuscripts, Boston Public Library. Addressed "for the Revd my dear Brother mr John Cotton, Pastor of ye Church in Plymouth." Top third of letter torn off.

From James Oliver, [2 March 1678?]

[BOST?] 2^{D} MARC[H]

MR COTTEN

Sir after my kind respects [....] may desire to hear of the last [....] being 17th feb came on [....] the lake where they be [many?] [....] are 200 mils short of Card [....] [illeg.] ye governer [....] to go after their [....] our Governer sent a letter [....] but it was not Com to his hand our [...] men have got ther wives and Children and the rest of the Captives ar ther saving and old man that formerly Lived at meadfeild who dyed by the way and a boy they was tired and froward whom the indayns say [illeg.] kild and was presently clapt in chains and is hanged for it. we [heard?] 2 Bunyms that came from [...] [with?] the [...] man we know no present Ground of fear with indyans the smalpox inCreaseth much in our town 3 ar dead sinc my Last to you [20] at Charles towne and [....] 4 [40?] ar returned and but on or two have it tha ar almost wel it is now Com into the [word left out] of this town no time ap[several words illeg.] hav [illeg.] [....]

Cotton Family Papers 8:2, Prince Library, Rare Books and Manuscripts, Boston Public Library. Prince's note: "To the Rev Mr John Cotton at Plimouth from Mr James Oliver of Boston. suppose March. 2. 1677/8. For ye small Pox was then prevailg in Charlestown & Mr willerd of Boston was not ordained till apr. 10. 1678." Letter badly mutilated.

From Thomas Walley, et al., [March 1678?]

To the Reverend elders of the church of christ in Plimoth to be Communicated to the church

Where as Mary Dunham the wife of Jonathan Dunham[1] is in relation to the church of christ in Barnstable being a child [of] that church hath made it her desire that shee may be dismissed to yor church of christ at Plimoth. We doe Commend her to yor watch and Care and pray you to receive her in the Lord that shee may be edified in faith and holiness to the Coming of the Lord to whose grace and blessing we Commend her and you and yor holy Administrations desiring yor prayers for her and us.

In the name and with the Consent of the church

Tho: Walley pastour
Henry Cob
John Aleman [Heman?] Elders

Cotton Family Papers 8:4, Prince Library, Rare Books and Manuscripts, Boston Public Library. Prince's note: "Mr Walley died March. 24. 1677/1678."

---

1. Probably the Jonathan Dunham and Mary Delanoy who married 29 November 1655. *Vital Records of Plymouth, Massachusetts to the Year 1850,* comp. Lee D. Van Antwerp, ed. Ruth Wilder Sherman (Camden, Me., 1993), 662. See also 20 July 1694.

From George Shove, [6 March 1678?]

Reverend S[r]

My syncere Love & Respects with my wifes to yo[r] selfe & M[rs] Cotton we are all at present in good health blessed be God & there are none dangerously sick in this place. but at Rehoboth the Mortalitie is renewed two were buried there the last weeke: the Lord grant them mercye & staye his holy hand for they are alreadie brought verie Lowe, & helpe us to fear his j[ud]gements. [we?] have no news here but what I suppose is with you. the [....] come sevenight there also [...] a fast at Wob[urn] [....] in order to the renewing [of t]heir Cove[nant] [....] Thatcher is to be there. M[r] [Keith] & [...] was to goe down that weeke if the Lord [....]. Not else at p[r]sent but desiring fellowship in yo[r] prayers I remaine S[r]

Y[r] affectionate friend & Bro.

G. S.[1]

Cotton Family Papers 8:3, Prince Library, Rare Books and Manuscripts, Boston Public Library. Addressed "the Rev[d]. M[r] John Cotton at Plimouth These." Endorsed "[...] Mr Shove March 7: 1677." Prince's note: "March, 6 suppose 1677/8 Taunton." Letter mutilated in lower center.

1. Prince's note: "ie George Shove."

[To Increase Mather], 21 & 25 March 1678

Barnstable March, 21: 1677:/78:

Revd & Deare Brother

I am now in pretious M[r] walleys study, Just going to the publick worship this fast day, his death is expected before the Morrow, a poore bleeding mourning church, the post goes for his son, in great distresse,

I am your Affec: Bro:

J: C:

our glory is almost gone,

ah poore plimouth Colony! wee conclude his death before this come to you.[1]

PLIMOUTH. MARCH, 25; 78:

DEARE BROTHER

The fast day above mentioned prooved soe rainy, that they sent not that day to Boston. on Friday morning I tooke my last leave of that Holy man of God, who yesterday about the time of his usuall going to the publick worship entered into his eternall Sabbath: In the whole time of his languishing he had sweet peace of conscience, the peace of God did rest upon that Son of peace, he told me [he] found as much need of christ as ever; I asked him what counsell from him I should impart to the ministry, his Reply was, he was not worthy to commend any thing to them, but said, his desire was, that the ministry would keep their garments pure & walke close with God, he added, methinks the magistracy is more decayed then the Ministry, yet I doubt not but the best minister in the Country sees a need to reforme. He did solemnely incourage me with hopes of a blessing upon my ministeriall labours; & said wee must part, but I leave you with confidence of meeting you againe with Joy: Many young ones at severall times whilst I was there flocked to his bed side, to whom he did with very great seriousnesse & solemnity of spirit give this counsell, that they should highly esteeme of & improove the Covenant God had made with them, it is, (said he) not a small thing for God to say, I am thy God, though some have despised it, I hope they are now of a better minde, the children of the church have peculiar promises made to them, & a peculiar interest in the prayers of the church which are for their owne members, these individuall words & many more did he more then once utter in my hearing last weeke to Church-seed; that blessed mouth is now silenced:

our church have appointed next wednesday for a solemne fast: His Funerall is on Thursday, where I thinke to be: I wrote to you last Monday, thinking my sons would soone have bin with you, but crosse winds have hindered, the first faire winde I hope you may have this & that; the messenger from B: to M^r^ walley called not at my doore yester evening, if he had, I had written & sent this by him.

Mather Papers 2:41, Prince Library, Rare Book & Manuscripts, Boston Public Library. No address; back of letter has apparently unrelated notes written in Mather's hand.

---

1. Thomas Wally died on 24 March 1678.

From Jonathan Tuckney,[1] 3 April 1678

Deare & much respected Cousen

Your very kind letter of Novemb 7 1677[2] came to my hand about three weeks since, which I [....] much rejoiced in, & do blesse God that I have so [....] you mindfull of me in so far distant a part of the wo[rld I am] glad that our letter-acquaintance is thus happily after so long intermission renewed; and indeed your answer to mine in 1660 (wch you mention in this last) I never received. Blessed be God that hath been so gracious to you as you intimate, in publique & private, ministerial & domestical respects. He who hath hitherto graciously, still please to goe on to do you & yours good in Christ our Saviour. As to myself I have not been a married man so long as you by 5 years; (marrying Novemb 16 1665) since when God hath given us seven children, foure sons, three daughters. whereof foure sons, one daughter living. But yet God doth not leave us without chastisement. My wife & youngest child being both ill at this present, & having been so for neer a fortnight, though not without hopes of recovery through mercy. The Lord fitt us all for His Pleasure & better us all by His Dealings. we & my mother in law (my Fathers 4th & last wife that had been wife to Dr Spurstow before) have lived in Hackney six year & a half. But I am not in the Ministry, only preach somtimes to help a friend now & then. ordination I would fain have if it might be without snares & difficult terms. of none of the Bishops is to be Expected without subscription & conformity, & of those of the Presbyterian Perswasion not without having some people constantly to labour amongst, which is hard to meet with, there being so many ministers Non-conformest that [...] ingrosse them. I have for my part Employment enough (till Providence [...] offer any other) in looking over & fitting out for the Press some of my Reverend deceased Fathers labours either in the Pulpit, or as Professor at Cambridge.[3] I have prepared for the Presse his Divinity—Readings & Determinations in the Scholes (at Cambridge) I hope they will be printed this summer. And against that they be out I hope I shall have ready His Sermons on the 45th Psalm, which Psalm he preacht over at Boston about 40 yeares prior. Its also some other things which [...] say its a thousand pities that they should [....] rixari. As to publick News that you desire, truly I [can] supply you with little at least of any that is good. Its the wonderful Mercy of God to this people how that from year to year still we have the Gospel of Peace & Peace with the Gospel; that we are not over=run with Popery; for doubtlesse that is the great desire & design of sundry (too many) of our great ones; especially since this great encreasing power of the French. We are, God knowes, a poor & peeled people; He grant we be not meted out to destruction. A great deal of pride & vanity, disention & enmity among Professors presage no good. O pray that God would amend & reform us, I am heartily [glad to?] read the additions (in yor letter) to my Cousen Mather's[4] Hist [....] with you being revived. The good Lord if it be His will sca[....] delight in warr; humble His people & prepare them for mercy [...] [be] stow it upon them I shall upon your desire take the freedom to write a few lines to my (now) Cousin Mather; hoping for a Return from him that may bring us into mutual acquaintance, which I shall be glad of. And I shall once more write to my aged Cousen Whiting.[5] Since my last died his Nephew our Cousen Mr Joseph Whiting of Boston[6] a good & usefull man. I pray you Deare Cousen Remember us in yor prayers, as I desire to do you & all yo^rs: My hearty & affectionate respects I pray to my Cousen yor Brother Seaborne. And still let me have the kindnesse so freely promised in yor last, of a Paper=visit yearly. Truly what God will do with his Church both here & abroad we canot say. Clouds gather apace & look very thick, threatening a storme. It is a doubtlesse [...] both duty & interest of all God's people to live by faith upon Himself Hab 3: 17: 18.[7] Micah 7: 7: 8, 9.[8] God help you & me & all o^rs & His to wait on Him & keep His way, which if He do, He will Exalt us, when the wicked are cutt off, we shall see it. Among the several Trials my Father before me & myself have had, one considerable one was the losse of my Father's Library in the dreadfull fire of London 1666. A very good library it was, & had been gathering many years, & cost deare; but lost then without recovery. God help me to study His word & my own heart. Indeed the losse was more to me in regard my Father had made good use of it his time & did not survive the fire foure years dying Febr 24 1669/70 but I that had <*such*> so much time before me might have studied it especially in this vacancy I am in from any publick & standing Employment. But fiat voluntas Domini.[9] My Father did buy a Library about a twelvemonth after the fire, which hath good bookes several, which I can (blessed be God) read & make use of. I have a Brother in law (that married my onely sister Mary 26 years agoe) Mr John Whittock a Non-Conformist Presbyterian Minister, lives in Nottinghamshire, a very good, able prudent man, who is ready to advise [....] any thing; & whom I usually see (either here at London or there[....]) once a yeare. <*He*> They have onely one child a son of about 17 a hopefull pious youth, that <*And*> studies university learning. Our eldest (Anthony) about 11 years old goes to schoole in London & is (I blesse God) pregnant for His time. But what to do with youth in this corrupt time of the Church & Universities we well know not. The Lord provide & direct. I have myself been out of Cambridge ever Since August 24 1662 for not [sub]scribing according to our Act of Uniformity. Happy you [in?] NE that are not pestered with those things [....] myself & weary you. God keep you, & [....] hands in His good work. with hearty salu[tations] to yo^rself & my good cousen. I commend you to God & am

yor much endeared Kinsman

Jonathan Tuckney

Hackney April. 3. 1678

Curwen Family Papers, American Antiquarian Society. Addressed "For his deare & much respected Cousen Mr John Cotton Minister of the Gospel at Plymouth in N. England." Endorsed "From my cousen Mr Jonathan Tuckney April, 3: 1678: Received, July, 20: 1678:" Several small holes, probably caused when Cotton opened the wax seal, and ink stains.

---

1. When John Cotton Sr. resolved to emigrate to New England, he resigned the vicarage of Boston, Lincolnshire. His cousin Anthony Tuckney (1599–1670) succeeded him in that place. By his first of four wives, Tuckney had a son, Jonathan (1639?–1693). As his letter reveals, Jonathan did not pursue the ministry, and he furnishes some reasons for his decision. One observer added that, although Jonathan was of good learning, it was "render'd useless by melancholy." *DNB*, s.v. "Tuckney, Anthony."
2. Not found.
3. Some of Tuckney's works appeared in print as *Forty Sermons* (1676); *Prælectiones Theologicæ* followed (1679). *DNB*, s.v. "Tuckney, Anthony."
4. Increase Mather.
5. Rev. Samuel Whiting (1597–1679), like John Cotton Sr., had come from Boston, Lincolnshire. He was pastor of the church in Lynn. Savage, *Genealogical Dictionary*, 4:520.
6. Boston in Lincolnshire.
7. Hab. 3:17-18: "Although the fig tree shall not blossom, neither shall fruit be in the vines; the labour of the olive shall fail, and the fields shall yield no meat; the flock shall be cut off from the fold, and there shall be no herd in the stalls: Yet I will rejoice in the LORD, I will joy in the God of my salvation."
8. Mic. 7:7-9: "Therefore I will look unto the LORD; I will wait for the God of my salvation: my God will hear me. Rejoice not against me, O mine enemy: when I fall, I shall arise; when I sit in darkness, the LORD shall be a light unto me. I will bear the indignation of the LORD, because I have sinned against him, until he plead my cause, and execute judgment for me: he will bring me forth to the light, and I shall behold his righteousness."
9. "The Lord's will be done."

From Thomas Hinckley, 29 April 1678

REVRD SIR

after my best respects to your self & mrs Cotten wth many thanks for all your great kindnes &^{c} These are to desire you to do your best to further our design, in obteyning m^{r} ffoster for our supply I have writ to him p joynt desire of our Church & Towne to pitty our needy condition wch m^{r} Lothrop carrys to him if the yarmoth vessell have winde to sayle to day elc bro: Huckins I think will carry it to morrow by land: pray (wth my respects affectionately to m^{r} Mather, ingage him, wth whom elce you thinke meet, to pmote that affayre for us I would be glad if he would give us a vissett as speedily has might be, <*that*> I being to be at Boston 23 of May shall have opertunity to wayt on him down ther, & if we cold know y[e] time he pitches on shall take care to send one to wayt on him up hither, in case he favors not to come by sea wth m[r] Lothrop yarmoth vessell. not elc now, being in hast but craving your earnest remembrances of us at throne of grace who desire not to forgett you I rest

y[r] affectionat friend & serv[t]

Tho Hinckley

Barnstable 29 April. 78

Cotton Family Papers 8:5, Prince Library, Rare Books and Manuscripts, Boston Public Library. Addressed "These ffor the Revrd and his worthily esteemed good friend Mr John Cotten Pastor of ye Church of Christ in Plimoth dd." Endorsed "From mr Hinckley, April, 29: 1678:."

Memorandum for a fast day,[1] 17 May 1678

The causes of setting apart this day for fasting & prayer, May, 17: 1678:

1: In pardon of all my sins & perfect cleansing from them.

2: For a blessing upon my ministry to the conversion & aedification of soules.

3: For spetiall direction and guidance from God unto and in the improvement of some meanes that may be effectuall through Gods blessing for the suppression of growing evills in this place, even among professors & espetially the sin of sensuality.

4: For a gratious supply to the bereaved Churches.

5: For sparing & healing mercy to my wife, now labouring under divers affecting weaknesses.

6: For mercy to my poore children, espetially for their soules that they may live before God, that they may be kept from temptations unto sin & in spetiall that my sons at Cambridge may be blessed in their learning & fitted for the Lords service, & that converting grace may be poured forth on all my children & servants.

7: That God would prevent the infectious desease from coming amongst us.

8: For mercy to the whole Israel of God.

Cotton Family Papers 8:6, Prince Library, Rare Books and Manuscripts, Boston Public Library. There is no signature on this document, but the handwriting is clearly that of Cotton.

---

1. In the records of the Plymouth church for 1678, Cotton wrote: "The chh set apart March, 27: as a day of Fasting & prayer for continuance of Peace healing the small px, & for sundry of our ministers that were languishing & for other mercies." *CSM*, 22:154. This memo is apparently Cotton's plan for a personal fast day as well.

To Cotton Mather, 11 June 1678

Plimouth, June 11: 1678:

Deare Cousen

I make noe question but it is your turne to speake, but it being the longest day in the yeare, I will spend a few minutes to salute you, & your deare parents, desiring & hoping that at the returne of this boat you will bestow a few salutatory lines upon me, Election newes wee have have none but omnia ut prius,[1] Mr Treats[2] sermon on Dan: 5: 27:[3] was very choice & esteemed by all Judicious worthy of great Acknowledgment: I shall be glad to heare that the Lord continues health in your family: Is the commencement & your commencing established?[4] Let us know whether the goods be come from o: E: my wife is daily ill, the Lord knowes what the issue will be: your fathers God love you & delight to blesse you, soe prayes

your truly loving uncle

John Cotton.

It is very long since I heard from Cambridge, pray if you can tell how my sons doe there, informe me, & whether the small pox be there? whom doth Charlestowne call? I would know whether Ratcliffe will take wheat for his worke.

Mather Papers 2:51, Prince Library, Rare Book & Manuscripts, Boston Public Library. Addressed "To my Beloved Cousen, Mr Cotton Mather, at his Fathers house, in Boston, be these presented."

---

1. "Everything as before."
2. Samuel Treat (1648–1717), an active missionary to the Natives on Cape Cod, began preaching at Eastham in 1672 and was ordained there in 1675. Weis, *Colonial Clergy*, 208.
3. Dan. 5:27: "TEKEL; Thou art weighed in the balances, and art found wanting."
4. Cotton Mather's Harvard commencement took place on Tuesday, 13 August 1678.

From Cotton Mather, [June 1678]

Hon^{r}ed s^{r}—You know I suppose how If a [illeg.] ye Eldest are Vocales, w^{n} ye rest either semi-vocales or mutes, Behold! how I make a virtue of necessity—Time & business have formrly forbad me to do y^{t} wch at present it but just pmits, ut canis ad nilum.[1]—

<*I am now in Cambridge—ergo if God see meet, my [several words illeg]*.>

It may be s^{r} you'l wonder at my brevity wch a quantum mutatus ab illo—Ille ego qui quondum[2]—I who once use to send by Every opportunity a whole Cartload of news, &c —& spin out like [illeg.] now to furle my sailes, & come just like Cato on ye stage, [Ere?] only to go off again.

But, sir, be pleased to know, I am now at Cambridge—& since it is so, w^{t} should the chief Errand of this epistle be? & the burden of each line, Exit of Each sentence in it, but w^{t} the martyr once—Pray, Pray, Pray—never more need than now—If residing in a place of much temptation, If being debarred ye special opportunityes of seeking and seeing ye face of god wch have once been enjoyed, If an Inconstant frame of sp^{t}, a deceitful hr^{t}, or in a word a cdition full of wants, mutato nomine,[3] be named a need of prayer, then I have gr^{t} cause to bespeak such a boon * * *

Mather Papers 2:51, Prince Library, Rare Books and Manuscripts, Boston Public Library. Written on the back of John Cotton to Cotton Mather, 11 June 1678.

---

1. "How you [I] play at nothing!"
2. "How changed I am from what I was formerly."
3. "By another name."

To Increase Mather, 15 & 16 July 1678

Plimouth July, 15: 1678:

Reverend & Deare Brother

It is soe long a time since I heard of or from you, that I am almost sick of it, & doe therefore greedily embrace this opportunity to salute you, hoping thereby also to heare of the Welfare of you & yours in this afflicting time by that infectious desease: through Gods great mercy it is a day of health with us, the Lord helpe us to improove it aright, that wee may not provoke him to turne our health into sicknesse: God hath gratiously blessed meanes for healing those distempers that were soe afflicting to my wife; soe that she hath now her health comfortably: It is a day also of spetiall mercy with me, through the rich & undeserved grace of God in christ, in respect of the sweet & hearty closing of the spirits of the godly with me in this Church,[1] & the great encouragement & advantage thereby I have to doe my Lords worke; I have found God by afflictions preparing mercy for me, my desire is, that by such choice mercies I may be duly prepared for Afflictions, which I have great reason to be in continuall expectation of:

The Church & people of Barnstable appointed a Fast last Thursday on purpose to beg of God to bow Mr Thachers[2] heart to accept their call; they sent to me to carry on the worke of that day which through Gods helpe I did: they are exceeding unanimous & hearty in their desires to injoy him, I never saw more affection manifested on such an account, I suppose this day will come one from thence to goe to M^r^ T: for his answer, I thinke you may doe God & his people good service in advising & perswading his father to be willing to gratify their desires which are soe earnest & serious: my selfe & wife present hearty Respects & love to you & yours; I suppose your son is at Cambridge: oh pray for my poore sons there[.] I beg your prayers for me & all mine, & rest,

your Affectionate Brother

John Cotton

I long for good newes of your Agents returne.

VERTE

JULY, 16:

Last night I was called out of my bed by one of my neighbours, who brought an Indian with him, who with the rest of Namasket Indians was this night run away from thence hither, by reason that yesterday a growne lad of Ketehte[qutt] (about 4 miles from Namasket) was fishing at the river & heard a gun & then more guns, upon which getting upon a hill not far from the wigwams he saw above 20 Indians assault those of Ketehtequtt & fire upon them & surround divers of them, he supposes all are taken or slaine; the flying Indians beleve the boy saith true; if our English at Namaskett, Bridgwater or Taunton who are all in a vicinity thereabouts hand us any confirmation of this story before sealing you shall have it, else it may passe for an Indian-tale; but because of what was done about Natik[3] wee are now prone to suspect some truth in such reports.

Before sealing, the truth of the matter comes to light, viz, a scout of Punkipaog[4] Indians coming to their countrymen fired their guns in way of salutation, the boy seeing this at a distance was frighted & fled with the other report; soe let all such stories vanish, if God have a favour for & please to deale gratiously with us:

Mather Papers 2:55, Prince Library, Rare Book & Manuscripts, Boston Public Library. Addressed "These For the Reverend, his Deare Brother, Mr Increase Mather, Teacher of a Church of Christ, at Boston." Endorsed " [. . .] C. July. 15. 1678."

---

1. Cotton's maintenance had to be approved by the town each year. A town meeting on 26 June 1678 agreed to pay him "four score pounds…on the same Conditions as it was performed the last yeer," which was one-third in "country pay"—wheat, butter, tar, or shingles; one-third in rye, peas, or malt; and one-third in Indian corn and wheat. *PTR,* 1:154, 157.

2. Rev. Peter Thatcher (1651–1727) was a Harvard classmate (1671) of jurist Samuel Sewall. At the personal invitation of Gov. Hinckley, Thatcher preached twice in Barnstable in 1678. The church there responded favorably and entered into negotiations with him to settle a ministry in Barnstable. *Sibley's Harvard Graduates,* 2:370-79. See the letter from Thomas Hinckley of 13 July 1680, below.

3. A reference to the recent capture by Mohawk raiders of twenty-two Natives at Magunkaquog, a "praying town" southwest of Natick. Jean O'Brien, *Dispossession by Degrees: Indian Land and Identity in Natick, Massachusetts, 1650–1790* (Cambridge, Mass., 1997), 65; Allen W. Trelease, *Indian Affairs of Colonial New York: The Seventeenth Century* (Lincoln, Neb., 1997), 237.

4. Punkapoag, located in modern-day Canton and Stoughton, Massachusetts, was the second of fourteen "praying towns" established in Massachusetts for Christian Indians. Richard W. Cogley, *John Eliot's Mission to the Indians before King Philip's War* (Cambridge, Mass., and London, 1999), 140-41.

From Thomas Hinckley, 15 July 1678

Rever^{D} & deare Sir

after my best respects p^{r}mised wth a thankfull acknowledgmt of your labor of love amongst us & many pticuler kindneses to my unworthy self, & mine, fro time to time, for requitall whereof I am forct to putt you over to him who only can richly supply you & yours, whatever may be lacking on our prts: sir I forgett not your kindnes p^{r} your man a good effect of all ill cause; (our Eld^{r} Chepman phraseth it) wch obligeth me to serve you on like occasion, & something further: in answer to your desire about ye yarn, the scotchman bought it for me but where I know not, it cost 14^{d} p ^{lb} as he informs but it must be reckoned as it falls and I suppose about 16^{d} p ^{lb} for either by mistake in ye waight there or loste by ye way in ye boat or how I know not, nor am I much solicitous about, but so it is that ye 20 ^{lb} is but 18 here. I received from my daughter wiburn (p ye boat w^{ch} & M^{ris} walley now came up in) 12 ^{lb} of like Irish yarn wch holds full wayt here, but where she had it or what it cost she informs me not. she will inform or buy some for M^{ris} Cotten if desired I doubt not. its usually to be had at M^{ris} Tappins or farnums but I suppose will cost more then 14^{d} p ^{lb} there, for I think ye scotchman bought it at first hand from ye mrchant. we are to have a Town meeting next 4th day whither ye business about m^{r} Thatcher was thought best to be referred: wth thanks for your advise therein desiring ye continuance of your fervent prayers to God for our generall & my p^{r}ticuler concerns respects to m^{ris} Cotten in haste (your man staying) I rest

yours affectionatly

Thos Hinckley

my wife p^{r}sents respects affectionatly to you both.

Barnestable 15 July. 78.

Pray Sir please to signify to my son Saml[1] at Sackonet p first opertunity that his oxen are come away hither.

Cotton Family Papers 8:7, Prince Library, Rare Books and Manuscripts, Boston Public Library. Addressed "These ffor ye Revrd & his worthily esteemed frind m^{r} John Cotten pastor of ye Church of xt at Plimoth dd." Endorsed "From m^{r} Hinckley July, 15: 1678:."

---

1. Samuel Hinckley (1653–1697). See 5 March 1696.

To Increase Mather, 26 August 1678

Plimouth August, 26: 1678:

Rev^{D} & Deare Brother

I wrote to you by my Cousen John last weeke, since which, deare Cousen Cotton hath bin our pleasant companion, he frequents every morning our Minerall spring & findes the sutable operation thereoff, if you had once tasted hereoff I beleive you will leave Linne for Plimouth, & then wee shall oft enjoy your good Company:[1] your son looseth not his time but is a diligent student; he is much delighted with this pleasant aire, & now & then intimates his feares of going into the Jawes of infection, but he ownes himselfe tui non sui Juris;[2] he is thinking & once said, he thought there might be some spetiall providence in his being here detained: my horses the 2 John Cottons have to Hampton whence I cannot soe conveniently transport him home by land, and I suppose it would not please you, neither am I willing, to send him home by the boats: I had much rather at their returne have a commission or at least permission for his stay till wee are weary of him, & that will be long enough; but if your fatherly wisdome & love say that he must returne to your house speedily, then at the returne of my horses I must (though agst my yea our affectionate desires) take care for his safe returne: Godly Mr. Baker dyed Aug: 22:[3] at night, was buried, Aug: 24:

About a fortnight since came to our Harbour a Privateer under the Command of one Capt Daniel, the Master, is Solomon Blacklach[4] son to the old man once resident in Boston, they stole away Rodes from New Yorke, I doubt many hellish abominations are here acted in secret by those who have not the feare of God before their eyes: they pretend a commission from the states of Holland & designe to take French vessels in your Easterne parts:

wee heartily salute you & our Sister, let me & mine have a constant interest in your prayers, I am,

your Affectionate Brother,

John Cotton

The small pox is increasing at Eastham, 4 or 5 are now sick of it since the man that dyed of it there. since John sunderlands[5] grand-son had that desease his owne son hath had it; they are both recovered, & none else there taken, through mercy: Mr Thornton hath begun & practised the Synods 5th Prop: in baptising sundry, there are 5 or 6 dissenting bretheren; your book of the 1st principles & de Bap:[6] I wish 20 of them in yarmouth, they might be of great use to establish the unsetled etc

If you could convey this to Deac: Eliot, Elder Bowles[7] might soone have it.

your son presents humble duty to you & his mother, love etc

pray send by this boat the footstoole I left & could not finde for want of sufficient morning light. Nath: I suppose knowes of it:

Mather Papers 2:60, Prince Library, Rare Book & Manuscripts, Boston Public Library. Addressed "These For the Reverend, his Deare Brother, Mr Increase Mather, Teacher of a Church of christ at Boston."

---

1. It is strange to think that a young Cotton Mather, or anyone else, would have come to Plymouth to "take the waters," but this seems to have been the case. The operation of the spring is not otherwise documented to the editors' knowledge, but there is a Watercure Street in the center of Plymouth that may suggest its original whereabouts.
2. "Bound to your rules, not to his own."
3. Rev. Nicholas Baker of Scituate died of "the stone" on 22 August 1678. Deane, *History of Scituate,* 182.
4. On 12 August 1678, the *James Frigate* entered Plymouth harbor, having come via Carolina and, most recently, New York. Solomon Blackleach, or Blackleich, "commander in cheiffe," Capt. Robert Daniel and one John Roads were aboard.Over the next several weeks the crew set about repairing and refitting the vessel, "theire designe unknown to the authoritie heer." Their evasiveness raised suspicions, the more so when Blackleach began surreptitiously recruiting sailors from ships in Boston. Fearing that Blackleach and company intended a privateering or even piratical voyage, and at the urging of Massachusetts magistrates, Plymouth authorities detained the vessel and examined the officers and Roads. They discovered that in fact Blackleach had no privateer's commission but had intended to use one issued to Daniel by the Dutch, and that Roads previously had been banished by Massachusetts for piracy. Furthermore, they learned that Roads had broken out of jail in New York and had come on board the *James Frigate* "in a private way." The case is recorded in *Plymouth Colony Records,* 5:265-70.
5. John Sunderland (1618–1703), a parchmentmaker of Boston, had belonged to the Artillery Company in 1658 but had fallen on hard times by 1672. He subsequently moved to Eastham. Savage, *Genealogical Dictionary*, 4:232-33.
6. The reference is to Increase Mather's *The First principles of New-England, concerning the subject of baptisme & communion of churches* (Cambridge, Mass., 1675).
7. John Bowles was an elder of the Roxbury church and the father of the John Bowles whom Cotton discussed in his letter to Increase Mather of 14 February 1679, below.

From James Keith, 28 October 1678

Bridgewater Octob 28 —78

Reverend & deare Sir

I have much desired but have been denyed opportunity, to Salute you by any Letter since the receit of your last[1] which is now some moneths ago. I return you many thanks for your kinde remembrance of me, in the papers you sent me, deare Sir I do blesse god for his grace towards you in y^t^ you are yet continued in such a comfortable capacity for his work & service when others are removed & Laid aside: it is sad & solemn y^t^ so many Lights are removed from the [illeg]; Mr Thachers' departure is a great breach upon the churches, & is like to be a step to further expretions of gods wrath in y^t kinde; god is punishing a gospell despising people, O y^t Al Xr[2] may know in this theire day the things which belong to theire peace, before they be hid from theire eyes. It pleaseth god in the way of his soveraignty & holiness still to hold me in rods of affliction, though his corrections are in measure. I hope I am somewhat better for the present, by the blessing of god upon the means improved but still under much indisposition to attend my publicke labours in regard of my bodily infirmityes. I have preached only twice since my return from Waymouth, I have but Little hope that I shall be able to preach generally this winter. we are like to be under great difficultyes in y^t respect. I have hade a great comfort hitherto in elder Bretts[3] assistance, but he is like to faile by reason of infirmity of body. Sir I long to see you here & to enjoy your labours one Sabbath, though I know you cannot leave your congregation & family w^tout difficulty, yet I must entreate you to think of it: it would be a great ease to me to be certifyed of your helpe & of the time of your coming, in the mean time let me entreate your fervent prayers to god for us, & for me y^t I may be able to sanctify the Lord under all those trials y^t are appointed to me: I expected my change before this time, but it pleaseth god yet to preserve my spirit by his visitation, whether the Lord hath reserved me for further service or further exercise I can not tell, but I am in his hand, & let him do wth me as it seemeth good to him. my selfe & my wife do tender our cordiall respects to you & Mistris Cotton, w^t hearty acknowledment of all your kindness, but I cannot now enlarge; commanding you to the [nih?] grace & neverfailing mercy of god I must take leave, deare Sir farewell in the Lord so prayeth

Your assurrd freind & affectionate though unworthy brother in the [....]

present my respects to elder Cushman

Curwen Family Papers, American Antiquarian Society. Addressed "For The reverend his affectionate freind Mr John Cotton pastor of the church of christ in Plimouth These." Endorsed "From m^r Keith october 28: 1678:" Hole along bottom margin obscures closing and signature.

---

1. Not found.
2. "Oh that all Christians."
3. Elder Brett; see the letter from James Keith of 30 October 1676.

To Cotton Mather, 15 NOVEMBER 1678

PLIMOUTH, NOVEMBER, 15: 1678:

MOST DEARE COUSEN

I greatly rejoyce in the goodnesse of God to you in that you are made whole, & I beleive you are as the Palme-tree, that your growth in grace will be more eminent by the late depression, Amen! It is good for a man to beare the yoke in his youth, & happy is that soule that can take the yoke of christ upon it. The gentlenesse of your Affliction & your soe speedy deliverance out of it (wherein soe much distinguishing grace doth appeare) layes you under a very great obligation to endeavour to your utmost to be doing for God, & the good Lord enlarge you therein. your letters[1] I received, but the bookes of which you write are in the hands of another boatman who is not yet come from Boston: In your next tell me what the binding of the two bibles cost, for they belong not to him that ownes the other, & I must righteously distribute the charges with my 2 neighbours: your letter, I thinke, answers all desired of you in my letters sent before I knew of your sicknesse, except Commencement Theses, which I pray send me some of, by the next for I have not one. The enclosed I intreat a speedy conveyance of for I earnestly desire him to meete me if he can at Mr. Norton's ordination, 27th of this Instant:[2] My selfe & wife most heartily salute you; soe doth John, Betty, Rowland etc your selfe & the rest of our Cousens:

The Lord blesse you & prepare you to be a rich blessing in your generation, soe prayes,

your affectionate Uncle,

John Cotton

pray send me word when your father writes to Cos: Tuckney, for I would send when he doth:

Mather Papers 2:65, Prince Library, Rare Book & Manuscripts, Boston Public Library. Addressed "These for his endeared kinsman Mr. Cotton Mather, at his fathers house in Boston."

---

1. Not found.

2. John Norton (c. 1651–1716), a graduate of the Harvard class of 1671, was ordained a minister at Hingham on 27 November 1678. *Sibley's Harvard Graduates*, 2:394.

From Cotton Mather, [AFTER 15 NOVEMBER 1678]

Having survived his own encounter with smallpox, Mather supplies his news-hungry uncle with a grim impression of the epidemic's recent effects in Boston.

I sh^{ld} fling a proh pudor![1] upon my delayes of doing you that service that duty dos as much oblige as you desire, but that I am made brazen faced by <*sufficient*> excuses sufficient to bear mee out.

I wonder w^{t} you Impute my non-Transmission of those things of yours wch are in my hands to. I know your Candor will not charge me wth Idleness, your Courtesy wl not Implead me for forgetfulness, & most of all, yor v^{ry} [your very] Reason wl not accuse mee of unwillingness to serve you in w^{t} I may, Even usque ad aras,[2] & if posible, there too. But if I am of age to speak for myself, Sickness, wch had ye first part in hindrance, was succeed by uncertainty of Conveiance, & y^{t} ag^{n} seconded by other Avocations—How frequently <*I have*> & unweariedly I have been engaged in seeking Plymouth boat, if noth. else, yet my old shooes will testify, who in y^{s} time, w^{n} Boston is become another Lutetia[3] (q. Luto suta) do proclaim y^{t} they wanted a pair of goloshooes—w^{n} traveling neer ye Dockhead. I w^{ld} bee more frequent in Letters Testimonial of my gratitude if I could but either fling salt on ye tail of Time, or get ye wind and Tide to bee favrable to my designs—wch possibly may in a sense bee before ye Greek Calend.[4]

Never was it such a Time in Boston, Boston burying-places never filled so fast, It is easy to tell ye time w^{rin} Wee did not use to have ye bells tolling for burials on a sabbath day Morning by sunrise, to have 7 buried on a sabbath-day night after Meeting, To have coffins crossing each other as they have been carried in the street, To have I know not how many Corpses following each other close at ye heels, to have 38 dye in one week, 6, 7, 8, or 9 in a day, Yet thus hath it lately been, and thus is it at this day, Above 340 have died of the small pox in Boston, since it first assaulted ye place, To attempt a Bill of Mortality & number ye v^{ry} spires of grass in a Burying place seem to have a parity of difficulty and in accomplishment. At first ye gradual m^{rcy} of God to my Fathers family was observeable & remarkeable, First, my Broth^{r} Nath.[5] gently smitten, and I more gently y^{n} Hee, & my Sr Sarah[6] yet more gently y^{n} I—But the order is broken on my Sr Maria[7] w^{o} on ye same Month & day of ye Month y^{t} my Fathr w^{s} v^{s}ted wth ye same disease 21 years agoe, was taken v^{ry} Ill, the Symptoms grievous and o^{r} fears gr^{t}, Sometimes Light-headed, but her Father prayed down mercy for her, and, her pox having turned a day or 2 agoe, shee is now so inter spemque metumque Locata,[8] that [hope] bares down the scales—So that of my Fathrs septenary of Childr: 4 have been visited. God fit & prepare for the 3 stroakes y^{t} are yet behind—

Sr, Let us not want y^e help of your prayers for all of us, especially for him w^o is not more your nephew y^n desirous to be your $serv^t$,

Cott.

Mather Papers 2:66, Prince Library, Rare Books and Manuscripts, Boston Public Library. Written on the back of John Cotton to Cotton Mather, 15 November 1678.

---

1. "Oh shame!"
2. "Up to/as far as the altars."
3. Lutetia was an ancient city on the site of Paris.
4. A "calend" is the first day of a Roman month. Since the Greeks did not use calends in their months, the assurance that a thing may happen "in a Greek calend" translates roughly to "when pigs fly."
5. Increase and Maria Cotton Mather's fourth child, Nathaniel (1669–1688), who became a classmate of Cotton's son Rowland at Harvard.
6. Increase and Maria's fifth child, Sarah, born 1671.
7. Increase and Maria's second child, Maria, born 1665.
8. "Poised between hope and fear."

To Increase Mather, 2 December 1678

Plimouth December, 2: 1678:

Reverend & Deare Brother

The Govr promised me to deliver my whole Indian Salary to any to whom I should Assigne it: I intreat you to take the trouble of delivering the note to him & receiving the money which is 22 or 23 pd I know not which certainely: I have hopes that 10 pd of it I May leave in your hands for your use upon the same account you had the 20 pd of Capt Hull; only I cannot at this time absolutely ingage it, because the hand of the Lord in this Infectious desease is now as neere my house, as Sanders his shop is to yours, & if it please God to visit my family I doubt it will cost me more then that in necessaries from Boston for such a time of triall; otherwise I shall not soone call for that 10 pd from you: I am uncertaine of an opportunity of sending againe this winter, & therefore doe at a venture charge this bill of 10 pd upon you, but I write not a word to M^{ris} Tappin about it, because you yet have it not; only I request you when you have received my money of the Govr to send to the widow to come to you to receive the money & to give you a receipt of it, & withall desire her from me, to give me soe much credit on her booke:

My last, in which I also wrote to P: as yet is by you unanswered, I would hope it will be successfull; if I heare it is not, if I live till after Feb: 17: I shall take speedy course to prepare for a sute at Aprill Court, the good Issue of which for recovery of Principall & Interest, good Lawyers doe assure me of: James Pemb: saith you are about selling your farme to G: White I suppose it is a mistake; my care hath bin, is & will be, if God spare life to help you to money as fast as I can for it, if you resolve to sell it; He speakes to me to know whether he may longer injoy the farme, but telles me not what termes my Brother Cotton propounds to him nor what you say thereabouts; I hope none of us will aske lesse then about 30 pd in silver per annum, for I finde this other pay at the Tenants termes comes not to much more then halfe the summe to answer my ends:

wee shall be very glad to hear that Cousen Maria doth recover more & more; wee begin to looke for our day of visitation because it is soe neere us; my Cousen John could be very glad to heare that all your family were past danger of it, for then he hopes his Deare Cousin Cotton would keep him company when he is sick of it: but that is too great a favour for us to hope for, yet a mercy wee should abundantly blesse God for in such a day of triall; however, our earnest request to you is, that you would now by writing communicate your experiences, & tell us what you doe every day from the time they are taken till the height & afterward, I doe account your observations from your owne practice May be more usefull then any thing else; if you also write the particulars you use, I will take care in season, God willing, to obtaine them: with due respects & love to you, desiring your prayers for us, that wee may be prepared to meete God, & that you may have a comfortable issue of your present trialls,

I rest, your affectionate Brother,

John Cotton

Lacksimons told me last weeke that Mr Pynchon hath brought over 20 pd due to his wife for 2 yeares rent from old Boston; if soe, why is not our 10 pd come also? pray informe me about it:

Mather Papers 2:67, Prince Library, Rare Book & Manuscripts, Boston Public Library. Addressed "These For the Reverend, his Deare Brother, Mr Increase Mather, Teacher of a Church of christ at Boston."

From James Keith, 15 January 1679

BRIDGWATER JAN. 15 —78.

REVEREND AND DEAR SIR

Although I have not heard from you for a long time neither hade opportunity to write to you, yet I do beare you still in remembrance, being under strong obligations thereunto by the bonds of love in christ Jesus. The occasion of my writing to you at present is from reports I have very lately heard, concerning some scandall & miscarriage of Robert Latham by excesse in drinking at your town,[1] whether you are acquainted with it I cannot tell, but I do heare that Mistris Cotton hath some knowledge of it, I would be certifyed concerning the truth of it, that we may know how to proceed in such a case: Although it is not pleasant to me, to be upon such work if it might be avoided, yet I look upon my self obliged in conscience to search it out for the vindication of the name of God & the honour of the gospell, I must therefore entreate you to enquire into it whether any testimony can be obtained from any of your town to prove the fact. Sir if you will please to take the pains to make enquiry, & to send me word by the first opportunity, it may be a good service to christ. deare Sir I need the help of your prayers, being still under restraint, by bodily weaknes as to the full exercise of my ministry. I cannot enlarge because of the bearers haste, our cordiall respects presented to your self and M[rs] Cotton, my kinde love to elder Cushman, commending to the never failing mercy of god in christ Jesus I rest

Sir Yours affectionately in the Lord

James Keith

Cotton Family Papers 8:11, Prince Library, Rare Books and Manuscripts, Boston Public Library. Addressed "For The reverend M[r] John Co[tton] Pastor of the church of christ in Plimouth. These." Endorsed "From M[r] Keith January, 15: 1678:"

---

1. At the 3 June 1679 meeting of the General Court, Robert Latham was fined ten shillings "for being twise drunke." *PCR*, 6:16.

From Seaborn Cotton,[1] 4 February 1679

Dearest Brother

I rejoyce that I have an opportunity to salut you, but am sorry, It is so short warning by ye bearer, that I have but time for a word or two. I blesse god that I heard of your welfare by your Letter received Jan 31.[2] & doe desire you to blesse God with mee for the health of my selfe & family The small poxe hath been in 2 familyes in our Towne, out of one of which then dyed 3 persons & 6 recovered The other Family had but one sicke in [it?] who is recovered (through mercy). The towne is generally in health in our neighbour Townes many have dyed of ye disease we desire to blesse god for his wonderfull sparing of us. Deare Brother, I thanke you for a promise of visiting us in the spring. I doe consent my son shall offeciate in your place at Lords day upon the condition you visit & helpe mee at Hampton my wife also Earnestly desires to see you. The bearer will not let me Inlarge, I crave the continuance of your prayers for me & [mine?] I hope am not forgettfull of you thus with Hearty love to your selfe & Sistur [illeg.] & wife, & to Couzene John &c.

I am your most Affectionate Brother

Seaborn Cotton

Hampton. Feb. 4. 1678

your Couzen Carre is safely delivered of a daughter, & in way of recovery

Hearty & Humble Respects & service to your Honored Governour & Lady
I trust once againe to visit your parts if you Continue there
your coming hither [illeg.] upon many accounts

Curwen Family Papers, American Antiquarian Society. Addressed "For the Reverend Mr John Cotton, Pastor to the Church at Plymouth." Endorsed "From my Brother Cotton February, 4 1678:" "Seaborn" is added in a hand other than Cotton's. Large tear along right bottom margin and one small hole.

---

1. Seaborn Cotton (1633–1686), eldest son of John Cotton Sr., received his name by being born at sea en route to New England. Like his brother after him, he preached in Connecticut following his graduation from Harvard (1651), but in 1657 he accepted a call from Hampton, now in New Hampshire, where he was ordained two years later. As he had required of Joshua Moodey, in 1684 Gov. Cranfield demanded that Cotton administer sacraments according to the Church of England liturgy. Rather than do so, Cotton absented himself from the colony until Cranfield left in 1685. Cotton died the next year. *Sibley's Harvard Graduates,* 1:286-93.

2. Not found.

To Thomas Hinckley,

14 February 1679

The campaign to fill Thomas Walley's place in the Barnstable pulpit was more than a year old at the time of this letter. Harvard graduate John Bowles (1653–1691) was apparently a candidate and had a strong advocate in Cotton. Unfortunately he had a stronger opponent in Gov. Hinckley. Here, Cotton appeals to his friend to give Bowles his support.

Plimouth February, 14: 1678:

Worshipfull & much Honoured Friend.

This last weeke came such uncomfortable tidings from Barnstable hither, that I knew not how to satisfy my selfe without troubling you with a few lines, I hope not proceeding from a principle inclining to medle with other mens matters, but from a sincere desire of the best good of that people who are, God knows, very deservedly deare & pretious to me; It doth indeed malé audire[1] with wiser then my selfe, that such discouragements should attend Mr Bowles; that such meane things should be soe taken up & presented as matter to alienate the affections of people from him; I am sure, the speakers doe greatly suffer in their names in more townes then this for their weaknesse herein, & your whole place I feare will be soe blemished thereby as that you will finde it more difficult to obtaine a minister next yeare then this; I need not tell you, worthy Sir, that it is a dying time with Preachers young as well as old, & it is very manifest, there is very great likelyhood of scarcity of ministers, & if I may without offense whisper it in your eare, I dare say, Mr M:[2] is far below Mr B: for learning & abilities, although his name be deservedly more pretious with those who knew his predecessours; that you are too heavy & weigh downe the whole towne (as is said) I freely say, that without doubt you may lawfully doe it in all cases generally, but I could upon my knees humbly beg of you, worthy Sir, that you would not only permit but contenance as much as you can with a safe Conscience a vote of your people for Mr B: who (I heare) are much more satisfyed with him, hearing how honest an answer was indeed sent from him to them at the returne of the messenger, though (it seemes) not soe thoroughly declared as should have bin: If upon a such toyes as these Mr B: should goe home without a renewed Invitation from the people, I doubt it would too deeply reflect upon their reputation & proove a great barre to future success in motions of such a nature; And Good Sir, (humbly againe & againe begging pardon of you for my boldnes with you) if you should appeare slow to promote a call for Mr B: out of a secret hope & desire to obtaine one yet More sutable (at least for your selfe) I verily feare you will finde your selfe uncomfortably disappointed, were it not much more desireable to waite upon God under his ministry & to follow the throne of grace with earnest prayers, that this man may be fitted to doe all that which (it may be) you rather expect in another;[3] Much Honoured in the Lord, I should be ashamed to looke you in the face, after soe much presumptuous writing to you, were I not perswaded in my heart (after humble seeking the face of God thereabouts) that the Lord called me thereunto; I know your candour is great, & your present Manifestation of it, I shall esteem it a great favor: my selfe & wife present due respects & service to you: Sir Cotton[4] presents his service to you: I have had noe newes from Boston a long time; The good Lord guide you in a right way, craving your prayers for me & mine,

I rest, Sir, your Worships servant in Christ

John Cotton

My love to Mr Bar: Lathrop[5] & his wife, & to Elder Cobb & his.

Hinckley Papers 1:13, Prince Library, Rare Book & Manuscripts, Boston Public Library. Addressed "These For the Worshipfull, his highly Honoured Friend, Thomas Hinckley Esquire, Magistrate, at his house, in Barnstable."

---

1. "Sound like slander."
2. The identity of "Mr M" is unclear.
3. Bowles was not called back, however. He later preached in Dedham and became the ruling elder of the Roxbury church in 1688. Turning to politics, he was a representative to the General Court, and he was Speaker of the House when he died of smallpox in 1691. *Sibley's Harvard Graduates*, 2:392-93.
4. Cotton's son John, still at Harvard.
5. Barnabas Lothrop (1636–1735) was a son of the Rev. John Lothrop (1584–1653), one of the first English settlers of Barnstable. Barnabas became a judge of common pleas and of probate, an assistant, and after the union with Massachusetts, a councillor in the administration of Gov. William Phipps. Trayser, *Barnstable*, 174.

From Increase Mather, 18 February 1679

DEAR BROTHER

I have delivred ye 10^{ll} to m^{rs} Tapp[an] <yor desire> according to y^{r} desire & I saw it set down in her hands. And 17^{s} to m^{r} Richards, who sayth you owed him 1^{ll} 8^{d}. Ensign Green hath not as yet called for his money.

Concerning ye Farms, y^{r} <*illeg.*> last l^{tr} but one, intimated as if you had no great desire of purchasing my Interest, nor regarded my Brotherly offer to you, whereupon

I advised wth some friends who perswaded me to petion ye county court for a division, because if my particuler Interest were known, some would give above 40^{ll} more y^{n} whilst in [Condem?]. I have [so?] acted accordingly, & [...] obtained from ye court what I desired. wthin y^{es} few dayes a gentleman y^{t} hath money enough, <*offered me*> offered me y^{t} 100^{ll} in money should be given me for my Interest, & 100 ^{ll} besides in money ingaged to me wth Intrest after the propertie of 6^{ll} [several words illeg.] <*illeg.*> payed, though I should sell it to him in Condem. How y^{n} could you think y^{t} 200^{ll} is more y^{n} yor Interest is worth? I have treated wth some Countrey men about it. one at Rumley Marsh telles me y^{t} my share is worth above 300^{ll}. A gentleman in y^{s} Town told me, y^{t} if it were a division th^{r} obtained, Hee doubts not but I may have 400^{ll} for w^{t} is mine at [Maddirioux?].

Paige has forfetted his bond to you & me to, not having brought his last payment wch was due to me. If you be minded to buy an House in Boston I will not be yor hindranc[e] though I can not think you are in earnest so [illeg.] as to throw away yor money so, where it may be a Tennant will not prsent y^{t} is desirable & ye Repairs quickly Eat out ye rent, & it may be fire consume al. I have always <*sd ye*> spoken ye same thing to you, viz. y^{t} I thought ye Farm was worth at least 300^{ll} And y^{t} I was willing you should have it 30 or 40^{ll} cheaper y^{n} another, And y^{t} as for yor money in Paige's hand, I would either take it in part of pay for ye Farm or if I sold it not to you, give you Interest for ye money. And you promised me y^{t} so it should be. I had rather <*illeg.*> borrow yor money y^{n} anothers upon some accounts. The Interest I'le pay you before hand as soon as I receive ye rest of ye money, if you please. or if you send Rowland to schoole at Boston againe, since I take him to be a towardly child I am willing to board him in my Family, & in y^{t} way justify you for ye use of yor money. I am not willing to sell ye Farm for halfe as much as it is worth, & so wrong my wife & children & make ye world laugh at me for a Simple Tom. And what more Brotherly tender to prsent to you, y^{n} I have done already respecting y^{s} matter I know not. Let me hear profitably by yor next whether you are Free to let me have ye money as Expressed or no, y^{t} so I may order my concerns Accordingly.

The Lord hath graciously stayed his hand as to ye smallpox in Boston. I know but of one in y^{s} end of ye Town sick. nor above 4 throughout ye whole Town. In many Countrey Towns, it is very sore. I hear y^{t} 50 are now sick in Woburn. Many of dorchester, Rocksburg, wenham, Newberry, Salsberry, Piscatewey where one man lost 4 daughters & 2 sons (one son left alive still) lately dead of ye small pox. I suppose you heer y^{t} Ammi Corlet is dead of y^{t} disease & Ephraim Angier Also mrs Angier sick of ye same distemper, & her Recovery very doubtfull. 3 of her Brothers dyed in Boston of ye very disease wthin y^{s} few moneths.

I blesse ye Lord, my Family hath bin well above 2 moneths: 6 of y^{e} [children] (all but Abigail) touched wth y^{e} <*dis*> [illeg.], though 3 of y^{m} so gently as y^{t} y^{y} had no need to lye by it. Let ye Lord alone have all ye glory. I am in haste being to p^{rch} ye Lecture y^{s}

Thursday, & much other work upon my hands. R^ts^ to my sister, & cousins, The Lord be wth you. I am,

Yo^r^ affectionate Brother

I Mather

Boston. Febr 18. 1678/9

Mather Family Papers, American Antiquarian Society. Addressed "These For the Rev^d^ my dear Brother Mr John Cotton, Pastor of ye church in Plymouth." Endorsed "[Fro]m Mr Mather Feb]ruary, 18: 1678:"

To Increase Mather, 12 March 1679

Plimouth March, 12: 1678:/79:

Reverend & Deare Brother

I wrote to you last weeke by Mr Saffin; one passage in your letter I forgat to speake to, viz, my buying a house at Boston, which thing indeed was a reality the last yeare, for I had Treaty with one (who is not likely long to injoy his house) about buying his house & land, which is very much for a Boston lot, neither doth it stand in much more danger of fire, then mine doth here; & I doe beleive if I had come to Boston this winter as I use to doe when the desease was not, I had made a bargaine for it: I therefore in what I wrote I pretended not a thing that was not; but by what I now say, I intend not any obstruction of proceeding with you, if you please (as I desired in my last) to set your lowest price you resolve to stand to, & how long you can waite for some of your money: Also let me know your minde about sute, for I am sollicitous to be in a way to recover the bond of P: if he have since paid you, I hope you have the bond safe for my use & service, by the commissioners or this boat I desire to heare from you: Last Monday afternoone Just upon the great Thunder-clap dyed our poore Treasurer,[1] that day six weekes he was taken sick with a feavour & Jaundice. Major Cudworth[2] labours under the same distempers & his condition is very doubtfull; the Lord raise up a succession of godly faithfull ones: With due love & respects to you & my sister, from my selfe, wife & cousen etc desiring your earnest prayers for me (who am but crazy & infirme) I rest,

your Affectionate Brother[3]

John Cotton

All of us present hearty love to Cous: Cotton, etc tell him wee thanke him heartily for our Almanacks; Wee are going this day to Treas:s buriall & ergo cannot write to him. I wish Ens: Greene had my letter, for I want his Answer, with the Catechismes I wrote to him for.

Mather Papers 3:10, Prince Library, Rare Book & Manuscripts, Boston Public Library. Addressed "These For the Reverend, his Deare Brother, Mr Increase Mather, Teacher of a church of Christ, at Boston." Some Latin notes by Mather on the address leaf.

---

1. Constant Southworth died on 11 March 1679. His will is dated 27 February 1679; his inventory was taken the following 15 March. Stratton, *Plymouth Colony*, 365.
2. James Cudworth (d. 1681) of Scituate was stripped of his office as deputy, his rank as captain, and his franchise in 1658 for "entertaining" Quakers, but eventually all three were restored. Early in King Philip's War, he was appointed to command Plymouth Colony forces depite his (accurate) protestations of incompetence. Elected deputy governor in 1681, he was sent to England to press the ministry for a colony charter, but he died soon after his arrival there. Stratton, *Plymouth Colony*, 275; George D. Langdon, *Pilgrim Colony: A History of New Plymouth 1620–1691* (New Haven, Conn., 1966), 197-98.
3. Relations between the brothers-in-law apparently became strained after this time; in a letter from Joseph Dudley to Increase Mather, dated 12 December 1681, Dudley refers to a "coldeness" between Mather and Cotton and urges a change of sentiment. Mather Papers 4:23, Prince Library, Rare Book & Manuscripts, Boston Public Library. One wonders if the financial issues concerning the Boston property that are outlined in the letters above had anything to do with the frostiness Dudley observed.

From Thomas Cooper[1] et al., 17 September 1679

At least Rehoboth was experiencing some good fortune during this "dying time with Preachers," as the next two letters relate.

To the Church of Christ at Plymouth

Grace—mercy and peace in our Lord Jesus christ be multyplyed

Reverend and Beloved

It is not unknowne to you. that notw^th^standing The Lords abundant goodnes to us, after our first bereavem^t^ in raising up one amongst our selves soe Emenently accomplished for ye greate worke of the Ministrye; yet for our greate unfrutfulnes and unprofitablenes under such glorious injoym^t^. The Lord most justly and rigteouslye againe bereaved us of our reverend & deare pastour, since which time The Lord hath caused us to expeariance the greate worth of the blesed injoym^t^ of his house (after wch we hoope our Soules ernastly breathe) by the want theerof, yet mixeing his smartest-chastisments with much pitye and greate compasion, and in a greate measure makeing up <*our*> (our allmost irrepairable Lose) with a new suplye sending us a person singularly quallified and furnished with gifts and graces for soe a greate a worke (for which indeed who is soeficent) an able workman rightly deviding the word of truth; a person well knowne unto many of you (viz) The Reverand Mr Samuell Angier[2] whome we have ellected in order to office amongst us; our Request therfore is that you would be pleased to Send your Messengers to be pressent wth us, and asistant unto us in the worke of Ordination which we intend (if God will) upon the 15th day of october next it being the fowrth day of the Weeke In the meane tyme begging your prayers for our Sollem preparation thereto, we commend you to the gratious direction of him whose p^{r}sence we desire may attend you in your atendance to this our desire And soe we Rest

Your Loveing Bretheren in the ffellowshipe of the gospell

Thomas Cooper sen^{r}
Daniel Smith[3]

In the Name and with the Consent of the Rest of the Church

Rehoboth the 17th
of Septembr 1679

Cotton Family Papers 8:13, Prince Library, Rare Books and Manuscripts, Boston Public Library. Cotton's note: "The messengers chosen & present at this ordination were the Pastour, Ruling Elder, m^{r} Samuel Fuller, Thomas Cushman Junior."

---

1. Deacon Thomas Cooper (d. 1680) was a prominent citizen of Rehoboth. James N. Arnold, *Vital Records of Rehoboth* (Providence, R.I., 1897), 817.

2. Rev. Samuel Angier (1655–1719) graduated from Harvard College in 1673. Early in 1677 he was approached by Gov. Hinckley to teach children in Barnstable, but he declined. He became pastor of the Rehoboth church in 1679, in the place of the late Noah Newman. A year later he married Hannah, the only daughter of Harvard president Urian Oakes. Sometime in late 1692 or early 1693, claiming poor health, Angier removed to his native Cambridge, resigning his position in Rehoboth. Eventually recovering his health, in 1696 he became pastor for the church in the part of Watertown that is now Waltham, in which capacity he served the rest of his life. *Sibley's Harvard Graduates* 2:422-28; Tilton, *A History of Rehoboth*, 96.

3. Daniel Smith (d. 1692), deputy and magistrate of Rehoboth. Arnold, *Vital Records of Rehoboth*, 876; *PCR*, 5:223.

From Samuel Angier, 27 October 1679

Rev^{D}. S^{R}.

These Lines would (being very desireous) persuad you of my (but reasonable) resolution, long agoe taken up, but since much strengthened & Confirmed, for Ever to remember your many oblidging courtesies: Time would faile me, to mention y^{e} [sev]erall particular acts, & ye praise worthyness of them: I can not but thinke of your late Kind visite, send a great cloud of thanks for ye same It was indeed great Kindness, ye day preceeding ye ordination y^{t} you minded me of those considerations soe suitable & needfull wch otherwise, I thinke would not have been sufficiently impressed on my thoughts: & very singular was ye respect your manner, in giveing ye right hand of fellowshipe did Evidence y^{t} if noe sooner, then on ye Last day of my life there should be an opportunity to make any suitable requitall, I should be ambitious to improve it.

S^{r} you may remember some discourse we had about ye administration of ye sacrament of ye Lords suppe, & ordination of Deacons; you know my unExperiencedness in those things; & therfore I hope you will not thinke amisse of my Ernest desire, but gratifying ye same in [....] a plaine, particular & distinct account, as to both y^{t} may fully informe my younge braine: I depend upon it & do not fear missing my Expectation; haveing soe large Experience of your great Candor & freindship: My greatest hearty respects to y^{r} selfe & m^{s} Cotton: greeting to all freinds as if [n]amed: I Ever remaine

your trusty servant & Endeared freind

Sam^{ll}. Angier:

S^{r} your prayers are my Constant desires:

Rehob: 27 octob: 79:

Cotton Family Papers 8:14, Prince Library, Rare Books and Manuscripts, Boston Public Library. Addressed "To the Revrd. Mr Cotton Pastor of ye Church of Christ in Plimouth: Q. D. C."

From William Bradford, 20 December 1679

As this and following letters suggest, the New England leadership was becoming uncomfortable with the renewed attention it was receiving from England.

Reverent Sir

I thought good to Certifie you in a line or tow of m^{r} Randals visiting o^{r} Governour:[1] who arived att. N. Yorke first, and came from thence last friday was a sevennight, who came from England in Octob last, who this day is gon to Boston, and hath taken posesion of Naraganset for his Majests: provence, as he came a longe, and visited Rhoad Island, and is bound furder as he saith for the Easterne parts: and Especially to Settle in Mason Interest:[2] whom he looks for over in the Springe: his Especiall buisnes now wth our Governor was to psent hime with letters from the Counsell of State, wherein they declare <*the*> his Majests kinde reception of o^{r} last letters by m^{r} Joles and that they were refered to the Comitte of forraine plantatons to make report of, and then a furder Answer to be returned: the Counsell have also sent divers Queres about the State of or Collonie to be with all Speed Answered, he brought a large Comission that Impowers Certaine Select Men of o^{r} Collonie with our Counsell to Sweare or Governor to be true to An act made a boute promoting of Sea afaires: formerly:[3] he Makes Speed to Boston: (where i thinke he will be little welcommed) to Settle his Majestes Commands before the Messengers come; who he saith was spedily to come away wth m^{r} Joles: having received their Instructions: so no More att psent tille I see you:

your Loveing frind Semper

M: B:

20 Desemb. 79.

Cotton Family Papers 8:15, Prince Library, Rare Books and Manuscripts, Boston Public Library. Addressed "ffor his Much Esteemed frind Mr John Cotton deliver This." Endorsed "From Major Bradford December, 20: 1679:."

---

1. Edward Randolph (1632–1703) first came to Plymouth in 1676 on a fact-finding tour for the Crown. Snubbed in Massachusetts, he received a better reception from Gov. Josiah Winslow, who decided that cultivating Randolph's friendship would be more in Plymouth Colony's interests. Langdon, *Pilgrim Colony*, 193-94; *ANB*.

2. See the letter from James Oliver of 27 March 1677, fn. Robert Mason was Randolph's cousin. Langdon, *Pilgrim Colony*, 193.

3. Parliament enacted the first of the Navigation Acts in 1651. These were not enforced in New England, but the Act of 1673 sought to change that with the establishment of salaried customs officers based in Boston. Edward Randolph returned to New England to become the first Collector of Customs for the port. Viola Florence Barnes, *The Dominion of New England: A Study in British Policy* (New York, 1923), 15-16.

From James Oliver, 29 December 1679

Boston 29: 10ber 1679

mr Cotton after respects prsented I mist the opertunyty by mr howland to give acout that on the 24th day in the morning our Comishners[1] arived at nantasket a sonday it provd 25 day mr Joseph Dudly went down with a vesel and A[rtillery] men and that night the [illeg.] the next day the went to our governs and our A[rtillery] Company, were all in arms and brought them to the towne hous wher a good Colashon[2] was provided and after 3 vole[3] the great guns were fire what ther returne is it is but doubtful but they are welcome [...] said the king Comands 2 more Comishoners [...] to Com over in six months, the parlymt [....] mercy prevent not so soone as mr [....] most alin prayd [illrg.] be in a toler[ ] [....]ersarys few frinds our help [....] of the Lord, our god [....] England mr [....] and [....]

Cotton Family Papers 8:16, Prince Library, Rare Books and Manuscripts, Boston Public Library. Addressed in Prince's hand: "To the Rev. Mr Cotton at Plimouth à mr James Oliver of Boston." The handwriting is Oliver's, considerably improved, but the paper is badly mutilated.

---

1. Edward Randolph and customs agents.
2. Collation, a light meal.
3. I.e., "volleys."

From George Shove, 15 January 1680

Taunton Jan. 15. 79/80

Revd & dear Sr

After a considerable time of deep silence, or intercourse hath a revivall by yours of 12th Instant,[1] which I recieved at Middlebro where I had some hopes I might have met you. I much reioce to hear of the goodness of God to you in building of yor house, & sparing yor dear Consort. My familee hath been v[i]sited with much illnes but hitherto verye mercifully, in that noe breach hath been made. my elest daughter of the sd stock is now soe visited [& is?] verye afflicted having had a feaver, attended with an Itching humor breaking forth all over the body [...] Cap [a pe?], but I hope not dangerous the rest in competent health, (blessed be God for his goodnes therin. Mr Keith is well, but things goe ill there still. there hath not been any late publick ch. progresse in dealing with the persons under offence. I had some opportunity with the Agents at Boston the last weeke. the generall News is the Duke of Munmouth is gone to Utricht in Holland,[2] & Yorke gone into Scotland,[3] Shaftsberrie formerly p^rsident of the Councell turned out of his preæsidentship.[4] the five Lords still in the tower,[5] the parliam^t prorogued by proclamation before the time of their session in octob^r till this Instant. Conventicles (about the Altyr at Least) generally Connived at. the Councell at Boston sat on Tuesday sevenight. a day of thanksgiving appointed on the 29th instant, and Generall Court & Assemble the beginning of the Next Month. the Letter he [...] sent them is sharp, yet Comending the prudent deportment of the Agents of [...] Comands are sent which will be of difficult observation. I heare there [...] o^r Govorn^r hath Letters but am unresolved of the Import. Randolphs Comiss[ion?] as to the four towns beyond Merrimack within Masons Claimes puts them upon great thoughts of heart. I met with Mr Moodie[6] & Maj^r Walden[7] at Boston who I percieve are under adept sence of their difficuties & danger they Looke upon themselves as o^r forlorn.[8] the Lord prepare them as us & all his people everywhere for troubles. the day begins to Looke verye dark & blacke. I am glad to hear of hopes of Unanimity at Barnstable if that be certaine that upon Mr Hinkleyes soe farr Condescending Mr Thatchers Interest is growing in ye hearts of the people the case is hopefull. Let mutuall prayers still be Continu[ed?] I present you & yor dear Consort with salutations from me & Mine a[....] am ever

[y^r] Assured friend

GS

I am much affraid of the death of a choice Man among us viz Mr Sam Smith[9] for whose continuance I desire your prayers private & publick.

Curwen Family Papers, American Antiquarian Society. Addressed "To the Reverend Mr John Cotton sen^r Pastor of the Church in Plimouth These p^rsent." Endorsed "... Mr Shove January, 15: 1679." Right margin badly frayed.

---

1. Not found.

2. James Scott (1649–1685), the illegitimate son of Charles II and Lucy Scott, was born during the exile of the royals. Created Duke of Monmouth and officially recognized by his father after the Restoration, he followed a military career. The Protestant party championed his succession to the throne over Charles's Catholic brother James, Duke of York, but Charles declared Monmouth's ineligibility and banished him to Holland in 1679. Monmouth later led the dramatic but failed attempt to overthrow James II. His forces were defeated at Sedgemoor, and the captured leader was executed 15 July 1685. Chris Cook and John Wroughton, eds., *English Historical Facts 1603–1688* (Totowa, N.J., 1980), 78.

3. James, Duke of York (1633–1701), the younger brother of Charles II, converted to Catholicism in 1669. In consequence, he was forced to resign his position as Lord High Admiral on passage of the Test Act in 1673. Sent abroad by his brother to avoid public hostility generated by the Protestant party, he returned in 1679 to become Lord High Commissioner to Scotland. Surviving attempts at impeachment and assassination, he was crowned King James II in February 1685. Cook and Wroughton, *English Historical Facts*, 71.

4. Anthony Ashley Cooper, first Earl of Shaftsbury (1621–1683), was a member of the Convention Parliament that welcomed the restored Charles II in 1660. He later fell from a position of favor with the king and became a leader of the opposition, intriguing with the Duke of Monmouth for the latter's succession to the throne. He helped fan anti-Catholic sentiment during the Popish Plot scare (1678) and was appointed President of Temple's new Council in 1679, but he was then dismissed for supporting the Exclusion Bill. Failing in his attempt to impeach the Duke of York as a Popish recusant in 1680, he was named in a plot to overthrow the government in 1682. In November of that year he fled to Holland, where he died two months later. Cook and Wroughton, *English Historical Facts*, 62-63.

5. In the hysteria following the Popish Plot, five Catholic Lords—Arundel, Powis, Petre, Stafford, and Belasye—were charged by the Protestant party with conspiring to kill Charles II. Arrested on orders of the House of Commons, they were held in the Tower of London to await trial. William Howard, Lord Stafford, was condemned and executed on 29 December 1680; Lord Petre died in the Tower; and the other three remained imprisoned there until 1685. The plight of these unfortunate victims of the Protestant party hardened Charles against the opposition and cost the Protestant party some public support. Antonia Fraser, *Royal Charles: Charles II and the Restoration* (New York, 1979), 360-61, 399-400.

6. Joshua Moodey of Portsmouth.

7. Major Richard Waldron (c.1616–689) of Dover, New Hampshire, was prominent in that colony's political and military affairs. He was killed in a Native raid during the first year of King William's War. Savage, *Genealogical Dictionary*, 4:390.

8. "Forlorn hope," or vanguard.

9. In 1672 there was a Samuel Smith in Taunton, who had a son born that year. Savage, *Genealogical Dictionary*, 4:132.

From [Nathaniel Mather?], 27 March 1680

Dublin. this 27th of ye 1st 1680.

[ ]ther

[....] yor Magistrates inclosed cause will [....] mislaid it so y^{t} at p^{r}sent I [...] indeavoured [...]. I heartily thank [....] mee. In yor ppositions wch you [...] [re] member one thing wch though for my [...] question vizt ye soules of godly psons [ ]ly upon their death yet I have known some some [...] Dr Tho. Goodwin who is lately deceased was of Meath in ye Kingdom as I have heard[1] [...] [g]odliest & most tenacious of orthodoxy of any [m]ember [illeg.] will not determine it onely before the ressurrection beata fruunter quieter [illeg.] I [illeg.] seemed to myselfe to wish y^{e} [...] little otherwise, y^{n} to descent in ye thing intended. [...] before mee I cannot instance.

[....] still as long as ye Lord shall continue both [...] to mee to hear from you. I can give [....] saw y^{t} through ye wonderfull ptection of & in ye injoyment of o^{r} liberty. How things goe [...] for London now certaynly & fully y^{t} I can write [...] bee big with expectation and our prlaticall cler[....] over a great way to meet y^{m}. In sunday of [....] have lately set up organs, and are [....] wch tis like [...] will follow) an altar to bee [....] Papists [....] their Mass in English [....]est of [En]gland & y^{t} year fell on y^{e} [....] pirations [illeg.] in their worp[2] is here [....] & Papists. A priest ordayned amongst [....] here tog^{er} but no presbyterian [....] laws but [....] been so ordayned doe [....] ordayned agayn by Bps. Wee [...] further searching [...] ye Plot, nor any thing [....] interest can keep off [....] design ag^{t} ye goverm^{t}.

Cotton Family Papers 8:17, Prince Library, Rare Books and Manuscripts, Boston Public Library. Addressed "To the Rev m^{r} John Cotton pastor of ye Chh in Plimouth in New England." Prince's note: "I suppose à The Rev. M^{r}. Nathaniel Mather, wos Father had married to s^{d} Cotton's mother." Letter badly mutilated.

---

1. Prince's note: "Dr Thomas Goodwin was Born at Rolesby in Norfolk on oct 5. 1600; ye eldest son of Richard & Catharine Goodwin, & sent to Cambridg Aug. 29. 1613. (his Life)." Underlining added by Prince.

2. Worship.

From John Eliot, April 1680

Beloved bro: Cotton

If you knew what a refreshing comfort it is to my heart, wch you sent me in y^{t} [...] leafe, it would be a spur to your heart to be diligent & accurate, to goe [on?] as you have so well begun, & I hope for the like helpe from you through the whole work of the Bible[1]—this one leafe hath afforded mee more help in that wrk of translation, then ever I had before from any English man. plus vident oculi para oculus[2]—w^{n} you come (if the Lord will) I shall give you an account of what help it hath afforded me, & we shall con[sider?] how to act herein for the future, the first [...][3] was printed of before I received this welcome leafe, but in all y^{t} follow I hope I shall make due use of your observations. I need not tell you y^{t} m^{r} Oaks is to be installed P^{r}sident,[4] the 4th of May, & m^{r} shepard[5] to be ordained the 5 day of May. I am glad to heare of your well faire, my respects to your yoakfellow let prayrs be mutual, to him who is o^{r} only help &c to whom I commit you & rest,

your loving brother,

John Eliot

Miscellaneous Bound Collection, Massachusetts Historical Society. Endorsed "From m^r^ Eliot senior Received, April, 16:1680." Addressed "for the [...] Mr Cotto[n] past[our] [...] plim[outh]."

---

1. In a letter to Robert Boyle, dated 7 July 1688, Eliot pays tribute to Cotton's facility with Native languages, asking Boyle to remit £10 to Cotton, "who helped me much in the second edition" of Eliot's famous Massachusett Bible. Eliot further hoped that two additional translations of his might be printed, "but I cannot commit them to the press without a careful revisal, which none but M^r^. Cotton is able to help me perform." *Sibley's Harvard Graduates,* 1:598.
2. "Two eyes see better than one."
3. Two or three words illegible.
4. Rev. Urian Oakes (1631–1681, H.C. 1649) emigrated to New England in 1634 and returned to England in 1653. After being silenced for nonconformity in 1662, he again sailed for New England. He became pastor of the church in Cambridge and was elected fourth president of Harvard College following the troubled tenure of Leonard Hoar. *Sibley's Harvard Graduates,* 1:183.
5. Rev. Thomas Shepard (1658–1685), son of the Rev. Thomas Shepard felled by smallpox, was installed in his father's place as Charlestown's pastor on 5 May 1680. *Sibley's Harvard Graduates,* 2:481-88.

From Samuel Wakeman,[1] 16 April 1680

FFAIRFIELD APR. 16TH 1680.

REVR^D^ & DEARE SIR

I somtimes in my sollitarie watches (in y^s^ my more lonesome state) call to minde those quondam days wherein I enjoyed ye Society of your m^ch^ esteemed selfe & other my old companions, & sometimes upon occasion looking over my long neglected papers I meete wth those letters w^ch^ (though somewhat distanced) our nearer neighborhood y^n^ now afforded & yett more lately there came to my hand two papers of verses upon ye deaths (woe worth y^t^ word) of m^r^ Walley & m^r^ Newman[2] ye one of wch was endorsed with ye harty respects of ye author in ye tender of it to my unworthy (& as I had thought utterly forgotten) selfe s^r^ I heartily thanke you (craving your excuse y^t^ it hath been thus long deferred) for so good a remembrance of me & were not y^t^ little little poeticall fancy I once had lost through disuse beyond all possibility of recovery such an occasion would have tempted me to have returned you somthing if not worthy your desert (wch how can it be) yet at least expresive of your pore friends desires. but ye case standing as it doth still failing to commend it must suffize silently to admire & lett me tell you y^t^ ye worke & labour of love towards these deare deserving & deservedly esteemed ones found upon y^t^ side for you in ye day of account wil be a far greater matter y^n^ thanks or applaus from men & in very deed upon ye occasion we may all sigh & say these & many ye like bereavemts y^{t} have of late befallen us in y^{s} land are very awfull ye Lord humble his people under these & all other tremendous strokes & give us who are yett left in ye worke y^{t} we may fulfil it working while it is yett day wth us, ye worke of our generation is upon us & it is our businese to serve it according to ye will of god wch the good Lord graunt. S^{r} I heare of you somtimes by my good friend & neighbor m^{r} Walker[3] & should be glad (if you please to favour me so far) to hear from you & there is one thing sir of wch I found of intimation in your verses y^{t} I would be bold to request of you y^{t} is m^{r} Newmans sermon on Jer. 6: 8th.[4] I know not whether it be in print or not if not if you can send it me in writing I am loth so m^{ch} to trouble you but surely in so doing you shall do me a great pleasure I preached upon a day of fast some years since upon y^{t} text & was in my meditations upon it somwhat perplexd & dissatisfied & have had a thirsting desire to have seene some body y^{t} had handled ye same subject in wch if you can helpe me you shall do me a piece of great satisfaction I have no commentarie of ye booke of Jeremy nor indeed know I of any it is my ignorance or else it is a booke y^{t} none have written upon if you know of any y^{t} have done to purpose upon it pray s^{r} signifie so m^{ch} to me Straites of time forbid me at present to enlarge unexpected businese faling in & ye going away of ye vessell being more sudden then was looked for I send y^{s} to your bro: m^{r} Mather by whome unlese otherwise provided you may make returnes & shall not now ad more but wth harty comendations to yours: & m^{rs} Cotten. That I am Cordiallit^{r}

Your very friend & serv^{t}. —

Saml Wakeman

Cotton Family Papers 8:18, Prince Library, Rare Books and Manuscripts, Boston Public Library. Addressed "Theesse for ye Revr^{d} m^{r} John Cotton pastor of ye ch of x att Plimoth." Endorsed "From m^{r}. wakeman April, 16: 1680:."

---

1. Samuel Wakeman (d. 1692) was one of seventeen scholars who left Harvard College without a degree in 1655. Thomas Prince expressly mentions him as one of five of that number "who afterwards made a very shining Figure in New-England." *Sibley's Harvard Graduates,* 1:16-17; Savage, *Genealogical Dictionary*, 4:388.
2. Cotton wrote two tributes in verse for Thomas Walley and Noah Newman, both of whom died in 1678.
3. Rev. Zecharaiah Walker (1637–1700), another of the seventeen scholars mentioned above, was pastor of the Second Church in Woodbury, Connecticut, from 1668 until his death in 1700. Weis, *Colonial Clergy*, 213.
4. Jer. 6:8: "Be thou instructed, O Jerusalem, lest my soul depart from thee; lest I make thee desolate, a land not inhabited."

From James Keith, 31 May 1680

BRIDGWATER MAY 31ST—80.

REVEREND & DEAR SIR

You must accept of these lines instead of a visit, for I am not now in any comfortable capacity to come & see you, as my condition is at present circumstanced. I have been sustained in some measure in the exercise of my ministry, through the power & mercy of a gracious god, ever since we parted at Taunton, untill the last sabbath. I finde my bodily infirmityes especially the fever so prevailing upon me of late that I am forced to breathe a while, not being able at present to attend upon my publick work. I intend god willing to go down to the bay, towards the latter end of this week & to make some stay there, to try whether a little rest & respite may be a means to raise me. I am waiting upon God to see what the Lord will do with me, & desire quietly to leave my self with him, who will never faile the expectation of those that trust in him. Sir I cannot now give you a particular account of our church affairs, in generall we meet with much trouble & opposition in the work of christ, the persons under offense are still hardened, the Lord humble them & give them repentance to the saving of their souls, if it be his holy will. there is little hopes of reconcilment, what the issue will be I cannot tell. the church is yet united through gods goodnes, none of the brethren dissenting that I know of one only excepted. We need your prayers. I pray Sir present my kinde respects to all the brethren whom providence may bring under your roof at this solemnity. I write in haste & cannot enlarge as I intended being prevented by company. Our cordiall respects presented to your self & Mrs Cotton, commending you to the never failing mercy of God in christ Jesus & earnestly desiring your prayers to God for [us?]

Sir Your affectionate frend & bro: in the Lord

James Keith

Cotton Family Papers 8:20, Prince Library, Rare Books and Manuscripts, Boston Public Library. Addressed "The reverend John Cotton pastor of the church of christ in Plimoth. These." Endorsed "From mr Keith May, 31, 1680:."

From the General Court of Plymouth Colony, 10 July 1680

To MR John Cotton Pastour and MR Thomas Cushman Elder of the Church of Christ att Plymouth, to be Communicated to that Congregation with all Convenient speed

The Generall Court haveing taken to theire seriouse Consideration the Great waight of those Concernes now before them; as alsoe the labouring Cause of God in the world; doe Comend it to all the Churches and people of God in this Collonie to sett apart to the last weddenesday in August ne[xt a]s a day of solleme fasting and prayer[1] wherein to seeke the face and favor of God to us and his whole [....] & Interest throughout the Christtian World and especially that the Lord would pl[ea]se to direct [....] owne and blesse that our waighty undertaking in Making [....]cation to our Sov^{r}: Lord the Kinge for the p^{r}servation Continuance & Inlargment of those Good privilidges and liberties[2] [....] and Civill [...] for soe longe a time wee have had the Comfortable [...] of; that we may find favor in *<his>* the eyes of our Kinge as a Testimony of y^{e} [....] Gracious owneing of us as his people in Covent^{n} with him [through his] [....] that God may be Intreated to be a wall of fier Round about us [....] in the middest of *<us>* this his wildernes People and [....] that the breaches that he hath made [....] in Any of [....] by a comfortable supply in the minerstys and that [....] may be advanced in our English Nations [....] and the [....] Kings Royall prson may be preserved from all [....] of Popish Adversaries and that all the Lords people [....] out of trouble; and that the Kingdoms of our Lord Jesus Christ [may be?] advanced and submited to every where.

By order of the Court Nathaniael Morton Secretary
Plymouth This 10th of July 1680.

Cotton Family Papers 8:21, Prince Library, Rare Books and Manuscripts, Boston Public Library. Letter badly mutilated in the center.

---

1. There is no record of this event in Plymouth colony, town or church records.
2. In the summer of 1680, Gov. Winslow received word from Secretary of State Henry Coventry that the King would be disposed, upon proper application, to grant Plymouth Colony a charter. Langdon, *Pilgrim Colony*, 194-95.

From Thomas Hinckley, 13 July 1680

Revr^D Sir.

our Elder desired me in his name to write these to you to entreate your favour so far as to pswade m^r Thetcher to preach for you next Lords day if it may be & that you would please to come ov^r to our help the same day for m^r Thetcher seemes not pswadable to preach any more here,[1] having preacht his farewell sermon last Lords day though unexpected to us to heare such that morning, many of us hearing nothing of it till that very day, but, that he would have helpt us whilst here he stayed m^r Crosby[2] is at prsent otherwise ingaged & none wth us in any capacity to be helpfull, so that we are likly if you cannot come; either to have no meeting at all on ye Lords day or a very thinn one & no other help for them except ye repeating of some of the Revr^d m^r Walleys former sermons wch it may be few may desire &c. Sir we greatly need your earnest prayers at ye throne of grace for us we by our sin have brought our selves into strayts its God only that can by repentance bring us out. the good Lord please to instruct every one of us in ye way he would have us go in & so see our wayes notw^thstanding all our pversnes & heale us (out of ye soverignty of his owne grace). in great hast wth respects to your self & consort & many thanks for all kindnesses I rest

yours obliged in effect as in affection

Thos Hinckley

Barnestab^l 13 July. 80.

Sir This day in ye afternoon the elder heard that m^r Thatcher had declared himself inclinable to preach for you next Lords day if you would come hither but he not favoring ye Elder so fare as to give him any hint of it he thought not of it to mean him hencf^th.

Cotton Family Papers 8:22, Prince Library, Rare Books and Manuscripts, Boston Public Library. Addressed "These ffor the Rev^rd & his very good ffrind m^r John Cotton at his howse in Plimoth dd." Endorsed "From m^r Hinckley July, 13: 1680:"

---

1. Despite repeated appeals from Barnstable during more than a year of negotiation, Peter Thatcher declined the pulpit there, settling instead at Milton in 1681. *Sibley's Harvard Graduates,* 2:370-79.

2. Regarding Thomas Crosby, see the letter from John Freeman et al. of 31 July 1672. By this time Crosby was apparently enjoying his new career as a merchant and had no interest in returning to the ministry.

Elizabeth (Ward) Saltonstall to daughter Elizabeth[1], 26 July 1680

July th. 26 80

BETTY

haveing an opertunity to send to you I could do no lesse then write a few lines to mind you that you carry your self very respectively and dutyfully to [serve?] Mris Graves[2] as though she were your mother and likewise respectively and loveingly to the children and servants and soberly in words and actions and be sure you keep your selfe diligently imployed either at home or at schoole as Mris Graves shall order you do nothing without her leave and asure your selfe it will be a great preservative from your falling into evill to keep yourself well imployed, but with-all and in the first place make it your dayly worke to pray earnestly to God that he would keepe you from all manner of evill. take heed of your discourse att all times that it be not vaine and foolish but know that for every idle word you must certerinely give an account to God another day. be sure follow your reading omit it not one day, your father doth purpose to send you some Coppies that so you may follow your wrighting likewise. I shall say no more at present but onely lay a strict charge upon you that you remember and practise what I have here minded you of, and as you desire the blessing of God upon you either in soull or body be carefull to observe the counsell of your parents and consider that they are the words of your loveing and affectionate mother

Eliz: Saltonstall

present my best respects to Mris Graves your Brothers[3] remember their love to you

Cotton Family Papers 8:23, Prince Library, Rare Books and Manuscripts, Boston Public Library. Endorsed "[....] much respected friend thes are to intreat [....]"

---

1. Elizabeth Saltonstall (1668–1725) was the daughter of Nathaniel and Elizabeth Ward Saltonstall. She was first married to John Denison (1666–1689), her brother Gurdon's classmate and the settled minister in Ipswich. Denison died in 1689, while Elizabeth was pregnant with their son, John. Elizabeth married Rowland Cotton in September 1692 and had eleven more children. *Sibley's Harvard Graduates*, 3:271-72, 277-86, 323-26.
2. Not identified.
3. Her brothers at that time were Gurdon (b. 1666), Richard (b. 1672), Nathaniel (b. 1674) and John (b. 1678).

To Samuel Treat et al., 21 October 1680

To the ch of x^T at Eastham
Gr: & Pe: from G: our Fath: from our L: J: x^T be mul:
Reverend & Dearely Beloved in our Common Saviour.

It being desired by letters from Elizabeth Mayo,[1] that she may have the approbation of this Church (whereunto she stands related by vertue of the Lords holy & gratious Covenant made & established with belevers & their seed, which Cov: was sealed to her in Bap:) to Joyne with your selves in laying hold of the Covenant of God, in order to her injoyment of full Communion in the holy ordinances of the house of G: wee doe hereby declare our rejoycing in the goodnesse of God who hath inclined her heart thereunto & freely dismisse her unto you, desiring you to [receiv]e her in the Lord unto Communion in all the holy [...] of God, according as you shall finde God satisfying [....]iences that she is one whom indeed the Lord [....] wee pray that she may be a living stone in [....] that she may be enabled to walke worthy [....] goodnesse unto all well-pleasing; And wee [....] you, that a rich blessing from heaven may [....] the administration of the things of God amongst [....] your furtherance & growth in all holines unto [per]fection; desiring also your constant prayers for us, we take leave & subscribe our selves

Your truly Lov: Breth: in the fa: & fel: of the Gosp:

J:C:
T: C:
with the cons: of the ch:

Plim: Oct: 21: 1680:

Cotton Family Papers 8:24, Prince Library, Rare Books and Manuscripts, Boston Public Library. Cotton's note: "supersc: These To the Rev^d m^r S: Treat Pas: of the ch: of x^t at Eastham." Cotton's copy of the letter. Mutilated on left margin.

---

1. Probably Elizabeth Ring Mayo (1652–c. 1691), who married William Mayo (1654–1691) of Eastham c. 1680. Clarence Almon Torrey, *New England Marriages Prior to 1700* (Baltimore, 1865), 500.

From John Alden[1] et al., 9 November 1680

Honered and beloved in our lord Jesus Christ brethren you Cannot be Ignorant how god by his wise pvidence was pleased to Remove from us by Death our Reverend teacher M^r^. holmes for some yeares past[2] (an humbling pvidence to us) but the lord of the harvest hath since beene pleased to smile upon us in our low estate (for wee have Cause to say, his mercy induers for ever) having sent amongst us another of his servants to be helpfull to us in the work of the ministry whose hart he hath framed and moulded not only to be willing to Joyne <*with*> us but allsoe to take ofice upon him these ar therfore to Crave your Christean assistance by sending your elders & mesengers to Concure with us in our work the 24th: Day of this instant (being the 4th Day of the weeke) which is the Day apointed by the church to Ordaine Reverend M^r wiswall[3] pastor of our Church, they not Douting of your christean Care and Redenes to Comply with our Request we take our leave & subscribe our selves your loving bretheren in Christ Jesus the church of Christ at Duxborrow.

John Alden
josiah standish[4]

in the name & with the Consent of the Church.
Duxborrow nov. 9. 1680:

Cotton Family Papers 8:25, Prince Library, Rare Books and Manuscripts, Boston Public Library. Addressed "To the Reverend Mr. Cotton Pastor of the Church of Christ att Plymoth to be communicated to the Church there." Cotton's note: "The church chose the Pastor, Ruling Elder, & two Deacons who were present at the ordination."

---

1. John Alden (c.1599–1687), the Pilgrim made famous by Longfellow's poem, helped establish the town of Duxbury in the early 1630s and resided there the rest of his life. Originally a cooper by trade, he also served for many years as an assistant in the colony government and was active in the church. Stratton, *Plymouth Colony*, 232-33.

2. Rev. John Holmes died on 24 December 1675. See the letter of 3 January 1676.

3. Ichabod Wiswall (1637–1700) was another of the five "shining Figure[s]" from the nongraduating Harvard class of 1655 (see the letter from Samuel Wakeman of 16 April 1680, n. 1). He taught school in Dorchester for three or four years before moving to Duxbury in 1676 to take the place of the late Rev. Holmes. In 1689 he went to England as an agent for the colony to secure a new charter. He failed in the attempt, largely due to Plymouth's inability to furnish necessary funds, and to the efforts of Massachusetts agent Increase Mather, who sought to have Plymouth joined to his own colony. *Sibley's Harvard Graduates,* 1:16, 560-61.

4. Josiah Standish (c. 1633–1690) of Duxbury, son of the famous Captain Myles Standish, eventually moved to Connecticut, and died there. Robert S. Wakefield, ed., and Russell L. Warner, comp., *Mayflower Families through Five Generations,* vol. 14 (Plymouth, Mass., 1997), 6.

From Thomas Hinckley, [December?] 1680[1]

1680.[2]

Sir if you think it best you may send these to M^r^. Angier[3] after your p^r^sall thereof, I leave it to your discretion as you shall thinke meet, or what elce you shall thinke good to write to him I thinke if God please to be at Plimoth on ye tuesday or wednesday of ye next week in order to answer ye Govrnors desire to meet at his house w^th^ [ye bay?] men about ye sale of mount hope &c.[4] or treaty about it on wednesday night afforesd & shold be glad to wayt on your self & him on friday following homeward to our Towne

T. H.

by reason of ye Treasurers comming down hither it stops bro: Huckins vissit of you.

Cotton Family Papers 8:26, Prince Library, Rare Books and Manuscripts, Boston Public Library

---

1. No address or endorsement, but Cotton is the most likely recipient.
2. Date added by Prince. Prince's note: "Before Gov. Winslows Death on Dec. 18, 1680."
3. Prince's note: "Then minister at Rehoboth (settled in 1679 Dceas^d^ [Removd?] in 1693) Bristol cwancea [Swansea], & settled in 1681."
4. After King Philip's War, Massachusetts and Plymouth quarreled over the right to Philip's lands in the vicinity of Mount Hope (modern-day Bristol, Rhode Island). Plymouth, especially, needed the land in order to settle the costs of the war. Gov. Winslow's policy of cultivating Edward Randolph apparently paid off: even as the colony rejoiced in its prospects for a charter, Plymouth celebrated the Crown grant that had awarded the entire disputed territory to the colony earlier in the year. Langdon, *Pilgrim Colony*, 194-95.

FIVE

"New England in Old England"

1681–1691

AS THE STUARTS TRIED TO REGAIN more direct control over their colonies, worries about Plymouth's future position in the empire appeared frequently in Cotton's letters, which often included information about the Plymouth and Massachusetts Bay colonies' ongoing negotiations with the Crown. Beginning with the suggestion that the king expected New England's agents to present themselves in London,[1] Cotton's correspondence reflects his understandable concern that Plymouth was not pursuing her own charter aggressively enough. Cotton chronicled Plymouth's official request for a charter in June 1685;[2] reported the arrival of Sir Edmund Andros and the fact that he commandeered a Boston church for Anglican worship;[3] detailed Edward Randolph's attempted land-grab;[4] and described Increase Mather's journey to England and back as the agent for Massachusetts.[5] Indeed, as late as June 1689, Plymouth did little more than send a petition to the Crown requesting a charter. Considering that Plymouth, unlike Massachusetts Bay, had never been chartered, this inaction seems surprising. Gov. Thomas Hinckley tried to raise funds to support Plymouth's petition, but the General Court refused to support the proposal. By 1690, Plymouth's future seemed to hang precariously in the balance of power between New York and Massachusetts. In February, the Massachusetts government paid for Ichabod Wiswall to join Mather as its agent. Wiswall was the settled minister in Duxbury, so he naturally represented Plymouth Colony's wishes as well when he sailed for England that year. Plymouth's decision not to send agents on her own behalf nearly guaranteed the colony's absorption by Massachusetts Bay or New York. As early as 24 June 1690, court records reflect Plymouth's delicate situation as she tried to retain her independence: "This Genll Court having information from England that the colony of Plimouth had been joyned to the government of New Yorke, but the same was prevented by the Reverend Mr Mather, who gave an accompt to Governr Sclater [Sloughter] how little service it would be to the people; we are also informed that after we were like to be annexed to Boston, but the same hindered by Mr Wiswall for the present; being also informed there is a possibility that we may obtain a charter for ourselves if we speedily address to their maties imploy a suitable person to manage & rayse sufficient moneys to cary the same an end." The Plymouth Court seemed doubtful that it would succeed and considered the request an opportunity to forewarn Plymouth colony residents about the imminent demise of their autonomy so that they could not claim ignorance later: "the Court thinking it their duty to informe the several inhabitants in the severall towns in this colony thereof, that they may not hereafter say they had no notice."[6] Mather, trying to protect Plymouth from New York, included the Old Colony in a draft Massachusetts charter in early 1690. While the letters below clearly illustrate Cotton's wish that Plymouth would actively pursue her own charter, he ultimately agreed with Increase Mather's decision to push for Plymouth's absorption into Massachusetts Bay. Cotton's support for Mather's efforts in London earned him many enemies in Plymouth, despite the fact that most Plymouth residents much preferred that the colony would become part of Massachusetts rather than join New York. Cotton's very public support of the resulting Massachusetts charter even caused him trouble years later, at least in his view. Concerns over the charter were reflected in later correpondence as well; see the letter of 31 January 1691, in which Cotton tried to envision the advantages of a union with New York. Cotton's penchant for rash talk, meanwhile, flourished throughout the charter crisis. For example, in a frank letter to Hinckley of 6 February 1691, Cotton goaded the governor to "stand forth & play the man." Convinced that Plymouth would be joined to New York, Cotton implored Hinckley to go to England to plead their colony's case directly with the Crown. Cotton wrote, perhaps disingenuously, that he might have overstepped his place with such candor: "Good sir, I have quite forgot myself." (Cotton's willingness to "forget himself" seems to have presented frequent problems throughout his life.) The three counties of Plymouth Colony were included as part of the Massachusetts Bay Colony in the latter's new charter, approved in London on 7 October 1691.

This group of letters also illustrates Cotton's considerable role as an "international news correspondent." His friends and colleagues clearly looked to him for information about the wider world beyond Plymouth Colony, especially nonconformist brethren who remained in England during the Restoration and faced increasing pressure from the Crown. Many letters in this section highlight the means by which Cotton shared information broadly, quickly and often with little comment. For example, Cotton nearly fully transcribed Cotton Mather's 20 December 1683 correspondence in a letter that he wrote seven days later to Thomas Hinckley.

Pastoral concerns reverberate throughout this collection, and in this section, news of Baptists,[7] a drunken excommunicate,[8] a surly group of parishioners,[9] an apology from a church member guilty of fornication,[10] letters of advice to and from ministerial colleagues,[11] and clerical salary concerns[12] reveal a minister busy with the quotidian concerns of a growing congregation and a mature network of colleagues. In addition, Cotton continued his mission among Native Americans in southeastern Massachusetts and worked on some new translations of Eliot's bible and catechism for the Society for the Propagation of the Gospel.[13]

As always, Cotton's naiveté about his correspondents' ability or desire to keep his words private evinces itself in these letters, as when he reminds Cotton Mather: "I would not have my name mentioned."[14] Surely Cotton knew that his letters traveled far beyond their intended readers, but he indulged in some lobbying efforts that highlighted both his stature within ministerial circles and his gossipy side when he tried to convince Jonathan Pierpont to accept the pulpit in Sandwich; —he even called Pierpont's father "the old man" with a "sullen temper" in one letter, only to supplicate to him in the next.[15] For all Cotton knew, the "old man" was reading it all.

---

1. To Thomas Hinckley, 13 January 1682.
2. General Court of Plymouth to King James II, 4 June 1685.
3. From Cotton Mather, 31 January 1687.
4. To John Chipman, 9 March 1688.
5. From Cotton Mather, 11 April 1688; To Increase Mather, 9 July 1688; To Increase Mather, 10 and 21 September 1688.
6. *Records of the Colony of New Plymouth in New England,* ed. Nathaniel Shurtleff and David Pulsifer, 12 vols. (Boston, 1855–61) (hereafter *PCR*), 6:259; George D. Langdon, *Pilgrim Colony: A History of New Plymouth 1620–1691* (New Haven, Conn., 1966), 234-40.
7. To Cotton Mather, 19 April 1681; To Cotton Mather, 6 January 1685.
8. To Thomas Hinckley, 13 January 1682.
9. From James Keith, 6 March 1683; To Cotton Mather, 11 March 1684.
10. From Bithia Sandy, 27 February 1684.
11. For example, from James Keith, 15 February 1686.
12. To Rowland Cotton, 2 September 1687.
13. From William Brattle, 16 July 1687.
14. To Cotton Mather, 19 April 1681.
15. To John Chipman, 25 September 1688; To Robert Pierpont, October 1688; From John and Ruth Chipman, 1 October 1688; To John Chipman, 5 October 1688.

From Jonathan Tuckney, 5 March 1681

Dear & much respected Cousen

yors of September [...] I received,[1] whereby I am glad to understand yor family [....] accession of a son to it;[2] and of my Cousen Mathers[3] then [.....]: It hath been a very sickly time all latter [part?] of last summer hereabouts. All of us in our family Except one child had been visited with a disease between an ague & fevor & some it hath returned to after intermisions. but blessed be God he hath made no breach upon us in our family. Though within these 2 years last past here in Hack[ney] 5 or 6 of our eminentest Godly men that were men of states too, & one faith[ful] minister Mr Jn Thomas Senior by name have been removed. The Lord [help us?] to improve these strokes aright. How publick affairs are you may bett[er] [be?] informed by Mr Epps:[4] but [wt?] great feares we are of Popery getting [...] Parliaments are so prorogued & dissolved that would do any thing [....] it, & to promote union amongst ourselves. A Parliament that had [...] to sit octob. 1679. were not permitted to sit till octob. 80 & after they [....], many Bills of Publick use were Jan. 19 dissolved by Proclamation[5] [...] of 5 Popish Lords clapt up about the Plot in 1678 one was tried & Executed[6] [...] now there is a Parliament summoned to meet at Oxford the 21 of this month[7] against which time there is no doubt but Plotts are laying to take them off there, & to set upon London too, as one house was fired Munday night last & thr[ee] or 4 burnt in it, a flax shop in Breadstreet. Our hope under God is in the City—Magistrates which this year are very couragious & resolute men. And what will be at oxford we must wait on God in reference to. there are in most places chosen those that were in the Last Parliament & were faithfull & zealous then. God send a supply to your Churches that were desolate, which I [should be?] glad to heare of as also of my Cousen Mather's perfected recovery. with our hearty salutations to you & yors, craving mutuall prayers, & mutual intercourse, I rest

yor affectionate kinsman

Jonathan Tuckney

Hackney March 5th 1680/81

Curwen Family Papers, American Antiquarian Society. Addressed "To his much respected Cousen Mr John Cotton Pastor of the church at Plimouth in New England These." Endorsed "From my Cousen, Mr Jonathan Tuckney March, 5: 1681: Received, June 4: Answered, September, 20:" Staining along right margin, two small holes in top third.

1. Not found.
2. John and Joanna's son, Josiah (1680–1756, H.C. 1698), was born 8 January 1680. John Langdon Sibley, *Biographical Sketches of Graduates of Harvard University, In Cambridge, Massachusetts* (Boston, 1873–) (hereafter *Sibley's Harvard Graduates*), 4:398-402.
3. Increase Mather's wife, Maria, had Hannah (1680–1700) on 30 May 1680. *Sibley's Harvard Graduates,* 1:437.
4. Possibly Daniel Epps (1623–1693), who emigrated to Ipswich, Massachusetts, in 1637. In 1674 his son Samuel (1647–1685, H.C. 1669) moved to London, where he died in 1685. Alternatively, the reference may be to Samuel's brother Daniel (1649–1722, H.C. 1669), of Salem. Father or brother may have been in regular communication with Samuel and therefore familiar with London news. James Savage, *A Genealogical Dictionary of the First Settlers of New England*, 4 vols. (1860–62; facsimile reprint Baltimore, Md., 1990), 2:125; *Sibley's Harvard Graduates,* 2:264-67.
5. In early 1679 the first general elections in eighteen years brought to Parliament not the new wave of support for which Charles II had hoped, but a government enlivened by an outspoken and determined Whig faction. Charles prorogued the March 1679 Parliament in May. The next Parliament, scheduled to meet in October of the same year, was determined to debate an Exclusion bill, aimed at denying the Catholic Duke of York any place in the Royal succession. Charles prorogued this Parliament before it ever met, and it did not sit until 21 October 1680. Chris Cook and John Wroughton, eds., *English Historical Facts 1603–1688* (Totowa, N.J., 1980), 88.
6. William Howard, Lord Stafford, was executed 29 December 1680.
7. The "Oxford Parliament" sat for only eight days, 21–28 March. The king had hoped to temper the fractiousness of the resentful Whig members by moving the Parliament to the Royalist-dominated university. Instead, the Parliament ended in bitterness and dismissal. Antonia Fraser, *Royal Charles: Charles II and the Restoration* (New York, 1979), 400-407.

From James Keith, 22 March 1681

Bridgwater March 22. —80

Reverend & dear Sir

Whether it be more strange to your self or to me that no letters have passed between us for so long a t[ime] I cannot tell. Although I reckon you owe me a letter, if I mistake not in my account yet I would have you to beleive that the reason why I have not written to you hath been want of opportunity, & if the reason of your not writing to me be the same (as I would hope it is) I am the better satisfyed: it is our comfort when other wayes of correspondence are denyed y^t we may meet at the throne of grace & pray one for another which I hope hath been our mutuall care according to the measure of grace received: it is the holy will of god yet to suspend me from the full exercise of my ministry as in times past by continued languishings & infirmityes of body, I have had but a [?] winter, though god hath upheld me in my worke in some measure throughout the winter, excepting one sabbath or two: I acknowledge my self unworthy to be improved in the lords vineyard, if it be his pleasure to lay me aside, & to cast me out as a dry branch, I must adore his soveraignty & unspotted justice: I hope it is my care & endeavour to understand the minde of god, both as to what concerns my self & his people under these solemn dispensations, O yt our hearts might be humbled & yt it would please god to return wt loving kindnes & mercyes according to the years wherin he hath been [affecting?]. I do very much marvell yt the honoured court hath appointed me to preach our next election sermon:[1] I would not decline any call of god, through unbelief, but if I should be no better than I am at present, it would be high presumption for me to undertake such a service, I desire to observe what may be of god in the call of his servants, but my bodily strength being so low I dare not at present give encouragment to expect yt service from me which is desired, I know our dear Newman[2] did labour under much bodily weakness [when?] he gave his last publiq testimony, but hade he been then under such an indisposition to speak as I am at present, he could not have performed: that little which I do is [with?] great difficulty, I have elder Breths help constantly in prayer before sermon I am hardly able to speak to hearing in this little congregation, it is therefore very improbable I shall be able to preach an election sermon. Sir I have made bold to write to good Major Bradford[3] yt you may be spoken to, to prepare for yt service, I presume there will be no hesitancy as to your order from authority, I must [?] acknowledge it is too much for me to desire yt you should stand as a [...] of my failure, but I hope your Respect to your freind, & much more your love to the work & service of christ will carry you above what inconveniences may therin attend you. I will endeav[our] to resolve you of at or before the election at Boston, it will be your wisdom to fixe upon a subject before, however things fall it will be no damage, I know your promptnes is such yt you may, by the help of the spirit of god, draw up in a short time that which may be suitable to such an occasion: dear Sir I beg your instant & fervent prayers to god on my behalf yt all the changes wc are appointed to me, may turn to my advantage through the supply of the spirit of Jesus christ, yt if god hath further service for me in the world I may be prepared for it or if otherwise he be calling me of the stage, I may be fitted for glory & eternall life: I have been long waiting for my change, & desire to be still waiting even all the dayes of my appointed time. I have nothing now to acquaint you with as to our affairs, our offenders are in statu quo theire freinds left them, the Lord forgive those who have been an occasion of theire hardening. my true love & respects presented to your self & Mrs Cotton, I must take leave, commending you to the grace of our Lord Jesus in whom I am

Sir Your assured freind & affectionate brother

James Keith

Sir present my respects to elder Cushman[4] to Mr Secretary & other freinds

Curwen Family Papers, American Antiquarian Society. Addressed "For The reverend Mr John Cotton pastor of the church of christ in Plimouth These/." Endorsed " From mr Keith March, 22: 1681:" Several small holes, frayed bottom edge.

---

1. James Keith may have given the Plymouth election sermon in 1681, but it was not published. William Brinsmead gave the Massachusetts election sermon in 1681 [Evans 298]. Charles Evans, *American Bibliography* (New York, 1941–1959), 1:51.
2. Noah Newman (1631–1676) was the minister in Rehoboth. Frederick Lewis Weis, *The Colonial Clergy and the Colonial Churches of New England* (Baltimore, Md., 1936), 149.
3. William Bradford (1624–1704) fought in King Philip's War and served as representative, assistant and deputy governor in Plymouth Colony. Savage, *Genealogical Dictionary*, 1:231-32.
4. Thomas Cushman, elder of the Plymouth Church since 1649.

To Cotton Mather, 19 April 1681

Plimouth April, 19: 1681:

Endeared Cousen

I have ever cause to acknowledge your love & care of my dear child;[1] & for that alone I oft owe you a letter of gratitude which though it be slender requitall, yet being the best I have at present I desire may be accepted: The immediate occasion of now writing is by you to acquaint your father, that this day past I spake with John Cooke,[2] who was a member & Deacon of this church in Mr Rayners[3] dayes, but for scandalous persisting in offense, he was Excommunicated; he hath since Joyned himselfe to the Anabaptist-society in Road Island of which Mr Clarke[4] was Pastour: I asked him, who sent him that booke superscribed To Brother John Cooke of Dartmouth (Russels booke[5]) he answered one of them in Boston; I asked him, whether he had ever bin at their Lords supper? His Answer was, Noe, but he had twice taught amongst them on two meeting-dayes, & that the church of which he was at the Island & that at Boston did hold Communion together upon all occasions; this J: Cooke never sought Reconciliation with this Church, Joynes to the Anabaptists at R: Isle, holds communion with them at Boston, I would not have my name mentioned, but doubtlesse it is an aggravation of their sin, who can admit a Justly Excommunicate to preach amongst them.

Due respects & salutations to your parents etc

Praying that you may increase with the increases of God, I rest,

your Affectionate uncle

John Cotton

Newes from o: E: would be a kindnesse:

Mather Papers 4:9, Prince Library, Rare Book and Manuscripts, Boston Public Library. Addressed "These For his Endeared Kinsman, Sir Mather, at his father's house, in Boston, ddd." Some unrelated notes by Mather on the address leaf.

---

1. Mather probably aided Cotton's son John (1661–1706, H.C. 1681), then completing his years at Harvard. *Sibley's Harvard Graduates,* 2:212-15.
2. John Cooke (1620–1695) emigrated with his father, Francis, on the *Mayflower* and served as deacon of the Plymouth church. Dissenting from the church as a Baptist, he moved to Dartmouth in 1676 as the first settled minister and established the first Baptist church in that community. In 1673, he represented Dartmouth in the General Court and was a chief magistrate. The Plymouth Church Records do not mention his excommunication, which Stratton believes dates to "sometime between 1656 and 1658." Eugene Aubrey Stratton, *Plymouth Colony: Its History & People 1620–1691* (Salt Lake City, Ut., 1986), 98-100.
3. John Rayner (d. 1669) graduated from Magdalen College (Oxford) in 1625, emigrated to New England in 1635, and served the Plymouth church for eighteen years. Savage, *Genealogical Dictionary,* 3:514.
4. Dr. John Clarke (1609–1676) emigrated to Boston from Suffolk, England, in 1637 after receiving his degree from Cambridge. After practicing medicine in Boston for two years, he settled in Newport (the Rhode Island colony) as the first minister of the First Baptist Church. He also served as an assistant and as treasurer of the colony, as an agent for Rhode Island in England from 1651–1663 and as deputy governor of the colony from 1669–1672. Weis, *Colonial Clergy,* 56.
5. Possibly William Russel's *Brief Account of the Proceedings Against the Six Popish Priests*, (London[?], 1680) [*Early English Books,* 2:1309; Wing L3484].

To Thomas Hinckley, 16 August 1681

Plimouth August, 16: 1681:

Much Honoured

These letters from o: E:[1] I found at Leift: Haywards at Boston & have had noe opportunity hitherto for safe conveyance, but I expect by Elder chipman[2] you may soone receive them: The Batchelors Theses I now send you, the masters Questions at present I have not,[3] the Salutator much lamented the death of Govr winslow[4] in his oration, & had prepared due gratulations for your Honour, but your absence prevented expression of them. old mris stoughton[5] was buried last wednesday: It is soe neere your going into the Bay, that I am the lesse sollicitous to insert newes from o: E: that most remarkeable is, the Petition from the Lord Mayor, Alderman, common councill of London to the K: for a Parl: etc: the Answer is very sharpe & reprehensory, bespeaking the strong influence of Popish Counsells; some other petitions were presented, stuffd with Adulations from southwark etc & had very gratious answers for their loyalty:[6] The Drought very considerable in England, Holland, France: I crave excuse for noe more inlarging with forraigne newes, you will be fully satisfyed at Boston shortly:

August, 31: is a day of Humiliation to be at Cambridge, carried on by divers ministers with m^r^ Nath: Gookin,[7] Mris Kingsman is shortly to be married to Deacon Sanders, who tells me he is but 75 yeare old:[8] I hope you will order your coming to Plymouth, soe as not to returne home till you have bin at the Commission-court; M^r^ shove[9] desired me to present his service to your Honour, soe did Mr Keith,[10] from whom you will heare a very satisfying answer to take off the many lyes & slanders in the Petition: my wife is not yet returned home; with my humble service presented to you & mris Hinckley, craving your prayers for me & mine, I rest, Sir,

your Honours obliged

John Cotton

The death of your son Rawsons child[11] I suppose is noe newes, the Lord doe them good by it: old m^r^ Jackson of Cambridge village,[12] blessed M^r^ oakes[13] was at his funerall a few dayes before his owne, Proh dolor![14]

Hinckley Papers, appendix 1:7, Prince Library, Rare Book and Manuscripts, Boston Public Library. Addressed "For the Honourable, Thomas Hinckley Esquire, Governour of Plymouth-Colony, these in Barnstable."

---

1. "Old England."
2. For Plymouth's elder, John Chipman, see the letter of 9 March 1688.
3. The class of 1681 included Cotton's son John III and Samuel Mitchel, John Hastings, Noadiah Russell, James Pierpont, John Davie, Samuel Russell, William Denison and Joseph Eliot. The questions are reprinted in *Sibley's Harvard Graduates,* 3:210-11.
4. Josiah Winslow (1629–1680) was the son of Plymouth's prominent settler Gov. Edward Winslow. Winslow was one of the students who left Harvard in 1642 in protest over the changed length of study. Josiah served as a representative to the General Court, an assistant, and commander-in-chief of the United Forces in King Philip's War. He was also one of the commissioners of the United Colonies of New England. Elected governor in 1673 after Thomas Prence's death, Winslow served until his own passing on 23 December 1680. Stratton, *Plymouth Colony,* 85, 102, 109-11, 113; *Sibley's Harvard Graduates,* 1:16.
5. Possibly Elizabeth Knight Stoughton, the widow of Israel Stoughton, who died in England in 1644, and the mother of Gov.William Stoughton. Torrey does not list a birth date for her, but Savage indicates that "the widow lived long." Savage, *Genealogical Dictionary,* 4:213; *Sibley's Harvard Graduates,* 1:194-95; Almon Torrey, *New England Marriages Prior to 1700* (Baltimore, Md., 1865), 715.
6. After dissolving the Oxford Parliament in March 1681, Charles was in no mood to consider seating another, especially since Louis XIV had just agreed to grant him a hefty subsidy, allowing him to do without Parliament in the immediate future. Fraser, *Royal Charles,* 407.

7. Nathaniel Gookin (1656–1692, H.C. 1675) was the minister in Cambridge (1682–1692). *Sibley's Harvard Graduates,* 2:474-80.

8. Torrey lists a marriage between Robert Sanderson (d. 1693) and Elizabeth Kingswill (d. 1695, aged 78) on 24 August 1681 in Boston. Savage confirms that a Robert Saunderson of Hampton and Watertown married a widow named Elizabeth and served as a deacon in Boston. Torrey, *New England Marriages,* 649; Savage, *Genealogical Dictionary,* 4:22-23.

9. George Shove (1634–1687, H.C. 1650, 1652) was the minister in Taunton (1665–1687). Weis, *Colonial Clergy,* 187.

10. James Keith (1643–1719) was the minister in Bridgewater (1663–1719). Weis, *Colonial Clergy,* 120.

11. Thomas Hinckley married widow Mary Smith Glover (c. 1650–1703) in 1660 in Barnstable. Her daughter, Ann Glover Rawson (d. 1730), and son-in-law, William Rawson (1651–1728), had six children who died young before 1681: Ann (b. 1674), Wilson (b. 1675), Margaret (b. 1676), Edward (b. 1677), Edward (b. 1678), Rachel (b. October 1679) and Dorothy (b. 8 August 1681). The family Bible indicates that all of the above children died in infancy, so Cotton is probably referring to the newborn Dorothy in this letter. Of their twenty children born 1674–1698, fifteen died young. Savage, *Genealogical Dictionary,* 3:511; 2:262; Sullivan S. Rawson, *The Rawson Family* (Boston, 1849), 14.

12. Edward Jackson was born c. 1604 in London, emigrated to New England in 1643 and purchased Thomas Mayhew's old farm in Cambridge Village, now called Newton. With two wives he had nineteen children. He also donated a large tract of land in Billerica to Harvard College. Jackson died on 17 July 1681. Savage, *Genealogical Dictionary,* 2:527-28.

13. Urian Oakes (1631–1681, H.C. 1649) died on 25 July 1681 after battling a "malignant fever" for several days. Oakes had been born in England, emigrated to New England in 1634 as a child and returned to England in 1653. After being silenced for non-conformity in 1662 during the Restoration, Oakes again sailed for New England. At his death, he was pastor of the church in Cambridge and president of Harvard College. *Sibley's Harvard Graduates,* 1:173-85.

14. "Oh Sadness!"

To Thomas Hinckley, 13 January 1682

Plymouth January, 13: 1681:

Much Honoured Sir

one Latine sentence from a Governour[1] Justly merits from me many sentences in way of Retaliation; & though at present I cannot send soe fully as I would, (my son being not to returne till the morrow) yet duty obliges to give you a hint of what from uncertaine rumors is this day turned into reall certainties by Capt Thomas, (whom I even now spake with, & who came lately from Boston) The King in his letter[2] doth take notice of their not sending messengers, but imputes it not to their disloyalty, yet expresly requires their attending his Command in that respect, & will not have his Authority slighted: It is taken for granted by Godly-wise, that the Immediate cause of the diversion of further harshnesse, was an Embassadour from the States of Holland, who (as God ordered it, & (as some suppose) was contrived by some Religious Protestants of the Councill) came in the very Instant when great Motions were on foote for regulations (or rather subversions) of Massachusets, & solemnly demands in the Name of the States, that his Majesty would forth with declare whether he were for Protestantisme yea or noe, they had waited long to know his resolution in that respect & could not, would not tarry any longer for his answer, they had suffered much by delayes, & now call for a speedy result; hence it was noe time to destroy N: E:[3] a place of Protestants, our peace is yet lengthened out & our pleasant things not taken away, upon this account publick thankes is given in sundry congregations in the Bay: Mr Randolph hath complained, that violation of the Kings Lawes respecting trade is connived at,[4] & that when he sues any on that account, he is forced to pay monyes (which is not the custome in such cases in o: E:[5]) & that he hath not Justice etc: the King writes on his behalfe, that they be carefull to doe him Justice, that he be heard without demanding mony of him, that his appeals to o: E: be allowed in case he be not satisfyed with any verdict etc. The Duke of Yorke hath as much acknowledgment in & from Scotland as his heart desires;[6] Papists have great hopes that the King will declare for them; the French King goes on doing mischeife:

old Mr Ting is dead:[7] the Awful hand of God in permitting Scandalous sinnes to breake forth here (I presume) is noe newes to you; Samuel Dunham,[8] a poore old Drunkard, God gave the church strength to purge him out; the Case of George Watson & his wife[9] was before the Church last Sabbath, & last wednesday, they show some signes of the beginning of Repentance, yet wee are generally agreed this next Sabbath to proceed to censure, & have appointed Feb: 8: for a day of Humiliation (the church alone) on the account of such sad outbreakings; pitty, Good Sir, & pray for this poore Church, that upon it may be engraven, Holines to the Lord.

My selfe & wife present our humble service to you and mris Hinckley, begging to be continually remembered in your prayers,

I rest, sir your Honours to Love & serve,

John Cotton Senior.

Mr Saltonstall hath a printed booke in vindication of the Protestants, & Capt Thomas hath many printed peices of newes, could I obtaine them I would soone transmit them to your Honour.

your letter to Mr Randolph I this day received, & shall send by the first.[10]

Hinckley Papers 1:27, Prince Library, Rare Book and Manuscripts, Boston Public Library. Addressed "These For the Honourable, Thomas Hinckley Esquire, Governour of his Majesties Colony of New Plimouth, living at Barnstable."

1. Not found.

2. King Charles had previously demanded that Massachusetts send agents to England who had been authorized to negotiate changes to the colony's charter. Colony officials had stalled the process by neglecting to do so. Exasperated, in October 1681 the Lords of Trade threatened Massachusetts with a writ of *quo warranto* if it did not send fully empowered agents immediately. Viola Florence Barnes, *The Dominion of New England: A Study in British Colonial Policy* (New Haven, Conn., 1923), 20.

3. "New England."

4. Massachusetts persistently ignored or thwarted the "Navigation Laws" passed by Parliament to regulate trade. Randolph, the court-appointed customs agent, enjoyed no cooperation from colonial authorities in his attempts to collect duties or enforce regulations.

5. "Old England."

6. In October 1679, James, Duke of York was packed off to Scotland as High Commissioner, in large part to remove his abrasive presence from the political hotbed of the Court. He did well in a difficult situation and returned to England in June 1682. Fraser, *Royal Charles,* 384, 418.

7. Edward Ting was 71 when he died on 28 December 1681 in Dunstable. He had been a merchant and brewer in Boston, married Mary Sears before 1640 and had fourteen children. Savage, *Genealogical Dictionary,* 4:356-57; Torrey, *New England Marriages,* 762.

8. Apparently after repeated warnings, Dunham, "failing by intemperance," refused to attend church and was "offensive" when the gathered church scolded him at a "private chh-meeting." Even after the congregants "exercis[ed] patience towards him for 2 Sabbaths more," Dunham refused to attend and, more importantly, was "not humbling himselfe." He was excommunicated, although two years later he "was reconciled to the chh." In 1688, Dunham "was burned to death in his house 24th Jan." Publications of the Colonial Society of Massachusetts *Collections* (hereafter *CSM*), 22 (Boston, 1920), 157, 252; *Vital Records of Plymouth, Massachusetts, to the Year 1850*, comp. Lee D. Van Antwerp, ed. Ruth Wilder Sherman (Camden, Me., 1993), 134.

9. Cotton's notes for 1682 suffered serious damage, but he wrote "[ ]son & his wife were called forth, [ ]onciliation, the brethren [ ] for a full [ ]manifestation." *CSM*, 22:250.

10. Not found.

From Cotton Mather, 19 January 1682

Boston 19d 11m 1681/2

Worthily respected Uncle—,

I promised to send you an Acct of what considerable News comes in ye late ships from England—I might have continued almost silent, & yett have kept my promise: there is so little Remarkeable that occurs; —The old word, yt wee were wont to have as ye First in Every seaman's mouth, in answer to ye Q. What News, —is still used, —All peace, & quietness—The story of ye Insurrection in scotland which wee had by Way of Holland,[1] is yt whereof I may say, as a scotchman upon another occasion did, It is but a Fable —As to what concerns N. E. in O. E.[2] The King hath sent a pretty favrable letter,[3] wherein yett Hee saies, Hee don't so accept o^{r} Excuse for o^{r} Not sending Agents, but that Hee expects wee should within 3 moneths (I think) yett do it, or incurr ye blott & guilt of Disloyalty—That which made Exceeding well for a moderate letter sent to us from His Majty, was, yt ye states of Holland sent over to England a somewhat rugged Embassadr who declared their Expectations yt ye King should now manifest Himself, whether Hee would join Cordially in ye protestant League, —or be a Friend to ye French K^{s} Interest[4]—This putt ye Court into an huge perplexity; & coming just at ye Time when o^{r} N. E. business was under Debate, it did so divert them yt they had not leisure to take Rigid notice of us—

In all other respects so farr as I can learn, things continue in statu quo prius[5]—Randolph is come with his family, —& has hired Mr Hez: Ushers house,[6] —where the Ministers wre wont to meet: —Heu! Domus Antiqua[7] &c—Of ye state of ye Colledge my Cousin will (I suppose) give you fuller Information in some Respects then I can—Si Vales, bene est, —ego [quoque] Valeo[8]—Excuse these Hasty Lines—written currente, & calente calamo,[9] —accept this small service, as from one not having an opportunity to do greater—present my service to my Aunt, —love to Cousens—and Continue to pray for

Your

C. M. —

Miscellaneous Manuscripts, The New-York Historical Society. Addressed "These For the Revd, —my Hond Uncle Mr John Cotton Pastor to ye Church in Plymouth." Endorsed "From my Cousen, mr Cotton Mather, January, 19: 1681:."

---

1. There had been anti-government revolts in 1679 and 1680, and the situation in Scotland remained volatile.
2. "New England in Old England."
3. See 13 January 1682.
4. The Dutch were naturally alarmed by Charles's close relationship with Louis XIV and hoped to clarify the ostensibly Protestant king's position.
5. "As they were."
6. Hezekiah Usher (d. 1676) was a Boston merchant and an early bookseller and publisher. Cotton may also be referring to Usher's eldest son, Hezekiah (1639–1696), who may have been in Lynn at this time and renting his Boston house. Savage, *Genealogical Dictionary,* 4:362-63; Isaiah Thomas, *The History of Printing in America,* ed. Marcus McCorison (1810; reprint, New York, 1970), 183-84.
7. "Oh! Old house."
8. "If you are well, it is well, and I also am well."
9. "With a hot and hurried pen."

From [Zechariah] Walker, 1683[1]

Rev^{D} & Dear Bro^{R}

Y^{rs} of ye 19th of January last I Rec^{d} & both by ye Contents & Dimensions of it, I perceived that it was a Winter Production, being of very little Growth. However I value it at a high Rate, ye Market always rising as things grow scarce. And just now it comes to Mind that the last Epistles of John are very short—You say that a great sum of Money should not have prevailed with you had you been within 40 Miles of Woodbury, to have returned home till you had seen me, I verily believe it—but you have taken sufficient Care y^{t} none shall have the Temptation, by keeping at a greater Distance. It's a fine easy Way to set still & appoint Others y^{r} Work. You add that you forbear Censuring &c And you do very well for—it is not safe for him who hath many Glass Windows, to throw stones at his Neighbors house, besides y^{t} Bulletts do Execution by a Rebound. At length You make a Master of your Martial spirits, & threaten to beat up my Quarters: but when? why so soon as you can get a convenient supply for your People: very ambiguous! If You mean only a supply for Ministerial Work, while you are abroad upon that Expedition, there may be some hope y^{r} Valour may be brought upon Proof: But if it must be deferred till all y^{r} Batchelors be supplied with convenient Wives, & your Maids with convenient Husbands, & such as either do, or think they want it with a convenient supply of Money, I shall not fear an Assault. In plainness I have so long in vain Expected a visit, y^{t} when you write of it, I Conclude you write in Jest, & y^{r}fore have answered accordingly, that ye Comment might Agree with ye Text.

Josiah Cotton, Manuscript "Account of the Cotton Family," Houghton Library, Harvard University.

---

1. In his "Account of the Cotton Family," Josiah Cotton prefaces this letter, "I shall next Transcribe some Passages out of 2 Letters from my Uncle Walker to my Father; One Jocose, ye Other: serious Dated 1683 & 1686." The second follows below.

From Josiah Rosseter,[1] 14 February 1683

GILFORD FEBRUARY 14: 1682

SIR

I sent to you[2] by henry wise[3] but he heard not whether you had Resevead it while he was there or not: I was drove to a short time in getting my Letters Ready for henry wise to bring to boston he being the Last opertunyty that I could heare of: what I did in hase or through weakenes pray pardon: I heare nothing conserning our ingland buisenes if doctor waldin[4] dos intend to try for if in england it will be very nesesary that you take some securyty from under his hand for his delevery of the mony to us if he gaine it or to delever up the writing to us if he gaine not the mony this is the Argment of those that understand those matters therefore if it be not to Late when this comes to your hands pray mind it: I have noe newse but could be glad to heare the sertainty of newse from england by your hand soe far as we can heare if it is Like to goe heard wt boston and soe wt us alsoe if the Lord prevent not the greate desines of the world: what neede have wee to prepare for those times that we may not be taken unawares the Lord help us soe to doe: I should be glad to heare from you by the bearer heare of Augustin: williams[5] an almonack[6] would be welcom: we are all prity well at this time my self wife and good thomas crittenden[7] Present our Respeckts to your self and wife our Love to all our cosens that are wt you cosen betty[8] intended to be maryead before now and soe possibly shee may have left you. not els but Rest yours to comand

Josiah Rossetter

Curwen Family Papers, American Antiquarian Society. Addressed "For mr John Cotten pastor of the church of christ att plimouth." Endorsed "From Brother Rosseter February, 14: 1682:"

---

1. Josiah is Joanna Cotton's brother, son of Bray and Elizabeth Rosseter. He married Sarah Sherman before 1677 and had moved to Guilford, Connecticut, from Killingsworth by 1682 at the latest. Josiah served as a representative from 1701 to 1711 and died on 31 January 1716. See 24 September 1669. Savage, *Genealogical Dictionary,* 3:577-78.
2. Not found.
3. Henry Wise (1655–1684) lived in Guilford, Connecticut. Savage, *Genealogical Dictionary,* 4: 614; Torrey, *New England Marriages,* 830.
4. Possibly Dr. Isaac Waldron (d. 1683), who lived and practiced in Portsmouth, Bristol and Boston. Savage, *Genealogical Dictionary,* 4:389.
5. Augustine Williams, of Stonington and Killingsworth, Connecticut, died before 1699. Savage, *Genealogical Dictionary,* 4:559; Torrey, *New England Marriages,* 818.

6. Cotton Mather authored the 1683 almanac *The Boston Ephemeris* (Boston, 1683) [Evans 351]. Evans, *American Bibliography*, 1:58.
7. Thomas Crittenden (1667–1754) was the son of Abraham and Susanna Grigson Crittenden. He married Abigail Hull (1669–1710) in 1690 and lived in Guilford, Connecticut. Savage prefers "Cruttenden." Savage, *Genealogical Dictionary,* 1:481.
8. Elizabeth Cotton (1663–1743), John and Joanna's second child and eldest daughter, married Rev. James Alling (1657–1696, H.C. 1679), the minister of Salisbury, in 1688. She was still living at home unmarried when Rosseter enquired after her in this letter. *Sibley's Harvard Graduates,* 1:506.

From Cotton Mather, 28 February 1683 [28 March 1682][1]

[. . . .]82

Honrd Syr!

Your Last[2] was very welcome: for it brought mee nothing but good Newes. —The Increase of Christs Church among you, must increase ye Joy of every well-principled Heart yt knowes it. —Really! The Report of one souls being brought to renounce Idols. —& Draw near to God in Christ, is to say no more, Worth hearing. —Happy N. E! where o^{r} gloriose Master has not yet broke up House! —

But will you not wonder that I <have> could find nothing but good Newes in your affectionate Lines, when some of ye first of 'em are, I have tasted deeply of ye cup of affliction this winter! —Nay. —but I don't recall ye word. —For you as well as David, will say, —It is good for mee yt I have been afflicted![3] —Surely! You have many a Time given yourself, & yours, & all your concerns, into ye Hands of God in Christ Jesus! What? And will you not Stand to His managements? Or will you imagine any other, but that, as not a Sparrow in your field, no, nor an Hair on your Head, falls to ye Ground without a concernment of His ever-watchfull Providence about ye Same,[4] So, Hee yt has performed all things for you, has dispos'd of 'em ten thousand times better then if you had carv'd for yourself —oh! for such gallant, & Lofty attainments, as to Love No creature wth a Distinct Love from ye Love of God. —& to have No Will distinct from ye Will of God! —But—facile omnes cum Valemus recta Consilia egrotis [damus][5]. —

Nay, —I do but pour water into ye sea, when one of my Low, & Dirty Spirit, goes to revive in you ye Noble Inclinacions, wherein doubtless you abound. —Only then, in ye upshot. —I can hear of No Ill befallen you, —for, Say to ye Righteous, It shall be well wth Him! &, o^{r} Light afflictions Work more glory. —&, Blow High, Blow Low, tis an ill wind indeed yt will not Blow good to them, When ye Promise sais, All things work together for good unto. —yea. — [. . . .] Comfortable Conclusion, yt Speaks [. . . .] reported to your sick Family, is yt [. . . .] [a]bundently confirm what has already [. . . .] ye rather, because of—Isa. 33. 24[6]— [. . . .] indeed, & ye whole Town almost, has been Visited wth ye Epidemical Cold. — (of which o^r^ youngest is now somewt dangerously ill—) —And I have myself smarted under it somewhat more then many of my Neighbrs. —for, I was kept a prisoner by it a matter of Three weeks. —& to my good D^rs^ apprehension, when I was first siezed wth my illness, —I was in some Likelihood of bidding my friends in this wearisome {I most truly, & feelingly call it, Wearisome} world, Good Night! —Nevertheless, I am abroad agn, tho: Labring (as a better Young man once did) under often Infirmityes. —& Likely (&, I sometimes think, —tho: I thank christ, without any a sticking affection—) to drop away when it is not expected. —only lett mee be found so doing. —& no body will be a Looser. —

So my pen Rambles! —But I must check its motions. —& only add. —That there is nothing of Newes stirring. —No, Not from England, in ye Last Vessels. —No, Not in one yt is now arriv'd from Rochel. —wth but Two moneths passage. —All things remaining as they were. — (h.e. The Earth removing. —& ye mountains carrying into ye midst of ye Sea, —& ye waters roaring & being troubled. —) Except I should say, That London has Lately been forc'd to part wth their Libertyes so far, as to admitt sherifs not of their own, but ye Courts Choosing.[7] —& what shall wee poor shrubs expect, when ye stately cedars crack!

Tomorrow, there is a Day of Prayer kept in o^r^ south-meeting-house. —& which bodes well, there is indeed a mighty Spirit of Prayer among us. —

I should be glad to hear from my Cousin Jno, —& should be willing enough to write to him, would he give mee any occasion. —o^r^ Church did about two moneths ago Pass an unanimous Vote. —desiring a Day might speedily be appointed for ye ordination of yt Same sorry Soul,[8] who, I Suppose, will no wayes comply wth ye mention'd address. But Who, I am sure does both need, & crave your daily prayers. —For I need not tell you, —my paper will Scarce give mee room, to tell you, Tis,

Your C Mather

William L. Clements Library, University of Michigan, Ann Arbor. Addressed "to the Revd (my Hond Uncle, —) Mr Jno Cotton Pastor to ye Church of Christ, in Plymouth." Endorsed "[. . . .]en Cotton Mather [. . . .], 28: 1682:." In a later hand: "(the date is probably March 28, 1682.)" Tear at top of page.

---

1. Mather's letter includes news of events that occurred in September 1682, so the date is more likely 28 February 1682/83.

2. Not found.

3. Several Bible verses refer to David's affliction, including 2 Samuel 16 and Psalms 132.

4. Matt. 10:29-30: "Are not two sparrows sold for a farthing? And one of them shall not fall on the ground without your Father. But the very hairs of your head are all numbered."

5. "When well, we all give correct advice to the sick."

6. Isa. 33:24: "And the inhabitant shall not say, I am sick: the people that dwell therein shall be forgiven their iniquity."

7. The king's attack on the Massachusetts charter was part of a much larger pattern. Invoking *quo warrento* often on minor pretexts, the Crown managed to reissue charters to a number of towns, including York, Colchester, Lyme Regis and even London. In each case, the king was given the power to veto the elections of officers. The result was the election of Tory sheriffs in London in September 1682. Fraser, *Royal Charles,* 422, 425.

8. Cotton Mather served as his father's assistant at Second Church in Boston (North Church) beginning in February 1681. He was called by North Church in December 1682, on 8 January1683 and on 3 August 1684. He was finally ordained after "many Days of *Fasting* and *Prayer*" on 13 May 1685. *Sibley's Harvard Graduates,* 3:7-8.

From James Keith, 6 March 1683

Bridgewater March 6 '82

Reverend & Dear Sir.

I received yours of Jan. 3.[1] & your last also of Feb.9[2] both which came to my hand diverse weeks after their date I thank [you] with all my heart for your affectionate remembrance of me under my affliction. I acknowledge myself a deep debtor to you & should have made some returns before this time, but that I have been shut up under many sorrows, being bereaved of diverse of my choicest friends. The death of our precious elder[3] is an irreparable breach upon this poor church & upon me. God hath removed him in judgement to this place. O that we were sensible of the Lord's controversy, & that it would please God to awaken us unto true repentance before the decree bring forth. I feared his removal some considerable time before God took him from us. His eminency in grace did prepare him for Glory. My hands are now much weakened in my work. How the Lord will dispose of me I cannot tell, but desire to roll the care of all my concerns upon him. I have been upheld this winter in some measure above expectation in my ministry; though I am still laboring under much infirmity of body. If the Lord will again suspend me from his work, I desire to submit to his sovereign dispose. My soul mourns for those abominations and grievous scandals which have lately broke out among your people:[4] but I rejoice to hear that God hath strengthened your heart and hands in the exercise of discipline and that you have been carried through such difficult work with Union & unanimity. The great affair of my dear friend, who is to me more than a father is not yet brought to an issue. The notion is earnestly followed by those who are concerned, but whether he will accept is a great question. Let us pray for him. I thank you heartily for my long and liberal election entertainment the last year. I cannot enlarge, being now going to Waymouth; heartily remembering Mrs Cotton, earnestly desiring your prayers for me, & commending you to the grace of christ, I rest

your real affectionate friend & unworthy brother in the work of the Lord

James Keith

John Davis Papers, Massachusetts Historical Society. Addressed "For the Revd Mr. John Cotton pastor of the Church in Plymouth." Endorsed "From Mr. Keith march 6. 1682." From a manuscript copy of the original.

---

1. Not found.
2. Not found.
3. William Brett emigrated to Duxbury, Plymouth Colony, from Kent by 1645 and was one of the original settlers of Bridgewater. Brett served as an elder in Keith's church, and occasionally preached in his absence, until he died in December 1681. Edward Mitchell, *History of Bridgewater, Massachusetts* (Bridgewater, Mass., 1897), 44, 120.
4. Keith is probably referring to disputes within Cotton's congregation, which Cotton later blamed on Satan, at least publicly: "Satan is always busy to make divisions in the ches, some differences fell out about this time in the chh..." In January 1683, Cotton was unwilling even to write about the dispute in the church records: "a church-meeting attended in the Pastors absence, after the conference, in which the Propositions made by the Pastour the meeting before were read, but the agitation & Issue of that meeting had best be buried in silence." By March 1684, Cotton agreed to seek the advice of neighboring churches. See 11 March 1684 below. *CSM*, 22:159, 251, 253.

To Cotton Mather, 13 December 1683

December, 13: 1683:

Deare Cousen

The enclosed[1] I received but yesterday, I hope it comes not too late for the presse; the two sons mentioned came to untimely ends, Thomas drowned by casting away of the boat in which he was; Benjamin[2] slaine with Capt Peirce;[3] concerning ought remarkeable towards the death of mr & mris southworth[4] I write not, only, I know there was a dismall darke cloud & a terrible thunder clap within halfe an houre of his death, mr southworth himselfe observed the great darkness & heard the thunder, for he asked if that noise was not thunder; <but> The Relation of this man is faithfull, he is a child of godly parents, both dead, his father but lately; I conclude your Revd father will give the substance of this Narrative an Imprimatur:

I hope you will hand me a few lines of winter-newes from Gen: Court, Elec: Preacher etc & something of my son John, if you heare of him, I cannot heare a word concerning him since I left Boston; my wife is at Taunton; Due salutations to your selfe & parents & my Cousens; The Lord delight more & more to blesse you with the best blessings; Pray for me & mine,

I am, your Affectionate uncle

John Cotton

Miscellaneous Bound Collection, Massachusetts Historical Society. Addressed "These for his Esteemed Kinsman, Mr Cotton Mather, Preacher of the Gospel at Boston."

---

1. Not found.
2. These seem to have been potential contributions to Increase Mather's work in progress on "Remarkable Providences." Neither the dead brothers nor the Southworths seem to have made it into Mather's published work, *An Essay for the Recording of Illustrious Providences*. See 13 December 1683 for a story that did.
3. Captain Michael Pierce (1615–1676) was killed along with fifty settlers and twenty English-allied Natives in the "Swamp Fight" that took place in Rehoboth on 26 March 1676. Noah Newman's letter to John Cotton describes the fight and lists the Plymouth Colony dead. See the above letter of 27 March 1676. Savage, *Genealogical Dictionary,* 3:430.
4. Constant Southworth died on 11 March 1679 and his wife, Elizabeth Collier Southworth, died in 1682. Constant Southworth's mother married Plymouth's Gov. William Bradford in 1623, and Constant served in many government positions, including those of treasurer and assistant; he also served in the Duxbury military company. Stratton, *Plymouth Colony,* 355-56; Savage, *Genalogical Dictionary,* 4:143.

From Cotton Mather, 20 December 1683

Honrd Syr

These Lines wait upon you to Thank you for yo [...] & to request you that since Mr W^s Narrative of [...] storm[1] is imperfect as to ye circumstance of ye [...] of ye Bricks by it you would please to Enquire of That, so as to [inform?] us ye next week, if it may be, because ye Boock at ye press will, I suppose then be finished.

I know not what else to add, But that persecutions of the Dissenters do Encrease in England[2] & to a marvellous heighth & many persons of all Ranks are forc'd to fly;

A gentleman, a Deacon of Dr Annesleyes Church,[3] yt is arrived here Last week, told mee, That there are Warrants out for Every Non-conformist Minister in the city of London. Two or Three Religios Noblemen are sd to have absconded in Scotland lately; In London, ye Common-Council having an Instrument sent them by ye King for them to sign their Resignation to His pleasure, retracted their old Vote of Compliance; & refused to do what was required in ye matter of submission.[4] Upon which His Majesty has Entred Judgment against ye Charter, & appointed instead of ye Mayor a Custos Civitatis, & in stead of ye Aldermen, a Number of pickt Justices to Supply their place.

In Hungaria there is ye most signal Revolution which this Last Age hath brought forth. The Male-contents, as they're called, have made most honourable Articles with ye Turks,—to pay them forty Thousand crowns annual acknowledgement, & for this to command on all occasions ye whole Turkish power to assist them—Hungary is not upon ye matter all Theirs. The Jesuits are not only banished That Kingdome but perpetually exiled from all ye Turkish Dominions. Count Techli is a King & ye Hungarians after his Death are to choose whom they please for his successor.[5] The churches have ye Libertyes of ye gospel againe & so have ye scholes. The suffering protestants return from all Quarters to their Ancient possessions. The Witnesses stand upon their feet, & prophecy [hear.] ye Great Voice from Heaven & the [light.] which is risen in that most Eastern part

[illegible line][6]

The Turks had allmost carried Vienna when an Army of germany, & Polanders with great losse to themselves, forced them to raise their siege.[7] Nevertheless in their march away they swept ye Countryes horribly & are Like to be at it again Early in ye Spring—

At piscataqua just now the Governr & Council have passed an Act That all above 16 years old shall not be debarred the Blessed Sacrament & That all children shall be christened & this after ye Liturgy-way, if it be desired by ye parents. and half a years Imprisonment, without Bond or Bail, is ye penalty of Transgressing ye sd Act.[8]

Here's enough to bespeak, & quicken your prayers &c&c&c

Who is to preach o^r^ Election sermon is not yett determined.[9] Neither is it, Whether [wee shall?] have above one Election more—

Curwen Family Papers, American Antiquarian Society. Addressed "To the Revd mr John Cotton Plimouth." Noted in another hand: "From my Cousen Coten Mather 20: Dec: 1683:" Hole in first page.

1. Increase Mather, *An Essay for the Recording of Illustrious Providences* (Boston, 1684) [Evans 372]. The incident in question is probably described in chapter 3, pp. 74-75, in which lightning severely damaged a house in Marshfield and killed one person in 1658. The identity of "Mr W" is unclear.

2. In the last years of his life, Charles II, the would-be absolute king, worked to quash any perceived challenge to his authority.

3. Samuel Annesly (1620[?]–1696), eminent Non-conformist divine, was named "Lecturer of St. Paul's" by Oliver Cromwell and briefly led the church at St. Giles, Cripplegate, before being ejected in 1662. *Dictionary of National Biography*, ed. Leslie Stephen and Sidney Lee, 63 vols. (London, 1885-1900) (hereafter *DNB*).

4. This represented more news concerning the reluctant surrender of London's charter. In June 1684, the justices of King's Bench ruled that the city's charter would be placed in the king's hands. Fraser, *Royal Charles,* 422.

5. The "malcontents" are probably the "Kurak," former soldiers, lesser nobility and outlaws angry about the Hapsburg inaction against the Ottoman invaders. Persecuted by Royal Hungary, they revolted in desperation, with Ottoman support. The Kurak of Transylvania were commanded by Imre Thököly, a young nobleman who led them to victory and a favorable armistice with Emperor Leopold I in 1682. Although he temporarily won autonomy for Transylvania, he was not a king. Peter F. Sugar et al., *A History of Hungary* (Bloomington, Ind., 1990), 115-16.

6. John Cotton transcribed Mather's news in his letter to Thomas Hinckley of 27 December 1683. In Cotton's transcription, the missing line reads, "of Europe is longed for westward by many, more than the day by the morning-watchers."

7. Emboldened by Thököly's successes against the Hapsburgs, Ottoman forces marched from Istanbul to invade Vienna. The famous siege began on 14 July 1683, but an alarmed Papacy brokered a holy alliance comprised of its own forces and troops from Venice, Poland and the Holy Roman Empire. The Ottomans broke off the siege on 12 September, with heavy losses. Sugar, *History of Hungary,* 116.

8. Massachusetts had purchased the Province of Maine from the heirs of Sir Ferdinando Georges in 1680.

9. Beverly's minister, John Hale (1636–1700, H.C. 1657), preached the election sermon in May 1684 on Judg. 3:1-2: "Now these *are* the nations which the Lord left, to prove Israel by them, *even* as many *of Israel* as had not known all the wars of Canaan; Only that the generations of the children of Israel might know, to teach them war, at the least such as before knew nothing thereof." Sibley suggests that the sermon was printed by order of the General Court, but Evans wrote that it was not printed. *Sibley's Harvard Graduates,* 1:509-20; Evans, *American Bibliography*, 1:59 [Evans 360].

To Thomas Hinckley, 27 December 1683

Plimouth December, 27: 1683:

Much Honoured Sir

Having lately received tidings of great import from a solid hand[1] I take my selfe obliged to present your Honour therewith.

"Persecutions of the dissenters doe increase in England etc to a marvellous heighth & many persons of all rankes are forc'd to fly, A Gentleman, a Deacon of D[r] Annesleyes Church that is arrived here last weeke told me that there are warrants out for every Non-conformist-minister in the City of London; Two or three religious Noblemen are said to have absconded in Scotland lately. In London the Common Councill having an Instrument sent them by the King for them to signe their Resignation to his pleasure, retracted their old vote of compliance & refused to doe what was required in the matter of submission, upon which his Majesty hath entered Judgment against the charter & appointed instead of the mayor, a custos civitatis, & instead of the Aldermen, a number of pickt Justices to supply their place.

In Hungaria there is the most signall Revolution which this last age hath brought forth: The Male-contents, as they are called, have made most honourable Articles with the Turkes, to pay them forty thousand crownes annuall acknowledgment & for this to command on all occasions the whole Turkish power to asist them; Hungary is now upon the matter all theirs; The Jesuites are not only banished that Kingdom, but perpetually exiled from all the Turkish dominions: Count Techli [Tekeli] is a King & the Hungarians after his decease to choose whom they please for his successour; The churches have the liberties of the Gospel againe & soe have the schooles; the suffering Protestants returne from all quarters to their antient possessions; the witnesses stand upon their feete & hear the great voice from heaven, & the light in which is risen in that most Easterne part of Europe is longed for westward by many, more than the day by the morning-watchers.

The Turkes had almost carried vienna, when an Army of Germany & Polanders with great losse to themselves, forced them to raise their siege, Neverthelesse in their March away they swept the Countreys horribly, & are like to be at it againe early in the spring"

God is doing great things in the world, he in mercy prepare us to meete him; With due service from me & mine to you & yours, requesting your daily prayers, I rest, Sir

your Honours servant

John Cotton

Hinckley Papers 1:54, Prince Library, Rare Book and Manuscripts, Boston Public Library. Addressed "These For the Honourable, Thomas Hinckley Esquire, Governour of New Plimouth Colony, living at Barnstable."

1. The "solid hand" is Cotton Mather's; the whole letter is a direct quotation from the previous letter, Cotton Mather to John Cotton, 20 December 1683.

To? [1684][1]

SIR

Our trialls are increasing now upon us, our Zions travell-throws are now upon her, she begins to be in paines, o pray for us who are become captives in our owne land, our persecutors are resolute, they study our ruine every day, they have invented noe lesse then 15 shamefull plots to turne upon us if they could, but have fixed them without any shew of colour, by which our signes doe hang in doubt over our heads day & night, sometimes they are putting one statute in force against us, sometimes another, sometimes our friends are indited for not coming to church by the twelve penny an[d] sometimes by the act of ten pounds a moneth, thousands excommunicated & many arrested upon it, wee are a prey to our common bayliffs who without any order can make lists of names & pretend them as orders from the sessions on purpose to make their advantage upon the feares & ignorance of our countrey christians:

In many places they are rifling the houses of the Lords people for being at meeting, pulling away goods from some unto whom bread should be given for their wants; our prisons they fill with the bodyes of the saints, they catch up our ministers whereever they find them within 15 miles of a corporation, two ministers are at this time in our Countrey prison, one of them made a prisoner for visiting the other; our charters of our corporations are given up in many places by a prevailing party with plans to alter the goverment of the place that it may convert to their proper purpose; In all our sufferings wee are denyed the benefit of all Law, & those statutes which were made against the Papists are turned upon us, & wee doe feare as soone as they can ripen things the Papists shall stand in our complexion & wee in theirs:

Bristoll is almost undone through the length of the troubles which have fallen upon them, they are forced out of the citty to worship God, 3 miles & more from the place, & cannot meete in quiet there neither; Lately as they met by a Rivers side to avoyd the pursuers which came out of Bristoll after them, the minister & one more run into the River, the man which run in with the minister is drowned, & the minister lay in a dying Conidtion for a moneth after, but I heare now he is Like to weather that point: Wee have the Act of Conventicles prosecuted against some for bare family-duties, such is the debauchery of the Informers & the readynesse of some Magistrates to receive their Informations; In many places they have sworne Commissions upon persons that could proove they had bin at the church in publick the same time, but noe redresse will be affoarded them upon any appeale; There is but one thing more wanting to compleat our misery which is endeavoured after as soone as things can ripen, & that is a Parliament & then wee expect totall banishment & confiscation.

Our misery is, that these things have made many to goe back againe that were once asistant to us in our wildernesse travells, which greatly raiseth the spirits of our adversaries, & straitens our hands that are left behind;

Our misery is, that wee draw not one way in our yoke, but have many of our brethren employed against us to plead Conformity Lawfull, who study to say more for our adversaries cause then they can say themselves;

Our misery is, that our late church-members which have left their fellowship through feare, are ready to accuse the rest, which stand as criminall;

our misery is, that wee dare not deal with our offending members for feare that in soe doing wee shall be indited in our publick Sessions for being offenders our selves;

Our misery is, that wee cannot visit our imprisoned brethren (in some places) for feare wee should be prisoners our selves;

Our misery is, that our ministers in private meetings are afraid to preach all truths lest treasonable passages should be sworne against them; our misery is, that our ablest sort of christians who have much of this world are pickt out one after another, & for words spoken are fined,[2] one twenty thousand, another 15000,[3] another 3000 pounds, & all to bring them to a condition not to be helpfull one to another; And Lastly (if I could tell when to write the Last evill of our misery) our misery is, that Arminianisme & Socianisme is like to be the prevailing Religion of our times; Oh where are the sounding of our New English bowels for old Englands ruines, our teares could drop for you in your late misery,[4] & our prayers were at worke for you in your then calamities; O pitty us, O pitty us in our straites, for the hand of God is greatly gone out against us, O that the eyes of our New English brethren would looke toward our [...] of our goods, O Looke upon our broken churches & bleeding ordinances, our imprisoned members & scattered ministers, oh that the cryes of our dying liberties & dying Gospel might fill your eares as loud as ever did the thunder from the clouds over your heads; oh the time was, when you had an Eliot[5] amongst you that could write to us in the Image of his bowels, styling it New Englands teares for old Englands feares; o bretheren are not our feares as great as ever, but where are your teares? May not a new calamity againe breake out upon you, which should it once more make you our debtors for prayers & teares on your behalfe, would you not count it a mercy that wee are your Lords remembrancers for you; O now pay your old debt to us first & for ought you know it may be a meanes to prevent your running upon a new score to us; o beg for strength & faith & patience for us, o beg that God would not make his Corrections any more tokens of his wrath to us; o beg for a spirit of Reformation among the Lords owne people, o wee cannot preach downe the pride of apparell amongst professors, o wee cannot preach down their worldlynesse & their Covetousnesse; o never were a people more glued to these sins then the professing people of old England are at this time; o that you might pray downe that which wee cannot preach downe; o beg a spirit of prayers & union for us, & that our God would not leave us in the Land of our nativity which by our sins wee have made the land of our Captivity; o the God of heaven stirre up your hearts for us & that you our friends would give him noe rest till he hath once more made us his praise in the earth.

Thomas Prince Collection, Massachusetts Historical Society.

---

1. Thomas Prince notes, "suppose 1684." This letter appears to be Cotton's transcription of another correspondent's letter.
2. Prince notes, "1683/4 Feb .6. Mr Hampden 40, 000."
3. Prince notes, "Feb. 14 Sr S. Bernardiston. 10, 000."
4. Prince notes, "in 1675 & 6," referring presumably to King Philip's War.
5. Prince crossed out "Eliot" and substituted "Hook." Prince is referring to William Hooke's *New England's Teares, for Old England's Feares Preached in a Sermon July 23, 1640, Being a Day of Publike Humiliation, Appointed by the Churches In Behalfe of our Native Countery in Time of Feared Dangers* (London, 1640).

To Mary Hinckley,[1] 10 January 1684

Plimouth January, 10: 1683:

Honoured & Deare Friend

A due sympathy one with another in affliction is a Gospel-duty; Gods bowels yerne towards his in distresse & could wee shew our selves the children of God by bowels of affection to the distressed, it would well become our christian profession; I am not able to doe or say what my heart is willing to expresse in this case; but, hearing that you are deeply dejected under the late bereaving stroake of Gods hand in your family,[2] I cannot but in Conscience of my duty to God & in compassion to you, whom my blessed father loved, & whom I much respect in the Lord, speake a few words that may by divine blessing tend to allay that excessive greife that hath taken hold of you; Consider, I beseech you what is done, & who hath done it, & why is it done? you have lost a deare gran-child by an ordinary desease, what is there in this more than the Common portion of the children of men; yea & of the children of God, you are not the first afflicted in this kinde, my owne deare mother besides the death of her owne, passed under this rod in the death of a pleasant gran-child of 8 yeares old, on whom her heart was exceedingly set; if God deale with you as with a child, you have hereby an evidence of your Adoption, you will not be cast downe because God seales his fatherly love to your soule by this Correction; God hath done what is done, & he did you noe wrong, his right was greater to that litle one then yours, it was Covenant-seed, & God hath made haste to accomplish all covenant-mercy to it, I hope this will not greive you; a babe embraced in the armes of Jesus christ, the Redeemer & shepherd of these Lambes, lyes safer & more comfortably then in the bosome of the most tender-hearted Gran-mother, will this greive you? What did you intend in the keeping of this child, if it had lived, certainly you meant, while it was with you to traine it up for the Lord; & did you not often pray for it, that its soule might be accepted in the Covenant of grace, all your good purposes, desires & prayers are answered in this, that it is safe in heaven, your worke is rewarded to the utmost of the wishes of your heart; & who can tell <how much> (but he that knowes all our hearts) how much you needed this Affliction & how much spirituall good God intends to your soule hereby; Weaning dispensations are very mercifull to a child of God, our hearts cleave too close to earthly injoyments, God, who is well worthy, would have more of our Affections; & happy is that affliction that is sanctifyed to cause the heart to be more in Love with God: upon my thoughts of your present visitations, I thought of Psal: 30:[3] & see noe reason but to thinke, that good David when he came into his new house had a dangerous fitt of sicknesse, which God sent to season his heart with more ardency, life & strength of grace & holinesse to dedicate himselfe & house unto the Lord, & I am verily perswaded, that is the worst harme God intends you by your present trialls, & when tried, you shall come forth as gold: I pray pardon my boldnesse with you, from you & your Mate, I have bin comforted & directed in an evill day, & therefore I owne myself your Debtor, though unable to discharge it; Thinke of Psal: 42: last:[4] the Father of mercies be your comforter & supporter, Soe prayes,

yours affectionately in our Lord Jesus

John Cotton

Hinckley Papers 1:57, Prince Library, Rare Book and Manuscripts, Boston Public Library. Addressed "These For his Worthily Esteemed Friend, Mris Mary Hinckley, living at Barnstable."

1. Mary Smith Glover Hinckley (1650[?]–1703), Gov. Thomas Hinckley's wife.
2. Prince's note: "This was Uncle & Aunt Rawson's 1st child, wc. died at its Grandfather Hinckley's, I suppose abt. ye 2 of Dec. 1683." Grindall Rawson (1659–1715, H.C. 1678) and Susanna Wilson Rawson's first child, Edward, was born 24 May1683 and died 21 November 1683. *Vital Records of Mendon, Massachusetts* (Boston, 1920), 491; *Vital Records of Medfield, Massachusetts* (Boston, 1903), 86, 168; Savage, *Genealogical Dictionary,* 3: 511.
3. Ps. 30: "I will extol thee, O Lord; for thou hast lifted me up, and hast not made my foes to rejoice over me. O Lord my God, I cried unto thee, and thou hast healed me. O Lord, thou hast brought up my soul from the grave: thou hast kept me alive, that I should not go down to the pit...Thou hast turned for me my mourning into dancing: thou hast put off my sackcloth, and girded me with gladness..."
4. Ps. 42:11: "Why art thou cast down, O my soul? & why art thou disquieted within me? hope thou in God: for I shall yet praise him, who is the health of my countenance, & my God."

From Bithia Sandy, 27 February 1684

To the Reverend Mr John Cotton, & Mr Thomas Cushman
to be communicated to the church of X^t^ at Plimouth,

I received a letter from you,[1] to warn me of my Sin, & call me to repentence in that, I had conjugal communion with him, who is now my husband, before our actual marriage, which letter I take kindly, at your hands, & I hope wil have a good effect upon me, though before that letter, I was under, plain & undeniable convictions, y^t^ in that matter I had sin'd against god, & broke his rule, & notwithstanding al endeavours from my owne heart, (or otherwise) to excuse it, yet I am conscious to my selfe, that I did evil in it, And after al my thoughtfulnes about it, I have no way left but to beg pardon, & look to him who hath said, y^t^ such as confesse & forsake their sin, shal obtaine mercy. I desire to greive & mourn for my sin herein, & to be greatly humbled under it, as it is a dishonnour to god, a scandal to the gospel, & greife & offense to you in perticuler, or any other christians. I desire the pitty & prayers of the whole church, to god for me, y^t^ my repentance may be sound, & that I may be found in Jesus x^t^ who doth sometimes wash & sanctifye, & accept of great sinners. I am thankful to the church, & elders for their care of me, & should be heartily glad to hear any further direction or counsel from you, & whether your care, & love towards me may be renewed, after so great a fall.

Bithia Sandy

<u>Bristol</u> Feb: 27: 83. 84

What is above written, & subscribed, is written & subscribed at the desire of her whose name is [underwritten?] as attests Benj: Woodbridge[2]

Thomas Prince Collection, Massachusetts Historical Society. Cotton's note: "This letter was read to the church, may, 2:1684: & well approoved of."

---

1. Not found, but the church records indicate that the letter was composed in late June 1683, a draft was read before the church on July 8, and the letter was sent after the church members agreed. Sandy was "guilty of fornication with him, whom afterward she married." After being "Admonished by the Elders in their name for her sinne" by letter, Sandy sent the above reply. The church heard the letter read aloud on 2 May 1684 and "well accepted" her repentance. *CSM*, 22:252, 255.
2. Benjamin Woodbridge (d. 1710) attended Harvard College but never graduated. He was ordained in Windsor, Connecticut Colony, where he served from 1670–81, and he served as the first settled minister in Bristol, Rhode Island Colony, from 1681 to 1686. He also ministered to congregations in Kittery (later Maine), in Portsmouth and in Newcastle (later New Hampshire), finally settling in Medford in 1698. Weis, *Colonial Clergy*, 234.

To Cotton Mather, 11 March 1684

Most Deare Cousen

you make me in your debtor by soe great a readynesse to comply with my desires in any thing, & sending me such good Epistles;[1] had your 2ond page had noe worse Intelligence then your first, I should have had lesse cause of greife then now I have; the Lord heale those breaches, & ours also: our Govr & Magistrates, being desired by the Church, did give some advice to us in a paper worthy to be written in letters of Gold (me Judice[2]), but our contentious Lord-bretheren deemed it not worthy of hearing the 2ond time or of desiring a copy to be left of it, which our Mag's did take notice of; the ch: went apart, & have chosen 5 ches to meete in Councill, 18th Instant, Barnstable, Taunton, Bridgwater, Duxbury, Marshfeild,[3] your & your fathers prayers will not be wanting, oh let them be more then ordinary, that I may finde mercy from God in this day; what further proceedings you heare of my Brother[4] & how it is with our son[5] there, please to informe; our salutations are respectively to each of our Relations with you; our fathers God love you, when will you come to us?

I am, yours Affectionately

John Cotton

Plimouth March, 11: 1683:/84:

I hope Mr Eppes hath my letter I left with you for Cos: Tuckney.[6]

Mather Papers 5:55, Prince Library, Rare Book and Manuscripts, Boston Public Library. Addressed "These For his much Endeared Kinsman, Mr Cotton Mather, Preacher of the Gospel, at Boston."

---

1. Not found.
2. "If I am the judge."
3. Evidently, the disputes that Cotton and Keith discussed in their letters of 6 March 1683 were not yet resolved. In January 1684, Cotton's church records reveal that "the church met & after the conference the Pastor propounded some grievances which he desired redresse of or release from office-worke, the Elder shewed discontent, & 1 or 2 more of the Bretheren, & there was no vote or issue put to anything propounded." By 7 March, the magistrates were involved and requested that Cotton appeal to neighboring churches for advice, which he did. After calling for a fast day to pray about their "present trouble," Lieutenant Ephraim Morton criticized Cotton, claiming that "he heard soe much in publick of differences, & that things were blowne up more that he heard all the weeke besides." *CSM*, 22:253-54.
4. Increase Mather was a Fellow at Harvard, 1675–1685. Weis, *Colonial Clergy*, 136.
5. Rowland Cotton (1667–1722, H.C. 1685) was at Harvard College. *Sibley's Harvard Graduates*, 3:323-26.
6. Jonathan Tuckney; see 5 March 1681.

From Edward Rosseter, 20 March 1684

Reverend duly & dearly Hono^d Cousen I do with great Integrity assure y^u that I take it as a very great and remarkable favour of the Lord to me to be thought fitt to have Correspondence with so worthy a person as your selfe which have had for some years together your letter of the 20th of Nov last[1] Came to my hands the 21 of ffebruary Which made a deepe as well as a double impression upon me some part I read with much delight & sattisfaction and other Could not read without many teares & much griefe should I take notice of every thing in yo^rs to give answer to it & a narative of what have accurred here & in ye nation since my last to you it would fill a very great vollume I may hint at some things which must not speake plainly to. But the Tables are turned In march the next moneth after mine to you A great persecution arose thorow out the land tho the storm was greater & more violent in some then other places and few places have had a greater share therin then this poor Town the rage & fury of very ill men upon very great mistaks to my personall Knolege have appeared exceeding great Its true to the Lords Everlasting praise be it we Enjoyed our blessed ministers and libertyes much longer then many other places did y^t were so numerous as we being abt 1500 y^t did meet & We were disturbed most Lords-dayes after March began but in Aprill thinking y^t heat over we ventured to the meeting House againe but prsently ye Mayor Came with his officers[2] who in fury brake down the great doores of the House & Wall y^{t} leads to it y^{t} was agt ye street & then laid all open after this his officers watcht it most Lords dayes y^{t} could have no meeting there & no other place would hold us for all to hear yet this House was built by his Ma^{t}ys Encoragment and we had his License for our own ministers and administering ye ordinances in our way which is not Contrary to y^{t} of ye Church of England for we had praying reading ye Scriptures & preaching as they have but have not the Service of the Church as they call it, But those Gratious blessed Glorious times are over for ye p^{r}sent And miserable dayes come Oh y^{t} I had A more deep sence of ye wrath of the Lord in this dispensation tis through the anger of the Lord y^{t} this Calamitous Missery is come we may read our sinnes in our punishm^{t} We had not such a due sence of the invaluable worth of ye great blessing of the Gospell and our unthankfullness and unfruitfullness for it & under it, such great stupendious Judgments are ye proper fruit of sin though it is true the Wisdom of God many times brings much good out of those Evills The good Lord helpe us to Consider our wayes and repent of all ye Evill found amonge us you know God Sometimes Executes judgments by way of Retaliation bringing a mans wayes upon his own head I may say without vanity no place in ye Land (in ye Land did I say) hardly in the world y^{t} enjoyed more then this place for Ministers I am sure for piety Holiness and Exemplary walking for all ministerall abillitys indifatigable indefatigable labours It is no Hyperbolicall Expression to say if any did Equalize none Exceeded them and there are yet a very Serious gratious people which as my dear ffather Alleine in his life you may se tells ye world y^{t} Considering how few Embrace ye wayes of Christ in good Earnest there were not a few such in y^{t} Towne But Alas Alas the greater part have gained no saving fruit upon there hearts which have often made me fear a dismall sunset of the day of Grace and Oh what Endless missery if grace in God & repentance in them prevent not are such like to fall into for such as are ye Lords All is well with them & must be so forever It must go well with the Righteous as the blessed God have promised .

In June a most astonishing (I wish it were not a Contrived) mischiffe happened to

to all dissenters in the Land a Company of vile men I doubt some discourses to murder the King three of y^{t} number were tried & Executed[3] therefore you may well say that the life of his Maty deserve prayer & praise Which I very heartely joyne in dayly & will say what in humane probabillity must looke for if his Life should be taken from the Earth before things are better setled the protestant Religion together with the lives of multitudes of its sincere & Zealous professors may go with it; Those will be rufull dayes indeed tho all y^{t} are gotten into ye Arke before such a deluge will be safe there were two great persons upon this accasion also tried & Executed perhapps you have there last speeches the first was the Excellent Lord Russell Son[4] & heir apparent to the great Earle of Bedford after him Coll: Sydny[5] the old Earle of Lecesters Son brother to him y^{t} is Earle now both deny the Treason charged on them Living & dying which you will see the plott of the three Executed with others not yet taken Oh the mischiffe it hath done to all y[e] serious dissentrs among us tho they were none & y[e] other Executed were Church men & not dissentrs yet because the dissenters chose them for the Severall last Parlam[t]s it is charged all on them and they are looked on & caled many of them as Enemies to the King and Goverment and Counted disloyall & I know not what not worthy to live tho when Bourne one of the Witnesses ag[t] the three being asked at the Tryall of one of them if the nonconformist Ministers were not Concerned in this business He answered on his Oath y[t] he asked Wist a Counseller another Witness if he should speake to them ab[t] it the said Wist answered no for that they had hindered all things of y[t] Nature Ever since Constantine the Greats time and truly I know none y[t] are more serious in praying for the Kings life then they are And which is more Its there & dissenters declared principles so to do & to be subject to y[t] Authority God in his Providence shall set over them I doubt no too many Rejoyce in this Providentiall dispensation having hereby an advantage to manifest their Rage & fury (that for want of accasion lay latent within) against better men then themselves you know the allwise God whose wayes of Providence are Allways Righteous tho often secret & unsechable for his wayes are in the darke & his footsteps are not known have made it the Constant Lott & portion of his people in this world to be following of the Lamb in the bearing his Cross & Suffering hard things upon mistakes as he did yet I would not be understood to laye y[e] blam but where I ought who Ever be y[e] Instrum[t] God is y[e] Authur of all afflictions ther is no evill in the Citty y[t] he hath not done it & allwayes Man suffereth for his Sin The great famine of hearing y[e] word purely preacht y[t] is now upon us y[e] Lord hath brought on us for I trust gratious ends He takes away the naturall stay & staffe of bread as you intimate yo[r] harvest to be much thined this last year And He may justly take away y[e] stay & staffe of our spirituall bread Its y[e] Lord y[t] have the placing & displacing our ministers those in y[e] Nation y[t] take not y[e] Oxford Oath must not live in five miles of any towne y[t] sends burgesses to Parlam[t] if they are taken the Justice have power to Commit them without Baile or maineprise for six monthes to prison & are liable to be sued by any person for [?] also for every offense So y[t] those Rev[d] persons related to me not being Sattisfied to take the Oath must not live here but if you please to writ to them I will take Care it shall Come to there hands Great thoughts of heart were in my selfe & many others for N.E. when heard of a Quo Warranto being sent agt your charter fearing it might be to y[r] prejudice of yo[r] Goverment not only in y[e] state but church also Indeed y[e] Great City of London & many more & Severall Townes have had y[e] like their old Charters broken[6] New given and such persons put out as some thinke were for y[e] happyness of K & Kingdom & others put in y[t] p[r]tend to be so tho I doubt it as well as multitudes besides. Tis Levelled agt dissenters all y[e] Land over such are in as have private meeting for y[e] worship of God I do not say Play Houses nor Whor[...] tho enough theire are of such in some places Even in oure Happy England and [...] many Ale Houses as now all dissenters are turned out (& those y[t] have no[...] for them put in) of all places of profit honour or trust I had allmost said yt [...] name off & might be blotted out from amonge us it grievs me for what you writ of a place Eastward of you where yr son ye minister was[7] It is a time here of great difficulty & my Bro yt often spake of going to N: E. is with others discouraged by what is seemigly Coming on you also for though things yet are faire & Calme & ye Generalty seem sattisfied yet if chang happen in yor Magestracy farwell to yor Glorious priviledges I Confess it would greatly comfort me to live neer yor selfe & my other worthy Relations with you if Could carry those here with me yt we might Love & Enjoy all together This year my youngest Sister Dorothy was married to a Scotts man a marchant Living now in this Town He is (as well as she) I trust one yt feares ye Lord they may do well together I may well sympathize wth you for ye Loss of your dear Sam[8] I have often known how sharpe a tryall yt is have had 4 one after another taken from me for I never had two sons living together My dear Sam Lives & is like so to do blessed be God Its one of my greatest Comforts to read in yor letter how many of my flesh & blood fears ye Lord with you some such are here also I thanke God I am truly agreived for my Aunt Hart[9] not knowing such a person as was in the world I am forward to helpe her all I can for her welfair & happyness both for time & eternity I give you my most affectionate thanks for your xtian Compassion to her in taking her into yor House may the gratious God make it [...] in Temporalls a tho[u]sand fold to you & yors if things were with me as formrly would do what become so neer a Relation but I have nothing really of my own but what is truely my Sonns left him by his Mother with whome I had 500ll but by bad debts & Losses in ye Trade of a mrcht to wch was bound have lost a thousand pounds in a few years & tho have as said yet I am in no want another relation of ye first degree affords me full support pray writ of her when you writ againe,

The Last Term Ending ffeb 12 many Excellant Gent in bonds about ye late Plott were discharged nothing being agt them but a Cry of ill men & the popish Lords in the Tower[10] there abt 5 years were admitted to Baile with ye Earle of Tyrone & Earle of Darby to appear the next Parlamt I might spend a [sheet more marques?] here but must forbear I forgot to mention in its right place what a Cry was agt this Towne in ye late plott severall were taken up & let go againe but hither Comes ye High Sheriffe of this County Lords & Govt & much ado here was searching up & downe for Armes in many dissenters Houses but nothing found & ye House I live in was searcht twice first for Armes & then my chamber Trunks & Chest for papers by said sherife & a kt & Baronet yt lives nere yt I opposed when he stood for Parlamt man but nothing but innocency found with me God forbid I should designe ye hurt of ye meanest man in ye world much much lesse ye King or Govermt I pray for ye happyness of both ye Kt Carried away many of my papers but nothing is in them to my prejudice they being abt Religion so that nothing have happened to me but for going to meetings to worship ye Lord & yet this seems ye great business now of this Kingdome Scarse a weeke passeth but we heare of meetings broken up & people Carried to prison

Cirtainly for Conscience sake I p^{r}sume your patience almost tired to read such a long hasty scrible yet could not thinke fitt to omitt [any?] of it as I said Could fill a vollem to tell only matters of ffact I have given [...] hints of what might have been larger in & my letter may be opened as I think yor last was to me before receved it & some are suffering deeply for writing speaking & printing nothing but truth my Relations brother in Laws 2 sisters with my selfe all Concurr in p^{r}senting you & all yo^{r}s & all o^r Relations in your Country our very dear Respects and intire Love & fervently pray an aboundant blessing from ye Lord may rest on your yo^{r}s and all relations as on my selfe which ends this from

Yo^r assurred most affectionate Kinsman in what may to serve you

Edw Rosseter

the 20th of March 1683

reading over my letter I observed y^t I neglected to tell you y^t in July after ye late Plott & ye Cry y^t was ag^t this place first the mayo^r a Knight & others got into ye meeting House takeing the advantage of y^t Criticall season brake down ye Pulpit & one Gallery & a litle while after ye same Mayor & other Gen^t Came & broke downe all ye 4 Gallerys in ye House y^t cost ye building besides ye House above 100ll & brought it on ye Cornhill & there burnt it with many a health to ye Confusion of dissenters and much hooping & roaring there was as you may read ye like Psa: 74:[11] And it was done in many other places as here burning the materialls of the Houses y^t there might be no more meetings yet ye House stands tho much threting to destroy it wholy

J. Davis Collection, Massachusetts Historical Society. Addressed "To the Reverend his duly honored Kinsman m^r John Cotten minister of the Gospell at Plymouth In New England." Endorsed "From my cousen, Mr Edward Rosseter, March 20: 1683:/84: Received, July, 9: 1684:" Note in a hand other than Cotton's or Rosseter's: "A Long letter ab^t State & church affairs in Eng-." Several small holes.

---

1. Not found.
2. With Tory sheriffs now in place, the Crown could more effectively persecute dissenters.
3. This was the infamous Rye House Plot, a scheme to assassinate both the king and his brother, the Duke of York, and seize London. What made this attempted coup different from the others was the involvement of high-level Whigs, including the Duke of Monmouth. The plot was betrayed, and York and the Tories used the incident and subsequent trials to flay the Whigs politically.
4. William, Lord Russell (1639–1683), a member of the "Country" party that opposed Charles II and one of the Rye House plotters. He was executed on 21 July 1683.
5. Colonel Algernon Sydney (1622–1682), long an ardent "Commonwealthsman" and opponent of the Stuarts. He was implicated in the plot and executed on 7 December 1682.
6. See 28 February 1683.

7. Cotton's son John Cotton (1661–1706, H.C. 1681) was at this time the temporary settled minister of Exeter, later New Hampshire. *Sibley's Harvard Graduates*, 3:212-15.

8. Samuel Cotton, John and Joanna's ninth child, was born on 10 February 1678 and died of scarlet fever on 23 December 1682. *Plymouth Vital Records*, 2.

9. Joan Hart descended from the Rosseter Family; see 8 November 1685. Savage, *Genealogical Dictionary*, 3:577–78.

10. See 15 January 1680.

11. Ps. 74: "O God, why hast thou cast *us* off for ever? *why* doth thine anger smoke against the sheep of thy pasture? Remember thy congregation, *which* thou hast purchased of old; the rod of thine inheritance, *which* thou hast redeemed; this mount Zion, wherein thou hast dwelt. Lift up thy feet unto the perpetual desolations; *even* all *that* the enemy hath done wickedly in the sanctuary..."

From Joshua Moody, 7 April 1684

Revrd Sr

Your double visit Epistolar[1] rec^d wth treble thanks. The Epistle of John ye Divine transcribed y^t it might not be lost, & kept by mee as a Grande Deposition, & remitted the Original by the same Bearer by whom yourself ventured it. I have need of all such Help & the Help of all the prayers of those that are [concerned?] in Sion. My poor pineing flock I pitty, not a sermon now for 9 L^rds Daies[2] but God can give Manna from heaven while food by [...] ordinary ways [...] suffering is hard, [...][3] than sinning. I desire I [...] able more [sensibly] & [feelingly] to speak of the App[...]of those Prison-Cordialls y^t the Scripture promises are full of. Tis easy to say, but hard to doe & feel, the Lord only can teach to profit, upon whom to cast his whole Burden is a Prisoners work. It is my lott to bee first, whose turn is next here only in whose hand o^r Breath & waies are knowen. Yo^r Bro. has been threat^d[4] but I believe will not be [so picked?]; either they'l let him alone or he will remove. Of yor Son, there is no Danger, hee does service safely, you need not fear his coming wthin theyr reach.[5] I wait for an Opportunity for safe conveying yo^rs to him, expect to see him the week, haveing but once lookt on mee these 9 weeks. If he comes not shall send his Letter, thô would rather see him. I see no way out (nor doe I use many thought about makeing a Way) [...][6], and perhaps not then [...] if they in whose house I am may obtain. But I [await] al theyr Wills thô in theyr hands. I much lament the sicknes of yor pious, prudent, hearty, kind Yoke fellow for whom I have a great Kindnes, & unto whom I am a great [D^r]. I heartily beg for yo^rsake (especially thô for every good woman a change for ye best [...] eligible) ye healing of her diseases & lengthening out of her life, having by wofull Experience known the Damage of such a bereavem^t[7] & [possebly] y^u may feel it more in some respects if it bee y^r Lot. I [...] at the healing [or preserving rath] the breach in yor church. Tell them its now an ill Time to quarrell, I would rather doe anything, part wth any thing,

yea stoop [...] only excepted) than be at strife at any Time but more eminently now as things are circumstanced [...] arise from o^r lusts, a little stooping [...] o^r Wills, [...] & a little yielde, selfe [...] especially at ye beginning w^d prvent such [...] of Mischief by strife (wch is in y^e [....]) y^t possibly much lab^r & expence & may not cure. The good Lord give prudence, [....] A [seald-Head] is soon broken. The God of Peace be with y^u, & ye peace of God [Rule over] y^u all. Rememb^r my [Bones] I am
yo^rs

Curwen Family Papers, American Antiquarian Society. Addressed "To the Revd Mr John Cotton Passor of the Church of Christ at Plymouth p^rst. per m^r Sam Prince QDC." Endorsed "From Mr Moody April: 7: 1684." Several holes and stained portions along fold lines.

---

1. Not found.

2. Joshua Moodey was under a kind of house arrest, ostensibly for non-conformity, and was prohibited from preaching. Gov. Edward Cranfield really wanted to punish Moodey for his meddling in tax collection and political matters and used laws regarding administering the sacrament to do it. Most recently, Moodey had used the pulpit to admonish a church member who bowed to Cranfield's pressure to swear an oath after trying to evade laws of trade. Moodey was released from prison only on the condition that he agree to leave New Hampshire, which he did. Everett Stackpole, *History of New Hampshire* (New York, 1916), 1:141-47; Nathaniel Adams, *Annals of Portsmouth* (Portsmouth, N.H., 1825), 78-80; *Sibley's Harvard Graduates,* 1:367-80.

3. Several illegible words.

4. Seaborn Cotton (1633–1686, H.C. 1651) was the minister in Hampton, later New Hampshire, from 1657 to 1686. Sibley suggests that Cranfield threatened to ask Cotton to give him the sacrament "according to the Liturgy" but did not because Cotton left for Boston. *Sibley's Harvard Graduates,* 1:286-93.

5. John Cotton (1661–1706, H.C. 1678) was preaching in Exeter, later New Hampshire, from 1684 to 1690 during Cranfield's attempts to enforce conformity in the colonies. According to Sibley, Cotton joined an armed protest against Cranfield. Despite this activism, Moodey reassured Cotton that his son was not in danger of arrest. *Sibley's Harvard Graduates,* 3:212-15.

6. Darkened, illegible line.

7. Moodey's first wife, Martha Collins (1639–1674), died before 1674. He married Mary Greenleaf (b. 1676) in 1696. Torrey, *New England Marriages,* 515.

From Jonathan Moodey, 8 April 1684

FROM YE PRISON 8 (2) 1684

REVD SR

After the sealing & before ye deptr of ye Bearer your son came down to give mee a visit & dd mee your first letter, & rec^d yours y^t came enclosed to me.[1] I thank you for yor formr letter also, & yor Affection[ate] Resentment of my Condition. I hope God will make it [...], & further his Gospell by my Confinemt thô it looks very sadly to see a flock of sheep wandering for want of a Sheprd. I have often thought God has been angry wth us all in N.E. both ministers & people for not due prizeing & improving o^r choice Liberties nor walking worthy of o^r [...] I am now in Prison preaching on ye text (Eph. 4.2)[2] the Lord help all his people to meet him seasonably; hee is in ye way & who can tell where he will stop? the Alarm is given, happy they y^t take it & stand upon theyr Guard. Sufferings are rightly called Trialls. What further y^e [...] has to exercise mee with I know not, but hitherto [...] not left mee destitute of his Mercy, & I hope he will perfect w^t concerns mee. Praise God & pray to him for mee. I shall not forget y^u nor yo^rs. $Renew^d$ $rememb^{ces}$ to yor good yokefellow to whom I & mine are so m^{ch} engaged, the Lord visit & revive her & doe for her in Body & souls al y^e [...] & does require.

I have discoursed yor son, and advized him to goe away to meet y^u [...] Election, wch y^u may expect, & hope he may return ag^n [...] people—

The Lord be with you, Rememt my bonds

y^r S^r

Curwen Family Papers, American Antiquarian Society. Addressed "To ye Revd Mr Jno Cotton." Endorsed "From Mr Moodey April: 8: 1684:" In a different contemporary hand "while in Prison." Several stains, and holes along left margin.

1. Not found.

2. Eph. 4:1-2: I therefore, the prisoner of the Lord, beseech you that ye walk worthy of the vocation wherewith ye are called, 2: With all lowliness and meekness, with longsuffering, forbearing one another in love.

From Jonathan Tuckney, 29 August 1684

Deare Cousen

Yo^{r}s of May 9[1] being occasionally at Cos. John
Whitings Hose or in the Bell in Lawrence[2] lane a very good man
I mett with having been there left by m^{r} Epps[3] a few dayes
after[.] I […] last wrote you in July.;[4] & having troubled
you so lately I may be the shorter now
That Breach you intimate made upon yor liberties in M^{r}
Moodey by Governour Cranfeild shews, what sence […]
would be at. [see it …] in psal 74.6,7[5] &c But tho if you read on that
[p]salm, you'l see ye faith & prayer of the Church begins to be [..] the 12th
verse.[6] & now we that ar zealous in prayer & humble &
holy in o^{r} lives as those good people of God then […] that, yea
what <not> not might we expect at the hand of our gracious
& Almighty Father who speakes as you have in Joel 2.
2c.[7] see the rest of the chapter. & Chapter 3^{d}[8] of the same
Prophecy. I am bold with you to point you [onely to places] by citing them, not
having time indeed at present to […] them.
Though we^{ll} my time is but scarce […]mentioning
Yo^{r} Brother Seaborn hath drawn […] this
<en> enclosed to him, which I […] in con-
-veying of & sending me in [Pli???] […] I may
for the future direct to him.
No <mor> more at p^{r}sent, but mutual salutation &
prayers. from

Dear Cousin yor affectionate kinsman

Jonathan Tuckney

Hackney Aug:29 1684

D. Cous. I am bold (in this to yo^{r}self) to insert this short Note to my good Cousin (yor Br^{o} Seaborn[9]). I <had> knew not how more conveniently to get it conveyd than by an own Brothers hand. Therfor I pray do me the kindnese. I would gladly maintain correspondence & with yor good Br^{o} Seaborn, as also my old Cous. Sam whitings eldest son;[10] I think he is of Bilerica. I had a letter from him in 1681. But my occasions pmit me not (in [?] train of time) to write to [ ] at this <Govt?> Govt. But […] it God [ ]

[?] vale in [ ] (mi) A [ ]

J.T.

Thomas Prince Papers, Massachusetts Historical Society. Addressed "For his deare & much respected Kinsman Mr John Cotton Preacher of the Gospel [torn]." Endorsed "From my Cousen, Mr Jonathan Tuckney, August, 29:1684: Received, November, 19:" Original is partially water stained, with a one-inch square hole in the middle patched on the back with a piece of printed text.

---

1. Not found.
2. Lawrence Lane can still be found off Cheapside, just east of St. Paul's Cathedral in London.
3. See 5 March 1681.
4. Not found. In left margin: "(as far as I at present remember) upon the 10th or 11th of that Month."
5. Ps. 74:6,7: "But now they break down the carved work thereof at once with axes and hammers. They have cast fire into thy sanctuary, they have defiled *by casting down* the dwelling place of thy name to the ground."
6. Twelfth verse: "For God *is* my King of old, working salvation in the midst of the earth."
7. Joel 2, chapter 2: "A day of darkness and of gloominess, a day of clouds and of thick darkness, as the morning spread upon the mountains: a great people and a strong; there hath not been ever the like, neither shall be any more after it, *even* to the years of many generations."
8. Third chapter: "A fire devoureth before them; and behind them a flame burneth: the land *is* as the garden of Eden before them, and behind them a desolate wilderness; yea, and nothing shall escape them."
9. Seaborn Cotton.
10. Samuel Whiting (1633–1713), pastor in Billerica, was the eldest son of the minister Samuel Whiting of Skirbeck, Lincolnshire, England. The Whitings emigrated to New England with John Wheelwright in 1636. Samuel Whiting Jr. graduated from Harvard in 1653 and in 1658 began preaching in Billerica, where he remained until his death. *Sibley's Harvard Graduates,* 1:363-66. *Vital Records of Billerica, Massachusetts to the Year 1850* (Boston, 1908), 200, 403.

From Henry Wainwright,[1] October 1684

REVEREND S[R].

y[r]: over Exact description of y[e] way Caused me to Erre y[e] day I Left y[u], for Comeing to y[e] hithermost house five miles on this side plimouth, I observed y[e] way on y[e] Left hand att y[e] Corner of y[e] fence, w[ch] Led me into a Wildernesse where I wandred among swamps & dismall solitary places, y[e] space of two houres or more, haveing Lost all manner of path, although y[e] Entrance (Like y[e] ways of sin) seemed to be a greatt beaten way, when I found my selfe so Bewildred, I would faine have returned to y[e] place where I Entred, But was altogether in a Confution, insomuch y[t] I almost dispaired of Ever getting out, fearing y[e] night might overtake me & there I might perish so I sought ye Lord for direction, & itt pleased him (by my observation of ye Sun) in a Litle time, to bringe me out, att ye very same place y^{t} I Entered, s^{r} I humbly Begg y^{u} would not any way take itt amisse, y^{t} I Acquaint y^{u} y^{t} ye Benefitt I received from y^{t} providence in ye spirituallizeing itt did Infinitely recompence ye trouble I sustained under itt, s^{r} I shall only satisfye y^{u} y^{t} I delivered y^{r} desires to ye m^{r} Baylyes,[2] & Earnestly Intreat to be accoumpted & alwais to Remaine, S^{r}

Y^{r} most Humble & ready serv^{t} to Command

Henry Wainwright

Thomas Prince Papers, Massachusetts Historical Society. Addressed "To the Reverend m^{r} Cotton, Minister of ye Gospell In Plymouth." Endorsed "From mr. Henry Wainwright Received, November, 1: 1684:"

---

1. Henry Wainwright.
2. Probably John Bailey (1644–1697), minister at Blackburn, Lancashire, who emigrated to Boston in 1683. Bailey served as minister to Third Church, Boston, the church in Watertown and First Church, Boston. Savage, *Genealogical Dictionary,* 1:94.

From Thomas King,[1] 3 October 1684

To the Church of Christ at Plymouth the Church, <The church> upon the North River in sittuate sendeth greeting in our Lord Jesus Christ wishing an increase of grace and peace in him,

Reverend and beloved The occation of these lines is To acquaint you: that the 15th day of this instant october is the tyme appointed for the calling & ordination of Mr Thomas Mighell[2] into the office of the ministry among us: if god permitt: And therefor desire the help of the Reverend Mr John: Cotton your Pastor with your <other> messengers to be helpfull to us: in that worke & wittnesses of our proseedings there in, thus desiring your Earnest prayers to god for us: in blessing & succeeding us in this weighty affair, we rest your brethren in Christ Jesus::

Tho: King: in the name of the church;

Sittuate october the 3^{d} 1684

Thomas Prince Papers, Massachusetts Historical Society. Addressed "To the Reverend Mr John Cotton, pastor to the Church of Christ at Plymoth dd these." Cotton's note: "In answer to this letter, the church chose, the Elder Cushman, & Mr Joseph Bradford to accompany the Pastour, which they attended:"

1. Thomas King (d. 1691) was a ruling elder in the Second Church of Scituate. King had emigrated to New England in 1635 at the age of 21. Samuel Deane, *History of Scituate, Massachusetts from its First Settlement to 1831* (Boston, 1831), 90; Savage, *Genealogical Dictionary,* 3:26.

2. Thomas Mighell (1639–1689) graduated from Harvard in 1663, taught grammar school in Roxbury (1666–1668) and preached in Milton (1669–1677) before going to the Second Church of Scituate in 1680. He assisted Rev. William Witherell beginning in September 1680 and refused ordination until Witherell died in April 1684, even though the church had offered him a call as early as July 1681. Mighell was ordained in the Scituate church on 15 October 1684. *Sibley's Harvard Graduates,* 2:144-46.

From William Hoskins,[1] — 8 November 1684

Reverend & dearly beloved Pastou^{r}, with ye beloved aged Elder the whome I dearly respect in christ Jesus, I had good hopes to have enjoyed your Commuion in ye ordinances of Christ in his publick worship this day, but am dissappointed my horse being out of ye way Haveing had seriouse thoughts in my selfe in refference to my wives Condition being weake & troubled with many Infirmities. I have endeavored to ease her & my selfe also of our remote living soe far from ye worship of god which is with much difficulty & sore destractions, & have removed her to Taunton, & I am following speedily if god will, I hope we are in gods way, & therefore doe earnestly request ye prayers of ye Church & people of god for us that we may have his presence with us & blessing upon us, that wee may walke close with god being stedfast in ye faith of ye gosple serving ye Lord & doing ou^{r} generation worke that we may glorify his name: my heart is with ye Church of Christ at Plimouth. but ye providence of god leads another way. I desier to retaine my Communion still with my old brethren & sisters and remaine a member of ye Church of Plymouth. soe for ye present I take my leave of all you my bretheren. desiring truth & peace Love & union may still abide with you, & ye god of peace still remaine amongst you. which is ye earnest desier of him

Who is you^{r} poor brother in ye faith of the gosple

William Hoskins

Lakenham 8th 9mo: 84:

Thomas Prince Collection, Massachusetts Historical Society. Addressed "To ye Reverend Elders of ye Church of Christ at Plimouth these P^{r}sent."

1. Probably William Hoskins (1647–1730), who was born in Plymouth, married Sarah Casewell (1658–after 1726) in Taunton and lived in that community. Or, his father, William (d. 1695), and his second wife, Ann Haynes. Savage, *Genealogical Dictionary*, 2:466.

To Cotton Mather, 6 January 1685

PLIMOUTH JANUARY, 6: 1684:

MUCH ENDEARED COUSEN.

I conclude you have had expectations to heare from me long before this time, & indeed if I had noe other buisnesse but to thanke you for your late courteous entertainment in your bed, good manners would have ingaged me ere now to have returned greatfull acknowledgments; but I deferred till I had used all lawfull meanes to obtaine the 50 pd for you, the unsuccessfullnesse of which I was not assured of till friday last; I am sorry that I cannot obtaine that which would have bin good for me to <receive> part with & you now to <part with> receive, but I am in hopes by March or April to obtaine that summe for you of one or another, yet dare not promise; Last weeke was with us very hard winter, & wee were ready to hope it was the very Quintessence & vitalls of it, but this weeke is as the last & hath brought us the greatest storme of snow of any this winter.

Through mercy, our family is well, & the towne generally; divers townes northward neere of us have lost an old good man or two this winter, as yet ours escape: I long to know what acceptance Mr Bernard[1] had amongst you, last weeke I heare he was very sick with feavour & ague at swanzey; they that call themselves the church there are soe offended that the towne were first in calling him that they will not heare him, but meete apart at Mris Myles's:[2] Due salutations from us to your parents, with your selfe & cousens, I rest, your Affectionate uncle,

John Cotton

If the Almanack-maker forget to put in when its full sea in Boston, it will be a great losse to us, as is the present want of it in the present Alm: for Jan: & Feb:

Let our prayers be Mutuall:

Thomas Prince Papers, Massachusetts Historical Society. Addressed "These For his Deare and much Esteemed Cousen, Mr Cotton Mather, Preacher of the Gospel, at Boston; ddd."

---

1. Most likely Thomas Barnes (d. 1706), who according to Weis came to Swansea as early as 1669, was ordained by the Second Baptist Church in 1693 and married Elizabeth Baker King in 1694. Weis, *Colonial Clergy,* 28; Torrey, *New England Marriages,* 44.

2. Mrs. Myles is probably the widow of minister John Myles (c. 1621–1683). Myles emigrated to New England in 1662 after he was silenced following the Act of Conformity, and first organized the Baptist church in Rehoboth. The Plymouth Court permitted the Baptist church to establish the town of Swansea in October 1667, and Myles was the beloved pastor there until he died in February 1683. Myles's successor, Samuel Luther, was ordained in July 1685. Cotton disliked the Swansea Baptist

church, as his note in the Plymouth Church Records illustrates: "Two of our members who lived at Swanzey sent to us to desire their dismissions to the chh there, the chh met Nov:18 & agreed the Elders should in their name returne answer in the Negative, because the brethren of Swanzey renounced communion with us or soe much as to be present when wee administered Infant-Baptism & did rebaptize our chh-seed." See 10 January 1671. *CSM,* 22:155. Weis, *Colonial Clergy,* 148, 130; Otis Olney Wright, *History of Swansea, Massachusetts, 1667–1917* (Swansea, Mass., 1917), 101-4.

From The General Court of Plymouth, 6 March 1685

To the Reverend Elders MR John Cotton pastour & m^{R} Thomas Cushman elder of y^{E} Church of Christ at Plimouth these to be comunicated to y^{E} congregation

This Court taking into Consideration ye state of affaires in this Colony & countrey as also of ye churches of Christ abroad in ye world & being deeply sensible of o^{r} manifold provocations of ye most <*high*> holy & mercifull God & [?] obstinancy therein notwithstanding all ye mercyes of God to melt & other means to reclaime & reforme us, as also of ye solemne dispensations of God whereby he seems to be saying, that as we are going on in o^{r} sins, so he is going on in ye way of his Judgments, so that we may justly feare no lesse in ye issue then a totall deprivation of o^{r} pleasant & pretious things which are so valuable & so necessary to o^{r} enjoyment & glorifying of god, but have been woefully slighted & undervalued by us—Doe therefore Commend it to all ye Churches & people of this Colony to observe wensday being ye 18th of this Instant as a solemne day of fasting & prayer; wherein to humble ou^{r} selves before ye Lord for all o^{r} declensions & Aposticyes & sinfull deportments towards ye God of o^{r} mercyes & neglecting in so great a measure ye end of o^{r} fathers Coming into this wilderness. & also to implore from God, that he Would poure out upon his people a spiritt of grave & supplication & thorough reformation, & divert Judgments impending, & yet own us as his Covenant people & bestow upon us ye blessing of this ensuing yeare in ye seasons thereof according to o^{r} necessities, & that all ye Lords people & intrest throughout ye world may be gratiously minded & secured as ye matter may require,

By order of Court

Nathaniell Morton Secretary

Plymouth 6th March 1684/5

Thomas Prince Collection, Massachusetts Historical Society.

From Edward Rosseter et al (fragments) April 1685[?]

friends as particularly named, [illeg.] leter to Cos Gilbert yor [...] a Candid answer. Concerning what I wish all due & most affectioan[ate] love and service to you I rest

Your very much obliged & very affectionate Kinsman

E. R.[1]

Reverend S^r[2]

For mee to bee large and particular, in giving you an account of our circumstances here, would be [...] [I reading?] my brothers, I find, have saved mee that labour. I heartily thank you for those gratious and affectionate lines you sent us, and doe greatly rejoyce to hear that your libertys are yet continued, and that the Gosple of Christ, is yet owned and countenanced among you[.] Our case in this respect, is most deplorable. Our liberties are gon, and all our pleasant things [ta]ken from us. Wee are a people in all probability upon the very borders of confusion. Wee are [re]duced to a red-sea distress, and truly (Sir) nothing less then a miracle can save us. For we [are] beset on every side, with as black and bloody a generation, as ever the sun saw, And I [fear?] in a few month time, you will hear of such a tragedy acted in England, that noe [chron]icle can hardly parallel. Popery and slavery severely threaten us. Mass is publicly [...] the kings chappel,[3] and if it were to bee confined within those walls, wee should [...] circumstances far better then now they are[.] What God will doe with us we know not. [...] to think, what dismall calamities are [st]ealing in upon us. Wee need your [...] owe to us, you are flesh of our flesh and bone of our bone, and therefor[e] [...][4] [p]romise you to ma[ke prayer]s dayly at the throne of grace, and [...][5] not enlage at present

Thomas Prince Papers, Massachusetts Historical Society. Addressed "To the Reverend & highly esteemed man m^r John Cotton Minister of the Gospel In Plymouth in New England [...] at m^r Shipways house [...]." Most of Edward Rosseter's letter is torn off and missing. The remaining letter is mutilated at the left and right margins and torn unevenly along the bottom. A fragment of another letter, in a third hand, is attached at the top of the document, apparently by Prince, with his note, "conclude ye 1st of April." This fragment seems to be part of a report of news from Europe but is not substantial enough for one to conjecture a single sentence.

---

1. Prince's note: "i.e. Edward Rossiter of Taunton in England see his Letter of March. 28. 1682."
2. This begins another letter in a different, unknown hand, immediately following the above.
3. Prince's note: "1st time—Feb. 8. 84/5."
4. Torn; part of line missing.
5. Torn; most of line missing.

General Court of Plymouth to King James II,

4 June 1685[1]

While wee your Majesties Loyall subjects of the Colony of New Plimouth, the most antient plantation of your Majesties dominions in this wildernesse are reflecting upon our great unhappynesse in the death of our late soveraigne your Deare Brother, who deign'd to looke upon us with a more propitious eye then on some other of these westerne Plantations, evidenced by his gratious letters of Febr:12th in the yeare of our Lord, 1679/80: whereby wee were incouraged to make our humble Application to him, & have received noe other then favourable returnes from him, giving us hopes to obtaine his Royall Charter etc as in said letters tendered, till the fatall death of his said Majesty put a death on those our expectations;[2] Wee say, while sorrowing over these things, wee could bethinke our selves of noe way under God soe rationall for the revivall of our hopes as by humble addresse to your Majesty, who being his Brother & successour may reasonably be thought Heire also to his favourable intentions & Royall purposes & promises by him declared in our favour;

Wee therefore take this opportunity being the first Generall Court of your Majesty held in New Plimouth since his late Majesties <decease> decease to congratulate your quiet accession etc & to signify our ready obedience to the order wee received from your Honourable Councill for your Majesties Proclamation:

And wee now become your Majesties most humble Suppliants, that in compliance with said Royall declarations & promises by soe gratious a Prince your Predecessor & Brother, you will gratiously please to grant us your Royall Charter, containing such Rights, Franchises & Priviledges, espetially religious, (which wee esteem more deare then our lives) as May be necessary for the good Government of this your Colony, & have bin humbly desired by us in former addresses, in which wee humbly crave your Princely clemency, & professe our selves <your> humble Petitioners on your Majesties behalfe to him by whom Kings reigne, that your Majesty may be under a Confluence of such divine blessings as may make your Reigne long & prosperous, soe pray

Thomas Prince Papers, Massachusetts Historical Society. This is a draft in Cotton's hand. Prince notes, "K Charles II Died Feb.6. 1684/5. Suppose this was drawn up at Plim Court in June 1685. The writing of ye Rev Mr John Cotton of Plimouth."

---

1. This petition is printed in "The Hinckley Papers," Massachusetts Historical Society *Collections*, 4th ser., 5 (Boston, 1861), 137-38. The copy we read was in Cotton's hand.

2. Cotton refers to the problems with Plymouth's charter, to which he will refer frequently in many of the letters that follow.

From Cotton Mather, 25 September 1685

But now,
my Ever-honrd Uncle,

Now some people will hang their Harps upon the Willowes. The great god hath given them the Wine of Astonishment to drink. The Newes wch was so fresh at your departure hence was a grievous abuse putt upon ye silly doves. First a Vessel comes in from England, which lying at ye Isle of Wight, & at Falmouth, received certain Intelligence that ye D. of Mommouth is utterly routed,[1] taken a Prisoner, and on ye 15th of July beheaded on Tower hill, undergoing his death with much magnanimity, refusing to make any answers to what was asked him on ye scaffold, saying, That hee came there not to speak but to Dy. Hee never had much above ten Thousand men most unarmed; had once beaten ye Ks. forces, but ye second time thro' ye ill-management of ye Lord Gray, hee was over-powered—thô hee himself, tis said, fought in his own person with incredible Valour till hee Lost ye Day. Tis suspected that Gray[2] was treacherous; for hee and one or two more be reserved for Discoverers of all that had any hand, and so much as a Little finger in ye Conspiracy. Rather for his Great Estate wch upon his Death wou'd have gone to his Brother.[3] And what use is now made of this attempt to ruine all Protestants, is obvious to any Considerate person, nor is it to be thought on wthout bleeding Lamentations. But since there comes in another Vessel from Scotland which brings hither some of Argyles men to be sold for slaves and they inform us That the Earl landed in a place where hee never could get much above a thousand men;[4] the forces of ye Kingdome being raised against him before he came on shore, & intercepting all passages so that they who had promised him their Assistence, fail'd him. Hee had a Little brush or two with his Enemyes—<*but*> once over-night, but their hearts were so taken from them, that before morning they Every one went to shift for himself. Argyle was taken in ye Disguise of a Grazier. and on ye Last of June, hee was beheaded at Edinburgh.[5] Some that are come over were present at his Execution. Wee have here a copy of his speech,[6] wch doth abundantly Justify & Augment the Opinion that wee had of him. I am sorry I cannot gett a copy of it to send unto you; but in due time expect it. His Death had this odd circumstance in it, that after his head was off, hee rose up on his feet, & had like to have gone off ye scaffold, if they had not prevented it.[7]

A standing Army is that wch both Kingdomes are now kept in subjection by. C. Kirk,[8] [...] is at Taunton; and there in cold blood hath butchered five-hundred people in that Fanatic Town.

You know what to think of those things and you are no doubt so much of a Protestant as to make this use of ye hideous calamities wch these things will occasion to all protestants, that you will quicken ye Importunate groaning prayers of your own people, and those that are in ye Neighbour Towns with due privacy and Discretion. Lift up prayers—Hee that does not now Arise & call upon god, & cry mightily is one of those sleepy sinners who make ye Times perilous. But you need not mee for your Monitor.

Remember mee with my due services to my Aunt & Respect to my Cousins; and to all Friends that Enquire after my welfare, especially to ye good [agd?] Simeon; your Elder to whom Tell my wishes, that he may not think of Departing till his Eyes have seen ye salvation of God.

I am, Your observant Kinsman

C. Mather

Boston, 25d 7m 1685.

Curwen Family Papers, American Antiquarian Society. Addressed and endorsed in a hand other than Cotton's or Mather's, "From Mr Cotton Mather Sept 25: 1685: For ye Revd John Cotton Plimouth."

---

1. The abortive Monmouth Rebellion ended with the rout of the Duke of Monmouth's forces at Sedgemoor on 6 July 1685.

2. Ford, Lord Gray of Werk (d.1701), fled England upon the discovery of the Rye House Plot. He commanded the rebel cavalry at Sedgemoor, but they failed in their crucial task of surprising the Royalist camp. Gray and his cavalry became confused and disordered and all but fled the battlefield. The suspicions of treachery may have been forgiven, for Grey was indeed spared in return for his confession and cooperation. Under William III he regained his fortunes, being raised to Earl of Tankerville in 1695, and First Lord of the Treasury in 1699. *DNB.*

3. Mather added this sentence into the margin without precisely signaling where it should be in the body of the letter.

4. Archibald Campbell, 9th Earl of Argyll (d. 1685), had already escaped likely execution in England for his opposition to Charles II and fled to Holland. When Monmouth raised his rebellion, Argyll took charge of an invasion of Scotland, which quickly dissolved. With his followers dispersing, he was captured and imprisoned. *DNB.*

5. Argyll was beheaded at Edinburgh on 30 June 1685.

6. Probably *An Account of the Most Remarkable fights and skirmishes between His Majesties Forces, and the late rebels... likewise the execution of the said late Earl, and Rumbold.* (London, 1685), *Early English Books*, 6:4374 [Wing A371].

7. The above-referenced account of Argyle's beheading does not include this "head-rolling" story, but his head was "affixed on the *Tolbooth.*" *Account of the Most Remarkable fights and skirmishes* (London, 1685), 8.

8. Colonel Percy Kirke (1646[?]–1691) had served under Monmouth in 1672 but was in the Royalist camp during the Rebellion. He was instrumental in the capture and supression of the rebels in Somerset after Sedgemoor and during the "Bloody Assizes" that followed. Although a hard man, the atrocities credited to him are largely fictitious or exaggerated. *DNB.*

From George Shove, 8 November 1685

To the Elders & Brethren of ye Chh In Plimouth The Chh in Taunton wisheth grace Mercie, & peace from God ye father & o^r Lord Jesus Christ.

Reverend & Beloved

We are certified that o^r sister Mrs Joan Hart,[1] now residing among you, doth desire letters of recommendation from us to you, in order to her fellowship with you in the holy ordinances of Christ: we do therefore here signifie to you that she was here orderly joyned to this Chh in full Comunion, & during the time of her continuance among us her Conversation was blameles, & since her removall from us to R Island we have not been acquainted with any thing scandalous concerning her, except her living so long without Comunion with any Gospell Chh; The evill wherof she being sensible of so farr as accesorie to any Neglect therin, & now willing to Continue no longer in such Neglect: we do cheerfully recommend & resign & Dismiss her to yor Comunion, beseeching you to receive her in the Lord as becometh saints for her edification, & Consolation, & we pray God on your behalfe that he will make his grace to abound towards you, to your enriching in goodnes, establishm^t & perseverance to the end, in which respects we dsire your Constant prayers for us also who are

Yo^rs in the Lord

G Shove[2] with the Consent of ye brethren

Taunto Nov.8. 1685

Thomas Prince Papers, Massachusetts Historical Society.

---

1. Emery suggests that Joan Harte was the widow of Nicholas Harte (d. 1654), who "was a merchant residing in Taunton in 1643, and afterward in Boston, and Warwick and Portsmouth, R.I." Shove wrote that she had lived in Rhode Island. If this is the correct Joan Hart, she died shortly after this letter was written, in 1685. Cotton noted that he had admitted Hart into the church: "Mris Joane Hart, recommended & dismissed to us from the church at Taunton." Emery and Savage also suggest that Hart was the daughter of Edward Rosseter, one of the earliest settlers of Taunton and the uncle of Cotton's wife, Joanna. Joanna's father, Bryan Rosseter, and Edward were brothers. See the letter of 20 March 1684, which suggests that Hart was then briefly living with the Cottons. Samuel Hopkins Emery, *A History of Taunton, Massachusetts from its Settlement to the Present Time* (Syracuse, N.Y., 1893), 740; *CSM*, 22:257; Savage, *Genealogical Dictionary*, 3:577-78.

2. For Shove, see the letter of 6 October 1673.

To Cotton Mather, 21 December 1685[1]

[. . . .] me 6 of the [. . .] Almanacks now [. . . .]ing, I will send you the mon[ey]

Dec: 21:

Deare Cousen

The Boat is long wind-bound, I request your care of all the enclosed,[2] but in spetiall this to M: Dennis,[3] I beseech you take care that it be given into her owne hand, for if her sad son get it, she will never see it, a poore, idle, lying, drunken wretch he is, & wee are forced to discard him, I pray, let some body give this letter into his mothers hand:

A sloop about 50 tun is soe cast up about mannamoiett, as that the Rogues are likely to be seized by our Authority, one of the men almost drunk, spake, a[s] the goods belonged to one Lord from Antego, whose neck they tyed a grin[?] about & threw him in to sea; it i[s] probably Richard Lord of Hartfor[d][4] guns great & small are aboard 10 men & 2 boyes; majer Freema[n] & Capt Thacher are by our [illeg.] gone to them: a further account look for daily:

Thomas Prince Papers, Massachusetts Historical Society. Addressed "These For the Reverend, Mr Cotton Mather, Pastour of a church, in Boston." Prince's note, referring to Mather: "ordained May. 13. 1685." Top and right side of letter torn.

---

1. Prince's note: "suppose this Letter was wrote Dec. 21. 1685 or 86."
2. Not found.
3. Probably Sarah Howland Dennis (d. 1712), the widow of Robert Dennis (d. 1691) of Yarmouth and Newport, Rhode Island. Family histories claim that both Robert and Sarah were Quakers. This could instead refer to Mary Lathrop Crowell Dennis, the wife of James Dennis of Boston. Torrey, *New England Marriages*, 215, 216.
4. Richard Lord (1636–1685) was married to Mary Smith (1643–1702) and lived in Hartford, Connecticut. He served as a representative for several years. Savage noted that he was "lost at sea in November 1685" but does not describe the mutiny. Savage, *Genealogical Dictionary*, 3:115-16.

From Cotton Mather, 28 December 1685

Boston 28.ᴰ 10.ᴹ 1685.

Reverd Syr; and much Honrd Uncle.

Many are ye Thanks Which myself, wth my Relations, have to return to o^{r} good friends at Plymouth for their many kindnesses to us. Thank Mrs Clark for her Fowls, & tell her that my Prayers for her are that shee may be gathered among the chickens under ye Saving Wings of ye Lord Jesus. My little Sister would Write her acknowledgements to her cousin & Name-Sake[1] for her pullet, but shee has not yett so pluck't it, as to gett a Quill from it, Wherewth to do her duty.

I send you a few Almanacks,[2] for which you shall pay mee in countrey-pay, I mean, with acceptance and love. God make ye next year as peaceable & plentifull to us, as this hath been. & obtain from us such an other Thanksgiving as o^{r} late free-will-offering in that kind; then wch never any was better attended in N. E. Wee have No Newes among us, but ye good Newes, that wee have None at all. Many Tokens for good there are in ye midst of us; Heaven grant daily more & more. One thing I find, to my own Joy unspeakeable. Since my beginning in a course of Catechising-Visitations, I find That there are more serious Young people far away then I could have imagin'd o lett Divine mercy increase ye Number of them. But no greater Joy could I easily have then that my Cousin, my Sister, my child, (What shall I call her?) your daughter Eliza Walked in ye Truth.[3] Present my hearty Love to her and tell her that I wish this sentence of her Lords were dwelling in her mind as if Written by ye point of a Diamond there, I love them that love mee, and they that seek mee Early shall find mee.[4] I have a Motion of a Match some time or other to propound unto her; a Match (for shee is old enough to be [timely?] married long ago) unto ye Lord of Lords, ye perfection of beauty, ye Joy of ye whole Heaven, ye immortal King, who is altogether Lovely; but my time at present is strangely devoured. Lett not my good Mother be forgotten in my salutations; tell her that I have sent her a peece of Honey-comb,–it came from ye upper canaan and flowes with milk & honey; and I Wish that shee would suck out every drop of the vast sweetness w^{ch} [is] in it; it is This. Our light Afflictions here, wch are but for a Moment, work for us a far more Exceeding & Eternal weight of glory.

I have Now a Jog to Leave off my scribble. I began wth Thanks to other people, I end wth some to you. I thank you for ye Blessings wch you bestow upon a poor, & yett painfull, Laborious, & yett disconsolate kinsman. Continue them; they are very gratefull, & I hope will not be altogether thrown away upon,

Syr, Your

C. M.

Autograph Letter Collection, Rare Books and Special Collections Division, McGill University Libraries. Addressed "To the Reverend Mr John Cotton." Endorsed "From my Cousen, Mr Cotton Mather, December, 28: 1685:."

1. Cotton Mather had two younger sisters who shared names with Cotton's daughters; both Elizabeth Mather (b. 1667) and Sarah Mather (1671–1746) were born after Cotton's daughters, Elizabeth (b. 1663) and Sarah (b. 1670).
2. Mather probably sent Samuel Danforth's *New England Almanac for the Year of Our Lord 1686....* (Cambridge, 1685). The first printing of the almanac was made in November 1685 and so carried the year 1685 as its publication date; the second printing was in March, so it carried 1686 instead. Mather clearly sent several copies of the first printing. Evans, *American Bibliography*, 1:68 [Evans 403, 404].
3. Elizabeth Cotton was John and Joanna's second child and their eldest daughter. She was born in Guilford, Connecticut, on 6 August 1663. Although Mather intimates in this letter that Elizabeth may have experienced saving grace in late 1685, she was not admitted as a full church member until 1688. Van Antwerp, *Vital Records of Plymouth*, 2; *CSM*, 22:261.
4. Proverbs, chapter 8, 17.

From Seaborn Cotton, [1685/1686][1]

Dearest Brother I have at last sent y^{r} son[2] home but I do request you to send him again, never was a man better belov^{d} of a People than he is—I think You can't do God better service than to supply the Hungry souls of Exeter wth his Ministry—still Importuning y^{r} prayers wth Fasting for me—I am y^{rs} verily

Seab^{e} Cotton

Josiah Cotton, Manuscript "Account of the Cotton Family," Houghton Library, Harvard University.

1. Josiah Cotton's manuscript is imprecise as to its date. He prefaced this letter and the one immediately following: "To ffinish this sheet I shall add some strokes out of a letter or two, from my Uncle Cotton to my Father, ye last of wch is Dated 1685/6 Which phaps might be ye last he sent—One of his Lett^{rs} concerning my Bro^{o} Jno." Josiah Cotton, Manuscript "Account of the Cotton Family," Houghton Library, Harvard University.
2. Seaborn Cotton is referring to Cotton's son John, his nephew.

From Seaborn Cotton, [1685/1686]

DEAR BRO^R –

Pray for us, as we desire to Pray for You – Many sick & dy about us, Pray, Pray, Pray, set apart one Day of Prayer at least for y^r Dear & Distressed brother – Deaths of our good Men I Mention not – Only it is Matter of Awful solemn Consideration wn the Righteous are taken away from ye evil to come, I hope many of us lay it to Heart – Dear Bro^r Pray for us as You do for y^r own; I am und^r great Presures bodily & ghostly, but my Hope & Confidence is in God All sufficient from whom I beg Help, To whom I commend You & Yours heartily; Our Fathers and Our Mothers God be our God & ye God of Ours for his Name Sake, & Let us all say, Amen –

Josiah Cotton, Manuscript "Account of the Cotton Family," Houghton Library, Harvard University.

To Cotton Mather, 21 JANUARY 1686

PLIMOUTH JANUARY, 21: 1685:

REVD & DEARE COUSEN

your last was very welcome, as every thing is that comes from you; The good effects of your being here are & are likely to be such, that I am sure you will never have cause to repent your last coming to Plimouth; blessed be God, you left a pretious savour that will render your next appearance amongst us a Joyfull day; your Almanacks I accept with thanks & love, the pay expected: wee sit longing (& yet trembling) to heare what newes Mr Jenner[1] brings, who this time 12 mo: brought tidings of the condemnation of the Charter etc but God can make, 86 as peaceable as 85: hath bin, Amen; the Lord increase tokens for good, a spirit of prayer is eminently soe; I rejoyce greatly to heare that God smiles upon your Catecheticall worke, I have, through grace, found a rich blessing in it. My ____ Eliza your ____ [2] hath bin lately & is still exercised with bodily illnesses, but I trust in free grace, soule-health will follow, Mr Love's last sermons[3] are her constant companion, keep her neere your heart when you are at prayer, she presents due love & Respects to you, & very thankfully accepts your tender Respect to her soule;

Y[our] good mother (as you are affectionately pleased to style her) threatens much to assault you by a paper-representative, I hope the good mood will shortly come upon her, you have her & my hearty Love by these presented, with due Salutations to parents & our Cousens; our Fathers God fill you more abundantly with his holy Spirit,

& crowne all your holy & painfull labours with that successe & blessing that your soule desires, & give you a cup brim-full of consolation in your most disconsolate houres; He will doe it; oh pray for him, (my Endeared Kinsman,)

who is, yours as his owne in neerest & strongest bonds

John Cotton

Cos: Dennis letter, deliver as the former.[4]

Mather Papers 6:1, Prince Library, Rare Book and Manuscripts, Boston Public Library. Addressed "These For the Reverend, his Deare Cousen, Mr Cotton Mather, Pastour of a Church of christ at Boston."

---

1. Thomas Jenner (d. 1699), ship captain from Charlestown, also served as artillery company captain. Savage, *Genealogical Dictionary*, 2:544.
2. This underlining is Mather's.
3. Christopher Love (1618–1651) was a minister in London. His final publication was posthumous: *Grace, the Truth and Growth and different Degrees... sum and substance of XV sermons...they being his Last... to which is added a funeral sermon* (London, 1677) [Wing L3159B]. *Early English Books, 1641–1700*, 2:989.
4. See 21 December 1685.

From Cotton Mather, 5 February 1686

Reverend Syr

In answer to your Athenian Enqueryes these Lines shall tell you That ye Last Vessel from England brings us these Accounts;

Concerning France. That ye persecution is grown horribly violent & bloody there. This one instance of popish cruelty Lately given will show ye rest—About forty persons (of some Quality, as tis s^d^) having privately shipped themselves to escape out of ye Kingdome were pursued & overtaken by some of ye Kings Frigats who immediately sett ye vessel on fire consuming it, & ye poor people in it. But which are worse Tidings far away, wee are certify'd That in Last September ye Number of French protestants wch had burn'd Roman-Catholics since ye beginning of this persecution is amounted to five-hundred-eighty-three-thousand and some add scores.

Concerning Home; That Multitudes of ye Rebels are Expected (one Alsop of Taunton in particular condemn'd to Dye) A woman that lived in Wapping, whom some of o^r^ people that know her are so vain as to rekon a Devout Religious person was burnt to Death for concealing some obnoxious folks. But in one Town (as this Ship receiv'd Intelligence when it lay at ye Cowes) a company of ye Rebels not yett siez'd being assaulted by ye Kings forces, made a sturdy Resistence till ye whole town came to their Assistance, & wickedly beat His Majestyes souldiers out of ye Town. What this may occasion wee can't yet understand.

Concerning o^{r}selves; That the Rose-frigate was ready to sett out, and Randolph haveing a commission for himself to be vice-president, Mr J.D. to be president and eighteen more to bee a council was gone as far as Canterbury in [much]state towards shipping himself therein. —

These are ye cheef things wch wth my service to my mother, & respects to my cousins, I have to gratify you with this information about

I am still yours as formerly

[no signature]

Boston
5d 12.m 1685.

Curwen Family Papers, American Antiquarian Society. Addressed "For The Revd John Cotto Plimouth." Endorsed "From my cousen, Mr Cotton Mather, February, 5: 1685:." Slight staining along fold.

From Samuel Treat[1] and Samuel Freeman,[2]

12 February 1686

Reverend & Dearly Beloved in our lord Jesus.

Wee Greet you Respectively in the lord wishing grace mercy & peace to be multiplyed towards you from god our Father and our lord jesus christ, incessantly praying & bowing our knees before the father of mercyes, that he would grant that you and <illeg.> poor Weaklings our selves may stand and abide perfect and compleat in all the will of god and be found stedfast and unmoveable in the work of the lord in this hour of the passion and tribulation of the gospel and kingdom of christ jesus, and a divine and heavenly blessing on all his holy institutions in order to the building of us up on our most holy faith and the confirming the souls of his disciples that the lot of sufferings may not be daunting to any of us.

Reverend and beloved it having pleased the onely wise god by the conduct of his all disposing providence to remove from our selves margaret Jackson[3] and to cast her lot of habitation among your selves, shee sometimes was not onely with us but is also of us in full communion having witnessed a good confession and whose conversation and communion whiles with us was commendable and comfortable, but she being removed from us (the which we may not Gainsay) and being more advantagiously under the opportunity of your holy watch and communion then of ours, and she desiring letters dismissive from us to the Church of Plimouth and we consenting to the providence and will of God therein, we therefore (you accepting of her) doe dismis and recommend her unto you in the lord desiring that you receive her in the lord as becometh saints and exercise towards her charity and watchfulness and the blessings of your sacred communion that she from time to time may need and be capable of; hoping & Desiring that she may approve her self one that knoweth heareth and followeth the voyce of the great shepherd in all his holy institutions and follow the lamb wither soever he goes and keep the words of his patience in this hour of tribulation; that shee and each of us may so approve our selves let us commit our selves to him that is able to keep us from falling and present us faultles before the presence of his glory with exceeding joy into whose everlasting arms we commit & commend you earnestly desiring that at what time soever your souls get up into the mount in dearest and nearest communion with god that then ye be not unmindful of us your poor brethren and companions in tribulation engaged in the like lot of conflicts that goodnes and mercy may follow us yea the rock with his refreshing streams may follow us through al our wildernes and [illeg.] like conditions enabling us to cleave to the lord with full purpose of heart.

So we bid you farewell
yours in the bonds of christian unity and charity

Samll Treat
Samuel ffreeman senir.
in the name and consent of this church

Eastham: 12th: feb: 1685:

Thomas Prince Papers, Massachusetts Historical Society.

---

1. See 10 October 1680.

2. Samuel Freeman was an elder at Eastham.

3. Margaret Jackson married Abraham Jackson Jr. in January 1685 in Plymouth, removed from Eastham, was dismissed from the Eastham church and joined the Plymouth church in full communion. *CSM*, 22:257.

From James Keith, 15 February 1686

Bridgwater Febr. 15. 1685

Reverend & dear Sir

I have received yours [of] [t]he 12 instant[1] & am glad to hear of your welfare, & do heartily acknowledge your love in your remembrance of me. I have waited for an opportunity all this winter to salute you by a few lines, but none hath presented till now. it is of the lords mercyes y^t^ we live, & y^t^ our libertyes of converse with him in his house, & our opportunityes of converse one with another are continued to this very day. Sir I thank you for your intelligence from Europe, which is the most full & particular I have hade. O y^t^ our hearts may be drawn out to a tender sympathy with our brethren, y^t^ we may improve the warnings the Lord is giving us by their sufferings to a solemn preparation for our day of fiery triall, y^t^ when it comes we may not think it a strange thing. I bless god for his presence with you in your afflictions, wee need not wonder y^t^ a lying tongue hateth those y^t^ are afflicted by it, considering what Solom: tells us prov. 26. 24.[2] 25. 26.[3] the slander of the tongue proceeds from hatred in the heart which when it is inveterate becomes implacable: devouring words, & practices are pleasing to the lying tongue. Ps. 52. 2. 3. 4.[4] men of unmortifyed lusts are restless. Prov. 29. 9.[5] & the more they meet with disappointments the more they hate which may be considerable in your case. it is good to observe the holy hand of god in all our reproaches, the Lord operates the tongues of our adversaryes, if they curse he bids them. we ought to pray for those by whom we are despitefully used & to wait patiently for the lord who will bring forth the righteousness of his servants as the light; though such exercises are greivous they are very light comparatively; let us remember those who endured cruell workings who were tortured & tormented not accepting deliverance of whom the world was not worthy, but much more let us consider our Lord Jesus who endured such contradiction of sinners; lest we be weary, & faint in our mindes, the hard winter hath obstructed my converse with my good neighbour. I have a great desire to go over to his lecture this week, the wayes are discouraging but may be I may venture. the lord hath been very gracious to me & my family in the difficulties of the season, we are all in competent health only under some exercise by colds. I have nothing momentous as to intelligence from hence to write at this time. Remember me to all freinds with you particularly present my service to the good deputy you know. I am sorry to hear of your good elders confinement, remember me heartily to him present my respects to L. Morton. I am glad to hear he hath stucke so close to you in your late troubles, if I was to see him I will thank him for it, you must accept of this at present for a return of your letter, thus desiring your prayers for me with a tender of my[...] selfe & Mrs Cotton I rest your [...] freind

Curwen Family Papers, American Antiquarian Society. Addressed "For The Revd Mr John Cotton Plimouth." Endorsed "From Mr Keith February, 15: 1685." Hole in top margin, staining along folds and at bottom right edge.

---

1. Not found.
2. Ps. 26:24: "He that hateth dissembleth with his lips, and layeth up deceit within him."
3. Ps. 25:26: "A righteous man falling down before the wicked *is as* a troubled fountain and a corrupt spring."
4. Ps. 52:2-4: "Thy tongue deviseth mischiefs; like a sharp razor, working deceitfully. Thou lovest evil more than good; *and* lying rather than to speak righteousness. Selah. Thou lovest all devouring words, O *thou* deceitful tongue."
5. Prov. 29:9: "*If* a wise man contendeth with a foolish man, whether he rage or laugh, *there is* no rest."

From the General Court, 6 March 1686

TO THE REVEREND ELDERS OF THE CHURCH ATT PLIMUTH

The dispensations of god to <*the*> his people being awfull & humbling: the Court Apoints the Last <*wednesday*> wednesday[1] of this Instant: to be sett apart as a day of publicke fasting & prayer: for their End: that wee may fall down before god in humble Confesion of all our sines whereby God hath been provoked to frown upon us: In Cutting short provision for man & Beast: in severall places: & by other providentiall threatnings: as also to Implore mercy from God: In Continuing our Choyce blessings to us: to prevent the spreading of any Infectious Deseases that hath allready been Aflictive in one part of the Country: & mercyfully hasten a Comfortable spring: after so long & seveer a winter: Blessing our seed time & harvest this yeare: & that god would have mercy on all his Aflicted people in the world: support them under: & give them seasonable deliverance out of all their Troubles: & that the kingdom of Christ may be Advanced throughout the world—

p^{r} order of Court

Nath:^{ll} Clarke, Secretary

Dated att plimouth March: 6th: 1685/6

Thomas Prince Collection, Massachusetts Historical Society.

---

1. The second "wednesday" is in John Cotton's hand.

To John Cotton (1661), 8 March 1686

PLIMOUTH MARCH, 8: 1685:/86:

MY DEARE CHILD

Hath the Lord had mercy on you & on us also, in restoring you to former health? how often hath God brought you neere to the gates of death & againe raised you unto life! oh, what bonds & obligations are upon you to be the Lords with your whole heart, who hath given you soe many lives! let your whole time & strength be now spent absolutely in the Lords service, that it may appeare this affliction & all the paths of God to you have bin in mercy: I need not tell you, how afflicting the tidings of your sicknesse was to us, noe doubt, you realized the overwhelmings of the spirit of you[r] tender mother; the tidings came to us on Feb: 19: on Feb: 26: I obt[ai]ned about 30 to Joyne with us in Fasting & prayer for you, & [the] bretheren did heartily & earnestly pray for you, the next morning early came a boate from Boston with a letter to us from Mr Moodey[1] with certaine tidings of your recovery, how ready is God to heare prayers, therefore will wee call upon him as long as wee live: Mr Moodey hath already sent us 5 letters[2] concerning you, expressing m[uc]h Christian sympathy with us, & shewing his earnest de[s]ire to comfort us & to ease our hearts in affliction for you, I & your mother take it exceeding kindly, & are greatly ingaged to him for his tender love & pitty soe manifested to us, when our spirits were greatly bowed downe: wee send our hearty respects & love to Capt Gilman & his wife,[3] with our abundant thankfullnesse to them for their great care of you & paines about you in this your distresse, the Lord gratiously reward them for it: your mother advises you, to purge your body well this spring: & to be let bloud also[4] the good Lord perfect healing mercy to you, & grant you saving good by all afflictions & mercies; all of us here heartily salute you with Love to Rowland & our relations where he lives; praying alwayes for the blessing of [...] rest upon you

[....] [Father John Cotton][5]

Thomas Prince Collection, Massachusetts Historical Society. Bottom margin is torn, center fold has several small holes, and left margin has one small hole.

---

1. Not found.
2. Not found.
3. Probably Judge Nicholas and Sarah Clark Gilman of Exeter, New Hampshire.
4. Purging and bloodletting were common healing practices in early New England. Joanna Cotton's medical training would have prompted her to instruct her sons to perform regular purges. Bloodletting was a more extreme treatment and generally performed only by practicing doctors. J. Worth Estes,

"Therapeutic Practice in Colonial New England," *Medicine in Colonial Massachusetts, 1620–1820, CSM,* 57 (Boston, 1980): 289-383.

5. Signature is in another hand, probably Thomas Prince's.

From Rowland Cotton, 13 August 1686

Boston Aug: 13. 16[86]

Hon. Sr

These are to Inform you that wee arrived at Boston about 6 a clock in ye afternone where I had no sooner came but I mett with Roger A[ ]ams[1] who told mee y^t^ he had [. . . .] according to your order, If y^t^ mr. white [. . .] gardner & mrs [. . .] were there att dinner, but did no [thanks?] m^r^ cotton tells me you shall pay for [. . .] Betty[2] laid att mrs Browns ye first night last night att uncle mathers,[3] too night at cotton mathers. mr cotton[4] goes for certain next wednesday sennet with his wife & frinds,[5] they are both present att y^s^ writing & affirm It—y^r^ marriage[6] will be this week or next according as y^r^ fancy inclines them—Mr Hutchinson has his letter[7] & mr mather. mr cotton sais my Bro Jno and mr Allin[8] will be down here to go up wth ym. mrs Ann tells mee yt Eleazur Russel courts abigall moody[9] & like to have her. I dont hear any news—uncle mather says If he comes to plymouth at all It will be ye week after next. He says If you do not preach for him, he will not go up. he will tarry att plym. but one week he says, & so you your self will not see him att all att plym: if he d[oe] not go to plym. he will [. . .] att watertown a week. he cant stay but a week he says because ye colledge is new setled Therefore seing his going to plymouth will be ye same week y^t^ I goe to Hampton and the same day These are humbly to Intreat you to lett some other way be for uncles company to plymouth, that so I may not goe with him. My humble duty to your self & your self wth love to B^rs^ & sisters presented I remain S^r^

your dutiful son

R.C.

Thomas Prince Papers, Massachusetts Historical Society. Addressed "For Mr J. Cotton in Plimouth." Endorsed "From my son Rowland August, 13: 1686:"

---

1. Probably Roger Adams (d. 1714), husband of Mary Baker (1653–1710), who lived in Roxbury. Savage, *Genealogical Dictionary,* 1:15.

2. Elizabeth Cotton, Rowland's sister.

3. Increase Mather.
4. Probably Seaborn Cotton (1633–1686), the groom's uncle.
5. Inserted word illegible.
6. Cotton Mather married Abigail Phillips (1670–1702) on 4 May 1686 in Charlestown.
7. Not found.
8. John Cotton, Rowland's brother, was preaching in Exeter with his uncle Seaborn Cotton. James Alling (1657–1696, H.C. 1679) was preaching in Salisbury. Evidently, the men were traveling together to attend Cotton Mather's wedding. Weis, *Colonial Clergy,* 62-63, 19.
9. Possibly Eliezur Russell, a Boston goldsmith, who seems to have died unmarried in 1690, since his will left his whole estate to his niece, Rebecca, his brother Jonathan's daughter, in Barnstable. Abigail Moody was the daughter of Rev. Joshua Moody and Martha Collins Moody, then living in Portsmouth. She died, also apparently unmarried, in March 1687. Savage, *Genealogical Dictionary,* 3:590.

From [Zechariah] Walker, 1686[1]

May it please God to teach us not to suffer such solemn Dispensations in vain—To lose Our dearest Comforts & to lose those Losses also will be intollerable. I presume you have heard how afflictive this summer has been to this Colony, partly by immoderate Rain & unusual ffloods, both as to time & measure, w[r]by many Hundred Bushells of Corn are gone to sea Unthreshed & much more spoiled at home: Partly by Epidemical sicknesses in Most Plantations, & still remain tho und[r] mercifull Abatem[en]t. It is God alone y[t] can teach us to Profit, & cause us to see why he Contendeth with us.

Josiah Cotton, Manuscript "Account of the Cotton Family," Houghton Library, Harvard University.

---

1. Josiah Cotton included this transcription in his manuscript "Account of the Cotton Family," and prefaced it, "The Other Letter was upon y[e] Loss of some Relation &c." In his manuscript, it followed immediately after an earlier letter in this volume; see "From [Zechariah] Walker, 1686." Cotton does not indicate the exact date, but Walker's reference to a difficult summer harvest informed our decision to place the letter here.

To Thomas Hinckley,

1–9 October 1686
[May–December 1686][1]

May it please your Honour

I made utmost haste this morning to finde you here, & am sorry for my disappointment; of late I have not bin soe sollicitous to hand aliquid Novi,[2] because Mr Moodey is constant in doing it to his son: Henfeild, Bennett & John Walley are newly arrived from London;[3] I saw a Letter that sayes, Sir Edmunds Frigatt was ready at the Downes to saile for N: E: & he was daily expected to come on board in order to his voyage hither:[4] the Army at Hounslow Heath is scattered to their winter-quarters: Rumors from the North of Ireland I dare not write: Sir, I missed mr Simeon Stoddard[5] yesterday as he was coming from the Preaesident,[6] who hath given him a letter to you,[7] which being of great concernment & Mr Dudley expecting my seeing you here told me its contents, which as neere as I can remember his words were to this purpose, viz, that he had a prisoner of yours in his custody, & expected you should call Powell[8] & any other witnesses before you & take their Testimonies against Joseph Nash[9] (I do not understand they should be sworne before you till the prisoner is in praescence) & send copyes of these evidences to him together with a man empowered by you to receive said prisoner & bring him to your Goale, for he must be tryed in the county or colony where the fact was done or words spoken: My Brother mather[10] & I were desired by the prisoners Relations to speake to the Pres: wee were both very carefull of reflecting on your Honour but it troubles me that I cannot viva voce[11] tell you how things are resented; while a pipe of Tobacco had bin taking, that wisest of men thinke might have bin done that would have saved many a pounds of charge to persons & Country, besides much trouble; I praesume it is hoped, that soe audacious an act as soe taking a man hence without warrant will have its due punishment by this Authority, if there be time for it before our doom comes. I could tell you an 100 things about this matter if I had time, but Mr Smith[12] is in post-haste it being Saturday; I take it for granted, & soe doe men abundantly wiser than I, that upon your receipt of the Presidents letter (which I only give you a forehint of) you will not deferre a day before you examine that Powell & any others in Plimouth, & make utmost haste to dispatch a messenger to fetch the prisoner hither, etc. I have not time to tell you how greivous it is to relations to have such a fellow to trample under his feet a government & thereby bring soe much trouble & losse to them that have not a shilling to loose: I trust, Good Sir, God will guide you wisely & uprightly to extricate your selfe out of these unhappy snares, & difficulties; how sim stodder will passe his letter I know not, but if it come here, I shall hasten it away, for the best friends of this our [...] pardon for my boldness, 'tis well its Saturday else before I finished this sheet, I feare I should have oversaid, if I have already, Deare Sir, at your candor cover it, intire respect to you hath extorted more than I dare thinke to doe when I began to write; I cannot detaine Mr Smith, in post haste

I rest, wester observantissime[13]

John Cotton

my paper met with a disaster,[14] I cannot helpe it now

Deacon Bright of Watertown[15] of 85 yeares old, waited upon the Gentlemen [...] on the late ordination day & yesterday by a cart was brought neere death, & was concluded to be dead before I left Boston

Earle of Powis, Lord Arundel, Lord Bellamy, Lord Dover are lately sworne of his majesties privy councill[16]

Thomas Prince Collection, Massachusetts Historical Society. Addressed "These for the honourable, Thomas Hinckley Esquire, Gouvernour of New-Plimouth Colony, Living at Barnstable."

---

1. In Thomas Prince's hand: "1686. between ye end of May & ye end of December."
2. "Anything new."
3. John Walley (1644–1712) was born in England and emigrated in 1686. See 10 August 1694.
4. Edmund Andros, Governor of the Dominion of New England.
5. Simeon Stoddard (1651–1730) served on the Provincial Council and lived in Boston. In the legal case that follows in this letter, the defendant (Joseph Nash) is Stoddard's brother-in-law. Savage, *Genealogical Dictionary,* 4:201; Richard Benson, *The Nash Family of Weymouth, Massachusetts* (Boston, 1998), 25.
6. Prince notes, "ie Joseph Dudley Esq—see ye Lettr followg."
7. Not found.
8. Evidently an eyewitness in the Nash case.
9. Joseph Nash was a mariner who married Elizabeth Holbrook before 1674 and Grace Stoddard before 1684. He was living in Boston in 1686, in which year he also owned land in Maine. Court records indicate that he appeared in the Superior Court of Judicature on 2 November 1686 "upon his recognizance, for speaking treasonable words against his Majestie —and no evidence appeareing to preosecute, was ordred to be discharged, giveing bond to be of good Behaviour..." *Records of the Superior Court of Judicature: Special Courts, 1686–1687* (copy), 13; Savage, *Genealogical Dictionary,* 3:260-61; Torrey, *New England Marriages,* 529.
10. Increase Mather.
11. "By voice."
12. The letter's carrier.
13. "Most respectfully yours."
14. Cotton is referring to the large stain along the lower left margin of his writing paper; he simply wrote on the paper that remained, justifying his text against the stain. Apparently the paper was still wet when he wrote the letter but was sufficiently dry by the time he signed his name, because his apology and postscript are written over the stained area.

15. The injuries Cotton described were ultimately fatal, and Henry Bright died on 9 October 1686 at the age of eighty-four. Bright had emigrated in 1630 with John Winthrop's fleet, settled in Watertown shortly thereafter, married Ann Goldstone in 1634 and had eight children. He served as Deacon of the Watertown church. Bright's death confirms the date of this letter as early October 1686. Savage, *Genealogical Dictionary,* 1:253.

16. Prince notes, "viz May. 17. 1686."

To Thomas Hinckley, 15 October 1686

PLIMOUTH OCTOBER, 15: 1686:

HONOURED SIR

Providence soe ordered that Mr Dudley's letter[1] (which I soe narrowly missed this day sevennight) lay wind-bound & came not to my hands till yesterday, which was an unhappy disappointment to mr Jacob Nash[2] (the prisoner's brother) who came hither on wednesday, concluding the letter to your Honour was arrived at its Port, but finding the contrary, Judged it vaine for him to goe Barnstable, thinking you would doe nothing without the President's letter, & therefore he returned home requesting my extraordinary care speedily to dispatch the letter, which I promised to doe by a messenger on purpose (if noe speedy way presented) out of pitty to a poore prisoner, whose confinement at Boston (by the villany (if I mistake not) of a wicked man) is very greivous to many considerable relations: Powell came on Monday to our Dep: Govr & told him, the Præsident had given Joseph Nash[3] a check, & intimated, as if he were returned to his owne home, all which is notoriously false; It is not for me to say, how greivous it will be taken at Boston if noe effectuall answer be returned to the Præsident's letter, till the time of your personall going to Boston, though it should be within 10 dayes; wiser then I conclude that you may (& hope God will immediately guide you to doe) that which may issue the whole matter long before that time; But if I am too bold, I know you have grace & candor enough to pardon me, it is not a pragmaticall-principle, but something better that now moves me; The messenger stayes,

I am, Sir, your Honours most observantly

John Cotton

Thomas Prince Collection, Massachusetts Historical Society. Addressed "These For the Honourable, Thomas Hinckley Esquire, Governour of Plimouth Colony at Barnstable."

1. This letter is referred to in 1–9 October 1696.
2. Carpenter and miller Jacob Nash (d. 1718) was married to Abigail Dyer (b. 1647) and lived in Weymouth; he fought in King Philip's War and served as a representative in 1689 and 1690. By 1694, he was listed as "captain." Richard Benson, *Nash Family of Weymouth,* 20-23; Savage, *Genealogical Dictionary,* 3:261-62; Torrey, *New England Marriages*, 529. See 1-9 October 1686 letter to Thomas Hinckley for the Nash case.
3. See the letter of 1–9 October 1686 for the Nash case.

To Rowland Cotton, 26 November 1686

Plimouth November 26: 1686:

Son Rowland

It was great pitty that you had not patience to tarry an houre, your selfe was the greatest looser, never did I finde Mr Stoughton more free to give me my Salary,[1] & in money too, & two such bags he had in his hand that I question not but if you had bin present he would have given you your latter ten pd, but because you were absent I said nothing of it: It is to me a great Marvell, that a quarter before your commencement is yet due [from] me, considering how much money [....] about that [ti]me, & now besides the [....] you had of Mr Stoughton I have [....] weeke paid three pounds seven sh[illings] to Mr Chickley for you, which you [...] have paid & not I: yet because I [...] for you to the utmost, I now doe [...] great wrong of your mother & the [...] order for the ward foure pounds at Cos: Mackart[y] [...] to pay our Colledge debts till the Commencement & as much since as it will serve for & deare child, doe not thinke I must make all my family any more to pine for keeping you at Colledge; you are now m^r of Arts, & if you are not fit now to begin to preach, I feare you never will;[2] Hasten home & study sermons & other things diligently, & doe not imagine that your staying at Colledge will helpe you out of debt, noe, it will bring snares on you & me, that wee shall not be able to get out of; you cannot (soe far as I now see) have any employ there to maintaine you, great motions are upon the wheele, if God succeed your uncle & he at his returne finde you a sober Christian he may doe you good, & your living at home this winter will be noe prejudice to you in that respect, but the contrary, if you sincerely give up your name to Jesus Christ as I hope you are about to doe, your lingering is some exercise to my spirit, but I hope the best; The Lord blesse you with <*the*> truth of grace & fix your heart with an invincible resolution not to degenerate from the God of your fathers: mother, sisters & brothers kindly salute you; come to your fathers house, where you shall have full maintenance, but abroad

I can not affoard it:

I am your Loving Father sollicitous of your best good,

John Cotton

Thomas Prince Collection, Massachusetts Historical Society. Addressed "These For Mr Rowland Cotton, at the College in Cambridge. Leave these with mr Elliston at Boston for Conveyance." Large tear along right margin, and staining throughout.

---

1. As one of the Commissioners for the United Colonies, William Stoughton (1631–1701, H.C. 1650) distributed Cotton's salary for his missionary work.
2. Cotton struggled to pay his several sons' college tuitions, and he implored Rowland to accept a paying pulpit rather than continue his studies past the Master's Degree he would soon receive. For a slightly later example of Cotton's tuition worries, see 2 September 1687.

From Cotton Mather, 31 January 1687

Reverend Syr.

I thank you for ye Kind Notice you continue to take of your Careless Kinsman. Instead of a Letter I do here enclose a Little printed pamphlet,[1] which I entreat your Acceptance of. I enclose also a few Written sheets, which I recommend unto ye perusal of my Cousin Rowland, as a specimen of ye method wch I could Wish his Theological studies might proceed in;[2] desiring that they may bee safely in convenient Time returned unto mee again.

I have no great affection for ye Writing of Newes. But, we are daily expecting to have one of o^r meeting-houses demanded by ye Governr who is very much disgusted (they say) by o^r Late untowardness,[3] when hee requested a meeting-house at his first Arrival. He gives much Content unto many people, if not unto all, by his mild & prudent Government, the Colledge particularly hee expresses a very obliging Kindness unto.

The Parlaim^t that was to sitt in Nov. is prorogu'd unto Febr[4]: The Turk is amazingly going down ye wind;[5] — [....] in England, tis s^d, may have their Liberty & protection from ye K.'s Broad-seal, if they will ask it; But they generally are unwilling to ask it. Present all my service, & Love, to my plimouth-mother;[6] & my Cousins. —

I am, Yours,

[Cotton Mather]

Curwen Family Papers, American Antiquarian Society. Endorsed "[...] my cousen [...] mather Received [Janu] ary 31: 1686:"

1. Mather probably sent one of his own recently-published tracts, most likely *The Call of the Gospel*, an execution sermon Mather preached on 7 March 1686 (Boston, 1686), or *Military Duties*, the artillery election sermon preached on 13 September 1686 (Boston, 1687).
2. Mather evidently suggested a course of theological study that Rowland could pursue at home without incurring further living expenses, which his father could ill-afford according to the letter above.
3. Sir Edmund Andros arrived in Boston in December 1686 and soon tried to find a space for formal Episcopal worship in Boston. The established churches were unwilling to share their meetinghouses for such a purpose, despite repeated requests. On Easter Sunday 1687, Andros finally forced the Third Church to share its meetinghouse, an uncomfortable arrangement that lasted two years, until the first King's Chapel was built on land seized from Boston's old burial ground. Andre Mayer, *King's Chapel: the First Century, 1687–1787* (n.p. 1976), 6-7.
4. Parliament did not sit again until January 1689, the Convention Parliament of the Glorious Revolution. Cook & Wroughton, *English Historical Facts*, 89.
5. The Ottoman Empire launched its last assault on Christian Europe in the late seventeenth century, marching as far as the gates of Vienna in 1683. However, after they failed to take that city, the Ottomans rapidly were pushed back through Hungary and Transylvania.
6. Joanna Cotton, Cotton's wife.

From Edward Rosseter, 10 February 1687

Sr

I have received two letter this year[1] from you for which I heartily thanke you the first I could not read without weeping to observe your affectionate simpathy with [us?] in our late most dolfull Condition therin Exprest, But Gods dispensations of Judgment were dreadfull and terrible and full of severity to sume yet to the most his mercys were as wonderfull in their preservation, And then that he should be so quick in the bounteous dispensations of his favours as to extend mercy to us in the midst of Judgments and restore us to peace and Tranquility after such an Amazing hurricane [that] passed over us is matter of wonder & call for gratitude. The other Intimates what I have along time feared Misserys begining to look in upon you; And may not the Lord say Concerning you as of them ye Profet you have I known of all the people of the Earth and you will I punish for all your inniquitys What place or Collony in the World have Enjoyed such holy & pious ministers such peacable sabbaths such plenty and purity of Ordinances without mixture of mens invent[ions &?] humane traditions

And may not I say as the [...] your wayes and your doings have procured those [...] unto you such have been your Miscariages, It have peirced my heart somtimes to hear what Odious Scandalls have broken out in your Country not by the Common sort of people but among Eminent professors Even they have been overtaken againe and againe with the Swinish Sin of drunkenness and Other Enormities such [as] Soloman intimates are fooles & mad to be the Instru[ments] of their Own ruin Is it not strang that he that is indued with Reason and understanding and Capable of knowing the nature and attending the Consequences of things should so greedily embrace the Cause & will not to be driven from it Whilst he hates the Effect as great a blemish as this Layes upon humane nature yet tis too True by sad and dolfull Experience amongs us faire men would seperate what Gods unalterable Law have joyned together Sin & Missery And the people know they Cannot have the One without the Other yet they will venture upon what they love though Cirtainely attended with what they Cannot Endure. You may well ask why such an Illiterate person as my Selfe should light a Candle to the Sun there is no flattery or hipocrisey in what I say But deare Sir I only touch what you are infintely better acquanted with then I can Express I mean the abominable nature of sin which the Scripture calls by the name of plague death & hell and the dreadfull Calam[ity] that first or last Without Sincere Repentance & reformation Cirtainely follow But this Course will helpe you and our [...] any people under stan I mean humilliation for past & present sins and unfeigned amendment will procure forfeited mercys abused wonderfull favours I have been affraid the Lords wrath is kindled againt y^u now Cirtainly you must set down this that the turning away of Gods wrath is of greatest Consequence If the Lord go on to be angry do what you can you will lose all your pleasant Enjoyments not only spirittual but temporall also. Oh that O and N:E then would cast away their lusts God hath no other quarrell against us or you He doth not afflict willingly. If we find out our beloved sins all of them & put them away who Can tell how soone the Lord may heale us & prevent farther misserys from overtaking us. Alass

Many Houses are Erected in the great Citty & other Citties & places in our Land & that Interest would be in the Encreasing hand. But tho there are many places ther but few that frequent them there is litle thriving in yt abominable I had almost said damnable trade

His Majesty have very gratiously sent a proclamation for the Moderate Presbeterians & Quakers to have full liberty of Conscience in Scotland[2] (& Its supposed the like will be granted for E & Ireland) as also the Papists these three are mentioned in it.

The dissenters have generally taken liberty all that nation over & many have Licenses from ye King so to do but the more wise & serious Christians are n[ot] without fear of what may follow but svents[3] belo[] God let us follow o^r presant duty & trust him with the Issue

You see how apt I am to be large when writing to my dear friend but will trouble you no farther but only to give you as desired the dear respects of my Worthy Brethren Sisters to your whole selfe and accept the like from

Yo[r] most intirely affectid Kinsman & Servant

E: R:

London in England The 10th of ffebruary 1686

Curwen Family Papers, American Antiquarian Society. No address remains. Endorsed "Mr Edward [...] 10: 1686: 1687:"

---

1. Not found.
2. James had long been keen to secure toleration for Catholics but found it was impossible to do so in England or Scotland without also addressing the status of Protestant dissenters. In February 1687, he published a "Letter of Indulgence" for both Catholic and Protestant dissenters in Scotland. He followed this in April with a "Declaration of Indulgence" for England also. Maurice Ashley, *James II* (Minneapolis, Minn., 1977), 196-97.
3. "Servants."

From William Brattle,[1] 16 July 1687

CAMB. JULY 16. 1687

REVEREND S[R]

After as happy & comfortable a Voyage as y[e] absence of our good Companions would allow of, We arrived at Boston, Thursday about 4 of y[e] Clock afternoon—& about Sun down I came to Cambridge & delivered to Lieut. Green[2] y[e] Primer w[ch] you sent by me, which y[e] Lieuten[t] sent this morn: to M[r] Eliot[3] whom I shall see too morrow & enform according to y[r] order: —By leaving Plymouth as we did, I had y[e] happinesse of being here time enough to pay y[e] last of Love to a couple who deserved y[e] same from me, I mean of accompanying to their graves y[e] corpes of my Good Aunt Eyrs[4] & our faithfull Stew[d] m[r] Bordman[5] who was buryed about Sun-down last night. M[r] Leverett[6] & my self are now going to Boston to acquaint M[r] Mather & his Excell:[7] wth y[e] Losse w[ch] y[e] Colledge has sustained, & I trust y[t] very speedily we shall have one provided to take care of us: —S[r]/ I give y[r] self & M[rs] Cotton my hearty thanks for y[r] late greate civility & kindnesse, Wish you & yours all happinesse—so Subscribe my self Rev S[r]

y[r] humble Serv[t]

Wm Brattle

Please to give my service to Mr Saltonstall[8] (if wth you) & to tell [....] him a 100 times [....] willing we should be [....]

Autograph File, Houghton Library, Harvard University. Addressed "For The Revd Mr John Cotton at his house In Ply^{m}."

---

1. William Brattle (1662–1717) graduated from Harvard in 1680, served as a fellow of the college for ten years beginning in 1686 and was ordained as pastor of the Cambridge church in 1696. Known for his "independence," especially from the powerful Mathers, and his willingness to dispute the Cambridge Platform, Brattle helped establish the Brattle Street Church with Rev. Benjamin Colman. Despite his prickly relationship with the Mathers, Brattle served as treasurer of Harvard College upon his brother's death in 1713. *Sibley's Harvard Graduates,* 3:200-207.

2. Samuel Green (1615–1702) emigrated with Winthrop in 1630 and settled in Cambridge. In addition to serving as captain of the town militia for thirty years, he was an important early printer in Massachusetts. Savage, *Genealogical Dictionary,* 2:305; Thomas, *History of Printing in America,* 54-71.

3. Cotton corrected Eliot's version of the catechism and the 1687 primer—see Thomas Prince's manuscript catalogue in which he placed a note about Eliot's Indian Bible, the 1685 version: "ye Rev Mr John Cotton of Plimouth being well acq^{d} wth ye Ind^{n} Lang^{g} was des^{d} by ye Ind^{n} Commis^{nrs} to correct Mr Eliot's vers^{n} of 1663; took this method—while a good Reader in his study read ye Eng Bible aloud, Mr Cotton silently looked along in ye same place in ye Indn Bible: & wh^{r} He thot of Ind^{n} words w^{c} He judg^{d} c^{d} express ye sense better, There He substituted y^{m} & this 2^{d} Edit^{n} is accord^{g} to Mr Cotton's correction."

4. Brattle's use of "Aunt" is a term of endearment and somewhat confusing. Dorothy Eyre was his sister's mother-in-law. His sister, Catherine, married John Eyre (1654–1700) in 1680. Dorothy and Simon Eyre emigrated from London in 1635 with several children and settled in Watertown. Dorothy died on 13 July 1687. Savage, *Genealogical Dictionary,* 2:133-34, 1:239.

5. Andrew Bordman died at the age of forty-two on 15 July 1687. *Vital Records of Cambridge, Massachusetts to 1850* (Boston, 1915), 2:475.

6. John Leverett (1662–1724) was a classmate of Brattle's at Harvard and the two men served as tutors together for more than ten years. When Brattle wrote to Cotton, Leverett and Brattle were traveling together to Boston to meet with Increase Mather, President of Harvard, about college finances. According to Sibley, Brattle and Leverett assumed control of the college during Mather's four-year stay in London to fight for the Massachusetts charter. Leverett later supported Brattle and Colman in establishing the Brattle Street Church. Although trained for the ministry, Leverett practiced law and served as a representative to the General Court, Speaker of the House, governor's councillor and judge of the Superior Court and, ultimately, president of Harvard College from 1707 until his death, much to the Mathers' chagrin. *Sibley's Harvard Graduates,* 3:180-98.

7. Dudley was chief justice of the new courts beginning in March 1687.

8. Perhaps Gurdon Saltonstall (1666–1724, H.C. 1684), then serving as a minister in New London, Connecticut Colony, or Gurdon's father, Nathaniel Saltonstall of Haverhill. Weis, *Colonial Clergy,* 181.

To Elizabeth Saltonstall Cotton and Rowland Cotton, 1 August 1687

Plimouth August, 1: 1687:

Daughter Betty

Son Rowland

That morning immediately after you went Theophilus[1] was taken violently sick with belly-ache, vomiting, & flux, but God in mercy recovered him before the sabbath; That day El: Churchel had a girle[2] & since Tho: cushman hath a boy[3]: My Lecture which should have bin on wednesday, I ordered to be this Monday, & old Mr Russell[4] comes from Barnstable to preach it: on the morrow I intend to goe for Bristoll & those parts, & sending Mr Danforth hither, shall stay at Taunton next Sabbath[5] & come home on Monday: soe that I hope Bro: Walkers[6] visit will be next weeke & that he will stay here the Sabbath ensui[ng]

Betty, you must finde out some contrivance [....] soone as you can, your mistick [....] doubtlesse lend you a horse for Rowland [....] you part of the way (& soe your uncle [....] may be to bring you quite home, consi[ ] [....] noble-spirited to you, there is noe [....] now & then on saturdays: Eph: Cole[7] will [....] but in his returne he will spend a weeke [....] & that will be too long for Betty to be on the [seas?] [...] try to the utmost for some other project: Betty, you must lay out a shilling, halfe pepper, halfe Indigo [&] bring it home with you for your mother: The Lord preserve you both & order all things well for you; all salute you; Rowl: looke carefully to your whole way at the Colledge & take heed of evill company, you know what will become of him who is a companion of fooles; I committ you to God & rest

your Loving Father

John Cotton

The shil: you may take up at Mr Ellistone's,[8] if he have the things; if he have them not, borrow the money I will repay it.

Betty, the shilling mentioned on the other side you must lay out besides the shil: your mother gave you to buy Allspice & Indigo, see that you bring them both.

Rowland, you send for all your things to be sent, but wee know not what things you meane, what old Cloathes you would have came in chest, what bookes, for I suppose there are but a few of your present Library that will be of present use to you; you may borrow of the Fellowes & use the colledge-Library: your Bible is here, if you like it you may take one of those new bound at Mr Wilkyes[9] & be carefull to send home the other by the first opportunity, your mother would know what shirts you have with you.

Theophilus is this morning taken ill againe, but not soe bad [as?] before as yet, God pitty & spare him. [Theophilus] is now better, bring him some ginger bread. [....] m^{r} Russell

Thomas Prince Collection, Massachusetts Historical Society. Addressed "These For Sir Cotton, at the College in Cambridge. Leave them with Mr George Elliston shopkeeper in Boston for conveyance as abovesaid." Large hole in right margin.

---

1. Theophilus Cotton (1682–1726, H.C. 1701) was the youngest of John and Joanna's eleven children, four of whom died either as infants or while they were very young. Van Antwerp, *Vital Records of Plymouth,* 2.
2. Eliezer and Mary Churchel had eleven children; their fourth daughter was named Jedidiah and baptized in 1687. *CSM,* 22:259; *Plymouth Vital Records,* 8.
3. Thomas Cushman Jr. (1637–1726) and his wife, Abigail Fuller Cushman (c. 1652–1734), had a son, Samuel. *CSM,* 22:259; Torrey, *New England Marriages,* 200.
4. Jonathan Russell (1627–1692) graduated from Harvard in 1645 and ministered to an often-contentious church in Wethersfield, Connecticut Colony, beginning in 1649. In 1659, he escorted a faction of the Wethersfield church to Hadley, Massachusetts Bay Colony. When he preached for Cotton in Plymouth, he was probably in Barnstable visiting (or perhaps even living with) his son, Jonathan Russell (1655–1711, H.C. 1675), who was the settled minister in Barnstable from 1683 until his death and the successor to the regicide Thomas Walley, whom his father had once hidden. *Sibley's Harvard Graduates,* 1:110-18, 2:455-57.
5. Cotton preached the Sabbath lecture in Taunton for Samuel Danforth (1666–1727, H.C. 1683), the minister of Taunton from 1687 until his death. Like Cotton, Danforth preached to Native congregations, worked for the Society for the Propagation of the Gospel and translated several works into Indian languages. *Sibley's Harvard Graduates,* 3:243-49.
6. Possibly Zechariah Walker, the ordained minister of the second church of Woodbury, Connecticut Colony, from 1668 until his death in January 1700. Weis, *Colonial Clergy,* 213.
7. Ephraim Cole was a blacksmith in Plymouth, married to Rebecca Gray. Savage, *Genealogical Dictionary,* 1:426.
8. George Elliston's shop was in Boston.
9. Richard Wilkins was a bookseller in Boston; he emigrated from Limerick with his son-in-law John Bailey, who had been forced out of his ministry for non-conformity. They settled in Boston by 1683. Only a few books printed in New England bear his name as publisher, and his shop did not carry books only, but presented a wide array of goods. His booklist leans heavily towards books for the ministry, "the learned and the gentry." Hugh Amory and David D. Hall, eds., *The Colonial Book in the Atlantic World,* vol. 1, *History of the Book in America* (Cambridge, 2000), 101-2.

To Rowland Cotton, 19 August 1687

Plimouth
August, 19: 1687:

Son Rowland

I wrote to you by Leift: Bryant[1] & to your Bro: John. Now by Mr John Lothrop. Pray minde the Bibles at Mr Wilkins,[2] if you keep one for your owne use you may, let the other be left at Mr Ellistons to be sent to us. I wrote you word of Mr Danforths ordination[3] at Taunton Sep.21: & about Bristoll, I hope you will be here about the time mentioned, send Johns letter[4] as soone as you can, all well & salute you, God preserve you

Your Lov: Fath:

J: Cotton

Thomas Prince Papers, Massachusetts Historical Society. Addressed "These For Mr Rowland Cotton, at Harvard Colledge, in Cambridge. Leave these with Mr George Elliston for conveyance."

---

1. See 1 August 1687. Lieutenant John Bryant and his wife Abigail lived in Plymouth with seven children. Van Antwerp, *Vital Records of Plymouth*, 11.
2. See the letter of 1 August 1687.
3. Danforth was ordained on 21 September 1687, as Cotton indicated.
4. Not found.

From John Cotton (1658–1710),[1] 26 August 1687

Reverend & Honoured S^R^,

I understood you designd a speedy journey to Boston soe should not have presumed to trouble you about ye barne so far as I am concern'd in it; I know y^t^ by lease we are not obliged to build a barne, but only to repair ye present, wch will as well, & to ye Tenants Satisfaction, answer ye end. I have therefore wrote to him so to do, & promised to repay him w^t^ shall come to my share—I wrote to y^r^self S^r^, about a division not of Affections but of ye farme, nor was it because I expect high advantages by it, or any at all joynd wth disadvantage to y^r^self—; I had rather loose than gain in such a way—; & innocent advantages I know no reason you have to begrudge me—I have a prospect of none (beside y[e] choice w[ch] God & nature hath given me) w[ch] y[r]self may not have in it as well as I—If you Expect orders to move in it, I have or shall leave w[t]ever of y[t] nature to y[e] managem[t] of the worthy Gentleman w[th] whom I have left y[e] matter of Election [&c] to y[e] Hon[d] Joseph Dudley Esq, from whom therefore you may Expect to hear it—Thus much S[r], as to business—.—I hope my good Aunt & cousins are well, give them my service & love—Your son is like to be in a wife[2] as happy as ever his ffather was, & y[t] will be very happy indeed—I should be glad if y[r]self & my Aunt would condescend to journey to Hampton, y[t] you might water y[e] seed you have formerly sown. Y[e] last short letter,[3] nor yet a gr[t] many more of y[e] same nature shall never tempt me, (I trust) to use any advantage injurious to y[r]self—If I had near such oppertunity, S[r] my principles teach me better, & therefore you may assure y[r]self of nothing but fair dealing from, S[r],

Y[r] honest nephew Jn[o] Cotton Alias y[e] son of y[r] Elder Brother Seaborne Cotton

Hampton Aug. 26. 87./

Curwen Family Papers, American Antiquarian Society. Addressed "To the Rev[d] M[r] Jn[o] Cotton Past[r] of the church at Plimouth." Endorsed "From my Cousen M[r] John Cotton, August, 26: 1687."

---

1. John Cotton (1658–1710) was the eldest son of Cotton's brother Seaborn and Dorothy Bradstreet Cotton. He graduated Harvard in 1678 and served as fellow of the college from 1681 until he was called by the Hampton, later New Hampshire, church in 1687. After many offers, Cotton finally agreed to ordination in 1696. (His widow, Ann Lake Cotton, became Increase Mather's second wife in 1715.) *Sibley's Harvard Graduates,* 3:1-5.

2. John Cotton (1661) married Sarah Hubbard of Ipswich, the daughter of Richard Hubbard and Sarah Bradstreet Hubbard, near the beginning of his six years in Exeter. *Sibley's Harvard Graduates,* 3:213.

3. Not found.

SIX

Salary Troubles in a Contentious Congregation

THE LETTERS BELOW ILLUSTRATE both Cotton's salary troubles and his often difficult relationship with the Cushman family. New England ministers seemed to complain regularly about their salaries, but Cotton's situation was certainly exacerbated by the policies of the new Dominion of New England. As part of enforced religious toleration, Sir Edmund Andros made the clergy completely dependent on money that the congregations would give voluntarily, instead of on a standard tax that would support a town's established church. Cotton had hoped for just such a tax "rate," for under the new policy Cotton's allies would help him to obtain a salary, but his enemies could choose not to support it. The records indicate a divided town: "it was propounded to the town whether they Judged them selves able to pay Mr Cotton the sume of 90 pd as they had done of late years the affirmative being put to voate but som hands were held up the Nagative vote being Called for many more hands were held up upon which it Was farther voted that the maintenance of the minster for this present yeare 1687 should be by the free subscription of Every one."[1] Cotton's salary suffered greatly under this new method.[2]

Making matters worse, church elder Thomas Cushman and Cotton often battled, as some earlier letters indicate.[3] Isaac Cushman, the elder's Cushman's son, would later prove even more bothersome to Cotton. In the 1690s, Isaac Cushman began preaching to the new church at Plympton, in part made up of defectors from Cotton's congregation. The younger Cushman was ordained by the Plympton Church in 1698, and Cotton claimed that his conflicts with Cushman were the main cause of his decision to leave Plymouth in 1699. Cushman also served as a deputy to the Plymouth General Court.[4]

1. *Records of the Town of Plymouth* (Plymouth, 1889–1903), 1:190-91.

2. To Increase Mather, 10 and 21 September 1688.

3. From James Keith, 6 March 1683; To Cotton Mather, 11 March 1684.

4. Frederick Lewis Weis, *The Colonial Clergy and the Colonial Churches of New England* (Baltimore, Md., 1936), 66; Eugene Aubrey Stratton, *Plymouth Colony: Its History & People 1620–1691* (Salt Lake City, Ut., 1986), 192, 276-77; George D. Langdon, *Pilgrim Colony: A History of New Plymouth 1620–1691* (New Haven, Conn., 1966), 221.

To Rowland Cotton, 2 September 1687

Plimouth September, 2: 1687:

Son Rowland

yours dated, Aug: 10: your uncle delivered,[1] Aug: 25: & by your writing for things to be sent to you, I perceive you had not received my two letters I sent you not long since,[2] an answer unto which I much desire, for if this motion to Bristoll[3] should succeed it would be greatly advantaging for your learning & save me much charge; & therefore I doe desire your coming home in order to being at Mr Danforths ordination this Sep: 21: & soe to Bristoll; & providence soe disposes that noe boates of ours are likely this moneth to fraight the[m] for Boston & soe your things cannot be sent you; I would gladly come to the Bay & speake with Roger but I see noe hopes of effecting it til about the second monday in october; it will be to me very accepta[ble?] if he can handsomely hinder a division of the farme & I not be seen in it, for I conclude a present division will be very damnifying to me & my heires: one Bible wee received; if providence [...] for your living at the Colledge, I hope if any gratuity be attaineable not to loose it by my present not coming: your un[cle] preached for me the whole Sabbath & went hence on Tuseday last Lydia Nelson's young daughter was buried[4] before it was a fortnight old. Aged Mr Alden I went yesterday to see, I judge he is on his deathbed;[5] your letter Aug: 12:[6] your uncle forgot to give it me till saturday Evening, Aug: 27: remember my love to Roger & tell him, I doe well approove of his designe to repaire the old Barne, so far as my Interest is concerned in it, viz, halfe: provided that it may last long enough to prevent any further trouble about a Barne; he will doe well to have cousen Johns consent to his motion also.[7] As for shingles I doubt not but to obtaine them, but I cannot by your lines understand the dimensions of them, you say short broad shingles 20 thousand, desire him to send me word, how many inches long & [last?] october be cut to send them to him; though I doe not understand about that. If I had any shingles by me I cannot gratify your particular request for want of a boate; the people a majority at towne meeting last weeke (Isaac Cushman being ring leader) voted downe a Rate, & appointed men for to get subscriptions for my maintenance this yeare, whether it will amount to 40 or 50 pd is uncertaine, & then I shall be poorely able to maintaine you at Colledge: I hope you have sent John his letter, when will he come & let us heare of the successe of his motion? I designe to send this by M^r will clarke to leave (as I did the 2 other) it Mr Ellistons for you, & next weeke Caleb Cooke[8] intends for Boston in a marshfeild Boate, by one or other, if it be possible, let us heare from you, my prayers are for you, that such grace may be given to you as you desire in your letters, the good Lord says Amen, mother & [sisters & brothers?] salute you

September, 6.

your Brother John meeting Mr Clarke on the road brought back this letter as also one from your selfe;[9] what you write concerning Mr Medcalfe his preaching at Bristoll[10] & your owne being comfortably settled at colledge inclines me at present to dispense with your staying there & to cease calling you to Taunton & Bristoll; only be you conscientiously carefull to improove your time with utmost diligence in your studies, that I may not have cause to repent the charge I am at to render you serviceable to your generation: your mother sent a pillow beere[11] by caleb cooke full of such things as you wrote for, the boat was soe full there was noe room to put your chest in: I suppose about the first week in october some of our owne boats will fraight for Boston, & then your Brothers things will come & ought else that is here necessary for you, my coming to Boston I designe, God willing about the tenth of october, soe long I stay, because I would see if I can get any thing to bring with me; I cannot adde to your 6 pence, only the 5 shil: you lent your Brother John I have repaid him, & have not soe much more in the world to give him, if it were to save my life: I have but a 1000 & 1/2 of shingles at my doore, choice ones, them I would have sent you by Caleb Cooke but he could not carry them: minde the matter to Roger & write to me thereabouts, if noe opportunity present before, you may be sure of one by some of the Gentlemen that come from Boston to our Grand Assize the last weeke of this moneth.

Betty sends you now three hankercheifs

Thomas Prince Collection, Massachusetts Historical Society. Addressed "These For Mr Rowland Cotton, Living at Harvard College in Cambridge. Leave these with Mr George Elliston for speedy conveyance." Torn right margin and water stains on bottom third.

1. Not found.
2. See above letters of 1 and 19 August 1687.
3. Rowland evidently received a call from the Bristol church.
4. The Plymouth records do not include this daughter of Lydia and John Nelson, who had two other children in 1683 and 1689. Lee D. Van Antwerp, comp., *Vital Records of Plymouth, Massachusetts to the Year 1850* (Camden, Me., 1993), 11.
5 Winsor's *History of the Town of Duxbury* mistakenly indicates that John Alden died on 12 September 1686, but Savage's *Dictionary* correctly states that he died on 12 September 1687. *Mayflower* passenger John Alden left Plymouth in 1631 and settled in Duxbury, serving the colony in both government and military affairs for more than forty-five years. John Cotton is believed to have published an elegy to Alden after his death, *Poem Occasioned by the Death of that Aged, Pious, Sincere-hearted Christian John Alden... who died September 12, 1687...* (Boston, 1687[?]) [Evans 426] Charles Evans, *American Bibliography* (New York, 1941–1959). Justin Winsor, *History of the Town of Duxbury, Massachusetts, with Genealogical Registers* (Boston, 1849), 55-63; James Savage, *A Genealogical Dictionary of the First Settlers of New England*, 4 vols. (1860–62; facsimile reprint Baltimore, Md., 1990), 1:23; Stratton, *Plymouth Colony*, 232-33.
6. Not found.
7. John Cotton, son of Seaborn Cotton. See the above letter of 26 August 1687.
8. Caleb Cooke (b. 1651) lived in Plymouth. Savage, *Genealogical Dictionary*, 1: 446-47.
9. Not found.
10. Possibly Deacon Jonathan Metcalf (1650–1727) of Dedham, Massachusetts, listed as a freeman in 1683. *New England Historic Genealogical Register*, 6 (1852): 173-76.
11. A "pillow beere" is a pillow case. *Oxford English Dictionary*, 2nd ed. (Oxford, 1989), 11:839.

From Walter Deane[1] et al, 5 September 1687

To the Reverend Pastor & Elder & our beloved Brethren of the Church of Christ in Plymouth we wish grace, mercy & peace.

R^{D}. & BELOVED!

Having appointed the 21: day of this instant Septemb. for the ordination of Mr Samuel Danforth unto the office of a Pastor over us, according to the order of the Gospell wee intreat yor prayrs to God for a blessing on us & him & yor joynt-Concurrence wth us herein; & for that end desire the presence of yor Revd. Pastor & Elder to witness yor consent & to joyn wth us in the prayr, & service of the day; & also of a Messenger from yor church, if you see meet. we purpose double exercise on y da[y] [...][2] you to suit yor coming in Complyance [...][3] of the plans for yor Enterteynm^{t}, [...][4] to o^{r} poor ability we have provided, you [...][5] acquainted at the house of Mis Shov[ ] [...][6] ever desire yo[ ] [...][7] in ye morning of the day appointed for [the] ordination. wishing [...] divine presence & blessing upon yor sacred Administrations, wee remaine

Yo^r^ affectionate Brethren

Walter Deane
William Harvey[8]
James Walker[9]
In behalfe of the Church

dated. 5^d^. 7^m^. 1687

Thomas Prince Papers, Massachusetts Historical Society. Addressed "To the Reverend Mr John Cotton. Pastor of the Church in Plimouth, to be communicated to ye Church." Cotton's note: "In answer to this letter the brethren chosen were George Bonum[10] & Nathaniel Ward,[11] who went with the Pastour to that Solemnity, the Elder went not:" Deep tear near middle of right margin.

---

1. Walter Deane (1612–c.1694), one of the original forty-six settlers of Taunton, emigrated from England with his brother, John, in 1637. He served as a selectman for more than twenty years, as well as a deputy to the General Court in Plymouth. Samuel Hopkins Emery, *History of Taunton, Massachusetts from Its Settlement to the Present Time* (Syracuse, N.Y., 1893), 39-40; Stratton, *Plymouth Colony*, 279-80.
2. Tear; one or two words lost.
3. Tear; two or three words lost.
4. Tear; two or three words lost.
5. Tear; two or three words lost.
6. Tear; two or three words lost.
7. Most of line illegible or lost to tear.
8. William Harvey (d. 1691) was one of the original settlers of Taunton and served as a selectman, representative to the General Court in Plymouth, constable, and surveyor. Emery, *History of Taunton*, 50-51.
9. James Walker (c. 1620–1692) was one of the early settlers of Taunton, although not one of the "forty-six purchasers." He emigrated as a teenager with his sister under the sponsorship of their cousin, John Browne. He became a freeman in 1650 and opened a tavern in 1679. Walker also served as a constable, deputy and selectman. Emery, *History of Taunton*, 85, 92; Savage, *Genealogical Dictionary*, 4:393-94.
10. George Bonum (Bonan), who often served as a surveyor in Plymouth, and his wife, Elizabeth, married in 1681 and had nine children by 1702. Van Antwerp, *Vital Records of Plymouth*, 4, 85; *Plymouth Town Records*, 1:184, 188, 194.
11. Cotton's church records read "Wood" in both cases, possibly Nathaniel Wood (b. 1652), the son of John Wood of Plymouth. Savage, *Genealogical Dictionary*, 4:627; Publications of the Colonial Society of Massachusetts *Collections* (hereafter *CSM*), 22 (Boston, 1920), 163, 261.

[To Rowland Cotton], 30 January 1688

Deare child

Yours by Tom:[1] received, wee blesse God for your recovery; Last Tuesday Sarah was taken[2] & hath had a very dangerous time of it, wee feared last Saturday would have bin her last in this world, but through mercy wee hope the worst is now past, wee long for your coming home but cannot send a horse, if the weather keep moderate, John Morton[3] will speedily come. This note to Capt Davis[4] carry to him & send an answer, & the thing I write to him for, send by Leift: Morton or by m^r^ will: Clarke. I now send 10 shil: you must give to Capt Davis & 5 shil: for your selfe: Tho: Hinckley left your letter at Mr Ellistons, that will direct you, give this letter to Mr Cooke & leave him not till he sends answer to the former letter & this also: get one also from [...] Cos: mather: God preserve you. All salute you, I am

your Lov: fath:

J: Cotton.

Jan: 30: 87: /88:

Multitudes more now full of measles in towne.

Thomas Prince Papers, Massachusetts Historical Society. Addressed "These For Sir Cotton, at Harvard Colledge in Cambridge. With 15 shillings. Per Leift: Morton Leave these with Mr George Elliston at Boston."

---

1. Not found.

2. John and Joanna's fifth child, Sarah, was born on 5 April 1670 and was named to replace an earlier daughter, Sarah, who died at age four in Guilford in 1669. Sarah survived the illness Cotton describes in this letter.

3. Lieutenant John Morton (1650–1718) settled in Middleborough, married Mary Ring in 1687, and had nine children by 1700. See the letters of 19 July 1676 and 9 July 1688. Savage, *Genealogical Dictionary*, 3: 244; *Vital Records of Plymouth*, 11.

4. Not found.

From Samuel Danforth,[1] 3 March 1688

March. 3. 1687/8

Revd Sr

Your loving lines datd feb. 24. 1687/8[2] I recd March 3d. following, but not by yt messenger you spake of & therefore Cannot accomplish yor desire in making returnes by his hand: but hope it will not be long before these do humbly present my service to you by some other means of Conveyance—I rejoyce yt God has to yor flock manifested so mch mercy in the midst of his severe stroke & that for yor own family you have had such Experience of divine Goodness in recovering to health, & succeding advice & Councell for the benefit of so many others also. I doubt not but that yor prayers will reach this poor Plantation also, among wm the Common Disease[3] spreads wonderfully beyond all Expectation; This morning I heard of the 36th person on wm it has seized. It has md a near approach to us in this house; the next neighbors (save one) on both sides of us being infected therewith. I have no other security agt it but humble Prayr to God to spare me, wch yet is not be md but wth submission to his will; wr I fortifyed wth some of yor deare Ladyes Advice & Directions[4] (to wm I present most humble service wth thanks for her gt kindness to me wn last at yor house) I should the mr couragiously prepare for a Conflict therewth wn God shall see meet to give it a Commission to seize me—

The Lives of all wth us who have had it are spared, thru' mercy: tho' by other Causes & diseases we have buryed 5 persons within this winter past.—As to yor kind & christian Expressions referring to or Ecclesiasticall Concernes, I thankfully embrace them together wth yor Cordiall Councell annexed: & beg yor prayers yt I may be kept humble & upright before God: who am unworthy to be a Reaper of his Harvest; the work is the Lords & its an awfull thing to be Employd in the servive of so holy & Jealous an one as or God is—for yor Satisfaction, Revd Sr, to wm I am obliged to gratify on all lawfull things to my powr, (as Gd shall direct me) I have annexed the Number of the persons admitted since ordination

1687. Nov. 6th—1: person.
Nov. 27—2: persons, of wch Mrs Elizab: Shove[5] was one
Dec. 18—6: persons.
Jan. 8 —3: persons.
Jan. 22—4: persons
Jan. 29—7: persons
Also March. 4.—5. persons to be received
March. 11—7. persons to be admitted (si Deo placit[6])

Leift Macey[7] has not yet offred himselfe but I am not wthout some Secret Expectation of him in time. There is a prospect of some more yet coming. Three persons besides these; found not acceptance at present wth the Church, but we pray for y^{m} & hope God will fitt y^{m} for Church fello'ship. It is s^{d} that he y^{t} soweth & he y^{t} reapeth shall both rejoyce together: I would off[er] this Quere for yor Candid Resolve, whether this (together) may not mean, Simul tempore as well as Simul Eternitate?[8] whether the snts in Heaven do not now kno' of this Addition to the Church, even at the same time wn the snts on Earth do kno' of it: So that there may be a Symphony of Prayers to Gd on this behalfe at the same time both for the Church militant & triumphant. There is another Text seems to favor this, nly,[9] That there is joy in Heaven at the Conversion of a soul: but I submit to wiser ju[dg]mts! begging yor prayrs, & kind Correspondence wth humble servic to yorselfe & all yours

I rest your unworthy ffr^{d}. &c

S. Danforth

S^{r} there is a report y^{t} one Mr Hoskins[10] an ancient persons of one of or Villages desires to remove hither will you favor me wth yor Judgment of the man & the matter

I was at Rehoboth February Lecture Mr Angier[11] was then well

I was at Mr Keiths[12] a fortnight after, who expected a Visit by this distemper Every day, but I have not heard y^{t} yet he labors under it.

Curwen Family Papers, American Antiquarian Society. Neither address nor endorsement remain.

---

1. Samuel Danforth (1666–1727, H.C. 1683) was the settled minister in Taunton from 1687 to 1727. Danforth also served as an Indian commissioner and compiled an Indian dictionary. John Langdon Sibley, *Biographical Sketches of Graduates of Harvard University, In Cambridge, Massachusetts* (Boston, 1873–) (hereafter *Sibley's Harvard Graduates*), 3:243-49.

2 Not found.

3. There was a serious measles epidemic in New England over the winter 1687–88. John Duffy, *Epidemics in Colonial America* (Baton Rouge, La., 1953), 166.

4. Joanna evidently offered medical advice in the February letter.

5. Mrs. Elizabeth Shove became a full member of the Taunton church on 27 November 1687.

6. "If it pleases God" or "God willing."

7. Lieutenant George Macey was the son of George Macey, one of the original forty-six settlers of Taunton. The younger George served as a selectman seventeen years, represented Taunton to the Plymouth General Court from 1672 to 1677 and progressed through the military hierarchy in Taunton during the last decades of the seventeenth century, serving in several wars. Conflicts between Macey and Capt.

Thomas Leonard escalated in the late 1680s, and by 1690, Maj. Thomas Whalley considered asking Cotton to convince Macey to step down: "Macey's party by virtue of the order of the Council are daily listing soldiers and take all opportunities to wheedle in all the youngsters they can, the other party look upon the proceedings not to be proper and so lie still...there is nothing that will tend to peace but for some (Mr Cotton &c) that have an interest in Macey to persuade for the peace of the town to lay down." A lengthy appeal from Leonard, "supposed to be forwarded to Mr. Cotton at Plymouth" in 1692, suggests that the division between Leonard and Macey continued. Emery, *History of Taunton*, 573, 85, 328-36.

8. "Not only for the moment (as well as) for all time."
9. "Namely."
10. William Hoskins; see 8 November 1684.
11. Samuel Angier; see 17 September 1679.
12. James Keith, minister in Bridgewater.

To Increase Mather, 8 March 1688

Plimouth March, 8: 1687:/88:

Revd & Deare Brother

I wrote to you this winter,[1] but know not whether you have received it; I waite with some earnestnesse of spirit to heare of the progresse of your Motions towards o: E:[2] resolving I must come & see you (if God permit) before your going; This day past, our congregation kept a Fast[3] with reference to the present visitation, soe that I am too weary now to write, but Rowl: going to night, I have but leisure to salute you & to request if the 5 pd for his scholler-ship[4] be attaineable, that you would now favour him with it to discharge his Colledge-debt; it would be a seasonable mercy from God to me if it be now to be had, if it cannot I desire to be contented, & must seeke some other way, but I conclude if it lye in your power, your brotherly kindnesse will helpe.

The distemper[5] is almost removed out of our towne, hardly any have escaped: Due salutations to you & all yours Respectively, o pray for me & mine, I am,

your Affectionate Brother

John Cotton

Mather Papers 7:4, Prince Library, Rare Book and Manuscripts, Boston Public Library. Addressed "These For the Reverend, his Deare Brother, Mr Increase Mather, Teacher of a church, in Boston."

1. Not found.
2. Increase Mather was planning a trip to England for the early spring of 1688 to try to convince the Crown of Andros's abuse of power in New England and to represent Massachusetts in her fight for a new charter. Michael G. Hall, *The Last American Puritan: The Life of Increase Mather, 1639–1723* (Middletown, Conn., 1988), 207-11. See also 11 April 1688.
3. "The chh set apart, March 7: a day of Fasting & prayer, on account of the measles in the winter & for the mercies of the yeare, & for continuance of & Gods blessing upon the meanes of Grace." *CSM*, 22:162.
4. Cotton's tuition concerns continued. See the above letters of 26 November 1686 and 2 September 1687.
5. Measles; see 3 March 1688.

To John Chipman,[1]

9 March 1688

March, 9 1687:/8: Plimouth

Good Friend

I have a selfish errand that invites me to salute you with this paper-messenger; my Deare mate (whom I know you have not forgotten) is troubled with her old distemper of the spleene, & therefore doth earnestly request you, & soe doe I on her behalfe, that according to your wonted way of shewing kindnesse to your friends, you will make diligent enquiry throughout all Sandwich & Barnstable for spleene-wort,[2] & get as much as you can possible, to send to her for releife in this her malady, it was the greatest helpe formerly of any meanes she used, & therefore wee intreat you what money soever it cost to get it, if you can heare of any body that hath bin soe carefull as to preserve it; moreover, my Dearest would have me assure you, that when the season of the yeare is come that spleene-wort is fit to gather, she doth resolve (if God permit) to visit you & that part of his Majesties Territory that is neere you & under your inspection, that she may her selfe see & gather soe necessary an helpe for the good of afflicted bodies:

wee both heartily salute you both, wishing you all prosperity,

I rest your reall friend perpetually

John Cotton

The Governour is going quickly his progresse to Pemmaquid;[3] M[r] Randolph hath petitioned for 700 acres of Land in Cambridge, viz, the Common & part of the Colledge-Lott.[4]

Thomas Prince Collection, Massachusetts Historical Society. Addressed "These For Elder Chipman, at Sandwich."

---

1. John Chipman (c. 1620–1708) emigrated by 1638 and became a freeman sometime between 1649 and 1658. He served as a grand juryman, deputy, selectman, and the ruling elder in the Barnstable church until he moved to Sandwich. Stratton, *Plymouth Colony*, 262-63.
2. Chipman's second wife, Ruth Sargent Winslow Bourne, was the widow of Rev. Richard Bourne, who had been thirty years her senior. Like Joanna Cotton, Ruth Chipman was a midwife and healer, and evidently the two women shared medicinal herbs. Thomas Prince, born into Ruth Chipman's hands, described her as "a little, lively smart gentlewoman of very good sense and knowledge, of the strictest piety." R. A. Lovell, *Sandwich: A Cape Cod Town*, (Sandwich, Mass., 1984), 121-22.
3. Sir Edmund Andros, the new governor of the Dominion of New England, was given authority over much of modern-day Maine, along with his other jurisdictions. He quickly made that power felt by attacking the home and trading post of Baron Jean-Vincent d'Abbadie de St. Castin in the Pemaquid settlement on the Penobscot. Historians suggest that the attacks on Dover, New Hampshire, in June 1689 and on Pemaquid in August 1689 were in retaliation for this aggression. Castin, the son-in-law of the Penobscot chief Modockawando, was a powerful intermediary between Natives and French in the area. Alan Gallay, *Colonial Wars of North America, 1512–1763: An Encyclopedia* (New York, 1996), 180-81, 549.
4. After Andros arrived, Edward Randolph became the secretary and registrar of the Dominion of New England. Randolph tried to exploit Andros's land policies to his own advantage: first he requested 500 acres of common land in Lynn, then 700 acres between Watertown and Cambridge. Both attempted land-grabs failed. Michael Garibaldi Hall, *Edward Randolph and the American Colonies, 1676–1703*, (Chapel Hill, N.C., 1960), 109, 113.

To Rowland Cotton, 10 April 1688

Plimouth April, 10: 1688:

Deare son Rowland

It was noe small exersise to me, that I found you not returned last weeke to Boston, I blame you not, concluding you had cause enough to stay; faile not to hasten word to us how it fares with your Brother & sisters as to the measles; & whether there be noe hopes of making his peace with Mr Mason; Major Walden told me of your travelling in it oh that there were a good issue; It seemes to me impossible, your Bro: should live any longer to doe service to that people, unlesse reconciled to him who is soe greatly offended with him, & therefore I heartily wish he would owne his failing in word or deed, that he may be againe at liberty to serve God & his people; send him my minde if you have opportunity, withall tell him, that I am willing to send Tim: to helpe him againe for some time, if I can heare of any freedome he hath to improve him & serve his owne interest. I spake not with Roger last weeke, but if I had I should have ordered him to deliver you three pds for the steward, & if I can but heare from you, I shall speedily <*to*> give you order to call else where for 4 pd to discharge Colledge-debts also: I am waiting to heare from you, all particular & generall newes, God preserve you, all salute you,

I am your Affection father

John Cotton

Doubtlesse Roger will now pay, if you aske him.

Next Sabbath John churchel & his wife & Eliz: Kenedy[1] are to be admitted into Church. Thomas Clark's wife is dead.[2]

Thomas Prince Collection, Massachusetts Historical Society. Addressed "These For M[r] *Rowland Cotton, at Harvard Colledge, in Cambridge. Leave these with M*[r] *George Elliston at Boston for conveyance."*

---

1. Plymouth church records list John and Rachel Churchel and Elizabeth Kenedy as "members admitted" in 1688. Kenedy was baptised at the same time. *CSM*, 22:261.
2. "Rebekah, the wife of our Brother Thomas Clarke, dyed, April, 4: she was not in full communion, a child of yarmouth church, & left in her owne hand-writing many gratious words that did fully evidence God was gratiously at worke with her soule, & that she was preparing for church-fellowship." Her grandparents included Rev. John Miller (1604–1663) who emigrated in 1634 and served as the settled minister in Roxbury, Rowley, Yarmouth and Groton. *CSM*, 22:262; Weis, *Colonial Clergy*, 141.

From Cotton Mather, 11 April 1688

Revrend and Dear Syr.

Last Saturday was with us a Day of many Fears, & of many Prayers.[1] Before y[e] Sabbath, o[r] good god answered y[e] Latter & removed y[e] Former. The Wind came about so far Easterly on y[e] sudden, That the vessels which were hastening after y[e] Ship of o[r] Hope, were forced into Nantasket, whil[e] that Ship very happily being gott a little beyond ye point, bore away, til about 6[h] p.m. When with y[e] Joyful Acclamations of all y[e] Ships company, o[r] Friend was received aboard, and <is gone> so hee is now gone, not Without fresh Testimony of gods presence with him. Praises, many Praises do wee now owe, unto y[e] keeper of Israel. The Designs laid against <o[r]> my Father, were very many and malicious. His pursuers (who are now Exposed unto all manner of Derision) had a particular Intent to sieze and search his papers, and this y[e] rather, because they had gott a Notion (How or Why, I cannot imagine) that hee had certain

Plymouth Papers with him. But, Blessed be ye Lord, Who has not given Him as a Prey to their teeth. A vessel is Within a Day or Two bound for London; by wch I shall send your Letter.[2] The public service my Father is upon, in carrying o^{r} Address of Thanks to ye King, makes it but an Equal Thing, as his other Circumstances make it a Needfull Thing, for us to do somewhat about Supporting his Personal Expences. I earnestly Recommend [....]to Your consideration and pro[....][3]

I thank you for your kind offers, about ye Sabbath you mention, & very readily Accept y^{m}. Let mee bee Remembred to my Friends, and in your Prayers. Wee are Well, Heaven make us good,—and mee especially, Who am,

Syr, Entirely yours.

11.^{d} 2.^{m} 1688.

Gazets of January tell us, That o^{r} Queen is with child:[4] That ye Pope & French King ar so at odds, that the Pope has Excommunicated ye French Embassador, & Interdicted ye Church in wch hee heard Mass at Rome:[5] That ye Swissers are like to Quarrel ye French, wch will bee a thing strangely affecting ye Circumstances of ye French Protestants.

That ye Grand Seignour, is deposed, by his Subjects, for his Ill government,—All wch are great Things.

Special Collections, University of Virginia Library. Addressed "To the Reverend Mr J. Cotton, Pastor of Plymouth." Endorsed "From my Cousen, Mr Cotton Mather, April, 11: 1688:."

---

1. Increase Mather sailed for London on 7 April. Hall, *Last American Puritan*, 210-11.
2. Not found.
3. Bottom of page torn, writing faint.
4. The queen's pregnancy was covered in the *London Gazette* (#2316, 26–30 January 1687).
5. This story is covered in the *London Gazette* (#2315, 23–26 January 1687).

To Rowland Cotton, 5 May 1688

PLIMOUTH MAY, 5: 1688

DEARE CHILD

Yours of Apr: 26: & 27:[1] came yesterday by Ed: Dotey,[2] I am glad 3 qrters are well discharged, if you minde Indian-studies, I hope what remain[s at?] the end of the commencement will be done by Mr stoughton;[3] Capt winthrop told me the goodness of your moderator: John Moses[4] dyed this day fortnight; [...] [G]oodwife King[5] is this day buried: wee had the Fast on Thursday[6] for Raine, & that day had plenty of it: you did well to h[ ]n newes of Exceter, now your mother concludes her daughters have it[7] & is much concerned for them, I expect Mr Moodey[8] to preach my Lecture next Wednesday, if it be possible: send word by him (however as soone as you can) how it fares with them: if I knew Mr Mason were at Boston, I would endeavour Joh[ ] peace, the 21st of this Instant I intend to travell towards Boston, 22d, to be at weymouth Lecture,[9] 23d to be at cambridge Lecture,[10] (I suppose it will be Wednesday morning before I arrive there) the sabbath ensuing I intend to be with your cousen at Boston, & in that weeke to doe all that is necessary, to fit you for your Commencement, quod [...];[11] & to goe to Cos: Tufts[12] then also; concluding the measles will keep my children from us till June, which indeed is our great affliction; salute, meo nomine[13] Mr Leveret [&] Brattle The Lord blesse you,

Your Lov: Fath.

J.C.

Your newes of Mr oakes[14] is good, but of—Gilman[15] very sad to us.

Thomas Prince Papers, Massachusetts Historical Society. Addressed "These For Sir Cotton, at Harvar[d] Colledge in Cambridge [torn] Leave these with Mr Elliston for conveyance."

---

1. Not found.
2. There are two likely Edward Doteys: Edward Jr. (b. 1664) and Edward (b. 1671). See the letter of 9 July 1688; Edward Dotey was also mixed up in the Clark's Island case. *Vital Records of Plymouth*, 4-5, Stratton, *Plymouth Colony*, 283-85; *Vital Records of Plymouth*, 4-5. Langdon, *Pilgrim Colony*, 220.
3. Cotton was evidently hoping that Rowland would pursue missionary work and receive some tuition help from the Society for the Propagation of the Gospel.
4. John Moses died on 22 April 1688. *CSM*, 22:134.
5. Ann King (wife of Samuel) died on 4 May 1688. *CSM*, 22:134.
6. "The chh set apart May, 3: as a Fast because of great drought, great raine came that very day & after, soe ready is God to heare the prayers of his people." *CSM*, 22:163.
7. Joanna was probably worried about the measles epidemic; see 3 March 1688.

8. Joshua Moody (1633–1697, HC 1653) was the settled minister in Portsmouth, New Hampshire, from 1658 until he moved to Boston's First Church in 1684, where he remained until 1693. He ended his ministerial career back in Portsmouth. *Sibley's Harvard Graduates*, 1:367-80.

9. Samuel Torrey (1632–1707) was Weymouth's settled minister when Cotton visited to hear the renowned preacher speak. Torrey attended Harvard but left without graduating when the college extended the course of study in 1656. He began his ministerial career in Hull and was ordained in 1664 in Weymouth, where he served as minister from 1656 until his death in 1707. Torrey was chosen to give the Artillery Election sermon in 1669 and the Election Sermon in 1674, 1683 and 1695. In 1684 he was also offered the presidency of Harvard College, but he declined. Weis, *Colonial Clergy*, 206; *Sibley's Harvard Graduates*, 1:564-67.

10. Nathaniel Gookin (1656–1692, H.C. 1675) succeeded Urian Oakes as the settled minister in Cambridge from 1681 until his death at the age of thirty-five. *Sibley's Harvard Graduates*, 2:474-80.

11. Three or four words illegible.

12. Mercy/Mary Cotton (1666–1715), daughter of Seaborn Cotton, was married to Peter Tufts (d. 1721). Seaborn and John Cotton were brothers. Torrey, *New England Marriages*, 758.

13. "Salute in my name."

14. Probably Thomas Oakes (b. 1644, H.C. 1662), who practiced as a physician in Boston, served as a representative to the General Court, and was its Speaker in 1692. Oakes also joined Increase Mather, Elisha Cooke and Henry Ashurst in London to fight for the restoration of the Massachusetts Charter in 1692. *Sibley's Harvard Graduates*, 2:130-32.

15. Possibly John Gilman (1657–1708) of Exeter, who served as a councilor under the Provisional Charter, a judge, and Speaker of the House. Savage, *Genealogical Dictionary*, 2:257-58.

SEVEN

Clark's Island

FOLLOWING JAMES II'S ACCESSION TO THE THRONE, plans for a unified Dominion of New England deeply affected Plymouth's independence and complicated the daily workings of the colony. In September 1685, Edward Randolph, charged with organizing the new government before Sir Edmund Andros's arrival, invited Thomas Hinckley, John Walley, William Bradford, Barnabas Lothrop and Nathaniel Clark to represent New Plymouth on the Governor's Council. After Andros arrived on 20 December 1686, the men were ordered to come to Boston for its first meeting. This centralization was challenging to Plymouth residents; journeying to Boston to pursue any civil case involving £10 or more, to administer all wills in excess of £50, and to settle all land suits was a hardship, especially in the winter. The expense for the men chosen as councilors quickly proved prohibitive; by March 1688, only Nathaniel Clark was attending the council meetings.

In addition to this change, Plymouth residents were introduced to other innovations, including quitrents and the dissolution of town meetings. Andros assumed the title to all lands that were not covered by earlier town grants, and even transferred some of the land to his own estate. In the letter below, Cotton referred to the governor's meddling when the rights were granted to a small island in Duxbury Bay. The town of Duxbury owned the title and kept the island as common land; however, Nathaniel Clark, a councilor loyal to Andros, wanted the property. In December 1687, Andros posted a notice inviting anyone who believed they had rights to the land to attend a council meeting in February 1688. Steeled for a fight, the town formed a committee to raise money to support a court battle "to defend there Rite" by establishing a rate—these are the funds Cotton outlined below. The committee consisted of Lieutenant Ephraim Morton, Joseph Howland, Joseph Warren, Isaac Cushman, Nathaniel Southworth, Joseph Bartlett and John Bradford. Andros was enraged by this fundraising and arrested the committee members. In July 1688, they were convicted and fined. Nathaniel Clark received clear title to the land. Edward Doty, who earlier had received woodcutting rights to the island from the town, was arrested for trespassing. Following the overthrow of the Andros government in April 1689, Clark was "declared to be a publicke enemy to (and disturber of the peace of) this colony," arrested and placed under a £200 bond. Plymouth voted to sell some town land to reimburse the committee members for any "Necessary Charges" they incurred while fighting for the island. The Town of Plymouth sold Clark's Island in 1690 to Samuel Lucas, Elkanah Watson and George Morton.[1]

The Clark's Island case became personal for Cotton in 1689. Dorothy Clark, Nathaniel's wife, was called before the Plymouth church in July on account of "her violent carriage to a child of the Pastors," and her "Joyning with & encouraging her husband to get Clarks island from the towne." The church concluded that she had an "evill frame of spirit" and that she had "pulled" Theophilus Cotton out of a tree and "then threw him over the fence." Furthermore, she was spreading rumors that Joanna Cotton had hurt her own son "by putting a key in his mouth caused his bleeding." Dorothy Clark claimed that she had heard about Joanna's abusive treatment from a "credible person" but would not "mention her Author," which prompted the church's "suspicion" that she was lying. When the church members asked Nathaniel to come to a meeting to defend his own and his wife's behavior, he refused. The church voted to "disown" him in July 1689.[2]

---

1. George D. Langdon, *Pilgrim Colony: A History of New Plymouth 1620–1691* (New Haven, Conn., 1966), 212-21, 225; *Records of the Town of Plymouth* (Plymouth, 1889–1903), 1:192-93, 197.
2. Publications of the Colonial Society of Massachusetts *Collections* (hereafter *CSM*), 22 (Boston, 1920), 265-67.

To Increase Mather, 9 July 1688

PLIMOUTH JULY, 9: 1688:

REVEREND & MOST DEARE BROTHER

Though Mr Foy[1] brought noe newes last Thursday of your arrivall, yet all your friends hope you are long agone safely at your desired Port, & in spetiall service for God & his Interest;[2] very awfull & considerable changes have attended Poore Plimouth since your departure from our Gurnett;[3] by reason of the motions de Clarks Island,[4] the Committee of 7 men chosen by the Towne to manage that affaire were at soe much charge as necessitated our people to ingage by free & voluntary subscriptions to reimburse them; & also to vote, the securing some lands till the money was paid to them; for this Lorkin fetches the 7 men with a writ charging they had resolved & raised money upon his Majesties subjects contrary to Law & the Towne Clerke, godly Deacon Fance for calling for the rate, & Mr wiswall for writing the paper to be subscribed; 3 pd, 7 sh: a man, besides all personall expenses, that Journey cost them, & M^r^ wiswall neere 20 shil: more, because he could not goe till a weeke after his first arrest by reason of lameness, Lorkin made him pay halfe a crowne a day for that week: all 9 are bound over to the superiour Court at Boston July, 31: & our godly brethren & neighbours are likely then to be considerably fined besides all costs of Court, etc: I hope by these ships you will have a more substantiall Narrative, or by the first opportunity after this approaching sessions; I was entered upon the good worke of Collection for something to be sent to a friend in o: E:[5] & should doubtlesse have bin successfull therein, but this blow hath soe blasted the designe, that there is not likely to be money enough to keep our best men out of prison without borrowing, unless God in mercy appeare to prevent the evills impending: how much wee need pitty & prayers is manifest, the good Lord appeare for his names sake.

Dear Sir last weeke good old Mr. Eliot showed me a letter he had prepared to send to Mr Boyle, in which he doth particularly mention my name, for helping him in Translating etc Shepards sincere Convert & sound belever,[6] & moves him to some particular acknowledgment of it; I greatly hope your Interest in friends to the Indian-worke may obtaine that for me that may greatly shorten my debt[7] to your selfe, which is all the grand worldly trouble I have, & unlesse this motion be successfull to attaine the end desired I must be forced to goe to o: E: if liberties continue, that I may have something to get out of debt; Much waiting is in N: E: for your letters, which if they be incouraging for young schollers to come over, I doubt the Spiritual famine you prophesied of will come speedily on this poore Land: My selfe & wife most heartily salute you, wishing you all possible prosperity & safety, Let me & mine be ever upon your heart in prayer; our good Elder presents due respects to you, & prayes hard for you, & soe doe thousands more every day: I take leave & subscribe

your very Affectionate Brother

John Cotton

*Mather Papers 7:25, Prince Library, Rare Book & Manuscripts, Boston Public Library. Addressed "These For the Reverend, his truly Honoured Brother, M*ʳ *Increase Mather." In a different hand: "London."*

---

1. John Foy (d. 1708) was a mariner in Boston. James Savage, *A Genealogical Dictionary of the First Settlers of New England*, 4 vols. (1860–62; facsimile reprint Baltimore, Md., 1990), 2:198.
2. Mather was in London lobbying for the new Massachusetts charter.
3. The Gurnet is a point of land at the northern entrance to Plymouth harbor.
4. See the editorial note preceeding this letter.
5. "Old England."
6. Thomas Shepard, *Sincere Convert, Discovering the Paucity of True Beleevers* (London, 1641); Shepard, *Sound Beleever, or a Treatise of Evangelical Conversion* (London, 1645).
7. It appears that Cotton received no "Indian pay" from 1684 to 1692. Until 1684, he earned £25 per year from the Society for the Propagation of the Gospel; beginning in 1695, his salary increased to £40 per year, and he received a raise the following year. MS 7946 New England Company: Accounts 1657–1731, Guildhall Library, London.

To Rowland Cotton, 13 August 1688

1688: Plimouth August, 13:

Deare son

I am sorry you soe much forgat your desolate Father as not to write a line by Mʳ Pierpont[1] to informe how, when & where you left your Mother, his memory could not containe to tell me any thing satisfying thereabouts, I thought you could not have bin soe unkinde, knowing how much I longed to heare of your mothers welfare & circumstances, & that Mr P: was coming hither; but children know not the heart of a father or husband: My bowels yerne over you & I have more than a 1000 thoughts how to dispose of you, I hope you are running m[e] noe more in debt at the Colledge, you had better have gone with your mother to Exceter;[2] My present thoughts are to board you at Charlestowne shortly, where you shall goe daily to Mʳ Morton for his

Instructions in Theology & other Arts,[3] I heare a singular Commendation of his way of Teaching how greatly beneficiall it is to Schollers; I cannot be at rest till you are in some way preparing to serve God; keep this to yourselfe at present, I beleve it will be much to your advantage if God succeed it. The Lord keep you from all evill, soe prayes,

your Loving Father

John Cotton

unlesse you are sure of this letter to your mother finding her at Exceter, keep it till she comes into the Bay, she must needs have it there. Respects to m^r^ Leverett & m^r^ Brattle.

Thomas Prince Collection, Massachusetts Historical Society. Addressed "These For Mr Rowland Cotton, with care deliver: Leave these with Mr Elliston at Boston for Conveyance." Thomas Prince's manuscript note: "By this Letter it seems as if Mr <u>*Jonathan Pierpont*</u> *is now Preaching at* <u>*Sandwich*</u>*." Right margin frayed.*

---

1. After graduating from Harvard, Jonathan Pierpont (1665–1709, H.C. 1685), kept a school in Dorchester, preached occasionally in Milton and was invited to the pulpit in Dedham. He declined the Dedham offer in December 1687. He would receive several additional offers by the summer of 1688, from New London (8 November 1687), Newberry (16 May 1688) and Northfield (22 May 1688), yet he would decline all of these as well. In April 1688, he was called to Sandwich but began preaching in Reading following some heavy lobbying at a ministerial funeral. In July he accepted his second degree at Harvard and returned to preaching in Reading despite Sandwich's call. See letters of 25 September 1688 and October 1688 for continued problems between Pierpont and the Sandwich congregation. John Langdon Sibley, *Biographical Sketches of Graduates of Harvard University, In Cambridge, Massachusetts* (hereafter *Sibley's Harvard Graduates*), 3:349-52.

2. Joanna was then traveling to see her son John, Rowland's brother.

3. Charles Morton was born in Cornwall, England, in 1627 and attended Wadham College, Oxford, graduating with a bachelor's degree in 1649 and a master's in 1652. After preaching in Blisland, Cornwall, for six years, he was silenced for non-conformity in 1662. Morton then taught school in Middlesex until he emigrated to New England in 1686. He ministered to the congregation in Charlestown from 1686 until his death in 1698. He also established a well-respected school there and served as vice-president of Harvard College from 1697 to 1698. Frederick Lewis Weis, *The Colonial Clergy and the Colonial Churches of New England* (Baltimore, Md., 1936), 146.

To Increase Mather, 10 and 21 September 1688

Plimouth September, 10: 1688:

Reverend & Most Deare Brother

After restlesse longing to heare of & from you, yours by the Isle of wight[1] affoarded much comfort to all that had bin praying for you; God that hath begun to show the greatnesse of his power & goodnesse, who can tell what he can, what he will yet doe for his poore people, & for his Names sake? when I read your lines, it came powerfully into my minde, wee ought to lay downe our lives for the bretheren, verily, Good Brother, if I am not greatly deceived you have fullfilled that scripture; before you went & since also I could hardly perswade my selfe that you would adventure into the Royall prescence with resolution soe to speake & declare as you have done, but I am now fully perswaded, that in a cloudy night, you had wrestled with the Angel by prayers & teares & prevailed for a blessing, & thence was strengthned thus to plead with man, the good Lord grant the Issue may be as comfortable as the beginning is encouraging; Well, my dearest Brother, whatever befall you or become of N: E: Interest, I am assured, all will have cause to, & all that feare God will, acknowledge, that you have now hazarded your life for the name of the Lord Jesus, & for the sake of His litle despised flock in this wildernesse; I doe not know nor did I ever heare that ever any one man run soe great a hazard attended with such circumstances for this people as you have done, it will adde to your crowne in the great day & for ever, whatever your trialls, conflicts & censures May be here; The Lord strengthen your heart & hands in his worke, & grant you in this your service, the blessing of Abraham, viz, to be a blessing to this whole land: How farre Plimouth case was carried the last superiour Court, I suppose you heard by Sir W: Ph:[2] as yet sub Judice lis est,[3] but hard measure is expected, if infinite power & mercy prevent not; our people are soe impoverished by the management of this unhappy Island, that the promises for my salary this yeare are thirty pounds short of what I had the last yeare,[4] & how much shorter the performances will be I know not, but hence it is that I can obtaine promises of very litle for o: E:, though something I hope will shortly be done, & a litle may be better then nothing: Some difficulty there was among the Commissioners many yeares agone about settling good old Mr Eliots salary, & once a lessening of it, he writing to the Corporation obtained a full establishing of his yearly revenue during life fifty pounds: the good man is hastning to his Journeys end[5] & telles me sincerely he hath none to betrust the worke with after his death but my selfe, if your occasions & interest invite to converse with the President & Treasurer, & you can obtaine fixing such a summe for me[6] at least when his worke is done, I hope you will soone be paid what I owe you, which is indeed the greatest externall concerne & difficulty I have in this world, & were it not for which I should not have troubled you with some lines as

I have done once & againe: God hath given a son to my John.

My Dearest Joynes with me in most hearty salutations of you, & prayers for you, wee beg your prayers for us & ours, I am,

your very Affectionate Brother

John Cotton

People being left to their liberty, maintenance of the ministry is likely to be brought to nothing very speedily.

verte

BOSTON, SEP: 21: 1688.

DEARE SIR

yesterevening came the ship from London with such tidings as filled the hearts of all that feare God with exceeding Joy;[7] how good a thing it is to trust in God, & to committ our way to God; the good Lord, who hath begun to show the greatnesse of his power & goodnesse, in mercy perfect that which concernes you and this his people by you, that being secured from your enemies, you may returne with fullnesse of blessing to this place, where constant & fervent prayers are going for you: I shall account myselfe not a litle obliged to you, if among your many freinds here, you will give me a line,

who am, Dearest Brother, yours most intirely

John Cotton

Mather Papers 7:30, Prince Library, Rare Book and Manuscripts, Boston Public Library. Addressed "These For the Reverend, Mr Increase Mather." In a different hand: "London."

---

1. Not found.
2. Sir William Phips.
3. "The case is under judgment."
4. Cotton had feared this would be the result of voluntary subscription; see his letter of 2 September 1687.
5. John Eliot lived nearly two more years, dying on 20 May 1690.
6. Cotton seems to have been angling to take over John Eliot's job, partly as a way to augment his decreasing salary.
7. Cotton is referring to news of the Glorious Revolution.

To John Chipman, 25 September 1688

PLIMOUTH SEPTEMBER, 25: 1688:

DEARE & RESPECTED FRIEND[1]

Mr Prince[2] & his wife & I had speech with [Mr?] Pierpont at his fathers house;[3] soe much I discerned as [gi]ves me cause to tell you, that not carrying those letters to the old man & to Readding church[4] are a principall cause of your non-successe; I am fully satisfied, that the call of that people to him & gaining his promise to be with them on the sabbath they agreed upon hath bin hitherto a fatall wound to your proceedings, & therefore it is a thousand pittyes that they had not that letter to show them the errour of their way:

And as for the surly old man, who is soe selfe-willed,[5] I am abundantly convinced, that if Redding had not stept in, you might have had a years triall of the young man;[6] Though I am not fond of any notions of my owne, who am a poore weake nothing, yet when I had impressions on my spirit to write those letters for you;[7] I did then beleve (& doe still) that they would have done more for your interest, then all that every man that went did or could speake: for however they might at Reding pretend to you great innocency, yet this is certaine, they did call a man to be their minister, who was then under promise to come to you on that account, & were not contented till he gave them an absolute promise to come to them from you on such a particular sabbath, herein the rule was greatly broken by them; & how lawfull it was for the young man to make such a promise to them under his then circumstances, I leave to after-consideration when the issue of your motions is further discovered:

And then for the old man, his sullen temper readily tooke advantage from personal discourses for further disgusts though none were given him, but if he had that or some such letter before his eyes to looke & chew upon when alone in his melancholy humors, it might have melted & mollifyed his sowre spirit, wee that were with him last friday did all Joyntly conclude it was high time those letters were prepared & sent to those mentioned; though your case be hazardous yet not desperate, in as much as the Elders of Boston & many others doe Judge Sandwich ought to have a triall of him for a time before any other people; It is certaine, though every body sees it not, there is some secret unfaithfullnesse towards you, that is a present wound, & therefore Faithfullnesse to God & to all concerned manifested in your letters may be of advantage to you.

I have therefore, Good friend, adventured to write an Epistle to the young man also, & if you will burne them all 3 together you shall not offend me, it will be quieting enough to my spirit, that I have desired & endeavoured to my utmost to promote the Interest of Christ among you: There is an ordination at Roxbury 3 weekes hence & I did desire young m^r^ Pierpont not to conclude against your call till that time; I intend then to be there;[7] but in the meane while; if you, & the good Christians among you will get together & fast & pray, & then dispatch such like letters to the Bay, it will greatly evidence your sincerity to God & man, & your reall sollicitude to advance the Kingdome of christ among you & who can tell but God may yet be intreated to grant you this mercy; Hearty love to you & yours, & to Mr Bassett,[8] praying for a gratious issue of this affaire,

I rest your truly Loving Friend

John Cotton

I would have some additions to the old mans letter, but I cannot frame them, because I have noe copy of that letter

M^r^ stuart is in such haste that I cannot write to M^r^ P: as I would:

Thomas Prince Collection, Massachusetts Historical Society. One small hole.

---

1. John Chipman was at this time the elder in Sandwich, apparently having left Barnstable, to help his "old friend" John Smith, who asked to be relieved of his duties in 1688 at the age of seventy-four. R. A. Lovell, *Sandwich: A Cape Cod Town*, (Sandwich, Mass., 1984), 129, 128.
2. Samuel Prince (1648–1728) was one of the merchants who enjoyed Sandwich's coastal access to Massachusetts Bay. He arrived from Hull in 1682, purchased land, became a freeman and served in various town offices. His second wife was Mercy Hinckley, the daughter of Gov. Thomas Hinckley. Lovell, *Sandwich: A Cape Cod Town*, 133.
3. Jonathan Pierpont's father, Robert Pierpont.
4. Although Pierpont was invited to Sandwich and was "accompanied by Elder Chipman" on his visit, he ultimately rejected Sandwich's call, partly because of his father's counsel. As Pierpont wrote in his diary, "My honoured Father was averse to my going to Sandwich." Pierpont was eventually ordained in the first church in Reading (Wakefield) on 26 June 1689; he remained there until his death in 1709. Ironically, Cotton's son Rowland settled as the minister in Sandwich in 1690. Lovell, *Sandwich: A Cape Cod Town*, 131; Weis, *Colonial Clergy*, 165; "Diary of Rev. Jonathan Pierpont," *New England Historic Genealogical Register* (hereafter *NEHGR*) 13 (1859): 255-58.
5. Cotton employed a less hostile vocabulary in the next letter, addressed to Robert Pierpont, the "surly old man" himself. See the letter below of October 1688.
6. According to Pierpont's diary, Cotton was right. The young minister was clearly struggling with his choice, for he wrote that, "I had inclinations to go to Sandwich" but admitted that "most were for my going to Reading." "Diary of Rev. Jonathan Pierpont," *NEHGR* 13 (1859): 257.
7. Ministers often gathered at ordinations, and Cotton was clearly hoping to lobby Pierpont on Sandwich's behalf at the Roxbury ordination of Nehemiah Walter. Cotton may also have been hoping to meet again with Pierpont's father, who lived in Roxbury.
8. Probably William Bassett III, grandson of Leiden Separatist and emigrant William, who served in Sandwich as a militia captain and colonel as well as a Register of Probate. For two of his letters during King William's War, see "The Hinckley Papers," Massachusetts Historical Society *Collections*, 4th ser., 5 (Boston, 1861), 214, 219; Lovell, *Sandwich: A Cape Cod Town*, 119, 147.

To Robert Pierpont,[1] October 1688

Sir,

wee are under an indispensible necessity by the humbling Providence of God in hitherto delaying to grant our desires in the injoyment of the ministry of your son, to make yet further application to your selfe & earnestly to request your friendly compliance with our motion herein; The more acquaintaince wee have had with him the more our hearts are carried forth towards him; you have already bin told that when he was last with us the church & Congregation did manifest to him their Joynt desires that he would accept of their call to labour here in the Lords worke, declaring & promising to doe for his support to the utmost of our ability; what particular summe is promised, wee resolve, God helping, shall faithfully be performed, and wee hope, through the blessing of God accompanying his labours amongst us wee shall be further enabled & enlarged to doe for him; many of the young generation with us are much affected with his Teaching, & doe earnestly desire to live under his ministry, wee therefore hope, through rich grace there will be a considerable harvest of soules, whom the Lord of the Harvest will by his hand gather in; Good Sir, be therefore intreated for the Lords sake & for the sake of a great number of soules in this place, to favour this our motion, & o that it were the will of God that noe other call may obstruct his acceptance of ours: It is manifest, you & wee all have noe cause but to be glad that his call to Northfeild[2] was not accepted by him, considering the mischeife since there done by the heathen; our motion seeming then more acceptable then that, & verily wee cannot but thinke that there is Just cause why our call should be hearkned unto & not that from Readding, be it soe, that they are unanimous in their call, & that there may be some other considerations more inviting to him to them than to us, yet wee beg you, as you are a christian, in the bowels of Christ to consider, that our call to your son & hopefull dependance upon him was while their Pastour was alive[3] hence wee apprehend they could not regularly make any motion to him, till our motion was brought to a full Conclusion; Further, they live neere the place of supply & can much more easily with grounded hopes of success looke out for helpe in their distresse than wee can;[4] wee all acknowledge, that conveniency must yeild to necessity, & that necessity must give way to extremity, that people are in necessity but wee are in extremity & wee have reason to feare if God deprive us of this mercy brought soe neere to us, it may proove the undoing of many soules & a desolating stroake to this place: There were sundry signall providences of God leading unto & carrying on this motion to your son, whom our hearts are much set upon, & if God should blast our hopes, wee dread the consequences thereoff; His soe soone returning to the Bay as it was contrary to our expectation soe it filled our hearts with greife & heavynesse; but wee hoped our interest in him was such (considering what expressions of Love wee had from himselfe) that he would soone returne to us againe; some of us had then thoughts of writing a letter to yourselfe, but because such of ours did accompany him, wee knew not but their personall speaking might attaine the end, but they all one after another returning not with an olive branch of peace & comfort in their mouths, but with the contrary even to this day, wee lye downe in the dust before God & desire to be more humble & vile in our owne eyes & sensible of our great unworthyness of any mercy, & as wee would be more quickened by the prayer of faith to looke to the father of mercies to bestow this blessing upon us, soe wee would still be endeavouing, if it be possible, to obtaine his returne to us; wee know it is Gods usuall dispensation to lay mercy under a sentence of death before the granting of it; that it may be the more prized when injoyed, & wee hope, the Lord intends noe other to us by hitherto frowning upon us in this matter: wee have once & againe bin solemnly seeking the face of God herein, & wee trust the prayer-hearing God will remember us in our low estate, because his mercy endureth forever & pitty us for his Name's sake & incline the heart of you & your yoke-fellow to deny yourselves (for his sake who gave his Life for the good of soules) soe farre as to give your son, as you have done to the Lord, soe to us in submission to the will of God: wee earnestly desire that you will spare him to us as lest for one yeare, & who can tell what cause may be of praise to God for the reviving of his worke in this place in such a time, & then neither you nor he will repent that you have thus adventured on the Lords account to spare your deare child soe far from you; All the discouraging returnes wee have hitherto had cannot silence us, wee must yet speake & plead for this blessing, it is for the life of soules that wee thus speake; & if God should yet say, wee shall not injoy your son according to our desire wee must & shall freely owne God is Just & righteous therein, but wee shall thinke that wee are not soe dealt with by man as becomes the Gospel, for while he had our motion under consideration, wee cannot beleve any other people could lawfully apply themselves to him, & had wee a due hearing of what wee have to say for ourselves in this matter, wee doubt not but all Men of God would conclude your son ought in Conscience to be ours for a time of competent Probation: Wee leave the matter with God & to your serious christian Consideration, humbly imploring wee may finde grace in the sight of God, & that you would at last condescend to give us a comfortable answer, for our Extremities are great & call for speedy releife; If God will deale with us as afflicted, overwhelmed David said, Thou hast lift me up & cast me downe; wee were lifted up in hopes of a choice ministeriall blessing but shall not injoy it, wee desire to say, the will of the Lord be done, but pardin us, if wee suggest to you that wee doe apprehend, that those who have hindred & continue to hinder our obtaining this mercy will not hereafter have cause to rejoyce in it: yet hoping in the mercy of God & waiting for his gratious appearances for us & commending our Brotherly love & respects to you, desiring an interest in your prayers, Love & candour, wee rest

your distressed brethren & friends

[unsigned]

in the name & with the consent of this congregation
sandwich october; 1688:

Thomas Prince Collection, Massachusetts Historical Society.

---

1. Thomas Prince notes, "This no doubt was wrote to the Father of m^r^ Jonathan Pierpont, by ye R Mr John Cotton Plimouth, for Elder Chipman & others of Sandwich."
2. For Pierpont's call to Northfield, see the notes on the letter of 13 August 1688.
3. John Brock (1620–1688, H.C. 1646) began his career in Rowley (1648–1650), briefly returned to Harvard to pursue his studies after completing both bachelor's and master's degrees and spent eleven years as the minister in Isle of Shoals, later New Hampshire, until 1662, when he settled in Reading (modern-day Wakefield) until his death in June 1688. *Sibley's Harvard Graduates*, 1:127-31.
4. Cotton seems to have been implying that Reading (modern-day Wakefield) should have had an easier time finding a minister because the town was closer to Harvard College in Cambridge—"the place of supply"—than Sandwich was.

From John and Ruth Chipman, 1 October 1688

FROM SANDW OCTOBER: 1: 1688

HONORED

and much respected sir: we received yours dated Septem,: 25:[1] for which we give you harty thanks but it would have been greater cause of Joy to us had you had better tidings for us; our harts are Cast down within us: and we need not enquire the reason: if we doe but think of our Condition: and ye frown of god yt is now upon our endevours for the mendment of our Condishon: and yt frown of god y^t^ is now upon our endevours for the mendment of our Condision: I have sent the paper you spake of[2] if you wil please to transcribe or mend it and send it back by this bearer: the church intends to send a letter to the old man: when m^r^ prince comes home: and m^r^ smith[3] ses he will set his hand to it: I am of your mind y^t^ those leters would have been very helpful in this Case: but we have none to giude us and any thing Comes of hard w^t^ us: many of us are sorowing under such disapointments: the god of al grace be plesed to give us wisdom to know how to cary in this dark day: y^t^ we may Justifie him in all who can doe us noe wrong: we find these tryals hard to bear: we returne to your self many thanks for al your pains and Care about our afairs: and desire the Continuance of your prayers for us who are your distressed freinds

John et Ruth Chipman

we present our respets wth harty love to your self and Mrs Cotten
I shoud inlarge but am in great haste

Curwen Family Papers, American Antiquarian Society. Addressed "these for the honored and much respected mr cotten teacher to the Church of plimouth deliver." Endorsed "From Elder chipman october, 1: 1688:"

---

1. See the above letter of 25 September 1688.
2. See the above letter of October 1688, to Robert Pierpont.
3. John Smith (1614–1710) emigrated to New England in 1630, preached in Barnstable on Long Island and settled in Sandwich in 1673. The Sandwich church had been without a settled minister for twenty years. Smith seemed well suited to the Sandwich congregation because of his moderate stance regarding Quakers, who made up a sizable portion of Sandwich residents. He was ordained in 1675 and remained in the pulpit until 1688, when he requested a dismissal due to his advancing age. See the above letter of 25 September 1688. Weis, *Colonial Clergy*, 189-90; Lovell, *Sandwich: A Cape Cod Town*, 109-11, 128-29.

To John Chipman[?],[1] — 5 October 1688

Plimouth October, 5: 1688:

My very Deare & truly valued Friends

I was yesterday abroad with the Elder to visit a sick woman (susanna Gardner,[2] a sister) soe that it was evening before I received your letter,[3] & I am this morning called upon by the bearer to hasten my answer & cannot take time much to deliberate; but according to your desire, I cannot say I have mended but I have altered the enclosed & have put in & left out as I thinke the circumstances of your case now call for; It is as every thing is that comes from me, weake & needs your candour & charity, but I am sure it comes from an honest heart to poore Sandwich; the latter passages in it that seem to reflect some fault upon those that are not friends to your motion, if you want courage & confidence soe to write, you may leave them out, but I thinke they are both usefull & necessary; God in mercy guide you; I conclude if Mr Prince be returned he may bring you as discouraging tidings as all others have done; yet not withstanding I cannot but apprehend it may be your advantage to venture all these letters to the old man & young[4] & to Redding, who can tell what impressions they may have? And if you will send one messenger more with these or such like letters, it may proove well, if yourselfe cannot, I shall be glad of M[r] Bassett, & embrace his company to Roxbury ordination, & soe make one triall more;[5] Get a company of christians together next weeke & pray hard, it may be God may be intreated; our hearty love to you both; with prayers for a gratious issue, I rest

yours Affectionately,

John Cotton

I am desirous to heare as soone as may be whether a man goes & when; for my time Roxbury is, God willing, oct: 15: Monday–morning. salute Mr Prince & Bassett.

Thomas Prince Collection, Massachusetts Historical Society.

---

1. Thomas Prince notes, "I suppose wrote to Elder Chipman of Sandwich."
2. In the vital records, Clerk Thomas Faunce listed a Samuel and Suzannah Garner, who married in 1682 and had three children by 1687. Evidently, Suzannah survived the illness Cotton mentions, because she later married Joshua Ransom on 10 March 1692, after Samuel's death on 3 September 1689. Lee D. Van Antwerp, comp., and Ruth Wilder Sherman, ed., *Vital Records of Plymouth, Mass. to 1850* (Camden, Me., 1993), 6, 86, 134; Savage, *Genealogical Dictionary*, 2:230.
3. See the above letter of 1 October 1688.
4. Robert and Jonathan Pierpont.
5. Cotton seems to have wanted William Bassett to join the lobbying effort in Roxbury.

To Thomas Hinckley, 28 NOVEMBER 1688

PLIMOUTH NOVEMBER, 28: 1688

HONOURED SIR

Being Last weeke at Boston; Mr Gardner came from London with letters from Bro: M:[1] saying, that Sir Will: P:[2] "being arrived he received the Petitions from Cambridge & Plimouth (another letter of his saith not, Plimouth but Mr Hinckley) which he was very glad of, & in a few days expected an opportunity to present them to his majesty, they came, (saith he) very seasonably to confirme the Information before given to the King of the oppression of his subjects;" I conclude mr moodey writes all weighty newes to his son & therefore save myselfe the Labour. I went to mr King & had from him the enclosed bill of costs, Mr Danforth[3] (who I suppose had as much hand in Cam's Petition as you had in Plim's) upon perusall tooke a copy, & because Capt Sewall was going immediately gave it to him & it went away last Thursday: All your former narratives passing safely to the King, I hope your account of the last troubles & oppressions of my neighbours will have the same successe, if you did send last weeke then C: Sewall hath them, if not I hope you will hasten to be ready for the next opportunity & send this bill of Costs also; Thrice 20 shil: for motion for Judgment is deemed cruell oppression[4] & many other particulars therein never heard of in any of the Kings Courts. Bro: M: hath borrowed 500 Guinneys; it will be great pitty if your neighbours take no reall notice of so as to asist therein, while he is acting our cause,[5] verbum sat:[6] with due service to you & yours, & respects to mr Russell[7] & his, I rest,

Sir, yours to serve

John Cotton

Worthy Mr St. sent by me his share of the Judges fee to our sufferers.
This bill must not goe of my handwriting.

Thomas Prince Collection, Massachusetts Historical Society. Addressed "These For the Honourable Thomas Hinckley, Esquire, at Barnstable." Right margin frayed and darkened.

1. Increase Mather.
2. William Phips.
3. Thomas Danforth.
4. For more concerning the skyrocketing court costs incurred during the era of the Dominion of New England, see 9 July 1688.

5. Cotton clearly supported Mather's charter efforts, a stance that he later regretted; see 6/7 July 1698.

6. "The word is enough."

7. Jonathan Russell, minister of Barnstable.

To Rowland Cotton, 29 November 1688

Plimouth November, 29: 1688:

Deare son

I wrote to you on Monday[1] by Leift Howland,[2] I now only adde, that wee doe earnestly & confidently expect your hastning home, and desire you also to send home by water all your glasse bottles, they will be a great use in bottelling up cider etc. Also bring me a new Almanack or two:[3] The foure pounds I ordered you to take for the Steward at Cos: Mackarti's[4] will discharge more of your colledge debt then you could desire or expect of me: All salute you, God blesse you,

soe prayes, your Lov: Fath:

J: C:

The Elder is very glad you are not gone Eastward, but are coming to us.

Bring home in the Boate all things you can conveniently, & 24 Mannitoowompae bookes[5]

your mother would have you minde m[r] Elliston of getting a good firking butter for us, he told me it was a groat a pd, I will send him the money for it immediately on receipt of the butter, let it be good & cheap:

verte

December, 3:

yours I received on Saturday,[6] am glad of your care to informe newes, I wish you may bring more good tidings of your uncle, also of your brother: I send you a cloak bag by J: Morton. Minde to doe all I write about on the other side, God blesse thee.

J: C:

Thomas Prince Collection, Massachusetts Historical Society. Addressed "These For Mr Rowland Cotton, at Harvard College, in Cambridge. Leave these with M[r] Elliston at Boston for Conveyance.

1. Not found.

2. Probably Joseph Howland; see 9 July 1688.

3. Probably John Tulley, *An Almanac for the Year of Our Lord MDCLXXXIX* (Boston, 1689) [Evans 499]; less likely, but possibly Daniel Leeds, *An Almanac for the year of Christian Account 1689* (Philadelphia, 1688) [Evans 446]. Charles Evans, *American Bibliography* (New York, N.Y., 1941–1959), 1:75, 82.

4. Possibly Thaddeus Maccarty (1640–1705) or his son, Thomas (Thaddeus?), who was a member of the Harvard class of 1691. Savage, *Genealogical Dictionary*, 3:139; *Sibley's Harvard Graduates*, 4:106-7.

5. Lewis Bayly, *Manitowompae Pomantamoonk Sampwshanau Christianoh Uttoh Woh An Pomantog Wnssikkitteahonat God*, (London, 1685) [Evans 383]. This is the second edition of John Eliot's abridged translation of Lewis Bayly's *Practice of Piety*. Eliot's first edition was published in Cambridge, Massachusetts, in 1665 by Samuel Green [Evans 95]. Evans, *American Bibliography*, 1:22, 63.

6. Not found.

EIGHT

King William's War 1689–1697

IN 1688 WAR ERUPTED BETWEEN French and English colonists (with their respective Native allies) along the northern border of Massachusetts Bay, in present-day Maine. By the summer of 1689, Britain had declared war on France, beginning the War of the League of Augsburg in Europe and King William's War in North America, but the colonists had already engaged in deadly frontier skirmishes.[1] The war was marked by sporadic raids on northern settlements along a border that had been left particularly vulnerable after April 1689, when many militia companies returned home following the overthrow of Edmund Andros's Dominion of New England during the Glorious Revolution. Increasing Native attacks like the "massacre" at Schenectady to the west prompted Massachusetts Governor Simon Bradstreet to call for an invasion of French Canada in the spring of 1690. Under the command of Sir William Phips, the combined colonial forces first focused on gaining Port Royal, Nova Scotia. Following their success, Phips pushed for an attack on Quebec, for which Plymouth Colony supplied 200 men, including fifty Indians. The October attack failed miserably, as English colonists were repelled by forces commanded by the Governor of Canada, Louis de Baude, comte de Frontenac. The English retreat in smallpox-infested ships suffered gale-force winds that blew some ships so far off course that they eventually landed in the West Indies.

By the war's end, French colonists and their many Native allies had raided Dover (July 1689), Pemaquid (August 1689), Schenectady (9 February 1690), Salmon Falls (18 March 1690), Falmouth, now Portland, (27 May 1690), York (5 February 1692), Wells (10 June 1692), Oyster River (July 1694), Groton (27 July 1694) and Haverhill (15 March 1697), among other settlements. The English launched retaliatory assaults on the Maine-Quebec border, such as the Battle of Brackett's Woods in 1689, and on Native forts near Brunswick on the Androscoggin River in September 1691 and on another fort near Lewiston shortly thereafter. The English had succeeded in capturing

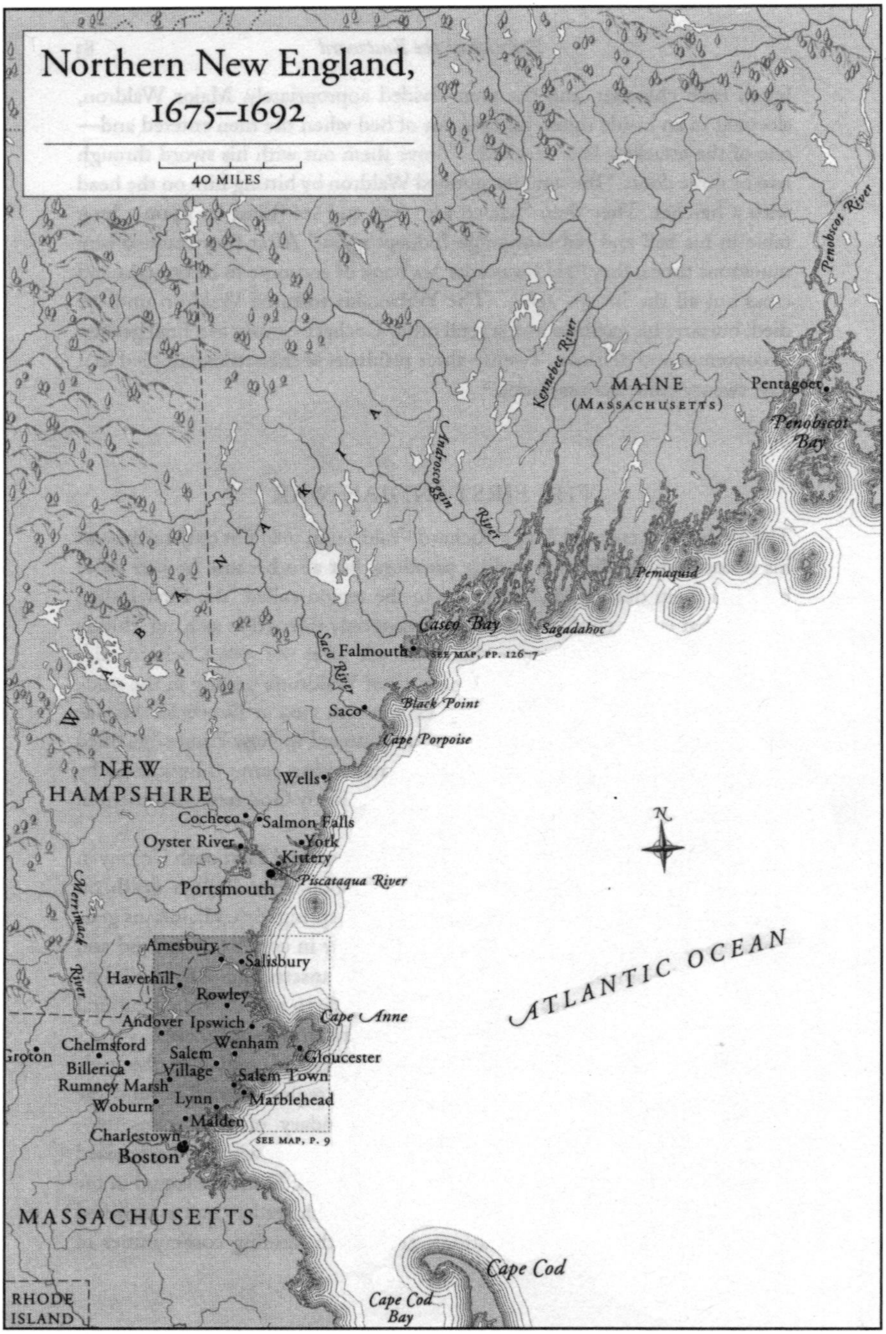

From In the Devil's Snare *by Mary Beth Norton, copyright © 2002 by Mary Beth Norton. Maps copyright © 2002 by David Lindroth, Inc. Used by permission of Alfred A. Knopf, a division of Random House, Inc.*

Port Royal only to endure its recapture by the French a year later. The Treaty of Ryswick (30 September 1697) concluded the war, which had ended in a stalemate, and restored all colonial possessions to their original status.

Many of the letters in this section include war news, especially since Plymouth Colony contributed both men and money to the war effort. In May 1690 the Plymouth Court ordered that sixty-two men under the command of Major John Walley join the combined forces of Massachusetts, Connecticut and New York at Albany, where they had gathered principally to defend the northern frontier.[2] Cotton also received and conveyed news concerning Major Fitz-John Winthrop's aborted mission to attack Montreal in the summer of 1690;[3] the desperate situation faced by families trying to live in border towns;[4] the attack on York in February 1692;[5] plans to construct Fort William Henry in Pemaquid beginning in 1692;[6] the raid on Oyster River in July 1694;[7] attempted peace negotiations at Fort William Henry in both 1693 and 1695;[8] the capture of Bombazeen;[9] attacks on Fort William Henry in 1696;[10] and Church's attempted raids along the Maine coast and Newfoundland,[11] among other war news. The taking and redeeming of captives on both sides was a primary war tactic, as it had been along the frontier since settlement began. Many of Cotton's letters described stealth raids, people taken, negotiations for their return, happy reunions, and even occasionally a daring escape.[12]

The war effort encountered resistance among Plymouth colony towns, several of which refused to send either men or money; in the years after the war, many towns struggled to pay taxes to the colonial government, which was desperately trying to cover soldiers' salaries.[13]

---

1. For example, see the letter below to Thomas Hinckley, 15 February 1689.
2. For more on Walley, see 10 August 1694.
3. From John Cotton (1661), 5 August 1690.
4. From Shubael Dummer, 13 January 1691; From Samuel Sewall, 22 February 1692.
5. From Samuel Sewall, 22 February 1692.
6. From Samuel Sewall, 22 February 1692.
7. To Rowland Cotton, 23 July 1694.
8. From Henry Dering, 12 August 1693; To Joanna Cotton, [29 May 1695].
9. To Rowland Cotton, 12 February 1695.
10. To Rowland Cotton, 4 March 1696; To Rowland Cotton, [after 7 August 1696].
11. To Rowland Cotton, [30 October 1696].
12. From Henry Dering, 20 August 1692; From Henry Dering, 12 August 1693; To Joanna and Rowland Cotton, [11] August 1694; To Joanna Cotton, [29 May 1695]; To Rowland Cotton, 13 November 1695; To Rowland Cotton, [14 May 1698].

13. Howard H. Peckham, *The Colonial Wars, 1689–1762* (Chicago, Ill., 1964), 25-56; Eugene Aubrey Stratton, *Plymouth Colony: Its History & People 1620–1691* (Salt Lake City, Ut., 1986), 133-34; George D. Langdon, *Pilgrim Colony: A History of New Plymouth 1620–1691* (New Haven, Conn., 1966), 226-32; *Records of the Colony of New Plymouth in New England,* ed. Nathaniel Shurtleff and David Pulsifer, 12 vols. (Boston, 1855-61), 6:208-57.

To Thomas Hinckley, 15 February 1689

Plymouth February, 15: 1688: /89:

Honoured Sir

It is noe small comfort to me, & to many here that feare God to heare of the Lords gratious recovering of you from your late sickness, he in mercy perfect his goodnesse in that respect & grant <in> according to the desire of your heart some blessed fruit to & in you & all yours both of the casting downe & Lifting up; God hath spetiall designes of grace in all his dealings with his Children; & as you have experienced of former, soe doubtlesse you will of this also, that it shall turn to your salvation through prayer & the supply of the spirit of Jesus Christ.

Sir, concerning the papers of which you speake,[1] Deac: Faunce[2] hath them ready, only waites for a safe hand to convey them by; God give successe to your endeavours to vindicate truth & obtaine Justice & reward your endeavours thereabouts: Concerning Newes, I wholly omit writing, because I conclude all & more then I know comes from M^r M: to his son:[3] 2 sleds at shipscott going homeward, the latter of them was assaulted, the Indians fired & killed one man, & wounded another who escaped, the dead they scalpt & went home triumphing;[4] Mr John Blake is dead.[5] & the only maiden-daughter of Capt Philips, sister to Cos: Cotton Mathers wife;[6] a dreadfull fine of 10 pd for Farewell; Jemison quasht his Indictment. Mr Stoughton writes me word,[7] that when he spake to you of 10 pd for me, it was without booke & by guesse, something I had much short of that summe but all is gone,[8] & some Indian creditors are not yet paid, I did hope for some from you till I had your letter, but I am content, having bin faithfull in that litle I received, but of this vivâ voce;[9] my wife is for Boston on monday; with our service to you & yours

I rest, Sir, your Honours to serve

John Cotton

Salute Mr Russell.

Hinckley Papers 2:27, Prince Library, Rare Book and Manuscripts, Boston Public Library. Addressed "These For the Honoured, Thomas Hinckley Esquire, at his house in Barnstable."

1. Unknown.
2. Thomas Faunce (1647–1746) was ordained a deacon of the Plymouth church on 26 December 1686. Publications of the Colonial Society of Massachusetts *Collections* (hereafter *CSM*), 22 (Boston, 1920), 161, 259.
3. See 28 November 1688.
4. War erupted between the French and the English along the northern border of Massachusetts Bay Colony (present-day Maine) in 1688, and French Catholic Indians attacked Pemaquid in August 1689; Haverhill also reported Indian attacks. After an official declaration of war, these skirmishes were considered part of King William's War. See the section above, "King William's War." Langdon, *Pilgrim Colony*, 226-27; Eugene Aubrey Stratton, *Plymouth Colony: Its History & People 1620–1691* (Salt Lake City, Ut., 1986), 132.
5. John Blake emigrated with his family as a child in 1630 and lived in Dorchester and Boston. Savage suggests that he died "early in 1689," leaving no children. James Savage, *A Genealogical Dictionary of the First Settlers of New England*, 4 vols. (1860–62; facsimile reprint Baltimore, Md., 1990), 1:192-93.
6. Cotton Mather's first wife was Abigail Philips, the daughter of mariner John and Catherine Anderson Philips of Charlestown. The "maiden-daughter" was most likely Catherine (b. 1672), since Mehitable (1667–1737) and Mary (b. 1676) were married by this time. Savage, *Genealogical Dictionary*, 3:412-13; Almon Torrey, *New England Marriages Prior to 1700* (Baltimore, Md., 1865), 350, 565.
7. Not found.
8. The New England Company account of 1692 noted, "To m[r] John Cotton for 3 years £40 p annu, & for the last year £ 50—170:00." By comparison, John Eliot received 100 for two years, and Hinckley received sixty-two for three years. MS 7946 New England Company: Accounts 1657–1731, Guildhall Library, London.
9. "By voice."

George Keith[1] to John Cotton, 1690

Here follow a few words of a Letter to *John Cotton*, called a Minister, at *Plymouth* in *New-England*.

John Cotton:

Having seen a few Lines from thy hand, attested by thee, and other two Witnesses, wherein thou and they declare, That in the Town of *Plymouth* in *New-England*, last summer, save one, ye heard me affirm, That the Scriptures are the Word of God. *My Answer to thee and them, is, That ye have not dealt fairly, nor as becoming true Witnesses, in this case; for every Witness should declare all the Truth, and conceal nothing of the Truth which they heard. Now this ye have not done, but diminished from my words, as your Consciences may bear witness, if your Memory be not bad; for I very well remember my words at that time, which were these, That I did acknowledge the true Sense of the Scripture to be the* Word of God, *and that in the same I was not singular in my Perswasion, from the people called* Quakers; *for* Samuell Fisher[2] *in his Book called,* Rusticus Academicos,[3] *that hath been in print upwards of twenty five Years, hath affirmed the same, to wit, That the true Sense of Scripture is the Word of God. And at that time I further said, That not everyone who had the Letter of the Scripture, had the Word of God, to speak properly, because they had not the true sense of Scripture, which none have, but such to whom it is given by the Spirit of God. I also did further affirm, That the Letter or words of Scripture may be called the* Word *in a figurative sense, as the* Map *or* Card *of* England *is called* England, *and that the Greek word is used in Scripture in divers acceptations.* All this, and more to the same purpose I spoke to thee at that time.

G.K.

George Keith, *A Refutation of Three Opposers of Truth, by plain Evidence of the holy Scripture...And a few words of a Letter to John Cotton, called a Minister, in Plymouth in New England* (Philadelphia, 1690), 73 [Evans 516]. Charles Evans, *American Bibliography* (New York, N.Y., 1941–1959).

---

1. George Keith (c. 1638–1716) was a prominent, and controversial, Quaker minister and writer. In 1677 he traveled on a missionary tour through Germany and Holland with George Fox, William Penn and Robert Barclay. In 1689 he settled in Philadelphia as headmaster of the William Penn school. Conflicts with other Pennsylvanian Quakers led to a splintering of the Quaker meetings in the 1690s and Keith's dismissal from the London Meeting. Eventually, he sought ordination in the Anglican Church and became an agent for the Society for the Propagation of the Gospel, attacking the Quaker church in his preaching and writing. Allen Tolman and Dumas Malone, eds., *Dictionary of American Biography* (New York,1957), 289-90.

2. Samuel Fisher (1605–1665) was a powerful nonconformist minister educated at Trinity College and ordained in Kent in 1632. He officially became a Baptist in 1643, but he had been associated with the Anabaptists for some years. A Baptist congregation invited him to become their preacher by 1649, and he engaged in vociferous oral and print battles over infant baptism. In 1654, he converted again, this time to Quakerism, following a visit by leading English Quakers William Caton and John Stubbs. Fisher began an active traveling ministry, journeying to Rome and Constantinople, among other places. He was imprisoned for his work and died of the plague in 1665 shortly after his release. His published works defending the Quaker faith were standard Quaker reading throughout the seventeenth century and beyond. *Dictionary of National Biography*, ed. Leslie Stephen and Sidney Lee, 63 vols. (London, 1885–1900) (hereafter *DNB*), 70-72.

3. Samuel Fisher, *Rusticus Ad Academicos In Exercitationibus Expostulatoriis, Apologeticis Quatuor. The Rustick's Alarm to the Rabbies: Or, the Country Correcting the University and Clergy, And (Not Without Good Cause) Contesting for the Truth, Against the Nursing Mothers and their Children in testimony of Truth Exalted.* (London, 1660) [Wing F1056].

From John Cotton (1661), 5 August 1690

PLIMOUTH AUGUST 5: 90:

HONOURED S^R^

On Saturday Evening about 16 houses besides warehouses and Bruehouses burnt at Boston[1] from ye Mill Bridge down halfe way to ye draw Bridge, Mr Rocks, M^r^ persons. No News of Indians; Major Winthrop was to march at ye head of ninteene hundred Mawquas[2] and Indians, with 600 christian from Albany to mount Royall,[3] Last tuesday morning, Canady is poor and discouraged Expect nothing but desolation. port Royall letters give ye account. ye fleete is to sayle to day. ye small pox as bad as ever.[4] printer Greene dead of it in thre days, his wive also dead.[5] Cous sarah peirce dead Last Saturday night,[6] An Lobloone pritty well of it. Cous conrys childe dead. Mr Hale saith God calls, ye Countrey cals, <*and*> Authority cals and christs Interest cals, and y^re^ sone doth and will goe to Cannady though his church and wife are unwilling.[7] Wise: Emerson: Overton:[8] no more as I know of. St Christophers retaken by our fleete: forty 3 men Lost in taking of it. A Brigonteene Last Saturday night from ffamouth England designed for New York arrived at Boston. Eleven weeks passage.[9] News very discouraging to our Late hectoring Enemys. King william gone to Ireland with a great ffleet. twenty thousand ffrench also Landed there.[10] King of france hath call in all pirates privateere, ye seas y^re^fore not dangerous. some thinke he hath a mind to step to white Hall to see whether an English Crowne will suite a french head. London Gazets say our Agents and Sr Edmonds Crew were safely arrived w^n^ our king was gone downe to his fleete, ye packquet Boat had a moneths passage thither, she Lewis and another are expected every hour. ye two sorts of Gentlemen were ordered to appear before ye committee of Lords for forreigne plan^ons^.[11] ye first thing alleadged against our fooes was ye seazing him y^t^ brought ye proclamation and imprisoning of him and using all means to keep it from ye knowledge of ye Countrey, witness being by; ye were found Gilty and so are committed, y^y^ are neither Lords nor Governours but Jaile [Bire?] and so like to remaine. S^r^. Edmons counsell desired our Agent to set y^r^ hands to ye Articles against him our councell said it was sottish and unresonable for it was New Engl not ye Agents y^t^ Articled againts y^m^. so y^y^ were Husht. Sr Hen Ashurst[12] Unk Mather[13] yt Agents had access in to her Majesty's presence and y^r^ Lips were graced with ye salutation of her Hand. as much respect manifested as can be desired we had Hanging over our affaire there[14]

ye Queen accounts us some of ye Best of Her subjects, and Gratiously saith we shall be dealt with as such. We are all well here, my mother Love to yourselfe ye duty of ye Rest. My Love to Brother

I rest your dutifull son

John Cotton

Curwen Family Papers, American Antiquarian Society. Addressed "These ffor y[e] Revend M[r] John Cotton A Barnstable." Endorsed "From my son John Received, August, 7: 1690:"

---

1. One of the major fires of colonial Boston, the 1690 fire destroyed at least fourteen houses as well as warehouses; it also consumed Samuel Green's printing press. Beginning at 2:00 a.m., the fire traveled across Mill Creek, increasing the destruction. *Memorial History of Boston*, ed. Justin Winsor (Boston, 1881), 388, 504.
2. Mohawks.
3. Fitz-John Winthrop and many Plymouth Colony soldiers participated in the attack on Montreal. See the above notes on King William's War.
4. This smallpox outbreak spread to Boston in October 1689 via a ship from the West Indies. The major epidemic continued to ravage Boston in 1690 and was rampant on the ships that carried colonial forces to attack Port Royal; in this manner the disease spread throughout New France. John Duffy, *Epidemics in Colonial America* (Baton Rouge, La., 1953), 48. Langdon, *Pilgrim Colony,* 232.
5. Samuel Green Jr. learned his trade from his father, Samuel, a Cambridge printer. The younger Green died in the smallpox epidemic in July and his wife, Elizabeth Sill, died a few days after. In August, Green's press was destroyed in the Boston fire of 1690. Thomas, *The History of Printing in America*, 83-84; *A History of the Book in America,* vol. 1, *The Colonial Book in the Atlantic World*, ed. Hugh Amory and David D. Hall (New York, 2000), 94; Savage, *Genealogical Dictionary,* 2:306.
6. Sarah Cotton Pierce was the daughter of Seaborn and Dorothy Bradstreet Cotton and married Richard Pierce on 27 August 1680. Pierce was a Boston printer who likely emigrated to the town after 1679 and before 1684. He continued to practice his trade until 1691, when he either began working for someone else, left New England or died. Isaiah Thomas, *The History of Printing in America, with a Biography of Printers & an Account of Newspapers,* 2d ed., ed. Marcus A. McCorison (1810; reprint, New York, 1970), 84-85; Amory and Hall, *The Colonial Book in the Atlantic World,* 94; Savage, *Genealogical Dictionary*, 3:430; John Langdon Sibley, *Biographical Sketches of Graduates of Harvard University, In Cambridge, Massachusetts* (hereafter *Sibley's Harvard Graduates*), 1:292.
7. John Hale (1636–1700, H.C. 1657) was the minister in Beverly from 1664 until his death. He served as the chaplain to the military expedition against Canada in 1690 from 4 June to 20 November over the strong objections of his congregation, to which Cotton alludes in this letter. One historian suggested that he served as chaplain because such "a large number were engaged" and "he was anxious to accompany them that he might watch over their morals." His son, Robert (1668–1719, H.C. 1686), carried out his father's ministerial duties in his absence. Frederick Lewis Weis, *The Colonial Clergy and the Colonial Churches of New England* (Baltimore, Md., 1936), 98; *Sibley's Harvard Graduates*, 1:509-20, 3:362-64.
8. John Wise (1652–1725, H.C. 1673) the minister in Essex, possibly John Overton, son of mariner Robert Overton (d. 1673), and John Emerson (1625-1700, HC 1656), the minister in Gloucester, all served as chaplains to Phips's 1690 expedition to Canada. Weis, *Colonial Clergy*, 233, 80; *Sibley's Harvard Graduates*, 1:485-87, 2:428-41; Savage, *Genealogical Dictionary*, 3:325.
9. Written in margin.
10. See Ichabod Wiswall's description of William's Ireland campaign in the letter of 17 October 1690.
11. James II had "ruined the Committee for Trade and Plantations." Michael G. Hall, *Edward Randolph and the American Colonies, 1676–1703* (Chapel Hill, N.C., 1960), 120.
12. One of the agents for the Massachusetts Bay Colony, Ashurst agreed to present Plymouth's petition for a charter, despite the colony's initial inability to support his efforts financially. On 3 March 1691 the

Plymouth Court finally voted to send Ashurst 50 guineas "that he would be pleased to use his care & endeavour to procure a charter from the King for a distinct government for this colony," and one hundred pounds sterling "towards the charge of procuring a charter as aforesaid" (*Plymouth Colony Records*, 6:260). Increase Mather repeatedly warned Hinckley that his hesitation was dangerous, as he did in a September 1689 letter: "You can never sufficiently requite Sir Harry Ashhurst for his concerning himself with such activity in your behalf. You must not think much to send over supplies of money for him to lay out to gratify some persons with for your benefit...My advice is, that you would raise money for that purpose, without any delay. You may do it too late: you cannot do it too soon." "The Hinckley Papers," Massachusetts Historical Society *Collections*, 4th ser., 5 (Boston, 1861), 211.

13. Increase Mather.

14. See the headnote "New England in Old England" on the Plymouth charter.

From William[?] Trail, 15 August 1690

[Beaumorise?] Augt 15. 1690.

Reverend & worthy Sir

I do take hold of the first opportunity I [have] had of writing to you, & of thanking you & yours for the kindness & [...] at Plimmouth in April last: I know [it was given?] me in the name of a disciple [the]refore whatever I be, it shall not lose its reward. We had a safe passage to [...], which I looked upon, more & rather at the gracious return of your own & your godly neighbors prayers for us, then of our own. The account of the publike affairs of these Nations, you will have from the prints, & from the report of those who carry our Letters to America. I am by good hands informed that our King W^{m} is a real godly man (a rare thing upon that throne) & has been a seeker of God since he was 8 years of age: I have seen & spoke with a serious godly Gentleman who was intimate with him when in Holland, to whom the then Prince, now King, did give a particular account of his case & exercise, & evidences of his piety; & indeed I think that the Devil & pope & Jacobites know too well that he is such a man, otherwise the English, Irish, Scotch & french hell-hounds would not have banded so against him. The Earle of Melvill (now his Majesties High Commissioner & chief Ruler in Scotland)[1] & severall others of the Nobility are known to be godly men: but there is a very wicked party in Scotland, who cease not to do what mischief they can, & there is a party of Highlanders in arms there & making disturbance: yet in Judah severall things go well, & others are mending; although many evil men & almost all the seducers are waxing worse & worse. I do kindly salute Mistress Cotton & your sons & daughters, & your praying serious friends & neighbours in Plimmouth, to whose kindness you know I am much obliged. I am not unmindfull of my promise to Mistress Cotton, but I have not had acess as yet to my fathers books;[2] yet I intend to send her either the book I promised, or (if I can not get it) a better of the same kinde. Those of the [Prelaticall preachers] that have not been as yet turned out by several State Acts of Parlt & Council in Scotland, nor yet by the rabble (who yet have turned out many) the presbytaries there are trying them, & turning out the scandalous & insufficient; so that few of that gang are like to be left in that Kingdom. So much at present [...] Sr

Your very much obliged Brother & Servt

W Trail

Curwen Family Papers, American Antiquarian Society. Addressed " For ye Revd m^{r} John Cotton In Plimth N England." Endorsed "From Mr Trail August, 15: 1690:" Two small holes and some staining.

---

1. George, 4th Lord and 1st Earl of Melville (1634[?]–1707), was made William III's commissioner to the Scottish Parliament in February 1690. *DNB.*

2. Possibly William Trail (1640–1714), minister at Borthwick, Midlothian, England, brother of Robert Trail (1642–1716), a noted Presbyterian minister. The books to which William referred in this letter belonged to his father, Robert (1603–1678), a zealous covenanter and one of the Scottish protestors, who ministered to the Scottish army in England in 1644. *DNB,* s.v. "Robert Trail." "Beaumaris" is a city in Wales.

From Cotton Mather, 17 October 1690

BOSTON. 17.^{D} 8.^{M} 1690.

DIE OB FRATRES MORTEM, ET MEMORABILI, ET MISERABILI.[1]

REVEREND S^{R},

Seeing of you, and (in ye want thereof) Hearing from you, are things, wch I count among none of my small Satisfactions. I do therefore particularly thank you for your last.[2] I bless God, for that Faith, wch has carried my Cousin Roland thrô his late Exercises, unto such an Issue; Lett him not imagine, that hee shall bee a Looser by any self-denial for ye Interest of God; the great God will see th[a]t hee shall bee no looser: One Sandwich will pro[ve] I am perswaded, worth Ten Dedhams to him, since hee has been determined by God, more than by himself, in his acceptance of ye calls that have been given him.[3] Remember me kindly to him.

The late sheet of Public Occurrences,[4] has been ye Occasion of much Discourse, it seems, about ye Countrey; & some that might as well have been spared. People had

& have a Notion, that I was ye Author of it. but as it happened well, ye publisher[5] had not one line of it from mee, only as accidentally meeting him in ye high-way, on his Request, I show'd him how to contract & Express ye Report of ye Expedition at Casco & ye East. However, ye Government, knowing that my Name was tossed about it, & knowing nevertheless that there was but One publisher, who pick't up here & there what hee inserted, they emitted a very severe proclamation against ye Poor Pamphlett, ye first line whereof thunders against Some, that had published that Scandalous Thing. This Accident gave a mighty Assistance to ye Calumnies of ye people against poor mee, who have deserved so very Ill of ye Countrey. The Reason, why I sent you not one of ye papers, was because I did myself at first agree in my Opinion wth such as Disliked ye two passages of ye Maqua's[6] & ye monster Louis; but I have since changed my mind. I now find, there is not a Word said of ye Maqua's, but what wee ought to say To y^m^, or else wee bring Guilt upon o^r^s[elves]. As for ye French Tyrant, nothing is mention'd of him, but as a Remote Report, and yett wee had ye thing in Print long ago: and hee is permitting ye Wickedest libels in ye World, to bee published of o^r^ K. Wm,[7] and for us to talk (as his good subjects here do) of being afraid of offending him, When wee are taking from him ye best Countrey hee has in America, is methinks a pretty Jest. But lett it go as it will; they that had a mind to make mee odious, have attained their End, wth as much Injustice as could well have been used; & a few such Tricks will render mee uncapable of Serving either God or Man, in N. England.

I do not know, Whether Harris will go on wth his Occurrences, or no; but if hee do, I shall Endeavour monthly to supply you. I look upon his Design, to bee a very Noble, useful, & Laudable Design; and some that you have heard Rail against it, might do well to Endeavour themselves to do something that may render y^m^ worthy to bee accounted Serviceable, before they discourage such Honest men, as those three or four (whereof, I tell you again, I was None) Ingenious men, frô w^m^ Harris had his Occurrences.

S^r^. Forgive ye Length of this Impertinent letter. I write this meerly for Want of Other Occurrences; whereof th[ere are] at this time a Great Scarcity; God Grant Good ones when they come.

Remember mee, to Relations wth you; and beleeve that I am,

S^r^, No Less Your Servant then Your Kinsman

C. Mather.

Special Collections, University of Virginia Library. Addressed "To the Reverend John Cotton, Pastor to ye Church in Plymouth." Endorsed "From my Cousen, Mr Cotton Mather, october, 17: 1690:."

1. "On the day, both memorable and miserable, because of the death of a brother."
2. Not found.
3. Rowland had recently settled with Sandwich's first church after rejecting a call from Dedham, preferring to be closer to his parents in Plymouth. *Sibley's Harvard Graduates*, 3:324.
4. Considered the first indigenous American newspaper, *Publick Occurrences Both Forreign and Domestick* was published on 25 September 1690 and was intended to be a regular serial. Focusing on local and colonial news rather than on international events, *Publick Occurrences* was silenced after only one edition, largely due to the war news it contained and the fact that it was published without official sanction. Editor Benjamin Harris implied in the paper that England's Native alliances ("Maquas") during King William's War had been unnecessary and unsuccessful, and he reported rumors that Louis XIV of France ("monster Louis") had been sleeping with his own daughter-in-law. Many people in Boston suspected that Cotton Mather was a central contributor—a claim he denied. Charles Clark, *The Public Prints: The Newspaper in Anglo-American Culture, 1665–1740* (New York, 1994), 71-73, 79-81.
5. Harris, a printer and newspaper publisher who left London in 1686, was the publisher of *Public Occurrences*.
6. "Mohawks."
7. "King William."

From Ichabod Wiswall, 17 October 1690

Dyers Court in Aldermanbury London: October: 17: 1690

Revd Sr you are the only person from whom I have received a line since my departure from N:E:[1] under which consideration I hold my selfe more especially obliged to returne you thankes And to give you an epitome of News. so much desired by you.—after one storme of six-weekes and 6 dayes: (with very little Intermission) we arrived at Bristoll. march ye 30: And by Land arrived at London April ye 5. The kings designe to goe persenaly into Ireland was a remora in the Buisines of y[e] patent. the king went from London June ye 4: and at y[e] River Boyne June ye 30 And July the 1 showed matchless valour,[2] And god Allmighty showed no less care in that wonderfull preservation of his Royal person After king James' flight king william Entered Dublin & having conquered many places besieged Limerick but being forced by great raines to raise his siege: he is returned back to England and was welcomed Septemb: 10 with great joy: witness y[e] many Bonefines trumpets: Bells Trumpets great gunes and fireworks employed that night with repeated huzzas & shouts in all parts of the City. Since his maties returne we are certainly Informed that Tyrronell: Lazune & Berwick with all the ffrench army are gon from Ireland to ffrance[3] despairing of any success there. Corke & kingsaile are surrendered to king william[4] & there is some sickness in Lymerick. so that it is hoped that all Ireland will be reduced this winter. many persons are flocking daily to Ireland to dwell there so general and most mens hopes of an absolute conquest there by king william. June ye 30 there was a sea fight in our chanell In which ye: Dutch and some few English behaved themselves like men: But such complaints rose against E: Torrington the English Admirall[5] that he is put in [...] and remaines in the former and in his roome three surren[dered?] viz: Sr John Ashbey Sr Richard Haddock: & Sr Tho: killegrens.[6] the Parliament began to sit October ye 2: And have voted many hundred thousands of pounds to manadge a war with ffrance next summer. The poore vadois have enjoyed wondrous mercys this Last summer. The massachusets [pat]ent is I hope in a faire waye to be compleated in a short time And poore plymouth might have been equaly happy (if they had not neglected their Opportunity.) by sending another Addresse to the king.[7] Here is nothing yet don for plymouth: & I shall tell you the reason if ever god bring me back againe to see youre face with ye faces of my other friends in N:E: which god in mercy hasten.) There have been some moving to annex plymouth: to New york: others to unite plymouth & the massachusets as one: both which at present seem to be stoped. And if the massachusets patent be granted this winter: it behoves plymouth to use their utmost care & diligence that they be not deprived of their Long enjoyed priviledges by their Oune neglect to Look out in season. Oh S^r^ bend your knees to the father of mercies that N:E: and partiqularly N:P:[8] may be once more happily setled and not returne againe to her Late bondage: you know not our present Circumstances: pray for us that we may not be Lead into temptation. nil nisi vota p supersunt.[9] The Torys Labour to fill mens eares & hearts with horror on the acco^t^: of ye pretended desolation and Confusion of N:E: and say the Land will be ruined except a generall Governor be sent! I believe some in N:E: will be ashamed when they heare the Extracts of their Owne writings. Sr Improve your Interest with the Governr for to hasten plymouth setlement. Remember me to mr Arnold:[10] to your good wife & children & to my plymouth neighbours as you have occasion partiqularly to Elder Cushman

The eternal god be your comon Refuge & cover poore plymuth in the hollow of hand where is the hiding of his power so prayes he who is S^r^ your ffellow labourer in xt.

Ichabod wisewall

Curwen Family Papers, American Antiquarian Society. Addressed "These for mr John Cotton junr at his house in plimouth." Endorsed "From mr wiswall october, 17: 1690 from England."

1. New England.
2. In the Battle of the Boyne, 1 July 1690, King William's Anglo-Dutch Protestant army defeated the Jacobite forces of the deposed James II. James was back in France within three weeks.
3. James Fitzjames, Duke of Berwick and son of James II (1670–1734), remained in Ireland until the fall of Limerick in 1691. Richard Talbot, Earl of Tyrconnel (1630–1691), and the French General Lanzun left Ireland on 12 September 1690. *DNB.*
4. In fact, it took a second campaign, in the summer of 1691, to pacify the rest of Ireland.
5. Arthur Herbert, Lord Torrington (1647–1716), commanded the Anglo-Dutch fleet in an engagement with a superior French force off Beachy Head on 30 June 1690. The allies fared poorly, temporarily ceding control of the English Channel to the French. Accused of cowardice or mismanagement, Torrington was subsequently arrested to stand court-martial on capital charges. He was acquitted of all charges but never received a command at sea again. *DNB.*
6. After Torrington's removal, command of the fleet was temporarily given to three admirals: Sir John Ashby (d. 1693), Sir Richard Haddock (1629–1713) and Henry Killgrew (d. 1712). *DNB.*
7. Wiswall clearly hoped that Cotton would use whatever influence he had with Hinckley to encourage the Governor to appeal to the King directly. As Wiswall saw it, Plymouth's silence would result in the colony losing its charter fight.
8. New Plymouth.
9. "Nothing except prayers remains."
10. Samuel Arnold (1622–1693) was the minister in Marshfield from 1657 until his death, and, before helping to settle that town, he was a representative to the General Court of Plymouth from Yarmouth (1654–1656). Weis, *Colonial Clergy*, 21; *Marshfield: Autobiography of a Pilgrim Town* (Marshfield, 1940), 27-28, 30-32.

From Increase Mather, 25 October 1690

London october. 25. 1690.

dear Brother

I have recd serverall lrs from you this sumer;[1] For wch I thank you. I have more yn once desired Mr Boyle[2] & other principal gentlemen cncrned in ye Indian Corporation yt yy would be kind to you. They ordered you 40 pound in silver.[3] Above halfe a year ago it was resolvd yt ye disposal of ye moneys due should be put into more hands yn one. yy were pleased to <*ask*> call for my Advice as to ye psons to be entrusted. I mentioned to you, mr Hinkley,[4] & Major Treat[5] - At Boston, Mr Bradstreet,[6] Mr Stoughton,[7] Major Richards,[8] & Mr [Marston?][9] yy are pleased to add one more wch I did not nominate, a Relacion of yors here.

I am [sorry?] you mention such a poor mean Argument as y[t] of y[r] debt to me. you do not know me if you think such Considerations will sway wth me. That money is due to my wife yo[r] sister, whom I must not see wronged.

I doubt[10] yo[r] Colony will be annexed to new-york [wch?] will not (I suppose) make you y[e] happiest Colony in N.E. I did once prvent it but I [?] Septimus [?] is able to do yor [illeg] part? then I (or an 100 more wiser yn I am) Can do you service. Rtr to my sister & to all yo[r]s.

I am, yo[r] affectinate Brothr

I Mather

Mather Family Papers, American Antiquarian Society. Addressed "To y[e] Revd M[r] John Cotton, pastor of y[e] church in plymouth New England" Endorsed "From my Brother, M[r] Increase Mather, october, 25: 1690:"

---

1. Mather may have been referring to Cotton's letters of 10 and 21 September 1688. This letter seems to have been a reply to comments in those letters.
2. Robert Boyle (1627–1691) was a noted English philosopher and scientist and a founder of the Royal Society. He also served as governor of the Society for the Propagation of the Gospel in New England, commonly called the New England Company (and hereafter called SPG), beginning in 1661. Although Mather seems to have been unaware of it, Boyle had resigned as Governor of the New England Company in 1689. *DNB*.
3. There are no accounts for Cotton's SPG salary from 1684 to 1692, but the 1692 account refers to Cotton's salary "for 3 years £40 p annu, & for the last year £ 50—170:00." MS 7946 New England Company: Accounts 1657–1731, Guildhall Library, London.
4. Gov. Thomas Hinckley.
5. Samuel Treat (1648–1717, H.C. 1669), minister at Eastham and Native missionary. *Sibley's Harvard Graduates*, 2:304-14.
6. Gov. Simon Bradstreet (1604–1697). Savage, *Genealogical Dictionary*, 1:236.
7. William Stoughton.
8. John Richards (d. 1694) lived in Dorchester and served as a lieutenant, captain and major, as well as a representative, speaker, assistant and judge. Savage, *Genealogical Dictionary*, 3:533.
9. Perhaps Manasseh Marston (d. 1705), a blacksmith who served as a captain and a representative to the General Court and lived in Salem and Charlestown. Savage, *Genealogical Dictionary*, 3:161.
10. "I suspect"—Mather again warned Cotton that Plymouth would be annexed to New York.

From Shubael Dummer,[1] 13 January 1691

YORKE JAN 13TH (90)

MR JOHN COTTEN

REVEREND SR

I received yours from Salisbury[2] & acknowledge your kind lines & particular remembrance of this poor place wherein Providence hath Cast my lot, it is a great favour of almighty god (& I heartily wish we ma[y] all see ye goodnesse of god in ye kindnesse of men) to stirr up ye hearts of his People with you to Contribute to ye necessity of ys poor townes.[3] you are ye fir[st] that have done any thing of this Nature ye lord Jesus I hope will accept it as done unto himselfe Amongst whome yr are some Alas yt so few that love him in sincerity. I desire though unknown to be Commended to those our neighbors & xtian freinds that have been ye promoters of & acters in this liberall Contribution & pray yt ye blessing promised to ym yt Consider ye poor may rest upon all yr heads & hearts & yrs after ym. Particularly unto Major church[4] of your Colony whome ye lord has been pleased to make an instrument of good service to this poor province both formerly & also Lately in taking those Captive Indians by which our Captives were redeemed & without whome I believe we should hardly have seen ye faces of any of ym. for what Cause is he no more Improovd I know not. yr are Many in our towne in a suffering Condition sundry Eastern peo[ple] that formerly & some this last Summer were driven from yr dwellings & have litle or nothing to live [...] Many widdows & fatherlesse ones & sundry of ym belonging to our church whose Relations helpes & guides were taken away in ye late spreading wasti[ng] sicknesse[5] which through mercy our neighbors at well[s] were not visited with. they in yt towne are General[ly] better to passe in outward [vessels?] yn we in our towne only they may looke upon ymselves in Grea[ter] danger because next to ye Enemy. but who kn[ows] where they may Come first. how ye Contri[bution] shall be disposed of whether to ye [...] must be left to your selves & good Reason [...] what may be appropriated to our town if y[ou] please to make mention of my Name together with Major Davis[6] or Captain Alcocke[7] or Lieutenant Preble[8] all or any of ys to receive & also to take care of ye dividing ye same as ye Greater need Calls for. Sr. pray for us yt if it be [the] will of god we may yet be preserved. but [...] for Sanctification of all affecting Provide[nce] & yt ye lord would please to disquiet those that [...] ye rest of our Captives & refuse to let ym goe.

thus in hast. for our thankesgiving is to morrow ye 14th day of this present Month & I am glad we heard of this Contribution that Among other acknowledgments ys may be one. ye lord be with you as he was with your father & as he has Gratiously promist Lo I am with you alway &c. I have Enclosed ye lett[ers] to Capt. Thomas[9] unsealed y[t] you may understand what they have written. Pray seal it & with all speed deliver it. Service to M[rs] Cotton.

Your friend & Servt. in xt

Shub: Dummer

Nichols Papers, Massachusetts Historical Society. Addressed "For y[e] Revere[d]. M[r] John Cotten Pastour of y[e] Church of x[t] in Plymouth y[s]."

---

1. Shubael Dummer was born in Newbury, Massachusetts, in February 1636 and graduated from Harvard in 1656. He was the settled minister to York, later in Maine, from 1662 until his death on 6 February 1692 during a Native attack that destroyed the town. In that same raid 160 people were either killed or carried into captivity. Weis, *Colonial Clergy*, 74. Cotton Mather, *Decennium Luctuosum* (Boston, 1699) in *Narratives of the Indian Wars, 1675–1699*, ed. Charles Lincoln (New York, 1913), 230-31; *Sibley's Harvard Graduates*, 1:471-75.

2. Not found.

3. Cotton's church collected money to send to communities ravaged by Native wars, including York. As Cotton noted in the church records, "This chh & people made a large contribution in the time of the warrs for the reliefe of those impoverished at & about Rehoboth; The like they did also in these wars & sent it to the distressed Eastward... This may truly be left on record, That upon any motion from the Elders for a contribution on such accounts, there was a great readynesse in the people to hearken thereunto & give freely & abundantly." *CSM*, 22:165.

4. Following a request from Massachusetts Governor Simon Bradstreet in July 1689, Benjamin Church agreed to recruit some Native soldiers and other Plymouth Colony volunteers to aid in defending the northern border against French and French-allied Native attacks, which had been raging since 1688. Church was one of the few veterans of King Philip's War who drew on his earlier experiences to command Native and English troops in the larger theatre of King William's War. He led men into the Battle at Brackett's Woods near Casco Bay in 1689 and commanded a second raid in the fall of 1690 at a Native fort near Brunswick on the Androscoggin River. Before the war ended, Church led two more assaults along the Maine-Quebec border, but Plymouth's participation in the war was half-hearted. Langdon and Stratton suggest that many colonists opposed sending Plymouth troops to fight in this war, largely due to a worsening financial crisis, reluctance to pay war taxes to support the effort and dissatisfaction over who would lead Plymouth troops. *Colonial Wars of North America, 1512–1763: An Encyclopedia*, ed. Gallay, 137-39; Langdon, *Pilgrim Colony*, 226-34; Stratton, *Plymouth Colony*, 132-35.

5. Smallpox epidemic.

6. John Davis served as a lieutenant, captain and major and lived in York. Savage, *Genealogical Dictionary*, 2:18.

7. Job Alcock (1638–1716) lived in York and served as a lieutenant, captain and Councillor in the first post-Andros government. Savage, *Genealogical Dictionary*, 1:21.

8. Abraham Preble (1642–1714) lived in York, and served as a lieutenant, judge and deacon. Savage, *Genealogical Dictionary*, 3:477.

9. Letters are not found; perhaps Nathaniel Thomas (1643–1718) of Marshfield, who was elected representative from Marshfield both before and after the new charter and served in King Philip's War. Savage, *Genealogical Dictionary*, 4:281-82.

To Rowland Cotton,

31 January 1691

To Mr Roland Cotton at Sandwich.

Plimouth. Jan. 31.1690/91

Dear Child

I know you long for newes: but w^n^ Hannah came, I had none to tell you. But Leift Colimore[1] being at Boston, was desir'd to go to such a man for Letters of great concernm^t^. He did, & came at Boston with y^m^ yesterday, & is this Day c^m^ hither on purpose to bring y^m^ Hither: & therefore you must This Day post y^m^ to ye Govr.

Broth^r^ Mather[2] hath written Letters to Him, & his son hath sent y^m^ enclos'd in his. Our Condition here calls with speed for a General Court. If it cou'd have been sooner, it had been well. Many Things in my Letters I cannot conveniently [write] but you may see y^m^ when you come. Couz mather[3] [says] y^t^ his Father understanding there was [....] Pl[imouth [...] in ye Gov. of New] York Comission [...][4] [joined][5]

The Act of General Indemnity [....] 1690, Pardoned all Treasons &c comm[....] English Plantations before ye last Feb[....] comprehended our late oppresors. Gov [looks like Sloughter, is a][6] modereate church man, & a good natured Gentleman[7]

England will this spring make a powerfull Invation upon France. The Duke of Savoy having restored ye Waldenses their Liberties, hath declared War upon France, & made som powerfull impression upon his adversaries.

Tell Mr Prince his Broth^r^ Thomas[8] is safely arrived in England. Capt Ware brought Mr Dudley, many passengers more, Mr Thomas Fairweather;[9] M^r^ [Sim]on Eyres[10] Mr Brenton, M^r^ [like Suckanam][11] who came to be Collector, Mr Barton [or Paxton][12] who hath brought much Riggin & can [supply all][13] ye Countrey. Capt Lewis, Foster, Prince, Bant &c suddenly expected. Much Powder is come. West & Palmer coming to New York. Randolph is desolate,[14] walking about [....] complaints how [....]ne [...][15] Hand was shot off [...][16] cos. mather's wife was [...] with ye small Pox, but Recovering. I shall soon see you after Feb.8. Salute Mr Prince & his wife, ye Elder[17] & his, Capt Basset.[18] The Lord bless & make you a Blessing

your Loving Father

John Cotton.

copy

Thomas Prince Papers, Massachusetts Historical Society. Addressed "To Mr Rowland Cotton at Sandwich." This letter is a manuscript copy in Prince's hand. The original, now lost, was apparently much degraded. The superscription habits more accurately reflect Prince's than Cotton's, who rarely employed superscription.

1. Anthony Collamore lived in Scituate, was born in England and married Sarah Chittenden in 1666. Collamore served as a captain in the militia and commander of the Scituate company and mastered his own trading vessel. He was shipwrecked near Scituate Beach and died on 16 December 1693 on a rocky ledge still known as Collamore's Ledge. Deodat Lawson published a broadside to mark his death, *Threnodia, or a Mournful Remembrance of Anthony Collamore* (Boston, 1694) [Evans/Bristol B 158]. Savage, *Genealogical Dictionary*, 1:432; Samuel Deane, *History of Scituate, Massachusetts: From Its First Settlement to 1831* (1831; reprint, Scituate, Mass., 1975), 131, 240; Roger Bristol, *Supplement to Charles Evans' American Bibliography* (Charlottesville, 1970), 12.

2. Increase Mather.

3. Cotton Mather.

4. Nearly entire line missing.

5. Prince left a space between this and the next line indicating six or seven lines missing; he wrote "torn out" in the space.

6. Prince's note.

7. Cotton seems to have been convinced that Plymouth had already been joined to New York and was stressing the positive side of this much-feared conclusion by praising New York's governor.

8. Merchant Samuel Prince (1648–1728) moved to Sandwich from Hull in 1682, married Mercy Hinckley, the daughter of Governor Thomas Hinckley, in 1686 and served in several town offices. Savage records a younger brother, Thomas, who was born in 1658, married Ruth Turner in 1685 and had three sons, but offers no other information. Russell A. Lovell, *Sandwich: A Cape Cod Town* (Sandwich, Mass., 1984), 133. Savage, *Genealogical Dictionary*, 3:487-88; Deane, *History of Scituate, Mass.*, 327-28.

9. Probably Thomas Fairweather, baptised in Boston on 12 June 1670. Thomas was the son of John Fairweather (d. 1712), who served as constable and captain of the Castle during the overthrow of Andros in 1689. Savage, *Genealogical Dictionary*, 2:138.

10. Probably Simon Eyers (1652–1695), who was born in Boston, educated with the financial help of his maternal grandfather, Comfort Starr, and settled in New Haven by 1685. Savage, *Genealogical Dictionary*, 2:133-34.

11. Prince's note.

12. Prince's note.

13. Prince's note.

14. Edward Randolph was kept under house arrest by the Massachusetts Council of Safety and in February 1690, under orders from the Crown, was sent to London to have his case heard before the Committee for Trade and Plantations. He was exonerated of all charges, but found himself unemployed. In August 1690, he briefly went to Ireland, then returned to some free-lance customs work in London and in February 1691 accepted a job as customs searcher in Barbados. Although he booked his passage to Bridgetown, he remained in London, hoping for a better job. By October 1691, he was made Surveyor-General in America. Hall, *Edward Randolph*, 128-35.

15. Line and a half missing.

16. Three quarters of a line missing.

17. John Chipman.

18. See 25 September 1688.

To Thomas Hinckley, 6 February 1691

Plimouth February, 6: 1690: /91:

Honoured Sir

Though an opportunity of speaking vivâ voce[1] may be at hand, yet I can noe longer check my desire of speaking to you by this paper-messenger; what my owne letters from Boston & o: E:[2] doe say, render me noe stranger to what was sent you from thence lately; Sir, I doubt not of your faithfulnesse & sollicitous care to promove the best interest of this poore Colony, who hath not only deserved ill from the hands of God, but have soe demeaned themselves to the Authority of their owne choosing, as not to deserve from man to say, I will be your Healer; yet, Good Sir, I hope you will overlooke all such discouraging considerations, & at this day stand forth & play the man for our God & for the cities of our God;[3] That wee are not in Col: Sclaters [Sloughter's] Commission (who, Mr. Dudley sayes is probably arrived at N: yorke before this day) is noe doubt true, that as yet wee are not conclusively disposed of at whitehall I take for granted, the Question then is, What shall wee doe? I doubt not but you have many a time this weeke made such an enquiry in your addresses unto God, & I know you are wont soe far too condescend as to aske some weake men their opinions; my experience whereoff quickens me to this present boldnesse in thus writing to your Honour; not that I am now ready to presume, in suggesting what seemes to be our present duty, but I make bold to say, that having had converse by letters & otherwise with men of wisdome, prudence & piety, I finde a notable inclination upon their spirits with great unanimity to move that your selfe would thinke favourably & complyingly of taking a voyage to o: E:[4] I believe none among us will be free to trust any but your selfe, & as for the many hundreds of pounds that must be collected to defray the charge of such an undertaking, I finde amongst us a great readyness (maugre all our great charges) to contribute largely thereunto, & the feares of going to N: yorke in most & the unwillingnesse of others to be under Boston, make them willing to any expences to prevent the same; I could almost be willing to thinke, that whatever improbabilities there were (as things were circumstance at whitehall) for us last yeare to obtaine a charter, yet a prudent messenger might (if there himselfe, with such friends as I beleve he would there finde) suggest such Arguments as would either obtaine a distinct charter or at least such priviledges & immunities in our affixing us to Boston, as would render our condition very comfortable; but alas, Good sir, I have quite forgot my selfe, when I first began, I only intended to suggest to your gratious consort that she should be willing to lend You to the Lord in soe great a service, if God shall call you thereunto, & hearing soe many speak much for it, I thought it but duty to acquaint you therewith, that your sedate minde may revolve it before you come hither; It falles in course (& for me unhappily) to be my Lecture-day, Mr Arnold[5] intends to be here, I wish Mr Russell[6] would come also if Mr Keith[7] come not, I shall have his lines, never did poore Plimouth (me Judice) need more helpe from heaven & earth than at this day; I know you have candour enough to pardon my boldnesse, I have oft experienced it; with due Respects & service to you & Mris Hinckley, commending you & this great affaire to the Wonderfull, Counssellour, desiring your prayers for me & mine,

I rest, Sir, yours humbly to serve

John Cotton

Capt Clap is dead.[8]

Hinckley Papers 3:34, Prince Library, Rare Book & Manuscripts, Boston Public Library. Addressed "These For the Right Worshipfull, Thomas Hinckley Esquire, Governour of the Colony of New-Plimouth, at Barnstable."

---

1. "By voice."
2. "Old England."
3. Clearly, Cotton still believed that Plymouth had a chance of retaining her charter, especially if Hinckley traveled to England himself. At the very least, he hoped that Plymouth would be annexed to Massachusetts Bay, not New York. Cotton was not the only one who questioned Hinckley's inaction regarding the charter. Plymouth's agent in London, Ichabod Wiswall, repeatedly questioned Hinckley's reticence, as he did in a July 1691 letter: "that Plymouth, under its present circumstance, should sit silent so long, (may I not say, sleep secure?) is a great riddle...if you desire to return to the late experience of the miseries of an arbitrary commissioned government, a little longer neglect of your opportunity may afford it." "The Hinckley Papers," 5:285.
4. The General Court of Plymouth did not send Hinckley; instead it voted in March 1691 to pay Ashurst, Wiswall and Mather for their work in London and asked that Ashurst "would be pleased to use his care & endeavour to procure a charter from the King for a distinct government for his colony." *Plymouth Colony Records*, 6:260.
5. Samuel Arnold (1622–1693) of Marshfield.
6. Jonathan Russell (1655–1711) of Barnstable.
7. James Keith (1643–1719) of Bridgewater.
8. Roger Clap (1609–1691) emigrated to New England in 1630 and served as lieutenant of the artillery company, and captain of the Castle from 1665 until Andros arrived. Savage dates his death as 2 February 1692, but this letter suggests that he died in February 1691. Savage, *Genealogical Dictionary*, 1:390.

From Cotton Mather, 14 September 1691

14^{D} 7^{M} 1691 Boston

Revd Sr

The short and Long & ye Truth, of o^{r} Intelligence from England is, That ye K. ye Last Day hee was at Whitehal, declared it his pleasure & purpose, that N.E.[1] should have charter priviledges Restored;[2] Nevertheless (s^{d} hee) 'I think it will bee for ye Welfare of that people If I send over a General, or a Govern^{r}, to Unite ye Territory & inspect ye Militia of it. However (added hee) I will not send any person, but one that shall bee acceptable to that people, & Recomended by their Agents here.' This notwthstanding, ye clerk of ye Council made a false Entry of ye Kings Order as if wee were to bee settled Like Barbados &c. at wch o^{r} Tories there grew mighty brisk. But before ye month was out, they grew down in ye mouth. The clerks forgery was discovered, & by Order, o^{r} Charter was finished (tho not yet sealed) by wch o^{r} Colony, unto wch ye Eastern parts[3] are added, have power to choose D. Govern^{r} & Assistents & all General Officers, on ye Last Wednesday, of every May; Only ye K. Reserves to himself, ye Liberty of sending a General for all ye United Colones: who nevertheless will have no power to do anything in o^{r} colony wthout ye Concurrence of o^{r} own Magistrates; nor can any Lawes be made, or Taxes Levied, wthout a general Court. There are several Additional priviledges in this charter, wch make it better than o^{r} old one; & o^{r} friends in England Express much satisfaction in it. This is now like to bee o^{r} settlement; but I suppose, Plymouth, which is so wonderfully sottish, as to take no Care of itself, is like to bee thrown in as a Province, wch ye Govern^{r} may have particular Instructions about. The K. you know chooses o^{r} Magistrates for ye first year, most of o^{r} old ones, are pitch'd on; some New ones are added, whose Names tis needless to mention; & Mr Stoughton will be ye first D. Govern^{r}. The Govern^{r} of ye whole[4] I suppose, I know,—but, multa cadunt intra calicem supremaqe Labra.[5]

I suppose p my next, I shall send you my, Little Flocks guarded against Grievous Wolves.[6] Heaven guard us all from all sorte of y^{m}. Remember mee to my Relations wth you. and pray for

S^{r}, Your Kinsman & Servt

[C] Mather

Mather Family Papers, American Antiquarian Society. Addressed "To the Reverend Mr John Cotton, Plymouth" Endorsed "From Mr Cotton Mather September, 14: 1691:"

1. New England.
2. The new Massachusetts charter was approved in London on 7 October 1691 and included all three counties of the former Plymouth Colony beginning with the 2 September draft. Langdon, *Pilgrim Colony*, 240.
3. The "eastern parts" included what is now Maine. Massachusetts had purchased the claims of Sir Ferdinando George's heirs in 1680 and naturally wished to retain the province.
4. Sir William Phips was appointed the royal governor of Massachusetts.
5. "Many things fall in between the cup and the edge of the lips."
6. Cotton Mather, *Little Flocks Guarded Against Grievous Wolves* (Boston, 1691) [Evans 563]. Mather's anti-Quaker tract was probably well received in Plymouth Colony, where Congregationalists often confronted Quakers in their towns.

From Cotton Mather, 8 December 1691

Dec. 8: 1691: Boston

Reverend S^{R},

I sent you a letter some weeks ago, wch I suspect by Yours to Day,[1] is not yett come to your Hands. My Newes-Papers were few, and those few that are worth your seeing are not now at hand. The most Considerable thing of all, I now send you not, because I am Reprinting of it; namely, The Blessed, Glorious, Ominous Union, between ye presbyterians & Congregationals.[2] Your dear Brother-in-Law,[3] was a Principal Author of that Long-Train'd Transaction; Whereof You may quickly see more.

I send you all ye Almanacks I have.

Mr Russel, will inform you about ye business of my Removal.[4] The story of my Father's having sent for his family, is false. If we have certain advice of Andros's Return to N. E. You will find half a dozen, or half a score of ye most Considerable persons in ye Countrey (who are yett Nameless) immediately to strike into England; <the> and they will not go, Except I accompany y^{m}. There will bee no other way to save All; and That way (for Certain Causes that must not bee mentioned) will certainly save All. The Gentlemen will not Fly, as o^{r} Fools call it, but go where o^{r} Tories would bee lothe to have y^{m} go. The Danger of things Coming to this pass, has made it necessary for mee to speak aforehand of my Inclinacions; for I shall not stirr, wthout ye Advice of ye Church I belong to; Others may go, with less Antecedent preparations.

But this Day, wee have Advice, that ye King was Returned into England; wch gives us Cause to hope that o^{r} Adversaries are still Clog'd. God clog y^{m} a Little further, and all will bee well.

Remember mee, to Yours, and pray continually for

New England Papers (#2833-z), Southern Historical Collection, Wilson Library, The University of North Carolina at Chapel Hill. Addressed "For ye Revd John Cotton Plymth." Endorsed "From Mr Cotton Mather December, 8: 1691:." In another hand: "his going to England."

---

1. Not found.

2. Mather was probably referring to the publication *Heads of Agreement assented to by the United ministers in and about London, formerly called Presbyterian and Congregational* (London, 1691) *Early English Books*, 8: 6448 [Wing H1282A]. Mather later reprinted parts of *Heads of Agreement* in his *Blessed Unions....together with a copy of those articles where-upon a most happy union has been lately made between....Presbyterians, and Congregationals, for that of United Brethren* (Boston, 1692) [Evans 621]. For some discussion of the union of Presbyterians and Congregationalists in 1690, and for Increase Mather's contribution to that agreement, see Carl Bridenbaugh, *Mitre and Sceptre: Transatlantic Faiths, Ideas, Personalities, and Politics* (New York, 1962), 23-34.

3. Increase Mather.

4. Mather never joined his father in London.

NINE

"Your Affectionate Father," 1692–1697

THIS PERIOD OF COTTON'S LIFE was characterized by relative ease. He enjoyed a happy congregation, successful sons who found clerical positions, daughters who married happily into ministerial families, healthy grandchildren with whom he was clearly smitten and increased acceptance into the highest ministerial circles in Boston. Cotton relished his role as father, and almost all the letters in this section highlight his devotion to family. Two remarkable letters he wrote with Joanna reflect all the desires that any loving parent would have—that their son Josiah should live well, remember God, study hard, make good friends, stay healthy and write letters home.[1] Joanna reminded her son of all the times that illness or accident nearly took his life and that he should "Love the great Physician that then healed your Body, Pray to him to heal your Soul." Another letter highlights Cotton's tender concern for his children; young Theophilus was away at school and sadly begged to come home after he was bullied and teased by some "Duxbury Boys." Theophilus's sadness clearly affected his father: "my parentall bowels yearned."[2] Joanna revealed her deep love in her letters as well. In December 1696, two young undergraduates at Harvard drowned while skating on the partially frozen Fresh Pond in Cambridge. She wrote to her son days after the tragedy, expressing how devastated she would have been if Josiah had been one of the drowned boys: "I can hardly bear to think how I should have born the affliction if it had been you."[3]

Cotton clearly enjoyed increased prestige in the mid 1690s, something his youthful transgressions precluded earlier in his career. In December 1696, he was invited to give the Wednesday lecture at Boston's Old South church; while he preached from the loftiest pulpit he had ever held, three parishioners became full church members and the powerful Reverend William Brattle "was very civill & courteous to me in entertainments etc." afterwards.[4] While the next section of letters details Cotton's fall, the last few letters in this section present Cotton at his most accomplished and confident.

Joanna spent much of her time during this period happily aiding her growing family, acting as midwife to her daughters and daughters-in-law and collecting and prescribing medicinal herbs—all of which reflect her considerable medical knowledge and experience. Like her husband, Joanna was clearly comfortable and confident in her role as mother, friend and caregiver.

Despite an official movement toward peace, skirmishes on the northern border continued, including a devastating attack on York on 6 February 1692, in which more than 160 English settlers were either killed or taken captive.[5] The 1693 peace treaty, signed by thirteen Abenaki sagamores at the newly constructed Fort William Henry in Pemmaquid, lasted only until the summer of 1694, when hostilities again erupted beginning with the attack on Oyster River.[6] News of captives being taken, and some who later escaped, intermittent concentrated attacks and persistent endemic violence on the northern frontier appeared frequently in Cotton's correspondence and suggested that the peace treaty did little to settle longstanding conflicts along the border.[7] Returning soldiers brought smallpox back with them after the official war concluded, leading to another epidemic in Massachusetts.[8]

Cotton received a few letters, primarily from Cotton Mather, detailing the witchcraft crises in Andover and Salem, but he wrote little about it himself.[9] He did share information about a foiled plot to assassinate King William in a 27 July 1696 letter to his son Rowland, based on two letters he received. While many letters in this section describe the world beyond Plymouth Colony, many of Cotton's letters focus on the important events of his neighbors, friends and family members. Marriage, death, sickness, education, local politics, local court activity and personal concerns commanded his attention much more frequently than did kings and generals.

---

1. Joanna Rosseter Cotton to Josiah Cotton, 19 February 1692; Joanna and John Cotton to Josiah Cotton, 2 December 1693.
2. To Joanna and Rowland Cotton, [11] August 1694.
3. Joanna Rosseter Cotton to Josiah Cotton, 14 December 1696.
4. To Rowland Cotton, 8 and 9 December 1696.
5. From Samual Sewall, 22 February 1692.
6. To Rowland Cotton, 23 July 1694.
7. From Henry Dering, 20 August 1692; To Rowland Cotton, 23 July 1694; To Rowland Cotton, 19 November 1694; To Rowland Cotton, 12 February 1695; To Rowland Cotton, 24 April 1695; To Joanna Rosseter Cotton, [29 May 1695]; To Rowland Cotton, [22 August 1695]; To Rowland Cotton, 13 November 1695; To Rowland Cotton, 4 March 1696; To Rowland Cotton, [6 March 1696?]; To Rowland Cotton, [after 7 August 1696]; To Rowland Cotton, [23 and 24 August 1696]; To Rowland Cotton, [30 October 1696].
8. From Henry Dering, 12 August 1693.
9. From Cotton Mather, 5 August 1692; From Henry Dering, 20 August 1692; From Cotton Mather, 20 October 1692; From Henry Dering, 28 January 1693.

Joanna Rosseter Cotton[1] to Josiah Cotton, 19 January 1692

My Dear Child[2] January 19. 1691/2—

I am full of fears lest you should forget God your Creator & Preserver, & Jesus Christ the Redeemer of poor Children, Christ loveth that Children should come unto him. I love them yt love me saith ye Lord & those that seek me early shall find me[3]—O my Dear—Seek the Lord whilst he may be found call upon him whilst he is near—Remember what God hath done for you, how often he hath saved your Body from Death, O Give him no Rest Night nor Day till he hath Saved your Soul from Hell—You read in Eccles: that Childhood & Youth are Vanity,[4] Beg the Lord to keep you by his Grace from Breaking any of ye Commandments; Pray continually morning & night before you sleep; Read the Word of God every Day, & beg of him to open your Heart as he did the Heart of Lydia,[5] that you may attend unto his Word, & lay up ye Word preacht & read in your Heart, Hide it there and that will keep you from Sinning against God. Labuor to get Grace & the Knowledge of Jesus Christ; Strive to Enter into the Strait Gate—Fear God & set him before your Eyes continually—When you are tempted to any Sin Say as Joseph did, How can I do this Wickedness & Sin against God?[6] and remember that Satan goeth about like a roaring Lion seeking whom he may Devour[7]—Flee all youthfull Lusts & Sins—Plead the Covenant with God tell him that he was the God of your Parents & Grand-Parents, and hath promised to be your God also; If you Seek him, he will be found of you, but if you forsake him he will cast you off forever—My Dear Child you may not sin as others do; God expects a great deal from you; He Hath bestowed abundance of mercy upon you; Therefore Let the Goodness of God lead you to Repentence, and the Love of God constrain you to love him again; Give that Life to him which he hath given you so often—That you may never forget those multiplied mercies, I will give you a catalogue of the most remarkable of them—God began to take you into his hands when you were but one Year & a half old; so willing was he to save you that he spared no Pains in trying you every way both by affliction & by Mercy—

Mercy 1. You were strangelly lame & quite lost the life of one leg, it was feared you would be a Cripple all your Days, but ye Lord wonderfully healed yu: O now Make use of all your Limbs & affections to run the Ways of Gods Commandments—

Mercy 2. You quickly after fell into a Tub of Water, & was brought in for dead, No motion or Life appearing for a considerable while: The Lord that is never weary of shewing Mercy Spared you then, O Bath your Soul in his Love.

Mercy 3. You were suddenly in two hours time struck blind & so continued thirty Hours, & by Degrees God opened your Eyes again, O beg of the Lord to open the Eyes of your Soul as he did the Eyes of Saul after he was blind

Mercy 4. You fell into our Well head foremost & none was by but your little Brothr Samuel (which I hope is gone to Heaven[8]). He could not help you, but God did help & save you, O Beg washing in the Blood of Christ

Mercy 5. You were in ye Street at Play, & there a Cart went over your Thigh; The Cart was full of Green wood & Iron bound wheels; and yet all your Bones may say who is God like unto Thee, Not one of them was broken

Mercy 6. You had a violent burning ffever which brought you almost to the Grave—O Love the great Physician that then healed your Body, Pray to him to heal your Soul

Mercy 7. You had another ffit of sickness which threatened your Life, but ye Lord heard Prayer for you; O that ye Lord would help you to see the Sickness of your Soul & heal & cure that

Mercy 8. You were most violently seized wth ye Bladder in the Throat;[9] of this your Bror Saml died, and many Scores of Children more, & God spared you; O Consider for what this distinguishing mercy was yours—You had Six Deliverances from Death by that Distemper; Thus the Lord delivd you out of 6 Troubles & out of 7 in two Years space; O my child let that Breath which God threatened to stop so often by that Distemper be spent in Praising ye God of yr mercies

Mercy 9. You remember how near you was to Death by the Hunt & ffall from a tree; There was but a hands breadth betwixt you & Death then, O the Goodness & Long Suffering of God;

Mercy 10 Dont forget how God saved you from Drowning at Barnstable—Render unto the Lord according to all the Benefits which he hath done unto you. Let not all ye Preservations be but a Reservation for further Wrath—My Son give God your Body & Soul affections & Desires—Resolve you will be his & for no other—Remember Joseph Jacobs youngest son but one; how his afflictions were all for his Souls Good—God hath waited on you, turn to him now lest when he comes again with another Sickness or Danger he will not spare you; and then what will become of Thee, My Dear Child; Pray & Ply the Throne of Grace for your Own Soul & for all Your Relations. Carry well to those with whom you live, Chuse good Companions, Hate Sin and Sinners, & Love God & Jesus Christ; This is the Prayer & Desire of Your loving Mother

Joanna Cotton

Keep you this Letter safe, & read it often, & Labour to get Good by it, or twill rise up in Judgemt against you

Josiah Cotton, Manuscript "Account of the Cotton Family," Houghton Library, Harvard University

1. Josiah Cotton (1680–1756) was John and Joanna's tenth child. Josiah was sent to Ichabod Wiswall, the minister in Duxbury, to learn Latin and to begin his formal schooling. Before beginning at Harvard in 1694, Josiah also studied with Jonathan Russell, the minister in Barnstable, and with Boston schoolmasters Joseph Dassert and Peter Burr. He was in Barnstable with Russell when he received this letter. John Langdon Sibley, *Biographical Sketches of Graduates of Harvard University, In Cambridge, Massachusetts* (Boston, 1873–) (hereafter *Sibley's Harvard Graduates*), 4:398-402.
2. In his manuscript account, Josiah Cotton introduced his transcription of his mother's letter: "I have many Letters of my Mothers full of kind Expressions & good advice; Three or four of which I shall transcribe—The first I receivd at Barnstable, being yn 12 years old."
3. Prov. 8:17: "I love them that love me; and those that seek me early shall find me."
4. Eccles. 11:10: "Therefore remove sorrow from thy heart, and put away evil from thy flesh: for childhood and youth *are* vanity."
5. Acts 16:14: "And a certain woman named Lydia, a seller of purple, of the city of Thyatira, which worshipped God, heard *us*: whose heart the Lord opened, that she attended unto the things which were spoken of Paul."
6. Gen. 39:9: "*There is* none greater in this house than I; neither hath he kept back any thing from me but thee, because thou *art* his wife: how then can I do this great wickedness, and sin against God?"
7. 1 Pet. 5:8: "Be sober, be vigilant; because your adversary the devil, as a roaring lion, walketh about, seeking whom he may devour:"
8. Samuel Cotton was born on 10 February 1678 and died on 23 December 1682.
9. Probably scarlet fever, which was identified in 1675 but was often mistaken for smallpox or measles. The symptoms include sore throat and fever, a rash and "the characteristic strawberry color of the throat and tongue." When severe, scarlet fever was usually fatal. John Duffy, *Epidemics in Colonial America* (Baton Rouge, La., 1953), 129-30.

To Rowland Cotton, 20 February 1692[1]

Plymouth, February 20, 1690/91

Dear Son,

This is my third epistle[2] to you this week. I hope all may fetch from you what news Mr. R hath in his letters, and what is in Mr Wiswall's last to the governour by Mr. Prince. Pray speak to Mr. Russell and the governour, if you see them at lecture next week, and let them give their judgment what answer to give in that clause to Mr Dummer's letter concerning the ordering of the contribution to each town. I suppose an equal division betwixt the two towns may give best satisfaction. After that lecture hasten those letters to me, for others need to see them. J Howland and J Nelson carried your mother briskly to Boston on Monday; they were at Roxbury by sunset. On Tuesday, John Allyn and a son of Capt. Bradbury's brought her a letter from son

Allyn,[3] signifying all (especially Betty[4]) were well on Monday morning, waiting and longing for her coming. Their horses they left at Winnesimmitt:[5] Thursday morning they designed thence to Ipswich, and this day to Salisbury, and the weather is very comfortable for their purpose. They brought news, that just before their coming from home they heard that (the particular place J.H. and J.N. who returned hither on Wednesday, cannot tell) there were seen tracks of snow-shoes of some hundreds of Indians, which hath occasioned those eastern parts already to run into garrisons. They say, Boston town hath not been so healthful these diverse years as just now it is. Old Capt. and Deacon Capen[6] died of the small pox at Dorchester this week. Mr Stoughton hath £600 from the corporation;[7] we may no doubt easily to have our salaries now. I have written to him by J. Morton who yet waits for fair wind. William Bret[8] hath sent you 15 pounds of hay seed, and a letter with it for 15 shillings: if you will order its conveyance to you, you may have it: we received it but yesterday. I had another letter from Boston, part of which I transcribe, because I expect not to see you quickly.

"I think I wrote you lately an easy word or two about a New England gentleman, lately returned to us from the other side of the water. My design (as well as the design of the gentleman in England, who enabled me so to write) was to prevent some intemperances, which I feared among ourselves; but I wish the word unwritten, for I can assure you, the curse, *Let him that is unjust be unjust still*, is dreadfully upon that person, and poor New England owes nothing to him but prayers to be delivered from his machinations; Nor would have I you too far trust the character I give of * for it may be said about the men of his way, *The best of them is a briar*.

"If you will take my opinion about your affairs, it will be useless to send your good governour to England. Sir Henry Ashurst (not to mention anybody else) will be more able to bring noble persons into your interests, than any one that can goe from hence; and half the money necessary to bear the charges of an agent from hence, would make Sir Henry capable of doing ten times the service for you. Besides, it will be a desperate thing for the old gentleman to run the hazard of being carried into France. The king hath ordered our charter to be drawn up, which was done accordingly, and he used so particular a conduct for the diverting of the intrigues our enemies might use to defeat his kind purposes for us, that we have all the assurance in the world, nothing but a miraculous and prodigous dispensation of the sovereign God can cause us to miss of it. Mr. D. never had opportunity to know what steps were taken for us, and the stories he tells about those things are but a branch of his designs to distract, enfeeble and affrighten his country, whom, I doubt, he has not yet forgiven. My father[9] obtained an order from the king to Sir G. Treby, the attorney general, and Sir J Somers, the solicitor general, and another eminent lawyer, to pass their judgment upon the validity of the Connecticut charter, and they gave it in, *That the charter was as good as ever it was, and the government there should proceed upon it*. This is the instrument now sent over to them, and I have newly transmitted it. If the Tories won't be quiet, they shall quickly see some things in print, which they will be ashamed of. As soon as my newspapers all come into my hands, I hope to send you a large parcel of them:" Haecille.[10]

Did I not repose great confidence in you, I would not thus write to you; but what you impart you will do it wisely, and not expose me or my intimate friend. The Lord bless you in your work, and make you grow daily more and more like J.A. Prepare a choice letter to thank your cousin Mather. I have sent to him by J. Morton, for your great book. His wife is abroad; his child hath had the smallpox and is almost well. Your sister and brother salute you; my love to you, etc.,

I am your Loving father

John Cotton

Your brother John hath preached two or three Sabbaths at the Bank.[11] Your mother so writes to me, and no more but he and his are well.[12]

Transciption from MHS Collections, 3rd ser., 1 (1825): 117-20. Addressed, "These for Mr. Rowland Cotton, Preacher of the Gospel at Sandwich."

---

1. The printed version of this letter suggests that it was written on 20 February 1690/1. The events Cotton describes in the letter indicate that it was written on 20 February 1691/2, so we have revised the date.
2. The other two are not found.
3. James Alling, Cotton's son-in-law.
4. Betty may have been awaiting Mary, born on 10 April 1692; see n. 1, above.
5. Modern-day Chelsea in Suffolk County, translated as "Swamp Hill." R. A. Douglas-Lithgow, *Dictionary of American-Indian Place and Proper Names in New England* (Salem, 1909), 179.
6. John Capen (1613–1692) emigrated to Dorchester and became a freeman in 1634. He served as an artillery company captain, deacon and representative from Dorchester. He died on 6 April 1692. His death date confirms the revised date. Savage, *Genealogical Dictionary*, 1:333.
7. The "corporation" refers to the Society for the Propagation of the Gospel, for which both Rowland and John worked.
8. William Brett (d. 1713) was the son of Cotton's friend, Elder William Brett of Bridgewater (see the letter of 6 March 1683). The younger William also served as deacon to the Bridgewater church. Savage, *Genealogical Dictionary*, 1:243.
9. This suggests that this letter was written by Cotton Mather, describing his father's work in London for the Massachusetts charter.
10. "Easily."
11. The "Bank" refers to the Strawberry Bank section of Portsmouth, in modern-day New Hampshire.
12. Written in the margin.

From Samuel Sewall, 22 February 1692

Boston; Febr. 22. 1691/2

Revrd Sir,

Yours of ye 15th Instt came to my hand the 18th following.[1] Doubtless your Remembrance of our [distressed?] friends at the Eastward,[2] will be a sacrifice very acceptable to God. When you please to send me the Money, I shall wait an opportunity for laying it out to ye best advantage of those to whom you shall order it. York is now in Extremity,[3] & ought to be chiefy regarded so far as I know. We begin to think long of [Weare?], be sure Mris Maccarty does. My Books are in him, when they come, you shall have ye refusal of [...] Major Hutchinson took his journey towards Portsmouth last Friday,[4] as Commander in Chief of our Forces, and to regulat Garrisons; Probably in a little time we may have his Opinion what is best to be done as to any Prosecution of the Enemy. Whatever method be agreed on, there will be no subsisting for us, except the other Colonies doe thorowly join with us and methinks there should be no haesitancy. Nam tua res agitur, paries cum proximus[5] [...] Capt Willie[6] is gott to ye Isles of Shoals with fourty souldiers; wch ye Inhabitants petition'd for, to be maintain'd at yr own charge. Capt Byfield[7] is come to Town to dwell with us again, Boston Trade being to him the more Eligible Mount of hope. My service to your self & Mrs Cotton, I take Leave who am,

Sir your friend & servt

Sam Sewall.

Curwen Family Papers, American Antiquarian Society. Addressed "For the Reverend Mr. John Cotton at Plimouth." Endorsed "From Captaine Sewall February, 22: 1691." Staining along folds.

---

1. Not found.
2. According to Cotton's church records, on 7 February he "moved & exhorted to a liberall contribution... for the [l]ife & Redemption of the captives lately taken at Yorke, & other [ ] Easterne parts in distresse: The...congregation made a very liberall contribution for the ends above." Publications of the Colonial Society of Massachusetts *Collections* (hereafter *CSM*), 22 (Boston, 1920), 273. See Shubael Dummer's above letter of 13 January 1691 for similar donations.
3. On 6 February 1692 French-allied Natives attacked York, and more than 160 settlers, including Shubael Dummer, were either killed or taken captive as they tried to reach one of the four fortified houses in the town. In deference to Benjamin Church's release of some Native women and children at Pejepscot in 1690, the Indians agreed to release the same number of English. *Colonial Wars of North America, 1512–1763: An Encyclopedia,* ed. Alan Gallay (New York, 1996), 812-13.
4. Maj. Elisha Hutchinson was made general commander of English forces in February 1692. Cotton Mather, *Decennium Luctuosum* (Boston, 1699) in *Narratives of the Indian Wars, 1675–1699,* ed. Charles Lincoln (New York, 1913), 227.

5. "For your business is attended to, when up against a wall."

6. Possibly Capt. Simon Willard (1678–1731), who had commanded Fort Loyal at Falmouth, Maine, in 1690, just prior to the French attack in May of that year. James Savage, *A Genealogical Dictionary of the First Settlers of New England,* 4 vols. (1860–62; facsimile reprint, Baltimore, Md., 1990), 4:555; Samuel Adams Drake, *The Border Wars of New England* (New York, 1897), 49. Note that Savage lists several other Willey men, as well.

7. Nathaniel Byfield (1653–1733) of Bristol served on the Plymouth Colony Council of War beginning in 1689. Benjamin Church, *The History of the Eastern Expeditions* (Boston, 1867), 40.

From Samuel Sewall, 11 July 1692

Boston; July, 11th. 1692.

Honrd Sir,

These are to inform you that the late Report we had concerning Wells as if that place were destroy'd is altogether a Mistake,[1] and that place is entirely well. It seems They had been clearing some Brush for their security which was laid in a heap & burn'd; and probably that was ye fire mistaken by the nocturnal Post, for Garrisons consum'd. The Thanksgiving will be kept here & in the neighbouring Towns I thought good to signify thus much to you, hoping it may be some Antidote against what I mention'd to Major Bradford[2] at ye White Horse[3] just before his going out of Town. The Govr attended by mr. Moodey &c is going to Kennebeck to design a place for setting a Fort,[4] & other prosecution of the war. We are well. service to your self & Mrs Cotton. Sir

your friend & Servt

Sam Sewall.

Curwen Family Papers, American Antiquarian Society. Addressed "To the Reverend Mr Jno Cotton at Plimouth." Endorsed "From Captaine sewall July, 11: 1692."

---

1. Wells was "in a practical sense the permanent eastern frontier of New England between 1690 and 1713." Remote from Boston, Wells suffered in both King Philip's War and King William's War. Allied French and Abnaki forces twice tried to attack the fortified village, in 1691 and in June 1692. Sewall's fears about Wells were, therefore, quite reasonable, albeit overstated. Wells was again attacked in August 1703 but remained inhabited and fortified. Gallay, *Colonial Wars of North America,* 792; Cotton Mather, *Decennium Luctuosum,* 232-40.

2. Maj. William Bradford.

3. Probably the White Horse Tavern.

4. Sewall was referring to the construction of Fort William Henry (Pemaquid, Maine), which Gov. William Phips began in 1692. Rev. Joshua Moodey, Thomas Danforth, Major William Vaughan and William Brattle accompanied Phips on his initial journey to Pemaquid to scout sites for the fort. The Crown pledged £20,000 to build "a menacing stone tower 29 feet high" above six-foot-thick walls. Protected by eighteen cannon, the fort was impressive. Gallay, *Colonial Wars of North America,* 348-49.

From Cotton Mather, 5 August 1692

BOSTON. AUGT. 5. 1692.

REVEREND S^R^,

O^r^ Good God is working of Miracles. Five Witches were lately Executed,[1] impudently demanding of God a Miraculous Vindicacion of their Innocency. Immediately upon this, O^r^ God Miraculously sent in Five Andover Witches[2] who made a most ample, surprising amazing Confession of all their Villanies and declared ye five newly Executed to have been of their company; discovering many more but all agreeing in Burroughs being their Ringleader,[3] who I suppose this Day receives his Trial, at Salem whither a Vast Concourse of people is gone; My Father, this morning among ye Rest. Since those, there have come in other Confessors; yea, they come in daily. About this prodigious matter my Soul has been Refreshed wth some little short of Miraculous Answers of prayer; wch are not to bee written; but they comfort mee wth prospect of an hopeful Issue.

The whole Town yesterday turned ye Lecture into a Fast, kept in o^r^ meeting house; God give a good Return. But on ye morning wee were Entertained wth ye horrible Tidings of ye Late Earthquake at Jamaica,[4] on ye 7th of June Last. When, on a fair Day, ye sea suddenly swell'd, & ye Earth shook & broke in many places; and in a Minutes time, ye Rich Town of Port-Royal, ye Tyrus of ye whole English America, but a very Sodom for Wickedness, was immediately swallow'd up, and ye sea came Rolling over ye Town. No Less than seventeen hundred souls of that one Town, are missing. besides other Incredible Devastacons all over ye Island, where Houses are Demolished, Mountains overturned, Rocks Rent and all manner of Destruction inflicted. The N.C.[5] Minister there scap'd wonderfully wth his Life. Some of o^r^ poor N.E. people are Lost on ye Ruines, and others have their Bones broke. Forty Vessels were sunk, - namely all whose Cables did not break but no N.E. ones. Behold, an Accident Speaking to all o^r^ English America. I Live in pains, & want your prayers. Bestow y^m^ dear S^r^, on

Your

C. Mather

What a filthy stir do they keep at Tauton[6] about their military Affayrs. Whereof You and I bear most of ye blame. be it Reasonable?

Mather Family Papers, American Antiquarian Society. Addressed "For the Reverend Mr John Cotton, Minister of ye Gospel in Plymouth" Endorsed "Cotton Mather 5: 1692:"

---

1. Sarah Good, Rebecca Nurse, Susannah Martin, Elizabeth How and Sarah Wild were tried and convicted on 29 June 1692 and executed by hanging on 19 July. *Witch-hunting in Seventeenth Century New England,* ed. David D. Hall (Boston, 1991), 280.

2. Between 15 July and 29 September 1692, more than forty Andover villagers were accused of witchcraft. Many confessed because of increasing pressure from family members: confessing witches survived, while accused witches who protested their innocence were executed. For the eventual recant of some of these "confessing" witches from Andover, see Upham, Charles W., *Salem Witchcraft, With an Account of Salem Village and a History of Opinions on Witchcraft and Kindred Spirits,* 2 vols. (Boston, 1867), 2:402-6. For the increasing problem of "confession" during the witch-hunt, see Bernard Rosenthal, *Salem Story* (New York, 1993), 42-45, 151-52.

3. George Burroughs, a former minister in Salem, was brought back from his new post in Maine to stand trial in early August. Found guilty, he was executed along with Martha Carrier, George Jacobs, John Proctor and John Willard on 19 August 1692. For Burroughs's role in the witchcraft trials, see Mary Beth Norton, *In the Devil's Snare: The Salem Witchcraft Crisis of 1692* (New York, 2002), 245-51.

4. The earthquake in Jamaica on 7 June 1692, destroyed buildings across the island but effectively leveled Port Royal: "within three minutes plunged half the town to the bottom of the harbor." Hundreds of people died, either drowned or buried alive in their homes, and the death toll grew during the rolling aftershocks that followed. Disease followed and added further to the numbers who died. Ministers naturally interpreted the tragedy as a payment for sinfulness, and several pamphlets were published in London that both detailed the horror and interpreted its meaning. Richard S. Dunn, *Sugar and Slaves: The Rise of the Planter Class in the English West Indies, 1624–1713* (Chapel Hill, N.C., 1972), 186-87.

5. Nonconformist.

6. Mather is probably referring to continued dissension about paying for King William's War and about who had been appointed to command local militias. Taunton was so divided over the matter of military leadership that in April 1690 the General Court of Plymouth voted to allow Taunton's men to sign up under either Capt. George Macey or Capt. Thomas Leonard, "in order to a present settlement of the militia...and for composing the uncomfortable differences that have been and yet continue there." Nathaniel B. Shurtleff, ed., *Records of the Colony of New Plymouth in New England* (Boston, 1855–61) (hereafter *PCR*), 6:237. Even this resolution angered many Taunton residents; see Walter Deane et al. to Hinckley (of 7 April 1690) and John Walley to Hinckley (of 16 April 1690), "The Hinckley Papers," Massachusetts Historical Society *Collections,* 4th ser., 5 (Boston, 1861), 234-38, 239-42.

From Henry Dering,[1] 20 AUGUST 1692

BOSTON AUG^{0}: 20TH: 1692

REV^{D}: S^{R}:

have yo^{rs} of ye 15 Instant,[2]—your son hath your [coat], —he is well and is as good a boy as most, I am greatly taken with him—

News—3 mast ships & a frigget come to Piscattaqua—& a Brigganteen to Boston—Writeings & printing declare, a hellish plott to destroy King W^{m} in fflanders, & ye Queen in England but discovered; Severall Lords Spirrituall & temporall in ye Tower[3] & other Prisons & the Parliam^{t}: to sett ye 14th June last, & these ships came from ye West the 15th day—the K: of ff Knowing y^{t} we had but 30: men of warr towards ye West sent out his fleet to fight us where ever they mett us—they ca[me] somthing neer us but ye wind comeing East, kept them from y^{t} p^{te} of our fleet, & brought ye rest of our fleet to y^{m} of ours wth ye Duch—& y^{n} we took the King of ffrances ord^{rs} to his fleet to return

so the ffrench Admirall came boldly on our Admirall Russell to the distance of about 3/4 of Musquet Shott & y^{n} Ingaged & from abt 11 a clock untill foure fitt briskly—& y^{n} being calme—towed away & we psued—y^{e}: ffrench have lost 23 of their capitall ships being burnt & sunck—the Rest beaten by a less quantity of our Ships then theirs[4] & had there been faire cleer weather its like we had destroyed them all for one of our Squadrons & the Duch did little by reason of ye foog & wind they were left on the ffr: coast while y^{m} y^{t} did fight came home & fitted, & are gon to them againe—have burnt 20: of their transport ships—K: James had many Irish & ffrench Ready to land In England, if encouraged—we & ye Duch have 800 Transport Ships ready

news from Newfound Land a week later, saith th[at?] King W^{m} hath Routed ye King of ffrances Armies, and taken 3 or 4 towns & goes on prosperously—& that our transpor Ships have Landed 2200 Soldiers in ffrance—y^{t} ye King of ffr is returned from his armie to Parris—sick of the gout,[5] y^{t} ye Emperour hath Slayn 10000 turks & taken 12000: more & a great deale more news there is but I Referr you to y^{m} y^{t} come hence—our Great gunns was fired for ye great Good news from England to manifest our Joy & thanks for Gods goodness to us therein—

no news yet from o^{r} Govr of w^{t} he hath Done

Mr John Usher come Lt Govr of New Hampshire[6]

Mr Burroughs & 4 more hanged yesterday; but did not Confess

more Witches brought in—& severall do Confess[7]

no Indians seen ab^{t} Wells since o^{r} Govr: went Eastward; he hath Sent out an armie, & is building a fourt:[8] Two Captives y^{t} were taken at Senectady,[9] run from ye ffr: Indians at Morriall,[10] say y^{t} ye Mohauks so annoy ye farmers y^{t} they dare not attend their Harvest—& had it not been for fish y[t] they did cetch, they must have deserted y[e] place & y[t] y[e] Senica Indians have killed 61 ffrench & ffr: Indians by an ambiscade[11]

since the above here is a vessel from o[r] Gov[r]. he landed at Casco bay but is now a building a fort at Pemmiquid & hath sent 400 Soldiers to meet with y[e] Enemie Eastwards

Curwen Family Papers, American Antiquarian Society. Torn along right margin.

---

1. The writer of this letter is most likely Henry Dering (1639–1717), who was a shopkeeper in Boston. Savage, *Genealogical Dictionary*, 2:41.
2. Not found.
3. Apparently there was a plot hatched by the French sieur de Grandval to assassinate William at his headquarters. The scheme was discovered in May 1692, and since Louis XIV and James II were both implicated, the news caused a sensation and many rumors. Stephen B. Baxter, *Willliam III & the Defense of European Liberty, 1650–1702* (New York, 1966), 301.
4. Admiral Edward Russell, Earl of Oxford (1653–1727), took command of the fleet in December 1690. He considered betraying King William and so avoided battle with the French until 1692. On 19 May 1692, the Anglo-Dutch fleet shattered a smaller French force near Cape Barfleur. *Dictionary of National Biography*, ed. Leslie Stephen and Sidney Lee, 63 vols. (London, 1885–1900) (hereafter *DNB*).
5. Some of this news was wishful thinking. Louis had indeed returned to Paris, but only after his armies had taken the city of Mons from the Protestants. William had been unable to raise the siege and had won no such smashing victories. Baxter, *William III*, 293-94, 303.
6. John Usher was a wealthy Boston merchant and bookseller who also served as the treasurer for the Dominion of New England and lieutenant governor of New Hampshire. *A History of the Book in America*, vol. 1, *The Colonial Book in the Atlantic World*, ed. Hugh Amory and David D. Hall (New York, 2000), 99.
7. See 5 August 1692.
8. See 11 July 1692.
9. The attack on Schenectady began during a fierce blizzard on 9 February 1690, when the residents left only snowmen as defenders of the pallisaded village, believing the weather to be their best protection. Sixty people were killed, twenty-seven were taken captive, and the survivors were left to flee twenty miles to Albany, with many dying en route. The raiding party returned to Montreal with all its captives, unharmed by the English-Mohawk forces pursuing them. An August 1690 letter from Peter Tillton to Massachusetts Governor Simon Bradstreet sought financial assistance for three escaped captives from the Schenectady raid, one of whom, John Webb, presented the letter to Bradstreet personally. Perhaps these were the same captives whom Dering described. Gallay, *Colonial Wars of North America*, 672-73; Tillton to Bradstreet, "The Hinckley Papers," 268-70.
10. Montreal.
11. This attack was probably in retaliation for the June 1687 French attack on the Seneca, in which several key Seneca villages were destroyed and the inhabitants were forced to flee. Although the Seneca had been French allies, that friendship had started to deteriorate in the late 1670s, and nearly twenty years of warfare between the Seneca and the French commenced in the 1680s. Gallay, *Colonial Wars of North America*, 684-86.

From Cotton Mather, 20 October 1692

Boston. Oct. 20. 1692.

My Kindest & my Dearest Uncle,

Your Thoughts for mee, I have alwayes prized; but I know not whether I ever wanted them so much as Now.

I now send You a Book, Written with as much Exercise of mind, as perhaps any thing, that Ever any pen of mine has meddled with. Pray Read it Critically, and Lett mee know whether you think, I have served, as you know I have designed therein to serve, God and my Generation.

There are fourteen Worthy Ministers, that have newly sett their Hands, unto a Book, now in ye press, Containing Cases of Conscience about Witchcrafts.[1] I did, in my conscience think, that as ye Humours of this people now run, such a Discourse going Alone would not only Enable o^r^ Witch-Advocates, very Learnedly to Cavil & Nibble at ye Late proceedings against ye Witches, considered in parcels, while things as they lay in Bulk, with their whole Dependences, were not exposed; but also everlastingly stiffle any further proceedings of Justice, & more than so, produce a public & open contest with ye Judges, who would (tho' beyond ye Intention of ye Worthy Author & Subscribers) find themselves brought unto ye Bar before ye Rashest Mobile.

For such Causes, & for One more, I did with all ye modesty I could use, decline, setting my Hand unto ye Book: assigning this Reason, that I had already a Book in ye Press,[2] wch would sufficiently declare my opinion: and such a Book too, as had already passed the censure of ye Hand wch wrote what was then before us.

With what Sinful & Raging Asperity, I have been since Treated, I had rather Forgett than Relate. Altho' I challeng'd ye Fiercest of my Accusers, to find ye Thousandth part of One Wrong step taken by mee, in all these matters, Except it were my use of all Humble & sober Endeavrs, to prevent such a bloody Quarrel between Moses and Aaron, as would bee Bitterness in ye Latter End; no other Fault has yett been laid before mee. At last I have been driven to say, I will yet bee more vile![3] And in quoting Math. 5. 9.[4] I have concluded, So, I shall not want a Father!

Since ye Trial of these unworthy Treats, ye persons that have used them, have endeavored such Expressions of Sweetness toward mee, as may make mee satisfaction. But for ye great Slander wth wch they have now fill'd ye Countrey against mee, That I Run Against my own Father, & all the ministers in ye Countrey; meerly because I run Between y^m^, when they are like Mad Men Running Against one another; they can make mee no Reparation; However my God will!

God has marvellously Blessed my poor Endeavours, for ye preventing of some Outrage, wch my Warm Friends, have been Running into; and I know, that God will Bless my Little Book, for further benefit that way: tho' by ye moane of somebody or other, is [co--er?] abroad under unhappy Disadvantage [of?] prejudice among ye people. I don't yett Repent of one word, that I have Written, nor won't it may bee, till you tell mee that I should.

My friends have now happily gained a point, wch has been long wished for; even for mee to become Unconsidered. I confess, Things become every day more & more so Circumstanced, as if my Opportunities of serving my Neighbrs were after a sort Expiring; alas, that I have made no better an use of y^m, while I had 'em! I seem now, to have Little to Do, but to Dy: and ô blessed bee ye Free-Grace of God, by whose Help, I hope, I can do That!

I begin to have a fine easy Time of it. & now I can, you see, write Larger Letters, than I use to do. I grow tedious; and I shall count you so too, if you don't write mee sound Good & Comfortable Words, as soon as you can.

God preserve You, and all yours, from a Crafty, Busy, prevailing Divel. Farewell. And think on

Your honest Cousen,

C. Mather

Ms. 1459, Rare Book and Manuscripts, Boston Public Library. Addressed "For the Reverend Mr John Cotton, Plymouth." Endorsed "From my Cousen Mr Cotton Mather october, 20: 1692:."

---

1. In August 1692, disturbed by the spiraling witchcraft accusations in Danvers, Salem and Andover, an association of ministers in Cambridge asked Increase Mather to investigate the accepted rules of evidence for use in witchcraft trials. By late September, Mather had drafted *Cases of Conscience Concerning Evil Spirits,* signed by fourteen other ministers. Mather's tract condemned the use of spectral evidence, which had been the primary means of convicting most of the accused men and women. Michael G. Hall, *The Last American Puritan: Life of Increase Mather* (Middletown, Conn., 1988), 256-64.

2. Cotton Mather's defence of the trials and of spectral evidence, *Wonders of the Invisible World*, was published just before his father's condemnation of the court's use of evidence and was received badly by a public that had grown suspicious of the trials. Peter Hoffer, *The Devil's Disciples: Makers of the Witchcraft Trials* (Baltimore, Md., 1996), 184-85.

3. 2 Sam. 6:22: "And I will yet be more vile than thus, and will be base in mine own sight: and of the maidservants which thou hast spoken of, of them shall I be had in honour."

4. Matt. 5:9: "Blessed are the peacemakers: for they shall be called the children of God."

From Henry Dering, 28 January 1693

Boston Jan^{ry} 28th 1692

S^{r}:

have yours of the 27 ult:[1] cannot procure y^{t} history yet; your Son Allins[2] lre I sent by a safe hand,[3] but w^{n} m^{r} Modey came, he brought me no answer, have sett you [...] Josiah to writeing, have putt him upon writeing to you & hereinclosed is a lre of his & two more to yourselfe,[4] he hath gott a bottle of Alix^{r}: & shall endeavour to send it wn this comes; y^{m} two Shipps were not from England

have yo^{rs}: of ye 11th Instant. but ye man y^{t} brought it did not call for an answ[er] I gave yor: son, the seven shillings you ordered for Robert Orchard[5] & ye other [...]

we are now at Febry 2^{d} & have yours dated yesterday,[6] we sent some soldiers to Pemiquid y^{s} winter, & last weake Capt. Wing[7] came to Boston with some of his Soldiers y^{t} ye Govr promised to release, & say y^{t} Geo^{r}: Heskill is kill'd (& 4 more wounded & are like to do well) at a place 3 leagues beyond Pemiquid wheither they went to fetch wood & timber ye pticulers of wch I leave the bearer to Informe you. Last night came in one came yesterday from Piscattaqua & brings noe news of any Ind[ians] your mate need not feare ye welfare of yor. children Eastward

no lres at m^{r}. Elistons.—y^{m} in prison upon Suspition of witchc[raft] are to be tryed at CharslTown tomorrow[8]—have told ye bearer something to tell you by word of mouth. All our due respects to you & yours

Y^{r} friendly Servt

Henry Dering

Curwen Family Papers, American Antiquarian Society. Addressed "ffor the Reverend M^{r}: John Cotton Pastor of the Church In Plymth p a friend q.d.c." Endorsed "From Mr Dering February, 2: 1692" Torn along right and left margins.

---

1. Not found.
2. Cotton's daughter, Elizabeth, married James Alling (1657–1696, H.C. 1679), the minister of Salisbury, Massachusetts, in 1688. *Sibley's Harvard Graduates,* 3:173-74.
3. Not found.
4. Not found.
5. Robert Orchard was a Boston merchant who had been involved in some controversy with the Court of Admiralty in 1666 and complained against the colony to the king in 1682. He married Sarah Blish of Barnstable (b. 1641) in Boston before 1668. Savage, *Genealogical Dictionary,* 3:314; Almon Torrey, *New England Marriages Prior to 1700* (Baltimore, Md., 1865), 545.
6. Not found.

7. Captain John Wing served as one of the first commanders at the newly-constructed Fort William Henry (Pemaquid) and was one of three colonial representatives at the 1693 peace talks at the fort. Mather, *Decennium Luctuosum,* 240, 251.
8. After passing a new witchcraft law modeled on Jacobean statutes, the General Court no longer accepted spectral evidence in witchcraft cases. On 3 January, a court comprising William Stoughton, Thomas Danforth, John Richards, Wait Winthrop and Samuel Sewall began hearing thirty-one cases. Twenty-eight defendants were acquitted, three convicted. Hoffer, *Devil's Disciples,* 89-90.

From Josiah Rosseter, 16 March 1693

GILFORD MARCH THE 16 1692/3

MUCH RESPECTED BROTHER AND SISTER

I would Return hearty thanks for your often writing to us and am glad to heare of our cosens being well disposed of in marigg: to satisfaction & desire it may soe be and soe contended with them content in that Relation will be a help to cary through many defecultys: which the world is now full off: it is wt us and I doubte not but in some measure soe wt you a very defecult time to Live in the world god in his providens shortens all our out ward enjoyments the freuts of the Earth faile much and every thing we by: is soe extreame deare heard hard geting along: in the world: but the Lord knowes what is best for: us I desire we may Learn by all his dispensations we have had a sore aflicting time this winter by a Raging dissease[1] sent in amongst us which caryed away about twenty persons in about five wekes time most of them heads of famelys: I shall give you an acount of some of them and theyr sudent dying at least some of them mr John Leet:[2] was the first he lay sick about seven days he dyed the 25 day of november: the next was Samuell Bristow[3] he was taken: sick in the Evening and dyed the next night being the thirtyth of november as Lusty strong midleagead man as most in the towne: the first day of desember dyead old goodman cook:[4] and the 5th: of desember dyed daniell Everth[5] and the sixt of desember dyed thomas wright[6] who has bene our sheapeheard this twenty years he lay sick not above foure and twenty hours the 7 of desember dyed Joseph Clayes wife[7] the 10 of desember a lusty young maide old permorlyes daughter the 16 of desember John spiniges wife[8] the same day daniell bishops wife[9]—the 18th day and tahann hill[10] dyed and alsoe a child in the same house the 20 day of desember Thomas blackly[11] dyed the 21 day tabythah byshop widdow[12] dyed the same day a young garle dyed the 25 day dyed goodwife wright whose husband was newly dead[13] before the twenty eight day John evert[14] and John turner wife[15] both dyed thus weare we dayly imployed in burying the dead and tending the sick: for children had very generally though most moderately and but short the same day that those two Last persons dyed was a day of fasting and prayer in publick wt us: and that which was Remarkably taken notis of was that there had almost none scaped death: that had been heard taken wt this violent fevor: or but two persons in the towne of which one of them was my negor servant and one young man more in the town: all old dyed that had that putread feavor: and now at this day of fasting there Lay seven persons violently taken in the same way of those that dyed before and all of them scapead wt Life and soe the dispensation wavead offe from us againe and I [hope?] not wt out some fruites of it by a consederable stroke upon young persons Looking godward more than has been wt us of Late & that it might increase: and in all this mortality god has sparead our famely: hetherto: which we have great cause to be thankfull for: we have now Living five sons and thre daughters and my wife expeckes another: before may next:[16] the Lord fit us for soe greate a work: that we may endeavor to bring them up in the nurture and feare of the Lord your famely lessens and ours increases: I could willingly put one of ours under your's and sisters tuition if you weare of the same mind and we could abtaine it but we Live soe Remote from you yet Let us not faile of your prayers for us that god would direcke us and teach us to walk aRight before him in all our wayes I am discoraged about ever comeing to see you being crasy and weakely ever sinse my Long Lamenes being disinablead for heard travell or heard Labor: and under many defecoltyes and tryals I did atemt a vissit Last sumer but not finding my self well and fit for travell alone and meting wt noe sutable company it put a stop to my coming to you: but pray Let us heare as often from you as you have opertunyty and I hope we shall doe the same that the Remembranse of soe neare and deare a Relation may not be forrgoten: wt myne and my wives due Respeckes to you both and Love to all our Cosens our oldest children present due Respeckes to you we all desire to se you

we are yours to serve and comand in what we may.

Josiah Rosseter

my wife Returns hearty thanks for a small token Resevead from her deare sister: by the hand of will Jones his wife[17] Last sumer.

Curwen Family Papers, American Antiquarian Society. Addressed "for the Reverand mr: John Cottenn Pastor of the Church of Christ att Plimouth Q.D.C. for convoyans Leave this wt mr Coten mather pastor of a church at bostonn." Endorsed "From Brother Rosseter March, 16: 1693:" Several small tears along right margin.

---

1. It is unclear which disease was afflicting Guilford; it may have been scarlet fever.

2. John Leete (1639–1692), son of Governor William Leete, died 25 November 1692. Torrey, *New England Marriages*, 460; Alvan Talcott, *Families of Early Guilford, Connecticut* (Baltimore, Md., 1984), 767.

3. Samuel Bristow (1651–1692). Talcott, *Families of Early Guilford,* 147.
4. Thomas Cook (d. 1692) lived in Guilford by 1639. Talcott, *Families of Early Guilford,* 248.
5. Daniel Everth (Evarts) (1638–1692). Torrey, *New England Marriages,* 254.
6. See the note concerning his wife's death, below.
7. Joseph Clay's wife was Mary Lord Clay (d. 1692). Talcott, *Families of Early Guilford,* 209.
8. John Spinning's wife (d. 1692) was Deborah Bartlett Spinning (1668–1692). Talcott, *Families of Early Guilford,* 1110.
9. Daniel Bishop's wife was Hannah Bradley Bishop (d. 1692). Talcott, *Families of Early Guilford,* 77.
10. Tahay/Tahan Hill (1659–1692) was married to Hannah Parmelee in November 1688. Savage suggests that they had no children, but Rosseter described the death of a child in their house. Savage, *Genealogical Dictionary,* 2:420; Torrey, *New England Marriages,* 372.
11. Thomas Blachley (1666–1692) was the son of Aaron (1644–1699) and Mary Dodd Blachley (1647–1683) of Guilford. Talcott, *Families of Early Guilford,* 105-6.
12. Tabytha Wilkinson Bishop (d. 1692) was the widow of Stephen Bishop (d. 1690). Talcott, *Families of Early Guilford,* 76.
13. Thomas Wright (1660–1692) died on 6 December, and Sarah Benton Wright (1650–1692) died on 25 December. Torrey, *New England Marriages,* 843; Talcott, *Families of Early Guilford,* 47.
14. John Evert (1640–1692). Talcott, *Families of Early Guilford,* 390.
15. Joanna Benton Turner (1660–1692). Talcott, *Families of Early Guilford,* 1176.
16. The Rosseter children to whom Josiah referred are Elizabeth (b. 1679), Josiah (b. 1680), Timothy (b. 1683), Samuel (b. 1686), Jonathan (b. 1688), Nathaniel (b. 1689), Sarah (b. 1691), Patience (b. 1692) and Joanna, who was the expected baby, born on 23 April 1693. Aside from these nine children, the Rosseters lost four children in infancy by 1693. Four additional children followed Joanna's 1693 arrival, and all survived childhood. Savage, *Genealogical Dictionary,* 3:578.
17. Abigail Morse Everett Jones was William Jones's wife, and they lived in Guilford. Torrey, *New England Marriages,* 427.

To Increase Mather, 23 March 1693

Plymouth March, 23: 1693:

Reverend & Deare Brother

your desire to know the true state of Affaires among the Indians & the number of those that receive the Gospel I shall now satisfy as far as my time reaches:

The Indians I preach to at waweantick (& adjacent villages of sepecan & mattapoisett[1]) are 36: At Namassakett, Kehtiticutt, Assawamsitt,[2] Quehehqussit[3] 50; charles their Teacher At Kitteaumutt[4] & thereabout 47: There are at Acushnett,[5] Ponigansett[6] & Coxitt[7] 130 in two Assemblies, in which is a church of 24 members, 10 men & 14 woemen, one of their Teachers, John is lately dead: At Sakonett[8] are

240 in 4 Assemblies, amongest which is a church consisting of 21 members; 9 men & 12 woemen Daniel, Simon, George, Joslin are the 4 Teachers there: How & by whom these two churches were gathered I at present know not certainly, only I understand, some of the considerable Indians of Martha's Vineyard churches were principally active in laying those foundations:

At Mattakeesitt (alias Namassakeesitt[9]) the sicknesse hath these two yeares last past bin soe deadly that the utmost of men, woemen & young Adult ones exceeds not (I think) 20: The spetiall meanes of the unsuccessfullness of labours among the Indians hath bin the English selling liquors to them, thereby they have bin extreamly debaucht, but in these places espetially about Acushnett & Saconett there are considerable number that are sober & hopefull, About a fortnight since I had about 60 hearers at Namaskett 2 days since (notice being given thereoff at my desire) I had about 90 Hearers there some came above 20 miles from Acushnett some above 40 from Sakonet of good carriage, who used their Bibles, 3 or 4 wrote after me (my text was Isa: 55: 3:[10]) & they had a very ingenuous savour & knowledge of what was spoken [re:] hearing of the word, coming to christ, & the Life there promised, & the blessings of the Everlasting covenant, it was to me very affecting to see them speak soe satisfyingly about these things & therefore I promised to come to them at sakonett this summer neer 60 miles hence with Gods leave, & they promise I shall see the 240, if they dye not before; I long to see you, but cannot yet come; without any foolish boasting, set aside blessed Mr Eliot, I cannot believe any man did or doth take half the bodily paines I doe with them in all the travelling part of the yeare, 32 miles forward & backward & 30 & 26 are usually my longest days travell & 2 or 3 houres spent with them, which is many a weary step to the flesh, it spends horses, money & spirits more then a litle (as my friends know) but I have cheerfully & constantly attended the worke of God amongst them; & have long since resolved soe to doe as God shall continue my strength & opportunities, though all rewards from man should cease; I am much calld upon & this weeke more then ordinary by many of their Teachers & Rulers, & this day while Major Bradford was sitting with me, 8 or 10 of them came & desire Coates, & this yeare providence hath soe ordered that I have not received one to give them, I only satsify them with a promise, that if any thing doe come to me for them, I will faithfully give it them; About 20 yds are left at Sandwich, Mr Treat,[11] Mr Mayhew,[12] Mr Tupper[13] having taken all the rest of the 308 yds: Sir, I have given you as true an account of the numbers of Indians as I can possibly procure, & I believe there is very litle or noe defect therein, in the revolution of this summer I may probably have a more perfect account to give of the state of those that are more remote; I hope you have called upon Mr Treat Mr Mayhew my son at Sandwich[14] & Mr Tupper for such an account from them also, & then the Gentlemen concerned will see how to proportion what is for the Indians, At this season of the yeare I have opportunities of having greater Assemblies because of fishing, which I am unwilling to loose, my absence I hope need not hinder any conclusion of sending hither what my Indians desire & expect; I record every opportunity of my being with them & have done above these 20 yeares which will evince I have not neglected my trust, & also in my booke,[15] how every yard hath bin distributed & to whom, hereby providing things honest in the sight of men, I wish every one of us betrusted in this way might yearly give an account of what we doe herein to those that betrust us: I seale not the enclosed to the Gentleman, that you may see I Judge the whole, desiring you to seale it & convey it: If you meet before I come (as I hope you may) you may be assured by these lines of my right to the 10 pd, if labour merit from man: Let me have your prayers that God would strengthen & blesse me in the worke; my son Revd: I know hath taken great paines to fit himselfe for this service, & laid out much money to learne the Language, & hath as yet only made & written sermons for the Indian Teachers to translate & deliver to them, his memory is not soe as with some others & therefore hitherto he hath not vocally preacht to them, but in truth he hath bin & is very conscientious in his endeavours about it, & if he finde in a litle farther triall, God denyes ability he will faithfully tell it you, but therefore for the yeare past I presume there will be noe scruple: other things I mix not with these lines,

I am your Affectionate Brother

John Cotton

Boston University Special Collections. Addressed "These for the truly Reverend, Mr Increase Mather Teacher of a church in Boston." Endorsed "March 23d 1693 Mr. Cottons Leter Number of the Indians he preached to 523 Indians." In the left margin of the first page is a column of numbers: 36, 47, 50, 130, 240, and 20, with the total 523 underneath.

---

1. Weweantic is an area in modern-day Wareham; Sippican is just to the west, in Marion, and Mattapoisett corresponds to the modern-day village of the same name, all on Buzzards Bay. Cotton probably made a circuit of preaching in these settlements.
2. All of these places are in modern-day Middleborough and Lakeville; see 14 September 1674.
3. Location is not clear.
4. An area southward from modern-day Manomet, in Plymouth, to Buzzards Bay.
5. An area at the head of today's Acushnet River in southeastern Massachusetts.
6. Apponagansett is a coastal area in South Dartmouth, Massachusetts.
7. In today's Westport, Massachusetts.
8. Today's Little Compton, Rhode Island.
9. Mattakeesitt/Namaaskeesitt is an area near the Duxbury/Pembroke boundary in Massachusetts.
10. Isa. 55:3: "Incline your ear, and come unto me: hear, and your soul shall live; and I will make an everlasting covenant with you, *even* the sure mercies of David."

11. Samuel Treat (1648–1717, H.C. 1669), minister in Eastham. Frederick Lewis Weis, *The Colonial Clergy and the Colonial Churches of New England* (Baltimore, Md., 1936), 208.

12. Experience Mayhew (1673–1758, H.C. 1720), son of Thomas Mayhew, minister on Martha's Vineyard. Weis, *Colonial Clergy,* 138.

13. Capt. Thomas Tupper Jr. (1638–1706). Tupper was the settled minister of Indian Church at Herring Pond in Sandwich from 1676 to 1706 and replaced his father, who had served the church from 1658 to 1676. Along with his work for the Society for the Propagation of the Gospel, Tupper served as a member of the Council of War, a town clerk, a selectman and deputy to the General Court from Sandwich. He was well connected in missionary circles as the son of Thomas Tupper Sr. and the husband of Martha Mayhew of Martha's Vineyard's missionary family. Cotton seems to have been suggesting that Tupper was resisting Rowland Cotton's ordination in Sandwich. R. A. Lovell, *Sandwich: A Cape Cod Town*, (Sandwich, Mass., 1984), 68, 191; Weis, *Colonial Clergy,* 270, 41.

14. Rowland Cotton.

15. Reference to Cotton's Native diary. See "Missionary Journal of John Cotton Jr., 1666–1678," ed. Len Travers, *Proceedings of the Massachusetts Historical Society* 109 (1998): 52-101.

From Henry Dering, 12 August 1693

Boston Aug° 12th 1693

Worthy Sr:

have yors: of 9 Instant,[1] shall send Majr Saltonstalls lre to Salem for conveyance[2] (if meet not wth: a fitt messenger hence) as did ye other two, & 3 dayes since sent him word of it,

no lettle Joy its hoped will come by peace with the Indians, wch I am ready to think wilbe now concluded honourably by ye Govr. who tooke mr Secretary with him & enough to make a Councill[3]—mr Alden[4] is lately come in & brought very good wheat from Menus—And 4 of ye men yt ye ffrench vessel of 16 gunns had this Spring taken at ye Eastward (& more men in 2 vessells), they say yt. ys. ffrench man lay 3 weekes in St. John River[5] with hi[s top] mast struck and landed there 120 barrells powder & above 2Ø of [....] chests of armes & 8 great Gunns for their fort wch is 30 leagues up the [....] years provision wth many fine coates for ye Indians all directly from ffrance, But its said yt Govr: Vilboons[6] Souldiers are all runn to Canada but 2.[7]/

The Sickness is mostly at ye North end of ye Towne; But not so many die as wn ye Souldiers came from Canada.[8] Severall Towns about Boston are [...] to be more Sicklier yn here in proportion. mr Burr teaches lattin in the schoole where mr Dorsett did.[9] all due respects to yorselfe & good mrs: Cotton

yors &c

Henry Dering

m^r^ Lutt of Nubery[10] hath promised to carry the things to Salisbury—/.
Casteen[11] hath by m^r^ Alden taken his oath to be [fore?] King W^m^ & Queen Mary, & saith he will act for us

Curwen Family Papers, American Antiquarian Society. Addressed "To the Reve^rnd^: m^r^ John Cotton In Plym^o^: These ddd Q.D.C." Endorsed "Mr Dering August, 12: 1693:" Several small holes.

---

1. Not found.
2. Not found.
3. Eastern Natives increasingly worried about winning the war, especially after hearing rumors that the Mohawks might join with the English forces. In August 1693, thirteen Abenaki sagamores attended peace councils at Fort William Henry. The English received generous concessions from them: "They agreed to submit to the English crown, restore captives, resume trade with the English, and to refrain from intercourse with the French." While this calm lasted only until the devastating summer raids in 1694, some Native leaders began to press for a more lasting peace. Gallay, *Colonial Wars of North America,* 349-50.
4. John Alden Jr. (1625–1702), son of the *Mayflower* passenger, was empowered by both the Andros government and the interim government that followed to carry out both official business and trade along the coast of northern New England. He frequently supplied northern outposts with men and munitions and often negotiated prisoner exchanges with the French. Mary Beth Norton implies that Alden's activities in Acadia and northern New England were sometimes unscrupulous and even traitorous. For more on Alden, see n. 7 below. Norton, *In the Devil's Snare,* 186-93.
5. The French helped maintain their colony in North America with provisions that they sent each spring. English forces increasingly tried to intercept these deliveries. For example, in 1695 Captain Eames was dispatched from Boston to disrupt the arrival of French stores; when he encountered a larger French fleet than he expected, he and his troops retreated after a brief conflict. The following year, the English tried again with a larger force but again retreated. Thomas Hutchinson, *The History of the Colony and Province of Massachusetts-Bay,* ed. Lawrence Mayo (Cambridge, Mass., 1936), 68-69.
6. Joseph Robineau de Villebon (1655–1700) was a native-born Acadian who was educated in France and first served in the French Army on the Continent. Returning to Quebec in 1681, Villebon began a rise to power, eventually serving as governor of New France, the official representative of the French king in North America. *Dictionary of Canadian Biography* (Toronto, 1966), 1:576-78.
7. Dering was probably referring to a botched prisoner exchange in May 1692. In 1691, John Alden's ship was captured by the French, and Alden, his son, Boston merchant John Nelson and the new governor of Acadia, Edward Tyng, were all captured. Alden was sent on parole to Boston to request the release of thirty French soldiers captured at Port Royal by William Phips in 1690. When Alden returned in May 1692, bringing just six soldiers to offer in exchange for his son, Nelson and Col. Tyng, the French governor, Villebon, sent two soldiers to meet him. Alden released the six soldiers on an island and abducted the two Frenchmen. Angry at what he considered to be poor military conduct, Villebon sent Alden's son and Col. Tyng to France. Nelson was first imprisoned in Quebec and later sent to Paris; he remained captive in France until late 1695, and then under bond to France until late 1697. Nelson did not return to Boston until the summer of 1698, while Tyng died in prison in France. Historian Louise Breen suggests that Alden's "greed" led to the failure of this prisoner exchange. *Dictionary of Canadian Biography,* 2:14-15; Hutchinson, *History of Massachusetts Bay*, 1:378-80; "Letter of John Nelson," Massachusetts Historical Society *Collections,* 3d ser., 1 (Boston, 1866), 196; *Diary of Samuel Sewall,* M. Halsey Thomas ed. (New York, 1973), 1:282-83; Louise Breen, *Transgressing the Bounds: Subversive*

Enterprises among the Puritan Elite in Massachusetts, 1630–1692* (New York, 2001), 200-206; Richard R. Johnson, *John Nelson, Merchant Adventurer: A Life Between Empires* (New York, 1991), 70-107.

8. Smallpox continued to afflict New Englanders, even when the numbers infected did not reach epidemic proportions. In 1690, 1692 and 1693, many New England towns reported outbreaks. For the epidemic among New England soldiers returning from New France in 1689–1690, see the letter of 5 August 1690. Duffy, *Epidemics in Colonial America,* 48-49.

9. Joseph Dassett (1666–1693, H.C. 1687) was a schoolmaster in Boston until his death. Peter Burr (1668–1724, H.C. 1690) took over Dassett's school until 1699, when he moved to Fairfield, Connecticut. He later served as deputy, Speaker of the House, and chief judge of the Superior Court. *Sibley's Harvard Graduates,* 3:389; 4:33-35.

10. Probably Henry Lunt of Newbury (1653–1709) or perhaps Henry Lunt (1669–1725), also of Newbury. Savage, *Genealogical Dictionary,* 3:131; Torrey, *New England Marriages,* 479.

11. Baron de Castin, Jean Vincent d'Abbadie (1652–1707), was born in France and began his military career in Quebec at the age of thirteen; he eventually married an Abenaki woman, the daughter of Chief Madockawando. D'Abbadie perfectly represents the multiple allegiances of many Acadians—he believed himself fully French and fully Abenaki but continued to trade with New England even while France and England were at war along the Acadian border. In 1690, he commanded the attack on Casco, and Gov. Phips felt that he was enough of a threat to warrant hiring French deserters to try to assassinate him in 1692. His headquarters on Penobscot Bay was uncomfortably close to New England's northern fort at Pemaquid. In this letter, Dering implied that d'Abbadie swore allegiance to the English Crown at John Alden's urging. An earlier attempt to bring d'Abbadie to the English side had failed; he was probably only pledging friendship and trade, something he had always enjoyed with New England merchants. In 1696, d'Abbadie commanded combined Native and French forces in the attack on Fort William Henry. *Dictionary of Canadian Biography*, 2:4-7, 14-15.

Joanna and John Cotton to Josiah Cotton, 2 DECEMBER 1693

DEC: 2: 1693

MY DEAR CHILD

Although I am absent from thee, Yet my Heart is with thee, & my Prayers for thee continually that God would have mercy upon thee, both Soul & Body & keep you from every evil way. Remember my Dear Josiah & never forget how many Lives God hath Given You, & be sure you give your Life to God, Fear God, & fear Sin Keep all the commandments—I charge you to Pray in secret & Read the Word every Day. Remember the Sabbath day to keep it holy—Follow your studies Faithfully—Chuse the best Company—Beg the Lord to keep you every Day, & call your Self to an acct every Night, what Sins in Word, Thought, or Action, You have committed that Day & Repent of them, & Mourn after Christ for ye Pardon of ym & for Grace to Serve God in Newness of Life—Your Name is Josiah, O that your heart were as tender as

King Josiahs—There is nothing will stand you instead when You come to dy but an Interest in Christ, Make Sure of it now while you are Young, the longer you live in Sin, the harder your Heart will be: Hear the Word—& Pray ye Lord Your Soul may profit by it—God loves ye Love of Youth & Christ Saith of Such are the Kingdom of Heaven.[1] My child dont throw this Letter away, but read it, & that which hath all your Delieverances from Death;[2] Read them often and Pray over them, & leave not your heart until you find a Change wrought, O what a comfort would it be to Your Parents to See you become a New Creature—Plead ye Covenant of the God of your Fathers & Grandfathers; He hath promised to be the God of ye Righteous & of their seed after them,[3] Give God no Rest until he hath blessed you with Spiritual Blessings—Be sober be Vigilant—Avoid all Temptations to Sin, This is the Prayer & earnest desire of your loving Mother—

Joanna Cotton

Dear Child, Hearken to all these holy counsells of your precious Mother then will God delight to bless you.[4]

Yr Loving Father

JC

And O that I might now Espy
Things that are for my Good
That so I may whilst call'd to day
Seek for Eternal Food
O Give Me Grace to Seek thy Face,
Now whilst I am in Youth,
That I may learn how to discern
All Falsehood from the Truth:
That nothing may turn Me away
From following the Lord,
But that I may both night & day,
Serve him with Hearts Accord
Make Me to go & run on so
As that I may Obtain,
What is my Mark the Heav'nly Ark,
Althô with Grief & Pain—[5]

Josiah Cotton, Manuscript "Account of the Cotton Family," Houghton Library, Harvard University. Cotton prefaced this letter in his mansucript: "Letter I recd wn I was at School in Boston."

1. Three gospels include the story of Christ and the children. For example, Luke 18:16: "But Jesus called them unto him, and said, Suffer little children to come unto me, and forbid them not: for of such is the kingdom of God." See also, Mark 10:14 and Matt. 19:14. Matthew also refers to Christ's request that believers become like little children: "And said, Verily I say unto you, Except ye be converted, and become as little children, ye shall not enter into the kingdom of heaven." [Matt. 18:3.]
2. Joanna is referring to another letter she wrote to Josiah; see hers of 19 January 1692.
3. There are many references to God's promise to Abraham and his seed; see, for example, Gal. 3:16, 29 and Acts 3:25.
4. Josiah prefaced this line, "To this Letter My Father has added..."
5. Josiah prefaced this poem, written on the reverse side of the letter, "I find a Small Poem Endorst on this Letter; The Defects whereof will doubtless be Excused, if composed by one not fourteen Years old—"

To Rowland Cotton, 22 January 1694

Plymouth January, 22: 1693: /94:

Deare Son,

By J. Morton I send my litle John Cotton a suck-bottle;[1] J: H: was not gone an houre from my house before J: N: came to me (who came from Boston late the night before), with tidings that his Bro: in Law, a Tr[ ] (he thinks Thomas) was lately killed with a cart, how is unknowne, for he went alone with it, very neere the path that turnes out of our road to Dorchester-towne: I received etc & ten pound is yours in my purse, this messenger (I know) would bring it faithfully, but I know not whether you are willing any hand should touch it till you come your selfe; when you come or send for it, bring an empty purse, for I have none to spare: my wife sends you a litle oyle of aniseed,[2] faile not to send home the <bottle> mioll by J: M: your childs now quietnesse without suck seems to Justify your mothers skill though she knows not when etc: you had best send speedily what is necessary for your shoos for I expect opportunity quickly; All the scraps that can be spared are now sent you for 'tother armpit: I need not say how welcome your Dearest & yours shall be to us when they come: If your Bro: have not Hes: & [?] either sell or lend J: D's & hand them presently; it will be but for 5 moneths, I will certainly make them as good then as they are now; a young woman kinde dyed suddenly at Hull (they say a Phipenny[3]) J: M: saith he will bring our Tick, I hope your Bro: will hand it to your house before his returne: Hearty salutes to you all from us all & prayers for you

your Affec: Fath: J: C:

John Waterman & his wife added to us yesterday by Dismistion from marshfeild. a bitter morning:[4]

Miscellaneous Bound Collection, Massachusetts Historical Society. Addressed "These For Mr Rowland Cotton, Preacher of the Gospel, at Sandwich." Endorsed in unknown hand: "Jany. 22. 1694 John Cotton." Prince's note: "In one of Jan: 27 He writes—The Govr (they say) bro't newes of ye small pox being among our enemies, wth ye Hostages."

1. Rowland was evidently trying to pacify his son, John, born on 15 July 1693.
2. The seeds or oil from the seeds of *Pimpinella Anisum*, or anise, were used primarily as a tonic for digestive disorders. Bateman's Pectoral Drops, patented in 1726 as a diaphoretic, included anise as an active ingredient. *Medicine in Colonial Massachusetts, CSM,* 57 (Boston, 1980), 331, 368, 369.
3. George and Elizabeth Fipiny's daughter, Sarah, died on 14 January 1694. The family had been living in Hull since at least 1683, having moved from Boston. George migrated from Weymouth, England to Hingham, Massachusetts, with his parents and siblings in 1635. Thomas W. Baldwin, *Vital Records of Hull* (Boston, 1911), 65. Savage, *Genealogical Dictionary*, 3:418.
4. Written along left margin. Cotton records the dismission and acceptance of John and Anna Waterman in the Church Records. *CSM,* 22:282.

To Elizabeth Saltonstall Cotton,[1] 29 January 1694

Plymouth January, 29: 1693: /94:

Much Endeared Daughter

I have thought it my duty, ever since I heard of the translation of your blessed Grand father to Heaven,[2] to write you a few consollatory lines; you have candour enough to pardon my hitherto omission: I need not tell you how ripe he was for heaven, & though the death of such pretious men of God & choice relations be a heavy losse to us, yet when wee consider their Happynesse & glory wee cannot but rejoyce therein; And therefore, Deare Child, turne every sorrowfull thought that you shall noe more see his face & heare his pleasant chearfull voice in this world, into affectionate contentment at the thoughts of that unspeakeable pleasure he now enjoyes among the spirits of Just men made perfect: I hope it will not be long before you & your pleasant babes will come & live with us, you have a mother & sister with me who salute you & to all whom you shall be most heartily welcome; co[...][3] & yours to God,

[your Affec]tionate Father

John Cotton[4]

Miscellaneous Bound Collection, Massachusetts Historical Society. Addressed "Thes For Mrs Elizabeth Cotton, at Sandwich." Bottom edge of letter mutilated.

---

1. Elizabeth Saltonstall Denison Cotton (1668–1725) was the daughter of Nathaniel and Elizabeth Ward Saltonstall. She was first married to John Denison (1666–1689, H.C. 1684), her brother Gurdon's classmate and the settled minister in Ipswich. Denison died in 1689 while Elizabeth was pregnant with their son, John. Elizabeth married Rowland Cotton in September 1692 and had eleven more children. *Sibley's Harvard Graduates,* 3:271-72, 277-86, 323-26.
2. Elizabeth's maternal grandfather, John Ward (1606–1693), was born in Haverhill, Suffolk, England, educated at Emmanuel College, Cambridge, and served as rector at Hadleigh, Essex, from 1633 to 1639, when he emigrated to New England. He was ordained in Haverhill, Massachusetts, in October 1645 as the first settled minister. He remained active as a minister and physician in Haverhill until his death on 27 December 1693 at the age of eighty-seven. Elizabeth's father, Nathaniel Saltonstall, had married Elizabeth, John Ward's eighteen-year-old daughter, in 1663. The Wards and Saltonstalls had long been "closely associated in local and colony affairs," and the marriage merely formalized their relationship. Weis, *Colony Clergy,* 214-15; *The Saltonstall Papers, 1607–1815*, Massachusetts Historical Society *Collections,* 80 (Boston, 1972), 49.
3. Torn; several words lost.
4. Signature in Thomas Prince's hand.

To Rowland Cotton, 18 May 1694

Plym: May 18: 94:

Deare Son,

Expect noe more 1/2 sheets; I am very glad of your Indian acceptation[1] & your next weeks work with them: Govr is returned;[2] Lord Cutts is not gone to Isle of Wight,[3] but his Leift Govr was going,[4] Mr Dudley; & his place is 500 per annum, besides what he will have while the Govr is absent, he writes he shall not come hither this yeare: Connecticott are likely to obtaine their desires at Whitehall: Mr Barnes saith it is his son Johns horse strayed from Jos: Bartlets,[5] he is at sea, & noe doubt, saith his mother he will pay the finder, & desires he may not be lost till the owner knows & speake his minde;

A small handfull of each herb, only of mouse ear[6] two handfulls, two quarts of beare boild to one, with this the Joynts are to be washed.

of the syrrup take 2 spoonfulls at a time morning & evening.

Mr Ruggles is a very desirable companion at bed & board & in the way: I told Mattakeesitt, they may expect me on that Monday,[7] & soe shall I to see you at J:

Bearstons[8] by one or two a clock at furthest. The Lord heale the Deare mother & its babe[9] & give you all all good, with all our heartyest salutations to you all,

I am, As ever etc

J: C:

R: R: is in haste:

Miscellaneous Bound Collection, Massachusetts Historical Society. Addressed "These For Mr Rowland Cotton, Preacher of the Gospel, at Sandwich." Endorsed in unknown hand: "May 18: 1694. John Cotton to me[,] Mary[,] John[,] J John Cotton[.] May."

---

1. Like his father, Rowland pursued an Indian ministry. Increasingly fluent in Native languages, Rowland preached regularly in Mashpah, near Sandwich, to more than fifty Native families. "Account of an Indian Visitation, A.D. 1698," Massachusetts Historical Society *Collections,* 1st ser., 10 (1809), 133.
2. Sir William Phips was the governor of Massachusetts from December 1691 until November 1694.
3. The Cutts family was prominent in both government affairs and shipbuilding in Portsmouth and Kittery. John Cutts was governor of New Hampshire (d. 1681); the title "Lord" may refer to his son, Samuel (1669–1698); however, John's brothers, Robert and Richard, also had sons who were active in the political and maritime affairs of the province. Everett Stackpole, *Old Kittery and her Families* (Lewiston, Me., 1903), 333-34; Savage, *Genealogical Dictionary,* 1:494-95.
4. Cotton's wording is confusing. If he were referring to New Hampshire's governor (he mistakenly referred to Cutts), he meant Samuel Allen, the wealthy London merchant and absentee governor of New Hampshire since March 1692. Allen's deputy and acting governor was John Usher, Boston's bookseller and a former member of Andros's council. Usher became deputy governor in August 1692. Everett Stackpole, *History of New Hampshire,* 4 vols. (New York, 1916), 1:166-67.
5. The Barnes family settled in Plymouth by at least 1633, and the elder John Barnes (this John's grandfather) was a merchant, brewer, innkeeper and land speculator. Barnes family members were also active litigants and often found themselves in legal trouble for excessive drinking, slander and general disorderliness. Clearly, runaway horses were one of their lesser offenses. Eugene Aubrey Stratton, *Plymouth Colony: Its History & People 1620–1691* (Salt Lake City, Ut., 1986), 240-41.
6. Mouse-Ear *(Hieracium Pilosella)* is a milky hawkweed that was used to treat lung disorders and asthma; it also has astringent and expectorant qualities that were useful in treating whooping cough. As Cotton suggested, the mouse-ear plant was collected and dried, then boiled into a tea. The milky extract from the leaves and stem was also applied directly to the skin to aid healing, especially of hemorrhoids. M. Grieve, *A Modern Herbal* (New York, 1931).
7. Generally, in referring to this place, residents of Plymouth meant land that became Yarmouth and Barnstable. "Mattacheese" or "Mattakeese" was translated as either "old fields" or "near the water." The Native inhabitants of the land from the west end of Yarmouth to the east end of Barnstable were called Mattakeset. Cotton probably meant that Barnstable's minister, Russell, was expecting him. Donald Trayer, *Barnstable: Three Centuries of a Cape Cod Town* (1939; reprint, Yarmouthport, Mass., 1971), 28-29.
8. Probably Joseph Bearse (b. 1652), who lived in Barnstable. His younger brother, James (b. 1660), is supposed to have died young. Savage, *Genealogical Dictionary,* 1:149.
9. Most likely a reference to Rowland's wife, Elizabeth, and infant son, John, who was born on 15 July 1693.

To Rowland Cotton, 22 May 1694

Plymouth May, 22: 1694:

Deare Son

Your Fath's letter[1] m[r] murdo brought me on Saturday, he came in m[r] John Lathrop,[2] with whom also was passenger, Preston[3] your Contemporary newly come from Barbados, he salutes you, wishes he could have seene you; there was also m[r] Collins of Newhaven[4] mr of a vessell & one Hall son in law to m[r] Prout[5] there, taken by the French in sight of Barbados, carried to Martineco, civilly treated there; seized by the Frigat, mr Collins sent word to N. haven of it, m[r] Pierpont writes to my Lady to get him released, she sends for the Capt, keeps him lovingly with her till he doth release him; After which he goes to the frigat side last Wednesday, tells Hall he will come next day & take him into a boat, Hall watches him, skips overboard in nothing but wastcoat & breeches, his hat in them, comes safe to the sloop, which I suppose this day is arrived at the Hianass:[6] Major Gold & his wife are dead,[7] not union at present for setling m[r] webb:[8] wee are afflicted to see in yours by R: R: that your family is soe afflicted, the Lord heale, support & sanctify all for good; I hope the illnesses will not arise soe high as to hinder your Journey on monday, I know of noe opportunity to send these & expect to write to you noe more this weeke & therefore in your next write with as much certainty as you can of your designe of meeting me at J: Bearstons on Monday; wee hope tomorrow or next day to see ours from the East,[9] though not a word have wee heard of or from them since they left Boston; A good Maide attaineable here is to us unknowne; wee 3 say to you all as alwayes, God Almighty ever blesse you all, soe daily prayes,

your Affectionate Father

John Cotton

A Ketch from Bristoll rumors of our East India fleet being taken by the French, because their convoy sir Francis Wheeler would not fight.

Miscellaneous Bound Collection, Massachusetts Historical Society. Addressed "These For mr Rowland Cotton, Preacher of the Gospel, at Sandwich."

---

1. A letter from Rowland's father-in-law, Nathaniel Saltonstall, was not found.
2. Probably this mariner was the grandson of emigrant minister John Lothrop (d. 1653) and son of John Lothrop (1645–1727) of Barnstable. Savage, *Genealogical Dictionary,* 3:120. See 10 August 1694 below.
3. There are two possible Prestons: Eliasaph Preston (1643–1707) of Stratford, Connecticut, or Joseph Preston (1646–1733) of New Haven, Connecticut. Savage, *Genealogical Dictionary,* 3:482-83; Torrey, *New England Marriages,* 602.

4. Savage lists both a William Collins who removed to New Haven and an Ebenezer Collins of New Haven, who married Ann Leete Trowbridge, Gov. Leete's daughter, in 1683. Savage, *Genealogical Dictionary,* 1:434-35.

5. Most likely Rutherford Hall (1675–170[?]), the son of Mary Rutherford Hall Prout (d. 1723), who died in Barbados. Hall's mother married John Prout (1648–1719) of New Haven in 1681. While Cotton described Hall as "son-in-law," modern readers would better understand "stepson." Torrey, *New England Marriages,* 606; Savage, *Genealogical Dictionary,* 2:332.

6. Hyannis.

7. Savage includes a Nathan Gold (Gould), who was the wealthiest man in Connecticut in 1670, served as an assistant to the legislature nearly every year after 1657 and died on 4 March 1694. A Connecticut militia officer named Nathan Gold was active in Leisler's Rebellion, and Torrey lists a Nathan Gold who died in March 1694, who was married first to Martha Harvey and then to Sarah Phippen and lived in Fairfield. These may all be the same man. Savage, *Genealogical Dictionary,* 2:286; Gallay, *Colonial Wars of North America,* 370; Torrey, *New England Marriages,* 308.

8. Probably Joseph Webb (1666–1732, H.C. 1684), who preached for a few years in Derby, Connecticut, and was ordained in Fairfield, Connecticut, on 15 August 1694. Cotton implied that the church was unsure of calling him, but he served Fairfield's congregation for nearly forty years. *Sibley's Harvard Graduates,* 3:301-305.

9. Cotton seems to have been referring to the anticipated return of Plymouth soldiers from King William's War.

To Rowland Cotton, 12 June 1694

Plymouth June, 12: 1694

Deare Son

I hope my saturday lines[1] came safe sub sigillo[2] to you, for I desired st. sK: to take them of Gibs: Sam: King[3] (Joannas Father) is dangerously sick of a feavour; m^r^ Alden who was left to take & bring captives is returned home without them, none being brought to him:[4] the Fr: Doc: is very sullen & surly at your mother,[5] & seems very strange, sending this by Est: Cole[6] to Dick, she told him it was from a stranger: Are you for your long Journey next Monday? Let me know that I may order my steps to accompany you to mattakeesitt on Tuseday morn: If you have Bro: walkers letter & the list of Counsellors,[7] restore them: you all have from us all our heartyest salutations; your Bro: Gurd:[8] was gone about 1/2 an houre homewards before your Fath:[9] received his letters from o: E:[10] by Herbert, of which you had some account; God blesse you all, soe daily sayes,

Your Affectionate Father

John Cotton

Your mother hath thoughts of speedy sending her bedtick to be wove with you, if you will take care about it & encourage her that it shall be well done.

Miscellaneous Bound Collection, Massachusetts Historical Society. Addressed "These For M[r] Rowland Cotton, Preacher of the Gospel, at Sandwich. Send word speedily whether the weaver will do it & when, for it is quite ready."

---

1. Not found.
2. "Under the seal."
3. Samuel King and Sarah Dunham King's (d. 1738) second child was Joanna (b. 1672). *Vital Records of Plymouth, Massachusetts to the Year 1850,* comp. Lee D. Van Antwerp, ed. Ruth Wilder Sherman (Camden, Me., 1993), 39; Torrey, *New England Marriages,* 439.
4. For Alden's role in prisoner exchanges, see 12 August 1693.
5. This suggests that there may have been some rivalry between midwife Joanna Cotton and Dr. Francis LeBaron. LeBaron was born in France in 1668 and was newly settled in Plymouth, working as a "chirurgeon," when Cotton wrote this letter. He appears to have maintained his Catholicism in New England, perhaps with the advantage of royally mandated religious toleration after 1692. He married and remained in Plymouth, and his son and grandsons also became doctors. See 6 August 1695. C. Helen Brock, "The Influence of Europe on Colonial Massachusetts Medicine," *Medicine in Colonial Massachusetts, 1620–1820, CSM,* 57 (Boston, 1980), 133.
6. Esther Cole Atwood married Medad Atwood (b. 1659) by 1686, and they lived in Eastham. Savage, *Genealogical Dictionary,* 1 425-26, 78.
7. The election of May 1694 saw the following men chosen as "councillors or Assistants" to the General Court from Massachusetts Bay: William Stoughton, Nathaniel Saltonstall, Bartholomew Gedney, John Hathorne, Isaac Addington, Jonathan Corwin, Daniel Peirce, Thomas Danforth, Wait Winthrop, Robert Pike, Elisha Hutchinson, William Browne, John Foster, John Pynchon, James Russell, Elisha Cooke, Samuel Sewall, John Phillips and Peter Sergeant. The men chosen to represent the former Plymouth Colony were William Bradford, John Saffin, Barnabas Lothrop, John Thacher and Nathaniel Thomas. *Acts and Resolves of the Province of Massachusetts Bay*, 7:43-44.
8. Gurdon Saltonstall was Rowland's brother-in-law; the two graduated a year apart from Harvard College. Saltonstall (1666–1724, H.C. 1684) served as the settled minister in New London, Connecticut, from 1687 to 1707, and as governor of the Connecticut colony from 1707 until his death in September 1724. Weis, *Colonial Clergy,* 181; *Sibley's Harvard Graduates,* 3:277-86.
9. Nathaniel Saltonstall.
10. Old England.

From Benjamin Smith,[1] 20 July 1694

Rev^D Sir:

This comes to Informe you that according to ye Discourse between Mr Mayhew[2] & yourself wn Lately wth you about meeting att succonesset[3] the last Monday in August in order to ye ordination of mr Dunham[4] amongst us wee Do pitch & agree upon y^t time (unles Mr Russell[5] do mean while timously give you & us word to ye contrary.) And do Desire such messengers from your church as you shall see meet to be then present with us to give us your help in this work of God.[6]

And wee do desire[7] according to your letter that you will resign to us your interest in him. This with Desires of your prayers for us is all att present from

Benjamin Smith

wo was appointed & Desired by the Rest concerned to signifye this unto you.

To be communicated to the Church.
Sandwich. July 20th. 1694–

Miscellaneous Bound Collection, Massachusetts Historical Society. Addressed "To the Rev^d: Mr John Cotton pastour of the chh of Plimouth." Cotton's note: "The church chose & sent the Pastor & Mr Fuller & at the vineyard, a church was gathered & m^r Dunham ordained Teacher, october, 11:" Prince's note: "Mr Dunham was a member of [...] dismissed from thence, in ordr to gather ye church at Ed[gartown]." A small tear at the bottom of the page interrupts Prince's note.

---

1. Benjamin Smith was the only son of one of Sandwich's early settlers, Richard Smith. Benjamin and his wife had eleven children between 1678 and 1704, but only the eldest son, Elkanah (b. 1685), survived childhood. Lovell, *Sandwich: A Cape Cod Town,* 153.
2. Experience Mayhew (1673–1758) was the newly settled minister on Martha's Vineyard in March 1694, and the grandson of the island's founder, Thomas Mayhew. Primarily concerned with Native churches, Mayhew traveled among Native settlements on the island and translated many sermons and doctrinal tracts into Native languages, which he had learned as a child. In 1695, he married Thankful Hinckley, Gov. Thomas Hinckley's daughter. *Sibley's Harvard Graduates,* 7:632-39; Weis, *Colonial Clergy,* 138.
3. Sakonessit is modern-day Falmouth.
4. Jonathan Dunham (1632–1717) was born in Plymouth and served as a missionary to the Natives in Saco, Maine, in 1659. Later he settled as a lay preacher—he did not attend college—in Falmouth, Maine, from 1679 until he received the call from the Edgartown church in 1684. Despite lacking a degree, in 1684 Dunham was ordained as a teacher in the church, where he remained until his death. Weis, *Colonial Clergy,* 74.
5. Jonathan Russell, minister in Barnstable.

6. Cotton's church records indicate that Dunham's request was read to the church on 8 April and Cotton's reply was approved on 22 April. The church also voted to send Cotton and elder Samuel Fuller to attend the ordination, which occurred on 11 October. *CSM*, 22:175.

7. "Desire" is written in Cotton's hand over the word "expect." See the letter of John Cotton to Rowland Cotton, 23 July 1694.

To Rowland Cotton, 23 July 1694

Plymouth July, 23: 1694:

Deare Son

I should be sorry if you should have cause to be sorry for a good wife that loves mine soe well; such is our affection to both, that wee have resolved that your Mother goes not to Boston at present for your sakes, I will take care to convey him to Camb. in the season[1] and your Moth: intends to goe when Yarm: & sandw: will give her leave; but we cannot consent to fetching your Moth: till your Dearest hath been a minute in travell,[2] only because of poore Theoph:[3] who is weake & ill every day, & wee feare the Jaundice is seizing him; were it not for his condition you might speed by Thursday, but that doth forbid, only if a reall Alarm be made, you may send when you please and my Dearest will run of all foure at an houres warning[.] your mother quite forgat salt which else she had certainly sent by J: N: but forbearance is noe payment, if the boat had a woodden tray, I suppose you found nutmegs in your starch: Seale this to sar. Tob:[4] if you please, but I hope she will desire you to read it to her: The word [expect][5] in B: S: letter[6] (which I suppose you wrote) was too bold, I expunged it & put in [desire][7] Salute Mr Rus: meo nomine[8] & a desire him to resolve immediately that noe obstruction be at that time, for if it be not that weeke, the Gen: Assem: is the next week after & Mr Mayh: will be come off[9] & noe seasonable opportunity will occurre before winter; I shall not read mine till the next sab: expecting to heare from Mr R:[10] before, at least by you: Tell B: SM:[11] wee must have a good sloop or shallop to convey us, not a small thing; our church, I doubt not, will doe all necessary to promote their settlement but if wee arrive there, wee shall try the matter for the church by previous examination; Also if any woemen desire to be of that church they should be prepared to covenant that day immediately after the church is gathered. The Govr went on Friday in the Galley & the None-such[12] is arrived at Bost. the same day: salutations & prayers etc The Lord be very gratious to thee my Dear Daughter, hope in his mercy;

Thy Affectionate Father

John Cotton

I wish B: S: would send to Yar:[13] also:

Tell Sar: Tob: the church expect to receive a poenitentiall letter from her in due time: you need not feare your wife calling this week, it will be neere a fortnight before 39 weekes[14] will be from begin: of Nov: The None-such hath retaken 2 of our vessels from the French; 2 killed at oyster river[15] but 40 persons in all carried away, saith J: Mur:

Miscellaneous Bound Collection, Massachusetts Historical Society. Addressed "These For Mr Roland Cotton, Preacher of the Gospel, at Sandwich.

---

1. Cotton was referring to the process of escorting his son Josiah to college.
2. John and Joanna's son John Cotton (1661–1706) was settled in Yarmouth and Rowland was settled in Sandwich. Joanna evidently spent much of her time traveling to assist her sons and their growing families. Rowland and Elizabeth Cotton were eager for Joanna to help them with the imminent birth of their daughter, Joanna, who arrived on 16 August 1694. Cotton asked that his son wait to call Joanna until Elizabeth was actually in labor—"travell." Weis, *Colonial Clergy,* 62-63; *Vital Records of Sandwich, Massachusetts to 1885*, ed. Caroline Kardell and Russell Lovell (Boston, 1996), 35.
3. Theophilus Cotton (1682–1726, H.C. 1701) was John and Joanna's youngest child. *Sibley's Harvard Graduates,* 5:30-37.
4. Probably Sarah Tobey of Sandwich. Cotton's church records for 1694 describe a church-child's sinfulness and his attempts to reach her, but he did not name her: "A chh-child fallen into sin, living else where the chh sent her a letter of Admonition, the yeare after she sent a letter signifying her Repentance which the chh accepted." By 1750, the Tobey family was one of the five largest families in Sandwich. *CSM,* 22:175; Lovell, *Sandwich: A Cape Cod Town,* 164.
5. Brackets in original.
6. Benjamin Smith to John Cotton, 20 July 1694.
7. Brackets in original.
8. "In my name."
9. Evidently, Experience Mayhew was due to leave Martha's Vineyard for the fall. Mayhew also represented his Native congregations at the General Court. *Sibley's Harvard Graduates,* 7:632-39.
10. Perhaps Jonathan Russell.
11. Benjamin Smith.
12. The *Nonesuch* was a man-of-war ship: *Acts and Resolves of the Province of Massachusetts Bay*, 7:828, 375.
13. Cotton wanted Benjamin Smith to invite the Yarmouth church to the ordination as well; his son, Josiah, was Yarmouth's minister.
14. Cotton seems to have been surprisingly well informed about his daughter-in-law's date of conception.
15. The town of Oyster River, later New Hampshire, was attacked by 300 French-allied Penobscots and Norridgewocks on 18 July 1694. While the town had fourteen garrison houses, many inhabitants were caught completely by surprise. In all, 100 English were killed and thirty were carried into captivity. Mather describes the attack in his narrative and suggests that "the Treacherous Enemy with a great Army fell upon that Place... and Kill'd and Captiv'd Ninety Four." Cotton vastly underrepresented the casualties. *Colonial Wars of North America,* 540; Mather, *Decennium Luctuosum,* 252-54.

To Rowland Cotton, 10 August 1694

Plymouth August, 10: 1694:

Deare Son

wee heare strange rumors of troubles in your county by feares of Indians, if there be any thing in reality you will certainly write me word of it; The Post is returned last night, the 2 frigats are come from O: E;[1] Nath: Lathrop[2] is come (they say) stooping like Pugsley[3] through distempers, 1 of the frigats to Boston, the other Eastward, this is all I heare next my heart, you must examine John Crocker[4] & John Goodspeed[5] who are upon the road coming (as the Post saith) by one of them I intend to send this, & here I stop my hand till some few houres passe over:

Noe Capt among us granted, & the souldiers say they will be hanged before they will stirre without one,[6] what they will say after breakfast you may read before the Page be filled; the letter[7] from Col. Sidney[8] & Maj: Walley[9] sayes they may have Negos for Leift: Deac: Faunce hath paid 5 pd to release his Joseph Holmes; with that money Dan. Ramsden is hired & goes,[10] James Winslow,[11] Joshua Barrow,[12] John Hawes[13] & Anthony Savory[14] seeme these as yet stand for our five:

11 a clock[15] The souldiers are now all going aboard & Josiah with them,[16] I doe affectionately salute my Deare Mate concluding she may be with you this evening; & soe to you & your Dearest, & Sarah & departing Josiah hand[17] duty and love,

I am in greatest haste yours heartily

John Cotton

Miscellaneous Bound Collection, Massachusetts Historical Society. Addressed "These For Mr Rowland

---

1. Old England.

2. Barnabas Lothrop (1636–1735), who served in many powerful positions in Barnstable and New Plymouth, was often chosen as representative on councils with his friend and ally Gov. Hinckley before and after Plymouth's merger with Massachusetts Bay. Lothrop and his first wife, Susan Clark, had fourteen children, including Nathaniel, who was born on 23 November 1669 and died in 1700. Amos Otis, *Genealogical Notes of Barnstable Families* (1888; reprint, Baltimore, Md., 1979), 1:180, 2:164, 167, 215-16.

3. John Pugsley of Harwich was injured in King Philip's War and was disabled for the remainder of his life. He evidently requested and was granted relief funds from the public treasury, for example, forty shillings from Plymouth in 1686. In June 1697 he appealed to the General Court for assistance and was granted £6 "for his relief," administered by Capt. John Thacher in trust. His petition indicated that he served in the military for two years, and during the "Long and bitter March up to and from Narrogansett &c he mett with an unhappy fall from off an horse by wch he broke one of his Lower ribbs & much hurt his back." His life was marked by an "unspeakeable deale of misery" and he was unable to work. In 1733, as one of the soldiers from Plymouth Colony who fought in the war, he

(or perhaps a son) received a grant of land in modern-day Maine. Given that Cotton used him as a metaphor, his disabled gait must have been rather public and pronounced. His name does not appear on any published lists of soldiers who served in King Philip's War. See also letter of April 1696. *PCR,* 6:189; *Acts and Resolves of the Province of Massachusetts Bay*, 7:154, 563; George Madison Bodge, *Soldiers in King Philip's War* (1906; reprint, Baltimore, Md., 2000), 439.

4. Probably John, the eldest son of Deacon William Crocker of Barnstable. John was born on 31 May 1637 and married, first, Mary Bodfish in November 1659, and then Mary Bursley in April 1663; he died in May 1711. Alternately, the reference could be to his son, John, born on 17 February 1664, who married Mary Bacon on 5 November 1702. The Crocker and Lothrop families were among the first settlers of Barnstable. Savage, *Genealogical Dictionary*, 1:474-75; *PCR,* 43; Otis, *Genealogical Notes of Barnstable Families,* 1:211, 200, 210-11.

5. John Goodspeed was the second child of Roger and Alice Layton Goodspeed, born in June 1645 in Barnstable. John married Experience Holley in January 1669 and had seven children. The Goodspeeds settled what is now known as Marstons Mills. Savage, *Genealogical Dictionary,* 2:276.

6. Conflict over local military leadership continued; see the letter of 5 August 1692.

7. Not found.

8. Col. Bartholomew Gedney of Salem; see the letter of 12 February 1695.

9. John Walley (1644–1712) was a prominent man in Plymouth Colony and served in a series of political positions both before and after 1692. His military prowess, however, did not match his political ambition: "John Walley is another example of a prominent politician given military responsibilities far above his abilities." He commanded New England's land forces during the 1690 attack on Quebec, but his "indecision and anxiety attack" caused him to wander around aimlessly and never order the attack on the city. His failure did not harm his political future, however; after the war, he served on the Governor's Council, as Commissioner of War (1693–1694) and as a judge of the Superior Court. While Walley never saw action again, he maintained the rank of major general of the militia. Gallay, *Colonial Wars of North America,* 770-71.

10. Deacon Thomas Faunce's sister, Patience, was married to John Holmes of Duxbury and they had eleven children, including Joseph. It seems that Thomas Faunce paid Daniel Ramsden to serve in the militia in place of his nephew, Joseph. Ramsden was born in Plymouth in September 1649, married Sarah and had four children from 1690 to 1700. (Ramsden's father, Joseph, was fined for drunkenness in 1671.) Savage, *Genealogical Dictionary,* 2:452; *PCR,* 7:135; Van Antwerp, *Vital Records of Plymouth, Massachusetts to the Year 1850*, 29.

11. Probably James Winslow, son of Nathaniel and Faith Miller Winslow of Marshfield, born on 16 August 1669. Savage, *Genealogical Dictionary,* 4:603.

12. John and Deborah Barrow of Plymouth had six children, including Joshua, by 1692. Savage, *Genealogical Dictionary,* 1:127.

13. A John Hawes appears on the list of freemen for Yarmouth in 1689; Savage lists a John Hawes of Barnstable who married Desire Gorham in October 1661, and suggests that he may have lived in Yarmouth. *PCR,* 206; Savage, *Genealogical Dictionary,* 2:380.

14. Anthony Savory was in Dartmouth as of 1686 and may have been the son of the Anthony Savory who was listed with the Freemen of Plymouth in 1643. Savage, *Genealogical Dictionary,* 4:28; *PCR,* 174.

15. Cotton wrote the time in the left margin.

16. See Cotton to Joanna and Rowland Cotton, August 1694.

17. "Send"?

To Joanna Rosseter Cotton and Rowland Cotton, [11] August 1694

SATURDAY MORN

oh My Deare, you that have run away soe far from me, are you now coming towards me? For that trick I will run on Monday morning as far t'other way & see when you & I shall meete if wee drive that stroak; but in sober sadnesse I am exceeding glad that God hath preserved thee Deare soule, in all thy wayes hitherto, He in mercy keep us safely till wee meete together here; Josiah went yesternoone with the souldiers cheerfull & well, they had a pleasant southerly breeze, & noe doubt arrived at the Castle in the evening & I believe this forenoone will be well at Boston: I went in the afternoone on purpose to see Theoph: who is well, but cryed most bitterly to me for a licence to come home this day,[1] I told him there was none but Sarah[2] to see & if he would stay till next Saturday I should be come from Bos: & perhaps you, but I left him poore lamb, with his back turned & he heavily bemoaning his condition & begging he might come home to day, My parentall bowels yearned, but I gave him noe hopes only of Sar's visiting him one day; He sayes they carry it well to him, all amisse I could get from him was, that the boys laught at him, there are 3 or 4 Duxb: boyes & he is alone & it may be they all set themselves to afflict him & his tender, proud spirit cannot beare it: Sarahs duty to you, my tender love to thee etc

I am thine ever as my owne

John Cotton

Capt Brigs[3] borrowed my stilliards[4] to weigh meat for etc & is gone to Bay with them, what did they cost?

Deare Son, yours last night rec:[5] If you had all the world in your power to give, you need not be at the charge to give it for your mothers tarrying with you till the day after delivery,[6] for if I meete her at my returne lat. end of next week it is as soone as I can expect to see her; Sar:[7] will be solitary but wee must get a solid man (I suppose) to lodge here; she is well, you both have mine & her hearty love; I thinke I forgot to tell you that Mr Hobarts lost son & a woman ran away & gat home,[8] the Indians being drunk, she sayes they were 30 & the English were neere them, had they come a litle further they might easily have taken & killed them all; mr Hob's maid hid herselfe under a tub in the cellar, the Indians were there, laid their guns on the tub, smelt her not.[9] write to me to Bost: J Rich: will goe hence early in the weeke, not on Monday, I hope for good newes from you there to transmitt to Haverhill:[10] God blesse you & grant mercy to Deare Betty etc soe ever prayes etc.

My great greife is that you have my Dearest soe long before you need her, & in lying in, when perhaps may be greatest need you cannot then enjoy her, but who can helpe it, you would send for her too soone:[11]

Miscellaneous Bound Collection, Massachusetts Historical Society. Addressed "These For Mris Joanna Cotton, at mr Cottons house in Sandwich." Prince's note at top: "suppose Aug. 94."

---

1. Now twelve years old, Theophilus, like his older brothers, received his early formal schooling first from Duxbury's Ichabod Wiswall and then from several Boston schoolmasters. It appears that he was still in Duxbury when Cotton wrote this letter. *Sibley's Harvard Graduates,* 5:30-37.
2. Sarah Cotton was born on 5 April 1670 and evidently was still at home in 1694. Savage, *Genealogical Dictionary,* 1:463.
3. Captain John Briggs lived in Scituate and served as a ship's captain. He also inherited his father's homestead upon Walter Briggs's death in 1684 and served in several town offices. Brigg's Harbour (Mishquahtuck) was named after his father, Walter, sometime before 1650. Samuel Deane, *History of Scituate, Massachusetts: From Its First Settlement to 1831* (1831; reprint, Scituate, Mass., 1975), 23, 225.
4. A Steelyard was "a type of balance scale, it consisted of a lever with unequal arms which moved on a fulcrum, the article to be weighed being suspended from the shorter arm with the counterpoise being slid along the longer arm until an equilibrium was produced." *Plymouth Colony Records: Wills and Inventories,* ed. C. H. Simmons (Camden, Me., 1996), 559.
5. Not found.
6. Rowland's wife was expecting a baby, Joanna, who was born on 16 August.
7. Sarah Cotton.
8. The Penobscot and Norridgewock raiding party that attacked Oyster River on 18 July 1694 divided following that attack. One portion, led by chief Moxus, continued south to attack Groton, Massachusetts, on 27 July. Twenty settlers were killed and about twelve were captured, including two of Gershom Hobart's children. One child was killed, and Hobart's captive son, Gershom, was ransomed four years later. This letter suggests that Gershom had escaped, but Cotton was mistaken. See 29 May 1695. *Colonial Wars of North America,* 540; Mather, *Decennium Luctuosum,* 253-54; *Sibley's Harvard Graduates,* 2:229-38.
9. Prince's note: "July. 27. 94 ye Indians fell on Groton, killed more y^n^ 20 carried away more yn 12—took 2 sons of ye R Mr Gershom Hobart, ye Minr y^r^."
10. Rowland's wife, Elizabeth, came from Haverhill, and much of the Saltonstall family was still living there.
11. For some comments on Joanna's midwifery skills, see Nathaniel and Elizabeth Saltonstall to Rowland and Elizabeth Cotton, 27 August–September 1694, *Saltonstall Papers,* 219-22.

To Rowland Cotton, 13 September 1694

Plymouth Sept: 13: 94

Deare Son

mine on monday[1] by J: Morey Jun: with 3 bookes for Mr Russell[2] I hope you have received; on Tuseday I went to Assawomsit & on wednesday I preacht a lecture to the English at midlebery[3] to prepare the brethren there to gather a church; Mr Danforth[4] hath begun to preach to the Indians, once or twice at Titticutt[5] & as often at Assawomsitt:[6] If you lanch not in this storme, I never expect to see the wind downe; it was his [...] that diverted the mercy from that people last yeare; If W: B:[7] have given offence let him ipso facto give satisfaction; if he hath not & yet T: T: remaine unsatifyed, let W: B: as a christian solemnly promise T: T: before you & any others that he will readily attend to the advice shall be given him by those that come to your ordination, & give said T: T: that satisfaction they shall say is regular; & this is enough, but to put by such a worke for such a cause, is but Satans designe to hinder the progresse of the Kingdome of Christ in that place:

Beck Cole this day hath a Boy;[8] Tell Sar: Tob:[9] our church expects a poenitentiall returne from her, asist her in it:

A Tobey told my wife yesterday that our Sarah was come to your house at which wee much rejoyce, longing to have her home; m^ris Thomas wants her extreamly day & night:[10] he being now at Boston; Next Sabbath Han: Jack: may be admitted & baptized,[11] will not Sar: come on Saturday & see it? What if she ride the mare, which your mother much desires to ride upon towards Bost: next Thursday? Our hearty love to you 3; your Dearest may take 4 or 5 pills of Rudii[12] or Coche, while it is working the child must not suck, when done working some body must draw her breasts; God blesse you all, soe prayes without ceasing,

Your Affectionate Father

John Cotton

Above 30 persons sick at Lakingham[13] of the feavor, & feav: & ague: A horse at Jab: Howlands[14] shop door dash out the braines of a child at once, of Jos: Sandy, which they had taken to live with them.[15] your mother saw the Physick with you ergo sends you none, take Rud: or Coche which she fanceyes best:

Miscellaneous Bound Collection, Massachusetts Historical Society. Addressed "These For Mr Rowland Cotton, Preacher of the Gospel at Sandwich."

1. Not found.

2. Jonathan Russell, minister at Barnstable.

3. The residents of Middleborough, Massachusetts, established the First Congregational Church on 26 December 1694. According to the church records and to this letter, Cotton had been consulted, and happily attended the church's gathering with four deacons and brothers of the Plymouth church. Samuel Fuller (1624–1695) had served as the settled minister beginning in 1678 and was ordained Teacher during the gathering ceremony. After Fuller's death, Thomas Palmer (1665–1743) ministered to the church beginning in 1696 and was ordained in May 1702. Described as "the most unfortunate ministry in the history of this church," Palmer divided the new church and was dismissed in June 1708 for "misbehavior and intemperance." Weis, *Colonial Clergy,* 259, 91, 157; *CSM,* 22:176; Thomas Weston, *History of the Town of Middleboro, Massachusetts* (Boston, 1906), 443-44, 309-10.

4. Samuel Danforth (1666–1727, H.C. 1683), minister at Taunton from 1687 until his death. Appointed by the Commissioners for the Propagation of the Gospel to preach to various Native settlements, Danforth also translated several sermons into Native languages and prepared an Indian dictionary. *Sibley's Harvard Graduates,* 3:243-49.

5. Now in Bridgewater, Massachusetts, along the Taunton River; Titicut was home to a group of praying Indians once led by John Sassamon.

6. Modern-day Lakeville, Massachusetts.

7. Probably William Brinsmead. Brinsmead attended Harvard from 1644 to 1647, when the college moved from a three-year to a four-year course of study for the first degree. Seventeen scholars were unhappy with the change in program length and left without obtaining degrees. After preaching occasionally in Plymouth, he was ordained at Marlborough in October 1666 and remained there until his death in 1701. Weis, *Colonial Clergy,* 41. *Sibley's Harvard Graduates,* 1:16, 560; Savage, *Genealogical Dictionary,* 1:254.

8. Ephraim and Rebecca Cole's second child, Samuel, was born in September 1694. Van Antwerp, *Vital Records of Plymouth, Mass To 1850,* 15-16.

9. See Cotton to Rowland Cotton, of 23 July 1694.

10. Perhaps this is a reference to Mary Appleton Thomas, who appears to have been a friend of Sarah Cotton's. Mary married Nathaniel Thomas on 20 June 1694 and perhaps wanted Sarah's company while her new husband was away in Boston. Sarah later attended the birth of Mary's first child; see the letter below of 25 May 1695. Torrey, *New England Marriages,* 735.

11. While Cotton's records do not indicate her admission into the church in 1694, his successor, Ephraim Little, listed "Hannah Jacekson The wife of Eliezer Jackson," as one of the women "that are of the church this 10th of March 1703." Cotton did note that four members were admitted in 1694, but he did not list their names. *CSM,* 22:193, 173.

12. Possibly Rhodie Rad, or rose-root, which Nicholas Culpeper recommended for migraines because it was "somewhat cool in quality." That same coolness may have alleviated sore breasts as well. Joanna may also have been suggesting Rhodium, which Culpeper recommended to "Encreaseth milk in Nurses." Nicholas Culpeper, *The English Physician Enlarged* (London, 1656), 11, 16.

13. Modern-day Carver, Massachusetts.

14. Jabez Howland (1644–1712[?]) was a blacksmith in Bristol. He also kept an inn and served as representative to the General Court in 1689 and 1690. Dorothy Chapman Saunders, *Bristol RI's Early Settlers* (Palm Bay, Fla., 1991), 100.

15. Elizabeth Sandy (1691–1694) was three and a half when she died "by a blow from a horse." She was Joseph and Bethia Lucas Sandy's fifth child. Saunders, *Bristol, RI's Early Settlers,* 121.

To Rowland Cotton, 24 September 1694

Plymouth Sept: 24: 1694:

Deare Son

J: Rickard came from Bost: on Saturday morning, noe newes; your moth's day of going is uncertaine as also the way by land or sea, but I conclude in 2 or 3 days she will depart; D[r] Sherman dyed last weeke: I was troubled to thinke how much raine you felt on Friday, but I am much more afflicted to thinke how sollicitous the enemy of soules is to hinder the worke of Christ with you:[1] what think you of a day of prayer, your church alone at your house, or your whole society publickly? next weeke is your Court & it cannot be, but I am willing for a spetiall good to change pulpits with you oct: 7: & suppose your Fast should be on Monday oct: 8: you can come from hence home by 10 a clock, & soe may M[r] Russell[2] & soe wee may all together spend that day, & not goe to Sackonessitt[3] till next morning & that time enough to reach the vineyard that day, if God please: If you approove of this designe & tell me soe I will then write to M[r] R:[4] immediately about it that at his Lecture you may conferre about it; & also to M[r] Prince[5] who may with Cap: B: promote it, all this is submitted to your censure, but I fancy something of this nature may doe well: wee are in expectation of your Bro:s coming daily to fetch his child; wee 3 salute you & yours most heartily, with uncessant prayers, I rest

your Affectionate Father

John Cotton

mr Prince much approoves of a church meeting, oct: 8: & prayer, he thinks you may doe well this next Sabbath to give notice to the Church of the meeting then to be: I yesterday told M[r] Mayhew,[6] it might be Tuseday morning before wee came to Sakonessitt:

A token for your Joanna.[7]

Miscellaneous Bound Collection, Massachusetts Historical Society. Addressed "These For M[r] Rowland Cotton, Preacher of the Gospel, at Sandwich."

1. Rowland's difficulties with his congregation continued. Although Cotton had ministered in Sandwich beginning in 1690, he was not ordained until November 1694, and raising his salary seems to have been a problem until 1696. Prior to obtaining a regular salary, Cotton seems to have solicited individual donations for his support, which evidently angered some of his congregants. *Sibley's Harvard Graduates*, 3:323-26.
2. Jonathan Russell, minister at Barnstable.
3. Sackonessit is modern-day Falmouth.
4. Jonathan Russell.
5. Samuel Prince (1649–1728) of Middleborough.
6. Experience Mayhew (1673–1758, H.C. 1720), minister on Martha's Vineyard. Weis, *Colonial Clergy*, 138.
7. Rowland and Elizabeth's daughter had been born just a few weeks earlier, on 16 August 1694. Kardell and Lovell, *Vital Records of Sandwich*, 35. This "postscript" was written on a strip of paper dated by Prince, "Plimouth—Sept. 24. 1694" and attached to the bottom of the letter.

From Samuel Fuller et al, 5 October 1694

To the Church of Christ in plimouth.
Reverend & well beloved in oure Comon Savior

we acknowledge with greate thankefullnes to God his greate goodnes to us in givinge us a naile in his holy place, vouchsafeing us the enjoyement of his holy ordinances; by youre acceptance of us to youre felloshipe; & we very thankefully acknowledge youre christian Care & love in cherishinge us under the wings of youre Communion as God hath given oppertunitie & deare Brethren, as it is a matter of humiliatione to us; that we have made noe better improvement of such Spirituall advantages; soe it is noe smale afflictione to us that oure dwellinges are soe remote from you that wee cannot soe (constantly & some of us through many bodely infimities but [vere?] rearely) attend those sealing ordinances which oure soules need for oure spiriuall oedificatione & growth in grace; we have therefore had many serious thoughts, wether God doth not Call us to gather into a distinct Church Societie, and to have one Amonge oure selves to Administer the holy things of God to us, the motion is weighty & we cannot but be sensible of oure insufficiency to manage soe greate a worke we therefor looke up to God for his directione & helpe being in Covenant with youre selves: we aske Counsel of the Lord att youre mouthe & praye you to afford us youre advice & assistance in this matter: there are some Bretheren of other churches livinge amonge us: whoe are desirus to Ingage with us in this worke & we hope allsoe some well affected neighbors whoe are settinge ther faces Zion ward, we humbly beg youre prayers to God, that God would build up his house amongst us & that we maye be prepared for soe greate a mercy & have grace rightly to improve itt & subscribe oure selves youre lovinge Brethren

Samuel ffuller[1]
Samuel Cudbert[2]
Samuel wood[3]
John Bennet[4]
Abiall wood[5]
middleberry

october 5. 1694

Miscellaneous Bound Collection, Massachusetts Historical Society. Addressed "To the Reverend Mr John Cotton. Pastor of the Church att plimoth. to be Communicated to that church. thes dd." Cotton's note: "The Church voted their consent to & approbation of this motion, oct: 21:"

---

1. Samuel Fuller (c. 1629–1695), son of a Mayflower passenger of the same name, moved from Plymouth to Middleboro, where he was one of the town "celect men," soon after King Philip's War. See the letter of 13 September 1694. Margaret Harris Stover and Robert S. Wakefield, eds., *Mayflower Families through Five Generations*, vol. 10 (Plymouth, Mass., 1996), 7.

2. Samuel Cuthbert was born in Plymouth in 1643 to Samuel Cuthbertson, an emigrant in 1623. Samuel died in Middleborough on 17 April 1699. Stratton, *Plymouth Colony*, 277.

3. Samuel Wood, born on 25 May 1647, was the son of Henry Wood of Plymouth. Samuel moved to Middleboro with his father as a young man and served as constable and selectman many times. Savage, *Genealogical Dictionary*, 4:625-26, 629; Weston, *History of the Town of Middleboro*, 63.

4. John Bennett was born in 1642 in Bristol, England, emigrated to Jamestown, Virginia, in 1665 and moved to Beverly, Massachusetts, in 1668. After a short settlement in Weymouth, Bennett moved to Middleboro in 1687. In addition to being one of the church's founders, Bennett later served as a deacon in the church, and as a selectman and town clerk. He died in 1718. Savage, *Genealogical Dictionary*, 1:167-68; Weston, *History of the Town of Middleboro*, 317-18.

5. Abiel Wood was another of Henry Wood's sons, born in Plymouth after 1654. Savage, *Genealogical Dictionary*, 4:625.

From Samuel Angier, 11 October 1694

[To t]he Rev^d^. Pastour, and our Beloved Bretheren of the Church of Christ in Plimouth—

[The Past]our & Bretheren of ye Church of Christ at Rehobo[th] Wish Grace, Mercy and Peace.

[B]eloved—Haveing Appointed ye 24 day of this October for the ordination of Mr Thomas Greenwood[1] [to the] office of a pastour among us, according to the order [of the Go]spell, we Intreat your Prayers to God for us & him—[...] Joynt Concurrence with us herein; and for that end [...] presence of your Reve^d^. Pastour with us on the day ap[pointed, a]lso that you wil send with him a messenger to witness [...]ent,[2] and Joyne with us in Prayers and the work. [ ] shall hear at Mr Greenwood's of the places provided after [ ]re, for Entertainment; and Intreat you to meet at his [..] ten of the Clock in the morning of the day appointed for [ ]ion. Wishing the Divine Presence with you and [ ]y upon your sacred Administrations, we Remain your [aff]ectionate Bretheren—

11:1694[3]

Samuel Angier[4] Pastour

with ye Consent of the Bretheren

Miscellaneous Collections, Massachusetts Historical Society. Addressed "To ye Rev^d^. Mr Cotton, Pastour of ye Church of Christ in Plimouth." Cotton's note, at bottom: "[I]n answer to this letter, oct: 21: the Church chose Brother Thomas Cushman to accompany the Pastor, who went at the time appointed:" The left edge of the letter is mutilated.

1. Thomas Greenwood (1673–1720, H.C. 1690) was ordained as minister to the Rehoboth Church on 24 October 1694 and remained in service to that church until his death. Weis cites the often noted, but mistaken, birth-year of 1670/1. Weis, *Colonial Clergy,* 97; *Sibley's Harvard Graduates,* 4:60-62; *CSM,* 22:175.
2. "In the event"?
3. "Oct." is penciled in under this date.
4. See the letter of 27 October 1679.

To Rowland Cotton, 18 October 1694

Plymouth october, 18: 1694:

Deare Son

Thanks to you both for the kinde entertainment; Bet: cl:[1] comes not, because her brother is come newly from sea; Dick is for his uncle a fortnight hence. your mother might have had many Easterne children, she hath brought us a boy, & 2 girles,[2] a third was not ready in the night she came away, but she comes in the next vessell, her designe was to supply you & John, if you please, they are promising girles o that you could be provided for the sabbath & lye with us to morrow night, for letters from Rehoboth call me to the ordination wednesday next[3] & I shall not see you if you stay till next weeke, & you shall first take your girle if you come & please my family being great with the addition of 3: you shall have all newes from your blessed mothers mouth; Mr Crosby is in post haste; you may tell Mr Russell[4] that Sam: Moodey[5] baiting in the way, his horse went from him with bridle, sadle, pormanteau, all his money, & linen in it etc not heard of <till> last Saturday, he well at Boston: my Resp: to Mr: & tell him I speedily desire to be sent me the Ministers paper he hath of mine, wee shall need it for midlebury: The crape you shall have; wee both with Sarah send you our hearty love, God blesse you & all yours

soe daily prayes your Affectionate Father

John Cotton

Mar: Dummer is dead:[6]

Biskets	0-1-0
Rum—0-1-0	
a gallon wine	0-3-6
more wine—	0-1-0
Rum -	0-1-0
more Rum	0-1-0
more—	0-1-0
more—	0-1-0
more—	0-1-0
more—	0-1-0
Borrowed mony	1-10-0
1 Gall wine	0-06-0
1 pint madera	
1 pint madera	
1 qut madera	
1 qut madera	

1 qut madera		
1 pint madera	4-6	
15 pd Beef—		1-10
		2-14-4[7]

Miscellaneous Bound Collection, Massachusetts Historical Society. Addressed "These For Mr Rowland Cotton, Preacher of the Gospel, at Sandwich. your Jacket is here."

---

1. Unknown; presumably "Betty," but no surname seems clear.
2. The "Easterne children" are Native indentured servants. David Silverman, "The Impact of Indentured Servitude on the Society and Culture of Southern New England Indians, 1680–1810," *New England Quarterly* 74 (2001): 622-66.
3. See 11 October 1694.
4. Jonathan Russell, minister at Barnstable.
5. Probably Samuel Moody (d. 1729, H.C. 1689), who preached occasionally at Hadley during 1693 and 1694 before turning to a military career by 1705 at St. John's, Newfoundland. Cotton described "baiting" him for Russell, which may mean that Russell was hoping to invite Moody to Barnstable in 1694, when Moody was still unsettled in a pulpit. Samuel Moody was also at Harvard when Rowland was a tutor. *Sibley's Harvard Graduates,* 3:406-9.
6. Probably Mary Dummer, who died on 5 October 1694. Thomas, *Diary of Samuel Sewall,* 1:321.
7. This account, in another hand, appears on the reverse of the letter.

To Rowland Cotton, 30 October 1694

Plymouth october, 30: 1694

Deare Son

Particulars at Rehob: & for woodstock to morrow ch: gathering & ord: of Mr Dwight[1] you must have viva voce:[2] C: Basset[3] was desired in presce[nce.] [Tel]l J: Morton & El: churchel to bring me some lette[rs fro]m Mr Ellistons but betweene 2 or 3 stooles att [...] for by land or sea I receive none as yet: send the [...] speedily, wee want it, your girles mother hath sent her [so]me tokens by Eph: Cole, they are here with us when you c[om]e: John Cole[4] by some fall in his boat last night hath bro[ken] his arme all to peices, as wee heare this morne from Joness river:[5] I have not time to write now to son John, wee are longing to see him (tell him soe) & if he c[ome] not this weeke, wee hope you will come both together to sup with us Nov: 7: one 1/2 000 of pins I send you, the other sort is not to be had; Ask C: Bas: why he brought not my letters: Lord in mercy direct in your case, the reproach of suspension beyond Nov: 21: will be greater then the evill of calling those 6 ches[6] to be present Nov: 20: & counsell & asist you in what they shall Judge best for the setlement of Gods ordinances amongst you: our Love & Sar: to you both, God blesse you all, soe prayes, your Affec: Fath:

J: C:

Sir Coleman says, Mr Brattl[e] came not to Rehob: because of his purpose to be at [S]and: ord:[7] Peg's sis: Betty is now living with Eph: Cole: my wife proceeds not about a girle for your Bro: John till she speakes with him[.] wee wish you both had your fish:

By Mr Athearne[8] the pins & a violl[9] of sweet Almonds,[10] warme it & drop into her eares as much as they will hold & put in black wooll, bring the violl againe, & another you have also soe says your mother:

Miscellaneous Bound Collection, Massachusetts Historical Society. Addressed "These For Mr Rowland Cotton, Preacher of the Gospel at Sandwich."

---

1. According to Sibley, Josiah Dwight (1671–1748, H.C. 1687) was ordained "about 1690" in Woodstock, Connecticut, but this letter suggests that he was ordained on 31 October 1694. His thirty-six-year ministry was plagued by poor salaries, contentious congregations, and accusations against him. In 1726, the church voted overwhelmingly to release him. He accepted a call to Dedham's third church in Westwood in 1735. *Sibley's Harvard Graduates,* 3:395-400.
2. "By voice."
3. See 25 September 1688.
4. While there are several possibilities, the reference may be to John Cole (1660–1748), who with Susanna Gray Cole (1668–1727) was found guilty of pre-marital fornication by the Plymouth Court in June 1688. Cotton noted in the church records that in April of that year, Susanna was "called before the church openly for fornication with John Cole before her marriage to him, she exprest some penitential words, & was laid under Admonition by the vote of the church." *PCR,* 195; Torrey, *New England Marriages,* 169; *CSM,* 22:261.
5. Jones River is in modern-day Kingston, Massachusetts.
6. "Churches."
7. Benjamin Colman evidently told Cotton about William Brattle's plans not to attend Thomas Greenwood's ordination in Rehoboth; he presumably did so in a letter, which has not been found. Apparently, Brattle planned to attend Rowland's ordination in Sandwich in November instead.
8. Savage refers to a Simon Athearn who lived on Martha's Vineyard, represented the island to the General Court in 1692, was married to Mary Butler on 4 October 1665 and died on 26 February 1711, at the age of seventy-one. His three sons were baptized in Barnstable. Savage, *Genealogical Dictionary,* 1:72; Torrey, *New England Marriages,* 23.

9. "Vial."

10. Nicholas Culpeper described how to make oils from several nuts, including sweet almonds, but he recommended an oil of bitter almonds to treat "such as are deaf," by dropping the oil "into their Ears" as Joanna suggested. Culpeper, *The English Physician Enlarged,* 211.

To Rowland Cotton, 1 November 1694

Plymouth November, 1: 1694:

Deare Son

Letters are come[1] to invite us to Mr Lawsons ordination,[2] 14th Instant, Mr willard,[3] Mr Norton,[4] Mr Cushion[5] are also sent to; & because that should be my Lecture & I had not the last, my present thoughts are to have my Lecture next wednesday, Nov: 7: & therefore if you & your Bro: have any thoughts of coming then, regulate your houres on that account; what made C: Bas: forget my letters? I am glad I have them, though none from you; I your moth: & sis: salute you both most heartily, with daily prayers,

I rest, your Affectionate Father

John Cotton

I am much thinking what I shall heare of your concernes next week; I shall speedily want the Paper de Toleration which Mr Russell[6] hath of mine, for midlebury church (I thinke) Dec: 12: will goe forward,[7] whatever yours will; If you have noe conclusion soe as to disperse letters next weeke for Nov: 21: it must then cease till next yeare & perhaps forever; Gods will be done: Dick is gone this morning in J: morton, last Tuseday betweene this & the ponds (probably about Ele-river[8]) his upper coat was lost off a horse, good homespun full'd cloath, puter buttons, close at the hands, perhaps some Indian found, aske to the utmost for it & at Moreys, that if possible, wee may have it to send the lad:

Miscellaneous Bound Collection, Massachusetts Historical Society. Addressed "These For Mr Rowland Cotton, Preacher of the Gospel at Sandwich."

1. Not found.

2. Deodat Lawson was ordained by the second church in Scituate (Norwell) on 14 November 1694. Prior to his calling to Scituate, Lawson had ministered in Edgartown (1681–1682) and in Danvers (1683–1688). He was dismissed by Scituate in 1698, having returned to England two years earlier. Cotton's

church records refer to Lawson's church as "chh at the North River." See the letters below of 22 August 1695 and 9 October 1695. Weis, *Colonial Clergy,* 124; *CSM,* 22:176.

3. Samuel Willard, minister at Old South Church, Boston.
4. John Norton (c.1650–1716, H.C. 1671) ministered to the Hingham church from 1678 until his death in 1716. Weis, *Colonial Clergy,* 152; *Sibley's Harvard Graduates,* 2:394-96.
5. Probably Jeremiah Cushing (1654–1706, H.C. 1676), who preached in Hingham and Haverhill before becoming the settled minister at the First Church in Scituate from 1691 until illness forced him to stop preaching in 1705. Weis, *Colonial Clergy,* 66; *Sibley's Harvard Graduates,* 2:498-99.
6. Jonathan Russell, minister in Barnstable.
7. See 13 September 1694.
8. The Eel River is in Plymouth, Massachusetts.

To Rowland Cotton, 19 November 1694

Plymouth, November, 19: 1694

Deare Son

I have Letters[1] from Coll. Allyn, Bro: Rosseter,[2] they all well; & from son Allyn[3] & Bradbury[4] dated Nov: 5: they all well, Capt Things death[5] was oct: 30: At Saco fort[6] 4 Indians came, madockawando[7] or his son one of them, 2 went into fort & stayed there whilst some English went out to speake with the other 2 Indians;[8] one of them bragd he had killed 22 English, the English killed them both & then they within the fort killed the other 2, all the scalps sent to Boston: Sam: Philips[9] (the bookseller) came last weeke from O: E:[10] the King not returned from Flanders; Jane Armitage is at our house for our son John, send him word of it with utmost speed that he may take some care to fetch her: Eluezer Rickard[11] & young Sam: King[12] were prest yesterday[13] Just before catechising; Letters[14] from Major Walley[15] are with me to goe to Major Thacher,[16] I suppose a presse is in it. But all this time we are distracted about next weeke pur orders for the Thanksgiving to be on Nov: 29: are come to us, it seems difficult if not impossible to divert that publick universall day; what to doe I cannot devise, you must talk with C: Bassett & your other brethren & freinds & if you could consult Mr Russell;[17] either your day must be on Tuseday, Nov: 27: (which perhaps may produce noe inconvenience) or on Dec: 5: the Lord direct in mercy, doe something in the matter with utmost speed; I hope in God it will be, though through many difficulties: Had I not mist of Ben: Eaton[18] this morn I might have had your answer by your Bro: Sal:[19] Hasten to some good Conclusion, wee 3 salute you both & with prayers, etc.

I am, your Affectionate Father

John Cotton

The more I thinke, the more I like Tuseday, if you can like it many here approove it, & then every minister may be at his owne home & keepe Thank-day, & you may have helpe too: perhaps you may have another Narrative truer about the 4 Indians, some say they found them to be spies:

Miscellaneous Bound Collection, Massachusetts Historical Society. Addressed "These For Mr Rowland Cotton, Preacher of the Gospel, at Sandwich."

---

1. Not found.
2. Josiah Rosseter, Joanna Cotton's brother, lived in Guilford, Connecticut.
3. James Alling (1673–1696), Elizabeth Cotton's husband and Cotton's son-in-law.
4. Cotton's daughter Maria (b. 1672) was married to Wymond Bradbury (1669–1734) and lived in Salisbury. *Sibley's Harvard Graduates,* 1:507.
5. Jonathan Thing (1654–1694) lived in Exeter and served on both the Grand Jury and as constable. According to Savage, there was a jury of inquiry into Thing's death, and it ruled that he was "shot by his own gun." Savage, *Genealogical Dictionary,* 4:279.
6. Along with the 1692 construction of Fort William Henry in Pemaquid, Maine, Massachusetts paid to build a fort across the river from Saco in what is now Biddeford. Gallay, *Colonial Wars of North America,* 349.
7. Sachem of the Penobscots, one of the leaders of the attack on Oyster River in July 1694. According to Thomas Hutchinson, Madockawando carried the scalps earned in Oyster River and presented them to Quebec's Governor Frontenac personally. See 23 July 1694. Hutchinson, *History of the Colony and Province of Massachusetts-Bay*, 61.
8. Drake describes this event in *The Border Wars of New England,* 104.
9. Samuel Philips was a bookseller in Boston who maintained a stock similar in size to those of his competitors Benjamin Harris and Michael Perry. Philips, like most Boston booksellers, specialized in English imports but increasingly also carried colonial imprints. Isaiah Thomas, *The History of Printing in America, with a Biography of Printers & an Account of Newspapers,* 2d ed., ed. Marcus A. McCorison (1810; reprint, New York, 1970), 185-86; Amory and Hall, *History of the Book in America,* 99-100, 104, 106.
10. Old England.
11. Eleazer and Sarah Rickard had three children, Sarah (b. 1688), Judith (b. 1701) and Lidiah (b. 1704), and lived in Plymouth. Van Antwerp, *Vital Records of Plymouth,* 28.
12. Samuel King Jr. (b. 1674) and Bethia King later married and had four children in Plymouth, Jonah (b. 1697), Sarah (b. 1699), Rebekah (b. 1700) and Samuel (b. 1702). He was the son of Samuel (b. 1649) and Sarah Dunham King (c. 1650–1738) of Plymouth. Van Antwerp, *Vital Records of Plymouth,* 24; Torrey, *New England Marriages,* 439.
13. Rickard and King were both evidently "pressed" (impressed) into military service on behalf of Plymouth.
14. Not found.
15. For Walley, see the letter of 10 August 1694.
16. Possibly Samuel Thacher (1648–1726) of Watertown, whom Savage describes as "leuit." Savage, *Genealogical Dictionary,* 4:272-73.

17. Jonathan Russell, minister at Barnstable.

18. Benjamin Eaton was the son of *Mayflower* emigrant Francis Eaton. He was married to Sarah Hoskins in 1660 and had at least one son, William, who died in 1691. Eaton had received land as part of the "first born" land donated by Maj. Josiah Winslow and Capt. Southworth. He qualified for free land in 1662 because he was a needy child born to parents who were in Plymouth by 1627. Stratton, *Plymouth Colony,* 182, 187, 205, 288.

19. Rowland's brother-in-law, Richard Saltonstall.

To Rowland Cotton, 21 November 1694

Plimouth November, 21: 1694:

Deare Son

Love carrys through many difficulties easily & makes heavy burdens light, but in very deed it is unparalelled selfe-deniall for your mother now to come, as she can tell you; Satans designe by Tob: (which in Hebrew is Bonum, but not soe in English at this time) I am amazed at & much more to heare of SM's dreadfull lye, that 4 of the ch:[1] never consented; Sir Grosvenor[2] sayes Mr R:[3] knows it to be false: your ch: meeting I should much feare the issue of, but that perhaps you may be too <late> lame to goe to it, but if you be at it, I presume you will call for noe vote, but if any opposers show their venemous spirit in the case; tell them you are not eager to take office, but are waiting upon God to know his minde & if those Elders etc next weeke advise against it, you will freely hearken to them: I went with your Bro: Sir Gr: (Mr Thomas went to Bos: with them) till Duxb: path & went on purpose to aske Mr Wiswalls[4] counsell, he is resolved, if God permit, to be with you on Tuseday & Judges the Thank-day should not at all divert your work Nov: 28: because yours was first notifyed to divers ches;[5] he cannot stay with you on Thursday but will spend it in travelling homewards, but perhaps I & some others maye preach for you then: but be you very carefull to be much with God for his helpe to prepare your ordination-sermon, for that must be; yours[6] by J: cl: received, I blesse God your heart is fixed in Gods way, to be at his disposall; perhaps Mr Prince may obtaine an act of councill for these ches that must attend you, to keepe the Th-day the weeke after; [...][7] salutations & prayers as ever,

from your Affectionate Father

John Cotton

My kinde love to Capt Bassett,[8] I hope God will helpe him now to carry it wisely at this ch: meeting, & if he have Thanksg: papers let him not disperse them till next weeke, he will incurre noe blame by soe doing:[9]

Miscellaneous Bound Collection, Massachusetts Historical Society. Addressed "These For Mr Rowland Cotton, Preacher of the Gospel, at Sandwich."

---

1. "Church."
2. William Grosvenor (1673–1733, H.C. 1693) was living with his widowed mother in 1694, when she purchased land in Brookline, and he was marked as "Gentleman" on the deed. In 1701, the family moved to Pomfret, Connecticut, and William was invited to preach by the town in Brookfield, Connecticut. He served as the settled minister in this frontier town from 1705 to 1708, despite repeated Indian attacks that undermined his efforts to form a church and took his brother's life. He eventually settled in Charlestown, South Carolina, where he died. Weis, *Colonial Clergy,* 98; *Sibley's Harvard Graduates,* 4:167-68.
3. Jonathan Russell, minister in Barnstable.
4. Ichabod Wiswall (1637–1700, H.C. 1651), minister at Duxbury from 1676 to 1700. Weis, *Colonial Clergy,* 233.
5. "Churches."
6. Not found.
7. Four or five words crossed out.
8. William Bassett, see 25 September 1688.
9. Cotton was suggesting that Bassett delay delivering requests from the General Court that congregations hold a general day of thanksgiving because it would coincide with Rowland's ordination.

From Samuel Cutbert and Samuel Fuller, 3 December 1694

To the church of christ in Plimouth

grace mercy and peace in oure Deare saviour

Reverend and Beloved

That God who hath the hearts of all in his owne hand havinge soe disposed that sundry of us are desirous to enter into church fellowshipe one with another that we may Injoy all the ordinances of christ for oure edificatione & growth in grace we have therefore agreed to sett apart the twenty sixt day of this instant December for humbling our selves before God & lookinge to him & waitinge upon him; for gratious success & blessinge; in gatheringe of the church; & then settlinge a teaching Elder amongst us. If the Lord shall please soe gratiously to smile upon us; It is heareupon oure earnest desire that you would send to us youre Reverend Pastor and some

Brethren to assist us in the mangement of this worke: that our faith & order maye be soe manifested as maye be to the Satisffaction of the churches of christ wee beg your prayers that God would prepare us for soe greate a mercy & that wee maye walke worthy of the vocatione wherewith we are Called & rest

youre Bretheren in Christ

Samuel Fuller[1]
Samuel Cutbert

in the name of those whoe desire & purpose with Gods helpe to proceed in this worke

Middlebury December 3: 1694

Miscellaneous Bound Collection, Massachusetts Historical Society. Cotton's note: "Members of Plymouth-church now to dismissed to this worke; Mr Samuel Fuller—Elizabeth his wife/ John Bennett—Deborah his wife/ Samuel Cutbert Esther, the wife of Ephraim Tinkham/ Samuel Wood Elizabeth, the wife of Eben-ezer Tinkham/ Abiel Wood/ & all their children. The church chose Deac: Faunce, Deac: Morton, Bro: Ephraim Morton & Bro: Eliezer churchel to goe with the Pastor on this service, They all did & on Dec: 30: the Pastor told the church how the worke was attended & perfected."

---

1. See 13 September and 5 October 1694; see also *CSM*, 22:176.

From Samuel Danforth, 5 February 1695

Tanton. Febr. 5. 94/5

Rev^d^ Sr

yo^rs^ of Jany. 25: I rec^d^[1] & wish all the Travellers between o^r^ Towns, were better spirted then to interrupt o^r^ Intercourse by theyr negligence to give speedy Transport to o^r^ Letters. But I am served so also wth respect to others. I sent a letter to Boston a month since & have no Answer to it yett. [Sckikard?] came safe to yor son who is in health. yor Request of a sight of my Indian Attempts[2] is a very kind offer: & the more kind because you presented me in yor offer of it who intended to have petitioned yo^r^selfe for such an intrest in yor Love. I have sent one of the Revd Mr Incr. Mathers sermons to you: I had writt some of it fair before yor letter came: but to shew you that it is not w^th^out faults I have mended diverse in it myselfe: & the more faults you shall please to mend, the greater your kindness will be to me: But as to yor Notion of any thing of mine Going to the Press: you are the first person who acquaint me wth it & I pray you to suppress the Notion or press it to death: I am not fond of such a thing, But have chosen to translate a printed sermon or two, in order to the sending of them to Cosen Rawson of Mendon[3] who has promised to correct them & thereby to approve himselfe a schoolmastr to me: But if you will joyn wth him in becoming part of a Tuto[r] to me you will oblige me highly & I shall endevor to testify my Thankfullness to you according to weak Ability. Thus Craving yo[r] prayers & Commending you & yo[rs] to Divine Mercy wth best service

I Rest Yo[rs] humbly & affectionately

Sam[ll] Danforth

Curwen Family Papers, American Antiquarian Society. Addressed "For the Reverend M[r] John Cotton sen[r] Pasto[r] of the church at Plymouth these." Endorsed "From mr samuel Danforth, February, 5: 1694:"

---

1. Not found.
2. Despite his protests, Samuel Danforth did publish his translation of Increase Mather's *Greatest Sinners Exhorted and Encouraged* (Boston, 1686) [Evans 415] as *Masukkenukeeg Matchesaenuog Wequetoog Kah Wuttoonatoog Uppeyaonont Christoh* (Boston, 1698) [Evans 832]. Charles Evans, *American Bibliography* (New York, N.Y., 1941-59), 1:70, 129.
3. Grindall Rawson (1659–1715, H.C. 1678) was the settled minister in the frontier town of Mendon from 1680 until his death. Active in Native missionary work throughout his life, Rawson translated several sermons into Native languages, preached to Christian Indians for twenty-seven years and joined Samuel Danforth on a tour of Native missions for the Society for the Propagation of the Gospel in 1698. He also served as a chaplain for soldiers on the Canadian expedition of 1691. *Sibley's Harvard Graduates*, 3:159-68.

To Rowland Cotton, 12 February 1695

Plym: Feb: 12: 94:/95:

Deare Son

I hope you have mine by Sam: Daniel[1] on Saturday; W. Thomas[2] (who carryed his sister) heard at Ipswich the Fort was found in hideous woods, when he came to Salem Col: Gidney[3] who came from Boston on Saturday told him etc on Sabbath-night that he had bin at the Examination of the Indians, Bumbazeen[4] was sullen & would confesse nothing, but Shipscott Johns[5] son or sons owned they had bin at the building of it, & being askt why they built that fort, answered it was to entertaine the French etc that were to come over the lake, soe that it is groundlesse to question the truth of that story; The terrible storme of snow made our Assembly on the sabbath short of 80, soe that twice in a way unusuall I am deprived of an opportunity to aske the church about my going to their Fast, I perceive my choice (yea almost all) my brethren are utterly against helping them, but if they were for it, God says it shall not be the snow being up to horse-belly generally each step, & I blesse God for putting the matter out of doubt by his owne hand: Their spirits, tongues & carriages are very perverse; on Saturday a vicars of Nantaskett[6] came in from the Cape laden with oyle, all well with them, a great preservation; our good Rebekah had a new daughter last Sabbath day;[7] your Journey to us is over for the present, you may not hazard life or health now to see us, I hope the snow will be gone before my next Lecture, <& desire neither you nor—>[8] you have our heartyest Salutations each of you from us 3 respectively & my daily fervent prayers,

who am, your Affectionate Father

John Cotton

Noe news or hopes of Mr Thomas till better wayes.

T: T: at Barnes's last friday show'd himselfe much to be a vaine-glorious foole,[9] boasting of his worth, abilities, knowledge, litle need to heare preachers etc made himselfe very ridiculous to the company which was numerous, Seth Pope[10] & W: cl: did stump & jeere him terribly & soe did others. I long to heare some good of your ch: meeting, methinks without him all might doe well. Melvin or Milton bring this.

Miscellaneous Bound Collection, Massachusetts Historical Society. Addressed "These For Mr Rowland Cotton, Pastour of the church at Sandwich."

---

1. Not found. Savage lists both a Samuel Daniel who was born in Watertown on 1 April 1674 and his father, who married Mary Grant on 10 May 1671 and died in 1695. Cotton was probably referring to the son, who married on 15 March 1694 in Boston. Savage, *Genealogical Dictionary,* 2:9-10; Torrey, *New England Marriages,* 203.

2. Probably William Thomas, son of Nathaniel Thomas of Marshfield.

3. Bartholomew Gedney (1640–1698) was a colonel, representative, assistant and judge in Salem. He served in elected positions under both charters and in Andros's council. Savage, *Genealogical Dictionary,* 2:240.

4. Bombazeen was one of the Native leaders who signed the 1693 Pemaquid peace treaty but also participated in the renewed warfare that followed as a French ally. In November 1694, he and two Native allies went to Fort William Henry under the flag of truce and were captured by colonial commanders. Bombazeen was taken to Boston, according to Cotton Mather, so "that he might in a close Imprisonment there, have time to consider of his Treacheries, and his cruelties." Mather included an "interview" with Bombazeen in *Decennium Luctuosum*. In November 1698, Bombazeen's petition for release after more than four years' confinement was heard by the Court, and, despite misgivings, it was granted. Mather, *Decennium Luctuosum,* 255, 256-58; *Acts and Resolves of the Province of Massachusetts Bay*, 7:601.

5. Sheepscoat John was one of John Eliot's praying Indians but had become a French ally prior to the war. John was one of the interpreters at the 1693 peace talks at Fort William Henry in Pemaquid. Mather credited him with the renewed efforts at peace in the spring of 1695. See the letter below of 29 May 1695. Drake, *Border Wars*, 105-6; Mather, *Decennium Luctuosum*, 251, 259.

6. George and Rebecca Phipenny Vickery (Vicars) probably had five sons who may have been shipmasters, George, Isaac, Israel, Jonathan or Benjamin. Savage, *Genealogical Dictionary*, 4:373.

7. Possibly Sarah Churchill, born on 10 February 1695 to Rebecca and John Churchill. Van Antwerp, *Vital Records of Plymouth*, 6.

8. Four and a half lines crossed out, of which only the first four words are decipherable.

9. Probably more about Thomas Tupper, Rowland's nemesis; see 13 September 1694 and 26 July 1695.

10. Probably Seth Pope (1648–1727), who was the son of Thomas and Sarah Jenney Pope of Plymouth and lived in Sandwich and Dartmouth. Savage, *Genealogical Dictionary*, 3:459; Torrey, *New England Marriages*, 593.

To Rowland Cotton, 22 March 1695

Plymouth March, 22, 1694:/95:

Deare Son

The Major Generall Winthrop[1] tells me that Sarah's hood is at Moreys found by Indian Squaws, I order long John to take & deliver it to you, admonish her not to loose it as she goes to Yarmouth on Monday, if it must cost yo[u] money to transplant her from your soyle thither I will reimburse you on sight of your bill of charges: I saw Theoph:[2] well yesterday & owe not for a day past: Jos: Bradford from Norwich[3] called at Cos. Maceys 'siah[4] wrote by him[,] is well & says he courted [...][5] Gustavus Hamilton ca[ ] [...] here he waites for his—(tha[t he del]ivered at cape Ane) toge[ther] [...] to buy salt at Ex[...]: he brought me a letter from bless[ed Mr] Trail dated Nov: 7:[6] & 2 choice English Physick bookes a token to your Mother; He much commends the King & affirmes the Queen to be far the best that ever was, a serious, cordiall, knowing protestant; he salutes all of you my children: Gustavus seeing 3 daughters when he was here 5 yeares since stared much on every female in my house but could not finde one of them, mris Sarah will loose his sweet fellowship: he lyes at Dol's a nest & cage of uncleane beasts & birds black & white night & day: I think to goe next weeke My selfe on Tuseday to fetch Jos:[7] home: Bacchus cannot, will not goe to service: El: wadsw:[8] paid at court 4 pd: Sam: Tilden[9] the same, & _____ of Bridgewater the same; Jos: Holmes[10] & Sam: Bartlet[11] came off with a check and court fees: Sam: Sprague[12] denyes fact & will be tryed by his peeres, his bonds continued till the next Court: old Tracyes[13] processe deferred till then also; because the Justices will first examine some points of law: Su: Ransom[14] got Authority to turne John Dotey out of his overseer-ship, & they chose James clarke & young Giles Guardians for her children & before witnesse tooke possession of her housing & lands & warned widow ('siah) morton[15] not to touch plow etc & soe the Court is ended:[16] My selfe & Dearest say, hearty love

I am, your Affectionate Father

John Cotton

J. morton says last Tuseday, the old ch:[17] chose Deac: Bridgham[18] & one Jackson (whom I know not) Elders & John Dyer[19] & David Copp[20] Deacons, 3 marblehead men over set & drowned 12th Instant.

I saw madam winslow & mris Pelham; Ned well in o: E:[21] a 1000 pd & more is due to them with mris Bellingham, which they have reason to think he will bring them this summer, James winst: is come home with his wife,[22] & John Clarke was last sabbath published to the younger sister (& is now to be [set?] up here) at which the Elder (his old sweet heart) much frets[23]

Miscellaneous Bound Collection, Massachusetts Historical Society. Addressed "These For Mr Rowland Cotton, Pastor of the Church, at Sandwich."

---

1. Fitz-John Winthrop (1639–1707), major, assistant commander of the colonial forces in King William's War, colonial agent and governor of Connecticut from 1698 to 1707. Savage, *Genealogical Dictionary,* 4:608.
2. Theophilus Cotton.
3. Joseph Bradford (1674[?]–1747) lived in Norwich, Connecticut, and was Gov. William Bradford's grandson. Savage, *Genealogical Dictionary,* 1:232.
4. Josiah Cotton.
5. Several words lost to a tear in the letter.
6. Not found. William Trail sent another letter to Cotton; see his of 15 August 1690.
7. Josiah Cotton.
8. Elisha Wadsworth (d. 1741) had married Elizabeth Wiswall in December 1694, and they lived in Duxbury. Torrey, *New England Marriages,* 769.
9. Samuel Tilden (1660–1739) married Sarah Curtice in 1694 and lived in Scituate. Torrey, *New England Marriages,* 742; Savage, *Genealogical Dictionary,* 4:301.
10. Possibly Josiah Holmes of Duxbury. Torrey, *New England Marriages,* 384.
11. Samuel Bartlett (d. 1713) was married to Hannah Pabodie (1662–1714 or later) and lived in Duxbury. Torrey, *New England Marriages,* 49.
12. Possibly Samuel Sprague, who lived in Duxbury and married Ruth Alden (1674–1758) in 1694. Or perhaps Samuel Sprague (b. 1640) who married Sarah Chillingworth and lived in Marshfield. Torrey, *New England Marriages,* 698.

13. Probably John Tracy (1633[?]–1718), who lived in Duxbury. Savage, *Genealogical Dictionary,* 4:320.

14. Joshua Ransom's second wife was widow Susannah Garner (d. 1735). The couple had married in 1692 in Plymouth. She had two living children from her first marriage to Samuel Garner (d. 1689) of Plymouth when she married Ransom: Samuel Garner (b. 1683) and Nathaniel Garner (b. 1685). She was apparently unhappy with John Dotey's role as guardian after Ransom died. Torrey, *New England Marriages,* 611; Van Antwerp, *Vital Records of Plymouth,* 6, 86, 134.

15. Josiah Morton died in 1694; his widow was Susanna Wood/Ward Morton. Torrey, *New England Marriages,* 522.

16. In much of the last section of this letter, Cotton seems to have been recounting business from the Court of General Sessions and Common Pleas in Plymouth. The records of this court from 1693–June 1698 no longer remain.

17. The "old church" is First Church, Boston.

18. Joseph Bridgham (1652–1709) served as a representative, and as both a deacon and ruling elder of First Church, Boston. Savage, *Genealogical Dictionary,* 1:249-50.

19. John Dyer (1643–1696). Savage, *Genealogical Dictionary,* 2:88.

20. David Copp (1635–1713) was Ruling Elder of Second Church, Boston. Savage, *Genealogical Dictionary,* 1:456.

21. "Old England."

22. James Winslow (b. 1669) married Mary Snow (d. 1717) and had at least two children, Seth (b. 1699) and Mary (b. 1701) in Plymouth. Torrey, *New England Marriages,* 829; Van Antwerp, *Vital Records of Plymouth,* 21.

23. It is most likely that Cotton was referring to the marriage of John Clark (d. 1712) and Rebecca Lincoln (b. 1674), who married on 14 May 1695 in Plymouth. John and Rebecca had five children and remained in Plymouth until John's death in 1712; Rebecca then married Israel Nichols. Among her eight siblings, Rebecca Lincoln had two older sisters, Mary (b. 27 March 1662) and Martha (b. 11 December 1667). Mary had already married Joseph Bates in 1684 when Cotton wrote this letter, so the jilted older sister he mentioned must have been Martha, who died unmarried in 1741. Torrey, *New England Marriages,* 157; Van Antwerp, *Vital Records of Plymouth,* 16; Savage, *Genealogical Dictionary,* 3:92-93.

To Rowland Cotton, 8 April 1695

Plymouth April, 8: 1695:

Deare Son

Mr Torrey is to preach the Election-sermon:[1] when you goe to yarmouth aske Mr otis[2] handsomely for my spur, I want it & shall be glad if he have lost it, provided he will by you send me a new paire: 2 French-men came from Port Royall, walkt through Boston-streets with a white flag towards Govr stoughton, about 30 leagues they drew a canoo over the Ice came to Pemaquid, thence by water to Piscataqua & soe in a sloop to Bost: they have letters from the Govr of Kebeck;[3] they say, 2 mrs of vessells are at st Johns that had bin taken by the Fr. their friends at Bost: feared they had bin lost till now or one of them: their names [...][4] welsh & sunderland:[5] neere your birthday (if not on it) the Q. dyed;[6] being sick but 4 days of the smallpox, quick & thick changes are much now expected: [...][7] your Moth: will doe as you desire; wee are sending to the shop for pins & peper, intending to send them now & horse reddish; & perhaps the life of Mr Norton & Mr Hooker,[8] which post back by the first; if the man that comes for Mar: Pr: intend to returne the same day he comes wee wish he would tarry till wednesday morn, but if he stays a night then let him come to morrow; The hurrys are soe great with 2 or 3 tailors these 2 days to fit out Jos:[9] that nothing can be lookt for or found for Bille, if he be ragged & wicked, it is what J: wat: said of their company, bec: poore & wick: wee may not have a min: wee are willing to lend the booke your wife desires if any body will bring it: old Mris Thornton[10] was buried last friday: Lord give rest to your deare mate; parents & Jos:[11] & The:[12] salute you all: a rich sabbath, all peace, 107 communicants, I long to heare of your sacr: whoever obstructs it, I doubt, will dearly repent it: God be with you all,

your lov: fath:

J: Cotton

Miscellaneous Bound Collection, Massachusetts Historical Society. Endorsed in another hand on reverse "1695 Jno Cotton to Rowland Cotton."

---

1. See 5 May 1688. Samuel Torrey published his 29 May 1695 election sermon as *Man's Extremity, God's Opportunity* (Boston, 1695) [Evans 739]. Evans, *American Bibliography,* 1:116.
2. Probably John Otis (1657–1727) of Barnstable, who served as a representative for more than twenty years, was on the Council for another twenty and married Nathaniel Bacon's daughter, Mercy, in 1683. Torrey, *New England Marriages,* 548; Savage, *Genealogical Dictionary,* 3:324.
3. "Quebec."
4. Several words crossed out; the first two seem to read, "Mr Thomas."
5. Cotton Mather described a brief sea battle between an English ship, manned by eight sailors and two servants, and a French ship with more than sixty men near Barbadoes in 1692. One of the seamen he mentiond was named Sunderland; he also referred to two more "that I now forget." The English sank the French ship in the 1692 battle, but this reference still may have been to the same Sunderland, who evidently was later taken captive by the French. Mather, *Decennium Luctuosum,* 239.
6. Queen Mary died on 28 December 1694. Rowland's birthday was 27 December. Barry Coward, *The Stuart Age* (New York, 1980), 338.
7. Several words crossed out, illegible.
8. Cotton Mather had recently published spiritual biographies of both Thomas Hooker and John Norton. Mather, *Johannes in Eremo, Memoirs Relating to the Lives of the Ever memorable, Mr. John Cotton, who dyed 23d. 10m. 1652. Mr John Norton, who dyed 5d. 2m. 1663....* (Boston, 1695) [Evans 724], and *Piscator Evangelicus. Or, the Life of Mr. Thomas Hooker* (Boston, 1695) [Evans 727]. Evans, *American Bibliography*, 1:114-15.

9. Josiah Cotton.

10. Probably the wife of Rev. Thomas Thornton of Yarmouth; she was the widow of a man named More, but her first name remains unknown. They married on 10 June 1683. Thomas Thorton was born in Yorkshire in 1609, educated for the ministry in England, silenced and ejected in 1662. He immediately settled in Yarmouth, where he served as a preacher and physician from 1662 to 1692. Like Cotton, Thornton ministered to Native congregations as well. Cotton's son John joined Thornton as a ministerial assistant and then served as his successor. Thornton retired from the ministry in 1692 and died in Boston in 1701 at the age of ninety-one. Robert and Ruth Sherman, *Vital Records of Yarmouth, Massachusetts to the Year 1850* (Camden, Me., 1975), 128; Weis, *Colonial Clergy*, 203; Marion Vuilleumier, *The Town of Yarmouth, Massachusetts: A History, 1639–1989* (Yarmouth, 1989), 9, 12, 23.

11. Josiah Cotton.

12. Theophilus Cotton.

To Rowland Cotton, 24 April 1695

Plymouth April, 24: 1695:

Deare Son

your packet received;[1] Are there such fooles as soe to esteem of Grosvenor?[2] Sir Cushing[3] I well like; I would hope some of yarmouth will be soe civill as to accompany him to or neere Sandwich & amongst them doubtlesse Sarah may be accomodated with a birth,[4] if they should not yet I would hope Sir Cushing will be soe kinde as to hand her safe to Sand:[5] & Plim:[6] also, I dare say Dr oliver[7] will not be displeased at it; pray write effecually that her returne at this time may by noe meanes be obstructed: Mr Br: left not your mother till she was as it were in sight of weymouth houses about the mill, which makes her being lost to me the more astonishing, but the good soule was doubtlesse musing deeply about what [illeg.] see) her letter relates to & sufferd the horse to turne head downe towards Hingham towne; I hope your Bro: John will be her companion homewards; J: Nelson[8] will (if he knows the individuall day) goe as far as weymouth to meet her: shute here from Maryland sayes 70 saile of Londoners at virg: G: Woolcott cryes (I suppose) because your mother told her she must send him back he was good for nothing: perhaps the other girle your Moth: talks on may be for us instead of Deb: Mackrill went in March, i:e: a firkin wee sent to Betty & Maria that lay all winter at Ellistons: I intend D: V:[9] to preach 2 sermons on the morrow, now (I thinke) all your queryes are answered: on Monday J: Morton came in the storme, noe letter, but besides divers other things of value there was a pillow beere full, I upon feeling said before the sailors, it was Guilford flax,[10] & soe I thought but when I opened it at home lo, it contained 13 pieces of Duke Hamilton in the forme of that flax, I suppose a parcell of your money purchased some of it, noe doubt you now will Judge you have a strong call to come hither next weeke:

This morning J: Rickard came in & brought many things for us: Mr Trails[11] 2 bookes etc & a letter from your mother,[12] which says, noe body must know of the scotch cloath, ergo Tale[13] when you come here: I suppose your wife may know now, & I am sure Sarah will when she comes home; your Mother was bound to Cambridge on Monday last: she hath not received halfe your Salary (she saith) which argues she hath some: she was not well on Sabbath night when she wrote: M^r^ woodbridge (I Judge the old man) is dead:[14] ours are all well at Salisbury: 2 men killd at saco,[15] she shall want a boat to put a girle aboard (for whom she says not) Tuseday (if faire) she intends home & hopes some man will meet her: my hearty love to you both, God blesse you all,

Soe daily prayes, your Affectionate Father

John Cotton

seale & haste away the inclosed:

Sam: Lucas[16] is this minute, P: M: arrived well with flying colors, he parted with 240 Bush: of graine at the vineyard & hath above 400 yet aboard & cider & some porke & other things, there is mercy in it to our poore who were brought very low:

Miscellaneous Bound Collection, Massachusetts Historical Society. Addressed "These For Mr Rowland Cotton, Pastor of the Church, at Sandwich Per Gallicum Doctorem."[17] Endorsed in a different hand "1695 John Cotton" and "To The Revd Mr John [sic] *Cotton, pastor of the Church of Christ at Sandwich." Cotton wrote around two tears in the right margin.*

---

1. Not found.
2. For William Grosvenor, see 21 November 1694.
3. Probably Caleb Cushing (1673–1752, H.C. 1692), who was born in Scituate and ordained in 1698 in Salisbury, where he remained until his death. Weis, *Colonial Clergy,* 65; *Sibley's Harvard Graduates,* 4:137-39.
4. There are two plausible explanations for this passage. Cotton's daughter, Sarah (b. 1670), may have been following her mother into midwifery. See, for example, 29 May 1695. Alternatively, daughter-in-law Sarah Hubbard Cotton, John's wife, may have been expecting a child. (One unverifiable Internet source referred to a child, Mercy Cotton, born about 1696.)
5. Sandwich.
6. Plimouth.
7. James Oliver (1659–1703, H.C. 1680) was a physician married to Mercy Bradstreet and lived in Cambridge. *Sibley's Harvard Graduates,* 3:198-99.
8. Probably John Nelson of Plymouth/Middleborough. See the letter of September 1696.
9. "God willing."
10. Flax fibers are used to make linen; presumably, Cotton was describing linen cloth from Guilford.

11. William Trail; see 15 August 1690.

12. Not found.

13. "Talley."

14. John Woodbridge was born in 1614, emigrated in 1634 and preached briefly in Andover from 1645 to 1648 before returning to England. After being ejected from his pulpit in 1662, he emigrated again to Newbury, where he ministered for a few years as an assistant to his uncle, Thomas Parker. He seems to have left the ministry before 1670 due to a "sad controversy" that "distracted the quiet of the church," according to Savage. Woodbridge also served as town clerk, schoolmaster, justice of the peace and magistrate, among other offices. He died in Newbury on 17 March 1695 at the age of eighty-two. Weis, *Colonial Clergy,* 235; Savage, *Genealogical Dictionary,* 4:631-32.

15. Cotton Mather referred to the "Falling of Two soldiers belonging to Saco Garrison into the hands of the Enemy, who Took the one, and Kill'd the other, some Time in March, 1695," but did not mention their names. Thomas Hutchinson referred to the killing of one soldier at the Saco fort and the capture of another. Mather, *Decennium Luctuosum,* 259; Hutchinson, *History of the Colony and Province of Massachusetts-Bay,* 65.

16. Samuel Lucas (1661–1716) was the fourth child of Plymouth's Thomas Lucas; he married Patience Warren in 1686. Savage, *Genealogical Dictionary,* 3:127; Torrey, *New England Marriages,* 477.

17. "By the French Doctor."

To Rowland Cotton, 29 April 1695

Apr: 29: 95:

Deare Son

Sam: Lucas was at meeting house doore but could not see ord:[1] because of multitudes; I thought Mr R's rashnesse in compelling an old vote a yeare or 2 since to serve for absolution will have ill effects; I shall be glad of a spur or 2: perhaps your cider boild & raw may be gone before I see sandwich, it would be a comfort to me to see your mate, but never since I had a house was I less willing to step out of sight of it then this last 1/2 yeare: Doth Gershom goe?[2] among the Halls, I shall much expect you to morrow P: M: faile me not, I have noe ch: meeting on wednesday, Amos yet tarrying at midlebury, I greatly hope for your Mother at this time & noe doubt your Bro: will now come also, to keep Mr Cushing I hope will be neddlesse: Sam: L:[3] brought above 700 Bush: neere 300 he unloaded at the vineyard, above 400 here, all gone on Friday & Saturday at 3 shil: per Bush: There needs another Fast, yea many such days to lament that wicked publication, beare your Testimony for God faithfully to them in private speedily & in publick ministry, feare not, God will blesse you in it; Be not partaker of other mens sins, keep thy selfe pure: I salute you both & your Bro: Sal:[4] the Lord Blesse you & all yours,

I am, your Affec: Fath:

J: Cotton

Miscellaneous Bound Collection, Massachusetts Historical Society. Addressed "These For Mr Rowland Cotton, Pastor of the Church, at Sandwich. Per m^r^ Murdo, Q: D: C:" Endorsed in another hand "1695 John Cotton to."

---

1. "Ordination"?
2. Perhaps Cotton was referring to Gershom Hobart; he mentioned him in another letter to Rowland, of 29 May 1695. News of Hobart's capture also appears in 11 August 1694.
3. Samuel Lucas.
4. Rowland's brother-in-law, Richard Saltonstall.

To Rowland Cotton, 11 May 1695

Plymouth May, 11: 1695:

Deare Son

you should have sent me word that you gave Mr Greenwood[1] 1 pd, after I had given him a peice at parting he told me upon my asking soe it was; wee hope much for newes of Capt Gorehams[2] successes, what came to R: Island the bearer can informe you, the Govr caused the Councill to sit on the Sabbath, but when Galley or Frigat went out wee heare not; J: Rickard is this day expected from Boston & then some newes perhaps may come worth telling from o: E: wee doe highly approove of your designe to be with us on Thursday night, & doubt not but the service you desire from the Tailor will then be accomplished: H: St: hath sent your Mother a letter: when you come she & you will agree about your portion of cloath; our love to you both Most heartily, God blesse you all, your

J: C:

Miscellaneous Bound Collection, Massachusetts Historical Society. Addressed "[These For Mr Row]land Cotton, Pastor [of the Church] at Sandwich." Bottom margin of paper trimmed at a later date, cutting off some of the address on the reverse.

---

1. Perhaps shipmaster and mariner Isaac Greenwood (1665–1701, H.C. 1685). *Sibley's Harvard Graduates,* 3:343.
2. Captain John Gorham or James Gorham, both of Barnstable, sons of Capt. John Gorham, who died in Swansea during King Phillip's War.

To Rowland Cotton, 13 May 1695

Plymouth May, 13: 1695:

Deare Son

This morne I met Ensigne Tracey[1] by M^r^ murdo's shop going towards you, I ran into shop & sent 2 open lines saying, your younger sister[2] was in sight, since that she is well come to us & is hard at worke making a topping, some head-tire[3] for your Dearest, wednesday or Thursday at furthest hither you must hasten, she cannot travell to see you being ______ she stays with us till this day fortnight, about next Monday comes her husband & takes her back when I goe to 'lection. you will finde the Tailor waiting upon you when you come: Ensigne Tracey left my 2 lines at moreys & is returned because M^r^ otis (with whom his business was) was coming this way, & brings me this message from Leift. morey, viz, that my horse (whom I turned upon the beach) was now with him, my earnest request to you is, that when you come you will not faile (whatever trouble & charge it is) to bring him hither, for I must secure him for my Boston-Journey, May, 27: M^r^ W: Clarke hath a letter for you (I know not from whom,) also here is a booke for you or your wife but that I keep till you come, it is about choice cookery; some persons have on purpose wickedly burnt Jones's river bridge last friday night;[4] your parents, sarah, maria, salute you both, God blesse you & all yours,

I am, your Affectionate Father,

John Cotton

Sir wm[5] had dispatcht all at court & was to come againe Govr but 6 days sicknesse, said Nay; yesterday Teacher & Pastor Mather from head to foot inclusively all in mourning apparell at the Ladys cost. cottons funerall sermon last Thursday upon o wheel,[6] yesterday on Neh: 2: 10[7] & his father on Isa: 57: 1:[8] all other particular newes your sister must tell you viva voce:[9] o my horse, let me see it by your hand & then you may hope for 10 pd & 2 pd:

Miscellaneous Bound Collection, Massachusetts Historical Society. Addressed "These For Mr Rowland Cotton, Pastor of the church, at Sandwich."

---

1. Probably one of the sons of John and Mary Prince Tracey of Duxbury, possibly Stephen, born in 1673, or perhaps John himself. Savage, *Genealogical Dictionary,* 4:320-21.

2. Maria Cotton Bradbury (b. 1672) was Rowland's younger sister and was married before 1693. Rowland's other younger sister, Sarah (b. 1670), was not yet married in May 1695. Torrey, *New England Marriages,* 90.

3. "Attire for the head; a head-dress." *Oxford English Dictionary,* 2d ed. (Oxford, 1989) (hereafter *OED*), 8:51.

4. On 29 May 1695, the General Court acknowledged the recent burning of the bridge and ruled that the inhabitants of Plymouth County should rebuild both the burned Jones River bridge and the decaying Eel River bridge. The residents could use "cuntry rates" to pay for the reconstruction and were "free from being charged towards the building any other bridg out of their Respectiue Townships." *Acts and Resolves of the Province of Massachusetts Bay*, 7:98.

5. Gov. William Stoughton.

6. Probably Cotton Mather, *Observanda—The Life and Death of the Late Q. Mary* (Boston, 1695) [Evans 726]. Evans, *American Bibliography*.

7. Neh. 2:10: "When Sanbalat the Horonite, and Tobiah the servant, the Ammonite, heard *of it*, it grieved them exceedingly that there was come a man to seek the welfare of the children of Israel."

8. Isa. 57:1: "The righteous perisheth, and no man layeth *it* to heart: and merciful men *are* taken away, none considering that the righteous is taken away from the evil *to come*."

9. "By voice."

To Joanna Rosseter Cotton, [29 May 1695]

Election-night Boston at Mr Adam Winthrops[1]
sitting by capt Appleton[2] & Mr Chris Philips[3] who salute you

My Dearest

Mr Capen[4] desires the benefit of my study & a Bible sutable to put his notes in order El: Churchel to be ready to set the Psalme if he cannot doe it himselfe, let him only have the litle Psal: Booke: Mr Torrey preacht an excellent sermon[5] on Hos: 1: 7:[6] In the Election Coll: Saltonstall[7] is left out & Coll: Shrimpton[8] is in his room; Mr Eliakim Hutchinson[9] is chosen in the room of dead Major Hooke:[10] Mr Bond[11] is speaker & Mr Dering[12] Clarke of the Deputies; List of votes, you must send all this newes to Rowl: & soe to son John:

Mr Stoughton,[13] 71:
Mr Danforth 79
X Coll Saltonstall 39
Coll: Pynchon 41
Mr Russell 66
Major Winthrop 74
Coll: Gidney 74
Mr Cooke 69

Mr Hathorne 58
Capt. Sewall 77
Coll: Philips 76
Major Browne 55
Mr Corwin 70
Mr Foster 64
Mr sergeant 49
Mr Addington 78
Major Pike 48
capt Peirce 68
Coll: Hutchinson 70
X Major Walley[14] 18

The Plimouth five Counsellors are as they were.[15] some Indians that went upon scoute have brought in 2 scalpes & 3 guns & they conclude that the third gun had an owner whom they sorely wounded or else they should not have found his gun noe newes of the snow frigat, it is greatly feared it is cast away upon rocks for want of a skilfull pilot: but the choice newes is that all the Easterne sachims but one (at least most of them) come to Pemaquid, & have brought in eight Captives, confest their great evill in fighting against us;[16] litle Gershom Hobart is one[17] (tell his Aunt Bradford soe) if an Easterly winde come they will be here to morrow this [time?] they much desire us to pardon them & to be at peace with them (perfidious wretches) & doe promise to bring in above 30 or 50 more within a moneths time, & they are gone for them, shipscott John[18] hath bin very active in this matter; Capt Marsh[19] hath made a truce with the Indians for 30 dayes soe they waite to see whether they will be faithfull or noe in that time: The freshmen are placed[20] The senior is Symmes, 2. Cotton (mirandum) 3. Mather 4. Willard. 5: Bradstreet etc: Josiah is well; wee came very comfortably & seasonably to Boston, Maria is well & goes on friday; Sister Ward is ill at Cos: Tufts,[21] her distemper is much in her legs: my heartyest love to you, & to Sarah, Salute Mr & Mris Thomas,[22] I did what I could to desire Capt Appleton not to goe till Friday but he is resolved to goe in the morning: The Lord comfort you,

I am, yours most Affectionately ever

John Cotton

Post my letter southward:

Capt Thomas hath desired Mris Prince not to goe to Plimouth because Mris Dummer is coming to nurse her,[23] but Mris Prince would come for all that if a vessell did present unlesse our Mr Thomas send to her not to come, their cradle is bought & your basket

Mr John Davenport is ordained Pastor at Stamford[24] young Mr Chancey[25] at

Pequonnuk: Mr Ruggles will tomorrow bring me my letter from Bro: Rosseter, hee & his & also Bro: Walkers all well saith minar of woodbury.

Mr Nathan Gold, & Capt Sellick new magistrates at connecticott,[26] Mr Andrews preacht their Election sermon[27]

Son & daughter in hast love to you all[28]

by goody fish this Letter I send you wher in is mirandum you must send it to your Bro Last munday Mrs Thomas was brought to bed of a brave boy before any was redy yesterday taken with black fits its mother the most Afectinate mother in the world allmost beyond bounds & thay may loose it[29] I & sara sat up all this night[30] J Ricard all most dead of the gout carid by 3 men from bed to fire neither eat nor slept I have been ther ever sins Tuesday at Litle better

hear is Cap Aplton Mr Capin preach on sabath mr dumer is com to be nurs great joy thay knew nothing of her beind brought to bed she coms to be nurs not els but prayers & lov

your mother

Joanna Cotton

Miscellaneous Bound Collection, Massachusetts Historical Society. Addressed, in John Cotton's hand, "These for M^ris Joanna Cotton at Plymouth," and in Joanna Cotton's hand, "For Mr Roland Cotton att Sandwich thes."

---

1. Adam Winthrop (1647–1700, H.C. 1668) was the grandson of immigrant John Winthrop. Following his graduation from Harvard, he spent some time as a merchant in England. Winthrop and his family returned to Boston in 1679 and he served as a representative to the General Court from 1689 to 1692. Named by the king to the first Governor's Council under the new charter in gratitude for his work against Andros, he lost in the first popular election in 1693. Winning every year after that, however, he served on the Council until his death in 1700. *Sibley's Harvard Graduates,* 2:247-49.

2. Probably Samuel Appleton (1624–1696), who led Massachusetts forces in King Philip's War. He also served as a representative to the General Court frequently from 1668 to 1692. An opponent of Andros, Appleton was imprisoned for his activity against the Dominion. Like Winthrop, he was named to the first Governor's Council but lost in the first popular election of 1693. See 23 September 1675. Savage, *Genealogical Dictionary,* 1:61-62.

3. Possibly Christopher Phelps of Salem, who married Elizabeth Sharp in July 1658. Savage, *Genealogical Dictionary*, 3:404.

4. Joseph Capen (1658–1725, H.C. 1677) ministered to the Topsfield Church from 1681 until his death. It seems that he was filling Cotton's pulpit during his trip to Boston for the election. *Sibley's Harvard Graduates,* 2:519-21.

5. Samuel Torrey (1632–1707, H.C. 1653–1656). See 5 May 1688. Cotton referred to Torrey's forthcoming election sermon in his letter of 8 April 1695.

6. Hos. 1:7: "But I will have mercy upon the house of Judah, and will save them by the Lord their God, and will not save them by bow, nor by sword, nor by battle, by horses, nor by horsemen."

7. Nathaniel Saltonstall (1639[?]–1707) served in many government offices, including those of representative, assistant, commander of the Essex militia and judge. He received the second lowest number of votes in this election; there were rumors that he had appeared at Council meetings drunk, which may have contributed to his loss. *Saltonstall Papers,* 53-54, 211-12.

8. Samuel Shrimpton (1643–1698) served as captain, on the Council of Andros, and on the Council of Safety in 1689. Savage, *Genealogical Dictionary*, 4:91.

9. Eliakim Hutchinson (d. 1717) was a wealthy merchant married to Sarah Shrimpton and served seven years in the new charter Council. In 1695, he was elected to represent "territory formerly called the Province of Maine," along with Samuel Wheelwright and Charles Frost. *Acts and Resolves of the Province of Massachusetts Bay,* 7:71; Savage, *Genealogical Dictionary,* 2:510.

10. Captain Francis Hooke (d. 1695) served in many offices, including that of the treasurer of Maine, and on the Council under both the old and new charters. He died in office on 10 January 1695. Savage, *Genealogical Dictionary,* 2:258-59.

11. William Bond (1625–1695) of Watertown served as a representative, a member of the Council of Safety and the first Speaker of the House under the new charter. He died in December 1695. Savage, *Genealogical Dictionary,* 1:210.

12. Henry Dering.

13. William Stoughton, lieutenant governor (acting governor).

14. Thomas Danforth, John Pynchon, Wait Winthrop, James Russell, Bartholomew Gedney, Robert Pike, Elisha Cooke, John Hathorne, Samuel Sewall, Samuel Shrimpton, Elisha Hutchinson, Isaac Addington, William Browne, John Philips, Jonathan Corwin, John Foster, Peter Sergeant and Daniel Pierce were elected as councillors (assistants) to the General Court on 29 May 1695. *Acts and Resolves of the Province of Massachusetts Bay,* 7:71.

15. William Bradford, Barnabas Lothrop, John Saffin, Nathaniel Thomas, and John Thacher were elected from "lands within the territory formerly called New Plymouth." *Acts and Resolves of the Province of Massachusetts Bay*, 7:71.

16. On 20 May 1695, several Native chiefs gathered at Fort William Henry at Pemaquid for peace negotiations. They also offered up eight captives, hoping for Native captives in exchange. Colonial representatives Col. John Philips, Lieut. Col. John Hawthorne and Capt. James Converse demanded the return of all English captives before considering their requests, so the talks abruptly ended. Cotton's optimism in this letter was premature. Despite desperate suffering, Native villages continued to mount attacks on frontier villages, and King William's War dragged on through 1695. Mather, *Decennium Luctuosum,* 259; Gallay, *Colonial Wars of North America,* 350.

17. For Hobart's captivity, see [11] August 1694.

18. See 12 February 1695.

19. Capt. John March had a varied military career, ultimately marked by dismal failures. In 1691 he led a doomed raid into Freeport, Maine, that was ambushed. He commanded Fort William Henry (Pemaquid) for a few years until he asked to be replaced by Capt. Pascho Chubb in early 1696. March led the September 1697 battle at Damariscotta, Maine, and later commanded forces in the 1703 attack on Pequawket and the 1707 battle at Port Royal, described as a "shameful failure." Gallay, *Colonial Wars of North America,* 413, 482, 577.

20. Thomas Symmes (1678–1725), Josiah Cotton (1680–1756), Samuel Mather (1677–1746), Josiah Willard (1681–1756), Dudley Bradstreet (1678–1714), Peter Cutler (1679–1721), Nathaniel Hubbard (1680–1748), Samuel Wolcott (1679–1709), Henry Swan (1679–before 1715), John White (1677–1760), John Fox (1678–1756), Richard Billings (1675–1748) and Oxenbridge Thatcher (1681–1772) were placed in this order by the faculty at the conclusion of the freshman year. *Sibley's Harvard Graduates,* 4:393-33.

21. See 5 May 1688.

22. Nathaniel and Mary Thomas.

23. Mrs. Dummer was going to Plymouth to attend Mary Thomas after the birth of her first child, expected shortly (see below).

24. John Davenport (1669–1731 H.C. 1687) began preaching in Stamford, Connecticut, in March 1693 after turning down an offer from East Hampton, Long Island, and was ordained in 1694. *Sibley's Harvard Graduates,* 3:369-74.

25. Charles Chauncey (1668–1714, H.C. 1686) was the first minister at Stratfield, Connecticut (now Bridgeport), ordained on 13 June 1695. He had ministered in neighboring Stratford since 1691, served as a military chaplain in 1690 and 1691 and probably ministered to the new town of Stratfield since its founding. *Sibley's Harvard Graduates,* 3:364-66.

26. Jonathan Silleck and Nathan Gold were elected as new assistants to the Connecticut General Court on 9 May 1695 as replacements for two recently deceased assistants, John Burr and William Pitkin. *Public Records of the Colony of Connecticut*, ed. Charles Hoadly, vol. 4 (1868), 138.

27. Samuel Andrew (1656–1738, H.C. 1675) was ordained in Milford, Connecticut, on 18 November 1685, after many years as a fellow at Harvard College. In 1699, he helped to found Yale College and served as its president. The election sermon appears not to have been published. *Sibley's Harvard Graduates,* 2:457-62.

28. This salutation and the section that follows are in Joanna Cotton's hand.

29. Midwife Joanna caught young Nathaniel Thomas on 27 May 1695. Nathaniel was the first child for Nathaniel (1664–1738) and Mary Appleton Thomas (d. 1727) of Plymouth/Marshfield. While the baby survived the illness Joanna described, he later died as a young child on 5 April 1699. Van Antwerp, *Vital Records of Plymouth,* 16; Torrey, *New England Marriages,* 735.

30. This offers another hint that Joanna may have been raising her daughter Sarah to become a midwife; see also 24 April 1695, in which Sarah seems to have been waiting for a birth. Sarah also appears to have been close to Mary Thomas (see 13 September 1694) and may have been attending the birth to help her friend.

From Samuel Willard, 19 June 1695

To the Elders & Brethren of ye Church of Christ in Plimouth
the Elder & Brethren of ye Church in ye South end of Boston, send Greeting

Rev^rd^, Honred, & Beloved.

These are to certify you, y^t^, wheras or beloved Sister, Rebekah Morton,[1] being by ye providence of God removed from us, & not likely to return agen to us; hath accordingly desired letters of dismission from us to you, among whom shee hath now for a considerable time conversed; wee, judging her removall to have bin regular & her desire proper; as being not capable of Immediate watch over her; here therfore consented therto, & do hereby declare & consent that shee should orderly become one of yor stated members; testifying y^{t} during her abode amongst us, ever since shee joyned in comun: wth us, her conversation hath bin without offense, & exemplary to our [best?] observation; & wee hope it hath not bin other since her converse among you;

Thus committing you to ye grace of God, wee remain,

yo^{rs} in ye fellowship of ye Saints.

Samll Wilard, wth ye consent of ye Brethren.

Miscellaneous Bound Collection, Massachusetts Historical Society. Cotton's note: "she was accepted, July, 21: 1695:"

---

1. Rebecca Morton was accepted as a church member by Cotton's Plymouth congregation on 21 July 1695. According to Savage, Ambrose and Mary Bumstead Dawes had a daughter, Rebecca, on 25 February 1666. Rebecca married Eleazer Morton of Boston and Plymouth in 1692 or 1693, following the death of her first husband, Benjamin Marshall, sometime after 1688. Cotton's church records indicate that she had been living in Plymouth at least since 1693, when her son Eleazer was baptized. He also noted that she was "a member of the third church in Boston" at the time of that baptism. Rebecca Morton would later become Cotton's final undoing in Plymouth. See the letter below of 18 June 1697. Torrey, *New England Marriages,* 522, 490; Savage, *Genealogical Dictionary,* 2:24; *CSM,* 22:280.

To Rowland Cotton, 26 July 1695

PLYMOUTH JULY, 26: 1695:

VERY DEARE SON

shall wee begin the old trade againe of Epistolizing? Let my first words be hearty salutations to thy deare mate, who was (& is) soe deare to me that I forgot the danger of my life 'twixt Sal's[1] & Hav:[2] that I might <*that I might*> see & converse with that choice mother who bore her, & I had a full recompense for all my toile & hazard in Journeying in what I there saw & enjoyed: it was wondred at, my sons going from my Lecture, I wish it may be soe noe more for more reasons then one, though now it could not be helpt, but the sermon then preacht might have bin of spetiall advantage to you, it was de service for Jesus Christ from Rev: 2: 19:[3] my heart is filld with thoughts of your church meeting to day, the good Lord be with you in it, as a Father I solemnly advis (I had almost said charge) you, noe longer to deferre the Lords supper, it seems to me scandalous the soe long omission of it, let T:T: & J:S: be devills incarnate,[4] yet doe you invite the church to the Lords Table, & if any will eat & drink their owne Judgement, its not your fault, feed christs sheep, I am confident T:T: glories wickedly in secret that you dare not have a sacrament bec: he is offended at W:B: suffer it noe longer to be soe; as for the offense of S:P: & W:B: against J:SM: certainly it is better to leave it with God to plead <*with*> that matter in his Conscience, it being done before your renewall of covenant on the ordination day, then to deprive a whole ch: of the sealing ordinances bec: of a particular offence: As for Baptisme, Administer it according to your light, it is you must give account to God of your ministeriall administrations, not the brethren: I know not what to doe, having promised sep: 8: for R: Island, if Barn:[5] councill be sept 4; know certainly of the Elder,[6] & if soe it be & that our ch: be sent to, hasten to tell me soe, that I may fix another sabbath for the Island (a fortnight before or after said time) & send Mr Danforth word of it. J: Morton is come this morning from Boston, noe newes, but much death of children, wentworth's is one;[7] I wish this minute I could post this letter to your hand: parents & litle brothers duly salute you all; God Almighty blesse you all & make you a blessing,

soe ever prayes your Affectionate Father

John Cotton

Gilbert is gone to o:E:[8] Frigats gone Eastward with Nath: Alden,[9] mate of Nath: Clark, their Pilot & Clarke thereby hindred his [way?]

Miscellaneous Bound Collection, Massachusetts Historical Society. Addressed "These For Mr Rowland Cotton, Pastor of the Church at Sandwich."

---

1. "Saltonstall's."
2. "Haverhill."
3. Rev. 2:19: "I know thy works, and charity, and service, and faith, and thy patience, and thy works; and the last *to be* more than the first."
4. Thomas Tupper seems to have continued his conflicts with Rowland. See 13 September 1694 and 12 February 1695. "JS" is probably James Skeff, one of the twenty members of First Church Sandwich when Rowland arrived. Rowland delayed administering the sacrament for nearly a year after his ordination in November 1694. Sandwich church records indicate that on 15 September 1695 "Mr Rowland Cotton first administered the Sacrament of the Lords Supper here." Between September 1695 and October 1721, Rowland administered the Lord's Supper 138 times. First Parish Church (Sandwich, Mass.), New England Historic Genealogical Society, ms. 638:291.
5. "Barnstable."
6. John Chipman was the elder at Barnstable.
7. Edward Wentworth, son of Samuel and Elizabeth Wentworth, was born on 5 February 1693 and died on 24 July 1695. *Boston Births, Baptisms, Marriages and Deaths, 1630–1699*, ed. William Appleton (Baltimore, Md., 1978), 209, 225.
8. "Old England."
9. Nathaniel Alden (d. 1702) married Hepzibah Mountjoy in 1691 and lived in Boston. Torrey, *New England Marriages*, 8.

To Rowland Cotton, [6 August 1695]

Monday Eve[1]

Deare son

Last Thursday your mother & Jos:[2] went to see Madam Winslow, & dropt Theoph:[3] at his schoole, on friday I went to them & all come home that night; this morning I accompanyed Jos: to Barkers, where (according to our friday agreement) wee mett Capt Thomas & Mr weld[4] who were his Pilots to Boston; At my returne I met L: Mory; Eph: Cole is this day come from B: a letter[5] from son Allyn[6] (datelesse) thus speakes. "were seene to drive about 30 cattle from Almsbury, our men followed till they discovered the enemyes fires, by which they guesse there are a great body, therefore dare not fall on them being themselves but a very few, they have sent to Newbury & Hampton for men, intending this night to march & fall upon the Enemy if they be not removed,["] Maria[7] still keeps up: wee know nothing of the shoos in the least; must those wretches keep you from sealing ordinances? I beleve you may end it without a councill; your mother is gone a visiting, I only (now very desolate) salute you & your Dearest, I wish I ever see you againe; I have written this day to Mr cushing[8] to come & supply my place Sep: 8:[9] I long to see you, & pray for you all,

& rest, your Affectionate Father

John Cotton

Elisha Holmes is publisht to sarah Bartlet,[10] Jos's youngest.

The Fr: K:[11] sends for all his subjects in America by which to redeem ours with him, our poore fr: Dr:[12] is fled Hinghamwards to steal his marriage[13] if he can:

Miscellaneous Bound Collection, Massachusetts Historical Society. Addressed, in another hand, "ffor the reverentt mr cotten in sandwich." In Cotton's hand, "Breife for James son of John Bull, Thomas, son of Judah, & Mary Thacher, in sally, sent to Plim: Dux: & Marshf: I suppose your county hath the same:"

---

1. Prince's note: "Suppose in Aug. 6."
2. Josiah Cotton.
3. Theophilus Cotton.
4. Thomas Weld (1653–1702, H.C. 1671) was the settled minister in the frontier town of Dunstable from at least 1679 until his death and served as a representative to the General Court in 1689. *Sibley's Harvard Graduates,* 2:388-91.
5. Not found.
6. Elizabeth Cotton's husband, James Alling.
7. Cotton's daughter, Maria Cotton.

8. Probably Jeremiah Cushing (1654–1706, H.C. 1676), the minister in Scituate from 1691 to 1705. Weis, *Colonial Clergy,* 66.

9. Prince's note: "Sep. 8. 95 is o & by his Letr of July 26. 95, He was to Preach at Rhode Island on Sep. 8."

10. Elisha Holmes and Sarah Bartlett married on 2 September 1695 in Plymouth and had eight children from June 1696 to March 1709. Torrey, *New England Marriages,* 383; Van Antwerp, *Vital Records of Plymouth,* 32-33.

11. "French King."

12. "French doctor."

13. The French doctor was successful. Dr. Francis LeBaron (1668–1704) married Mary Wilder (b. 1668) of Hingham on 6 September 1695, and they had three children, James (b. 1696), Lazaros (b. 1698) and Frances (b. 1701). See 12 June 1694. Torrey, *New England Marriages*, 458; Van Antwerp, *Vital Records of Plymouth,* 16-17.

To Rowland Cotton, [22 August 1695]

THURS MORN:[1]

DEARE SON

I am going to keep this day with R: Rans:[2] your 3 letters came yesterday[3] P: M: & the booke; you did well to be thorough with Mr sm: I am confident your ch: may without sin passe an act of forgiv: & obliv: I ever told you all before ordination ought not to be repeated: if He second you, let it passe, though Tom: say noe: Cucumber wee have none at all, & which is worse, Mris Thomas's hogs at marshfeild eat up 50 & soe none can come from thence; The Garrisons distance I know not: soe much to your first: for the 2ond & 3d: some of my letters I have copyes of non immerito;[4] your mothers folio is in part here: melvin is mistaken, it was a garrison-house & as you heard & more, too much in these straites to transcribe: Though the goose & pig be eaten, if I be well & not too weary on friday morning I will strive to come to you & stay till Saturday morning, I have bin soe contriving all this weeke & wish I may not be disappointed; sep: 4: I mount D: V:[5] for R: Island: old Mris Thomas's[6] breast in a most dreadfull, dangerous condition,[7] her sister French hath lanct it, the issue is much feared: There is a rumor (I cannot say its true) that Honnywells Garrison (I thinke it is at Saco) is destroyed & every soule belonging to it,[8] I hope it is not soe, ergo report it not for a truth; your mother was fetcht yester afternoone to Lydia Bartlett (once Griswald) she is in her 7 moneth, feared to have a dead chid within her,[9] soe that I most solitary, doe only salute you both. Mr Lawsons Father is dead[10] in o: E:[11] last sabbath but one he preacht on My Father etc. in Kings:[12] I heare 300 pd is left him, & he talks of going to fetch it, & is preparing a vicar till his returne, viz,

Sir (Eph:) Litle,[13] who is to preach for him next Sab: but one. Sir Tom: gives 30 pd to Dr. Cutler[14] & lives with him for his skill: I leave this sealed with Patience to send if a hand present in my absence; God blesse you all,

soe prayes, your Affectionate Father

John Cotton

Miscellaneous Bound Collection, Massachusetts Historical Society. Addressed in pencil in a modern hand, "To Mr Rowland Cotton, Pastor of the Church in Sandwich."

---

1. Prince's note: "Aug. 1695—Aug 22 or 29."
2. Probably Robert Ransom, either the father (d. 1697) or son (d. 1723), who both lived in Plymouth. See 29/30 April 1697. Torrey, *New England Marriages*, 611.
3. Not found.
4. "Not undeservedly."
5. "God willing."
6. Deborah Jacob Thomas (1643–1696) was the wife of Nathaniel Thomas (1643–1718) and lived in Marshfield. Her sister, Hannah Jacob Loring French (1640–1720), was married to Stephen French and lived nearby in Plympton. Savage, *Genealogical Dictionary*, 2:534; Torrey, *New England Marriages*, 735, 285.
7. Lancing or "opening" an infected breast of a lactating mother was usually a last resort, after herbs and frequent manual expressions of milk to relieve sore, blocked ducts had failed to ease the pain. Breastfeeding difficulties were a common reason for midwives to revisit patients, even nearly a year after birth. Laurel Thacher Ulrich, *A Midwife's Tale* (New York, 1990), 112-13, 196-97.
8. Cotton Mather was referring to an incident at Saco in August 1695: "Sargeant Haley, Venturing out of his Fort at Saco, Stept into the Snares of Death." Mather, *Decennium Luctuosum*, 260.
9. Lidiah Griswold Bartlett delivered her second baby, Samuel, on 29 August 1696, according to Van Antwerp's *Vital Records*. This may have been the baby Joanna was helping to deliver, since Thomas Prince was unsure whether this letter had been written on 22 or 29 August and Antwerp may have been mistaken by one year. Otherwise, the baby referred to in this letter did die and Lydia had another one a year later on nearly the same date, which seems less likely. Van Antwerp, *Vital Records of Plymouth*, 14.
10. Deodat Lawson's father was Rev. Thomas Lawson of Denton, Norfolk, in England. Deodat emigrated to New England and served as the minister in Edgartown and Danvers before accepting ordination in Scituate's second church in November 1694. He was dismissed by that congregation in 1698, when neighboring clergy advised Scituate to begin looking for a new minister, given Lawson's prolonged absence of more than two years "merely for secular advantages, and taking no heed to the ministry which he hath received of the Lord." Evidently, Cotton had heard correctly about Lawson's proposed travel plans. See the letter below of 9 October 1695. Weis, *Colonial Clergy*, 124; Savage, *Genealogical Dictionary*, 3:63-64; *Old Scituate* (1921; reprint, Scituate, Mass., 1970), 171.
11. "Old England."
12. Possibly 2 Kings 2:12: "And Elisha saw *it*, and he cried, My father, my father, the chariot of Israel, and the horsemen thereof. And he saw him no more: and he took hold of his own clothes, and rent them in two pieces."

13. Like many young graduates, Ephraim Little (1676–1723, H.C. 1695) first worked as a schoolteacher in Plymouth. Following the second adultery accusation against Cotton in 1697, Little replaced him as the settled minister there. *Sibley's Harvard Graduates,* 4:248-52.

14. Dr. John Cutler came to Massachusetts from Holland and settled in Hingham before 1674. He served as a surgeon in King Philip's War and taught Boston's most prominent doctor, Zabdiel Boylston. Historian Philip Cash credits Cutler and other European-trained physicians for an increasingly "professional" medical community in early eighteenth-century Boston. Here Cotton alludes to the mentoring that Cutler performed for New England's doctors-in-training. Philip Cash, "The Professionalization of Boston Medicine, 1760–1803," *Medicine in Colonial Massachusetts, 1620–1820, CSM,* 57 (Boston, 1980), 73; Brock, "The Influence of Europe on Colonial Massachusetts Medicine," 124.

To Rowland Cotton, 27 August 1695

Plymouth August, 27: 1695:

Deare Child

your mother on my horse & I on another went to the Funerall of good Mr Fuller[1] yesterday, she is soe pleased with my Nagg that she resolves to ride single upon him to Bristoll next weeke, & if you run up on Monday to looke upon us & stay one night wee shall not be angry with you for it: Deacon Bennett[2] at the grave desired the towne to repaire to the meeting house in order to calling a minister, they did soe, & unanimously called J: C:[3] (the 2 first letters of my name) & gave him the Call (for you may be sure he would not faile to be there ready for it) they chose the Deac: & Jos: Vaughan to subscribe a letter in their names to our church for approbation & license that Amos may improove his Talent amongst them; Their letter I shall read to our ch: at the Sacrament & noe doubt a License will be granted by us, only the munponsetites[4] did cleave to him yesterday, spake to divers of midlebury not to call him, because they had spoken first & are almost distracted for feare they should loose soe great a treasure: some of us (who mourne heartily & cannot but soe doe for the death of soe godly a man) stand admiring that our Extremity should be Gods opportunity to show mercy to this church & rescue us from all difficulties de Eldership: oh that God would send me good newes of your concernes at your meeting (if you are to have one) Midlebury had 4 sacraments, the 4th was Aug: 18: when death was upon him but God helpt him to doe all the worke of that day & his next Sabbath he kept in heaven, saying on Saturday, Aug: 24: (on which day he dyed an houre before sunsett) blessed are they who are prepared to keep an everlasting sabbath: your parents heartily salute you both; God blesse you & all yours,

soe daily prayes, your Affectionate Father,

John Cotton

Mr Fuller was Just 66 yeares of age.

old G: Hoskins is not yet deadly sick,[5] but I thinke the wife of Eph: Tilson[6] is: Rob: Ransom continues in his good frames:[7]

Miscellaneous Bound Collection, Massachusetts Historical Society. Addressed "These For Mr Rowland Cotton, Pastor of the church at Sandwich." Cotton's note: "The man supposed to be lost etc after wandring some days (wee heare) came alive to some remote house of weymouth."

---

1. Samuel Fuller (1624–1695) ministered to the Middleborough church from 1678 until his death on 17 August 1695. Before becoming a minister, he served as an elder in Cotton's Plymouth congregation. See 13 September and 5 October 1694. Weis, *Colonial Clergy*, 90.
2. John Bennett (d. 1718) was one of the church founders in Middleborough and a deacon. Savage, *Genealogical Dictionary*, 1:167-68.
3. According to Cotton's church notes, the church in Middleborough called Isaac Cushman (1648–1732), the son of Plymouth's elder, Thomas Cushman, and an elder himself. Cotton's congregation met on 1 September and heard that Cushman had two calls. The Plymouth church "manifested generally...their desires not to part with him, but that he should be an elder here in his blessed Fathers room," but also stated that he should go "where the orderly providence of God should call him." Rather than proceed to Middleborough or remain in Plymouth, Cushman instead joined the "New Society," or the splinter church at Plympton. Cotton did not accept this split easily, but a reconciliation was reached in the summer of 1696, when "every one of us expresse our consent hereunto by an universall lifting up of our hands, & this was declared to be a finall issue of this matter & all differences that had thereby bin occasioned amongst us...mutual forgivenesse of all past offences." The New Society at Plympton would not become a fully separated church until October 1698, so Cushman temporarily remained a deacon in Cotton's church. Cotton would later claim that his conflicts with Cushman encouraged him to leave Plymouth in 1699. See 2 September 1687. *CSM*, 22:177-79.
4. Settlers around modern-day Monponset ponds in Halifax, Massachusetts.
5. William Hoskins Sr. died on 7 September 1695. See 8 November 1684 and 3 March 1688. Van Antwerp, *Vital Records of Plymouth*, 135.
6. Elizabeth Hoskins (b. 1646) married Ephraim Tilson (1636[?]–1715) on 7 July 1666. Savage suggests that Elizabeth was William Hoskins's daughter and that she did not die in 1695. Van Antwerp, *Vital Records of Plymouth*, 665; Savage, *Genealogical Dictionary*, 2:466.
7. Robert Ransom evidently struggled emotionally; Cotton later wrote about his attempted suicide. See 29/30 April 1697.

To Rowland Cotton, 9 October 1695

oct: 9: 95:

Deare son

yours by The:[1] calls for noe answer; on monday Betty & Will: went I accompanyed to Barkers & then went to Indians: N: South: went beyond Bearstows to pilot them past hazardous paths, young winslow (sam: Lillys apprentice) & Midlecott[2] (whose uncle is dead & hath left his father 700 per annum, & who is going in wilson for o: E:[3]) were fellow-travellers with ours; Amos did spend the Sab: at Ben: soule's[4] they had a large contribution for him: Mr Lawson told his ch:[5] last Sab: he was bound for o: E:[6] would provide a supply, they continuing his stated salary, he would provide & maintaine a preacher, the matter to be issued next Sab: & he would then name the man[.] at the next house to that meeting house Capt Studsons wife[7] (a Hingham Hawks) riding to the worship, her daughter behind her, fell downe (its feared) her skull is broken, it lyes all bare on her forehead as broad as palme of hand, she was alive on Monday, but very dangerous: Bartlets Cod fish is as neere Sandw: as Plim: almost, & perhaps you may see him as soone as I except on Sabbaths; I have mackarill ready for your Bro: in a cask of mine, & I will give him as much as I leave for my selfe, if a convenient opportunity present for conveyance; Is it not best for your sacr:[8] to be the sab: after the Fast (I ever deemed it a choice preparative) & then Mris Fish may be admitted[9] before: Carpenters rattle upon my house: W: told me he would visit us before xtmas, & spake words very pleasing to me at parting, I am of your minde concerning him, & am glad you wrote as you did it made—looke t'other way & swallow with a smile: Parents & sister duly salute you both, God blesse you & all yours & deale gratiously with your mate in the houre of need.

I am, your Affectionate Father

John Cotton

Gibson lay at Mris clark's, I am now ready to send when a man appeares. our boats this morn say they have catcht 6 or 7 Bar: of Mack: yesterday:

Good child, if you would not have us starve, faile not to buy a firkin[10] of butter & two fatt cattell, wee must stick at noe price, doe as for selfe: the butter one of our boats may take at Boston for us; your mackarill went on monday, forgotten on saturday, but a fathers care etc.

Miscellaneous Bound Collection, Massachusetts Historical Society. Addressed "These For Mr Rowland Cotton, Pastor of the church at Sandwich."

1. Theophilus Cotton; not found.
2. Richard Middlecott emigrated from Wiltshire and in 1672 married into a well-established New England family; his second wife, Sarah, was John Winslow's daughter and Miles Standish's widow. His three daughters married equally powerful men in the colony. He served on the Council under the new charter but lost in the first popular election and died in 1704. Savage, *Genealogical Dictionary,* 3:205.
3. "Old England."
4. Benjamin Soule (1665[?]–1729) married Sarah Standish (1667–1740) in 1693 or thereabouts and had five children in Plymouth. Torrey, *New England Marriages,* 693; Van Antwerp, *Vital Records of Plymouth,* 36.
5. See 1 November 1694 and 22 August 1695.
6. "Old England."
7. Capt. Benjamin Stetson (1641–1711) of Scituate married Bethia Hawke (b. 1644) on 15 August 1665 in Hingham, and they had ten children. Benjamin served as a representative to the General Court both in Plymouth and in Boston after the consolidation of New Plymouth and Massachusetts Bay in 1693. A record of Bethia's death has not been found, and Benjamin did not marry a second time, so the authors suspect that Bethia survived the accident that Cotton described. Torrey, *New England Marriages,* 706; Savage, *Genealogical Dictionary,* 4:183; George Lincoln, et al., *History of the Town of Hingham* (Hingham, Mass., 1893), 3:294.
8. "Sacrament."
9. Mrs. Fish was admitted to First Church Sandwich on 8 December 1695. First Parish Church (Sandwich, Mass.), New England Historic Genealogical Society, ms. 638:1.
10. A firkin is a small wooden keg.

To Rowland Cotton, 25 October 1695

Plimouth Oct. 25. 95.

Dear son

God was good to us yesterday.[1] my text was Isa. 3.8.[2] D.[eacon] Fance prayed before my sermon PM

Mr Brown yt kept shop neer Capt Wing's dyed lately.[3] One man dyed at ye castle of ye small pox. Its supposed, That Disease, or a worse is in Wing's Lane, saith El Churchil.[4]

Letters from newfoundland bring Letters to Byfield of admiral Russel's successes. From Josiah I transcribe—"Poor Jacob & several others of ye schollars[5] which came from newberry, have lost all their Things: ye vessel being cast away, [ ] Goods lost; ye men saving their Lives."

Miscellaneous Bound Collection, Massachusetts Historical Society. Prince's note: "In ye Handwrit[g] of y[e] Rev M[r] John Cotton of Plimouth: but y[e] Bottom torn away & lost." From a manuscript copy in Thomas Prince's hand.

---

1. Prince notes: "1695. Oct 24 was ye Gen Fast."
2. Isa. 3:8: "For Jerusalem is ruined, and Judah is fallen: because their tongue and their doings *are* against the Lord, to provoke the eyes of his glory."
3. John Brown (1665–1695) of Newbury died following a brief Native captivity. (Wing was one of the commanders at Pemaquid in Maine.) Cotton Mather decribed the event: "On Oct. 7, the Indians entered the House of one John Brown at Newbury, carrying away Nine persons with them...The Captain Retook all the Captives; but the Indians, in their going off Strook them all so Violently on the Head with the Clubs... that they afterwards all of them dyed... Some of them Lingred out for half a year, and some of them for more than a whole year...at last they Died, with their very Brains working out at their Wounds." Savage, *Genealogical Dictionary,* 1:266, 271; Mather, *Decennium Luctuosum,* 260.
4. Eleazer Churchill.
5. Josiah Cotton was at Harvard; the students from Newbury at Harvard in 1695 were Richard Brown (1675–1732, H.C. 1697), Daniel Greenleaf (1680–1763, H.C. 1699), Moses Hale (1678–1744, H.C. 1699) and Samuel Moody (1676–1747, H.C. 1697). *Sibley's Harvard Graduates,* 4:336-41, 356-65, 472-76, 476-78.

To Rowland Cotton, 13 November 1695 [1 October 1695]

WEDNESDAY BEFORE LECT:[1]

DEARE SON

your mother is better something since she burnt her leg, but is hurried extreamly for want of a sempster;[2] Theoph: hath had a very sad bout since the sabbath with the throat-distemper,[3] now through mercy better; Patience went on monday night & Sarah would be a very welcome helpe to her moth: but wee rejoyce that she does you soe much good & for your sakes call not for her as yet: I doubt your considerable respite will not be long: If 'sias come not before I arrive there I intend to hasten his coming with your horse, doubting your charg in keeping him will prove too heavy, doe you write to M[r] Br:[4] to hasten his coming to serve you: The Embryo hopes of being here Nov: 24:[5] revive me & your moth: o for a confirmation by saturday, to save further trouble etc: Capt Hammond was very honourably treated by the Fr: Govr[6] at Kebeck[7] & sent home without any ransome:[8] it is said divers preachers have promised to supply winnetuxitt[9] this winter, M[r] weld[10] next Sab: Lawson,[11] & some say M[r] cushing[12] but (I hope not) M[r] Thomas is come home & hath brought neere 300 pd in goods: Hope Besbidge[13] dyed yesterday, & M[r] Isaac winslow[14] is dangerously sick, Dr Bailey[15] hath bin with him: Thursday fore noone; Elder chipman is with me & advises me to speak to M^r smith,[16] now in towne to supply your pulpit at the time mentioned, which I was afraid to doe lest you should deem it inconvenient, but the Elder thinks it will doe well, I deferred sealing my letter till mr sm: came to my house but he stayes soe long at Mr Thomas's that I must finish; the Elder tells me M^r Pr: hath brought a hanger on for his fath: H: cost but 36 shil: doe you see it & aske the price & if you like it for me, tell me where I may get such a one:[17] J: Rich: saith Jos:[18] said on saturday that he intends to come home next week on your horse, but I had rather you could sell him, however if you doe not I intend to hasten him hither, if God carry me thither: your parents & Theoph: salute you all 3: with prayers etc I am,

your Affectionate Father,

John Cotton

I have desired M^r sm: he denyes me not nor promises but I beleve he is exorable, faile not to accomplish it speedily & write of it:

Just now I am told sad newes that draws teares, Deac: Clark's pretious godly wife who was at our house last sabbath, was taken ill the night before last & dyed[19] this morning, Lord awaken us, only [Frn?] Dr[20] with her:

Miscellaneous Bound Collection, Massachusetts Historical Society. Addressed "These For Mr Rowland Cotton, Pastor of the church at Sandwich."

---

1. Prince notes, "suppose Oct. 1. 95." See n. 19 below for a different date.
2. "Seamstress." *OED*, 14:963.
3. "Throat-distemper" was a combination of diptheria and scarlet fever that erupted in several epidemics in New England during the seventeenth and eighteenth centuries. James Cassedy, "Church-Record Keeping and Public Health in Early New England," *Medicine in Colonial Massachusetts, 1620–1820, CSM*, 57 (Boston, 1980), 253.
4. Perhaps William Brattle (1662–1717, H.C. 1680, 1703). Brattle was not settled as the minister in Cambridge until 1696, so he may have offered to help Rowland. See the above letters of 16 July 1687 and 30 October 1694. Alternatively, Cotton may have been referring to William Brinsmead (d. 1701, H.C. 1644–1647), who had preached in Plymouth from 1660 to 1665 and was the first ordained minister in Marlborough starting in 1666. See the above letter of 13 September 1694. Both men were Cotton's friends. Weis, *Colonial Clergy*, 38-39, 41
5. Perhaps Cotton was referring to his daughter-in-law's pregnancy, then in its final weeks. Elizabeth Cotton, Rowland and Elizabeth's third child, was born on 3 November 1695, so if Cotton's date was correct, the "embryo" arrived a few weeks early. Kardell and Lovell, *Vital Records of Sandwich*, 35, 1371.
6. "French Governor."

7. Cotton Mather described Hammond's unusual ordeal: "on July 6 Major Hammond of Kittery fell into the Hands of the Lurking Indians...Hammond was now aboard a Canoo, intending to put ashore at Saco; but some of the Garrison-Soldiers there, not knowing that they had such a good Friend aboard, inadvertently Fired upon the Canoo; and so the Indians carried him clear away. They transported him at length to Canada, where he met with Extraordinary Civilities; Count Frontenac, the Governor himself, nobly purchased him of his Tawny master, and sent him home to New-England, by a Vessel, which also fetch'd from thence a Considerable Number (perhaps near Thirty) of English Prisoners." Prince's note on the manuscript was evidently copied directly from Mather's text. Mather, *Decennium Luctuosum*, 259-60.

8. Prince's note: "July. 6. major Hamond of Kittery fell into ye hands of ye Indns wo carried him to Canada, [where] C. Frontenac treated him very civilly & sent him home by a vessell wc fetched near 30 English prisoners."

9. Modern-day Plympton, Massachusetts.

10. See 6 August 1695.

11. Deodat Lawson had evidently not yet left for England when Cotton wrote this letter. See the above letters of 22 August 1695 and 1 November 1694.

12. Either Jeremiah Cushing (1654–1706, H.C. 1676), minister at Scituate, or Caleb Cushing (1673–1752, H.C. 1692), not yet settled. See the above letters of 1 November 1694 and 24 April 1695. Clearly, Cotton's opinion of Cushing had changed since the spring. Weis, *Colonial Clergy*, 65, 66.

13. Hopestill Besbedge (often written as Bisbee) was born in Scituate in 1645 and in 1680 married Sarah King (b. 1650) in Hingham. Torrey, *New England Marriages*, 71; Savage, *Genealogical Dictionary*, 1:171.

14. Isaac Winslow Jr. (1670–1738) survived this illness and married Sarah Wensley on 11 July 1700 (Cotton Mather officiated). Sherman and Sherman, *Vital Records of Marshfield*, 22, 390.

15. James Bailey (1650–1707, H.C. 1669) ministered in Danvers and Killingworth, Connecticut, but after 1691 worked mainly as a physician; he died in Roxbury after a lengthy and debilitating illness. Weis, *Colonial Clergy*, 24-25; *Sibley's Harvard Graduates*, 2:291-99.

16. Probably John Smith (1614–171[?]), who was the minister in Sandwich from 1673 until his retirement in 1688 and may have returned (reluctantly it seems) to help Rowland. See the above letters of 25 September and 1 October 1688. Weis, *Colonial Clergy*, 189-90.

17. Perhaps "a contrivance by which a rope, chain, or hook is used to suspend something." *OED*, 6:1089.

18. Josiah Cotton.

19. Elizabeth Crow Clark, Deacon Thomas Clark's wife, died on 13 November 1695. This death establishes the date of this letter. Van Antwerp, *Vital Records of Plymouth*, 135; Torrey, *New England Marriages*, 159.

20. Evidently, only Francis LeBaron, whom Cotton consistently calls "the French doctor," attended Elizabeth Clark when she died.

To Rowland Cotton, 18 November 1695[1] [28 October 1695]

MONDAY MORN [1695[2]]

DEARE SON

J: Morton from Bos: on Sat: night says Capt Hammond[3] (who was taken that weeke I was at salsbury) is one come from canada, they immediately carried him to Kebeck.[4] The fr:[5] man that took Col: Page's sloop, Phippenny, stephen of Connecticott, went Eastward & found James [Couch?] with butter & cheese, who went further East to take in spars for masts & took all from him but his masts & sold him his sloop againe. Theoph: is come home & tarries this week because M^r^ W: goes this day to Bost: In a word send me word, whether you can preach here Nov: 24:[6] without much inconvenience to your deare & family & M^r^ Sm:[7] doe for you & noe inconvenience, if it might be, the 7 pd will then be paid, but if it cannot tolerably be, I shall not expect or desire it of you, I see noe hopes of returning the same week because of Cos: Cotton with Roger, & with M^r^ stoughton & colledge etc & shortdays etc & therefore must send supply if I can from the bay, wee 3 salute you 3. God Almighty blesse you all,

soe prayes, your Affectionate Father

John Cotton

A letter & sol's whisk I sent by Mr Pr: what newes in Mr Br's letter? it is very cold:

Miscellaneous Bound Collection, Massachusetts Historical Society. Addressed "These For Mr Rowland Cotton, Pastor of the Church at Sandwich."

---

1. Prince's notes speculate that the letter may be dated "Oct 28 or Nov 4, 11, 18." When read in context with other letters, especially that of 13 November 1695, the later November date is more appropriate.
2. "1695" was added by Prince.
3. See 13 November 1695.
4. Prince notes, "Maj. Hammond was taken July. 6. 1695."
5. "French."
6. Prince notes, "Nov. 24. 1695 is . [sunday]."
7. John Smith; see 13 November 1695.

To Joanna Rosseter Cotton, 21 November 1695

Boston Nov: 21: 95

My Dearest Portion in this Life

It is as pleasant riding as at midsummer, I know not that ever I had a more comfortable Journey in all my Life hither, I lodged at Mr Torreys[1] who is very happy & cheerful in his new Enjoyments, on Tuseday I spoke with Mr Stoughton[2] who candidly resented my suggestions & said, he would have some man prudently say those things to the Assembly: I have not yet spoken with the speaker, but if it may be, it will be good to delay this businesse till Mr shirtliffe[3] comes, who hath a good interest in many Deputies, I hope he will come speedily in J: Morton, my love to him & tell him I say soe: cos: weld[4] (they say) is gone by sea to marshfeild & will not preach to them till he hath spoken with us at Plim: I conclude he will be with you & you need not my counsell what to say to him, but that figleafe will not hide their nakednesse from the eyes of wise men:[5] mr st: hath ordered an 100 & ten yds for Rowl:[6] & Tom:Tup:[7] to divide betwixt them, he hath ordered an 100 yds for me which if Mr Cooper come to his warehouse this morning I intend to put aboard J: Mor: A Rheme of paper, a bundle of Bibles a 3d of spectacles, a 4th of Inkhornes is already aboard. If you please to accept the gilt bible, I bestow it upon you, if it were all gold it were not too good for thee, the contents you love; oh my Deare, till I sat with Mr st: I never thought of the 4 letters I left upon the cupboard in parlor; hasten them to me; Letters from son Allyn[8] say, all ours are well, the day before he wrote arrived our packet of letters in which was yours to Mris stockman: Betty addes to Sarah 2 lines, E: F: married to Mary W:[9] Henry French to Betty Colins,[10] Mris Coffin (Peters wife of Exceter) is dead:[11] Cos: John writes to me of his son to be simon or Thomas which I please,[12] & Joynes with me in ordering Roger to depart the farme, my Lady Phips desires to buy it of us: Josiah is with me & all is well with him; I cannot send him with the horse this weeke because I have not yet spoken with the Fellows & am unresolved what to doe with him: I send my love to all my childrne, if you can convey it, son Rowl: God blesse with & to you all on the Sab: Mack: Ellis: Ber: have his Turkeys but can you send none for me to give? I hope with Gods helpe to still our unsatisfyed ones, Mr Torrey speaks up to the case; After Lecture Mr H's case is to be heard before the Elders; Capt Dudley, his Bro: Jos: Sir Ballantine gone in the fleet last sab: from Pascat: too: E: Eldred[13] & Macarty are come in here againe; some defect in the new ship:

Miscellaneous Bound Collection, Massachusetts Historical Society. Addressed "For mris Joanna Cotton at Plymouth with an 100 yds of Duffils." [14]

---

1. Samuel Torrey, minister in Weymouth. See the above letter of 5 May 1688.
2. Lt. Gov. William Stoughton had been the acting governor since Phips's death in February 1695.
3. Presuambly William Shertliff (1657–1730), who was born in Plymouth and married Susanna Lothrop (1664–1726), the daughter of Barnabas Lothrop, in October 1683; they had fourteen children in Plymouth and Barnstable. Torrey, *New England Marriages,* 672; Savage, *Genealogical Dictionary,* 4:92.
4. See 6 August and 1 October 1695.
5. Reference to Gen. 3:7: "And the eyes of them both were opened, and they knew that they *were* naked; and they sewed fig leaves together, and made themselves aprons."
6. Rowland Cotton.
7. Thomas Tupper.
8. Elizabeth Cotton's husband, James Alling.
9. The only marriage that fits these initials is that of Edward French to Mary Winsley, of 17 September 1695 in Salisbury. Torrey, *New England Marriages,* 284; Savage, *Genealogical Dictionary,* 2:205.
10. Henry French married Elizabeth Collins on 7 November 1695 in Salisbury. Torrey, *New England Marriages,* 284.
11. Abigail Starbuck Coffin had married Peter Coffin (1630–1715) in 1657 or thereabouts and died in Exeter, New Hampshire. Peter Coffin served in King Philip's War; he was elected to serve as a representative to the General Court, chosen to be a councillor and appointed to serve as a judge on the Supreme Court of New Hampshire. He does not seem to have remarried after Elizabeth's death. Torrey, *New England Marriages,* 166; Savage, *Genealogical Dictionary,* 1:419.
12. Cotton evidently favored the name Thomas for his cousin's fourth child. "Cos John" was John Cotton (1658–1710, H.C. 1678), the minister at Hampton, son of Seaborn and Dorothy Bradstreet Cotton. The baby, Thomas, was born on 28 October 1695 and baptized on 26 April 1696. Cousin John's, wife, Ann, may also have favored Thomas as an honor to her father, Thomas Lake. Savage, *Genealogical Dictionary,* 1:463-64; *Sibley's Harvard Graduates,* 3:2-5.
13. Elisha Eldred (1653–1739) was the son of William Eldred of Yarmouth. Savage, *Genealogical Dictionary,* 2:107.
14. Duffle is "coarse wollen cloth having a thick nap or frieze." *OED,* 4:1108.

To Rowland Cotton, [December 1695][1]

Thursday

Deare son

wee shall rejoyce to heare of Josiahs safe arrivall with you: yours of sat:[2] came yester-eve. Mr R:[3] could have told you a story worth hearing about the French at the [?] & capt Hammond[4] which Mr Moodey[5] told us the first day of our being at Boston, but I cannot tell it you: James Barnabey[6] (G: Barrow[7] his mate) came with their shallop safe yester-eve; J: Bar's thumbs almost frozen but like to doe well: The main masts of J: Morton & John Doyl mr of John [Cole's?] are down (whether cut or spent wee yet know not) yester, P.M. went 6 men in the new sloops skiffe with [drams?] & food to releive & help them, our Bay is all frozen over: my deare wife is washing this bitter cold day; wee are sorry sar's Journey to Yarmouth was not last week; her returne, & all of you next weeke, is much desired & expected, wee suffer more then a litle by selfe-deniall; Thanks be to God for your health: God continue his mercy to you all, wee both affectionately salute you all; Mr Thomson[8] is a none-such, and a universall vote for him last sabbath,[9] he is gone, but noe doubt will soone returne; munponsett's[10] meeting this weeke to hear their Grant etc; I know of noe hand to convey these but waiting,

rest your etc

J:C:

I thank you for [your] good Labours here Lately & fault not your taking the [bi] ble & inkhornes you well deserve it: Mr stoughton told me he had ordered an 100 yds for you & Tup to divide, I suppose it is aboard one of your sloops

Friday morn

I rejoyce to see J: [...] who will stay a 1/4 of an houre for these

Capt Thomas tells me that Mr Thomson intends to be with them about the end of Febr or 1st of March for noe conveyance of his wife, 5 children etc till then, our 2 boats came in yester-eve. J: Morton at J: Doyls sen: & young John nearer sturtevants, their dangers & feares were considerable, noe damage but J: Mortons main mast cutt downe, & Tho: Morton's ague if not frozen in feet & legs & very full of pain will: shirtliffe[11] is going by land to Boston this morn:

your two[12] by John Chipman Last night, I have but one Tulleys Almanack,[13] John Usher[14] gave it me; your mother hath often sent you word for paine of head & teeth, plaisters to the face, oyle of penny royall.[15] wee hope it is not the old trade the very first weeke after the month is out: I blesse God for Josiah's safe arrivall, as to orders, the cause of my sending him to you was only to serve you, that you might have your owne horse, it was only to pleasure you that I kept him to bring it from cambridge for you desired it, else he had come in our boats home the week before, & divers shills I had saved thereby; if 'siah hath not yet carried Sarah to yarmouth, I wish a horse might be fitted to doe it for they will be very much Troubled if they see her not, & if our mare may bring him hither ward. I suppose she will goe home of her selfe, any charge you are at for his or her coming home or going to yar: I will freely reimburse: if he goe Southward, wee cannot expect you till our Court weeke but by all means let that be the furthest; through mercy wee are all very well, & salute all our children, commending you to God; I rest

your Affectionate Father

John Cotton

the Physick now comes, your moth hath but litle but she spends enough for 2 portions for a child here is also Mr Thomas's cloath If your Bro: Rich:[16] had said a word to me that he would have had your horse; Jos: should not have come on it, he weares a curld wigg & told me, he intended New London or Sandwich but was unresolved which Just now your mother minds me of sending my horse for Jos: to come home upon, if I can get J: Morey to convey him, I will, & if he be fitted round for Ice upon my acnt; I hope every one will be suted & pleased

Miscellaneous Bound Collection, Massachusetts Historical Society. Addressed "These For Mr Rowland Cotton, Pastor of the Church at Sandwich." Several small holes and severe water damage have darkened manuscript.

---

1. Prince's note, "Dec. 95, or January. 95/6. Sr Little took his 1st Degree in 95." The Massachusetts Historical Society has catalogued the letter as January 1696.

2. Not found.

3. Jonathan Russell?

4. See 13 November 1695.

5. Joshua Moody.

6. James Barnaby was born in Plymouth, married Joanna Harlow and had two children in Plymouth, James (b. 1698) and Ambrose (b. 1706). Savage, *Genealogical Dictionary*, 1:117. Torrey, *New England Marriages*, 42.

7. Savage does not list a "G Barrow," but *New England Marriages* lists a George Barrows, who married Patience Simmons on 14 February 1695 in Plymouth. They remained in the town. Torrey, *New England Marriages*, 47.

8. Edward Tompson (1665–1705, H.C. 1684) first ministered in Simsbury, Connecticut, from 1687 until the summer of 1691, apparently without ever being ordained. In 1691, he began preaching to a splinter congregation from the western portion of Newbury, Massachusetts, much to the dismay of Newbury's town fathers. Continued conflict prevented Thompson's settlement into 1695, when he

accepted a call from Marshfield, Massachusetts. He was ordained on 14 October 1696. *Sibley's Harvard Graduates,* 3:306-9; Weis, *Colonial Clergy,* 205.

9. Prince's note: "Mr Edward Thompson ordained at Marshfield Oct. 14. 1696."

10. Modern-day Halifax, Massachusetts.

11. See the letter of 21 November 1695.

12. Not found.

13. John Tulley, *An Almanac for the Year of our Lord, MDCXCVI* (Boston, 1696) [Evans 776]. Evans, *American Bibliography*, 1:122.

14. See 20 August 1692.

15. Extract of pennyroyal (*mentha pulegium*) was usually administered as a tonic. Like feverfew, pennyroyal was primarily used to treat menstrual or postpartum complaints. Ulrich, *A Midwife's Tale,* 355, 357; *Medicine in Colonial Massachusetts, CSM,* 57:376.

16. Rowland's brother-in-law, Richard Saltonstall.

To Rowland Cotton, 4 December 1695

Plymouth December, 4: 1695

Deare son

I have bin contriving to get home your horse & thought to send it by the pedlar, but I am almost resolved that Josiah shall bring it; your mother hopes & desires it may not be long before our Sarah come home, & soe say I, she wants her cloaths, receipt book & pillian, she saith, if any of you be taken with a paine in your side you must not let blood first, but take Physick:[1] Two books, Mr Torreys sermon[2] & Dep: Gov Jones's verses are yours, & the other two are for your Bro: John; it is a time of litle or noe newes the grant of munponsett obliges them to get a learned minster;[3] I have last Sab: propounded the Lds sup: to be that day fortnight, solemnly calling upon all concerned to endeavour to discharge duty & seeke satisfaction etc All my children south ward I hope to make welcome next weeke; your mother on sab: morn was fetcht to Hannah Morton (Finney)[4] whom all Judged to be dying, & came not home till Monday eve; she is better; Also to Mary Holmes[5] was your moth: fetcht last weeke who is very ill: The man who brought your letter last week frighted your moth: by telling that one of the family was very sick, wee hope you are all well: this is a very confused heap of lines for one newly come from Bost. but I have nothing worth imparting. wee doe heartily salute you all, & praying for you,

I rest, your Affectionate Father

John Cotton

Miscellaneous Bound Collection, Massachusetts Historical Society. Addressed "For Mr Rowland Cotton."

---

1. While she seemed to caution Rowland in this letter, Joanna's use of bloodletting varied; see for example, the letter of 8 March 1686, by which she advised her son to "let blood." Like many physicians, Joanna believed that blood-letting should be practiced in conjunction with pharmaceuticals. J. Worth Estes, "Therapeutic Practice in Colonial New England," *Medicine in Colonial Massachusetts, 1620–1820, CSM*, 57 (Boston, 1980), 300-301, 303.
2. For Torrey's election sermon, see the above letters of 8 April and 29 May 1695.
3. See 27 August 1695.
4. Hannah Phinney Morton (b. 1657) married Ephraim Morton (1648–1732) ca. 1677 in Plymouth and they had five children from 1677 to 1685. Hannah survived this illness, dying in 1731. Torrey, *New England Marriages*, 522; Van Antwerp, *Vital Records of Plymouth*, 27.
5. There are many possibilities, but the most likely follows from Thomas Faunce's town records for Plymouth: "Mary Holmes, daughter of Mr. John Holmes of Duxbery, decd 8 March 1695/6." Her illness, therefore, may have lasted three months or more. The Duxbury vital records refer to a Mary Holmes, daughter of Josiah and Hannah, born on 5 November 1674. Van Antwerp, *Vital Records of Plymouth*, 135. *Vital Records of Duxbury, Massachusetts, to the Year 1850* (Boston, 1911), 93.

To Rowland Cotton, 4 March 1696

March 4th 1695/6 wednesday morn.

Alas, my Deare children,

Edward French[1] is just now come to my house with a dolefulle letter from deare [B]etty Allyn,[2] whose husband[3] is [from?] the dry gripes fallen into a Leth[argy] always asleep unlesse forcably awaked & immedietely falls aslee[p agai]ne, senslesse, knows not what he saith, is not outragious it is ten d[....] mother is going to salisbury this evening as far as Barkers, poore Betty [...] her Brethr[....]

[...] recovered last sa[bbath fort]night [some?] Indians (sagamores some) appeared with a flag of truce at Pemaquid, Capt chubb[4] went out to them without armes man for man Indians askt for Rum & tobacco, Capt said noe its sab: day, they said, wee will have rumm or wee will have rume & you too, 2 Inds laid hold on the Capt then he called to his men to fall on for Gods sake, then he made signes to his men to come from the fort one of the English had a hatchet under his Coat, took it out & kiled an Indian, & then they killed 2 more Indians & took another live & wounded another (supposed) Mortally, then many of the enemy came neere & the English retreat[ed?]

& [...] all safe to the fort, only a rumor as if one of oure [...] the [they?] killed, w[ ] is since [ ]ad [illeg.] Love to you all, let [prayers?] [illeg.]

Cotton-Prince Papers, Prince Library, Rare Book and Manuscripts, Boston Public Library. Addressed "These For Mr Rowland Co[tton] at sandwi[ch]." Letter badly mutilated along folds.

---

1. See 21 November 1695.
2. Betty Allyn was Cotton's daughter, Elizabeth Cotton Alling.
3. Prince's note: "Rev. James Allen." James Alling (1657–1696, H.C. 1679) ministered to the church in Salisbury from 1682 until his death on 3 March 1696. Alling was married to John and Joanna Cotton's daughter Elizabeth. Elizabeth married Alling's pastoral successor, Caleb Cushing, in March 1699. Weis, *Colonial Clergy,* 19; *Sibley's Harvard Graduates,* 3:173-74.
4. Pasco Chubb assumed command of Fort William Henry at Pemaquid after John March resigned. In February 1696, as Cotton described, he foolishly ordered the killing of several Native chiefs (including Egeremet and Abenquid) who had come to the fort to discuss prisoner exchange, igniting renewed hostilities later in the summer. See the letter below of September 1696. Cotton implied that the Natives struck first and that Chubb acted in self-defense. Most contemporaries and historians have disagreed and criticized Chubb's rash actions. Gallay, *Colonial Wars of North America,* 350, 137; Mather, *Decennium Luctuosum,* 261-62, 270; Drake, *Border Wars of New England*, 108.

To Rowland Cotton, [5 March 1696][1]

Thursday A: M:

Deare Son

I heare J Baker is expected hourely from Hull, homewards, ergo I make ready; yours by Mr. Carey[2] I have but though multitudes are come by moreys, not one word of that letter, prethee send noe more to be left there, for they hardly ever come seasonably: I thanke your wife for thoughts of Diet-bread; your Deare mother went yesterday about noone; Nico: carried her to Mr Southworths & I suppose must carry the cloak bag to Boston on my horse, & mr S: carryes her to Bost: but morey not sending your letter, hence wee have noe account whether your Aunt will come shortly hither which was an exersise; A Hatch was Pilot to Mr Kene & one Gold who came to our doore & your mother is likely to have their company all the way, for they went hence together; know then (if you don't already) that Mr Kene (the Tailor) knows you very well & was very sorry Hatch would not pilot them to your house: He & Gold were Passengers in Parker, who with shute & the prize they left safe in Providence,

Mr Burrough's daughter & all very well, one of the ships lost a mast on the coast; the prize is there condemned; they came in Nath: Parkman's sloop[3] to Tarpolian Cove,[4] & in his chest he hath a letter for me from Cos: Rosseter[5] at whose house he was often in Taunton, mr Harford & mr warren & theirs all well; By Ens: Tracy I wrote to you[6] on Tuseday, Sam: Hinckley[7] after his sweat on monday tooke Physick of us yesterday, I have not heard this morning how he doth: I salute you both & pray for you all,

who am, your desolate father

John Cotton

Postscript; sam: H: Just now sends Is: Lathrop[8] to me to desire me to be at sand:[9] next sab:[10] & you at Bar: that mr Russell may preach here;[11] but I cannot leave this family, he is sending for mr Rus: if you will goe to Bar: & he promise to come to you, it will doe well:

Cotton-Prince Papers, Prince Library, Rare Book and Manuscripts, Boston Public Library. Addressed "These For mr Rowland Cotton at Sandwich."

---

1. Prince's note: "suppose. Mar. 5. 95/6."
2. Not found.
3. Nathaniel Parkman (b. 1655) was a Boston mariner like his father, Elias (d. 1662), who was lost at sea. Savage, *Genealogical Dictionary,* 3:359.
4. On Naushon Island, Buzzard's Bay, Massachusetts.
5. Presumably Josiah Rosseter, but the letter has not been not found.
6. Not found.
7. Probably Samuel Hinckley, the son of Governor Thomas Hinckley. Samuel was born in February 1653 and married Sarah Pope in November 1676 in Barnstable, where they had eleven children. He died on 19 March 1697. Otis, *Genealogical Notes of Barnstable Families,* 2:38-40.
8. Isaac Lathrop (b. 1673) was the son of Meletiah and Sarah Farrar Lathrop of Barnstable. Savage, *Genealogical Dictionary,* 3:121.
9. Sandwich.
10. Sabbath.
11. It seems as though Jonathan Russell (the minister in Barnstable) and Rowland Cotton (the minister in Sandwich) were merely exchanging pulpits.

To Rowland Cotton, [6 March 1696?][1]

Friday, p: m:

Deare Son

your mother went accompanyed with Mr Southworth & will: Barnes upon M^r^ will: Clarks horse, they lodged that night at Barkers, Thursday morning (soe well was your moth:) that they were at Cushings before our mr Thomas came thither but from Capt Jacobs, he saith, last Sat: morn: Cos: mathers Hittabel dyed,[2] it was in bed with a nurse & crowed pleasantly about break of day, the nurse fell asleep & about sun rise the child was found dead lying on her arm; Court likely to be dissolved this weeke; J: Bradford is come home, the Judges Mr Dart: Coo: Sew:) intended to lye at Barkers on monday night, soe that if your Bro: & others come not till Tuseday morn, you will be time enough before court begins, but if you come on monday morn you shall both be very welcome: Bring the books you have borrowed though my dearest be gone, I hope she will returne, but I saw her bowels so yerne to poore Betty,[3] that in a few minutes she exprest her resolves to goe this difficult Journey, designing (if possible) to carry Dr oliver[4] along with her; Isaac Lobdell[5] was at son Allyns Feb: 23: & from Bost: sent me a kinde letter of his illnesse; the Enemy did kill one of our English by a shot in the head; & young Alden at Port Royal bought a fraight of wheat, but he discerned soe much of the French Privatteers who are there frozen very hard (who did us the mischeif last yeare & are preparing shallops for next summer that with airs will fly like the wind) that he fled away without his wheat that he had paid for lest vessell & wheat should all be taken away, 2 English captives <were taken> ran away with him; noe doubt a Sagamore was one killed by our capts Bagonett, divers Mowhawks 20 or 30 are with our Easterne enemy, one was in this company; J: Rickard reacht the Castle on monday night, the Lathrops reacht but to Scittuate: noe harm de platter: Desolate I with sol: & Jos: salute you both: God blesse you all,

your Affec: Fath:

J: C:

old mr. Bulkly (our oldest minister) lately dead.[6]

Pembertons seems to beare the bell for all Dudley & Mather.

major Townsend is speaker,[7] Jewett[8] came not time enough: Leift Allyn was to come to Bost: this day for your moth: maria was sick (as wee heard) but is gratiously recovered; a vessell this week from N: York with pease, bread & flower which is now 18 sh an 100 pd: By Elisha Hedge[9] convey to your Bro: all news with our Love, his is well, I would now seale & give it El: H: but that I hope for will: Barnes to night with more newes from your mother.

W:B: is come,[10] your moth: well at Bost: son Al:[11] much as he was: Dismall destruction of vessels, poore fishermen, neare 20 dead bodies found, salem, marblehead, Ipswich vessels, math: says, & perhaps Isle of shoals also: a Newbury vessell cast up at Nantasket beach, men all saved, vessell like to get off & noe damage to goods.

Cotton-Prince Papers, Prince Library, Rare Book and Manuscripts, Boston Public Library. Addressed "These For Mr Rowland Cotton, Pastor of the Church at Sandwich."

---

1. Prince's note: "suppose March. 6. 95/6."
2. Mehitable Mather was Cotton and Abigail Mather's sixth child, born after April 1695, and is described only as dying "young." Horace C. Mather, *Lineage of Rev. Richard Mather*, (Hartford, Conn., 1890), 79.
3. Their daughter Elizabeth was grieving for her husband, James Alling, who died on 3 March, but Cotton's postscript indicates that he didn't know that Alling had died. See the above letter of 4 March 1696.
4. Probably Dr. James Oliver (1659–1703, H.C. 1680) of Cambridge, who worked as a physician following his graduation. *Sibley's Harvard Graduates,* 3:198-99.
5. Isaac Lobdell (1637–1718) was a freeman in Plymouth in 1673 but also resided in Hingham and Hull. The letter he sent to Cotton has not been not found. Savage, *Genealogical Dictionary,* 3:102.
6. Edward Bulkley was born in Bedfordshire in 1614, emigrated to Boston in 1635 and briefly attended Harvard College but did not graduate. He first ministered in Marshfield from 1642 to 1656 and then accepted a call from Concord, where he served from 1659 to 1694. He gave the Artillery Election Sermon in 1679 and the Election Sermon in 1680; neither was published. He died on 2 January 1696. In the left margin of the letter before "old," Cotton drew a hand pointing to "old." Weis, *Colonial Clergy,* 45.
7. According to Samuel Sewall, Penn Townsend was elected Speaker of the Massachusetts House on 28 February 1695/6. Thomas, *Diary of Samuel Sewall,* 348.
8. Nehemiah Jewett (1643–1720) lived in Ipswich and was married to Exercise Pierce (1647[?]–1731); he served as a representative for Ipswich from 1689 to 1694 and was speaker in 1694. Savage, *Genealogical Dictionary,* 2:549.
9. Elisha Hedge (1642–1713) lived in Yarmouth, where Rowland's brother John (1661–1706, H.C. 1681) was a minister from 1691 to 1705. Torrey, *New England Marriages,* 363; Weis, *Colonial Clergy,* 62.
10. This second postscript was written beneath the address.
11. James Alling, Cotton's son-in-law.

To Rowland Cotton, [April 1696?][1]

Saturday Morn:

Deare Son

As to your monday night letter,[2] I can assure you, it is noe small greife to me & your mother, her utter inability to doe you service, it would greive your heart to see her, every day droopings by reason of bodily infirmities, soe weak she is that a litle loud word almost undoes her, o that God would open a doore for your Dearest to see her parents, sarahs thoughts or words of her Journey a week before signify nothing of obstruction in the least, she is only afraid if you goe now she shall loose your good company then: my sinking mate said last night she thought she must soone send to John to fetch home his & to Betty not to send hers, she cannot beare the least noise: The markt sentence in your mothers letter[3] is worthy to be written in letters of gold, wee can all feale to its truth, Happy, o thrice Happy are they that have an interest in & their affections fixt upon those things that they cannot be deprived of! I intend to write to salisbury by 'sias who (the Tailors having now finisht for him) is now ready for the first faire winde in Eph: Cole: I say not how welcome yours shall be for more than a night notwithstanding her desert of the little parlor:

Barbados newes came only (as far as I yet heare) by your J: chipman, I doubt its too true; Capt Thomas came last week from salem, litle hopes of his wife;[4] mr Noys[5] better, but returnes not yet to his pulpit, J: Emerson[6] preacht for him on the Fast etc old Mr Philips hastning to his end,[7] as Col: Gidney[8] (who was with him on the Fast) tells Cap: Tho: If I can perswade Mr Dexter to hasten away, I think to send Theoph: now, who may on monday goe from you to Bar: & call upon the damsell to get ready while he steps to yarmouth & returnes to call her on Tuseday morning, I hope the child may have company, you will be tender of him; The books your moth: hath not perused & is willing a litle longer to detaine them: wee etc most heartily salute you both, with prayers etc

I am your affec: fath

J: C:

The vile Su: And: broke prison the night before last, sheriff Bradf: not yet come to us from Bost: ergo the Hue & cry not yet gone; wee suppose he brings some orders from L. Govr for Exec: but too late for the young beast.[9] your mother intends to send the Physick now, if she can get strength & time before they mount. Js: Cush: buries today a son not 5 weeks old,[10] it is his third successively dying before Bap: the second was that sabbath wee were at the vineyard: J: Nelson stoops (more than Pugsley[11]) with the gout; you sent right notes.

seale this letter for The: to carry; I soe right bec: Math: Fuller[12] came since you spake to Mary & tells her relations here that she is for her trade now, a sudden change from what you wrote, I hope wee shall obtaine this quarter at least, your moth: being soe weak & Sar's mar:[13] had not you bet best write too, being near witnesse of her promise

Trumpet for John & 8p. silver: Bone lace for Joanna, Thread lace for Betty. stomacher[14] for their mother.

The least portion for Joseph; my wife sends three portions more, if two <are> will work enough for John Prince, you may keep the other portion.[15]

Cotton-Prince Papers, Prince Library, Rare Book and Manuscripts, Boston Public Library. Addressed "These For Mr Rowland Cotton, Pastor of the Church at Sandwich."

---

1. Prince's note: "suppose April. 96."
2. Not found.
3. Not found.
4. Nathaniel Thomas's (1643–1718) wife, Deborah Jacob, died on 17 June 1696 in Marshfield. Savage, *Genealogical Dictionary,* 4:281-82; Torrey, *New England Marriages,* 735.
5. Probably Nicholas Noyes (1647–1717, H.C. 1667), the minister in Salem. Weis, *Colonial Clergy,* 153.
6. Probably John Emerson Jr. (1670–1732, H.C. 1689), who was preaching in Manchester, Massachusetts, from 1695 to 1697. He preached in Salem as the settled minister from 1697 to 1699. Weis, *Colonial Clergy*, 80.
7. Prince's note: "R Mr Philips of Rowly D Apr. 22. 96." Samuel Philips (1625–1696, H.C. 1650), the minister in Rowley, died on 22 April 1696. Weis, *Colonial Clergy,* 164.
8. Col. Bartholomew Gedney of Salem; see 12 February 1695.
9. On 10 March 1695/6, Susanna Andrews, a single woman living with her parents in Lakenham, was indicted for murdering her newborn twins in September 1695. Her parents, John and Esther, were also indicted for hiding Susanna and secretly burying the dead babies. Massachusetts Archives, Suffolk County Files, Reel 20, vol. 37, #3279.
10. Isaac and Rebekah Cushman had six living children by 1696; the last recorded birth was that of Fear, born on 10 March 1689. The last three children, all of whom died as newborns, seem not to have been recorded. Van Antwerp, *Vital Records of Plymouth,* 11.
11. For this "Pugsley" reference, see 10 August 1694.
12. Matthew Fuller (1663–1744) lived in Scituate/Barnstable. Torrey, *New England Marriages,* 289.
13. Cotton was worried about losing his servant, Mary, especially since his daughter, Sarah, married William Bradbury on 16 March 1696 and was no longer living at home. Torrey, *New England Marriages,* 90.
14. "A waistcoat" or "medicated cloth applied to the chest" or "an ornamental covering for the chest...worn by women under the lacing of the bodice." *OED*, 16:753.
15. These last two postscripts were written beneath the address.

To Rowland Cotton, 27 July 1696

Plymouth, July, 27: 1696:

Deare Son

on the Fast day a Post said at Bost: that divers ships were seene in Ipswich Bay which hastned the Capt & his souldiers to the castle that evening, but they were only the mast ships, 2 frigats, & 2 more merchantmen who are arrived at Pascataqua

From Cos: Cot: Mather I transcribe as followeth.

"Designing that my whole country shall have the story of the miraculous things (which are numerous) attending the defeat of the late invasion I must pray your patience & pardon that I cannot now recite the particulars. The miscarriage of the Plot[1] has marvellously united the nation, there is a most incomparable good Parliament, whereoff Sir Paul Foley is the Speaker.[2] The King is gone over to Flanders, the Lords Justices mostly the same or the like with what were last yeare; not above 8 or 10 are yet executed for the late treason & those not Noblemen,[3] but the Triall of the Traitors is daily going on. They enter into an Association to revenge K: Williams death (if untimely) all the nation over;[4] The Parliament is by an Act made capable of (not dissolution, but) meeting & sitting immediately on the Kings death & for halfe a yeare ensuing;[5] The Earle of Bellamont is not yet coming[6] & I suppose, except he can have N. Yorke in his Commission he will not come at all; A most horrible calamity, yea dissolution is come upon this miserable country for want of an Agent, by the disallowance of soe many of our Lawes, the rejection whereoff is now signifyed unto us with reasons fetch'd from certaine contested clauses here & there occurring in them. Poor Mr. Dudley's 2 sons are not heard of, the Lord be favourable to their distressed Father!" Haecille.[7]

From Cos: Sam:[8] thus;

"upon discovery of the late Plot severall 100s have bin clapt into prison amongst which they have tryed 8 who thereupon have paid their last debt to nature;[9] Fergusson is one of the imprisoned & 'tis Judged will be executed I doe not heare of any dissenters besides him in the conspiracy. The conspiracy was strong & the designe desperate; the French clergy had advanced a considerable summe which they lent to K: James for fitting the expedition <for> from France; many French merchants had loaden vessels with the most saileable goods for England but the discovery has put an end to their merchandise & their goods returnd on their hands againe, & had the Plot succeeded they would have had a good price for their wares but now must be content to keep them in France; The Plotters that have bin executed doe cleare K: J: & Lewis[10] from knowing any thing of their designe to Assassinate his Majesty & they may beleve it that can. The Nation is generally & more then ever right for the present Government, the Parliament <is> are strong for the good of the Nation, Sir P: Foley is speaker, a Gentleman whom I have seen & know to be a true Englishman; They (i: e: the Parliament) at their first opening the sessions appointed a day of Humiliation & prayer for the blessing of God on their Counsels, which has bin out of date for 40 <year> etc years past, they say, there is a number of them strongly set for repealing & taking off the Sacramentall Test[11] (which has hindred many persons worthy of civill & sacred employment from having it) but what steps that have taken is not yet certainly known here. The K: being about to goe for Flanders has appointed severall Noblemen to be the Lords Justices amongst whom Admirall Russell is one.[12] The Duke of Leeds (Darby that formerly was)[13] is not one of them; In Generall Things have a better prospect then ever heretofore since the war began; I doe not heare of considerable action by sea more then wee had newes of before.

Mr Ben: Coleman[14] writes from Engl: an account of his being taken & having lost soe much as his very manuscripts through the barbarous Rascality of a French Preist that was on board the Privateer that took him, I call it barbarous because they stript him starke naked, I term it rascality bec: 'twas a Preist that kept his writings, sermons etc from him though with the violation of a promise given to restore them upon Mr Colemans giving him a piece of Gold that was concealed in the heel of his shooe which when the Idolater had gotten into his clutches, he had noe more to say to my friend; Mr Whittingham[15] (who came over with capt Gillam)[16] says Mr Coleman is well accepted in London though he have not any settled imployment in a particular congregation as yet.

There was an Artificer in France that to show his ingenuity made a Clock that at the time of the striking of the houres, it did by the cunning of the worke discover severall Princes one after another doing obeysance to Lewis & one particularly represented his Brittannick Majesty & had ordered it soe that it should stoop lower than the rest to signify greater submission But (very ominously I hope) the machine by the overstraining of the wheel strook downe the image of Lewis which it was to pay its respect unto, Lewis the K: hearing of this sent the workman to prison for it though it was by accident & not by designe of his that soe it was; receive as much of this relation as you thinke fitt, it causes a great deale of laughter & am apt to thinke the main stroakes of it are true.

In Scotland a great many persons on a Fast day were signally converted by the preaching of a minister at Edinburgh which has caused much discourse & is lookt on as a signe for good. My Lord Bellamont designes to come this summer,[17] the former character of his good will to the country does continue & I hope it will be accordingly when he comes over As to N: E: many of our Lawes are repealed in Engl: & an exception is taken at our Colledge Charter bec: there is noe mention made of visitors to overlook them, distinct from the Corporation, which is of the same nature with our overseers heretofore. (I the scribe faulted this in the very day I heard the charter.)

Mr. Whittingham tells me Coll: Dudley does almost despaire of his sons[18] which went in Maintrue, there was a rumor of his being taken into France but it vanished, it is much to be lamented that 2 persons of our acquaintance should be thus lost as there is great reason to feare they are; Mr Whittingham was one of (the late) Mr Thos: Mackartyes bearers to the grave who dyed of feavor last December: The ships Gillam, Ems, Thackston came in on sabbath (his letter was dated July, 18:) which caused an Alarm P: M: I preacht A: M: at the south & was forct to give over twice by reason of a cry of fire, but at last wee went on pretty quietly: Doe not vouch all that is written to be absolutely true, allowance is to be given in telling a story, though I beleve that the maine things are soe: If this account satisfy not as to fullnesse please to give me more particular Articles of Inquiry & I shall be ready to give as speedy answer as may. Duty etc & Remembrance to all kinsfold nearer to or further from you;" Haec Ille:[19] If you want any particular information more, tell me soe, & I will send for it, for my owne part I am much filled & comforted with soe much & soe good Intelligence & resolve to maintaine a good Correspondence with him on this account.

Some persons were hurt at Deare Island by that Monday Thunder The foremast of J: Cole fell upon J: Greys shoulder & some ropes were soe about his midle that he was halfe overboard & in great danger of drowning, he desired publick thanks for his deliverance, poore man! It was a blessed sacrament day to many, & 3 children baptized my text was Isa: 33: 17:[20] I propounded to have a ch: meeting & left it till next sab: to fix the time which you may conclude will be Aug: 19: when you must preach my Lecture; marshfeild intend ordination in october,[21] the ch: have appointed Sept: 9: to be kept as a preparatory Fast & Deac: Ford came to me on Saturday in the Name of the Ch: to desire me to preach on that day once, & I have promised, D: V:[22] to doe it: J: Sturt:[23] etc came on sat: but said not a word of ours there, but yesterday P: M: I askt him & then he could tell me a female was borne,[24] our very great love to our children etc there: the like to you both, God blesse you & all yours; I am,

your Affectionate Father

John Cotton

Dear Daughter, if your Dearest be kept to yarmouth this day, may it not be best for James Lewis the bearer[25] to take the letter of you after you have read & sealed it againe & carry along to meet the owner that soe yarmouth & Mr Lathrop & Mr Russell may have what is newes.[26]

I want time to read what I have written.

I looke for Jos:[27] every day, Theoph:[28] writes to him they were safely housed at Traceys before the raine & after it got well home.

Cotton-Prince Papers, Prince Library, Rare Book and Manuscripts, Boston Public Library. Addressed "These For Mr Rowland Cotton, Pastor of the Church at Sandwich."

1. In February 1696, informants revealed a plot to assassinate King William III during one of his regular hunts in Richmond. The act was roughly to coincide with the landing of a large French invading force then gathering at Calais. The plot was foiled, and fourteen alleged conspirators were seized. The timely movement of forces from the Netherlands to England and the dispatch of the fleet to the Channel also frustrated the invasion plans. When the dual threat was revealed, the Whigs naturally aroused as much patriotic fervor as possible, "uniting" the nation against foreign intrigues and invasion. Baxter, *William III*, 336-37.

2. Sir Paul Foley (1645[?]–1699) was Speaker of the House of Commons from 1695 to December 1698. He was known as an upright, impartial man, unspectacular, but respected. *DNB*.

3. At least three of them, however, Sir John Friend, Sir William Perkins and Sir John Fenwick, were knights. Baxter, *William III*, 337, 343.

4. Days after they heard the news of the assassination plot, the Commons and some Lords formed a "General Association for King William," a patriotic vigilante group promising revenge against all "unfriendly" elements if William were killed. Baxter, *William III*, 337.

5. This move was obviously designed to fill any power vacuum left by an assassination and to prevent a Jacobite coup.

6. Richard Coote, Earl of Bellomont (1636–1701) came to North America as the governor general of Massachusetts, New York and New Hampshire and served as captain-general of the militias of Rhode Island, Connecticut and the Jerseys. The hope behind these multiple office holdings was that Bellomont would be able to coordinate the military activities of the northeast colonies and enforce the Navigation Acts more effectively. For his pains, he received almost nothing but trouble, especially from New York and Massachusetts. *American National Biography*, ed. John A. Garraty and Mark C. Carnes (New York and Oxford, 1999).

7. "Easily."

8. Samuel Cotton.

9. See n. 1, above.

10. Perhaps, but James's son, the Duke of Berwick, was clearly involved; it would have been surprising if James and the French King had not known something of the scheme. Baxter, *William III*, 337.

11. The Test Act, passed in 1673, barred anyone who did not subscribe to the rites and doctrines of the Church of England from public or military office. The Act was particularly aimed at the Catholic Duke of York, but it affected dissenting Protestants as well.

12. See 20 August 1692.

13. Sir Thomas Osborne, Earl of Danby (1631–1712) became Duke of Leeds in 1694. *DNB*.

14. Benjamin Colman (1673–1747, H.C. 1692) preached briefly in Medford and planned to join in missionary efforts in Carolina. However, he emigrated to England instead, in 1692, eventually returning to Boston in 1699 to help establish the Brattle Street Church. Sibley includes an account of his capture at sea. *Sibley's Harvard Graduates*, 4:120-37.

15. Possibly William Whittingham (d. 1672), a merchant of Ipswich and Boston.

16. Probably Captain Benjamin Gillam (c. 1663–1706), mariner of Boston.

17. See n. 7 above.

18. See n. 8 above.

19. "Easily."

20. Isa. 33:17: "Thine eyes shall see the king in his beauty: they shall behold the land that is very far off."

21. Edward Tompson (1665–1705, H.C. 1684) was ordained in Marshfield on 14 October 1696. Weis, *Colonial Clergy,* 205.

22. "God willing."

23. Either John (1658–1752) or Joseph (b. 1666) Sturtevant; both lived in Plymouth. Torrey, *New England Marriages,* 720.

24. Possibly Abigail Cotton, daughter of Rowland and Elizabeth, born on 9 July 1696. Laverne C. Cooley, *Short Biography of the Rev. John Cotton & a Cotton Genealogy* (New York, 1945), 34.

25. Probably James Lewis (1664–1748) of Barnstable. Torrey, *New England Marriages,* 463.

26. "Yarmouth" refers to John Cotton, Cotton's son; Nathaniel Lathrop (1669–1700) lived in Barnstable, and Jonathan Russell (1655–1711, H.C. 1675) was the minister in Barnstable.

27. Josiah Cotton.

28. Theophilus Cotton.

To Rowland Cotton, [after 7 August 1696]

Thursday

[Dea]re Son

[You]rs by Tom: West[1] I received, I was sorry to be diverted but [I] being a stranger I was compelled to goe downe to him [wh]ich I intended not to have done to any that day whilst the breth: [we]re gone to Mr T: I cannot release you from preaching, for he [will?] not come, though his wife is recovering; they have had full [disco]urse with him, he is strong that I must be the man,[2] but [ ]rly averse to their inchurching; in his letter to me[3] are these words; [....] noe difficulty in the case itselfe as it lyes before the ch: [...] [dou]bt not but God will direct you to a comfortable issue. [...] words are encouraging, all the rest you must see & heare [whe]n you come, God in mercy bring you with a blessing:

[....] bring dreadfull tidings from the East;[4] The two Fr: frigats [...] Paxtons[5] went to Pemaquid, there also was a party by [...] of the Enemy, (how many 100s I heare not certainly) [....] carried 12 great guns ashoare & planted agst the weakest part of the garrison, what the English were doing all that time or sleeping or worse I know not; Required us to surrender, capt Chubb refused, the Fr: Gen:[6] told them he would send 4 bombs, he did soe as he said, the 1st some considerable distance from the fort, the 2ond nearer, the 3d yet nearer, the 4th toucht the fort, as he told them it should; wee then yeilded upon these Articles, viz, that wee all should passe out of the Fort each man with all that was his owne & goe safely aboard a vessell for Boston, the termes were accepted;[7] the Indians demand halfe the English of the Fr: Gen: as their due [he?] sayes noe, I have engaged them Liberty & will keep my [wor]d, the Indians beg hard to have 6 English men & [....]all C: chub to make amends for those they [lo]st by [....] denyes them, they beg hard for 4: he gives [th]em [....] a number are detained (how many [I] k[now] [....]ton (who they say) Lost not a man [....] Boston sent by the Enemy & [....] them againe, unlesse [....] Frenchmen with us be returned to them;[8] It is said there was not po[wder?] enough to shoot above twice from the fort, some [....] sold it to the enemy; Hinckley (that brought [....] said a Post came on saturday that said the Fr[ench] were come over the Lake, had killed about 300 [...] & had cut up their Corne; All the out-planters west & north are in dreadfull danger & may expect every where to be assaulted & that speed[ily.] God is very angry with poore N: E: I conclude [....] thoughts that all Major church's measures mus[....] he will not dare to goe with soe small an Ar[ ] [....] Indians, there will be enough to meete him, if [....] Lord pitty & guide us: for Kit to succeed is astonis[....] in my creed, their charter (I beleive) is yet good & [...] Bellamont is an Irish Title, though my Lord Cook [....] English man, but certainly it is noe other Govr coming to us;[9] I suppose Kit came away before the Frigats & mastmen [...] made him say Guber: was on the waters, I can hardly thinke [...] other frigat is coming with him this summer: yesterday [....] Howls oxe, worth 6 or 7 pd, dyed of a surfett, eating [...] English Grasse; I am glad you are soe innocent, [....] that your Bro: be soe too: A generall practicall tru[th?] [....] very welcome, I cannot then preach: your mother [...] as well or better then she hath been th[ese?] many m[onths? We] both salute you both; I know not [....] for [...] convey this, but am now ready [....] Jos: [...] letter of his long passage & th[....] [ta]ken by [...] of Charlestowne; God blesse [....]

soe daily prayes;
[....] Fa[ther]

Sprague much jeer'd
T: W: yesterday in my house for his black coate:

Josh: morse brought your Leathers to my house & takes nothing for them: This scotch letter[10] was soe ill written that I can hardly make good English of it, the outside is, A powerfull Conversation by the powerfull Spirit in Scotland, Good wife Kenedy brought it from Boston & sent it to me.

Cotton-Prince Papers, Prince Library, Rare Book and Manuscripts, Boston Public Library. Letter torn on left edge & at bottom. Letter is in Cotton's hand.

---

1. Not found.
2. Weymouth's minister, Samuel Torrey, evidently would not come to fill his pulpit on 19 August 19. See the next letter.

3. Not found.
4. The following is apparently a transcription.
5. Prince's note: "ye Newport man of war." This probably refers to the beginning of the attack on Fort William Henry, which began on 5 August 1696, when the French attacked and won the English ship the *Newport*, commanded by Captain Paxton, in the Bay of Fundy. Mather, *Decennium Luctuosum*, 262; Gallay, *Colonial Wars of North America*, 350; Drake, *Border Wars of New England*, 110.
6. "French General."
7. Following Chubb's decision to kill the Native sachems who came to the fort to discuss prisoner exchange in February 1696, hostilities erupted again in King William's War. Chubb surrendered the fort one day in early August 1696 during a siege by French soldiers and their Native allies. Mather and other contemporaries criticized Chubb for what they considered to be his cowardice in surrendering. Gallay, *Colonial Wars of North America*, 350, 137; Mather, *Decennium Luctuosum*, 261-62; Drake, *Border Wars of New England*, 111.
8. The transcription appears to end here. Prince's note: "Pemaquid Fort surrender'd by Chub Aug. 5 or 6. 96."
9. Richard Coote, Earl of Bellomont (1636–1701) became the governor general of the provinces of Massachusetts, New Hampshire and New York and served as commander of the joint forces of those provinces as well as of Connecticut, Rhode Island and the Jerseys. See also 27 July 1696.
10. Not found.

To Rowland Cotton, [23 & 24 August 1696][1]

MONDAY P: M: BY J: MO: SEN:

Read this First

DEARE SON

If your horse proove lame W: C: will yelpe & yell out his complaints to every one notoriously, but I am glad you are soe well Mounted & sorry you saw not the finback;[2] speedily send word to Mashpau[3] that your Lect: must be on monday, for if I come not to you to morrow (as I beleve I shall not) you may expect me next monday or Tuseday without faile, if God permit: (our sacr: is to be next sab: as well as yours) you will accompany me as far as I goe southward: since you went I recall that I preacht at Bar:[4] oct: 30: wee wonder that C: Mole is not yet returned, but expect him certainly this eve; young Sam: Prince came hither on saturday & saith on Friday morn the Fleet went Eastward he saw them 2 leagues off, only Capt Emes[5] is not gone, some say its from cowardise, others say falsnesse, some say he pleads the King hath sent his orders to him to convay the mast ships home, & if he should goe & be taken what would become of the mast ships & how should he answer it to the K: if they be taken going

home? our fishermen catch very much mackarill: your mother is considerably ill night & day ever since you left us: wee both salute you both God blesse you all, I am,
your Affec: Fath:

J: C:

J: mor: sen: is rated to me 14 shil: he hath given me but 10 shil: & he saith he will give you 10 shil: & I must expect noe more: Aske Mr Rus:[6] whether he be willing for Eastham Lecture next week: Its said your new horse is intolerably bad to keep, take heed of loosing him.

Tuesday; J: M: staying till now I recall & open interponere.[7]

Last night C: Mole came, on Thursday night he called Govr. St.[8] out of bed who treated him very courteously, after midnight he called his wife up at charlestowne, who had buried a child of 9 months old since his departure;[9] C: Elmes [Emes] is gone some houres after the fleet but in a very ill humor, the cause is Envy, he scornes to goe under a Commorode[10] (a cramp word but I thinke I say it right) it seems the biggest of the new come Frigats is Admirall, but he would have bin Adm: himselfe, but Authority ordered it otherwise, it is concluded he would soone overtake the rest: one of capt Mole's prizes was unladen & prized & then made the fireship now in our fleet: Partridge is not yet arrived in N: E: only they have newes that he is coming Le: Govr instead of usher, who was very huffy with Mole because he would not carry his prizes to Pastacaqua for condemnation, threatned to seize etc but Mole is above danger from him: The Law of o: E: now is that which will be attended as soone as Mole gets to Boston, (who is gone aboard & now weighing anchor) when the prizes are condemned The King must have a fifth part of the goods, in order to which a Commissioner is to be chosen by the Authority to see a Just division & to take the Kings part, & then all the rest of the goods & all the prizes are to be delivered to capt mole for him & his partners.

He sayes, that he heard yester-morning, a Post had brought newes in the night of damage done by the enemy at wells,[11] particulars he knowes not; he heares nothing of our Army: Divers of the Barbadoes fleet are arrived; not yet all, but litle Rumm: your mother is fetcht this morning to Joseph warrens youngest child,[12] dangerously sick of vomiting & flux: Reb: Morton hath a living son[13] this last night, all hopeful.

Cotton-Prince Papers, Prince Library, Rare Book and Manuscripts, Boston Public Library. Addressed "These For Mr. Rowland Cotton at Sandwich."

1. Prince's note: "Suppose in 1696, Aug," but see 25 August 1696, n. 1, which fixes this letter's chronology.
2. A finback whale (*Balaenoptera physalus*) is the second largest whale and has a distinctive flat head and a throat marked by deep furrows.
3. The Indian Congregational Church in Mashpee had Native preachers only from 1682–1729, after the death of Richard Bourne and before the arrival of Joseph Bourne (1701–1767, H.C. 1722). Weis, *Colonial Clergy,* 36.
4. Barnstable.
5. The fleet, consisting of three men-of-war and two armed merchant vessels, sailed in pursuit of Iberville's victorious ships following the surrender of Fort William Henry. One of the captains, Eames, encountered a more vigorous French fleet than he expected and retreated. See 12 August 1693. Drake, *Border Wars of New England,* 112.
6. Jonathan Russell, minister in Barnstable.
7. The Tuesday installment was written on a second, smaller sheet and was enclosed in the Monday portion.
8. William Stoughton.
9. Edward Mould, son of Captain Samuel and Mary Mould (Moulds), was born on 8 October 1695, and died on 1 July 1696. Roger D. Joslyn, *Vital Records of Charlestown, Massachusetts*, (Boston, 1984), 168, 172.
10. Commodore.
11. Prince's note: "June. 24: 1696— 3 men & yr wives kill'd by Indians at Wells." On 24 June, Thomas Cole and his wife were killed by Natives as they were returning home to Wells, Maine, with neighbors following a visit to York, Maine. While Prince noted that "3 men & yr wives kill'd by Indians at Wells," Mather implied that only Cole and his wife were "slain." Drake suggests that Cole, his wife and two others were killed. Two days later, on 26 June, an assault on nearby Sagamore Creek and Sherburne's Plains left fourteen settlers dead, four captured and the settlement in flames. Stackpole includes a list of the people killed and captured. Mather, *Decennium Luctuosum,* 261; Drake, *Border Wars of New England,* 108-9; Stackpole, *History of New Hampshire,* 186-87.
12. Mehitable and Joseph Warren's newborn daughter, Priscilla, arrived on 19 June 1696. She survived this illness and was engaged to Lemuel Drew in 1751. Van Antwerp, *Vital Records of Plymouth,* 23, 145.
13. The published town records list the birth of Nathaniel Morton on 24 August 1695 instead of 1696, mistaking the year by one. Van Antwerp, *Vital Records of Plymouth,* 31.

To Rowland Cotton, [25 August 1696]

WEDNESDAY A: M:

DEARE SON

J: morey sen: hath 2 letters for you: yesterday:[1] Mr Melvin brought me a letter[2] from Jos: but noe newes in it: Amongst the many English & scotch dead of the sicknesse at Barbados,[3] Dr Williams & his wife are reckoned; he lived at Newhaven & at charlestowne & Boston since: T: Palmer[4] had a fall off his horse at Boston which detained him till last Saturday, then he came to Midlebury, but had soe much paine & illnesse that he could not preach on the sabbath & he is yet at Isaac Howlands[5] ill & feverish, what answer he intends to give I heare not, but it is said that compton voted for a minister & that Palmer hath now a Major vote of that towne & their new minister the minor; Mr Melvin saith his Bro: simon[6] bid him tell me, that Mr Wadsworth is shortly to be ordained, he hath forgot the day but he thinks it is this day fortnight.[7] I resolve D: V:[8] to be at it, & if soe, then I must seasonably tell Marshfeild, they must not expect me that day; I tell Mr Melv: of my purpose to be at yarm: on Tuseday & to goe to Eastham weds: morn; he saith he will be our companion thither; wee both salute you both, God blesse you all,

I am your Affec: Fath:

J: C:

Dispatch your Indian Lecture on Monday without faile for I hope that day to see you: Mr Nath: Clark is taken by the Fr: & another vessell that came out with him, he is at Pettaquabull & may soone be expected here.

HAC [HELDEN?] 4TH EPISTLE, WEDNESDAY, P: M:[9]

SON

Aske this Dr Read newes from Andover of Abbott & Blancher kiled, & a man & 3 Children carried from Haverhill[10] which (he saith) Johnson of Haverhill told him major Hincksman hath laid downe his place & Mr. Ting of Dunstable is Major.
I have but a minutes time

Cotton-Prince Papers, Prince Library, Rare Book and Manuscripts, Boston Public Library. Addressed "These For Mr Rowland Cotton, Pastor of the church at Sandwich."

---

1. See 23 and 24 August 1696.
2. Not found. Probably Samuel Melvin/Melyen (c. 1675–1711, H.C. 1696). Melvin's family was among the most important in New Netherland; his father moved to Boston in the 1680s. After graduation, Melvin first taught school in Hadley; he later ministered to the First Presbyterian Church in Elizabethtown, New Jersey. *Sibley's Harvard Graduates,* 4: 298-300.
3. Probably yellow fever; epidemics of "bleeding fever" ravaged Barbados in the 1640s and the 1690s. Dunn, *Sugar and Slaves,* 303.
4. Thomas Palmer (1665–1743) was the settled minister in Middleborough beginning in 1696. Although he never attended college, he was ordained in 1702. After his dismissal in 1708, he worked as a physician until his death. Cotton was alluding to Middleborough's pending decision whether or not to hire Palmer as its minister. Weis, *Colonial Clergy,* 157.
5. Isaac Howland (c. 1650–1724) was the youngest son of emigrant John Howland. He was an innkeeper and lived in Middleborough; he also served as a representative to the Plymouth Court several times before 1692. Savage, *Genealogical Dictionary,* 2:479.
6. Both Sibley and Savage suggest that Samuel Melvin had a sister, Abigail, and a brother, who is unamed.
7. Prince's note: "Mr Wadsworth was ordained on Sept. 8. 1696." Benjamin Wadsworth (1670–1737, H.C. 1690) was ordained in Boston's first church on 8 September 1696. Weis, *Colonial Clergy,* 212.
8. "God willing."
9. This "epistle" was written on a very small scrap of paper, folded and sealed, without address, apparently enclosed with the letter preceding.
10. The captives were probably Jonathan Haynes and his five children, who were captured from Haverhill on 15 August 1696. See 30 October 1696 and 14 May 1698. George Wingate Chase, *History of Haverhill* (Pub. by the author, 1861), 184-85.

To Rowland Cotton, [before 7 August 1696?]

Plym: Tuseday A: M:

Deare Son

By Abr: Hedge[1] I saluted you yester-morn:[2] soone after came Jos: Dun: & Sam: Sturt: to tell me in all their names that they were ready to attend the ch: to converse with us when ever a ch: meeting should be appointed[3] for that end: I intend Aug: 19: my Lecture day for that service, & you shall then preach for me, unlesse it appeare more adviseable that I desire & obtaine Mr Torrey[4] to doe it: yours of sat: P: M:[5] per I know not whom I received yesterday at breakfast: not one word of Thaddeus, he is given up for lost: the 3 ship mrs were now only passengers, Gilbert spake with Col. Winthrop in o: E:[6] he was not well; to Sir Litle was in Paxton chyrurgions mate: It is saintloe that is infirme with his wounds: Sturt: came to fetch Sir Litle to be a qrter of this yeare with them[7] & he is gone; yesternoone sailed hence John Cole & John Grey[8] his mate & fraighter, & in him, Mr Elliston Murdo, John Dyer[9] (Han: Mortons husband) Goodwife Kenedy[10] (to see her husband at the castle) Martha Cole & Lydia Grey[11] whose businesse is to buy her wedding cloaths, caleb Loring[12] (which whom she now stands posted) being gone by land to meet her there, but the storme, blacknesse, thunder & lightning was soe terrible & she soe laden with wood & lying on one side, that I perceive it is much to be feared what is become of them; yesterday came Theoph: with oxenbridge Thatcher[13] (Josiahs contemporary) to see us, & went back not long before the thunder etc I feare they were sorely drencht, long to heare how they escaped, I suppose you know your Presbury[14] had his legs shot off in Eames[15] & dyed: I intended here to stop & finish tomorrow for Betty Nye,[16] but Just n[ow] comes in Mr Atherne; your parents send you both our heartyest [...] the Lord blesse you & all yours

soe prayes your Affectionate Father

John Cotton

The Thunder & Lightning killed in Mr. Barnes's Pasture one of his best oxen & a new milch cow & barkt a tree that was betweene the two dead beasts:[17]

Cotton-Prince Papers, Prince Library, Rare Book and Manuscripts, Boston Public Library. Addressed "These For Mr Rowland Cotton, Pastor of the Church at Sandwich."

---

1. Abraham Hedge lived in Sandwich and Yarmouth and was the son of William Hedge. Savage, *Genealogical Dictionary,* 2:400.

2. Not found.

3. Cotton was alluding to the split of the Plymouth church that occurred following a 19 August church meeting. A group of members, led by elder Isaac Cushman, wanted to establish a separate church in early 1696. Joseph Dunham and Samuel Sturtevant (1654–1736) were two of the departing members. Cotton was initially opposed to the action, but by September Cushman and Cotton reconciled, and Cushman became the first minister of the new church in Plympton. *CSM,* 22:176, 178-79.
4. Cotton was going to ask Weymouth's minister, Samuel Torrey, to preach for him on 19 August, when he planned to address the splinter congregation.
5. Not found.
6. "Old England."
7. Samuel Sturtevant escorted Ephraim Little (1676–1723, H.C. 1695), who was teaching school in Plymouth, to serve as a temporary minister to the splinter congregation in Plympton. See 22 August 1695.
8. Likely John Cole (1660–1748), who was married to Susanna Grey (1668–1727) and lived in Plympton. Possibly John Grey (b. 1661) of Plymouth who was married to Joanna Morton, or John Grey, who married Susannah Clarke, of Harwich. Torrey, *New England Marriages,* 169, 320.
9. John Dyer (b. 1672) married Hannah Morton in June 1694, and they lived in Boston. Torrey, *New England Marriages,* 237.
10. Probably Elizabeth Kennedy of Plymouth, who was going to see her husband, Alexander. Savage, *Genealogical Dictionary,* 3:10.
11. Martha Cole (c. 1672–1718) was married to Nathaniel Howland (d. 1746) in March 1697 in Plymouth. Torrey, *New England Marriages,* 395.
12. Caleb Loring (1674–1732) married Lydia Grey (1678–1771) on 7 August 1696 in Plymouth. Torrey, *New England Marriages,* 474.
13. Oxenbridge Thacher (1681–1772, H.C. 1698) was the eldest son of Milton's minister, Peter Thacher. He was a Harvard classmate of Josiah Cotton's, but evidently also friends with Theophilus. *Sibley's Harvard Graduates,* 4:417-19.
14. William Presbury was born in Sandwich in 1664 to John Presbury (1640–1679), but no source lists his death date. Charles Banks, *History of Martha's Vineyard* (Boston, 1911–25), 3:410-11.
15. "Eames" refers to Captain Eames. See 12 August 1693.
16. Elizabeth Atwood/Wood Nye, was the wife of Caleb Nye (1658–1704) and lived in Sandwich. Torrey, *New England Marriages,* 542.
17. This postscript was written under the address.

To Rowland Cotton

[30 September 1696?][1]

<Thurs> Wednesday

Deare Son

Deacon Ford[2] hath brought letters to me for our chh to send our messengers to their ordination[3] oct: 14:[4] I wish I knew how you intend to order your Journey to us in order to your being at that solemnity, your mother resolves D. V:[5] to goe thither at that time: Sir Litle's Text[6] was, Thes: 5: 6:3 his sermons have a good Commend, there was a competent contribution for him, & they are very desirous of constant enjoyment of him during Mr Lawsons absence, he only hath promised them this next sabbath & tells me he will not leave his schooling here & take the work there; He also tells me, that old Mr Cushing told him he had a letter from his son Caleb[7] informing of his purpose to come this week or next to see him, if soe then wee shall doubtlesse see him here or at Marshfeild; Love, prayers etc

your etc

J: C:

Cotton-Prince Papers, Prince Library, Rare Book and Manuscripts, Boston Public Library. Addressed "These For Mr. Rowland Cotton at Sandwich per Indum."

---

1. Prince's note: "Suppose Sep. 30. 96."
2. Possibly Michael Ford (d. 1721) of Marshfield. Savage, *Genealogical Dictionary,* 2:183; Lysander Salmon Richards, *History of Marshfield* (Plymouth, 1901), 2:102-3.
3. Edward Tompson (1665–1705, H.C. 1684) was ordained in Marshfield's First Church on 14 October 1696, where he remained until he died. *Sibley's Harvard Graduates,* 3:306-10; *CSM,* 22:179.
4. Prince's note: "Mr Edward Thompson ordain'd at Marshfield Oct. 14. 1696."
5. "God willing."
6. Although Ephraim Little was a schoolteacher in Plymouth at this time, he often filled in for other ministers in southeastern Massachusetts when they were away. In this case, he substituted for Deodat Lawson in Norwell after Lawson departed for England. Little's text that day was "Therefore let us not sleep, as do others; but let us watch and be sober." For Lawson's extended and controversial absence, see 22 August and 9 October 1695. *Sibley's Harvard Graduates,* 4:248-52.
7. John Cushing (1627–1708) lived in Scituate and served as a representative from Plymouth Colony under both charters, among other positions. His son, Caleb (1673–1752, H.C. 1692), accepted the pulpit in Salisbury in 1698 and married Cotton's widowed daughter, Elizabeth Cotton Alling, in 1689. Savage, *Genealogical Dictionary,* 1:489-90; *Sibley's Harvard Graduates,* 4:137-39.

To Rowland Cotton, [5 October 1696][1]

MONDAY

Deare son

yours by S: Br:[2] rec: Nath: Chh:[3] laden for Yarmouth went hence on saturday, I suppose it was for your Bro: Oct: 14:[4] was fixed by the chh for M[r] Tomp:s ord[ination]: & Capt Tho: told me our chh was to be sent to, as yet their letters are not come, whether they come or noe I doubt not but the ordin: will be at that time, unlesse cap: Tho: send word he cannot leave the court etc to come home; Newes confidently anexxed here that he is to marry Mris Doleberry;[5] Letters by way of Madera, 2 packets to the two Govrs, Bost: & Connec: from o: E:[6] another great Plot to destroy the King in Flanders is discovered, soe major Bradford told John Rickard,[7] but noe man is yet come from court to tell more; the Govr of Barbados is dead[8] & M[r] Bond (My Bro: by Egginton) is now Govr,[9] he is highly prized there & esteemed too good, they feare for them long to injoy him: a Privateer from Jamaica-side hath brought in 5 or 6 prizes to Road Island or thereabouts; your parents salute you both, soe doth Theoph: now here: Love to Cos: Sals: It is conclused the Fleet set saile yesterday[10] from New castle: Ele: Rogers came last night from Bost: & sayes, not a word of newes from the Army; I commend you all to God,

& rest, your Affectionate Father

John Cotton

Her Education at Major Richards' made me give her his name. Will M[r] Moodey lye that night with you or us? Bathshua Harlow is published to Richard Seares.[11] By Will: Thomas, comes this minute, I am assured the ordination will be next week:

Miscellaneous Bound Collection, Massachusetts Historical Society. Addressed "These For Mr Rowland Cotton, Pastor of the Church at Sandwich."

1. Prince's note: "suppose Oct. 5. 96."
2. Not found.
3. Probably Nathaniel Churchill of Plymouth, son of Eliezur (d. 1716) and Mary Dotey Churchill (d. 1715).
4. Prince's note: "Oct. 14. 96 is [symbol for Wednesday]." See the letter of 30 September 1696.
5. Nathaniel Thomas married Elizabeth Wilkes Condy Dolberry (d. 1713) on 3 November 1696. Torrey, *New England Marriages*, 735.
6. "Old England."
7. John Rickard (c. 1652–1726) of Plymouth.

8. Francis Russell died in 1696 after serving as governor for two years. Russell, brother to the Earl of Oxford, brought his family to Barbados, and all died from fevers. Robert Schomburgk, *The History of Barbados* (1848; reprint, New York, 1971), 307.

9. Francis Bond had served as a member of Russell's cabinet and was the senior council member on the island when Russell died, so he became the acting governor until December 1697. Sir Ralph Gray (1661–1706) assumed the governorship in December 1697, arriving on the island in July 1698. Schomburgk, *History of Barbados*, 307-8.

10. Prince's note: "[symbol for Sunday]. Oct. 4."

11. Bathshua Harlow married Robert Seares on 21 October 1696 in Plymouth. Torrey, *New England Marriages*, 659.

To Rowland Cotton, 19 October 1696 [10 October 1696][1]

MONDAY

Deare son,

the inclosed[2] is worthy of your reading but too much to transcribe send it me againe; Doe you know that Mr John Appleton (Mris Thomas's Brother) is colonell in his uncle's room?[3] that Leuit Coll: Wade is dead[4] & a wainwright in his place? Isaac Little[5] is made a Justice & of Quorum last night the wolfe (our sheep lying out) killed foure out of my six & bit the fifth, & 13 killed 4 or 5 wounded out of Eph: Cole's[6] 24: Salutations from us to you all etc prayers etc:

yours etc

J: C:

Saffin is turned out from being Judge of Bristoll court.[7]
John Morton hath a son today, great Joy[8]

Miscellaneous Bound Collection, Massachusetts Historical Society. Addressed "For Mr Cotton at Sandwich." Thomas Prince's note: "Col Wade D[ied] Oct. 4. 96."

---

1. Prince's note: "Suppose Oct 10. 96." See n. 8 below; the date should be 19 October 1696.

2. Not found.

3. John Appleton (1622–1699) of Ipswich served in many public offices in Massachusetts, including that of lieutenant colonel. His sister, Mary (d. 1727), was married to Nathaniel Thomas (1664–1738) of Marshfield/Ipswich. His uncle Samuel Appleton (1624–1696) had served as lieutenant colonel and had recently died, on 15 May 1696. Savage, *Genealogical Dictionary,* 1: 60-62; Torrey, *New England Marriages*, 735.

4. Thomas Wade (1650–1696) of Ipswich died on 4 October 1696. Savage, *Genealogical Dictionary,* 4:379.

5. Isaac Little (1646–1699) lived in Marshfield and was the brother of the minister Ephraim Little, a regular replacement for Cotton's pulpit in Plymouth. Savage, *Genealogical Dictionary,* 3:99.

6. Ephraim Cole of Plymouth.

7. John Saffin (c. 1634–1710) served in many government offices, including as a judge in the Superior Court in 1701. He moved to Bristol in 1690 to marry his third wife, the widow Rebecca Lee. Shortly afterward, he was appointed the first judge of probate in Bristol. Governor Dudley removed him in October 1696. Savage, *Genealogical Dictionary,* 4:3-4.

8. John and Mary Morton's fourth child, Ebenezer, was born on 19 October 1696. Van Antwerp, *Vital Records of Plymouth,* 10-11.

To Rowland Cotton, [30 October 1696][1]

FRIDAY MORN

DEARE SON

I write longing & waiting for an opportunity to tell you that yesterday P: M: Sol: & her husb: & Mol: are come safely to us & that on Monday or Tuseday at furthest they intend your house & thence to Yarmouth for night & Molle saith if her 2 brothers will goe next week to Boston she will never come to see you more; wee heare son John's building is not finisht & thence I conclude he cannot come, & I perceive that Mr Brattle's ordination day will speedily be fixt[2] & I beleive you will be willing to attend that: As for newes, they must tell it you; Haines & his eldest son[3] ran from the enemy, the son got to [saco?] fort & told them that his father was coming but spent able to travell noe further, they went 5 miles & fetcht him safe in a wheelbarrow, its thought he is too much spent to recover; they say it is but 2 days Journey to Indians, 50 fighting men, an 100 squaws & papooses. probably Major chh[4] is designed for them, for they have much [be]aver, corne & other good things: chh hath taken the grea[ ] [...] & much plunder at some fort with bailes of Eng[lish] [...] etc: one English sea-man dyed of sicknesse, he hath bin fighting some where, how many they killed is unknowne, one Frenchman kiled had a letter in his pocket that came from the bay informing that chh was coming[5] & his whole designe; this minute comes in Judith (now) Tubs[6] to carry these, & sol: calls to me & sayes you must goe up to Cos: Cottons ordination[7] which will be Nov: 19 or 26: & that time I must marry Cal: & Bet:[8] they say it is soe intended, faile not to write to me, (if opportunity present before the sabbath as I beleive it will by Tho: Howland & James Winslow who went yesterday to Eastham & intend back tomorrow) whether you & your Bro: divert your bay-Journey, if you doe then I will give notice of the Lds sup: to be Nov: 1: whilst my children are here: much more newes is talkt but you must have it vivâ voce,[9] rumors that L: Govr Partridge[10] & those ships from o: E:[11] are taken; your parents, sisters, Bro: W: all respectively salute you, with prayers, etc

I am etc, your etc

chh hath fought with whom & where I know not, some of his souldiers have flesh-wounds: they were at St John's but did noe hurt to the Fr:[12] there & I think received none:

Miscellaneous Bound Collection, Massachusetts Historical Society. Prince's note: "Mr John Cotton was ordained at Hampton, Nov. 19. 96." Right margin frayed, several small holes, darkened and stained.

---

1. Prince's note: "Suppose Oct. 30. or Nov. 2. 1696."
2. Prince's note: "Mr Wm Brattle was ordained at Cambridg Nov. 25. 96." William Brattle (1662–1717 HC 1680) was ordained in Cambridge on 25 November 1696. Weis, *Colonial Clergy,* 38-39.
3. For the Haines captivity and escape story, see the letter of [14 May 1698].
4. Major Benjamin Church led raids along the coast of Maine and into the Bay of Fundy, where French settlements offered plunder and opportunities for victory as he burned small French outposts. He hoped to attack the central Native settlement at Norridgewock, but his commander Colonel Hathorne would not allow it. Instead, Church raided a small French fort on the St. John River, which provided some stores but was no great victory. Gallay, *Colonial Wars of North America*, 138; Drake, *Border Wars of New England,* 112-16.
5. The English tried to retaliate against the French, who were successfully destroying all the English settlements on Newfoundland beginning in November 1696. Stoughton sent ships and troops led by Colonel Hawthorn and Major Church to Newfoundland to confront d'Iberville's forces, but they failed. See the letter of 29/30 April 1697. Gallay, *Colonial Wars of North America*, 350, 377.
6. Judith Prince Barker married William Tubbs (1655–1718) after 1693 in Duxbury. Torrey, *New England Marriages,* 756.
7. John Cotton (1658–1710, H.C. 1678) was ordained in Hampton, New Hampshire, on 19 November 1696. Weis, *Colonial Clergy,* 62.
8. Cotton's widowed daughter, Betty Cotton Alling (1663–1743), did not marry Caleb Cushing (1673–1752) until 14 March 1699. Evidently, Cotton thought the marriage was more imminent than Cushing did. Torrey, *New England Marriages,* 199; *Sibley's Harvard Graduates,* 4:137.
9. "By voice."
10. William Partridge, born in Portsmouth, succeeded John Usher as lieutenant governor of New Hampshire when he returned from London by February 1697 with a commission dated June 1696. Partridge had been treasurer of the colony and was a wealthy and transatlantically known shipwright and merchant. Although Usher had complained about the poor salary granted him as lieutenant governor, and had even appealed to Governor Allen in London to come to New Hampshire, he was surprised by Partridge's seizure of power. Usher later claimed that Partridge's assumption of the lieutenant governor's position was illegal. Stackpole, *History of New Hampshire,* 1:196-202.
11. "Old England."
12. "French."

To Rowland Cotton, 8 and 9 December 1696 [10 and 11 December 1696]

Monday

Deare son

on Friday morn I came from Boston, some horses had made a good track for me; at milton Eben. Allyn overtook me & rode with me to monotticutt bridge, diverting to his uncle's, but when neere cushing's he & his Bro: James overtook me a little before sunsett & that evening betwixt 6 & 7 wee came very comfortably to Barkers & the next morning home, my passage was as good as ever, Gratias Deo:[1] Maxwell was buried at Cambridge on Wednesday,[2] the bearers were the 2 first seniors of the <*each*> the 3 first classes, cooke,[3] stoddard,[4] symmes,[5] Cotton,[6] Dummer,[7] Belcher;[8] these had white skarfes & gloves, the 2 fellowes & Mr Pemberton[9] had black sckarfes & all the schollers had gloves, the mourners were Mr Boreland, murdo, smith & daughter & other scotch Merchants; Eyres on Thursday borne by Hutchinson (the coll's son)[10] & Tom: Dudley[11] (Pauls son) who lives with Mr Eyres, Dummer & Belcher sophimores, Bradstreet[12] & winthrop[13] Freshmen, who had as the former & all the schollers betwixt 50 & 60 Grad: & under Grad. had gloves; 'sias came not to this because of a tumor in his chin: your Bro: Rich[14] was there, he salutes you both, but was ingaged to returne to Haverhill, your parents are there well, he hopes to see you next weeke: the circumstances of their drowning at fresh pond Nov: 30: I write not,[15] Mr R:[16] might informe you: Gen: Court full of confusion, upper house send downe Non: con: to the lower with their vote to send an Agent for the old charter, a motion much derided. colledge-charter Danforth & cooke are perversly set against,[17] last Monday Boston-ministers were in councill, Mathers & willard[18] spake smartly & vexed those selfe-will'd ones: my lecture is this wednesday: wee both send you both our hearty parentall Love, God blesse you & all yours soe ever prayes,

your Affectionate Father

John Cotton

Sam: cooper, Nath: Hancock & his wife, Andrew Boreman & his sister (Mr Ben: w's friend) were all propounded for chh Fell: while I was in the pulpit, Mr Brattle was very civill & courteous to me in entertainments etc & pleasant maxwell & Eyres were my spetiall attendants from sat: to mond: & a few houres after left the world.[19]

Tuesday; I waite for Eben: Allyn; who (w:c: saith) courts Beck Rus:[20] a mirum![21] cos: Hannah mather is likely to marry John oliver[22] a cooper (as well as wymand) his father was son to mris Jackson of Newtowne, mother to mr Neh: Hobart's wife;[23] the

John oliver in catal: Grad:[24] was his Grand-father: Theoph: came Joyfully last friday home, & your mother is daily fitting of him for Boston by Tailors etc o that some man in your parts had a horse to lead to the Bay, that The: might ride on, wee are not fond of his going by sea: Ele: Rogers & Jabez warren[25] are waiting for a passage: Is mris Treat dead?[26] Theoph: salutes you all:

Miscellaneous Bound Collection, Massachusetts Historical Society. Addressed "These For Mr Rowland Cotton, Pastor of the Church at Sandwich."

---

1. "Thank God."
2. Prince's note for the two funerals that Cotton describes: "suppose [symbol for Wednesday] Dec. 2, [symbol for Thursday] Dec. 3. 1696." On 30 November 1696, William Maxwell, a sophomore at Harvard College, drowned with his freshman colleague, John Eyre (1682–1696), while skating on Fresh Pond. Maxwell was the son of a prominent merchant in Barbados, and Eyre was the only son of John Eyre, Esq., justice of the peace in Boston. The funerals were 3 and 4 December. *Sibley's Harvard Graduates,* 4:480-81, 520-21.
3. Elisha Cooke (1678–1737, H.C. 1697). *Sibley's Harvard Graduates,* 4:349-56.
4. Anthony Stoddard (1678–1760, H.C. 1697). *Sibley's Harvard Graduates,* 4:381-83.
5. Thomas Symmes (1678–1725, H.C. 1698). *Sibley's Harvard Graduates,* 4:411-17.
6. Josiah Cotton (1680–1756, H.C. 1698). *Sibley's Harvard Graduates,* 4:398-402.
7. Jeremiah Dummer (1681–1739, H.C. 1699). *Sibley's Harvard Graduates,* 4:454-68.
8. Jonathan Belcher (1682–1757, H.C. 1699). *Sibley's Harvard Graduates,* 4:434-49.
9. Ebenezer Pemberton (1672–1717, H.C. 1691) was librarian at Harvard College from 1693 to 1697, a tutor from 1697 to 1700, minister at Old South Church in Boston from 1699 to 1717, and a fellow from 1707 to 1717. *Sibley's Harvard Graduates,* 4:107-13.
10. Colonel Elisha Hutchinson (1641–1717) had three sons who may have carried John Eyre's coffin: Thomas (b. 1675), Edward (b. 1678) and Elisha (b. 1681); none attended Harvard College. Savage, *Genealogical Dictionary,* 2:510.
11. Thomas Dudley (b. 1680) was the second son of Paul and Mary Leverett Dudley. Both grandfathers were governors of Massachusetts Bay. Savage, *Genealogical Dictionary,* 2:76-77.
12. Simon Bradstreet (c. 1680–c. 1715, H.C. 1700) was the son of Samuel Bradstreet, who practiced medicine in Jamaica. When his father died in 1682, Simon and his three siblings were raised in Boston by their grandfather, Governor Simon Bradstreet. *Sibley's Harvard Graduates,* 4:514-15.
13. John Winthrop (1681-1747, H.C. 1700) was the son of Waitstill Winthrop, grandson of Governor John Winthop. *Sibley's Harvard Graduates,* 4:535-49.
14. Richard Saltonstall, Rowland's brother-in-law.
15. Classmate John Barnard's eyewitness description of the drowning is in Sibley's account of John Eyre. *Sibley's Harvard Graduates,* 4:520-21.
16. Jonathan Russell, minister at Barnstable.
17. From 1686 to 1689 and from 1692 to 1708, Harvard College's traditional charter was "in abeyance" because Massachusetts Bay also lost its charter. The General Court of the Province of Massachusetts

Bay granted a new charter of 1692 that established a corporation led by a president, treasurer and eight Fellows, but the king dissolved that charter in 1696. A new charter accepted in 1697 was similarly dissolved by the Crown in 1699. *Sibley's Harvard Graduates,* 4:12-13.

18. Increase Mather, Cotton Mather, Samuel Willard.

19. Cotton suggests that he was with the young undergraduates in the days before their drowning.

20. Ebenezer Allen (d. 1730) married Rebecca Russell on 14 April 1698 in Barnstable. Torrey, *New England Marriages,* 9.

21. "Ah, remarkable!"

22. John Oliver married Hannah Mather (1680–1700) on 28 January 1697 in Boston. Torrey, *New England Marriages,* 544.

23. The groom's father, John Oliver (1644–1683[?]), was the son of Elizabeth Newgate Oliver Jackson (d. 1709) from her first marriage to John Oliver (d. 1646, H.C. 1645). Elizabeth was also mother of Sarah Jackson, who married Nehemiah Hobart (1648–1712, H.C. 1667) on 21 March 1677 in Cambridge. Savage, *Genealogical Dictionary,* 3:309-10; *Sibley's Harvard Graduates,* 1:102-6; Torrey, *New England Marriages,* 377; Weis, *Colonial Clergy,* 107.

24. "Graduation catalogue."

25. Eleazer Rogers (1673–1739 or later) and Jabez Warren (d. 1701) were both seamen who lived in Plymouth. Warren drowned in 1701. Savage, *Genealogical Dictionary,* 4:426; Van Antwerp, *Vital Records of Plymouth,* 136; Torrey, *New England Marriages,* 632.

26. Elizabeth Mayo Treat had died on 4 December 1696 in Eastham. She was the wife of Samuel Treat (1648–1717, H.C. 1669), the minister at Eastham and Cotton's colleague in Native ministry. *Sibley's Harvard Graduates,* 2:304-14.

Joanna Rosseter Cotton to Josiah Cotton, 14 December 1696

Dec[r] 14. 1696

Dear Chil

By your [fat?] Bro[r] I send these Lines, Live & Love like Broth[rs] now & always— O my child what if it had been your Portion to have been drowned with your companion?[1] Consider seriously where you should now have been: The good Lord sanctify it to you for your thorough converson. now new strive lest Death sudden Death find you unprepared; It may be God sent this dreadfull Providence on purpose to awaken many schollars & you in particular— Read Zeph 3.7.[2] When any are cut off as those two were, God saith surely thou will fear me, thou wilt receive Instruction: The Lord grant it may be so lest a worse thing come unto you. Pray constantly to God to keep you by the power of his Grace from Temptations to Sin of every kind—call to mind what God hath done for you…how often God spared you & took away others— Dont think they were greater sinners than you Nay but Except you repent you will likewise Perish....You are indebted to God & have nothing to Pay Cry unto him who can Perform all things...O the poor Lads [Maxwell & Eyre] from perfect Health into Eternity in a few minutes, that thought no more of it than you. Never, never, never let this Providence be forgotten by you. I can hardly bear to think how I should have born the affliction if it had been you. The Lord pity the poor Parents—Dear Child I charge you not needlessly to venture on Water Land or Horse. and ye good Lord be your Keeper here & to Eternity. Which is the prayer of your afflicted Mother

Joanna Cotton

Josiah Cotton, Manuscript "Account of the Cotton Family," Houghton Library, Harvard University.

---

1. Joanna is referring to the drowning of Harvard undergraduates William Maxwell and John Eyre. See the 8/9 December 1696 letter above.
2. Zeph. 3:7: "I said, Surely thou wilt fear me, thou wilt receive instruction: so their dwelling should not be cut off, howsoever I punished them: but they rose early, *and* corrupted all their doings."

To Josiah Cotton, 18 January 1697[1]

Plymo Jany 18. 1696/7

Dear Child

I have not written oft to you of late but I have to yr Bror The: and have ordered him to show you all my Letters & therein directed ye Same good Counsell to you as unto him & ye more especially to you considering not only you have lived some more years than he, but also the Place you live in & the Company you Daily converse with may expose you to more & greater Temptations; The Night after the Fast, Your Mother (whose heart as well as mine is tenderly thoughtfull of & solicitous for your best Good) dreamt you were dead, but we hearken not to Dreams: My Waking thoughts concerning you are often very awfull lest you should be left of God to any sin that may Dishonour his name & wound ye Peace of your own Conscience, & bring Shame & Ruine & Misery upon your both Body & Soul forever. Divers days have I kept in Strict Fasting & Prayer in my Study on Purpose to beg Mercy at the hands of God for thy poor soul & I am restless & desire to be continually so in Pleading & Wrestling with God that he would bestow Converting Grace upon you, and that will keep you by ye Grace of God from ye Power of sinfull Temptations: I am glad you have one of your Uncles Sermons; how awfully doth he therein speak of more dreadfull things to befall the Colledge & what can be more terrible than such sudden Deaths but Sin;

To be given over to vile affections, to be given up to the Plague of a filthy Heart—you know what Solomon saith Prov. 13.20[2] a Companion of Fools shall be destroyed. The snares of evil Company are very dreadfull & dangerous; sinners entice one another to such Evils as are very suitable to the inward corruptions of the Heart—My Dear Josiah a Child of many & signal Preservations and of many Prayers, I thank God I know of no scandalous Sin you are addicted to but I am jealous over you with a godly jealousy lest Satan should prevail against you by any of his unwearied Solicitations to Destroy You. Be very diligent in your studies, Read & Meditate upon Petr 5.8.[3] Make Conscience as for your Life of Secret Prayer & Reading the Word Morning & Evening; If you live in the neglect of Prayer, You will grieve ye Holy Spirit, & provoke God to withdraw his Restraining Grace from you, & wo to you if God shall depart from you. Dear Son I hope better things for you tho. I thus Speak. When I was lately upon my Knees pouring out my Soul with many tears into the Bosom of God on your Behalf (as well as for Theophilus & the Rest of Mine) I found a Strong impulse upon my Heart to set Pen to Paper & thus, to Write to you—The Lord accompany the same & all other means of Grace, the Ministry of the Word you Enjoy, with the Power of his Spirit for your effectual awakening & the Saving Good of your precious soul. Your mother sends with me her hearty Love to you, Lord hear & accept in Christ—I am your affectionate Father—John Cotton

P.S. Be a good Husband of your Time and Money—and ye Lord Preserve you.

Josiah Cotton, Manuscript "Account of the Cotton Family," Houghton Library, Harvard University.

---

1. Josiah introduced the letter in his account, "My Father, as I hinted before, wrote a multitude of Letters, of which I have preservd but two that he wrote to me, the first when I was at Colledge."
2. Prov. 13:20: "He that walketh with wise *men* shall be wise: but a companion of fools shall be destroyed."
3. 1 Pet. 5:8: "Be sober, be vigilant; because your adversary the devil, as a roaring lion, walketh about, seeking whom he may devour."

To Rowland Cotton, 29/30 April 1697 [September 1696][1]

Thursday A: M:

Deare Son

yesterday I wrote by John Dunham;[2] C: Mold & Eph: Cole are getting horses to goe to Scauton neck[3] to look after a castaway boat, ergo I prepare to send these with your 5 1/2 peices, C: mackartys gift, an apron to your Dearest; your mother sends a Lace to her if she please to accept soe small a token of her love & some ginger-bread for the Lambs: T: P:[4] on Luk: 14: 14:4[5] preacht the most pittifull, leane sermon, nonsensicall, corrupt etc that (I think) I ever heard: newes I transcribe;

"A ship lately arrived at virginia, which came from London the latter end of Febr; sayes; 1: This yeare the confederate forces were to be augmented 30000 English, 20000 Dutch, 20000 Imperialists, 10000 Spanish, & if the French King will not ratify the Articles of the Plenipotentiaries the sweedish King will appeare at the Head of 30000 sweedes: 2: That the King designes to be in the camp a moneth sooner then usually: 3. A French Jesuite came to Roterdam with bills of exchange to take up a great deale of moneys, & the merchants there wondering that such a fellow should take up such great summes of money, suspected him, & put him on the rack, he confessed he had a designe upon the life of the King, & soe he hath received condigne[6] punishment: 4: King James took leave of the French King & came out with a fleet of ships for Holland, Scotland or Ireland but Sir Cloudsley Shovell with a fleet of ships drove him into Brestt:" Mr Bridgwater[7] came home last weeke, many Fr: vessels about Barbados, so that wee may feare what will become of our Brigantine that went hence Apr: 22: Ele: cush's wife[8] continues in dreadfull horrors, the 4 cushmans & other neighbours spent yesterday in prayer with her sent for Mr Wiswall[9] to come & Joyne with them but he told them he was not well; & would not come I suppose He knew it was Lect: Ele: cush. did most earnestly send for me last night & I intend to goe by & by, being this morning sent for by our friend J: Nelson[10] to make his will, he had a sad night, dreadfull load at stomach, sick at heart, I doubt[11] he must dye; the night before last poore old Robert Ransom[12] attempted to strangle himselfe with an hankercheife but was prevented, it is too probable he will not leave till he hath sent his soule to the pit; his despairing horrors are soe great; Carrett seed wee have none, wee are contriving next week to carry your trade to Rob: Barkers[13] with some of our owne; your mother will see at Mr Thomas's about the cloath; If you should lend J: Den's winchester[14] I would be security for its being returned as good as it is or its value, for Theoph: writes they are 5 shils: at the shop & truly that is hard for me now to spare. The: says "pure sport, pure sport the Quakers preach at Bost: almost every day, & some woemen, one opened her mouth soe wide that a six penny loaf might be thrust in;" (I suppose it was Paitons sister[15]) he hath had a latine letter from Peleg W:[16] very good & arch, but the old man made it all, hacille:[17]

sat with her on Tuseday night till near break of day, I suppose soe it will be tonight: wee all salute you both, ut moris est;[18] Sam: Harlows eldest son[19] is very sick: His man Tho: Doty[20] prest, Johnson of Jos. churchel,[21] Arthur Harris[22] (Abiel shirtliffs[23] man) Ned: May (J: sturtevants) & Elisha Cobb,[24] this last hath paid his 5 pd: The Lord blesse you all; I hear noe horses can be gotten for C: Mold etc Capt Call,[25] Deac: of Charlestowne is dead, I end & leave it for a passage if any present while I am gone to the sick,

your Affectionate Father

John Cotton

Friday

yesterday I went to J: Nelson, who was rationall enough to make his will & dyed[26] in the night an houre or two before day; Mris Stone & Cos: Deb: are Just gone she was noble here: The funerall is to be to morrow, Mr Thomas came home but yesterday & saith noe doubt a fleet of English men of war are gone to retake Newfoundland;[27] Capt Chubb.[28] to be tryed for his life last Wednesday; Hedge hath carried yours from your Bro: John to R: Island & now gave it Jos: I perceive divers purses are alike filld: your mother hath taken up by [...] 2sh: 2p a yd, perhaps Mr T. may abate the 2p: I hope El: Hedge will bring them safe to you: It is now sat: morn:

Here is a rough copy of your mothers to the Colonell,[29] but it is soe intermixed that you may not see it until you come hither; Those from the Col: you must send againe, for she will not part with them: on Thursday told Rob: Ran: made like violent attempts to strangle himselfe but was prevented, caveat netertium tempus:[30] My cold & hoarnesse [hoarseness] hath bin very bad all this weeke & soe continues that Sir Litle[31] preaches here once to-morrow.

If it be possible procure an Almanack[32] & send for the Dr: I am going my selfe to see if El: Hedge will carry these things, the litle bundle of tokens well sowed up, I doubt not but he will take the 6 yds of cloath, if he cannot, we will keep till an opportunity.

My wife bought a remnant of Lace for 2 caps, she sends an inch more then she leaves for her selfe & lest it should not be long enough she hath put a bit at the end, the remainder of which is for a cap for Betty, the coat is for Joanna, the box for litle John: To you a bitt of chocolatt. a bit of Lace for Sarah for a Cap: send your Bro: the o: E:[33] newes, the other I have written, but have not time for that:

Cotton-Prince Papers, Prince Library, Rare Book and Manuscripts, Boston Public Library. Addressed "These For Mr Rowland Cotton at Sandwich."

---

1. Prince's note: "After Aug. 1696." See n. 29 below; the date should be 29/30 April 1697.
2. John Dunham (1649–1697) lived in Barnstable. Savage, *Genealogical Dictionary*, 2:81.
3. In Sandwich, on Cape Cod.
4. Prince's note: "Palmer."
5. Thomas Palmer, the new minister at Middleborough, preached on "And thou shalt be blessed; for they cannot recompense thee: for thou shalt be recompensed at the resurrection of the just."
6. Condign: "worthily deserved, merited, fitting, appropriate, adequate." *OED*, 3: 682.
7. Torrey refers to a Thomas Bridgewater, who married Elizabeth Mackarta in 1696 and lived in Boston. *New England Marriages*, 97.
8. Eleazer Cushman (1657–1723) married Elizabeth Coombs on 12 January 1687 in Plymouth. Elizabeth survived this illness and lived until at least 1723. Savage, *Genealogical Dictionary*, 1:491; Torrey, *New England Marriages*, 199.
9. Ichabod Wiswall (1637–1700), minister at Duxbury. Weis, *Colonial Clergy*, 233.
10. According to Thomas Faunce's town records, John Nelson died on 29 April 1697 at the age of fifty-four. Nelson and Cotton were neighbors, and Cotton had sold land to Nelson a few years earlier. Van Antwerp, *Vital Records of Plymouth*, 135.
11. By, "I doubt," Cotton means, "I suspect."
12. Innkeeper Robert Ransom (c. 1630–1697) died on 14 December 1697; there is no evidence that the death was a suicide. Torrey, *New England Marriages*, 611.
13. Robert Barker (1651–1729[?]) lived in Scituate. Elizabeth F. Barker, *Barker Genealogy* (New York, 1927.)
14. "J Den" is probably John Denison. H. (Hugh) Robinson (1584[?]–1655), *Scholae Wintoniensis phrases Latinae=The Latine phrases of Winchester-schoole : corrected and much augmented with poeticals added : and these four tracts, viz. I. Of words not to be used by elegant Latinists, II. The difference of many words like one another in sound or signification, III. Some words governing a subjunctive mood not mentioned in Lillies Grammar, IV. Concerning [chreia] and [gnom¯e] for entring children upon making of themes / by N. Robinson...; published for the common use and benefit of the grammar-schools. 5th ed., with many additions.* (London, 1667). The Mather Library at the American Antiquarian Society has a copy of this Latin language conversation and phrase book. See also 10 May 1697.
15. Carla Gardina Pestana explores the way in which Congregationalists dismissed Quakers as "other"—less threat than object for ridicule—by the late seventeenth century in *Quakers and Baptists in Colonial Massachusetts* (New York, 1991), 149-58, 160-64.
16. Letter not found. "Peleg W" is probably Peleg Wiswall (1684–1767, H.C. 1702), son of Duxbury's minister Ichabod Wiswall. Theophilus and Peleg were evidently friends; Theophilus was already at Harvard, and Peleg would begin his studies in 1698. *Sibley's Harvard Graduates*, 5:176-79.
17. "Easily."
18. "As is the custom."
19. Samuel Harlow's (1653–1734) eldest son was John, born on 19 December 1685. He survived this illness and died on 30 January 1771. Savage, *Genealogical Dictionary*, 2:356.

20. Probably Thomas Doty (b. 1679) of Middleborough. Savage, *Genealogical Dictionary,* 2:62.

21. Joseph Churchel lived in Plymouth. His servant, Johnson, was impressed for military service.

22. Isaac (d. 1707) and Mercy Latham Harris's eldest son was Arthur, born probably between 1668 and 1670 in Bridgewater. Savage, *Genealogical Dictionary,* 2:362.

23. Abiel Shurtleif (1666–1732) lived in Plymouth. Torrey, *New England Marriages,* 672.

24. Elisha Cobb (b. 1678) was the son of John and Martha Nelson Cobb of Plymouth. Savage, *Genealogical Dictionary,* 1:413.

25. John Call (often spelled Cole) was born in England in 1635, settled in Charlestown by 1656, served as a deacon, and died on 9 April 1697. Savage, *Genealogical Dictionary,* 1:329-30; Torrey, *New England Marriages,* 131.

26. See n. 11 above. This confirms the date of this letter as 20/30 April 1697.

27. After destroying Fort William Henry in August 1696, the French fleet, led by Pierre Le Moyne d'Iberville, sailed for Newfoundland. From November 1696 to April 1697, Iberville's forces leveled thirty-six English settlements and killed or imprisoned nearly 900 people, nearly eradicating the English presence in Newfoundland. Gallay, *Colonial Wars of North America,* 377, 350; Drake, *Border Wars of New England,* 114-16.

28. Prince's note: "Chubb surrender'd Pemaquid Fort in Aug 1696." The defeated commander of Fort William Henry, Pascho Chubb, returned to Boston and was imprisoned until March 1697, awaiting court-martial. He was released as *persona non grata* and returned to Andover, where he and his wife were killed in a Native attack on 22 February 1698. Mather described their deaths as "Vengeance" by enraged Natives, although he refrained from criticizing Chubb's decision to kill the peace delegation. See the letter of 4 March 1696. *Colonial Wars of North America,* 350, 137; Mather, *Decennium Luctuosum,* 261-262, 270; Rowland Cotton to John Cotton (1693–1757), 1 March 1698, Miscellaneous Bound Collection, MHS.

29. Not found.

30. The Latin should read, "caveat ne tertium tempus," which translates as "let him be warned not to try it a third time."

31. Ephraim Little.

32. John Tulley, *An Almanac for the Year of our Lord, MDCXCVII* (Boston, 1697) [Evans 815] or, less likely, Daniel Leeds, *An Almanack for the Year of Christian Account, 1697* (New York, 1697) [Evans 785]. Evans, *American Bibliography,* 1:123, 126.

33. "Old England."

To Rowland Cotton, [10 May 1697][1]

MONDAY A: M:

VERY DEARE SON

yours by J: B: received early,[2] the candid resolves of you & your Dearest are most affectionately received, & wee doe thanke you as heartily as if wee had seen her here, though her prescence would have bin exceeding pretious, her token wee gratefully accept & dispatcht a 3d part of it before breakfast, tasting much of the sweetnesse of her love therein; Lord reward her kindnesse: Truly Betty's coming was a great mercy, & I purpose on wednesday (if God continue to adde to your mothers health, who (through rich mercy) is much better then she was on Friday, though very weak & faint & her soule bowed downe with greife almost to death) to goe along with Betty to Bost: & now you know you must preach here twice on the sab: & as for Sir Litle[3] I am confident there is noe danger in the least of disappointment; Preach Repen: or faith, de xt, but yours on Luk: 14:[4] will doe very well; wee hope your Joanna[5] is better; I now expect you not this morn, but if you should come I know I shall blesse God for it, however Gods time is the best I desire to wait patiently for God, I hope to see you at Bost: next week, & pray & hope that God will make you a spetiall blessing in this houre: This morn J: R: from B: The: says, "some thinke (though none chosen May, 8:) that Mr Dan: of Dorch: is to preach Elec: serm:[6] Great preparations for war in O: E:[7] [ventures?] for peace. A Galley came in on Friday one of [...] with bombs, granades, powder for the Country, K: sends fleet to retake Newfoundland[8] Phesy of Braintree set in the pillory[9] for working on a Fast day, & for speaking Treason & fined 10 pd (if I understand his character) he said noe King but K James etc.: He saith you wrote to him, you had sent winchesters phrases[10] to Plim: & begs me to hasten them to him; this you have not done ergo pray save me that money of buying if you can your sloop will be ready: Goods fall mightily & are like to fall for a word of them is come"; our hearty love & thanks to you both for love showed & intended; my cold that hath lasted above 3 weeks is as bad or worse than ever, were I this day to preach I could in noe degree be heard, Bettys due love also: with prayers etc

yours etc:

J: C:

I expect Mr Prince every minute bec: of your letter, Ruth Barrow[11] sick of the feavor ever since sat: Morn: Ami willis[12] taken yesterday at meeting time home sick: Leift: Arnold very bad almost a weeke, yesterday a litle better; the majors [...] the first prayer P: M: yesterday went sick out of meeting: none seem neer death with [...]

Miscellaneous Bound Collection, Massachusetts Historical Society. Addressed "These For mr Rowland Cotton, at Sandwich." Left margin frayed, two small holes, stained and darkened overall.

---

1. Prince's note: "Suppose 1697, May 3 or 10."
2. Not found.
3. Ephraim Little.
4. Luke retells Jesus's parable of the wedding guest and becoming a disciple of Christ. Ironically, Samuel Sewall would later refer to this chapter of Luke when he heard of Cotton's second adultery accusation and wrote about it in his diary: "Salt is good: but if the salt have lost his savour, wherewith shall it be seasoned? It is neither fit for the land, nor yet for the dunghill; *but* men cast it out. He that hath ears to hear, let him hear." Luke 14:34-35. See Sewall's comments about Cotton as "Unsavoury Salt" of 30 September 1697 in Thomas, *Diary of Samuel Sewall*, 1:378.
5. Rowland and Elizabeth's daughter, Joanna.
6. John Danforth (1660–1730, H.C. 1677) was the minister in Dorchester from 1682 until his death. He did preach the 1697 Election sermon, but it seems not to have been published. *Sibley's Harvard Graduates*, 2:507-14.
7. "Old England."
8. See 30 October 1696 and 29/30 April 1697.
9. William Veasie was found guilty of speaking "factious and seditious words" against the king and his government in Massachusetts Bay, and of working on a day of Thanksgiving, 18 June 1696. The central witnesses to the case recounted his crimes: Veasie said "he did not know but there was a great deal of sin comitted in setting apart Days of Thanksgiving & Humiliation...that the King had granted Liberty of Conscience, and that King James was his Royal Prince, and that he did not know how this King came to the crown, and that the Crown belonged heires by succession. That it was an ill thing to kill a man privately, but he that went into France & fought him (intending King William as the Deponent understood) did like a man....[when they departed] he returned to his plow." He was sentenced to the pillory. Veasie seems to have joined with neighbors to conduct Episcopal services and was one of the founders of the Braintree Episcopal Church. In 1702, he was elected as a representative from Braintree; apparently, when his criminal past was recounted, he was ejected from the House. Massachusetts Archives, Suffolk County Files, Reel 21, vol. 38, #3443; *Acts and Resolves of the Province of Massachusetts Bay*, 7:332.
10. See 29/30 April 1697 for an earlier reference to "Winchesters."
11. Ruth Bonum Barrow lived in Plymouth; she had married Robert Barrow in 1666. Savage, *Genealogical Dictionary*, 1:127.
12. Torrey lists an Amy Wyllys (1625–1698/9[?]) who married John Pynchon (c. 1625–1703) and lived in Springfield. *New England Marriages*, 608.

To Rowland Cotton, AFTER 26 MAY 1697 [19 MAY 1697][1]

WEDNESDAY MORN:

DEARE SON

yours by M^r^ Pr:[2] received, newes from o:E:[3] you must have vivâ voce[4] next week at the metropolis; mr John Hubbard[5] came hither on Monday night & bought all the Fish for Coll: Shrimpton, offering 20 shil per Quintall certaine; he says Mr Moodey languishes,[6] could not get to meeting P:M: last sab: stomach & sleep almost wholy gone from him.[7] Cos: Walter[8] to preach Artil: Elec: about 11 houses lately burnt at Easthampton with lightning; yester morn Capt Thomas & his wife were here, returned at eve: Blathwait writes de Bellamonts coming, its said the law is abolisht that limits choice of Repres: in their owne towne: Boston at first chose Townsend,[9] Bifeild,[10] Leg,[11] but Foxcroft[12] who was next not having the major part of Electors, they voted againe & Deacon Bridgham[13] hath it; Eph: Litle[14] for marshfeild, John Cushing[15] for Scituate, likely to be a very new house; your mother is better, but languishes very much; yours by Done; old Mris Thomas heard Sir Litle[16] say he was to be at Sandwich next sab: also I sent a letter[17] yesterday to confirme him in our confidence he would then come: (I wish I could speak with you first. why can you not be here on friday night or Sat: noone)? I resolve not to goe with Betty to morrow, but to stay till Monday, having noe voice to preach, soe that you must preach twice whilst I sit by, & if I goe to Bost: with you, it will be noe losse to you: parents & betty salute you both with Cos: Sal: God blesse you & all yours, if I could contrive it I would meet you at Eph: Mortons,

I am, your Affectionate Father

John Cotton

It was well done that your Bro: came to see us.

son John is asleep, & coming to M^r^ clarks, Mr Kethcatt[18] shows me 2 letters[19] for you, what newes is in them, let me know to morrow; I could give a 100 pd, if I were worth it to speak with you, God helpe you now to doe for etc this is subsigillo[20]

Miscellaneous Bound Collection, Massachusetts Historical Society. Addressed "These For Mr Rowland Cotton, at Sandwich.

---

1. Prince's note: "Suppose 1697, May 19." But the election news that Cotton retold indicates that he wrote this letter after 26 May.
2. Not found.
3. "Old England."

4. "By voice."

5. Probably the prominent merchant John Hubbard (d. 1710), who resided in Boston and Ipswich. Savage, *Genealogical Dictionary,* 2:484.

6. Joshua Moody (1633–1697, H.C. 1653) died in Boston on 4 July 1697 while seeking medical advice for "complication of distempers." *Sibley's Harvard Graduates,* 1:367-80.

7. Prince's note: "R Mr Jonno Moodey Died July 4. 97."

8. Nehemiah Walter (1663–1750, H.C. 1684) was the minister in Roxbury from 1688 until his death. He preached the Artillery Election sermon in 1697, but it seems never to have been published. *Sibley's Harvard Graduates,* 3:294-301.

9. Maj. Penn Townsend (1651–1727) served in the artillery company and as a representative to the General Court under both charters, also as Speaker. Savage, *Genealogical Dictionary,* 4:318-19.

10. Capt. Nathaniel Byfield (1653–1733) served in the artillery company, as a representative under both charters, as Speaker of the House, and as a judge in multiple courts. Savage, *Genealogical Dictionary,* 1:325-26.

11. Capt. Samuel Legg was elected as one of four representatives, or deputies, from Boston on 26 May 1697. *Acts and Resolves of the Province of Massachusetts Bay*, 7:148.

12. Francis Foxcroft (c. 1657–1727) served in several official positions, including as a representative to the General Court. Savage, *Genealogical Dictionary,* 2:197.

13. See 22 March 1695.

14. Ephraim Little. *Acts and Resolves of the Province of Massachusetts Bay*, 7:149.

15. John Cushing (1627–1708) emigrated to New Plymouth as a child and served as a selectman, representative and assistant of Plymouth Colony, as well as a representative under the new Massachusetts Charter in 1692 and 1697. Savage, *Genealogical Dictionary,* 1:489-90; *Acts and Resolves of the Province of Massachusetts Bay*, 7:149.

16. Prince's note: "Sr Little took his 1st Degree in 95."

17. Not found.

18. Probably Robert Cathcart (c. 1650–1719), an innkeeper who settled on Martha's Vineyard in 1690. Banks, *History of Martha's Vineyard*, 2:41-42.

19. Not found.

20. "Under the seal."

TEN

"Scandal in Plymouth," 1697–1698

THE FIRST LETTER FRAGMENT BELOW describes the reaction of the Plymouth church to allegations that in 1697 Cotton was again guilty of adultery, in this case with a church member, Rebecca Morton. While this letter indicates the congregation's support for Cotton and its desire that he remain its pastor after the adultery accusation, Cotton did leave Plymouth in the wake of the scandal. The church records are vague on his eventual departure: "The aspect of providence from this time was such that made way for the Pastor & chh to part from one another without reflexion upon the chh his worke seeming now to be at an end; sundry chh meetings wee had, one day of Fasting & prayer together in publick in which the 2 next neighbour-ministers were desired to asist in carrying on that worke who did soe & the brethren after that kept some in one house, others in another, a day of prayer; the issue of all meetings & agitations was, a councill was called the chh from the ches of Weymouth, Duxbury, Bridgewater, Taunton & Barnstable, who met & Judged it best that the Pastor should cease his worke amongst them & the chh dismisse him with such expressions of their love & charity as the Rule called for."[1]

Many of the letters that follow offer clues to Cotton's own interpretation of the scandal, especially his belief that this accusation was whipped up by his enemies to punish him for supporting Mather's charter in 1692, which cost Plymouth her independence. He described the accusation at length in his letter to Joanna of 6 and 7 July 1698, suggesting that when Mather returned with the new Massachusetts Charter that included Plymouth Colony, many of their neighbors were enraged: "(from their godly zeale & reall Conscience) did raile at him & revile him for falsenesse, treacherous dealing yea & wickedness to take them in to be slaves." They felt especially betrayed, according to Cotton, because it was Mather—a friend—who had made the deal. Some even damned Mather to hell: "old Mather would go to hell shortly for all his wickedness." Cotton claimed that when he "gave many a severe rebuke" and defended Mather, he earned their venom, too. He suggested that these are the "persons that have bin most against me." After Cotton's death, one contemporary, shipbuilder Thomas Coram, agreed and argued that Cotton suffered "as much Injustice... in that abominable Proceeding against him as those other Innocent men who were Murdered on account of the Pretended Witchcraft."[2] To others, Cotton seemed to vacillate on the adultery issue, confessing one moment, and, according to Cotton Mather's diary, denying all wrongdoing at another.[3]

With his career in peril, Cotton also frequently wrote about his financial concerns in regard to his own daily needs as well as those of his two sons still in college, Josiah and Theophilus. At the same time that he tried to track down past salaries owed to him, he attempted to convince friends to help his sons pay their bills.[4] He described his own correspondence in this period as "sorrowfull."[5] Cotton clearly was hopeful that he could remain in Plymouth's pulpit but worried that the Boston ministers would effectively remove him, and his letters reflect his uncertainty: "I am yet wholy unresolved what course to take."[6] He continued preaching to Native churches,[7] traveling to visit friends to lobby on his own behalf, and working within his considerable network to secure a pulpit,[8] but he also acknowledged that more powerful ministers might prevent his settling anywhere. A new tone infected Cotton's letters in this period—desperation: "I have a 1000 thoughts but think I shall doe nothing at all but lye downe under my burthen till I dye... think, think, think, pray, pray, pray."[9]

Joanna became increasingly ill in response to her husband's alleged infidelity, and Cotton's letters described her sicknesses.[10] He begged their sons to help care for her. Cotton wrote letters to try to cheer her and to remind her that, "God comforteth those that are cast downe." He even asked her to pray to God to show him "spetiall mercy." There are hints in these letters that he was guilty of something, especially when he referred to Joanna; in a 1698 letter to Rowland, with whom Joanna was then living, he asked his son to pass on his "most tender & affectionate Love to my deare wife... Deare soule, the Lord be her Comforter." Wishing she would return to him, he described her as the one "in whom all my life & all the comforts of it are soe much bound up."[11] This second adultery scandal turned Joanna into a transient in her children's homes as she moved from child to child, living with them, rather than with her husband. The decision often to live apart led to some hurtful gossip—"considerable aspersions"—among their Plymouth neighbors.[12]

1. Publications of the Colonial Society of Massachusetts *Collections* (hereafter *CSM*), 22 (Boston, 1920), 180.
2. Arthur Lord, "Rev. John Cotton of Plymouth," Publications of the Colonial Society of Massachusetts *Transactions* 26 (1924–1926): 79-81.
3. *Diary of Cotton Mather, 1681–1708*, ed. Worthington Chauncey Ford, Massachusetts Historical Society *Collections*, 7th ser., 8 (Boston, 1912), 277.
4. From William Brattle, 19 October 1697.
5. [To Rowland Cotton, 30 October 1697].
6. [To Rowland Cotton, 30 October 1697].
7. To Rowland Cotton, 18 February 1698; To Rowland Cotton, [17 June 1698]; To Rowland Cotton, 29 June 1698.
8. To Rowland Cotton, [14 May 1698]; To Joanna Rosseter Cotton, 6 and 7 July 1698; To Joanna Rosseter Cotton, 8 July 1698.
9. To Rowland Cotton, [2 July 1698].
10. To Rowland Cotton, [2 February 1698]; To Rowland Cotton, 18 February 1698.
11. To Rowland Cotton, [May 1698].
12. To Joanna Rosseter Cotton, 8 July 1698.

[To Rowland Cotton, 18 June 1697][1]

PRESENT AT THIS CHURCH-MEETING THIRTY FIVE BRETHREN.

The church having met together on June, 18: 1697: to consider of the sad & scandalous reports that had bin raised & spread abroad concerning some miscarriages in the Pastor towards Rebekah Morton, having heard her charges & the Pastors particular vindications of himselfe from all those scandals & his confession of one, declare themselves bound to take up satisfyed with Him according to Rule in reference thereunto & manifest their desires that he would continue to carry on the Lords worke among them as formerly.

This abovewritten was the vote of the church the day abovesaid by lifting up of hands, the contrary vote was called for & not one lifted up his hand:

POSTSCRIPT P:M:

since I finisht my letter I received a letter from Theoph: of June, 15:[2] which says nothing of mony, but that the Indians have destroyd 2 persons at Hampton,[3] your mother hath bin from the time of her rising worse then ever she was since I knew her, soe that I much question the Lawfullnesse of your tarrying long before you see her, I wish she be alive when you come:

Miscellaneous Bound Collection, Massachusetts Historical Society.

---

1. These two slips of paper were apparently enclosures in a June 1697 letter that is now lost.
2. Not found.
3. On 9 June 1697, John Young was killed, his son was wounded and Luke Wells was taken captive during a foiled attack on Exeter, New Hampshire (Hampton). Charles Bell, *History of the Town of Exeter, New Hampshire* (Exeter, 1888), 220.

From William Brattle, 19 October 1697

CAMB. OCT: 19: <u>97</u>

REVD SR

Yours first & 2^{d} I have rec^{d},[1] & heartily wish by word or deed I could serve you:

As to Theophilus, He carries it well, & I have a respect for him; Thô as to y^{r} proposal of Boording him to be sure for ye present there is no room for it; I have denyed some already & dare not think of any such thing: I hope to get him out of Commons & to obtain for him a place at one of ye Tables ere long:[2]

I shal resign his Class to Mr Pemberton[3] within a day or two & doubt not but y^{y}'ll have a good Tutor in him.

As for accommodating y^{r} sons by disbursing for them &c I have hitherto done it; <*But*> And wish I could do it further But I must confess, that w^{t} wth disbursments on ye house & w^{t} with disbursmts for houshold stuff &c I am so straitned & at some times distress'd for want of mony, that I dare not encourage y^{r} dependance upon me: The Stew^{d} will expect his Quarter Bills to be paid; & unless I had mony in my hands I cannot possibly answer his Expectation, & it is a vain thing to dissemble it. I would straiten my self ye more for y^{r}self at this juncture considering y^{r} circumstances, But all will not do; Since ye 14.10 d I have disbursed 11: 6 d which makes—1.6: 4 d It being for y^{e} [sweeper], Wood, a Book binding, [...] & to Boston for Siah: The 2 Bills are 3.2.11

<u>3.4.3</u>

6.7.2 which I wish I could clear but cannot for want of mony. I pray G^{d} be with you & yours. I am Revd S^{r}

Y^{r} Friend & H. Servt

W Brattle

Curwen Family Papers, American Antiquarian Society. Addressed "To ye Revd Mr John Cotton Minr of ye Gospel In Plymouth." Endorsed [from] will [Brattle] october, 19: [1697]." Manuscript badly torn along left margin.

1. Not found.
2. Here began Cotton's attempts to settle college debts for Theophilus (H.C. 1701) and Josiah (H.C. 1698). Brattle's willingness to help had limits: "I dare not encourage yr dependance upon me." Many of the remaining letters in this collection reflect Cotton's fears that he would not be able to pay for Josiah and Theophilus to finish their studies, given his own difficulties.
3. Ebenezer Pemberton, tutor at Harvard.

[To Rowland Cotton, 30 October 1697][1]

SAT: MORN AM:

DEARE SON

Bas: might have bin soe kinde as to have brought all my letters to my house, as well as have left them at Thomas's, & then he might have seene your desolate mother & have brought you the letter[2] which I sent you by Rus: yesterday: Jos: writes[3] that Mr Brattle was ill & not at meeting last Sabb: & that they feare a fitt of sicknesse & that will put off his marriage[4] next week: Freshmen are placed, corwin is first Theoph: the sixth, weld & wiswall the 2 last:[5] Mr Pemberton began last Monday to heare the Freshmen recite, quickly more alterations are expected, He sayes their classes have almost done reciting & askes whether he may live with you this winter, his tarrying at Coll:[6] signifies nothing longer then next week: your Aunt writes, that my sorrowfull letters & my wives to Cos: Cott: will move the hearts of some concerned to doe what they can for us; she says, they heare a good character of Theoph: a good report from some of their chh & there is great hopes he will be taken care of: I hope Cos: Math:[7] will take him this winter & for Jos: if he live at home he may doe well if he be told what must be the matter of his studies: [....] minister; you [...] think) to encourage [....] write to Bro: Math:[8] it will doubtlesse soften his heart & may move him to take some care of Theoph: & much intreaty of them may prevent my being interdicted Ind: work; I was with them & preacht at Ele-river[9] on Thursday (there I spyed Bas:) & it seems as acceptable as ever; & intend mattakeesitt[10] next weeke D: V:[11] Fish came not till this morning & Tho: Howland[12] had before he came sold that cow which he told you I should have, but he promises to bring me a very good one from home after his returne; it now raines hard & I expect not to send this today; wee 3 salute you both, God blesse you & all yours, pray hard for your distressed Father

J: C:

I am yet wholy unresolved what course to take as to a Journey or abiding this winter, but I am through divine helpe resolved to be utterly quiet & not to stirre a step in mooving for present Reconcil: with the chh, though I know noe more of them then I did, yet I doe conclude there must be such a Life in me as may, (being told to them abroad) obtaine their helpe & direction in that affaire, but I promise my selfe noe good from man, but God can doe every thing:

Miscellaneous Bound Collection, Massachusetts Historical Society. Sheet cut along bottom margin, parts of several lines lost.

---

1. Date according to Prince.
2. Not found.
3. Not found.
4. William Brattle married Elizabeth Hayman (1677–1715) on 3 November 1697 in Boston. Almon Torrey, *New England Marriages Prior to 1700* (Baltimore, Md., 1865), 94.
5. George Curwin (1683–1717, H.C. 1701) was first in his class from his entrance until his graduation. Cotton's other placements are inaccurate. Thomas Weld (1684–1704, H.C. 1701) was placed tenth (out of nineteen) when he arrived and graduated eighth. Samuel Wiswall (1679–1746, H.C. 1701) began college ranked sixteenth, fell to eighteenth and graduated in sixteenth place. John Langdon Sibley, *Biographical Sketches of Graduates of Harvard University, In Cambridge, Massachusetts* (Boston, 1873–) (hereafter *Sibley's Harvard Graduates*), 5:26, 124-25, 126-29.
6. "College."
7. Cotton Mather.
8. Increase Mather.
9. Eel River is in Plymouth.
10. Mattakeesitt is the area near the Duxbury/Pembroke boundary in Massachusetts.
11. "God willing."
12. Probably Thomas Howland (d. 1739), the son of Arthur and Elizabeth Prince Howland of Plymouth. James Savage, *A Genealogical Dictionary of the First Settlers of New England,* 4 vols. (1860–62; facsimile reprint, Baltimore, Md., 1990), 2:479.

To Rowland Cotton, 1 February [1698]

Tuesday Feb: 1:

My very Deare son

Sir Litle[1] came home on sat: on sabb: noone he gave me a Booke under seale from Bro: Mather,[2] it was sir W: Phip's his life[3] dedicated by Mr Nath: Mather to Earle Bellomont,[4] & an attestation de Authore (whose Name is not in the Title page, nor need it) by said Mr Mather, Mr Howe & Mr Matthew Mead; I see not that ought else is in it but what you read in the manuscript, & therefore suppose you will not long for it: All the letter I had was the enclosed (in the Booke) noe superscription to it, noe inscription, noe subscription, you see the desire & expectation of the Libeller; neither is there a word who sent the Booke, but Jerusha wrote on the outside of the Paper, For Mr J: C: at P: I would see God in all these things; but I cannot tell how to answer his expec: for it was Mr Treat & Mayhew[5] that gave information of many of these 24 Assemblies & Teachers & I know not how to gaine them now; if I tell him he must send to them to know it may be he will be vext; send me the Libell againe: Text was, Ps: 126: 5[6] all to comfort under afflictions; He sat at my Kitchen fire all sab: noone: says Capt Turells widow dead[7] & her son John Barrels wife, who was Capt Legs daughter,[8] also George Monkes[9] & one grand child of Elliston by their daughter[10] dead & the other at the point of death, soe Judged, 15 lay dead last Tuseday, 7 more then neere it, a very fatall time at Boston & at Roxbury sad: these colds & coughs are the visible malady, Physitians have not yet found out the hidden wound, suppose the fogs last fall the cause: I sent not one letter by him but he went to Mr T: who wrote by him to Bro: Math:[11] I suppose on purpose to usher him into his royall presence; as he came back he called upon Mr T: who told me he would write to me but Eph: could not stay because neere night & his company waited for him to reach Hingham: I shall now daily look for his lines, o Lord prepare me for them, I expect noe good: This day the Major hath ordered Kenedy's & others to appeare at Jael's to be examined about Nan: Ramsdens death, a great assembly goe thither; noe doubt guilt of much cruelty:[12]

yours by T: H: I received this morning,[13] I did receive your minimam, answered all by Lew: what of mine invited your answer you unsealed not your letter to insert: now to your inside, I heare not whether Bass: or any else hath brought Ephs book: you say Nuptiae—celebrandae,[14] I am very sorry & soe it mater for your family illnesses, Lord in mercy heale you all, last night our Joanna had an ill cough & stopping in her throat, she takes Physick today, it is now working very well: All your passages of newes were wholy new: you did well to write them for I am desolate & heare litle. Hannah roares dreadfully fearing her mother is dead, a litle hopes, because there is another widow

King Lives also neere Mris wantons, if you know ought certainly informe us; Is it Boston-Browne by the Dock? is Killio the rich man? you cannot come to us before you shall be very welcome, you may waite & hope for good, but I see nothing but death, only God can show wonders to the dead: Jos: longs to come to you but cannot get a horse, else he soone would: his schoole is a litle increased by John Wood & Rich: Holmes, etc;[15] He with his parents salute you: I rest, with prayers etc

your sorrowful father

John Cotton

Capt Pope is likely to recover[16] at Ellistons. Newes from Court may come before a hand to carry this

This minute yours by Mr Peper[17] is come; wonder not, my Deare child, that I now minde it, one universally forsaken is apt to observe & feare the worst in every thing: I beleive with my soule you are as you say: I am glad you Bro: R':s buisnesse is ended at Bar:[18] I beleve never such a winter in N: E: since I was borne; They sled wood over the ferry & carry provisions to the Castle, & goe to Nantaskett on the ice: Not a stick of wood had I about a fortnight since, then Rich: seares[19] sold me a cord from his doore, that is spent & when I began this letter I had not a stick to get supper, but Deac: Wood[20] just now brought me a sled load, wee have burnt Nicho's trundle-bed & some pillars of mr Corlets bedstead, God yet provides: what heard you at Barn: in that hour or 2 fit to suggest? Lord heale your mate & lambs: Jan: 23: was sacrament day at the North chh cotton & sam were both soe ill they went not to meeting, their Father preacht [all] day & administered;[21] A man went on the ice to Hingham he skipt over one hole [...] A man at the ferry fell in but escaped drowning, hee & sir Litle.

It is said some drowned adventuring on the ice in Bristoll ferry, Justice church there lost horse & sadle, himselfe escaped:

Miscellaneous Bound Collection, Massachusetts Historical Society.

---

1. Ephraim Little.
2. Increase Mather.
3. Cotton Mather, *Pietas in Patriam the life of His Excellency Sir William Phips, late Captain General and Governour in Chief of the Province of Massachusetts Bay... by one intimately acquainted with him*, (London, 1697), *Early English Books*, 8:6379 [Wing M1138].
4. Prince 's note: "Dated Apr. 27. 1697"

5. Samuel Treat (1648–1717, H.C. 1669), minister at Eastham, and Experience Mayhew (1673–1758, H.C. 1720), minister at Martha's Vineyard. Frederick Lewis Weis, *The Colonial Clergy and the Colonial Churches of New England* (Baltimore, Md., 1936), 208, 138.

6. Ps. 126: 5: "They that sow in tears shall reap in joy."

7. Capt. David Turrell's wife, Mary Colbron Barrel Turrell, died on 23 January 1698. Savage, *Genealogical Dictionary*, 4:343-44; Torrey, *New England Marriages*, 760; *Boston Births, Baptisms, Marriages and Deaths, 1630–1699*, ed. William Appleton (Baltimore, Md., 1978), 1:238.

8. John Barrel (b. 1657) married Isabella Legg (1672–1698) on 14 September 1693, and she died on 22 January 1698. Torrey, *New England Marriages*, 45; Appleton, *Boston Births, Baptisms, Marriages, and Deaths*, 1:238.

9. Cotton seems to have been implying that some relation of George Monk's died. Mary, the daughter of Christopher and Mary Monk, was born on 26 March 1694 and died on 25 October 1697, but George Monk was not Christopher's father, at least according to Savage. Tavern keeper George Monk of Boston's Blue Anchor tavern himself died later this year, on 7 September 1698. Monk was one of Boston's most favored tavern keepers, and his establishment had one room that often hosted sessions of the General Court and the Superior Court. Cotton may simply have been mistaken. David Conroy, *In Public Houses: Drink & the Revolution of Authority in Colonial Massachusetts* (Chapel Hill, N.C., 1995), 14, 18; Savage, *Genealogical Dictionary*, 3:224; *Acts and Resolves of the Province of Massachusetts Bay*, vol. 7, 564; Appleton, *Boston Births, Baptisms, Marriages, and Deaths*, 215, 227, 238.

10. Jonathan Elliston died on 6 November 1697, but Cotton stated that the deceased was his grandchild through his daughter, who would not have been named Elliston; the records do not list another death that would fit Cotton's information, which may have been mistaken. Appleton, *Boston Births, Baptisms, Marriages, and Deaths*, 238.

11. Increase Mather.

12. In June 1698, Thomas Ramsden of Duxburough was presented for "neglecting to give evidence to the Grand Jury when summoned" and charged a fine. There may have been a connection to Nan Ramsden's case; however, court records for this period have been lost. David T. Konig, *Plymouth Court Records* (Wilmington, Del., 1978-1981), 1:224.

13. Not found.

14. "Weddings are to be celebrated."

15. Cotton's son Josiah became a schoolmaster in Marblehead in the fall of 1698; perhaps he was teaching there or elsewhere on a temporary basis. *Sibley's Harvard Graduates*, 4:399.

16. See 18 February 1698.

17. Not found.

18. Barnstable.

19. Richard and Bathshua Seers married in Plymouth in 1696 and remained there to raise their five children. *Vital Records of Plymouth, Mass To 1850*, comp. Lee D. Van Antwerp, ed. Ruth Wilder Sherman (Camden, Me., 1993), 17.

20. Savage refers to John Wood, who was a Deacon in Marlborough; Torrey lists a John Woods (1641–1716), who married in Marlborough. Savage, *Genealogical Dictionary*, 4:627; Torrey, *New England Marriages*, 834.

21. Cotton and Samuel Mather (1674–1733, H.C. 1690) were too ill to hear their father, Increase Mather, preach.

To Rowland Cotton, [2 February 1698]

WEDNESDAY

This morn at break of day, your mother had an ill fitt of vomiting, is now well: Justice wadsworth was with the Major at the examination yesterday,[1] all is ended, it was manifest Nan had hard usage but dyed in one of her fitts:[2] Jos: heares of a sturges that will lead a horse & sadle back, perhaps he will come upon it to you, if his cold increase not too much, if he doe I beleive you must convey him back with Nath: Clarke behind him to see his father; wee cannot hire a horse because etc.

N is set next to J: Den: before your Betty & Sarah, is he [wo]rthy of such honour?

Miscellaneous Bound Collection, Massachusetts Historical Society. Addressed "These For Mr Rowlan[d Cotton] at Sa[ndwich.]"

---

1. See 1 February 1698. John Wadsworth was sworn in as a justice during the General Sessions in August 1692. *Plymouth Court Records, 1686–1859*, 1:219.

2. No evidence of Nan Ramsden's life remains; for Cotton's impression of the case, see his letter of 1 February 1698.

To Rowland Cotton, 18 February 1698 [6 March 1698][1]

FRIDAY
NIGHT

DEARE SON

Capt Pope (& his son Tho: both recovered here) I spake with, who tells me that Mr Melvin & Green are at Mr Barnes's, I therefore now write, hoping in the morn to give these to them: poore Joshua Prat (who soe replyed to your Bro: John) dyed on wednesday[2] & was buried to day, I was not with him till a few houres before his death; his speech began to faile as to sentences, words he spake, seemed affectionately to desire my prayers with him & when ended, his sense thereoff: I went from him to John & Ele: churchel[3] in whose families hardly a person well, each of them with much christian candour desired the like, which I durst not refuse; this day came Andrew ward,[4] Mr of a sloop (one of Midletowne) to me full of distresse of soule, I hope God is preparing him for spetiall mercy; your deare mother had some releife 2 or 3 dayes, yesterday Rob: Bartlet fetcht her to his very sick family, but that which compelled her going was, he had a lovely boy borne on wednesday[5] both its feet bending inwards, likely to be a cripple, she bound up etc lay there all night, came home early, & ever since hurried, by Jos: churchel for his son John,[6] will Harlow & Ben: Warren for their wives,[7] & Will: Ring for his child[8] fetcht her on horseback & mercy wood she must cupp a 2ond time,[9] the first was 2 days agone, thus is she tired with serving, Lord strengthen her I wish she be not Laid up to morrow, she was never more willing to doe & run as now: Litle J: Barnes almost sunsett brought me your letter[10] by Fish which next I answer I cannot mourn for Tob's death, because I think you are glad; I never knew till now my cowes name, but she is young & if she have a good stomach I intend to pay for it: I see not the least prospect of getting wood when this is spent, as it will by monday (I think) I blesse God for beginnings of recovery with yours, His mercy perfect it: If it must be in April, God give you a blessing then in your mother. For writing, printing, softning, I desire to say, the will of the Lord be done: I suspect Mr Stoughton expects my writing for the money, I wish you (if you think I should) would endite me a letter, for I know not how to frame one; was it friend or foe, knave or honest person that thought it would be very well for us to keep etc. who can say, God will not shew wonders to the dead! though I am ready to say, there is noe hope; sir w:s Life[11] the major hath not yet sent home; If God save me in the new triall at T: H's, I thinke it best to lye still & not move a step to T. or M's for any present issue: the 18 are, 1: Kitteaumutt (alias the Ponds:) 2: Mattakeesitt: 3. Titticutt. 4: Assawamsitt: these were mine: 5: Mashpau. 6: monument. 7: Acushnett. 8: Coaksitt, 9: & 10: two at Sakonett. 11: chappaquidgick. 12: Nashamoiett: 13: Sengekontackitt: 14: Toikimmy or Nashuakemmuck: 15: Tackanio: (alias Gay Head) these 5 at the vineyard: 16: & 17: at Nantuckitt: 18: Saukatuckitt, where I preacht last August: surely Mr Treat, Gookin & Thacher can make up the rest: when Assize comes God direct for the best: I have a sermon on that Text, if I can finde it to night; I will send it now. If I should burne barne, it would cry like cutting the trees: I have noe Almanack, nor will I buy one though I might at N: T:'s because I never did, neither shall you for me; the old tells sun rise & for moone I send to see J: Rick's at full or change & that is all I want it for, ergo I charge you not to spend a penny for one, but if one be given you, then I will accept your gift not else: Fish is gone by & I lost sending letters to Bost: the former Green or this or Melvin, pray engage to call on me at their returne: wee both salute you both; God heale, save & blesse; John Short's only child is dangerous, Tom: Litle is with her.[12]

Miscellaneous Bound Collection, Massachusetts Historical Society. Addressed, not in John Cotton's hand, "The Revd Mr Rowland Cotton, Ministr at Sandwich, Pr mr Melvin: QDC."

1. Prince's note: "Suppose 1697/8 March. 6."
2. According to Thomas Faunce's town records, Joshua Prat died on 16 February 1698, so this letter must have been written on 18 February 1698, not March 6, as Thomas Prince suggested. Van Antwerp, *Vital Records of Plymouth*, 135.
3. John Churchill (d. 1723) and Rebecca Delano Churchill (d. 1709) had five children, aged eleven months to ten years. Eleazer Churchill (1652–1716) and Mary Bryant Churchill (1654–1715) had eleven children; the oldest was twenty-two. Van Antwerp, *Vital Records of Plymouth*, 6, 8; Torrey, *New England Marriages*, 153; Savage, *Genealogical Dictionary*, 1:386-87.
4. Probably the eldest son of Andrew Ward (1647–1691) and Trial Miegs Ward, born in 1669 in Killingworth, Connecticut. Savage, *Genealogical Dictionary*, 4:406-7.
5. Robert and Sarah Bartlett's fourth child, a son, was born on 16 February 1698. The unnamed baby died on 20 February 1698. Van Antwerp, *Vital Records of Plymouth*, 13.
6. Joseph and Sarah Churchill's eldest child, John, was born on 3 July 1678.
7. William Harlow (1657–1712) and Lydia Cushman Harlow (1659–1717[?]) probably called Joanna to assist in the birth of their seventh child, Mary, or their eighth, Isaac. Ben Warren (b. 1670) and Hannah Morton Warren (1677–1715) had their first child, Benjamin, on 15 March 1698; they evidently needed prenatal advice from Joanna. Van Antwerp, *Vital Records of Plymouth*, 8, 18; Torrey, *New England Marriages*, 344; Savage, *Genealogical Dictionary*, 2:357.
8. William Ring and Hannah Shirmon Ring had only one living child in 1698; their second child, Hannah, was born on 26 May 1697. Van Antwerp, *Vital Records of Plymouth*, 17, 86.
9. Mercy Wood died on 4 March 1698. "Cupping" was a common procedure to draw out infection: "The operation of drawing blood by scarifying the skin and applying a 'cup' or cupping-glass the air in which is rarefied by heat or otherwise." Dry-cupping was designed to raise the infection without scarring the patient. Van Antwerp, *Vital Records of Plymouth*, 135; *Oxford English Dictionary*, 2d ed. (Oxford, 1989) (hereafter *OED*), 4:134.
10. Not found.
11. Prince's note: "Sr W Phipps Life Dedicated Apr. 25. 97."
12. Thomas Little (1674–1712, H.C. 1695) was a physician and merchant who lived in Marshfield until 1699, when he settled in Plymouth. *Sibley's Harvard Graduates*, 4:253.

To Joanna Rosseter Cotton, 16 April 1698

2ond letter now to you: April, 16: 1698:

My most Deare

I thanke you for the remembrance of your Love, I know you have more then you expresse; wee have attended your orders in every thing, the barbaries at ready, & halfe the Anniseeds, & the things to make cabbagenets[1] & lastly, the 2 bottoms of black woosted;[2] wee only want a hand to convey them safely to you: Deare Heart, when cast downe, read, Psal: 42: 5:[3] 11:[4] & 43: 5:[5] the booke of God is full of cordialls for you, even for you, though your soule too often refuses to be comforted; you will much refresh your deare children if when you come from your chamber & have bin soe much conversing with God you will be cheerfull in conversing with them; with God all things are possible, & nothing is too hard for him, when a soule to its owne apprehension is cast out of Gods sight, yet there may be a looking towards his holy Temple; the God that comforteth those that are cast downe, refresh you with the Consolations of his holy spirit, & give you to see the Joy of his salvation; I leave you in the armes of everlasting mercy, & affectionately intreating that you will daily poure out your soule to God for spetiall mercy to be vouchsafed to me,

I rest, yours whilst I am

John Cotton

Is there not to be found 3 or 4 choice, spetiall christians with whom you may keep a day of fasting & prayer? I know Mris Prince is one; my children can tell you. Daniel Davis[6] (he that eat with James Allyn at our house who perhaps came now to visit Betty Dotey[7]) saith, that 2 are dead at Saybrook this winter, one of them a chauker, 14 at Hadham, above 40 at Fairfeild; & that Andrew ward is still very bad at Boston:[8] the 2ond candle will last us one night more.

I perceive by Tom: F: last evening that they are most wretchedly set to quarrell away a good peice of land on this side the stone, but they will not intrench an inch upon J: Rickard, I am weary of my life in this meshech,[9] son Rowl: must buy this land & let him manage the case for I hate to have to doe with them; Turne over leafe:

I have tryed this morning & I finde as neere as I can ghesse that from J: Rick's fence to the stone is 6 or 7 paces more then from the stone to Eph: Cole's barne, soe that if they hold their vile resolution to have halfe of my present enclosure three or 4 paces the chh-agents will rob me of, if son Rowl: can indeed attest on oath that L: Morton, war: etc did set that stone as boundaries 'twixt my land & the chh's, as I am very confident they did, it will be a good lift; Capt Howland one of the 3 is yet alive

& it is said, he also is able soe to assert, if I can see him I intend to aske; noe dog was ever more weary of turning spit then I am with these malignant—o Lord deliver. I wish Mr Prince might come from the Bay today, that these letters may be gone to you; crafty Tom whose other men, & noe lesse then 4 because it was soe vast a tract of land (a litle garden spot) he will hide himselfe, but most venemously instigate, for he invents that the stone was set only to range the highway not to divide 'twixt chh & me; a horrid falsehood. I beleive my every day black upper coat growes soe rotten & teares daily that I feare I cannot possibly weare it many dayes longer, what shall I doe? here is noe body to mend it, neither can I weare my stuffe[10] one over my thick troopers Coat, if I can finde a wastcoat in your chest fit for me to weare under my searge Jacket then I beleive I must use it & weare the stuffe coat my deare one sent; Doe you want any herrings? it will be our dinner today. Tom: F: also said, as if there was noe bound mark at the other end therefore noe doubt it was only to range the street, I could not say ought to it then, but even now I went to the fence 'twixt Clarke & me & there is also another stone for the boundary at that end which will show their falsenesse & venom:

Miscellaneous Bound Collection, Massachusetts Historical Society.

---

1. Cabbage-net: "a small net to boil cabbage in." *OED*, 2:745.
2. Woosted: "a wollen fabric or stuff made from well-twisted yarn spun of long-staple wool combed to lay the fibres parallel." *OED*, 20:581.
3. Ps. 42: 5: "Why art thou cast down, O my soul? and *why* art thou disquieted in me? hope thou in God: for I shall yet praise him *for* the help of his countenance."
4. Ps. 42: 11: "Why art thou cast down, O my soul? and why art thou disquieted within me? hope thou in God: for I shall yet praise him, *who is* the health of my countenance, and my God."
5. Ps. 43: 5: "Why art thou cast down, O my soul? and why art thou disquieted within me? hope in God: for I shall yet praise him, *who is* the health of my countenance, and my God."
6. Probably Daniel Davis (b. 1673) of Concord, Massachusetts, who married Mary Hubbard in 1699. Torrey, *New England Marriages,* 205; Savage, *Genealogical Dictionary,* 2:21.
7. Elizabeth Doty Morse (b. 1676) was the daughter of Plymouth's John (1640–1701) and Elizabeth Cooke Doty (1649–1692); she married Joshua Morse in Plymouth in December 1698. Elizabeth Doty Oaksman was the daughter of Plymouth's Edward (c. 1643–1690) and Sarah Faunce Doty; in 1698, she had already married Tobias Oaksman and lived in Marshfield. Which Betty Davis went on the visit is unclear. Van Antwerp, *Vital Records of Plymouth,* 4-5; Torrey, *New England Marriages,* 227, 521, 542.
8. See 18 February 1698.
9. Probably a variation of "meash" or "masshe"—"to become enmeshed or entangled" or "to entangle, involve inextricably." *OED*, 19:647.
10. "Woolen fabric." *OED*, 16:984.

To Joanna Rosseter Cotton, 19 April 1698

April, 19: 98:

My Deare

M[r] Prince is gone over to M[r] Barne's, in his cloak bag are 2 browne papers, in which are Barbaries, 2 bottoms of black woosted, Anniseeds & all for cabbage nets wee could finde; In discourse with him, he tells me yesterday M[r] Tor:[1] talkt much with him about me, & he would have me goe some where and be retired & not yet issue my case here: Tor: thinks that whilst I am here they will unite the more against me, & says also, I can be in noe straits, having noe body to maintaine but you, only having lived soe well all my dayes, it seems hard to be shortened,[2] abundance of talk he had, & said that in time I might have imploy else where, but never here, which he needed not to have said, for I would not stay here for the world, if I could helpe it, only this new discourse confirmes me in a resolution to cry night & day to God to have pitty on me, & if possible, to dispose, that as soone as you are returned home, I may have some retiring place out of the noise of this Babel: Deare soule, pray for me without ceasing,

who am, Thine, in depths of Affliction

John Cotton

Tor: said, I had a farme to maintaine me:[3] Let son know these things, & give both your thoughts.

Miscellaneous Bound Collection, Massachusetts Historical Society. Addressed "These For Mris Joanna Cotton, now at Sandwich."

---

1. Samuel Torrey (1632–1707), minister in Weymouth. Weis, *Colonial Clergy*, 206.
2. One and a third lines crossed out.
3. Two words crossed out.

To Rowland Cotton, [May 1698][1]

Deare son

This Thursday morning Mr Lord[2] came unthought of to my house, he lay at Mr Barnes's; I pitty your bad throat & have told him you will certainly engage him for the Sabbath; Mr Morton was buried[3] this day fortnight; I wonder Mr Prince spake not of it; he can modestly & well tell you all Caralino-storyes; He preacht for Mr Willard[4] last sab: A: M: & at charlestowne, P: M: he is in haste, I have not to adde, but my most tender & affectionate Love to my deare wife, of whose being better I long to heare, Deare soule, the Lord be her Comforter; The same God heale you, & give deliverance to your mate & hasten me that good tidings that there may be noe obstruction of her returne in whom my life & all the comforts of it are soe much bound up; faile not, I pray to write your account of the transactions with the Agents & send me a coppy thereoff, Tho: Howland[5] will speedily plow & plant my ground, mater's direction may doe well; Hannah is better: Last Tuesday Mr Brattle Fellows, Schollars, i: e: the seniors (such as 'Siah etc) all at a great feast at Mr Leveretts new house in Cambridge; my hearty Love to you both, I thank you & pray God reward you for your filiall respect this weeke & formerly to your desolate father

John Cotton

make him promise you before he goes to Barnstable, for your throat needs ease, as well as your other trialls call for it: God blesse all yours:

Miscellaneous Bound Collection, Massachusetts Historical Society. Addressed "These For Mr Rowland Cotton, Pastor of the Chh at Sandwich."

---

1. Prince's note: "Suppose 1698. May." Information in n. 3 below suggests that this letter was written in early May.
2. Joseph Lord (c. 1672–1748, H.C. 1691) was an early settled minister in the Carolina colony, beginning in December 1695. After establishing the settlement on Ashley River, called Dorchester after Lord's home congregation, Lord returned to Boston to encourage emigration, arriving on 16 April 1698. Clearly, Lord thought that Cotton would be willing to consider such a move. He also married Abigail Hinckley, Gov. Thomas Hinckley's daughter, on 2 June 1698 in Barnstable. *Sibley's Harvard Graduates,* 4:101-6.
3. Charles Morton (1627–1698), minister in Charlestown from 1686 to 1698, died on 11 April 1698. Weis, *Colonial Clergy*, 146.
4. Samuel Willard (1640–1707, H.C. 1659), minister at Boston's Old South church. Weis, *Colonial Clergy,* 227-228.
5. See [30 October 1697].

To Rowland Cotton, [14 May 1698][1]

SATURDAY, A: M:

DEARE SON

By Patience that lives at young J: Moreys, I sent you yesterday an account of all that was then told by Theoph: but he is a kin to you & newes comes deliberately from him; Mr Cush: & he met at Lewis's the great bridegroom & bride, A Salem-Browne (a son of him who married Bailey) with Mr Burrough's daughter,[2] what a brave match is that! young Haines is returned to Haverhill[3] & says the Indians knockt his father on the head & were about to kill him, he pleaded hard for his life & told them his running away from them was because his father would, else he would have staid etc they spared his life, & I wish they may not catch him a 3d time: he sayes the squaws & young ones are gone up to plant corne, the men are come downe to doe mischeife; They have newly killed a man at yorke, & carried away 2 or 3 persons:[4] At quechecho a new married man saw two Indians looke in at his window; Another English man abroad had a gun with him to kill birds & he did see an Indian in the bushes, but they saluted not one another: Mr Tappan is likely to obtaine Mr Gerish's daughter:[5] Tho: Lambert gave me your pacquet,[6] To begin with son John, I perceive his heart was warme, it seems a litle too harsh (but tell him not that I say soe) his intimation that his mother had not obtained that compleat conquest over a hasty spirit in Judging, I am sure if he had over his, he would not have soe written of her who is a mirrour of patience;[7] I perceive they were ill in his family, am glad they are better: Arent you dull, my child, that you know not his meaning about his losse, looke againe & you will see what wee saw at first glance, viz, the losse of ours, i:e: of our visiting you at Sandwich, because sick: your mother smiled heartily at that passage & beleives it to beare all truth, viz, about the butter, but truly, I never heard word of Delano nor his butter to this day since he first wrote of it, pray tell him soe that he may not in the least expect a supply from it; I hope for new daily. Indeed his lines are too red; for gauls I beleve you should read Galls, but seeing it is an appearance only (though I confesse too great) passe it by with a brotherly, Jocose animadversion, & our parentall love to them etc & also from Theophilus who says that Hincks & a woodbridge from Cos: Hampton now are added to their classis:[8] Cos: Cott: Math:[9] told The: that Mr Willard would appeare his good friend which makes me conclude that I shall finde mr Brattle's words true, that M^r^ W: would see for kindnesses among his friends: Now for your letter; my wife keeps fixt for you, it is well she is here, by the helpe of Tailors, to fix Theoph: to goe to Coll: by Tuseday night; As yet I am unprovided but doe hope on friday or saturday to convey my wife to you, for I cannot beare your not going Northward, not that I expect much good if any for my selfe, but there will be good for Theoph: I am perswaded: I will cease to write of bounds, but all other proprietors are well, enough satisfyed & will never stirre more if the chh make noe disturbance; it was towne-agents laid out land for the chh as well as for the others ergo it will stand: what my need may be of mony I know not, I see you expect a miracle or my starving; God can doe every thing, I wish I had noe greater exercise then to provide for this life, though that may be difficult enough: I professe I have forgot the Ques: be you sure to tell me as you passe along: I beleve the Law forbids Elders: I heare not of my cow: It is Dick Hubbard who married Dr Clarks daughter,[10] Randolph would not suffer him to goe for o: E:[11] because he produced not sufficient bonds-men that the King should have his dues, ergo he tooke Corne etc & came to N: E: Sister doth meane (I am confident) more of Cos: simonds then you think; Heartlesse when God hides his face from our prayers, I thought by that she meant she had prayed to have some heart there turned to favour me but findes it not, Lord shine in Christ: she told Theoph: she had a sugar-loaf to send my wife by the first vessell; I take as litle pleasure in M[r] Deerings[12] acting as you can, but Theoph: says, he speakes very kindly to him & if noe body else will etc he will doe it himselfe, but for some of these great men, espetially L: Gov: I knew had utterly spoiled my market there, but when you are there, you will setle all in the right channell; Theoph: sayes Cos: Cottons wife is now at Bost: & son will is to come next week & hath promised to bring her home; he is not like to be at 'Lect: but Mr Cal: Cush:[13] will & he will certainly, if called, give Mr sewall good incouragement to promote The's education in this way; Theoph: knowes not that I discerned him last night neere 1/4 of an houre in secret prayer in his bed-chamber, I hope God is in his soule; I know of noe hand to convey this today, but now it is ready; mris Freeman saith he comes to fetch her on Monday, misse him not; on Tuseday they returne, I shall then minde you as I doe every day, if I live till then: wee all 3 salute you both; the Govr intends to speak with the Mowhawks before his returne & that is well; with prayers etc, etc, etc

J: C:

Mr Clark of Exceter goes upon Crutches still: Mr Thomas bought Truworthy's sloop full of salt (i: e the salt in it) & they are daily unloading it, it is here 3 shil: a bush: 14 or 15 shil: a hogshead:

This minute appeares the bearer.

Mr Noyes of salem is to preach the Election-sermon;[14] I beseech thee Goe & heare him. Old Goodman Fellows of salisbury[15] is dead & old Goodwife Eastman,[16] son will: sayes son Johns Chest of drawers will be ready by the Commencment to send to him.

Miscellaneous Bound Collection, Massachusetts Historical Society. Addressed "These For Mr Rowland Cotton, at Sandwich."

1. Prince's note: "1698 suppose may.14."

2. Captain John Brown (b. 1672) married Sarah Burroughs on 21 April 1698. Brown's father, William Brown of Salem (d. 1716), married Rebecca Bayley on 26 April 1694, after his first wife, John's mother, Hannah Corwin Brown (1646–1692), died. William Brown served in many government offices, including as a member of Edmund Andros's council. Sarah Burroughs was the only child of Francis Burroughs, a merchant in Boston. Savage, *Genealogical Dictionary,* 1:278, 310; Torrey, *New England Marriages,* 107, 109.

3. Jonathan Haynes (c. 1646–1698) was captured with four of his children—Mary (b. 1677), Thomas (b. 1680), Joseph (b. 1689) and Jonathan (b. 1684)—on 15 August 1696. (See the above letter of 30 October 1696.) The raiding party split up and Jonathan Sr. and Thomas were taken to Maine, from whence they escaped, while the other three children were taken north and sold to the French. Mary was later "redeemed," but Jonathan and Joseph settled in Canada. The event to which Cotton refers in this letter occurred on 22 February 1698, when the Natives who burned Andover returned home by way of Haverhill. Jonathan and Thomas Haynes were again attacked; Jonathan was killed, probably because he was too aged to travel, and Thomas was captured. He again escaped. Savage, *Genealogical Dictionary,* 2:389-90; George Wingate Chase, *The History of Haverhill* (Haverhill, Mass., 1861), 184-85, 201-3.

4. Cotton Mather described the event: "...on May 9, 1698, the Indians Murdered an old man, at Spruce-Creek, and carried away Three Sons of that old man, and wounded a man at York." Cotton Mather, *Decennium Luctuosum* (Boston, 1699) in *Narratives of the Indian Wars, 1675–1699*, ed. Charles Lincoln (New York, 1913), 270.

5. Christopher Toppan (1671–1747, H.C. 1691) did not marry Joseph Gerrish's (1650–1720, H.C. 1669) daughter, Elizabeth; she married Joseph Green (1675–1715, H.C. 1695) in March 1699. Instead, Toppan married Sarah Angier on 13 December 1698. *Sibley's Harvard Graduates,* 2:299-304; 4:113-17, 228-33.

6. Not found.

7. Three lines crossed out.

8. Samuel Hinckes (d.[?] 1759, H.C. 1701) joined Theophilus's class during the final quarter of the freshman year. Ephraim Woodbridge (1680–1725, H.C. 1701) joined the class a year late, and Samuel Woodbridge (1683–1746, H.C. 1701) joined the sophomore class. *Sibley's Harvard Graduates*, 5:69-73, 129-34.

9. Cotton Mather.

10. Boston mariner Richard Hubbard (d. 1699) married Dr. John Clark's daughter, Elizabeth, on 9 November 1697. Savage, *Genealogical Dictionary,* 2:485; Torrey, *New England Marriages,* 397.

11. "Old England."

12. Probably Henry Dering (1639–1701), a Boston shopkeeper. Savage, *Genealogical Dictionary,* 2:41.

13. Caleb Cushing.

14. Prince's note: "[symbol for Wednesday] may 25. 98." Nicholas Noyes (1647–1717, HC 1667) preached the Election Sermon on 25 May 1698, published as *New England's Duty and Interest* (Boston, 1698) [Evans 850].

15. Samuel Felloes died on 6 March 1698. *Vital Records of Salisbury, Massachusetts*, (Topsfield, Mass., 1915), 557.

16. Sarah Smith[?] Eastman (1621–1698), the widow of Roger Eastman (1610–1694) of Salisbury, died on 11 March 1698 in Salisbury. Savage, *Genealogical Dictionary,* 2:93; Torrey, *New England Marriages,* 240.

To Rowland Cotton, [17 June 1698][1]

Friday nigh sunsett:

Loving son

This morning I sent a letter[2] to my wife by Eph: wampam who said, he knew you well: since I had yours[3] by S: Br: & immediately sent away the Cloath to Theoph: by J: Rick: De Grind & Danf:[4] if you come at Will: Nummuck,[5] it seems well that you advise him to be ready at Sandwich to meet them or at Moreys & to accompany them to his meeting house at the Ponds, he is now all the Teacher they have, though not every Sabbath, & he can obtaine a competent Assembly for them, but the death of old wannoo & occanootus[6] hath much altered that appearance which was in their day very great; As for Mattakeesit let them finde it as it is, it was once a full Assembly & large, but death hath brought it low: Namasket, another of my Assemblies is wholy forsaken: Assawomsitt & Titticutt I have been much with but not since Mr Danforth hath taken them; I doe not desire you to send the mony for the plums, I owe you much more kindnesse; welcome next Monday, Lord order every passage of that day to be mercy to me, & her & us all, yea & every day, yea & for ever; faile not my deare of coming, nor you offending her at that day for a 1000 pd, feare not her being mett, but I will not bring her over that bridge for all that mony, but some body will, I hope: my expectations then to see her will be as absolute & positive as it is lawfull or possible to be as to contingencies: I suppose, I have gained the heart of Mr Dexter for ever; he was making a hideous moane to borrow a horse to marshfeild; W: Cl: would not, Barnes would goe with him; J: D: was much provoked I said nothing, but I thought he was your neighbour & as he was passing along riding on his owne this way I met him & told him he should have mine[7] o the inexpressible ravishment of his soule at my kindnesse & the promises of requiting my love, he will call this eve for this & the roots tyed up in a cloath: I hope he will not spoile my horse, he said, he must be at Yarmouth by tomorrow noone, ergo I had pitty: he will, noe doubt, tell you his resentments hereoff: the brigantine is come now to load; sam: Litle[8] spake with Theoph: last night, well at Boston: Heartyest Love to my dearest, parentall to you both; God blesse you all & litle Nath:

I am, your Affectionate Father

John Cotton

Will Raws: & Dan: come & see me & invite me with them to mattakeesitt

Miscellaneous Bound Collection, Massachusetts Historical Society. Addressed "These For Mr Rowland Cotton, at Sandwich. cum tribus radicibus. Quid ait frater tuus ad novum filium: Die saturnii mane hora octava: vicinus tuus cum equo iam rediit & maximas reddit gratias."[9]

1. Prince's note: "Mr Grindal Rawson & Mr Samuel Danforth spent ye Time in visiting ye Indians, in 1698, a May. 30. to June 24. Suppose in 1698, june 17."
2. Not found.
3. Not found.
4. de/"about" —The Society for the Propagation of the Gospel in New England appointed Grindal Rawson (1659–1715, H.C. 1678) and Samuel Danforth (1666–1727, H.C. 1683) to visit Native settlements from 30 May to 24 June 1698. Their report is printed in Massachusetts Historical Society *Collections,* 1st ser., 10 (Boston, 1809), 129. *Sibley's Harvard Graduates,* 3:164, 244.
5. According to a 1693 document, there were two men named William Nummuck, one designated "jr." and associated with the Native church in Sandwich. Jeremy Bangs, *Indian Deeds: Land Transactions in Plymouth Colony, 1620–1691* (Boston, 2002), 560-62.
6. Wanoo and Occanootus were neighbors at Manomet and appear frequently in Plymouth town and colony records. They both served on the Native jury for the John Sassamon murder trial in 1675. Clearly, they were both firm supporters of missionary work among the Natives. Nathaniel B. Shurtleff, ed., *Records of the Colony of New Plymouth in New England* (Boston, 1855–61), 5:168.
7. "(Back he ran to Barnes & took him)."
8. Samuel Little (1655–1707) lived in Marshfield. Savage, *Genealogical Dictionary*, 3:99.
9. "With three roots. What your brother said to the new son: early on Saturday at the eighth hour: your relative returns with a horse and sends back the greatest thanks."

To Rowland Cotton, 29 June 1698 [22 June 1698][1]

WEDNESDAY P: M:

DEARE SON

It is not easy to think what tremblings were upon your mothers heart & feares as to your dearest, whom she soe left, & what comfort & ease it was to her spirits to heare from you by Cap: B: that God had given such a reviving, God make you & us truly thankfull for such sparing mercy; by massey I wrote to you:[2] since which I heare of the death of Mris Jeffries,[3] the only child of Esq: usher: Letters from Theoph: say, that Breck being turned out, being one of the 5 (sir Litle[4] saith, Deming, Holman were 2 more of them,[5] they are all pardoned upon a confession-making) he is now waiter at the Batchelors table, that saves some mony: Jos:[6] writes noe newes, only promises to be sparing in his expences: 13 to commence with Jos: & about 15 or 16 masters,[7] sir Litle is one, but not the Dr: Sir Price[8] in o: E:[9] hath sent to be one & will have it though absent: Sir L: says, Mr Bradstreets ord: is now fixt to be the week after commenc:[10] I suppose Praeses ordered that: Mr Dering writes that Doc: Cooke is my exceeding good friend & that Bro: M:[11] will doe well by Theoph: the 1st I beleve, the

2ond, Lord say Amen to it: I have some hopes it may be soe: It was very wisely done of you to order [Row?], etc to come first hither, for all Indians were here; they put up horses at Nath: clarks bespoke quarters there & came most seasonably to my house by day light, as soone as wee had done supper, (a good mutton pye etc) they tooke a pipe, mater[12] would not see them then, I gave them a cup of small beare drawne 1/2 an houre before for supper: wee walkt & found Indians, they ordered them to come with my leave to my house this morn, Charles <*preach*> prayed then sang, Raws: preacht from Ecle: 12: 7:[13] for part, Charles ended with prayers &c, betwixt 50 & 60 auditors: John wannoo[14] told them Tup:[15] lyed, pannoowae kuttoawonk, to say Kitteaumutt was his they were only & alwayes Mr Cottons Indians; now 10 families, about 50 adult & many children; as for Mattakeesitt, I told them, death had thin'd their numbers, but the Major could speak to that; he had much discourse in private with Danf:[16] soe had M^r^ wadsworth,[17] I beleve they both spake much good for me, but I promise my selfe none from it: I spake not a syllable to Danf: of etc nor he to me, nor did I offer a cup of ought this morn: they are gone directly to Taunton: I beleve they cannot pray Ind. this morn they toucht her: your hot love to mater was great to post to J: Bs, I am glad C: Gor: hindred you; I beleive you askt her pardon where noe sin was: Court newes you must have of C: Bas: I know not nor aske any. not any sleep last night for bugs, mater run towards day to [Cod-'s?] bed & had some hours sleep, I none, she is almost killed in taking paines to kill them this day; she writes to you & tells you what she sends; hearty love & prayers, God perfect healing grace & mercy to yours,

I am etc.

Miscellaneous Bound Collection, Massachusetts Historical Society. Addressed "These For Mr Rowland Cotton, at Sandwich."

---

1. Prince's note: "1698. suppose June. 22 or 29." See the letter of 2 July 1698 to confirm the later date for this letter.

2. Not found.

3. Elizabeth Usher Jeffries (1669–1698), wife of Boston merchant David Jeffries (1688–1742), died on 27 June 1698. She was the only child of John Usher by his first wife. Usher served in many government offices, including that of lieutenant governor of New Hampshire. Savage, *Genealogical Dictionary,* 2:539; 4:363.

4. Ephraim Little.

5. Robert Breck (1682–1731, H.C. 1700), David Deming (1681–1746, H.C. 1700) and John Holman (1679–1759, H.C. 1700) were classmates who seem to have participated in an event that *Sibley's* calls a "riot." John Veazie (1681–1701, H.C. 1700) and Daniel Dodge (1677–1720, H.C. 1700) also joined in the "class riot." *Sibley's Harvard Graduates*, 4:515-18, 518-19, 523-26, 532, 519-20.

6. Josiah Cotton.

7. Thomas Symmes, Josiah Cotton, Samuel Mather, Joseph Willard, Dudley Bradstreet, Peter Cutler, John Fox, Nathaniel Hubbard, Samuel Wolcott, Henry Swan, John White, Josiah Torry, Oxenbridge Thacher and Richard Billings comprised the Class of 1698. The master's students in 1698 were Walter Price, Richard Saltonstall, Nathaniel Saltonstall, John Hubbard, Simon Willard, Abijah Savage, Oliver Noyse, Thomas Blowers, Ephraim Little, John Perkins, Jedidiah Andrews, John Robinson, Joseph Green, Joseph Morse, all classmates of Harvard 1695. *Sibley's Harvard Graduates,* 4:393, 218-19.
8. Walter Price (1676–1731, H.C. 1695) was traveling in Europe during the 1698 commencement but defended his master's question—on the suitability of monarchy—and was granted the degree, listed first in his class. *Sibley's Harvard Graduates,* 4:270-71.
9. "old England"
10. Prince's note: "was not ordained till Oct. 6. 98." Simon Bradstreet (1671–1741, H.C. 1693) was ordained in Charlestown on 26 October 1698 after a "fierce dispute" led by Increase Mather, who opposed his ministry. Although Bradstreet began preaching in Charlestown in 1697, he was reticent to accept a settled position amidst the congregation's turmoil. This probably explains why his ordination took place later than Cotton suggested in this letter. *Sibley's Harvard Graduates,* 4:154-56.
11. Increase Mather.
12. "Mother."
13. Grindal Rawson preached on Eccles. 12:7: "Then shall the dust return to the earth as it was: and the spirit shall return unto God who gave it."
14. John Wanoo (Wauno) was a Christian Indian in Plymouth, who ministered to converted Natives and was empowered by William Bradford "to decide small differences among them." "Account of an Indian Visitation, A.D. 1698," Massachusetts Historical Society *Collections*, 1st ser., 10 (Boston, 1809), 134.
15. Thomas Tupper.
16. Samuel Danforth.
17. Benjamin Wadsworth.

To Rowland Cotton, [2 July 1698][1]

Deare Son

It is still saturday morning, & when I came from writing to you[2] by Jos: Rider at Barns's, I espied David Loring,[3] & going home R: Har: hollowed me & gave me yours, to which by D: L: take answer; mercy Dunham brought for you my Thursday lines:[4] I think I approoved your totall silence de Yarm:[5] but I doe as highly (if not more) approove your present lines, & soe doth mater[6] now awake; John & his mother were soe peremptory de majore etc that it seems to me (as it doth to you) impossible almost but that He etc would heare me; mater is only for my telling them to morrow, that (as you say) I was invited for this sabbath, but went not becaúse I would not offend them, & not to say, I am for the next also, but leave the case more generall; I am in a very great strait, seeing hazards both in accepting & in refusing; it is most manifest by Jos: Rid:[7] that I am really expected there today; my not coming now (I think) cannot hurt me but show some self-deniall; their being destitute to morrow[8] may perhaps advance their hunger for the next sabb: if I visit all my children next week, I can returne before Sab: to your home, if encouragements are not competent; though I beleive some compliance with D: F: etc here would save me from Tor:[9] etc well enough: I wish you had these my 2 letters before wat: & Bar: come back today, but I feare you will not: I hope your Bro: will hold his Toungue de Argts, its pitty he knew of it, but it could not be avoided: Cal: Lor:[10] saw Theoph: well on Thursday; He & Dav:[11] saw your Bro: yesterday at 2 a clock p: m: ride by Pet: Jacobs,[12] they lay at The: Cush's[13] that night, & soe escaped all the rain etc If you will speak to Rus:[14] de [promise?] doe as your wisdom shall think best: your parents salute you both, Lord blesse you all,

I am, your Affectionate father

John Cotton

The fire at salem was soe, the drawer ran up frighted to see the rum on fire & then it was too late to quench, major Browne's, Hurst's etc. burned.[15]

If Jos: Rider be not gone, what if you wrote a line to tell of her husband going well after raine from T: cush's, & what you think of my visiting her; A line from Maj: & M[] would say much

Miscellaneous Bound Collection, Massachusetts Historical Society. Addressed "These For Mr Rowland Cotton at Sandwich."

---

1. Prince's note: "Suppose July. 2. 1698. (no 2.)."
2. See the letter of 2 July 1698.
3. David Loring (b. 1671) was the son of Thomas and Hannah Jacob Loring of Hull and lived in Barnstable. Savage, *Genealogical Dictionary,* 3:117-19.
4. See the letter of 29 June 1698.
5. "About Yarmouth."
6. "Mother."
7. Joseph Rider; see the letter of 2 July 1698.
8. Three words crossed out.
9. Samuel Torrey.
10. Caleb Loring (1674–1732) lived in Plymouth and was David Loring's younger brother. Savage, *Genealogical Dictionary,* 3:117; Torrey, *New England Marriages,* 474.
11. David Loring; see above note.
12. Peter Jacobs (b. 1668) lived in Hingham. Savage, *Genealogical Dictionary,* 2:534.
13. Theophilus Cushing (1657–1718) lived in Hingham. Savage, *Genealogical Dictionary,* 1:489, 491; Torrey, *New England Marriages,* 199.
14. Probably Jonathan Russell.
15. Prince's note: "1698. of June. 28. a Fire at Salem yt burnt Several Houses." See 2 July 1698.

To Rowland Cotton, [2 July 1698]

Saturday[1]

Deare son

I hope to heare from you today by Jos: waterman or by Rob: Barow;[2] I commend your prudence in a totall silence de Yarmouth, but am extreamly surprized this morn, coming over to speak with Abiel shirtliffe[3] to buy some corne (Judging he was come back with his sloop but he was not himselfe) Mr B: & his wife aske me if I goe to Yarm: today, & tell me Joseph Rider[4] told them, he thought I would, for they had desired it & said Rider being but at John Barnes's I stept thither, & askt him, why he spake of such a thing, he replyed, mris miller[5] told him, that the Major & her husband desired my son to speak to me to come & they lookt for me today; well, deare child, I can deny my owne interest for Gods Holy Names sake, I goe not now, but I am in a dreadfull strait; Mr wiswall (though he knowes noe particular place) yet sayes, Mr Tor: & Mr Math: will take offence if I preach any where,[6] but himselfe wishes I had free liberty soe to doe, & he goes on Monday with Peleg[7] for admission into Colledge, o that you could speak with his seasonably; He thinkes some kinde of indulgence in the generall from the bretheren tomorrow, would salve the matter & make all safe, I have a 1000 thoughts but think I shall doe nothing atall but lye downe under my burthen till I dye; Lord pitty, help, direct; think, think, think, pray, pray, pray till Monday & then speak, whether I had best goe see my children southward next week: mater asleep, love, prayers, etc,

yours etc.

J: C:

A great fire at salem it is said, by Rumm catching fire, or fire-rum in Mr Gidneys cellar, five houses burnt, 2 blowne up, major Brownes one of thes:[8] If Johns letter be not gone to his wife,[9] send it by this man. Is it best to venture a word to D: F: & soe etc. to morrow! I think of Prov: 16: 3:[10]

Miscellaneous Bound Collection, Massachusetts Historical Society. Addressed "These For Mr Rowland Cotton, at Sandwich."

---

1. Prince's note: "1698 Suppose July. 2. Fire at Salem was on June. 28. 1698."
2. Joseph Waterman (1643–1712) or perhaps his son, Joseph (b. 1677), both living in Marshfield. Robert Barrow, the husband of first Ruth Bonum and then Lydia Dunham, lived in Plymouth. Savage, *Genealogical Dictionary,* 4:432, 1:127; Van Antwerp, *Vital Records of Plymouth,* 10.
3. Abiel Shurtleif (1666–1732) was the son of William and Elizabeth Lettice Shertliff and lived in

Plymouth. Savage, *Genealogical Dictionary,* 4:92; Van Antwerp, *Vital Records of Plymouth,* 18.

4. Probably Joseph Rider (c. 1644–1718), who lived in Yarmouth, or his son, Joseph, born on 22 December 1676, also from Yarmouth. Savage, *Genealogical Dictionary,* 3: 540; Torrey, *New England Marriages,* 625.

5. Perhaps Margaret Winslow Miller, wife of John Miller (1632–1711) of Yarmouth, son of Yarmouth's minister, John Miller (1604–1663). Torrey, *New England Marriages,* 509; Savage, *Genealogical Dictionary,* 3:209.

6. Ichabod Wiswall (1637–1700), minister at Duxbury (1676–1700.) Samuel Torrey (1632–1707), minister at Weymouth, and Increase Mather (1639–1723, H.C. 1656), minister at Second Church, Boston, did not want Cotton preaching in Massachusetts Bay. Weis, *Colonial Clergy,* 233, 206, 136.

7. Peleg Wiswall (1684–1767, H.C. 1702) was the son of Ichabod and Priscilla Pabodie Wiswall of Duxbury. *Sibley's Harvard Graduates,* 5:176-79.

8. Salem's "Great Fire of 1698" occurred after dark on 28 June. The fire began in Timothy Lindall's warehouse on Essex Street and destroyed the homes of Samuel Prince, William Browne, John Pilgrim and William Hirst. In order to stop the spread of the fire, the Hathorne House on the corner of Essex and Liberty streets was blown up. In all, £5000 worth of property was lost, more than half of it from merchant William Browne's warehouse. Sidney Perley, *History of Salem, Massachusetts* (Salem, 1926), 3:347-50; Savage, *Genealogical Dictionary,* 2: 240-41.

9. Not found. Cotton's son John married Sarah Hubbard, daughter of Richard and Sarah Bradstreet Hubbard of Ipswich, during his time in Exeter, New Hampshire. *Sibley's Harvard Graduates,* 3:213-14.

10. Prov. 16: 3: "Commit thy works unto the Lord, and thy thoughts shall be established."

To Joanna Rosseter Cotton, 6 and 7 July 1698

Sandwich July, 6: 1698:

My Most Deare

It is commencment day, almost sunsett, I hope Mr W: Clark will call here & bring these; God brought me very comfortably hither; My daughter will doe very well; all the children are well; Nurse Jenkins as full of Love, respects & charity as ever: I have not bin out of my chamber this day only for family-prayer; the Elder came to me last night & was full of tender manifestations of his good will; He Judges I ought noe longer to lye still; He moved Capt Green of Maldon (who did to him expresse much respect to me) that they would send me a call from Maldon, because Mr Wigglesworth[1] is almost leaving his work; soe much was the Elders heart upon it, that he moved it to Mr Raws:[2] etc when here, Raws: did reply, the Elders in the Bay might not be for it, & that (noe doubt) will be found true, if Bro: M:[3] heare of it: however the Elders love to me must be acknowledged; he telles me when he heard the first draught, he told Mr Tor:[4] he could not set his hand to such a paper, Tor: replyed if he would not then none must, if not all, Tor: also told the Elder, he namely, the Elder was much eyed & would be minded what he did & said, & it is most certaine, had not Mr T. bin there, it had not bin as it was, but God saw it best for mee I desire to be silent before him: the Elder freely ownes, he did concurre with Mr Wiswall[5] in such a sentence as he would have, but nothing would doe to hinder what was: The Elder also says, that he hath told Mr Russell,[6] it was too severe & the like, & Mr Rus: *<addes>* says, he was desirous & endeavoured it might be otherwise: Elder also seems very well pleased at the Permit the chh gave last Sabbath, & thinks it to be a great matter & is very willing I should preach here next sabb: (for Mr Smith[7] says, he will doe nothing unlesse in his owne house) I almost think the Elder will goe with me to morrow to Barnstable, if not as far as yarmouth, & be as active to promote my restoring as some have bin to doe the contrary; my thoughts are very awfull, if things are not fully encouraging at yarm: I shall returne on saturday; I hope my son John will not come home before the sabbath, if he doe then I am sure there will be noe worke for me there, but if he come part of the way, he had best stay at this house & here will be a pulpit ready for him. I am much concerned for son Rowl: though I doubt not God will helpe him wisely to answer his uncle:[8] if the Ques: be why am I the worse for being a kin to him?[9] the Answer is, upon his coming from o: E:[10] with a charter taking in Plimouth, our people were all in a rage at him, Josephus, J: War: J: Brad: & many more of the bretheren (from their godly zeale & reall Conscience) did raile at him & revile him for falsenesse, treacherous dealing yea & wickednesse to take them in to be slaves, etc. Josephus himselfe said that, if it had bin open, wicked enemies had done it he could better have borne it, but to be thus betrayed & sold by seeming friends etc such things moved my spirit & my respect to my deare Brother ingaged me to give many a severe rebuke to such things & upon that account these persons that have bin most against me were provoked at me ever since: & when another man came home from o: E: he made it his worke (as you know) to traduce Bro: M:[11] & lay him very Low, even as to his moralls as well as his unworthy betraying of Plimouth Colony, in soe much that good people have said partly in your hearing & often in mine, they did formerly Love his books & had such & such a one, but now hearing he was an apostate, a wicked man etc they threw them aside & could not endure to read them. these things imbittered my spirit, also to heare a man say, old Mather would goe to hell shortly for all his wickednesse & the like, I have with all my might freely & heartily borne my Testimony for him agst such unjust reproaches & slanders, & I know & soe doe many more that for this I *<was>* suffered much prejudice with many; yea, I am sure with 2 cheif men in the Councill, one of whom said *<often>* to me more than once, it was a mystery to him, that God suffered his owne children to goe on with the reigning of the sin of pride in them etc soe much did He say agst father & son in slighting of them, yea very much despising the son, that my speaking contrary hath bin to *<o much>* my damage however it is in other respects: my hearty love to you, my desire is that you will send this very letter under sufficient sealed covers to be left with Mris Mackarty for him, that he may make what improvement he pleases of it, he will doe not hurt with it, & it may be some passage or other in it may be of some use: Daughter hands you her duty; I hope J: Rickard is not gone, but you will write & send these also by him: Pray for, Thine as his owne

John Cotton

Daughter says to son Rowl:

buy 10 pd of cotton wooll, I now seale with her love to him, hoping M^r sprague[12] may bring this & you will soone convey it to Bost by land or sea: some from yar: say, I am much expected to preach there: the good Lord direct pray hard, ingage M^r stone[13] to see me:

July, 7: I heare this morning M^r clark passed by yesterday, which I am very sorry for, I must now waite for M^r sprague & shall have this sealed for him; Mr Dexters action is deferred till next court,[14] I wish my son had this letter: when showres cease I am ready: My daughter loves her husband, all is well here.

Miscellaneous Bound Collection, Massachusetts Historical Society. Addressed "These For Mris Joanna Cotton, at her house, in Plimouth."

---

1. Michael Wigglesworth (1631–1705, H.C. 1651) was plagued by ill health throughout his ministerial career in Malden, and he often had assistance from other ministers. The church voted in March 1698 to pay for some help for Wigglesworth, but Cotton was not chosen to assist or replace him. *Sibley's Harvard Graduates,* 1:259-86.
2. Grindal Rawson.
3. Increase Mather.
4. Samuel Torrey.
5. Ichabod Wiswall.
6. Jonathan Russell.
7. John Smith (1614–171[?]), former minister at Sandwich, who still resided in the town and occasionally assisted Rowland Cotton. See 25 September 1688.
8. Increase Mather.
9. Cotton believed that this second adultery accusation was political—that he was being punished for supporting Increase Mather's charter, which dissolved Plymouth Colony, giving Massachusetts Bay control over southeastern Massachusetts. During the charter negotiations, however, Cotton praised Mather's efforts; for example, see the letter of 10 and 21 September 1688.
10. "Old England."
11. Increase Mather.
12. Possibly Samuel Sprague (b. 1640), who served in many local government positions in Plymouth Colony. Savage, *Genealogical Dictionary,* 4:156.

13. Possibly Nathaniel Stone (1667-1755, H.C. 1690), who returned to Massachusetts in the summer of 1698, began preaching in Harwich and married Governor Hinckley's daughter Reliance on 15 December 1698. *Sibley's Harvard Graduates,* 4:79-82.

14. Probably the protracted case involving John Dexter, a miller from Sandwich. Dexter was being sued by Capt. Thomas Tupper, Thomas Tobey, Zechariah Jenkins and Israel Gannet of Sandwich because he trespassed on a neck of land called Shawnee Neck (Scituate), which was given to the inhabitants of Sandwich in 1639 for common cattle grazing. In 1695, Dexter plowed the land, planted corn & put up a gate, trying to claim ownership. This complicated land dispute took more than three years to settle. See Suffolk County Files, Reel 22, vol. 39, #3525, Massachusetts State Archives.

To Joanna Rosseter Cotton, 8 July 1698

Yarmouth July, 8: 1698:

My Dearest

A large Epistle[1] I left for you at sandwich, & after I was come from thence, I was told that James Warren[2] was at the Elders, which made me thinke he might take that letter for you, I hope he did not, I would not by any meanes it should miscarry or be opened by any one in the world[3] but you first; I met Mr Sprague, who promised me to call for it & deliver it to you with his owne hand; As soone as I had fitted my horse it fell a raining, soe that I could not stirre till sun about 2 houres high in the evening, I called at Mr Hinckleys doore,[4] Mr Whippo's,[5] Mr Lathrop's but did not alight any where; spake with Ensigne Hawes[6] neere his house & good Peter Thacher[7] came running over his fence to salute me with great affection, hoped to enjoy me etc. by day alight I arrived here, daughter presents her duty to you, she & the children are all well; Deac: Josiah Thacher[8] had bin here the night before to see if I was come, daughter sayes, she heares not of one man in all the towne but is glad & willing I should preach here, only Bassett[9] that loves noe minister: Elder at parting advised & encouraged me to be ready & if from the people in the meeting house assembled any came to invite me then to accept it: It is a rainy morning againe: I spend this day here as I did last wednesday at son Rowl's: only hearing W: Barnes & J: Watson are going home to day from Mr Hedge's, I thought it necessary to salute you & againe to bespeak your fervent prayers for me that God would lead me in a right way because of my observers; I long to heare from you by mr stone *<daughter gives you love daily>*

I am, Thine most affectionately whilst I am,

John Cotton

I spake with mercy Dunham at Mr Whippo's, & since I came hither Mr M: telles me, she hath vindicated you & me from some considerable aspersions, grounded upon your living soe long at Sandwich[10]

Miscellaneous Bound Collection, Massachusetts Historical Society. Addressed "These For Mris Joanna Cotton, at her house, in Plymouth."

---

1. See the letter of 6 and 7 July 1698.
2. James Warren (1665–1715) was married to Sarah Doty (b. 1666) and lived in Plymouth. Van Antwerp, *Vital Records of Plymouth,* 9; Savage, *Genealogical Dictionary,* 4:424.
3. Cotton was concerned about the 6 and 7 July 1698 letter because he wrote at length about how his Plymouth neighbors reacted to Mather's charter, which included daming Mather to hell and initiating a virtual boycott of Mather's publications, among other things.
4. Prince's note: "I was Then at the House, & Door & saw Him. T. Prince." Plymouth colony's last Governor, Thomas Hinckley (1619–1705).
5. James Whippo, first married Gov. Hinckley's daughter Experience and then to Abigail Hammon, who lived in Barnstable. Savage, *Genealogical Dictionary,* 4:507.
6. There are two likely choices: John Hawes (d. 1701), who lived in Barnstable and Yarmouth, and Joseph Hawes (1673–1752), who lived in Yarmouth. Savage, *Genealogical Dictionary,* 2:380; Torrey, *New England Marriages,* 354.
7. Peter Thacher (1665–1736) was married to Thankful Sturgis and lived in Yarmouth. Peter was the eldest son of John and Rebecca Winslow Thacher of Yarmouth. Torrey, *New England Marriages,* 733.
8. Josiah Thacher (1667–1702) was married to Mary Hedge and lived in Yarmouth. Josiah was the younger brother of Peter Thacher, mentioned above.Torrey, *New England Marriages,* 733.
9. Probably Nathaniel Bassett (c.1628–1711), who lived in Yarmouth at least since 1672.
10. Joanna's decision to live away from Cotton had clearly caused some rumors, which evidently worried Cotton.

[To Joanna Rosseter Cotton], 8 July 1698

8 July 1698[1]

SECOND LETTER FROM HENCE

Deare soule

It hath bin a very rainy friday, but amongst others Mr Miller[2] came to visit me, & telles what a concurrence there is in the hearts of all people to desire my preaching if reports be true, there is very great gladnesse upon the account; I sit downe astonished, & am musing whether it be a beginning of mercy & deliverance or a lightning before death; my heart melts in the sense of the present manifestations of divine compassions, let the issue be what it will: All that heare what the Bretheren did say, viz, that it should be noe offence, are most excessively pleased & fully satisfyed that their motion is of God: I begin now to think God may accept me to doe some service for his name on the morrow, Lord in mercy prepare me for it & accept in Christ; I conclude there will be with some a strange resentment of it, I wish my son in the Bay might have what I wrote before & now, & say & doe as he pleases; He will not come from thence till that day. I hope you may have opportunity by land or sea to send: He may know his neighbours have lost the whale, the Jury have now given it to Nausettmen:[3] It is said, many of Barnstable will be here this sabbath: Lord, what will thou have me do?

Some will readily think & say, it was some trick of my sonnes to bring it to this, but it will be very unjust for they tell me here, how they discerned it to be very surprizing to my son when it was first motioned, neither did he doe or say any thing to promote it, he was affected to heare such persons mention such a thing not in the least expecting it; he was wholy passive in promoting it; Bretheren here said it one to another, & did wonderfully unite in it, but my son is very innocent: I wish Cos: John Cotton[4] & Mr Brattle[5] knew these things from my sons

Miscellaneous Bound Collection, Massachusetts Historical Society.

---

1. In Thomas Prince's hand.

2. Probably John Miller (1632–1711), the son of John Miller (1604–1663), Yarmouth's minister (1647–1662). Savage, *Genealogical Dictionary,* 3:209; Torrey, *New England Marriages,* 509; Weis, *Colonial Clergy,* 141.

3. Beached whales were valuable property, and courts often decided ownership. Plymouth Colony stipulated which portion of each beached whale should go to the colony treasurer, finder, cutter, and property owner. In 1654 in Weymouth, the General Court of Massachusetts Bay divided the animals in three, granting equal thirds to the "countrje," the "toune of Weimouth," and "the finders." A Barnstable case went through several appeals. In March 1694, the Superior Court of Judicature in Plymouth ruled against three men, Samuel Lewis, William Weeks and Thomas Boweman of Falmouth, who claimed that a whale beached in Falmouth was wrongfully taken from them by Gov. William Phips. The case was reviewed in Bristol in September 1694, and their evidence was rejected. But, in December 1695, they were granted a new hearing of the case before the Supreme Court of Judicature in Plymouth. Evidently, they won. *Plymouth Colony Records,* 11:61, 66, 114, 132-34, 136, 207-8; *Records of the Governor and Company of Massachusetts Bay*, ed. Nathaniel Shurtleff, vol. 4, part 1 (1650–1660) (Boston, 1854), 191; *Acts and Resolves*, vol. 6, *Private Acts, 1692–1780*, 13.

4. Hampton's minister, John Cotton (1658–1710, H.C. 1678), was Seaborn and Dorothy Bradstreet Cotton's son, and Cotton's first cousin. Weis, *Colonial Clergy,* 62.

5. William Brattle.

ELEVEN

"Leaving Massachusetts and Exile in Carolina," 1698–1699

WHILE COTTON HAD CERTAINLY HOPED to receive a call from a church in southeastern Massachusetts, Charlestown, in the Carolina colony, was the only place that welcomed him. The leading merchants of the town, many with decidedly checkered pasts, and Reverend Joseph Lord, Plymouth Governor Thomas Hinckley's son-in-law, eagerly sought Cotton's services. The powerful Boston ministers encouraged him to accept the call, undoubtedly glad to be rid of their problem altogether.[1] The letters below illustrate Cotton's decision to leave, the preparations for his departure and his emotional parting from his wife, children and friends.

Joseph Lord's wife, Abigail Hinckley Lord, was thrilled with the idea that her former neighbor, Joanna Cotton, would be joining her in Carolina.[2] But Joanna clearly struggled with this decision: "mother seems not to know what to do abt coming to you."[3] It is quite surprising that Joanna even felt she had a choice to make, that she felt she could refuse to accompany her husband. John's letters suggest that he expected her to join him after he settled in; other letters suggest that Joanna never really wanted to go, nor felt that her health would even permit it.[4] After Cotton died, Cotton Mather wrote that Joanna's dilemma was finally solved: "Your Distress, about your Voyage to Carolina, being thus at an End."[5] Son Rowland wrote that he, with some of his congregation, were considering joining Cotton in Carolina;[6] Josiah also seems to have thought about settling there as well[7]—or at least, that is what they wrote to him, perhaps merely to console an undoubtedly lonely father.

Cotton sailed for Carolina on 7 December 1698. Joseph Lord described their three-week voyage as "pretty comfortable." They encountered neither storms, nor "any great matter of sea-sickness." When they arrived, both ice and Anabaptists awaited them. Lord wrote that Cotton would likely settle at Charlestown and receive the "right hand of fellowship" in his new congregation on 15 March 1699.[8] Cotton's son Josiah referred to a journal that his father kept in Carolina—"which I have in my hands"—

that is now lost.[9] The diary fragment below, transcribed by Josiah, details Cotton's pastoral work in Carolina, which echoed his earlier experience with the struggling Plymouth church. Letters sent from Carolina also demonstrate Cotton's continued penchant for networking and gossip.[10] The final letters in this collection describe his death during a yellow fever epidemic in September 1699 and include some reactions to the sad news that came both by letter and street gossip.

---

1. To Rowland Cotton, [16 July 1698].
2. To Rowland Cotton, [16 July 1698].
3. From Rowland Cotton, 25 April 1699.
4. From Joanna Rosseter Cotton, 13 July 1699; To Rowland Cotton, [8 August 1699].
5. Cotton Mather to Joanna Rosseter Cotton, 23 October 1699.
6. From Rowland Cotton, 25 April 1699.
7. To Josiah Cotton, 1 August 1699.
8. Joseph Lord to Thomas Hinckley, 21 February 1699, "The Hinckley Papers," Massachusetts Historical Society *Collections*, 4th ser., 5 (Boston, 1861), 304-5.
9. Josiah's transcript is included below as "Diary entries by John Cotton, 11 December 1698–14 September 1699."
10. To Rowland Cotton, [8 August 1699].

To Rowland Cotton, [16 July 1698]

SATURDAY MORN[1]

DEARE SON

Gods wayes are past finding out; when I came home I found Mr Robert Fenwick[2] at my house, where he had waited divers houres for me with his call subscribed by Govr Blake,[3] some of his Councill & sundry the inhabitants of charlestowne:[4] their promises amount to about 67 pd annually: Mr Allyn[5] & Mr Willard[6] send me a letter under their hands encouraging me modo quodam[7] to goe, advise me to get my dismission from the chh & desire the countenance of the Councill (I suppose they meane that of Mr T's[8]) I have written to Mr Keith[9] by the mason who goes today & desired by him an answer on monday; I am going to Duxb:[10] & if Mr W:[11] will encourage & send a line to the chh, then I purpose to morrow to move by the chh for my dismission; Mr Lord[12] much encoura[ges?] me to goe, Mris Lord grasps your mother[13] by the [...] & is ready to leap [out?] of her skin for Joy [....] told him, he being [....] was not [....] to subscribe the le[....] put off) [....], his uncle might [....] though the warning was short, & encouraged him, [...] he should not meet with mr Torrey & have his [....] -rence yet to come forward to me: M^r^ T: he did speak [....] his words were, he left it to the Boston ministers: mat[er?] [....] before had strange []kings of light in secret [....] nected to be satans delusions, & in the morning [....] & duty such like impressions on her [heart?] [....] & the Gentleman comes to the doore; wee are [...] in a maze & muze, Mr Dering writes to me much [...]ing; Mr Wilkins hath much spoke for it: Mr Willar[d] [...] postscript, the vessell will saile the latter end of [...] very [...] what [....] & thanks to you [...]

yours

J: C:

I would send Jos:[14] Just now to you with the letters but I must show them to mr W:[15] if any [....] I come back, I leave these for you, if not, Jos: must come as you can p[ur]pose & your [...] you must come away with Mr Rus:[16] & goe to the Bay & setle every t[h]ing for me. I promis & [...] without faile to send my answer to him next thursday or friday at furthest & [...] to keep the vessell 2 days of the week after for me: [several words illeg]

Miscellaneous Bound Collection, Massachusetts Historical Society. Addressed "These For [...] Cotton, at Sandwich." Prince's note: "1698 . Apr. 16. R Mr Joseph Lord arrives at Boston à S. Carolina. June. 2. marries mrs Abigail Hinckley at Barnstable. Nov. 15. sails wth m^r^ W & Mr John Cotton à Boston." Bottom half of letter badly mutilated.

---

1. Prince's note: "He was at yarmouth July 9 & 10 & not got to Sandwich ye 11 & this mt be wrote ye [symbol for monday] after. 1698 Suppose July. 16."

2. Robert Fenwick (d. 1725[?]) was born in England and began his working life as one of the "Red Sea Men," privateers who raided merchant vessels in the Indian Ocean. Forced to remain in South Carolina on bond, he eventually acquired land, largely by importing six slaves to settle in the province. At its largest, his property included more than 3,000 acres. He also ran a sawmill near Dorchester, Cotton's settlement. His public offices eventually included those of tax assessor, representative to the Assembly, militia captain, and justice of the peace. *Biographical Directory of the South Carolina House of Representatives*, ed. Walter B. Edgar (Columbia, S.C., 1977), 2:246-47.

3. Early colonial South Carolina seemed plagued by poorly chosen and corrupt proprietary governors, and Joseph Blake (d. 1700) was one of the worst, "one of the most notorious customs racketeers in colonial America." He served as governor in 1694–95 and from 1696 to 1700. Walter Edgar, *South Carolina: A History* (Columbia, S.C., 1998), 90, 93.

4. Prince's note: "i.e. in S. Carolina."

5. James Allen.

6. Samuel Willard.
7. "Me in a certain measure."
8. Samuel Torrey.
9. James Keith, minister of Bridgewater.
10. Duxbury.
11. Ichabod Wiswall.
12. Joseph Lord invited Cotton to join his missionary efforts in the new Carolina colony, and Cotton accepted. See the above letter of [May 1698]. Another minister, Hugh Adams (1676–1748, H.C. 1697), joined Lord and Cotton in Carolina. Adams married in Carolina, not returning to New England until 1706. John Langdon Sibley, *Biographical Sketches of Graduates of Harvard University, In Cambridge, Massachusetts* (Boston, 1873–) (hereafter *Sibley's Harvard Graduates*), 4:103, 321-36.
13. Abigail Hinckley Lord, Governor Thomas Hinckley's daughter, was undoubtedly well known to Joanna Rosseter Cotton, and she seems to have been eager for Joanna to move to Carolina also.
14. Josiah Cotton.
15. Ichabod Wiswall.
16. Jonathan Russell.

To Rowland Cotton, [30 July 1698][1]

LATR END OF JULY. 1698, MR JOHN COTTON OF PLIMOUTH WRITES TO HIS SON RC[2]

"Mr Thomas says—This is ye story of m^{rs} Bellevant. a man w^{o} diverse months Before had some Provocation à woman, see ye Dafter but, took Her to be ye Person, & shot at Her (she walk^{g} before Him) wth his Pistoll. It took Part of her sleeve: she ran into a shop; He after Her, shot a Bullet y^{t} went through her Back that came out before Her. When He saw her Face, He cried; Lord have mercy! this is not ye Person. He ran away, was soon seized, pleaded Distraction: No doubt is hanged long agoe. It was printed in Old England, & will be Here.

Mr Nelson came out when this ship did, in a Brigantine for NE.

Mr Thomas says: His couz Ad winthrop[3] told him, The Case at Sudbury was, Mr Sherman w^{d} t^{k} in a woman y^{t} h^{d} b^{n} vicious: 2 Brownes cheif men opposed: He with ye chh l^{d} y^{m} under Admonition: ye Council advise ye chh to t^{k} it off, & Brownes h^{v} ye Day

Mr Prince most ingenuously writes to me[4]—Mrs Prince is a penitent observer"

Miscellaneous Bound Collection, Massachusetts Historical Society. Addressed "To Mr Rowland Cotton at Sandwich." Endorsed in an unknown hand: "1698 From Jno Cotton."

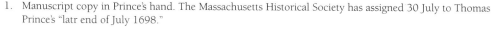

1. Manuscript copy in Prince's hand. The Massachusetts Historical Society has assigned 30 July to Thomas Prince's "latr end of July 1698."
2. Rowland Cotton.
3. Either Adam Winthrop (1647–1700, H.C. 1668) or his son, Adam (1676–1743, H.C. 1694). *Sibley's Harvard Graduates,* 2:247-49, 4:209-14.
4. Not found.

To Rowland Cotton,[1] 24 October 1698

PLYMOUTH OCTOBER, 24: 1698:

MY DEARE SON

This moment this bearer brought me a choice letter[2] from your Dearest[3] (who last week sent me 2 caps) I wonder I heare not a word from you this morning by honest Ele: Churchel,[4] who saw you yesterday at meeting; here I am in a poore desolate condition, not knowing what to doe, stirre I cannot one foot till I heare from you, though I am now ready to come at 2 houres warning, if God sayes come, if he sayes, stay, his will be done, J: Rick: & El: Rogers,[5] are ready for the first faire winde & Jos:[6] & his chest is to come in one of them, but I will not send any thing of mine, if they goe before you send to me; I wrote to you on friday by John Marsh,[7] but the [...] kept him here till saturday, soe that he [...] to keep Sabbath at Hingham, I hope by [....] he hath given you my letters, which I [...] you will soone deliver as directed; if the foule weather hinder the vessels Loading, I may be soe ready as not to hinder them for me; I desire to rest in the will of God; your Bro: John will be here to night; parents salute you, o that I knew what God will doe in this matter: Jos, Love to you,

I am in utmost haste, your Affectionate Father

John Cotton

mind your mothers Physick & marblehead:

Miscellaneous Bound Collection, Massachusetts Historical Society. Hole along left margin.

1. "For Mr Rowland Cotton, now at Boston" in Prince's hand at top of page.
2. Not found.
3. Rowland's wife, Elizabeth Saltonstall Cotton.

4. Eleazer Churchel.
5. Eleazer Rogers (1673–1739+) lived in Plymouth. Almon Torrey, *New England Marriages Prior to 1700* (Baltimore, Md., 1865), 632; *Vital Records of Plymouth, Mass To 1850,* comp. Lee D. Van Antwerp, ed. Ruth Wilder Sherman (Camden, Me., 1993), 31.
6. Josiah Cotton.
7. Not found.

To Rowland Cotton,[1] 25 October 1698

Plymouth October, 25: 1698:

My Deare son

your letters of Friday & two of Saturday I received[2] Monday night, & your Monday letter with one of saturday came by M^r^ crosby & done this morning, the Lord knowes what a five days & nights wee lived from M^r^ L's[3] letter till yours came last night; Capt. Bennett from London is here & Mr Rankin (I thinke is his name who married widow Butler[4]) a ship mr but now a passenger being bound by land, I venture these lines by: preparing every thing I can get butter living fowles etc. I have noe porke; there are gone from Ele-river about 10 Turkeys of James Warren's in Tobias Oakes man,[5] I cannot speake with the owner or skipper, but noe other appearing, I wish Mr Fenwick[6] knew of them, that they might some of them be bought for the designe: I hope you had my letters by John Marsh & that Mr Rus:[7] had his before he comes homeward, I hope you will finde they doe noe hurt. I am astonished to heare that your uncle[8] should say, there is noe discouragement can it be true? My son John came hither last night, yours were then all well; you have bin a faithfull, tender child to your distressed parents, the Lord God of heaven remember it for ever & reward it in mercy; If wee saile not before the sabbath, I wish Cos: Tuft would bring me a horse to goe on saturday eve to his house, or that I might goe to the Castle; God direct, you will think what to doe for the best in that respect: I intend, God willing, if weather hinder not to come towards you on Thursday morning & hope to reach Cos: Mathers that night. Your place is provided for on the sabbath ergo doe not resolve to leave me soe soone as friday, if I must tarry longer, I know not how to live without you:

If you like the enclosed, seale & give it to this desireable man: parents & 2 brothers salute you, God Almighty blesse you,

I am, your affectionate Father

John Cotton

you say not, what says sister, I ghesse what; I feare C: sewall is slow in it:

Miscellaneous Bound Collection, Massachusetts Historical Society.

---

1. "For Mr Rowland Cotton now at Boston." in Prince's hand at top of page.
2. Not found.
3. Not found. Perhaps letters from Joseph Lord.
4. Andrew Rankin married Grace Newcomb Butler (b. 1664) in April 1692 in Boston. Torrey, *New England Marriages,* 611.
5. Tobias Oaksman (1664–1750) was married to Elizabeth Doty (1673–1745), and they lived in Marshfield. Torrey, *New England Marriages,* 542.
6. Robert Fenwick; see 16 July 1698.
7. Jonathan Russell.
8. Probably Increase Mather.

To Rowland Cotton, 3 November 1698

Boston November, 3: 1698:

My very Deare sonne,

Whom I pray the God of heaven to blesse with all, but espetially with spirituall blessings in Christ Jesus; you may easily Judge that the exersises of my spirit are such that I am not soe capable of taking such a solemne farewell of you, as otherwise I would, you are a son whom God hath made a blessing to me & noe small comfort in all my trialls & difficulties, a fathers blessing therefore you deserve & have & shall have for ever; I commit you & all yours into the hands of God our Father in Christ, & doe very heartily salute your deare yokefellow, blessing God every day for his mercy in providing such a Companion for you, the Lord continue her a rich blessing to & with you for many yeares, that you may Live together as heires of the grace of Life: All particulars as to my selfe etc I have written in a large letter to my deare, mourning dove; I suppose sometime or other you will see it: I finde universall love & respect & many kindnesses as if there had never bin ought afflicting, soe good is God; wee waite only for a faire winde, if these raines & Easterly windes should continue 5 dayes longer, oh, how glad should I be to see you on monday night, but I hope & desire Gods hastning to smile on the voyage with winde & weather & despaire of once seeing you here before I goe; I am your Debtor for all your dutifull care in Journeying & doing soe much for me, I have noe way to requite it in part, but by bestowing 20 shil: on you from Roger which, I desire you to accept when payable; all my other, viz, son John & my 3 daughters have had as much now: you Living neerest, I pray you (which I know you will doe) asist your deare mother in all her affaires & comfort her to the utmost: farewell, my deare children, the Lord be your portion forever,

I am, your affectionate Father

John Cotton

How reviving will a line from you now be?

I told M^r sewall, perhaps you & your mother would desire the Judges in March to helpe her to my Arrears: He gave me one of Mr Noyes's sermons[1] & says, each towne is to have some by order of court, in that way I hope you will have one, soe your mother may have mine I left with you; farewell, farewell, my son, my son!

[2]I thought it might not be amisse to whisper this is your eare, that there might be noe expectations of impossibilities:

Miscellaneous Bound Collection, Massachusetts Historical Society.

1. Probably copies of Noyes's recent election sermon, printed as *New England's Duty and Interest* (Boston, 1698) [Evans 850].

2. Two lines crossed out.

To Rowland Cotton, 9 November 1698

Boston November, 9: 1698:

My very Deare Son

I that am wont to write soe often to thee, know not how to goe aboard without once more saluting thee, my loving & faithfull child: I hope God will helpe me to remember & never to forget the wormwood & the gall,[1] as also your coming last spring, I very easily discerne your meaning: A paire of Mr Bailys gloves I send you & a paire to your Bro: John with my Love: I have not worne them, the good man did a Litle: There will be very great need of your being fatherly in looking after the concernes of Theoph: the reasons I give are in my letters to your mother, all which you may read; I doubt not your care in looking upon my papers left in the basket & asisting my dearest in all she needs; My Bookes & all Manuscripts, pray let none be lost that may be of any use, but soe preserved among you my deare ones, that I may have them againe if God bring me hither; I finde as much love & respect as heart can desire; I doe desire you wisely to stand your ground as to M^r^ T:[2] set aside the word chh & yeild not an ace to him, for all is right you said & cause enough for it, & now Deare child, the God of all grace be with thee & blesse thy soule, body, wife, children & in all respects, & make thee a rich blessing to many soules; my most hearty Love to you & your Dearest; Let the wheel of prayer be ever going for me,

I am, Thy Affectionate Father

John Cotton

salute the Elder & Mr Russell:

Miscellaneous Bound Collection, Massachusetts Historical Society. Prince's note: "Nov. 15 Cotton sails à Boston NE fr Charlstown, S. Carolina."

---

1. References to "wormwood and gall" appear in several places in the bible. For example, in Jer. 9:15: "Therefore thus saith the Lord of hosts, the God of Israel; Behold, I will feed them, *even* this people, with wormwood, and give them water of gall to drink." In each example, wormwood and gall mark a people cast out of God's favor. See also Jer. 23:15; Lam. 3:15, 19; Deut. 29:18.

2. Probably another reference to Rowland's continuing troubles with Thomas Tupper. See 13 September 1694 and 12 February 1695.

Diary entries by John Cotton, 11 December 1698–14 September 1699

[HE] set sail for Carolina on Tuesday Novr 15th 1698—where he arrived Decr 7 following: and I find this Ejactulation on that Day in his Journal (which I have in my Hands) 'O Lord make me a Blessing here...' Here he set himself to do all the Good he could & was very abundant & successfull in his Labours—He gathered a Church & was Settled Pastor of it March 15. He set up Catechising, Precht a Lecture once a fortnight, Had private meetings, private Fasts alone & with Others, Made frequent visits to the Sick, opposed Gainsayers, Satisfied the Doubtfull & was ye Instrument of Edifying and Quickening many Saints & Converting many Sinners. In the short time of his continuance amongst them there were many Baptized & about 25 New members rec^d^ to full communion. He had abundant Respect shown him especially by those that were Good, & also by some that were Great, even ye Govr himself. He was there counted Worthy of & Reciev[d] double Honour—

Dec[r] 11 The first Sabbath after his arrival I find him breathing forth his Desires in this manner—'Lord humble me & make me a Blessing indeed to many Souls' on that Day he preacht on Matt 1.21[1] and many seemed Affected—

Ag[n] January 2 After his Recieving a Considerable sum for his Labours, he writes thus, Lord make me thankfull for outward Supplies, but above all Prosper his Work in my Hands & make me Faithfull & Successful therein

Feby 21st He writes thus,'I catechised 26 Persons Some of the Damsels after Catechising got alone in a chamber & Prayed together having been much affected with what they had heard. The good Lord carry on these Beginnings to a sound Work of conversion. The Eldest of y[m] was not 13. Some about 10 & under a Good Incouragement to feed Christs Lambs—

March 10 The Gov[r] had yesterday at my motion ordered me to Discourse him this morning, I did so & had all desireable Incouragemt as to his approbation of our Church Proceedings next Week—

March 13. Much Distrest in Spirit, Cast down with thoughts of my approaching Work—

March 15 The Day of Church Gatherng, I preacht Psal. 137.5.6[2] We were five hours at meeting, I read y[e] Confession of Faith; The Church by lifting up of Hands chose me to be their Pastor, we read & by Standing up assented to y[e] Solemn Coven[t] w[ch] we had before subscrib[d] wth our hands Mr Lord gave the Right hand of Fellowship in the name of their church many were much affected and Blessed God, etc.

April 28. Church fast kept at M[r] Jones's I Pray'd & then preacht on Isaj: 53.6—God was graciously present with us in all the Work of the Day—

May 2 A Day of Thanksgivinbg the Church kept publickly for our Gospel Enjoyments, Settlement of the Church &tc. I preacht on 1 Thess. 5:18—

June 16 The Church kept a fast at Madm Simmons's in Preparation for y[e] Sacramt A.M. I preacht on Matt 15:25[3] (Mr Fenwick[4] &c Prayed) P.M. on 1 Cor: 11.28[5]—I read M[r] Denings Letter to y[e] Church[6]—& am to return their Thanks to him for his Christian Love & Respect therein—the Letter my Wife sent to the Sisters of y[e] Church in answer to theirs to her[7] was then publicly read—

July 28 The Chh kept y[e] fast at M[r] Alexanders I preacht A.M. on Psal 73:28[8] then S[r] Adams prayed &c. I preacht P.M. on 1 Cor 11:28[9]—I propounded to the Church to Consid[r] seriously of & Prepare for y[e] Choice of Elders & Deacons—

Sepbr 4—Many taken Sick in Town. I went & Spake to divers of y[e] Ch to Quicken them to prepare for y[e] Lords Supper, & Discourse with them about their Soul concerns—

Septr 8th Our Ch Fast at M[r] Jones's for Preparation to the y[e] Lords Supper I Preacht A.M. Psal 85:6[10] P.M. 1 Cor 11:28[11]—I spoke with Six more & agn wth seven more agn wth Eleven more &c about Preparation for y[e] Sacrament Many were much affected with y[e] Prayers & Sermons of this Day. It was now a very Sickly dying Time Septr 10 I then Spake wth two more of y[e] Church as on y[e] Six preceeding Days—I preacht A.M. on Psal 36.8[12] P.M. on James 4.14[13]—38 Communicants of y[e] Ch 9 absent—Much of Gods Grace & Glory appeared this Day to many Souls in Sanctuary administrations

Septr 13. I preacht on Colos. 3.2[14] Set y affections &c

which I suppose was y[e] Last sermon that he ever preacht—

My Father kept a Journal or rather a Diary of Remarkable from the time of his going from New England to Septr 14. 1699 which was but four Days before his Death—a great sickness & Mortality that begun at Charestown Aug[t] 17.1699 (wherein no less than 176 Persons died) carried off my Father Septr 18: 1699 in y[e] 60th year of his Life to the great Loss & Grief of y[e] People

Josiah Cotton, Manuscript "Account of the Cotton Family," Houghton Library, Harvard University

---

1. Matt. 1:21: "And he shall bring forth a son, and thou shalt call his name Jesus: for he shall save his people from their sins."
2. Ps. 137:5-6: "If I forget thee, O Jerusalem, let my right hand forget *her cunning*. If I do not remember thee, let my tongue cleave to the roof of my mouth; if I prefer not Jerusalem above my chief joy."
3. Matt. 15:25: "Then she came and worshipped him, saying, Lord, help me."
4. Robert Fenwick; see 16 July 1698.
5. 1 Cor. 11:28: "But let a man examine himself, and so let him eat of *that* bread, and drink of *that* cup."
6. Not found.
7. Neither letter was found.
8. Ps. 74:28: "But *it is* good for me to draw near to God: I have put my trust in the Lord God, that I may declare all thy works."
9. 1 Cor. 11:28: See note 7 above.
10. Ps. 85:6: "Wilt thou not revive us again; that thy people may rejoice in thee?"
11. 1 Cor. 11:28: See note 7 above.
12. Ps. 36:8: "They shall be abundantly satisfied with the fatness of thy house; and thou shalt make them drink of the river of thy pleasures."
13. James 4:14: "Whereas ye know not what *shall be* on the morrow. For what *is* your life? It is even a vapour, that appeareth for a little time, and then vanisheth away."
14. Col. 3:2: "Set your affection on things above, not on things on the earth."

From Rowland Cotton, 25 April 1699

PLIMO: TUESDAY ALMOST MIDNIGHT APRL. 25: 1699.

DEAR SIR.

I suppose this is my Eighth Letter[1] to you, my Last sent to one M^{r} sanford, att Boston, a gentleman wo very civilly [to]ld Tho Smith yt If any of us w^{d} send he would conveye This morne. Rob. Harpr:[2] brought me your letters[3] & from mother some account of you &c & her design to go boston tomorrow Early. & yt a vessell would sayle speedily to you &c out of Duty therefore & respect unto you not only as a father but as a friend & benefactor. I came this Evening hither. altho I have bin very ill for some time, & am now so much, I can hardly hold this pen—O Lord pitty me & be gracious to my dear family. amen—your letters to my self wife & mother I have read but can only give you a short Genll word.

I am astonished & melt with Joy att ye wonderful grace of God to you & the Good souls with you. o yt I had such busines at Sandwich, wee seem to be sealed up. my wife sends you hearty duty Joan allin is with us. Elder & wife, prince & wife Bassett &c much salute you & rejoice. bass intends to write Mary[4] is ravisht & blesses you much—some of our town talk much of coming over If could gett a living in Carolina. wee cant conceive wt you mean as to [m^{rs}?] Dominus &c wt is the matter. shee seemed choice. mother goes boston morrow whom I desire to send you all that is sendable—wee hear yt Betty is married. may 15.[5] (ye day yt o^{r} Govr setts out from york [to us?]). Bro Jno & I purpose East if God Pmitt. Phaps I may then write to you p pensilvania If I can. mother seems not to know what to do abt coming to you[6] I tell her she must go next fall. I suppose sheel write you her mind. tho if you Intend shee shd come you must send word what shee must bring from hence out of ye house &c—pray God Increase & continue your strength & succes. I can add no more. now save only hearty service to ye worthy mr fenwick[7] & his Lady tho unknown. & very true duty to yorself begging your constant prayers & blessing on me & mine

I am Yor unworthy son,

R. C

where in ye world is yor Cuz Joseph Whiting—. tis now past midnight—my dear wife expects childing June or July.[8] James warren[9] has bought Tom Littles[10] house—

Cotton-Prince Papers, Prince Library, Rare Book and Manuscripts, Boston Public Library.

---

1. None of the others have been found.

2. Not found. Robert Harper lived in Sandwich with his wife, Deborah Perry Harper. Savage, *Genealogical Dictionary,* 2:358; *Vital Records of Sandwich, Massachusetts to 1885*, ed. Caroline Kardell and Russell Lovell (Boston, 1996), 1:22.
3. Not found.
4. Possibly Nathaniel Bassett (1628–1711) and his wife, Mary, from Yarmouth. Torrey, *New England Marriages,* 50.
5. John and Joanna's widowed daughter, Elizabeth Cotton Alling, married Caleb Cushing (1673–1752, H.C. 1692) on 15 March 1699. *Sibley's Harvard Graduates,* 4:137.
6. Joanna clearly struggled with her decision about joining Cotton, and most of the remaining letters refer to her difficult choice not to join her husband in Carolina. In September 1699, according to a letter from Theophilus to his mother, Increase Mather wrote to Joanna "wrin he said he advised you to goe to Carolina." But then he closed the letter by asking his mother to "send word whether, or when you Intend to goe to Carolina." Theophilus Cotton to Joanna Rosseter Cotton, 12 September 1699, Miscellaneous Bound Collection, Massachusetts Historical Society.
7. Robert Fenwick, see the letter of 16 July 1698.
8. Abigail Cotton was born on 9 July 1699. Joanna refers to this birth in the following letter of 13 July 1699. Kardell and Lovell, *Vital Records of Sandwich,* 35.
9. See 8 July 1698.
10. See 18 February 1698.

From Joanna Rosseter Cotton, 13 July 1699

PLIMOUTH JULY 13 1699

MY DEARE

Your Letter of the 22 of May[1] I received on Saturday before commencement. Was glad to hear of your welfare the Lord continue it: sinc that a story is at Boston & all about the towns al though I heard it not til that you were dead it was talkt on 3 weaks or a month ago at Hingam you say you drempt I wear dead but yet the Lord strangly kepes me alive. I for the most part Live a diing life by reson of weaknes siknes & solitary Afflictions your Children are yet alive John never saw your Letters till lattely & hath not yet an opertunity but will & mr miller hath writ you one Letter[2] & now remembers his respects & Love Rolands wife hath brought him an Abigall on Lds day last all well you may know that I am very weak for I Could not go thither he durst not fetch me Josiah Theophilus & mariah are now heare with me son Cush[3] was hear yesterday staid but one night in town brings his wife next month poore Sarah is brought to bed of 2 sons william & John[4] baptised on the last Sabbath but one before the 2cond was born tooke her leave of Husbands & all her frinds wors of 2ond then ever of the first of all her children I now heare are sick deadpall good

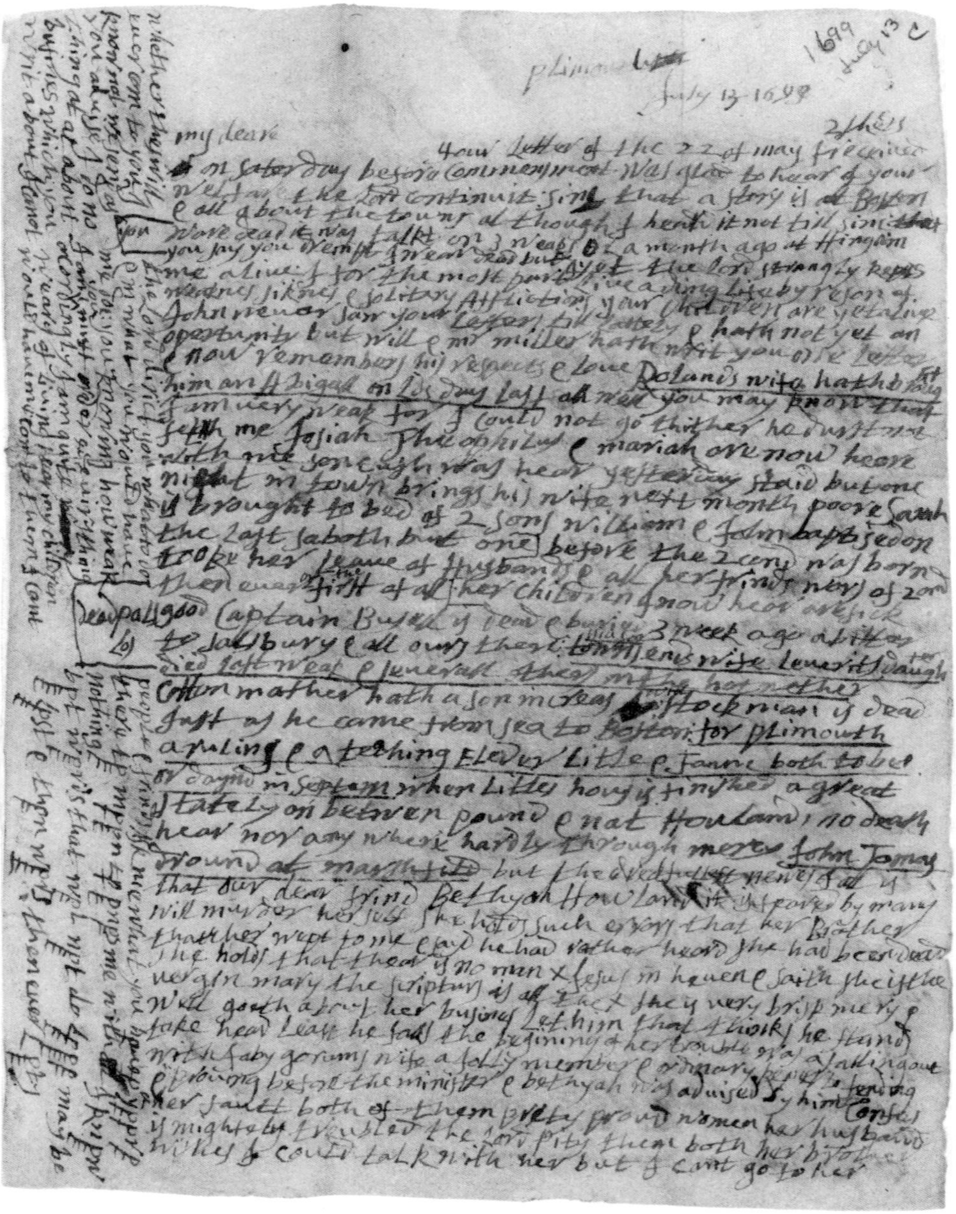

Joanna Rosseter Cotton to John Cotton Jr., July 13, 1699.
Courtesy of the Massachusetts Historical Society.

Captain Busall is dead[5] & buried 3 weak ago a bitter los to Salsbury & all ours there: Major townsends wife Leverits daughter died[6] last week & severall others in the hot wether Cotton Mather hath a son increas[7] [will:?] stockman is dead[8] Just as he came from sea to Boston: for plimouth a ruling & a teaching Eleder Litle & Fanne both to be ordaynd in Septem[9] when Litles hous is finished a great stately on betwen pound & nat Howlands, no death hear nor any where hardly through mercy John Tomas dround[10] at marshfeld but the dreadfullest newes of all is that our dear frind Bethyah Howland[11] it is feared by many will murder herself she holds such errors that her Brother thatcher wept to me & sayd he had rather heard she had been dead. She holds that thear is no man X Jesus in heven & saith she is the vergin mary the scripturs is all the X she is very brisk mery & well goeth about her busines Let him that thinks he stand take head Least he fall the begining of her trouble was a falling out with Jaby gorums wife a Jolly member & ordinary keeper to tending & proving before the minister & bethyah was advised by him Confes her fault both of them prety proud women her husband is mightely troubled the Lord pity them both her brother wishes I could talk with her but I cant go to her

I beleve nobody will give me anything hear for tables bedsteds cupbords chirs stools nor any thing els not one farthing come in of arears nor never will I beleve there is none in the world in my condition the [...][12] of my hart are [...] open every [accont?] inward & outward yet I must [...]

I sit in darkness pray for me & let all that feare god pray I leave you with the Lord & remaine your Afflicted & poor sickly wife

Joanna Cotton

my Love & respects to all your frinds
as though I named them to you
shall I take my dismission and to who

I shall never come with out you come or send such as will be equovolent both men & a woman to fech me your oysters came safe & good so did everything

I weare sent for to salsbury & wear at cos John Cottons he is glad to hear of your welfare & wishes you would [...] [loveingly?] to the church men and all other parswations won them by [...] I beg & your good example trust none no not the best men there [...] Tom Faunce the good Lord be your keeper some say have a [...] of the men [...] he prove a thorn in your side this people are [...] now at [...] then ever mr [...] & would not [help?] me goe to you for it will be so agoone quickly Lord [forbid?] think what I must go through the Lord strenthen me with strength in my soule fairwell I wish you well in my owne soule

JC

whether thes will ever com to you I know not we send as you advise I do no thing at al about busines which you writ about I canot the Lord direct you what to do & in what you would have me doe: you knowing how weak I am you must order & doe eviry thing acordingly I am quite weary of living hear my children would have them come to them I cant

people & frinds Ask me what you heare [...] your there to [...] me with I know nothing but words that wil not do [...] may be lost & then wors then ever L pty[13]

Miscellaneous Bound Collection, Massachusetts Historical Society.

---

1. Not found.
2. Not found.
3. John and Joanna's son-in-law, Caleb Cushing.
4. Sarah Cotton Bradbury (1670–1733) gave birth to her second set of twins, John and William, on 30 June 1699. Her first set was born on 23 March 1698, but only Samuel survived, and he died young. Despite Joanna's impression that delivering the second twin this time was so difficult that she "tooke her leave of Husband & all her friends," Sarah gave birth to nine more children between 1701 and 1716. *Vital Records of Salisbury, Massachusetts* (Topsfield, Mass., 1915), 26, 27, 530.
5. Salisbury's Captain William Buswell died on 21 June 1699 at the age of seventy-three. Savage, *Genealogical Dictionary,* 1:319.
6. Mary Leverett Dudley Townsend, the wife of Penn Townsend (1651–1727), was buried on 5 July 1699. Savage, *Genealogical Dictionary,* 4:318-19.
7. Increase, Abigail and Cotton Mather's sixth child, was born on 9 July 1699. *Sibley's Harvard Graduates,* 3:41.
8. William Stockman (b. 1675) was the son of John and Sarah Pike Bradbury Stockman of Salisbury. Savage, *Genealogical Dictionary,* 4:199.
9. The church records indicate that the congregation "sett appart october the 4 99 to Elect & ordain Mr Ephraim Little to be their pastor & Thomas Faunce to be their Elder." Publications of the Colonial Society of Massachusetts *Collections* (hereafter *CSM*), 22 (Boston, 1920), 188.
10. John Thomas Jr. (1649–1699) was the son of early Marshfield settlers John Thomas and Sarah Pitney Thomas. When he drowned he left no heirs, so his considerable property passed to his nephew, John. *Marshfield: Autobiography of a Pilgrim Town* (Marshfield, Mass., 1940), 138-39; Torrey, *New England Marriages,* 735.
11. Bethia Thacher Howland (d. 1725) was the wife of Jabez Howland (1669–1732) of Plymouth and Duxbury. Joanna referred to Bethia's "brother thacher." Bethia had only one brother alive in 1699, John (1639–1713) who lived in Yarmouth. Savage, *Genealogical Dictionary,* 4:270-72; Torrey, *New England Marriages,* 394, 733.
12. Joanna embellished her words in this section of the letter and her extra marks and slashes have rendered some of the words illegible. It is unclear whether these slashes were decorative or attempts at privacy. Most of the ellipses reflect one or two words that are indecipherable.
13. This final section, from the "JC" on, was written as a postscript along the left margin of the first side. Like the final part of the second side, Joanna embellished many of the letters with slashes that obscure them, making several words illegible.

To Josiah Cotton, 1 August 1699

Charlestown in South Carolina Augt 1, 1699

My very dear Son[1]

I have written every Letter that I intend now to Send to New-England, & Reserved yours to the very last, not because you least deserved my Remembrance, for I freely confess you have done much to merit my greatest Favour, and I shall retain a real affectionate Memorial that you were the only person that visited me last Jany from N.E.

You testify your natural affection in Rejoicing at ye Good of your Father, & you did very well to go to Boston & Dispose of Letters &c. Only my child where did you learn to say Sunday? I am sure not of your Parents; I have so corrected that Word here that none of my People dare any more use it in my Hearing—I am glad to hear you have a numerous Family; The Lord give you Wisdom & Grace to Educate y^{m} in all Respects so as may Glorify God & Render you very acceptable to that People—If you come with your Mother You will not need money to Pay your Passage I think. It is a great Mercy y^{t} you are in a way to live Comfortably there, which makes me afraid to unsettle you by Removing hither; That Passage of yours You know not how soon you may be a Preacher—is very Refreshing to me; Hoping God in mercy will direct & quicken you to those studies y^{t} may capacitate you for such special service to his Name, & here will be need enough of such; your Mother, Bro^{r} & Friends must weigh everythng, & the good Lord direct for the best. I believe I should Indulge your tarrying hence one year longer, were it not that the most intolerable Burden of your dear & precious Mothers Parting with so many dear Children, would have some Ease & abatement by your Company—I know how dear you are to her, & what Records she hath kept in Writing & in her Heart of Gods signal appearances to you: words; O that all might Ingage your heart to be for the Lord & him alone & that forever—If you find that Place full of Temptations, so it is every where; But O Pray in Secret night & day unto God, that you may be kept from every evil Way & Work: Look narrowly to your Thoughts in Secret; Let not an evil Thought be allowed in You—Your Doxology in the Close of your first Page hath a very gratefull Resentment with me. Mr Fenwick[2] I believe will write to you, he hath an intire Love & Respect for you, & is very much for your coming—God hath so graciously Settled me that I dur'st not favour one thought of unsettling—the Lord give you true Grace & purge your Heart from all sin, & make you a Blessing & dispose graciously for you in all Respects. I am your affectionate Father.

John Cotton

Josiah Cotton, Manuscript "Account of the Cotton Family," Houghton Library, Harvard University

---

1. Josiah introduced the letter in his manuscript account: "The other Letter I recd at Marblehead from Carolina, which was ye last I had from my Father & is as follows—"

2. Robert Fenwick; see 16 July 1698.

To [unknown],[1] 1 August 1699

Beloved Friend—The first Lines of my Letter to your Bro^r^.—Take as written to your self -- for as was he so were you loving & faithfull to me in every Condition—A Reward of Grace be given to you both, from ye Lord on y^t^ Acct. I remember you heartily Wisht my Lott might fall out not far from you & exprest your charitable hopes that my service might be profitable where God should Dispose of Me; I have reason to bless God whilst I live & forever for wt. God hath wrought for & by me, an unworthy Creatire—I am well satisfied with ye good Providence of God in bringing Me hither—A holy Minister from some Part of New-England wrote to me that I was sent from thence by <u>Prejudice</u> & Purchased here by <u>Prayer</u>; I know Man meant it unto Evil (I mean some Men) but God meant it unto Good to save some (O that it might be Many) souls. My Love to You & y^r^ good Yoke Fellow, the Lord Bless you both wth all Manner of Blessings & all your Children; I shall be very glad to hear y^t^ Converting Work goes forward amongst You, & y^t^ Peace & ye Power of Godliness is much advanced in ye Church—&c.

Josiah Cotton, Manuscript "Account of the Cotton Family," Houghton Library, Harvard University.

---

1. John Cotton introduced the letter in his manuscript account of his family: "To fill up this Vacant Page I shall Insert a Letter from my Father to a Man of Plym° Church & Town, Dated from Charlestown in South Carolina—Aug^st^ 1—1699—."

From Joseph Lord, 7 August 1699

Revd Sir

I am Exceedingly Obliged to you for yor readiness to stand up in Vindication of my Lettr[1] as well as of ye Cause it pleaded for & I take notice of some things in yor Answr [to?] that Lettr of Mr Scriven's[2] wc might have been Advantageously & to ye Purpose inserted in my Rejoindr; Yet Pray Sir don't take it amiss, if I tell you yt I think one thing in it cannot be Defended: [Viz. That a Child may close wth Christ in a Promise] (I speak of it, because if any such thing shd be so sd or written to the Adversary, he will take advantage by it to Insult) Mr [Dan]niel Rogers will be against you in such an Assertion; And I cannot see yt Luke [1-1[3]] will Prove it: For Christ may take Possession of an Infant by his Spirit wn there is no Act of Faith in ye Infant laying hold on Christ in a Promise. Mr Brinsly[4] in his Vindication of ye Doctine & Practice of Pedobaptism[5] has a Passage to ye Purpose. As also (if I mistake not) Mr Marshal, in Answr to Tombs.[6] My Latter is not yet Gone to Mr Screven. Joseph Summr,[7] ye Intended Bearer, & Moses Way,[8] were both taken into full Communion wth ye Chh, Yesterday. How Mattrs stand wth Respect to our Delinqts ye Eldr (wc, I think, is going down) will give you an acct. In one of yor Lettrs you spake of three Deaths at Barnstable, wreas [whereas] we had an acct of but one: Viz: Elizabeth Allen.[9] News of ye Colledge & Courts, I suppose, you had; as also of ye Death of Madm Phillips[10] of Charlstown &c. othr nes from N. Engld. I had none, but only some generally known things if you cannot be wthout Information of. I am Suspicious yt our Neighbor Hawks is inclining to ye Anabaptists: because, Preaching (yesterday, was Sev'n night) on yt Passage of Isa. 49.8.[11] And give thee for a Covent of ye People;. In my Use of Information one Inference was, Hence they yt Exclude Infants from an Interest in ye Covt, exclude ym from Salvation. Because yy [they] exclude ym from Christ ye Author of Salvation Act. 4.12.[12] wc he had manifested Dissatisfaction abt, as an Inference wc he did not see into. O Passe graviera, Dabit Deus hu quog; finem;[13] But so long as we have enemies abt us we must Stand to our Arms. I Cease, being in haste, only Saluteing all Friends, & Subscribing my self

Yours in Christ,

Joseph Lord

Dorchestr in Carolina
Aug. 7. 1699.

Clements Library, University of Michigan. Addressed "To ye Revd Mr John Cotton, Pastor of ye Church at Charlstown in Carolina, Deliver &c." Endorsed "From Mr Lord August, 7: 1699:" In another hand: "to John Cotton."

---

1. Not found.

2. Baptist William Screven (d. 1713) emigrated from Kittery, Maine to South Carolina by 1696, when he purchased one thousand acres of land near Charleston. Screven, who had arrived in Maine in 1668 from England, had married Bridget Cutt(s), the daughter of a wealthy shipbuilder, in 1674. Screven's zeal for Baptist doctrine did not prevent his serving in several local political offices. In January 1682, the Baptist church in Boston granted Screven the right to establish a Baptist church in Kittery. The Congregationalist churches were angered by Screven's proposed church, and he was fined, imprisoned and ordered to leave Maine in 1682. Despite that order, he seems to have remained in Maine until early 1696, when he left for Carolina. The congregation he led near Charleston, which was the first Baptist church in South Carolina, adopted the London Confession of Faith, which marked them as Particular Baptists. Joe King, *A History of South Carolina Baptists* (Columbia, S.C., 1964), 10-14; Leah Townsend, *South Carolina Baptists, 1670–1805* (Baltimore, Md., 1974), 5-12.

3. Luke 1:1: "For as much as many have taken in hand to set forth in order a declaration of those things which are most surely believed among us."

4. John Brinsley (1600–1665) attended Emmanuel College, Cambridge, and was ordained in 1624, only to be ejected from his pulpit for nonconformity in 1627 and again at the Restoration. *Dictionary of National Biography*, ed. Leslie Stephen and Sidney Lee, 63 vols. (London, 1885-1900) (hereafter *DNB*).

5. John Brinsley, *The Doctrine and Practice of Pedobaptism Assserted and Vindicated* (London, 1645.)

6. Many authors, including Stephen Marshall (1594[?]–1655) published replies to John Tombes's (1603[?]–1676) three-part printed attack on infant baptism entitled *Anti-paedobaptism* (London, 1652–57). Tombes published a response to Marshall's criticism, *An Examen of the sermon of Mr. Stephen Marshal about Infant baptism in a letter sent to him* (London, 1645). For another example, which included Marshall's criticisms of Tombes, see Richard Baxter, *An Answer to Mr. Tombes his Valedictory Oration to the People of Bewdeley. Plain scripture proof of infants church membership and baptism being the arguments prepared for and partly managed in publicke dispute with Mr. Tombes at Bewdley on the first day of Jan. 1649: with a full reply to what he then answered and what is contained in his sermon since preached… which I saw, against M. Marshall, against these arguments: with a reply to his valedictory oration at Bewdley…* (London, 1653) [*Early English Books,* 834:13]

7. Joseph Sumner (b. 1674) emigrated to South Carolina from Dorchester, Massachusetts, in 1695 with his parents, Deacon Increase Sumner and Sarah Staples Sumner, and his uncle Samuel Sumner, aunt Rebecca Staples Sumner, and their large families. William Sumner Appleton, *Record of the Descendants of William Sumner, of Dorchester, Mass.* (Boston, 1879), 3-4.

8. In 1695, Moses Way (1672–1737) left Chelsea, Massachusetts, for South Carolina with his newly-widowed mother, Joanna Sumner Way, and his two brothers, Aaron and William. He lived in South Carolina until his death. Joseph Sumner (see n. 8 above) and Way were cousins; Joseph's father and Moses's mother were siblings. A. Dane Bowen, *Henry Way (1583–1667) and Descendants* (Baltimore, Md., 2001), 118-21.

9. Elizabeth Allyn (1681–1698) was the daughter of Samuel Allyn and Hannah Walley Allyn of Barnstable, and she died on 23 December 1698. "Barnstable Vital Records," *The Mayflower Descendant* 2 (1900): 213.

10. Katherine Phillips, wife of Colonel John Philips (d. 1726), died on 24 February 1699. *Vital Records of Charlestown, Massachusetts to 1850*, ed. Roger Joslyn (Boston, 1984).

11. Isa. 49:8: "Thus saith the Lord, In an acceptable time have I heard thee, and in a day of salvation have I helped thee: and I will preserve thee, and give thee for a covenant of the people, to establish the earth, to cause to inherit the desolate heritages."

12. Acts 4:12: "Neither is there salvation in any other: for there is none other name under heaven given among men, whereby we must be saved."

13. The passage is from Vergil's *Aeneid* (book 1, line 198). As Vergil wrote it, "O passi graviora, dabit dues his quoque finem." "I have suffered rather painfully, god will give an end to this, too."

To Rowland Cotton, [8 August 1699][1]

PAG, 5:

[De]are son,

[...] [acci?]dentally met with this letter[2] from M^r^ E:[3] to M^r^ P:[4] [....] among our friends privately; I send it to you, partly that your [.....] mother & have one pleasant diversion with it whilst you are together, partly (though I cannot desire you to goe to salem on purpose yet) that you would use some meanes if possible to know of Mr Eppes whether Mr Pierpont sent him an answer to that letter, if he did I beleive it was as arch as his & I wish wee might have a copy of the answer to make us cheerfull here when your deare mother comes & send this also back againe that the right owner may have it; I will not expatiate on the 3 particulars; there is <u>much</u> truth on both sides, but <u>all</u> is not true on any side: of gaming; I will tell you a story; Mr Allison (son in Law to <u>Mr</u> wilkins[5] a sad debauche gamster, say not soe from me) hath issued out 2 writs agst one Dacres for debt, the one is a debt of five pd mony, the other twenty six pd, both due by bill; Playing together Dacres lost both games at Dice etc & the custom is, when a man hath lost to give bill to the winner to pay the money; these Actions are to be tryed before Judge Bohun,[6] Aug: 8: & one Capt Daisly sues the same Dacres to this court for fifty pd debt on the same account; & noe doubt the Plaintiffes will recover their debts; I spake the other day to Lantgrave Morton[7] (who of all the Councill is my most ingenous friend, comes to heare me each sabbath he is at towne & alwayes gives me one or 2 visits & though noe subscriber, yet freely gives me divers pounds) whether it were lawfull to allow such a debt, he pleasantly replyed, the Parliament of Engl: did allow such debts recovered provided they did not exceed an 100 pd, & he doubted not but the Judge would give it, soe that I see noe room for me to beare my Testimony agst such wickednesse; the Defendant pleads, the Plaintiffe cheated in the games: the poore man (above named) being neere death in towne went into the country for his health & soe far recovered as to requite Gods kindnesse with thus gaming & is come to towne to prepare for the happy court, having noe other way to get money; the place where these games were played was next door to the house where he lives of whom I have already written & I have reason enough to Judge that he was spectatour & actor therein: I hope you have the comfortable tidings (soe it is generally here) that poore Randolph is close Prisoner in Bermudas, the Govr Mr Day is a very hotheaded man (& Govr Blake who first told me of Rand's imprisonment, said he would certainly humble him before he had done with him[8]) & his mittimus[9] was upon suspition of his designing some evill agst the Government, the poore wretch could get noe money here, though he used base, sneaking tricks to trepan some merchants & ship masters, & is not likely to get much where he is; I doubt not your abundant [...] care to say & doe every thing that may accomodate your pretious mother in advancing this designe of her passage hither, which is most bitterly distressing to me when I think of her parting with so many of her limbs (as I may call her) but is it possible to be avoided? oh noe! Lord strengthen her faith, then all will be [well?] & God will restore by her much comfort & mercy to me; out of Cos: Mathers [...] you must heare our chh-trouble de Arthur Dicks, but his discovery & [...] [prove] much to our advantage, though for a time it was humbling to me & us a[lso?] I have written to you for 2 farmers already, I must send for a third, for my good Mr Jones hath a plantation neerer then M^r^ [Crotheres/Crosheyes?] a very choice one, Just over the water agst our very house, & I am sure a diligent, faithfull man would have a rich bargaine of it, & he might come to meeting every sabbath, the passage ordinarily would not be halfe an houre; good child, Labour in this matter, what I say for the encouragement of any will proove reall & more then I say, rather then lesse, I would not expose you to travells or losse of time about this affaire, but take all opportunityes that doe occurre to enquire & soe far to encourage, he will spare 2 negro's to serve upon good termes; Major Boone[10] had lately his white man who was his overseer bitten by the toe as he was swimming his toe bit off, it is supposed he was by that creature kept under water & soe [drowne]d I propounded another for chh-fellowship last sabbath to [....] if you have noe occasion to goe that way, he may [....] to send one in answer & may transcribe it for me: Th[....] most all quarters of the world & then is noe newes any where [....] soone have it, If I should baptize a Jew professing Christ, I ghesse who will [...] a Boston-lecture, perhaps it may be ripened before the ship goes: Mr Nicholas Trot,[11] a Kings Atturney Gen: here, telles me Rand: wrote letters to the King agst Govr Day, Day intercepted them & therefore clapt him up, but he sayes, noe doubt Day will speedi[ly] be turned out by the coming of a new Govr, & then Rand: will ruine Day for thus abusing him.[12] might I beg one favour of you? i:e: never to have a <u>Nero</u> in your family one day longer, he was soe horribly vile & infamous that I cannot beare the name in an[y] of my families, Cesar, Cyrus, Hector, & a 100 more are a 1000 times better, I hope you will change his name for my sake, who have in every thing done to the utmost for me; A state[ly] gowne of sad stuffe such as Bro: M: or his son weare, made & brought with your mother will cover my meaner clothes on the sabbath: As to the Jew (it being now Aug: 7:) say nothing, because he is gone into the Country & I have not since spoken with him & also some of the chh [officers?] have bin tampering with him to get him to accept the signe of the cross, soe that the issue is very uncertaine; All conclude here that Pyrates will depart the American coasts before your mother comes to saile, Lord preserve her,

& strengthen her faith; Every week, these divers weekes hath brought in a vessell & within these 4 dayes, 4 are come in, salt is here but 1 shil: 3 penc: a bushel; Mr Jones telles me he know Mr Pierpont did send an answer to Mr Eppes & read it to him, I hope you will not faile to send both to me. Aug: 8: 2 vessels come in today one from Pensilvania & the other from the Bay of etc: the Jew is come to me this morning lively in his good motions, soe that now I forbid not your speaking of it as you please: These way & Bacon order their bills to Linne, soe that it will be but one trouble, [you?] will not faile to asist your deare mother in getting the same, & let all be don according to my desire soe far as may stand with other necessities & conveniences. My hearty love to you & your deare mate, the good Lord delight to blesse you & all my deare Lambs your children; To his rich grace I commend you all, & rest

your Affectionate Father

John Cotton

Mr Cocks, who brought me hither, hath this last weeke most basely & sordidly reflected upon Mr Fenwick, & reviled him without any Just cause, & called him privateer[13] & used many other wicked expressions, he was vext because [...] Bridgham had given commission to Mr F: to minde his part of the [...] & fraight, this cocks is a rotten Anabaptist never comes to our meeting [but?] to heare Gilbert Ashley,[14] little did I thinke he would have prooved soe unworthy a fellow, yet I think to write to you by him next week, or by Mr Adams the merchant of Robert Meares's ship, who intends to come with him, this Mr Adams married Mr Dean Winthrops daughter[15] of Pullen Point, cousen Germane to Mris Thomas of Plym: he always comes to our meeting & carryes it civilly to me: Mr Bennett of N:E: in a great fly boat from Barbados wants but a high tide to bring him over the barre to us: poore Mr Allison dyed Last saturday & now court sits today, but he cannot prosecute his two actions against Dacres (a villaine that came with Randolph) the one was for [5] pd, the other for 26 pd, which Allison won at gaming, but hath none [...] ever [...] meares (who came full of logwood) his ship is condemned for rotten & is to be bur[ned?]

Miscellaneous Bound Collection, Massachusetts Historical Society. Many small and several large mutilations along all margins.

---

1. Misdated "May 5" by the Massachusetts Historical Society.
2. Not found.
3. Eppes.
4. Pierpont.

5. Joseph Alliston/Allison married Comfort Wilkins before 1693. He died before this case went to court; see the note below. Torrey, *New England Marriages*, 14.

6. Chief Justice Edmund Bohun was commissioned in May 1698 but had a tempestuous relationship with the proprietary government. In the fall of 1699 the Lord Proprietors warned him that his inability to get along with Gov. Blake was because he had "done things imprudently and irregularly"; they further reminded him to accept only his fees and "not to show too great a love of money," implying that Bohun had accepted inappropriate funds. While living in Carolina, Bohun corresponded with the Royal Society of London, to which he sent seed, plants and dried butterflies illustrating the flora and fauna of Carolina. He died in the same yellow fever epidemic that killed Cotton. Edgar, *South Carolina: A History*, 178; *History of South Carolina*, ed. Yates Snowden, 5 vols. (Chicago, 1920), 1:126, 130, 132. As he did so well in Plymouth, Cotton struggled to remain connected, even on the frontier of the British mainland colonies.

7. Joseph Morton (d. 1721) was the son of Gov. Joseph Morton and came to the Carolina colony with his father by 1681. He inherited his father's considerable property, and, by the time of his own death, owned nearly 5,000 acres and seventy-six slaves. "Landgrave" is a title granted by the proprietors. In 1697, Morton was chosen as a judge of the Vice-Admiralty court, but his tenure was colored by an accusation that he profited personally from his judicial decisions regarding merchant vessels. When his bid for the governor's office was defeated on a technicality, he became an outspoken critic of the government, even while serving as an elected gepresentative. Edgar, *Biographical Directory of the South Carolina House of Representatives*, 2:475-76.

8. See n. 12 below.

9. A warrant of commitment to a prison.

10. John Boone (1645–1711[?]) came to Carolina from Barbados by 1673 and was granted two hundred acres. Although he became a more substantial planter, he first made a career as a Native trader and Native slave dealer. His public service was marred by illegal slave trading, piracy and theft, leading to his forced removal from the Grand Council; when he was elected to the Assembly in 1706, he declined to serve. A major in the militia, he became a member of the anti-proprietary party. Edgar, *Biographical Directory of the South Carolina House of Representatives*, 2:88-89.

11. Nicholas Trott (1663–1740) arrived in South Carolina in May 1699 after serving as attorney general in Bermuda. With a commission as the first attorney general in Carolina, he became an outspoken critic of Governor Joseph Blake and Joseph Morton. In 1700, Trott was suspended and eventually arrested by Blake, despite having recently been elected to the Assembly. He continued to hold political office in Carolina and gain great personal power, serving as Speaker of the House and Chief Justice. He is also known for his legal work, especially for compiling *The Laws of the Province of South Carolina* (1736). David Ramsay, *History of South Carolina* (Newberry, S.C., 1858), 2:275; Edgar, *Biographical Directory of the South Carolina House of Representatives*, 2:681-84.

12. In November 1698, Edward Randolph left New York and sailed for Charlestown as a surveyor general under orders from the Board of Trade to investigate customs racketeering. He spent the winter of 1698-99 in Charlestown and was in Bermuda by April. Samuel Day was the governor of the royal colony of Bermuda but had only been on the island for about a year when Randolph arrived. Randolph tried to re-administer the oath of office, but Day refused, arguing that he had already taken the oath in England. This seemingly minor incident ignited Randolph's systematic attack against Day, largely through letters sent to the Board of Trade. In these letters, Randolph claimed that Day's crimes ran the gamut— from wasting gunpowder to announce his arrivals and departures by cannon to drinking orange juice from the King's Chapel chalice. Copies of the damning letters that Randolph had written to the Board of Trade were secretly supplied by Randolph's clerk, and they infuriated Day. After verbally attacking Randolph over his newly-appointed customs collector in May 1699, Day threw Randolph in jail. Other damning letters against Day flooded the Board of Trade, and Randolph's attempts to unseat the corrupt governor enjoyed great support in London. Michael G. Hall, *Edward Randolph and the American Colonies, 1676-1703* (Chapel Hill, N.C., 1960), 191-97, 201-2, 211, 221.

13. Actually, Robert Fenwick was a privateer before he came to Carolina, despite Cotton's indignation. See 16 July 1698.

14. Gilbert Ashley was living in South Carolina by 1691 and served in the Assembly in 1695, and as a justice of the peace. Edgar, *Biographical Directory of the South Carolina House of Representatives,* 2:43.

15. Eliah Adams (d. 1708) married Priscilla Winthrop (b. 1669) by 1698 in Boston. Torrey, *New England Marriages,* 3.

From Joseph Lord, 5 September 1699

Revd Sir,

Having been hindered from saying so much before by Lettr, These Lines may Inform you y^t I am bettr Satisfied about ye Defensibleness of ye Actual Faith of Infants,[1] altho' Mr Daniel Rogers is so Positive to ye Contrary, y^t his words are, "Pitifull is their shift who have no bettr way to stop an Anabaptist's mouth, but to say an Infant may have Faith.["] But w^t my mind is on those Scriptures y^t you Produced, I have not liesure now to write fully. But there is another thing, in w^c I w^d desire you to give me Grounds of yor Opinion. The Eldr Informs me y^t you signified it to be yor mind, y^t Children of ye Chh are not to be Excommunicated. Agt w^c having s^d y^t it seems to me y^t ye Nature of the thing Requires, not Exclusion from ye Chh, but a rendering y^m [... Heathens publicans], w^n [...[2]] do that requires ye Highest Censure y^t ye Chh can lay upon them; Since ye Chh [...[3]] y^m into that Visible Interest in God w^c they [have?] it seems but Rational y^t, upon their visibly casting God off, ye Chh shd. Pronounce y^m wthout such Visible Interest: I must desire you to send me w^t defect you see in my plea, & what Grounds ye Contrary Judgmt is founded on.

If w^t I mean be not avidt. to you (for I write in haste), I shall be ready to explain my self, w^n you signify so much to me, It being my desire y^t in y^t [...] unto we have attained, we may walk by ye same [...] & speake ye same thing.

I have sent my Rejoindr to Mr Screven's Lettr, to Mrs [Gates?], for her Perusal, & to be transmitted from thence to him.

My self & Wife Salute yor self Mr & Mrs Jones[4] & [all o^r] friends, w^c aftr Desiring yor Continued Prayrs for us all, is [...[5]] from him who is in Reality

Yors in the faith of Christ

Joseph Lord

Dorchestr
Sept. 5. 1699

Yors of Aug. 17.[6] gave me an acct. of a strange piece of Preposterousness; y^{t} a Covent sh^{d} be sealed before it was mad[e] And a Circimstance [...] w^{c} you tell me of [...] ye Pr[....] who (as it is [....] saluted by [....]

Clements Library, University of Michigan. Addressed "To ye Revd Mr John Cotton Pastor of ye Chh at Charlstown, Deliv^{r} &c." Endorsed in an unknown hand "[ ] 1699 from Rev Joseph Lord of Charlestown S.C." Tear along right edge.

---

1. For his initial query to Cotton about infant baptism, see Lord's letter of 7 August 1699.
2. Tear, one word missing.
3. Tear, one word missing.
4. Possibly John Jones (d. 1730) and his wife, Mary. Jones was granted at least 460 acres of land in Berkeley County in 1717 and helped to lead a popular revolt against the Council in 1727. Edgar, *Biographical Directory of the South Carolina House of Representatives,* 2:372.
5. Tear, one word missing.
6. Not found. The letter was most likely Cotton's reply to Lord's letter of 7 August 1699.

From Cotton Mather to Joanna Rosseter Cotton, 23 October 1699

Boston. 23. 8m 1699

My dear Aunt

You have erred unto God in your Distresses: Behold how Hee Extricates you!

Wee can Expect no Vessel from Carolina this Winter, and I suppose there is none going from New England thither.

By way of N. York wee have Letters of Advice from thence. They inform us, That by an infected Vessel, arriving <*there*> at Charlestown, ye horrible plague of Barbados was brought into the Town. About ye Latter End of September, it had been there, Little above a fortnight. In this Little Time, it had made an Incredible Desolation; I think many above an Hundred were Dead; and so many more Lying at ye point of Death, that ye Dead were carried unto their Graves in Carts.

<*They*> Mr Fenwick, and others Write, that all the ministers in Charlestown, were Dead; but they mention the Death, of their Precious Pastor, my Uncle, as the most Killing Disaster, they had yett mett withal. In their Confusion they tell us not ye precise Time of his Death; nor do they relate any circumstances of it, only That hee lay

sick Two Dayes, and hee Dy'd the Third. which is the period whereat the sick of that pestilential Distemper use to dy. That circumstance will make you think of Lazarus; and you'l join with mee in hopes, That my Uncle was one whom the Lord Loved.

I need not say unto you, how near the Death of so beloved a Friend goes to the Hearts of his Relatives in this Town and in a special manner to mine. I had not many Friends on Earth; Like him.

But in the midst of o[r] Sorrowes, on this deplorable occasion wee have not only the general Consideration of Christianity to bee o[r] Consolations; but wee have a peculiar satisfaction in the Lords accepting my Uncle to Dy with Honour, in the Service of the Gospel and Kingdome. As it was no great mercy (I beleeve) unto plymouth for their Laborious, and Good-Spirited, and well-Tempered Pastor to be driven from them, so it was a great Mercy unto my Uncle, to bee Employed in gathering a church for the Lord Jesus Christ, in a Countrey, that had never seen such a Thing, from the Beginning of the World. Wee understand from all hands the hee was extraordinarily serviceable to the Interests of religion, and that hee Enjoy'd Great Esteem and as Great Success. And now at Last, being so Little short of Sixty, and having seen his Children, all so far, and so well, brought up, their are in all these things very sensible mitigations of o[r] Calamity in Loosing him.

[Ho]wever none of these things, make it cease to bee a calamity and an Affliction, which calls upon us to Humble o[r]selves, and prepare for o[r] own approaching Change, and abound in agreeable supplications.

Your Distress, about your Voyage to Carolina, being thus at an End, I pray the everlasting Husband of the Widow, to Direct you and Comfort you, in Every other Distress, (for One seldome comes alone,) and give a comfortable Issue to all. So I subscribe, and approve myself

Your kinsman & servant,

Cotton Mather

Miscellaneous Bound Collection, Massachusetts Historical Society.

From Theophilus Cotton to John Cotton,

26 October 1699

octob: 26. 99.

Dear Bro

yesterday morning I came away from plimouth got in here about sun sett, and going up to [Morse-es?], I met with m^{r} Tom Smith, who told me he was sorry for my Loss, w^{t} Loss saith I? why saith he hant you heard yet, no said I why said he y^{r} father is Dead, o never was I struck into such Amasement in my Life he told me also y^{t} y^{r} was an 100. 50 dead in it says as all ye ministers of ye town are Dead, with a plague wch a Barbadian Brought y^{r}; [...] Lived over 3 Dayes y^{n} y^{y} Recove[reed] father died 3rd day o Lord Lett it be for our good. ye newes came by ye way of new york. I have heard no more about it <*about &*> yet. I am going to Deacon Bridgams, he hath Letters from thence. I must End Bec: Hodge is just agoing.

I Remain your Loving Bro

T. Cotton

I am att a great stand w^{t} to Do, I have a great mind to go to plimouth.

Miscellaneous Bound Collection, Massachusetts Historical Society. Addressed "To ye Revd. M^{r} .John Cotton att yarmouth with all possable speed I pray. p m^{r} Hodge Q.D:C." Prince notes, "In a Letter à m^{r} Josiah Cotton at Marblehead of nov. 9. 1699 to his Br Rowland, He writes 'ye Death of my Father, w^{n} he was wonderfully imployed for ye conversion of souls, was far distant à my Thoughts—I wonder m^{r} Fenwick had not writ more particularly in his Letter about it (for he only says—our Precious Cotton is Dead.

PEDIGREE CHART OF COTTON-MATHER-ROSSITER CONNECTIONS

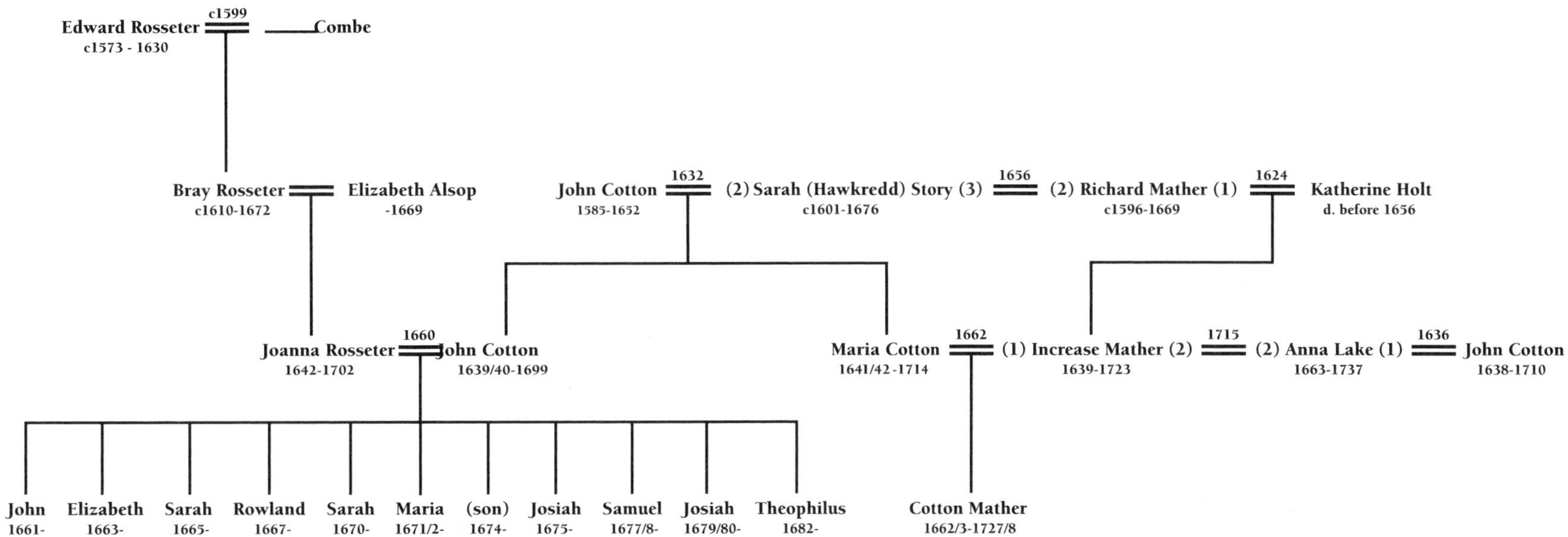

Courtesy of Robert Charles Anderson

INDEX